DOING
THEOLOGY
IN TODAY'S
WORLD

DOING THEOLOGY

IN TODAY'S WORLD

Essays in Honor of Kenneth S. Kantzer

JOHN D. WOODBRIDGE

THOMAS EDWARD McCOMISKEY

EDITORS

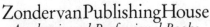

ZondervanPublishingHouse
Academic and Professional Books
Grand Rapids, Michigan

A Division of HarperCollinsPublishers

Copyright © 1991 by John D. Woodbridge and Thomas Edward McComiskey

Requests for information should be addressed to:
Zondervan Publishing House
Academic and Professional Books
1415 Lake Drive S.E.
Grand Rapids, Michigan 49506

Library of Congress Cataloging-in-Publication Data

Doing theology in today's world : essays in honor of Kenneth Kantzer / John
Woodbridge and Thomas McComiskey, editors.
   p. cm.
   Includes bibliographical references and index.
   ISBN 0-310-44730-5
   1. Theology, Doctrinal—History—20th Century. 2. Fundamentalism.
I. Kantzer, Kenneth S. II. Woodbridge, John D., 1941–   . III. McComiskey,
Thomas Edward.
BT80.D65   1991
320'.01—dc20   91-19112
                                                CIP

Edited by Leonard G. Goss and Gerard Terpstra

Printed in the United States of America

91 92 93 94 95 96 /   / 10 9 8 7 6 5 4 3 2 1

This edition is printed on acid-free paper and meets the American National
Standards Institute Z39.48 standard.

CONTENTS

INTRODUCTION

If theology is the human attempt to think aright about God, then doing theology should be one of the most exciting and attractive enterprises we could ever undertake. For what is more important than knowing God, his ways, and his perspectives?

And yet in the last decade of the twentieth century the study of theology is not in especially good repute even among devoted Christians. Theological texts appear incapable of escaping the obviously heavy imprint of their creators' own presuppositions. A number of such works seem inextricably tangled in vexing epistemological questions regarding how we determine any theological statement to be valid.

Many laypersons have long since rendered a negative judgment against "theology." The word evokes for them images of huge musty tomes written in an arcane language that only professional theologians can decipher. Laypersons often assume that "theology" is not "practical," that is, not capable of giving answers to their queries about life's pains and sorrows. What relationship could possibly exist between "theology texts" and the uplifting words of faith and comfort they find in Holy Writ?

The present volume acknowledges the panoply of "bad press" under which theology presently rests. For example, J. I. Packer sagely responds to complaints drawn up against the doing of systematic theology. At the same time the basic premise underlying this volume is the conviction that theology can be—indeed, ought to be—pertinent and spiritually uplifting and that a study of it can contribute much to the spiritual health of the Christian churches. One of the great tragedies within various Christian communions is that large numbers of believers do not sense that good theology has much to do with the life of the Spirit and with the way things really are as God views them.

We believe that a fresh look at how theology is being pursued as the Christian churches approach the dawn of the third millennium is not only a worthwhile enterprise but also an indispensable one. The vantage point from which we seek to gain this perspective is that of evangelical Protestantism. For this reason a preponderant number of authors in this work are evangelical Protestant writers. This perspective accords with the theological stance of Kenneth S. Kantzer, who is honored in the volume. Dr. Kantzer has been one of the principal shapers of evangelical theology in the second half of the twentieth century.

On the other hand, evangelical Protestant Christians need to know how theologians from other traditions view the study of theology. We are grateful, therefore, that a number of writers who do not share these evangelical convictions graciously consented to explain how they think theology should be pursued. In consequence, this volume provides a wide range of views concerning how theology is being done in today's world. Its principal focus, however, does remain evangelical Protestant.

In the first section evangelical Protestant scholars describe the contributions various disciplines make to the study of theology, at the same time attempting to put together a helpful approach to the doing of theology. In the second section evangelical Protestant scholars explain the distinctives of their particular tradition's approach in doing theology. In the third section theologians who do not identify with these convictions seek to explain the distinctives of their approaches to the doing of theology. In the final section, Dr. Kantzer provides a summary analysis of his method of doing theology and interacts critically with a number of the essays in this volume.

It is our hope that this volume will contribute to the strengthening of the Christian churches not only by demonstrating that the study of theology is indispensable but also by providing helpful suggestions concerning its pursuit. If it fulfills this intent, this volume will serve as a fitting token of appreciation to honor Kenneth S. Kantzer, who spent much of his life so unstintingly in teaching generations of students to value and love evangelical theology and his Christ.

A TRIBUTE TO
KENNETH S. KANTZER

WALTER C. KAISER

Every once in a while there steps onto the historical stage a person who seems to have been given an unusually significant part to play in shaping his or her generation and even generations to come. Kenneth S. Kantzer will be remembered as one of these unique persons.

After observing Kenneth Kantzer's life and work for thirty-five of his seventy-four years of life, I would like to try to put into perspective the ways this man affected our generation because he dared to do what others thought impossible.

The greatest legacy Dr. Kantzer has achieved can be found in the impact of his teaching upon thousands of men and women. His love for the classroom and his mastery of the art of exciting theological students to excel will be forever etched in the hearts and minds of two or three generations of scholars, pastors, and missionaries who represent a community that is truly worldwide in extent.

In the minds of most of the people who have known him, however, Kenneth Kantzer is one of the foremost architects of the evangelical resurgence in the last half of the twentieth century. He started on that road in 1963 when he accepted the post of academic dean of a newly renamed and completely restructured graduate school, Trinity Evangelical Divinity School. His achievement is seen not only in the growth of that school, though that was impressive enough, but also and especially in what the school has come to symbolize and the fresh challenge it has created for a dormant conservative theology that had languished for a number of decades. Although at least one other evangelical school had succeeded in pioneering the way before Kantzer's efforts, he was able to avoid both extremes of the evangelical movement and to chart a middle course without jettisoning the central theological affirmations that conservative theology upholds.

Space does not permit me to document properly the areas where this Distinguished Professor of Systematic Theology has exerted a major influence. It is enough to say that he was a major force in bringing together and shaping the single doctrinal plank of the Evangelical Theological Society (now numbering some two thousand scholars with advanced graduate degrees and in its forty-fifth year of existence). For the first thirty-five years of his teaching career he also performed administrative duties. Only those who worked beside him in those early days can appreciate the time and energy these duties demanded. At Trinity he acquired for the colleagues who served under him a generous sabbatical program that few other institutions have made available to their faculties.

Some of Kantzer's own major accomplishments in theology have been his editorship of *Christianity Today*, the coeditorship of the important volume *Evangelical Affirmations*, and his leadership of a provocative series sponsored by the *Christianity Today* Institute.

Few have mastered the ancient, modern, and biblical literature on the theology of Scripture, general revelation, and apologetics better than this evangelical theologian. Following a seminal sabbatical year of study (1954) in Germany and Switzerland, he became one of the scholars most sought out in the evangelical community regarding the doctrine of Scripture. His leadership in this area was clearly discernible in the now famous "Lausanne Covenant" and in the various statements issued by the International Conference on Biblical Inerrancy.

The mark of the man, however, is not in his achievements, for he would humbly wish to credit them to the honor and the glory of his Lord. Although he has written books of lasting value and has enthusiastically communicated excellent and memorable notes to his classes, he will be remembered most by those who knew him for the substance and the authenticity of the prayers he uttered at the beginning of each class, committee, or faculty meeting. Here was the true man at work with his Lord while his God worked in him.

It will be difficult to write the history of the evangelical movement and its impact on the culture of the second half of the twentieth century without giving a large portion of the discussion to Kenneth S. Kantzer. The shape that evangelical theology took during this period (especially in the areas of the doctrine of Scripture, natural theology, and apologetics) will often coincide with the length and and breadth of the shadow of this man of God for our times, Kenneth S. Kantzer.

Section I

DOING THEOLOGY: THE HELPING DISCIPLINES

1

IS SYSTEMATIC THEOLOGY
A MIRAGE?
AN INTRODUCTORY DISCUSSION

J. I. PACKER
REGENT COLLEGE, VANCOUVER, BRITISH COLUMBIA

Here, first, is a parable.

Parched and weary, the desert traveler sees before him an oasis of shimmering water. Thankfully he heads for it, but as he moves toward it, it vanishes. How come? Well, it was a mirage, only a mirage, just an illusion of reflected light. There is no genuine water there. There never was any. For all its attractiveness to thirsty wanderers, the oasis is not in fact real. Bad news!

And here, now, is the interpretation.

For eighteen centuries Christian thinkers have pursued a discipline—variously called *first principles* (so Origen), *wisdom* (so Augustine), *theology* (so Thomas Aquinas), *Christian philosophy* and *doctrine* (so Calvin), *dogmatics* (so Reformational and Roman Catholic teachers since the seventeenth century), and *systematic theology* (so American Protestant teachers since the nineteenth century)—that seeks a full and integrated account of all Christian truth. Books developing this discipline have borne a variety of titles—*enchiridion* (handbook), *ekdosis* (exposition), *sententiae* (opinions), *summa* (full statement), *commentarius* (survey), *loci communes* (topics of shared concern), *institutio* (basic instruction), *medulla* (marrow, as in bones), *syntagma* (arrangement), and *synopsis* (overview), among others—and have been put together in many different ways. All mainstream exponents of the discipline, however, and all without exception till the opening of the nineteenth century, have been sure that it yields genuine knowledge of God, first cognitive and then relational, being based on God's own revelation of truth about himself as the lover, seeker, and savior of lost mankind.

But today spokesmen for a certain type of Protestantism, one that emerged out of the self-styled Enlightenment and that its critics refer to as liberal, radical, modernist, or revisionist, challenge this confidence. They allege that the ordered knowledge of God that Roman Catholic, Eastern Orthodox, and Reformational Protestant teachers have set forth with (be it said) striking agreement at most points is like the oasis in the parable. Because it is clear and coherent and claims to be absolute and final truth, coming from God himself, it cannot but allure the wayfaring mind. But, say the challengers, it is in fact an illusion, a mirage, an illegitimate objectifying of opinions—in plain words, a fantasy, an unreality, a vast mistake, a giant fraud. Theology (so they say) cannot relay to us revealed truth, for there is no such thing; it can only describe, correlate, interpret, and criticize or justify intuitions and guesses about God that are found in the churches; and it is high time that, by facing this fact realistically, we cut theology down to size.

Are the critics right? This chapter attempts to weigh their claim.

SYSTEMATIC THEOLOGY UNDER FIRE

Our question might be posed as follows: Can systematic theology exist? At a surface level, of course, the question is silly: obviously it can exist, because it does. Teachers like Kenneth Kantzer impart it at universities and seminaries all around the world and have been doing so for centuries. The publishing of books and journals to advance it has become a sizeable industry. Do not these facts settle our question? Alas, no, for it is being asked at a deeper level. It is the integrity of the theological process, as classically conceived, that is at stake. Let me explain more fully.

The historic claim for systematic theology is that it is a *cognitive science*—that is, a way of knowing its subject-matter (in this case, the words, works, will, and ways of God) that produces analyzed, tested, and integrated conceptual formulations, to which is given the status of known facts. This body of knowledge is held to derive more or less directly from God's own active self-disclosure to human beings in the past—an activity involving the giving of verbal messages and teachings through chosen agents and supremely through God's incarnate Son, Jesus Christ, and the embodying of this material in permanent form for us in the canonical Scriptures. In this revelation, so classical theology affirms, God introduces us to ourselves as creatures given existence so that he and we might live eternally in love together, and explains to us that through our corrupt and corrupting self-will we have lost his favor and evoked his hostility. But the matter does not end there; central to God's revelation is the good news of the redeeming love whereby he has quenched his own wrath against us through the atoning death of Jesus and now offers himself to us to be our reconciled heavenly Father, who will pardon us, renew us, and bring us to everlasting glory. Humbly and thankfully to receive this biblical instruction and to live by it in faith, hope, and gratitude, so the classical claim continues, is the basic form of homage and worship that we owe to our Creator, and systematic theology has strategic importance for us because it crystallizes and conserves the life-giving revealed truth.

Clearly, however, if the authenticity of biblical revelation is queried, or its cognitive (mind-to-mind) character denied, the scientific status of systematic theology, along with the veracity and value of its declarations about God and godliness, are at once undermined; and that is the situation we face today. Revisionists insist that, whatever else the biblical tradition can do for us, it cannot give us objective knowledge of God—conceptions, that is, that are guaranteed true because God himself is vouching for them. Why not? Because God does not in fact use language to tell us things in the way that the older theology supposed. Literary criticism of the Bible is supposed to make this obvious. What we have in the Bible, say the revisionists, is an assorted mass of myth, legend, folklore, fantasy, and educated guesswork regarding God, all shaped to a greater or lesser degree by the prejudices and pressures of bygone cultures. None of this can be normative for us in our own current cultural milieu. So theology should give up its proud claim to be stewarding and safeguarding universal truth and settle instead for the humbler role of describing religious phenomena from a standpoint of universal cultural relativism. The Bible's testimony to God should be read as a testament of human religion rather than an attesting of divine revelation; it should be read as an expression of human thoughts and imaginings about a God who is really silent and withdrawn, rather than of God's thoughts about and words to a human race that is really blind and deaf to his approach, as the older view of theology affirmed. Theology must adjust to the fact that we have no word from God in any ordinary, natural, specifiable sense.

This view is put forward in the name of reason, but our first response must be that on the face of it it involves a quite unreasonable attitude to the Bible. For, first of all, the Scriptures of the Old and New Testaments display a pervasive internal unity, being bound together by a faith in the God of creation and covenant that all the writers of the books can be shown to share. And, second, these books do embody unambiguously a pervasive claim to be telling truth that abides because it comes directly from the God who does not change. No serious reader of the Bible can dispute that the Scriptures tell a single story, the tale of how mankind's Creator became mankind's Redeemer through Jesus Christ; nor can such a person dispute that according to both the story itself and the personal belief of the writers who record, explain, and apply it, the Creator has used human language to make known his holy will for mankind and the plan of salvation that he is currently executing. Any revisionist who overlooked these things would show himself an ignoramus. The usual revisionist move, however, is to question whether we should take seriously the biblical account of God telling us about himself and ourselves; whether believing and building on it methodologically, as classical theology has done, does not involve us in self-deception about the way God actually is—whether, in short, the habit of receiving all Bible teaching as from God, just as Jesus and his apostles received all Old Testament teaching as from God, does not lead to a cloud-cuckoo-land of clear and coherent notions that are, as a matter of fact, false to reality. The suspicion is that systematic theology as classically done absolutizes the relative, formalizes the ineffable, claims to know the unknowable, canonizes the imaginary, ossifies the transient, and misses what is really real and authentically spiritual. Many in the mainline Western churches are sure that this kind of theology, in all its historic mutations (Orthodox, Roman Catholic, Lutheran, Reformed, Wesleyan, Dispensationalist, etc.), is flawed and misleading in this way. Hence they see it, as was said above, as a delusive mirage—an unfruitful aberration, time-honored but wrong-headed and culture-bound, a great time-waster, and in the final reckoning baggage to be left behind.

Where did such radical skepticism about the historic path of Christian systematic theology come from? In general terms (and in this introductory discussion I am deliberately being general), it came from the two watershed assumptions whereby the European Enlightenment shook itself free from ecclesiastical control. The first assumption was that God is mute, without speech, so that Scripture is not in any substantial sense his word. The second assumption was that Western reason, well trained in post-Renaissance philosophy, can determine what is true and false with regard to God and man's relation to God. The audacity of the first assumption and the provincialism of the second are clearer to us today than they were to anyone two hundred years ago. Born and cherished among the deists and rationalists of the seventeenth and eighteenth centuries, these principles of method moved out into the mainstream to preside over the ablest Protestant theology of the nineteenth century and in due course to take control of most of the older theological teaching institutions and denominational bureaucracies. As a result, in many circles of theological study today the rightness of these methodological assumptions is simply taken for granted, and no other way of doing theology is understood or thought viable. In these circles classical systematic theology is replaced by novel alternatives put together on some form of empiricist-experiential-speculative-agnostic basis, each such theology representing a different way of desupernaturalizing and scaling down traditional Christian beliefs; and the pluralism thus created is hailed as a sign of theological health. Against this still-swelling tide of modernity only Orthodox, Roman Catholic, and Anglo-Catholic theology, which appeal to the church's historic consensus, and evangelical theology, which appeals to the self-interpreting authority of the Scriptures, can ever hope to stand.

The revisionist tide is kept flowing today partly, at least, by the continuing influence of a belief that pervades all Western and Westernized society at a presuppositional level, namely confidence that universal evolutionary progress is actually occurring everywhere; setbacks are only temporary, and no hiccups can finally upset the apple cart. The fruit of this faith (for faith is what it is) is the all-too-familiar mind-set for which the newer is the truer, only what is recent is decent, every shift of ground is a step forward, and every latest word must be hailed as the last word on its subject. In theology today the evolutionary paradigm rides high, and the field is full of progressives who, however much they doubt the viability of this or that popular option, clearly cannot conceive that the old paths might mark out the wiser way to go. I do not dispute that ongoing discussion in the academic theological community may bring genuine benefit by laying out possible options and exploding unsound theories, nor that this double benefit may properly be called progress at surface level—progress, that is, within the currently accepted paradigm for theological study. But I venture to suggest that the evolutionary paradigm itself, which invites us to welcome all shifts in theology as aspects of progress from strength to strength, is out of place here; nothing justifies it, only conceit prolongs it, and the ruinous effect of revisionist theology on mainstream church life during the past century must surely call into question the mind-set that has sustained it. If, however, evolutionary expectation in theology be judged an illusion—a mirage, in fact—then it is neither atavism nor obscurantism, but simply Christian good sense, to suggest that no real wisdom can emerge in theology without a paradigm shift back to the time-honored mental method for this study. What is that? It is the method that starts with a humble recognition that God the Creator, the God revealed in Jesus Christ, introduces, identifies, and authenticates himself to us through the teaching of Holy Scripture, and that our finite, sin-scarred minds know him only as we accept and internalize that teaching.

For more than half a century after the First World War Karl Barth pointed theology in this direction; but the obtrusive oddities of his exegesis and theological construction limited his influence, and overall the Protestant pendulum still swings in the direction of speculative and, by older standards, skeptical subjectivism. Books like Thomas Oden's *After Modernity . . . What?*[1] and the present volume seek to change that state of affairs; whether they can succeed, time alone will show.

THE NATURE OF SYSTEMATIC THEOLOGY

My own hope (I make no bones about it) is to see systematic theology of the older Christian type, more specifically of the older evangelical type, rehabilitated; and the first step to this end, as it seems to me, must be to clarify afresh its own ideal for itself, an ideal which, I find, is not always well appreciated. Nothing in this world is perfect, and it is not hard to find shortcomings in every theological system that has ever appeared. But defects in theological systems are of two sorts, some involving a wrong method and others resulting from failure to meet the demands of a right method, and it is observable that exponents of classical systematic theology, past and present, are often criticized for failures of the second kind as if they were failures of the first kind—failures, that is, that reflect some deficiency in the method being followed. Thus, for instance, the black-and-white theology that calls itself fundamentalism is often criticized for being impossibly and intolerably biblical, whereas the truer criticism would be that its purpose of being utterly biblical is entirely right, but its spirit of embattled rationalistic defensiveness has never allowed it to be quite biblical enough in practice. To counter such misdirected criticisms I will now try to spell out in some detail what those who currently practice classical systematic theology are actually up to.

The aim of this theology, as we have seen, is to function as a science: that is, as was said before, to give the world a body of analyzed, tested, correlated knowledge concerning God in relation to his creatures in general and to mankind in particular. The method whereby it pursues its aim requires the student to be conscientiously Bible-based, Christ-centered, and church-oriented, with a sustained life-changing and world-changing interest. These perspectives of concern hang together, and Bible-based thinking requires one to embrace them all, as all major systematic theologians from Origen on have in fact done. The method itself—which Thomas Oden calls the *conciliar* method, Reformed theologians often label the *churchly* method, and I claim as the true *evangelical* method—involves setting up a three-way conversation in which the Christian heritage of understanding, which is called tradition, is given a place alongside the head-scratchings of today, both in the church and outside it, for generating and guiding interpretative reflection on the inspired Scriptures. The overarching question is, How may we best state and apply the complete Christian faith, topic by topic and as a whole, in the light of current interests, doubts, assumptions, perplexities, questions, protests, and challenges? Answers to that question, and to all the specific questions into which it breaks down, are built up as the Scriptures are searched and exegeted, as the problems of insiders and the wonderings of outsiders are listened to, as the church's past approaches to the problem areas are reviewed and assessed by biblical teaching, and as that teaching is allowed to interrogate us in its own terms about our thinking, believing, and behaving. Into this process Roman Catholics introduce the aberration of treating tradition at key points as an infallible interpreter of Scripture, Protestants of the so-called liberal-evangelical type introduce the aberration of picking and choosing within the body of biblical instruction, and conservative Protestants sometimes introduce foreshortenings of the process itself. Aberrant models of the method must not, however, be identified with the method itself, just as a regular limp must not be identified with a healthy walking style.

What was almost a benchmark account of the discipline, as evangelical Christians a century ago conceived it, came from the pen of B. B. Warfield in 1896, in an essay entitled "The Idea of Systematic Theology."[2] There Warfield delineated systematic theology as a science using the data of Scripture, as clarified through direct exegesis and biblical theology in light of historical theology, to crystallize revealed knowledge of God— a knowledge that becomes progressively more exact and full as under God's providence successive conflicts with heresy beat out the truth, and that is constantly operating as an invitation, guide, and spur to the practice of faith in and fellowship with the crucified, risen, and reigning Lord Jesus Christ.

Let us be sure that we have the measure of this formulation. When Warfield spoke of systematic theology, he was distinguishing it from exegetical theology and historical theology, both of which on his view lead up to it; from practical theology, which on his view is informed by it; and from apologetics, which on his view clears the way to it by giving reasons to believe that God is real and the Bible is revelation.[3] When Warfield spoke of exegesis, he meant the discipline of answering the question, What did the various Bible writers mean their envisaged readers to learn about God's will, work, and ways from each passage that they wrote? When he spoke of biblical theology, he meant the discipline of answering the question, What is the total message of each biblical book and writer and unit of material on each of the topics they deal with, and what is the message of Scripture as a whole about it, and by what stages was this total message revealed? When he spoke of historical theology, he meant the many-sided exploration of how Christians of the past perceived and expressed the various elements of the biblical faith. What Warfield offered overall was a masterful mainstream statement of the Reformational idea of proper theological procedure as it presented itself to a fine mind toward the close of the Christendom era, when it was still possible to think of Christian faith and philosophy as a community commitment, of Christian theology as the growing point of Western culture, and of the Christian theological enterprise as the supreme human endeavor.

As a door swings on two hinges, so the classical view of systematic theology turns on two basic ideas, both directly Bible-based, and both obviously fundamental to Warfield's conception of theology as an ongoing science. The first hinge is the concept of human beings as made in God's image, so that they can reason about facts and values, form plans, and receive messages from, respond to, and communicate with other minds through language, as God himself does. Whatever more of meaning exegetes may find in the thought of God's image in man (and there is an ongoing dispute about this),[4] no one can doubt the correctness of taking it to mean at least this much. Then the second hinge is the concept of the Bible as the word of God—which is a two-sided idea, meaning on the one hand that the entire didactic content of the Bible is given by God for the instruction of mankind, and on the other hand that the text itself is God-given and has in it more of truth and wisdom than any church or individual has ever yet grasped. The systematic theologian's goal must accordingly be to use his mind to grasp and state in order as much as possible of all the things that God teaches in Scripture, so as to be able then to go to God knowledgeably in the exercise of faith and prayer and to discern his will in each situation for the practice of faithful obedience. Thus theology is to be "earthed" in life, according to William Perkins' striking definition of it, four centuries ago, as "the science of living blessedly for ever."[5]

For any real advance toward this goal a humble, teachable, praying heart, and the illumination of the Spirit that God gives to those who ask for it, are both required, and theologians in the classical tradition have usually made much of this fact. No one ever gave it more vivid expression than Luther, and his declaration of it is worth quoting at some length.

> I want to point out to you the correct way of studying theology, for I have had practice in that. . . . This is the way taught by holy King David . . . in the one hundred nineteenth Psalm. There you will find three rules, amply presented throughout the whole Psalm. They are *Oratio* (prayer), *Meditatio* (spiritual reflection), *Tentatio* (spiritual conflict: *Anfechtung*).

Firstly, you should know that the Holy Scriptures constitute a book that turns the wisdom of all other books into
foolishness. . . . Therefore you should straightway despair
of your own reason and understanding . . . kneel down in
your little room (Matt. 6:6) and pray to God with real
humility and earnestness, that he through his dear Son may
give you his Holy Spirit, who will enlighten you, lead you,
and give you understanding.

Thus you see how David keeps praying in the above-
mentioned Psalm, "Teach me, Lord, instruct me, lead me,
show me," and many more words like these. Although he
well knew and daily heard and read the text of Moses and
other books besides, still he wants to lay hold of the real
teacher of the Scriptures himself. . . .

Secondly, you should meditate, that is, not only in your
heart, but also externally, by actually repeating and comparing . . . the words of the book, reading and rereading them
with diligent attention and reflection, so that you may see
what the Holy Spirit means by them. And take care that you
do not grow weary or think that you have done enough
when you have read, heard, and spoken them once or twice,
and that you then have complete understanding. . . .

Thus you see in this same Psalm how David constantly
boasts that he will talk, meditate, speak, sing, hear, read, by
day and night and always, of nothing except God's Word
and commandments. God will not give you his Spirit
without the external Word; so take your cue from that. . . .

Thirdly, there is *tentatio, Anfechtung.* This is the touchstone
that teaches you not only to know and understand, but also
to experience how right, how true, how sweet, how lovely,
how mighty, how comforting God's Word is, wisdom
beyond all wisdom.

Thus you see how David, in the Psalm mentioned,
complains so often about all kinds of enemies, arrogant
princes or tyrants, false spirits and factions, whom he must
tolerate because he meditates, that is, because he is occupied
with God's Word. . . . For as soon as God's Word takes root
and grows in you, the devil will harry you, and will make a
real doctor of you, and by his assaults (*Anfechtungen*) will
teach you to seek and love God's Word. I myself . . . am
deeply indebted to the papists that through the devil's raging
they have beaten, oppressed, and distressed me so much
. . . they have made a fairly good theologian of me, which I
would not have become otherwise. . . .

There now, with that you have David's rules. If you study
hard in accord with his example, then you will also sing and
boast with him in the Psalm, "The law of thy mouth is better

to me than thousands of gold and silver pieces" (Ps.
119:72). . . . And it will be your experience that . . . the
longer you write and teach, the less you will be pleased with
yourself. When you have reached that point, then do not be
afraid to hope that you have begun to become a real
theologian. . . .

If, however, you feel and are inclined to think you have
made it, flattering yourself with your own little books,
teaching, or writing . . . if you perhaps look for praise, and
would sulk or quit what you are doing if you did not get it—
if you are of that stripe, dear friend, then take yourself by the
ears, and if you do this in the right way you will find a
beautiful pair of big, long, shaggy donkey ears. . . .[6]

Have the demands of humility and the dangers of pride in
theological study ever been more strikingly expressed? I doubt
it. Luther's insight into what is involved in understanding
spiritual things spiritually does not, however, stand alone;
Warfield ends his essay with a comparable emphasis, phrased
as follows:

. . .The systematic theologian is preeminently a preacher
of the gospel . . . he needs to be suffused at all times with a
sense of the unspeakable worth of the revelation which lies
before him as the source of his material, and with the
personal bearings of its separate truths on his own heart and
life; he needs to have had and to be having a full, rich, and
deep religious experience of the great doctrines with which
he deals; he needs to be living close to his God, to be resting
always on the bosom of his Redeemer, to be filled at all times
with the manifest influences of the Holy Spirit. The student
of systematic theology needs a very sensitive religious
nature, a thoroughly consecrated heart, and an outpouring
of the Holy Ghost upon him, such as will fill him with that
spiritual discernment, without which all native intellect is in
vain.[7]

Warfield's style is not Luther's, but in sentiment they converge.

By quoting the testimony of these two evangelical giants to
the spiritual demands of theological study, I effectively narrow
my focus of concern to the rehabilitating of the evangelical
version of that older type of theology that revisionists dismiss
as a mirage. That narrowing is intentional, for at this point with
regard to both the content of the theology and the spirituality of
theologizing the ways really do divide. In evangelicalism the
sense that I, whom the great and glorious God calls to serve
him by theologizing about him, am naturally nothing but a

guilty sinner, a damned fool, and a lost soul, and yet have an assured acceptance and intimacy with God through justifying grace, is clearer and more vivid than in Roman Catholicism and Orthodoxy (which, considering the historic weakness of both those traditions on justification by faith, is only natural). Hence evangelical theologians, when compared with others, seem extraordinarly insistent on their natural insufficiency for their task and at the same time extraordinarily confident that through God's enabling grace their theology is right. These twin emphases express justification by faith on its intellectual side and are characteristic of the reformed Augustinianism that is the mainstream evangelical heritage in both doctrine and spiritual life. Believing that this reformed Augustinianism, which both Luther and Warfield exemplify, is Christianity at its purest, I will henceforth concentrate on discussing the way to reestablish the credentials of evangelical systematic theology specifically, leaving Catholic and Orthodox versions of the supposed "mirage" theology on one side.

Rehabilitating evangelical theology requires more, of course, than applauding the spirituality of its exponents. It requires also that the rationality and coherence of the parts of the system within its overall theistic frame be demonstrated. That demonstration belongs to the understanding that faith rightly seeks; for where inner coherence is not seen, credibility is diminished. I now offer two sample demonstrations (space precludes more): I will show the coherence of the two hinge concepts discussed earlier with the larger biblical outlook.

Regarding the first hinge concept, the image of God in man, the demonstration is plain and compelling and involves no controversy. All versions of Christianity hold that God's purpose in creation was that he should be known, loved, and glorified by his human creatures and honored in their life together by their love for each other. But for this to be possible, human beings had to be able to relate to God and others in a personal way, and this required that they be capable of being addressed and instructed, and of thinking, feeling, and loving; and it is God's bestowal of these capacities that the concept of creation in God's image primarily proclaims. No Christian disputes that.

By contrast, the second hinge concept, the status of canonical Scripture as the totally true and trustworthy word of God, is widely disputed among modern Protestants, as we have seen. Nonetheless, the demonstration of its coherence with the rest of the Christian system is no less plain and compelling than the one just given. The need for God to give us a fully inspired, reliable Bible follows from the once-for-all character of God's redeeming work in Christ, whereby in Jerusalem, Palestine, on a date in A.D. 30 or 33, God reestablished his purpose in creation by having Jesus die for mankind. All developed cultures know that oral tradition is not fully trustworthy for transmitting facts and their explanations, so that anything of permanent importance, requiring exact statement, needs to be put in writing; only so can accuracy and long-term accessibility be guaranteed. For God, having established a way of salvation that depends on knowing facts about Jesus of Nazareth, to then give the world written material that provides this knowledge and that can be used as a touchstone to decide between rival versions of Christian belief would seem to be necessary wisdom; for God not to do this, either by giving us nothing written at all or by supplying written material that cannot function straightforwardly as a guide to faith and life in Christ (which is what both Roman Catholicism, with its appeal to tradition, and radical Protestantism, with its selective subjectivity, say in effect that he has done) would seem to be inexplicable unwisdom—in fact, folly. Early Patristic and later evangelical theology have constantly maintained that God was wise in this matter, and it is in no way unreasonable to endorse that verdict today. Belief that the Bible is complete, clear, true, and trustworthy is theologically coherent and prompts praise; of the doctrine that Bible teaching is untrustworthy to a degree and/or obscure, neither of these things can be said. Without going into the many specific reasons for receiving the canonical Scriptures, in all their humanness, as the word of God, guaranteed reliable by the Father, the Son, and the Spirit, it can be stated categorically that on grounds of theological coherence alone the evangelical view of Scripture leaves its rivals standing.

AUGMENTING WARFIELD

Was Warfield's account of systematic theology, then, the last word on the subject? No; it now needs to be augmented in five ways at least, in light of the new questions, emphases, and angles of vision that have opened up in theology during the past hundred years.

First, it needs to be stated that a dimension of *mystery* is inescapable and must be acknowledged whenever we set ourselves to think about God. By this I mean, not that there is anything necessarily and intrinsically unclear in what God has revealed in the Bible, but that we must always proceed on the basis that there is more to God's being, work, and purposes than we have been told, or could grasp if we were told. Calvin's illustration of God accommodating himself to human capacity by using the equivalent of baby-talk when telling us about himself is surely very apt.[8] A person with a brain like Einstein's cannot, in talking to a three-year-old, share all the thoughts in his mind, and those he does share must first be much simplified and then expressed in ways that fall far short of the full reality being referred to. We should see ourselves as like three-year-olds in relation to our Creator as he teaches us from his written word; what he tells us, however coherent and clear as far as it goes, can never be assumed to be exhaustive. D. A. Carson illustrates this felicitously, writing as follows:

> I am not saying that the Bible is like a jigsaw puzzle of five thousand pieces and that all five thousand pieces are provided, so that with time and thought the entire picture may be completed. Rather, I am suggesting that the Bible is like a jigsaw puzzle that provides five thousand pieces along with the assurance that these pieces all belong to the same puzzle, even though ninety-five thousand pieces (the relative figures are unimportant for my analogy) are missing. Most of the pieces that are provided, the instructions insist, fit together rather nicely; but there are a lot of gaping holes, a lot of edges that cry out to be completed, and some clusters of pieces that seem to be on their own. Nevertheless, the assurance that all of the pieces do belong to one puzzle is helpful, for that makes it possible to develop the systematic theology, even though the systematic theology is not going to be completed until we receive more pieces from the one who made it. . . . Meanwhile, even some systematicians who believe that all the pieces belong to the same puzzle are not very adept puzzle-players, but sometimes force pieces into slots where they don't really belong. . . .[9]

That reminder of our limited powers, along with the initial reminder of the limited nature of God's revelation itself, must ever be borne in mind as we labor in systematic theology.

Second, it needs to be stated that limitations are imposed on systematic theology by the *analogical* nature of biblical and Christian language about God. Some of the best work here has been done since Warfield's day, and we should not fault the Princeton theologian for sharing his era's unawareness of the logical problems of theological speech that linguistic analysis and cultural hermeneutics would later raise. But there is a crucial point to be made here; stated simply, it is as follows:

Human beings live a life that is derived; dependent; limited in space, time, and power; never fully integrated; and always morally flawed, and all the words in all human languages that relate to human existence are signifying and speaking of a life of that kind. God's life, however, is different; it is underived, self-sustaining, infinite and eternal, unlimited by any of his own creatures, totally integrated, transcending space and time, perfect in holiness and righteousness, purity and love, wisdom and fidelity. This means that whenever we find Scripture—that is to say, God in Scripture—taking nouns, adjectives, and verbs from the common stock of human language to express to us who he is and what he has done, does, and will do, and whenever we ourselves use nouns, adjectives, and verbs to tell each other what we found God teaching us about himself in the biblical documents, those nouns, adjectives, and verbs must be partially redefined, so that they will never ascribe to God the restricted and sinful type of existence that marks mankind. How is this to be done? The rule is that from each word's ordinary, everyday meaning all that reflects human limitation and imperfection must be excluded, and into that ordinary meaning the thought of divine perfection must be imported, according to the specific teaching of Scripture as to what precisely this perfection involves.[10] Theology that fails to do this, and thus allows itself, in Aquinas' terminology, to speak of God *univocally* rather than *analogically*, will thus be in a deep sense incompetent and misleading, laying itself open at point after point to the error of conceiving of God as if he were a limited being like ourselves. Much popular theology is, and no doubt always has been, incompetent in this way, and when systematic theology allows itself to go beyond Scripture (or even cast it off) and become speculative, it regularly lapses in similar fashion. It is vital for the health of systematic theology that we should be on the watch for such lapses, and when we detect them we should make an issue of them and labor to weed them out; otherwise genuine unreality, in the sense of noncorrespondence to what is—the mirage-factor!—will become a mark of our theology, as our radical critics think it is already.

Third, it needs to be stated that the method of theological *theory-forming* implicit in Warfield and explicit in his mentor, Charles Hodge,[11] is inadequate and misleading. In its own day, it was offered in order to show that theology as a science is exactly on a par with the physical sciences, the procedures of which had already established themselves in many minds as normative for knowledge of any kind, and the unrealism of Hodge and Warfield reflects the unrealism of turn-of-the-century science about its own procedures. Their account ran thus: systematic theology operates by *induction*. As the natural scientist first collects all the facts and observations relevant to his inquiry and then distills from them the universal regularities ("natural laws") that they exhibit, so the theologian first collects all relevant biblical affirmations on the matter in hand and then draws from them generalizations about God, man, and the world in relation to each other. Since Warfield's time, however, it has come to be generally acknowledged that this concept of scientific method, which was supposed to guarantee total objectivity, does not correspond to what scientists actually do— so one does not impugn theology's claim to be a science by recognizing that this is not in truth theology's method either! In the natural sciences, subjective—that is, personal—factors enter from the start into the selection of data, the forming of hypotheses, and the devising of means to test them; hunches and educated guesses play a key role in scientific advance, with observational data then being sought to confirm or confute the guesswork. This procedure is sometimes called *retroduction* rather than induction, because in it the theory is brought back to the world of facts for verification, rather than being definitively inferred from a set of facts already known (how?) to comprise all the data needed for forming the theory. And in systematic theology the story is the same.[11] Most of the work consists in practice, not of producing new formulations at all, but of testing and adjusting old ones—old theories, that is—in light of fresh questions, both logical and factual, that have emerged, and of fresh precision that has been achieved in exegeting the biblical material. Nothing in theology is ever so clear and certain as never to need reexamination, and Warfield's vision of an ever-growing deposit of tested, accredited, and definitively established theological results (one thinks of the ever-growing mountain of tested and accredited butter in the European Common Market) seems somewhat out of line with reality.[12]

Fourth, it needs to be explicitly said that every proposed theology must vindicate itself as a *hermeneutic*, that is, a way of understanding both the message of the whole Bible, viewed as wisdom from God, and ourselves and our lives as interpreted by that wisdom. To be hermeneutically adequate, a theology must exhibit three qualities together. First, it must show itself to be a *canonical interpretation* of the canonical Scriptures, in other words a comprehensive synthesis of all the Bible's relevant didactic content, so far as this is known at present. Second, it must pass muster as a *contextualized communication* that sets forth understanding of the significance for life of the truth it presents within the frame of the cultural milieu into which it is being fed. Third, it must prove itself as a *heuristic hypothesis*, that is, a guiding presupposition which, when made basic to further Bible study, deepens insight into the meaning and force of particular passages and so becomes the means whereby fresh truth comes to light (for it is always the case that, as the pilgrim pastor John Robinson long ago said, God has yet more light and truth to breath forth from his holy word). Failure to pass this threefold hermeneutical test will reveal a theology as less than it should be in its totality, whatever virtues are visible in its particular theories and parts.

Fifth, it needs to be stated that the systematic theologian's biggest problem is always *himself*—that is, the unmortified arrogance and continuing darkness of his own intellect, which leads him unwittingly, in perfect sincerity and often with painstaking labor, to offer God's people theological constructions that are unbiblical, man-centered, culturally determined, unpractical, undevotional, undoxological, Spirit-quenching and self-aggrandizing—theological constructions that in effect put God in a box of one's own manufacture, claiming in effect to master him by knowing exhaustively what he will and will not do. Theologians who allowed themselves to speak as if they had God in their pocket would indeed be presenting a mirage of unreality! But the true systematic theologian will be carefully, prayerfully watching himself all the time so as to avoid doing any such thing.

COUNTERING THE ATTACK

From the vantage point established by what has been said so far, I now return to the critique of classical systematic theology from which this chapter took its rise. How is the claim that such theology is necessarily a deceptive and misleading mirage justified by those who make it?

The reasons given rest on the Enlightenment assumption of the muteness of God, to which reference has already been made, and boil down essentially to two.

The first is that the canonical Scriptures cannot in any case function as a source of instruction about God in the way that systematic theology requires them to do. This is said not just because natural and historical science is thought to have exploded the idea that Scripture speaks truth about matters of fact; more fundamentally, it is said because different sections of the material are thought to offer a whole series of theologies that are out of accord with each other. So any clear, coherent that systematic theology claims a biblical base will certainly be misleading, for it will have been produced by mishandling the evidence and ignoring the contradictory pluralism that Scripture actually exhibits.

The second reason given is that any particular systematic theology will be the product of an historical and cultural process that is incurably relativistic. The shape and substance of all ideas, including theological ideas, that any persons or communities at any time take as truths are held to be conditioned by the surrounding culture in such a way as to make it impossible for them to function transculturally as abiding standards. It is argued that there is no such thing as transcultural truth and that failure to see this shows only that one does not understand the inescapable relativism of the historical process.

Can such reasoning be countered? Yes, I think so, and at more than one level.

To start with, it can, I believe, be shown that the Bible's alleged pluralism is a mirage—that is, an unreality, an appearance that on closer approach dissolves away. Exegesis that is genuinely empathetic and logically alert—remembering, first, that in Scripture as elsewhere different words may be used by different people to make the same point; second, that in Scripture as elsewhere the full significance of statements about God appears from the practical responses to God that are called for; third, that God in his self-glorifying purpose is the real theme of every biblical writer in every book, chapter, and verse; and fourth, that the New Testament itself notes a series of divinely planned differences between the Old and New dispensations—can cogently demonstrate the theological coherence of the many-stranded canonical material and has in fact been doing so ever since the days of John Calvin, at least.

Then, further, it may be observed that the critique of normative theology cancels itself out. If its relativistic basis be accepted, then it cannot itself have normative force, nor can any revisionist theology have normative force. To assert the paradigm of historical relativism in order to negate the universal claim of one proposed form of rationality is to negate the universal claim of all proposed forms of rationality, including that which affirmed the paradigm in the first place. Asserting this paradigm makes it irrational to ask, expect, or even want anyone to agree with you about any question of truth. Sauce for the goose is sauce for the gander; you are not God, and you may not think of yourself as standing outside that relativistic process that you claim everyone is inside. To the historical relativist, we may say: your own assertion of historical relativism is a strictly nonrational act, a culture-determined accident, and there is no reason why anyone should follow you in it. Thus the a priori argument for denying that a normative theology is possible destroys itself.

Forceful as these considerations are, however, something yet more decisive remains to be said. The strongest reason for rejecting theological revisionism lies in the basic fact on which Christianity rests, namely, the incarnation of God the Son. For the New Testament writers and all who follow them, the Incarnation, fully and finally displaying God in a totally human life, was the climax of a long revelatory process in history and is the critical norm for future thought and speech about God for as long as this world will last. The Lord Jesus Christ, we may say, is divine revelation in paradigmatic form, the form to which all other divine revelations correspond. Spelling this out, we may affirm the following propositions about God's self-revelation to sinful mankind:

1. *God uses language* to communicate with us. God incarnate was a rabbi, a teacher, a talker, and a language-user, and when he spoke, God was speaking. A priori doubts, rife since Kant, as to whether God could or would use language to tell us things, and whether therefore Holy Scripture could possibly be his verbal word to the world, are thus resolved. God uses language.

2. *God reveals truths* about him and us. Jesus taught truths about God and mankind throughout his messianic ministry.

3. *God's self-revelation, made at one point through one person in*

the space-time history of this world, can be, and in fact is, God's word to all mankind in every place at every point of time henceforth. No cultural change affects this.

4. *The giving of God's revelation is something distinct from the receiving of it.* Jesus is the revelation of God whether he is received as such or not, just as the Bible is the word of God whether it is acknowledged as such or not.

5. *God has authenticated the Old Testament and the witness of the apostles* as a rule of faith and life. This authentication is embedded in Jesus' teaching, just as reception of it is modeled in his submission to the Old Testament throughout his ministry. These words and teachings of men are to be received as also, and equally, and primarily, words and teachings of God.

6. *The personal, relational knowledge of God that fallen humanity needs rests on knowing about Jesus Christ.* It is by becoming his disciple through faith and repentance that sinners enter the kingdom of God, which is the sphere of salvation. The central task of preaching and theology is thus cognitive communication of the facts about Jesus. This remains true at all times, in all cultures, and under all circumstances.

I sum up my discussion, therefore, like this: Jesus Christ, who as God incarnate is God's final self-disclosure, is the criterion for judging theologies. By this standard the Bible-based, Christ-centered systematic theology of the historic Christian mainstream is in principle justified, while the revisionist theologies that dismiss this theology as a mirage, yielding no sure knowledge of God, and are skeptical of all cognitive communication from God or about God, are found wanting. Logically, they can maintain their critique of cognitive systematic theology only by denying the authority of Jesus the divine teacher, and this requires them to deny the Incarnation itself and redefine Christianity in terms that exclude direct personal worship of Jesus—as in fact some of the clear-headed exponents of revisionist thinking actually do. The mirage in this situation, the real unreality and the genuine delusion, is not the historic belief that what Francis Schaeffer called "true truth" about God is contained in and expressed by biblically faithful systematic theology, but the supposition of the revisionists that they are talking of the way things really are when they deny this. It would be a happy thing were this mirage more widely recognized for what it is.

NOTES

[1]Thomas C. Oden, *After Modernity* . . . *What?* (Grand Rapids: Zondervan, 1990—a revision of *Agenda for Theology: Recovering Christian Roots*, 1979).

[2]B. B. Warfield, "The Idea of Systematic Theology," in John Jefferson Davis, ed., *The Necessity of Systematic Theology* (Grand Rapids: Baker, 1980), 127–67 (reprinted from *Presbyterian and Reformed Review* [1896]: 243–71); idem, *Studies in Theology* (1932; reprint, Grand Rapids: Baker, 1981), 49–87.

[3]Warfield, "Idea of Systematic Theology," 142–47; idem, *Studies in Theology*, 63–68.

[4]See D. J. Clines, "The Image of God in Man," *Tyndale Bulletin* 19 (1968): 53–103; idem, "Image of God" in Sinclair B. Ferguson and David F. Wright, eds., *New Dictionary of Theology* (Downers Grove: InterVarsity, 1988); Anthony A. Hoekema, *Created in God's Image* (Grand Rapids: Eerdmans, 1986), 11–101; Philip E. Hughes, *The True Image* (Grand Rapids: Eerdmans, 1989), 3–69.

[5]William Perkins, *Workes*, 1626, I.11 (from *A Golden Chaine*).

[6]From Luther's "Preface to the Wittenberg Edition of Luther's German Writings," trans. Robert R. Heitner, in *Luther's Works* (Philadelphia: Fortress, 1960), 34: 285–88; slightly amended.

[7]Warfield, "Idea of Systematic Theology," 164–65; idem, *Studies in Theology*, 86–87.

[8]See J. I Packer, "John Calvin and the Inerrancy of Holy Scripture," in John D. Hannah, ed., *Inerrancy and the Church* (Chicago: Moody, 1984), 166–67; Ford Lewis Battles, "God Was Accommodating Himself to Human Capacity," *Interpretation* 31 (1977): 19–38.

[9]D. A. Carson and John D. Woodbridge, eds., *Scripture and Truth* (Grand Rapids: Zondervan, 1983), 91–92.

[10]Basil Mitchell states how this rule will work: "A word [in Scripture, and then in Christian theology] should be presumed to carry with it as many of the original entailments as the new context [i.e., the full biblical and theological context] allows, and this is determined by their compatibility with the other descriptions which there is reason to believe also apply to God. That God is incorporeal dictates that 'father' does not mean 'physical progenitor,' but the word continues to bear the connotation of tender protective care. Similarly God's 'wisdom' is qualified by the totality of other descriptions which are applicable to him; it does not, for example, have to be learned, since he is omniscient and eternal" (*The Justification of Religious Belief* [London: Macmillan, 1973], 19).

[11]See, on this, John Warwick Montgomery, "The Theologian's Craft," in *The Suicide of Christian Theology* (Minneapolis: Bethany, 1970), 267–313.

[12]See Peter Toon, *The Development of Doctrine in the Church* (Grand Rapids: Eerdmans, 1979), 70–73.

2

THE ROLE OF EXEGESIS IN SYSTEMATIC THEOLOGY

D. A. CARSON
TRINITY EVANGELICAL DIVINITY SCHOOL,
DEERFIELD, ILLINOIS

Among the many ingredients that go into making a good systematic theologian is the ability to keep a large number of intellectual balls in the air at the same time. The systematician is concerned about saying something true, insightful, and in proportion with respect to other elements of systematic theology. Some account must be taken of the long history of theological study, of other attempts to articulate the same subject matter, of the bearing of contemporary thought on both the content and the form of the subject, of the systematician's biases and blind spots, and, if the systematician holds a high view of Scripture, of whether or not what is said is in conformity with the Bible—or, better, accurately reflects the content and emphases of Scripture, but in contemporary garb.

THE PROBLEM

Unlike balls whirling through the air by the juggler's skill, the various ingredients that constitute systematic theology are not independent. Drop a ball and the other balls are unaffected; drop, say, historical theology and not only does the entire discipline of systematic theology change its shape, but the other ingredients are adversely affected. Without historical theology, for instance, exegesis is likely to degenerate into arcane, atomistic debates far too tightly tethered to the twentieth century. Can there be any responsible exegesis of Scripture that does not honestly wrestle with what earlier Christian exegesis has taught?

In the contemporary discussion about the nature of theology, there is more than one way to drop a "ball." It is as easily done by defining the ball out of existence as by simply dropping it and letting it go. For example, a theologian may simply "drop" historical theology—i.e., take as little account of it as possible; but a theologian may also define exegesis in such subjective terms that Scripture is never a canon, never more than *my* reading, which has as much and as little warrant as anyone else's reading. Historical theology has thereby been rendered entirely inconsequential to the interpretive task. Or systematic theology itself may be defined in such a way that its content is not in any sense constrained by Scripture. Scripture becomes a legitimate contributing element, but no more controlling than, say, the disciplines of historical and philosophical theology. And thus Scripture itself has been defined. It is not itself revelation; at best, it contains or hides a revelatory word.

A very high proportion of the unease in the discipline of systematic theology today is generated by the mutually contradictory definitions under which different systematicians operate. Attending meetings of the Society of Biblical Literature and the American Academy of Religion is a bit like showing up uninvited at Babel a few minutes after God's judgment has fallen: it is enormously stimulating to listen to scores and scores of small groups of people talking their own language but somewhat disconcerting to recognize that the project on which they are said to be engaged has largely ground to a halt.

This chapter makes no pretensions about reversing Babel. The aim is more modest: to work through in an introductory way just what exegesis ought to contribute to systematic theology and the extent to which exegesis itself ought to be shaped and constrained by systematic theology. I will be defining the most important terms as I go and interacting with some alternative proposals so as to lay bare some of the points of dispute lurking behind the conflicting definitions.

We begin, then, with *theology*, what Maurice Wiles calls "the elusive subject."[1] At its most rudimentary, it is disciplined discourse about God,[2] and thus is properly parasitic on religion, on the experience of God. This is not, as we will see, a catastrophic capsize in the seas of subjectivism, for even revelation is, from the human perspective, an experience of the

God who is not only "there" but who has also disclosed himself. But in a hypothetical world where everyone is an atheist, where no one ever experiences God, there could be no theology. Or, to put the matter positively, disciplined discourse about God, unless it is entirely negative, assumes that some people, at least, have come to know him in their experience, or to know something about him, or at least to know some people who claim to know him or to know something about him.

With so broad a definition, disciplined discourse about virtually any experience of the numinous can be labeled theology. By the same token, one can meaningfully speak of "Muslim theology" or "Roman Catholic theology" or "existentialist theology." Before attempting to define systematic theology, it is important to think through what might be meant by *Christian theology*. For many, Christian theology is theology (as broadly defined above) undertaken in the heritage of Christendom. Thus when Voelkel, building on the work of Wilhelm Herrmann, develops one form of existentialist theology, he sees himself as setting an agenda for the development of Christian theology within the university environment.[3] Such an approach, I think, is impossibly generous. It is not *Christian* theology unless it is disciplined discourse about the God who is central in the Christian religion—the God and Father of our Lord Jesus Christ, the God who is the transcendent Creator, the God who is personal, the God who speaks, the God who has revealed himself supremely in the person and work of Jesus of Nazareth.

Now I have not yet spoken of revelation, nor of the way Christians come to receive revelation as revelation. Indeed, a great deal of contemporary Christian theology, as defined so far, directs its "disciplined discussion" to these points. For instance, in a recent book Stephen Sykes surveys Schleiermacher, Newman, Harnack, Troeltsch, and Barth with respect to the interplay found in each of these theologians between "inwardness" (i.e., inward religious experience) and the external doctrines and ecclesiastical forms of religion.[4] He argues that the "essence of Christianity" is bound up with this tension. True enough. What he does not address, however, are *which* doctrines must be raised for consideration, and which must be dismissed as misguided or heretical. As Sykes has framed himself, Arius and Joseph Smith could both happily be admitted to the "essence of Christianity." In short, today a vastly disproportionate amount of Christian theology scurries in circles around the threshold of the discipline. It talks about the methods, tensions, hermeneutics, and shape of Christian theology, but it does not help Christians know what to believe, and why. Some simply deny that there is any stopping place: Christian theology can be done only "on the way"[5] through life, refusing to stop anywhere: not at negation, since that would lead to agnosticism, and not at the historical givenness of Christian revelation, since that would be to absolutize it and thus to divinize the past.

By now the problem of revelation has become acute. In the past, the "biblical theology" movement told us that revelation was in event, not in word. Others taught us that the word of God is not Scripture but operates through Scripture to make its own impact on the receptive soul. But for many, the rise of the new hermeneutic has so relativized even these minimalistic visions that many theologians either cease being *Christian* theologians, in the sense defined above, or else, aware that there must be some "givens" but nervous about articulating them, they focus endlessly on method, and thus compound the problem by catering to the pluralism of the age.

Thus there is a profound sense in which one of the purposes of Christian theology is to address the question, What should Christians believe? Even if the synthetic answers it produces can never attain the finality and authority of the revelation itself, it is exceedingly important that Christian theologians maintain this orientation. Christian theology must of course address questions dealing with what has traditionally been called prolegomena; but mature Christian theology refuses to devote all its attention to prolegomena, as if the theologian's responsibilities have been fully met when there has been endless talk about how to "do" Christian theology but nothing discussed outside the realm of prolegomena. One might as wisely make vast preparations for an enormous enterprise that does not exist.

Robust Christianity is uncomfortable with the vague assumption that there are givens out there somewhere, when those givens are so rarely expounded. In line with the central tradition of two millennia of Christian belief, it is important to believe and teach that God has revealed himself in events and people: he is not nearly as terrorized by the scandal of historical particularity as are many Christian thinkers, nor can he possibly be seduced by the suggestion that to hold this position is to divinize the past. In space-time history he himself has spoken through his own appointed prophets and ensured that his revelation would in due course be inscripturated so that the message of his redeeming love would be made known to the ends of the earth. Above all, he has revealed himself in the person of his Son, the unique revelation of the Father, the self-expression (λόγος) of God, Jesus of Nazareth. Jesus became flesh, a Jew who lived at a particular time and place. By his death he displayed ultimate obedience to his Father and achieved the defeat of death by bearing the penalty that would otherwise have justly fallen on his people. By his resurrection he demonstrated that he was not the God-condemned criminal many observers thought his crucifixion proved him to be. Far from it: his sacrifice was accepted by the Almighty, and he himself was exalted to the Father's right hand, whence he bequeathed his Spirit on his people as he had promised. Even now he rules, as the Father's sovereignty is mediated exclusively through him until the final enemy is destroyed. All this, and much more, is entrusted to his people in the Scriptures, which not only provide the human witness to the historical dimensions of this revelation, but also themselves constitute God-breathed revelation.

That, or something like it, stands at the heart of "mere Christianity." One could add a few more details, talk about the nature of the church, change the emphasis here and there, and still not lose the principal point: Christianity is a revealed religion. And that means that *Christian* disciplined discourse about God, Christian theology, must be discourse whose subject matter is finally and irrevocably constrained by that revelation.

Three points deserve clarification before the next step in definition can be profitably undertaken. First, although God has revealed something of himself by what has traditionally been called "general revelation"—that which is found in nature and in the conscience, however tattered, of each human being by virtue of having been made in God's image—and although that revelation has a real if limited role to play in making God known (Ps. 19; Rom. 1), its contribution to Christian theology is necessarily limited. Indeed, even what we think about the potential of general revelation is largely controlled by God's special revelation. Although it is entirely proper to speak of God's disclosing himself to us in the events and people of Scripture, and supremely in the person of his Son, in practice this forces us back to Scripture, the written revelation of God, for we have little or no access to the events and people apart from Scripture.

Second, every *Christian* theologian ought therefore frankly to delineate just where he or she perceives the locus of revelation to be. It is the malaise over that responsibility that has engendered so many discussions that skirt the principal substance. I cannot here assign space to defend my understanding of the matter, but the relation between exegesis and systematic theology cannot be explored without delineating what is to be "exegeted" (to coin a verb). I hold that the locus of God's special revelation is the Bible, the sixty-six cannonical books, reliable and truthful as originally given. Nor is this the upstart conservatism of a desperate reactionary: it is, overwhelmingly, the central tradition of two millennia of Christians.[6]

I am of course aware that this view receives short shrift in some quarters. Partly to ensure that my understanding of these issues is not obscurantist or glib, I have tried to read widely in these areas in recent years and to assist in articulating an adequate doctrine of Scripture for the end of the twentieth century—one that deals fairly with Scripture and addresses the concerns of the contemporary world of scholarship.[7] Whatever degree of success has been achieved, others must judge; it would be a relief, however, not to have to read more remarks like those that dismiss what is the central tradition of the entire church on this matter as "a false position which cannot be defended except by those impervious to reason."[8]

Third, the language was carefully chosen when I argued that Christian theology must be discourse "whose subject matter is finally and irrevocably constrained by that revelation." The language is flexible enough to allow that Christian theology may include more (but certainly not less) in its subject matter than the fundamental datum of Christian revelation, but tight enough to insist that whatever further data are introduced it is the Christian revelation that must utterly control the discourse. For example, if Christian theology chooses to talk about, say, sin or the Holy Spirit, then much of the actual substance of the discourse will emerge from the revelation. Extrabiblical concepts of sin or Spirit may be examined, and various models may serve as vehicles for contemporary expression, but the substance of the discourse will derive from the datum of Christian revelation (as I understand it, Scripture). If, however, Christian theology chooses to talk about, say the potential for ecological disaster in Puget Sound, or politics in Managua, the *control* must be with Scripture, even though the *substance* may largely derive from other sources. In other words, Christian theology properly addresses more than those subjects explicitly treated in Scripture, but where it does so it remains Christian theology only where the truths of Scripture have a bearing on the subject and remain uncompromised. Where the subject is virtually removed from Christian revelation, except in the most derivative sense (e.g., in discourse on quarks), the subject can no longer be said to be Christian theology. Conversely, where Christian revelation does have a bearing on the subject, perhaps major, but is shelved or diluted or compromised in favor of control from another discipline or authority, then at some point the discourse ceases to be Christian theology.

Biblical theology is an expression used in an extraordinarily wide variety of ways. In this chapter it is understood to be a subset of Christian theology, a subset bounded in two ways. First, its subject matter is exclusively biblical. At root, it is the result of the inductive study of the text of Scripture. Second, it organizes its subject matter in ways that preserve corpus distinctions. It is less interested in what the New Testament or the Bible says about, say, the sovereignty of God, than it is in what Paul (or Isaiah, or John) says about this subject. When such distinctions are observed, then biblical theology may be interested in probing common points or differences in perspective among the biblical corpora, but the distinctions themselves are never lost to view. This means, in turn, that biblical theology is organized chronologically, or, better, salvation-historically (another admittedly slippery term!)—both within any one corpus (e.g., What development is there in Paul?) and from corpus to corpus.

Systematic theology, then, is Christian theology whose internal structure is systematic; i.e., it is organized on atemporal principles of logic, order, and need, rather than on inductive study of discrete biblical corpora. Thus it can address the broader concerns of Christian theology (it is not merely inductive study of the Bible, though it must never lose such controls), but it seeks to be rigorously systematic and is therefore concerned about how various parts of God's gracious self-disclosure cohere.

Perhaps it needs to be made clear that by insisting that systematic theology is organized on "atemporal principles" I do not mean that any systematician can reasonably expect that his or her work will so transcend time and culture that it remains definitive at all times and places. There is a degree of subjectivism in all human reflection that must be faced (and which is discussed below). By saying that systematic theology is organized on "atemporal principles" I mean that the questions it poses are atemporal—not that the questioner occupies a spot outside time, but that the focal concerns are logical and hierarchical, not salvation-historical. Likewise the answers evoked by such questions are atemporal in their structure, not in any pretensions about the definitiveness or finality of their form.

Thus systematic theology asks and answers such questions as, What is God like? What does the Bible say about election? What are the necessary elements in a truly Christian marriage? How are the competing demands of justice and mercy to be worked out in the church of which I am a member? Who is acceptable to God? and so on.

Of course, any one of these questions may need breaking down into many component parts. Consider, for example, What does the Bible say about election? It will become necessary to ask what the various biblical corpora say on the subject and how these diverse emphases may be fitted together. But systematic theology will also want to know how election fits into the broader biblical framework of the sovereignty of God and what bearing it has on (or how it is shaped by) biblical teaching about personal and corporate accountability. At some point the systematician will want to learn something about how this subject has been handled throughout the history of the church, how the critical passages have been interpreted, and what the outcomes have been in every area of life, thought, evangelism, and godliness. And at each stage the systematician will want to check results against the meaning (I use the term advisedly) of Scripture.

That brings us to a definition of *exegesis*. It is the analysis of the final-form of a text, considered as an integral and self-referring literary object.[9] Several things flow from this definition. Exegesis is not source criticism or redaction criticism, though it may contribute to both. The text on which exegesis is performed is a *literary* object. This means that, so far as this definition is concerned, one may speak of the exegesis of a metaphor, but not of a nonliterary symbol; one may speak of the exegesis of an integral, written message, but not of a series of oral reports (unless and until they are reduced to writing).

That the text is self-referring does *not* mean that the text cannot refer outside itself (in that case there could be no exegesis of historical documents, i.e., documents that refer to real events in space-time history), nor does it deny that extratextual study may have some bearing on the analysis of the text (a point made clear in its simplest form when archaeological study or the examination of comparable texts sheds some light on the meaning of a word in one particular text). Rather, it means, at the least, that the text itself must exercise control as to its meaning. Exegesis is not the listing of possible parallels, however much light such parallels may shed on the text.[10]

More importantly, the definition is broad enough that it refuses to identify exegesis exclusively with one particular discipline. Second-year Greek students may think of exegesis in terms of parsing, word study, syntactical analysis, and the like, but in reality exegesis is never so limited. Responsible exegesis will certainly resort to linguistic analysis, both lexis (analysis of the vocabulary) and syntax (analysis of the way words are related to each other). But it will also analyze the text at the level of the clause, the level of the sentence, the level of the discourse, and the level of the genre. It will seek to be sensitive to idiom, literary technique, metaphor, and lines of argument. It will ask how truth is conveyed in the rich plethora of literary genres found in the Bible.[11] It will be aware that in each of these disciplines there are competing theories that must be taken into account. For instance, a grammatical approach will soon raise questions about what grammar is, not necessarily as an end in itself, but in order better to analyze the text. In one's grammatical analysis, is it best to rely on nineteenth-century categories, simply because they are well known? Does Chomskyan transformational grammar prove enlightening? Is the verbal system temporally based, or should aspect theory be applied?

In short, exegesis is open-ended. It is not the sort of thing about which one can say, "I have completed the task; there is no more to do." Of course, in one sense that is exactly what *can* be said if what is meant is that the exegete has come to the end of the text. The exegesis is complete, *at that level of analysis*, when the entire text has been analyzed. But exegesis itself is not a mechanical discipline with a few limited steps that, properly pursued, inevitably churn out the "right answer." On the other hand, progressively sophisticated levels of exegetical analysis may rapidly illustrate the law of diminishing returns!

Exegetes with this view are quite happy to speak of discerning the author's intent, provided it is presupposed that the author's intent is expressed in the text. Only in this way can the intentional fallacy be avoided. There is no other access to the author's intent than in the text. Even if we accept the view that the author's intended meaning is not *exactly* the same as the meaning of the text, it can be shown that in most instances the two are so closely related that little practical difficulty arises on this account. Nor does any difficulty arise from anonymous texts: readers infer the (unknown) author's intention from what he or she wrote; indeed, at a theoretical level coherence of a text is guaranteed only by the assumption of authorial intent.[12]

Biblical exegesis is exegesis of biblical texts. The question at issue in this chapter then, is how biblical exegesis is to be properly related to systematic theology. It is important to say at the outset that every Christian who thoughtfully asks a question such as "What is God like?" and then turns to the Bible for an answer is involved with this question. If the Christian is at all disciplined in his or her thinking, he or she is, to that extent, a systematician, a systematic theologian. The person of great erudition differs only in degree. And for both, the relationship between the exegesis of the biblical text and the formulation of systematic theology is more than a theoretical question best reserved for academics with nothing better to do and a fair bit of time on their hands. The question, in the end, is how we are to talk and think about God.

What remains in this chapter is to probe some of the contemporary questions that bear on the relationship between biblical exegesis and systematic theology.

EXEGESIS AND HERMENEUTICS

The subject of hermeneutics is currently in enormous ferment and creativity. At the risk of reductionism, it can be divided into two areas.

The first area has as its aim the explication of how to analyze a text, how, in fact, to do exegesis as it has just been defined. Older works adopt a fairly strict subject/object distinction: "I" the subject, the knower, learn the principles of how to read "it," the object, the text. One thinks, for example, of standard works like those of Terry[13] and of Ramm.[14] In such treatments the term *exegesis* is usually considerably narrower than its use in this chapter. It tends to refer to what I would call *grammatical* exegesis—i.e., that part of the exegetical task that turns on knowing the languages of the original text and handling them responsibly. *Hermeneutics* in that framework then addresses all the other perceived interpretive challenges. The books of that period still deserve to be read; indeed, a few from that tradition are still being written.[15]

Still within this tradition in that they largely preserve the subject/object distinction are many books that tell us how to "do" exegesis but whose focus is less on the meaning of "literal" or on how to handle typology than on source criticism, form criticism, tradition criticism, redaction criticism.[16] Recent developments in the same heritage have tried to plug several noticeable "holes," such as the urgent need to benefit from literary criticism[17] and to integrate findings from linguistics. Such books can be quite elementary and introductory;[18] others display considerable maturity.[19] From the perspective of the definition of "exegesis" developed here, these topics are not all of a piece. Literary criticism contributes directly to the "final-form analysis" of a text; source criticism does not. Indeed, one may view source criticism as prolegomenon to exegesis—though in practice one cannot do source criticism without exegesis, and (sometimes) vice versa. But the point we must observe here is that all of these hermeneutical considerations operate within the framework of the subject/object distinction already outlined.

Before leaving these kinds of books, I cannot too strongly emphasize that the tools they provide the student are extraordinarily important and are ignored to the interpreter's peril. True, there have been many competent theologians without a first-class command of Hebrew and Greek, *but all things being equal*, the interpreter or theologian with a solid grasp of the original languages will prove more enriching and precise than the colleague without it. Not every theologian has even a rudimentary understanding of the contribution of sociolinguistics to semantics, or of literary theory, or of relevant historical background, and so forth; *but all things being equal*, the person with these and other competencies enjoys decided advantages. Those with the highest view of Scripture will always have the highest incentive to develop all those tools that assist in the task of understanding what Scripture says.

Far more complex, though frequently quite speculative, are those "experimental" works that bring together a number of conferees to "read" set biblical texts. The aim is to bring different and, let us hope, complementary areas of competence to bear. One scholar will read the text—i.e., will attempt an exegesis of the text—on the basis of modern rhetorical theory; another will apply historical-critical methodology; still others will apply various social sciences (psychology, sociology, and the like).[20] These works stand at a crossover point: each exegete, consciously or unconsciously, is maintaining the subject/object distinction, but the very fact that the different perspectives that are being brought forward are bound up not with distinctions in the text but with differences in the various readers shows that the new hermeneutic has made its influence felt.

That brings us to the second major branch of hermeneutics, sometimes referred to, rather generically, as the "new hermeneutic." At bottom it is based on the destruction of the subject/object model, the "I/it" model. At its most extreme, it insists that each subject is so different in the total package of "pre-understandings," knowledge, biases, competence, and cultural values brought to the exegetical task, that each analysis of the text will be different from all others. Indeed, because human beings are in transition, my reading of the text today may be rather different from my reading of the text tomorrow. This makes the aim of the exegetical enterprise, not the discovery of the meaning of the text, but such interaction with the text that it makes an impact on me. A "language-event" takes place, generating not so much understanding of the text as self-understanding.[21] The further development of "deconstruction" need not detain us here. It is enough to observe that it goes beyond notions of meaning in the text and of competing individual meanings to analytical procedures that generate conflicting meanings within the text and thus destroy each other. It is a kind of hermeneutical nihilism.

This modern development affects not only biblical exegesis but virtually every field in which people are interested in analyzing texts. Literature, history, sociology, psychology, anthropology—all have felt the tremendous impact of the new hermeneutic.

What has not always been observed, however, is the way these two principal hermeneutical models, these ways of doing exegesis, both mirror and contribute to two quite different views of the relationship between biblical exegesis and systematic theology. The reason is not hard to find. On the one hand, those of extremely conservative framework tend to think of systematic theology as the synthesis of the results of all responsible and appropriate exegesis. In their view, exegesis is an entirely neutral discipline that discovers meaning in the text, or, more precisely, discovers the meaning of the text. Systematic theology then assembles the aggregate of these discovered meanings; biblical exegesis thus determines systematic theology. Among such conservatives, there is precious little place for historical theology, except to declare it right or wrong as measured against the system that has been developed out of one's own exegesis. Similarly, there is far too little recognition that the systematic theology one has adopted up to any particular point in the exegetical process exerts profound influence on the exegesis itself.[22] A person profoundly committed to, say, a pretribulational view of the rapture is unlikely to find anything but verification of this view in 1 Thessalonians 4:13–18, no matter how "objective" and "neutral" the exegetical procedures being deployed seem to be.[23] Not only can a hermeneutically alert opponent find reason to differ with the exegesis, but he or she can usually identify the questionable steps that have led to the circularity.

On the other hand, those who have been rather too greatly influenced by the new hermeneutic do not detect any straight line of control from biblical exegesis to systematic theology, but a legitimate (indeed, unavoidable) circularity. Reading the biblical texts spawns ideas, which are banged around with other ideas until they synthesize in systematic theology. At any point in exegetical practice, one's antecedent grasp of systematic theology is part of the "grid" that filters out what one does and does not "hear" in the text and what one does and does not allow to prove influential to one's thought, even if it is "heard." At some point the Bible becomes of marginal influence; it merely provides the linguistic pegs on which to hang a lot of systematic thinking about God, thinking whose essential shape derives from elsewhere. One cannot but be amazed that the biblical index to the German edition of Tillich's three-volume *Systematic Theology* requires a mere two pages.[24] In the same way, far too much of contemporary reader-response theory (variously called reception aesthetics or reception theory, from German *Rezeptionstheorie*),[25] is so tied to the autonomy of each individual modern reader, and so removed from the first readers and from any possibility of there being meaning *in the text*, that the subjectivism is staggering. We are not, after all, talking about various personal responses to a great novel in a discussion group of a literature class. We are talking about literature that is historically located, literature *designed* to be read by concrete individuals and groups, literature that frequently *refers* to events and people that can be located in the historical continuum—quite apart from its claim to be *revelatory* literature.

In the real world, however, neither hermeneutical extreme has any real prospect of prevailing. Indeed, it is possible to think of the new hermeneutic as, in part, an overreaction to the opposite error, the positivism that refuses to recognize how relative and culturally conditioned our opinions are. Today very few informed thinkers unhesitatingly adopt either extreme, at least not without some caveat. At one end of the spectrum, if a conservative scholar such as Larkin insists that there is objective meaning in the text and that this meaning can be discovered, he will also make frequent allowances for the cultural bias that must be recognized and handled at every stage of the interpretive process.[26] But at the other end, most recognize that if the new hermeneutic is pushed to its logical extreme, the outcome is solipsism. No one will be able to commune with anyone—not even the proponents of the new hermeneutic who expect the rest of us to read and understand their books. Since that view is so manifestly ridiculous, even some deconstructionists are backing away from it. LaFargue, for instance, may still hesitate to speak of a determinate "meaning" to a text, but he is happy to talk of a determinate "substantive content" and to insist it is knowable.[27] Sophisticated discussions of the new hermeneutic are available, discussions that integrate the best of its insights while attempting to create models to show how it is possible for objective content to pass from the "horizon of understanding" of one person to the "horizon of understanding" of another, or from the "horizon of understanding" of a text to the "horizon of understanding" of the exegete.[28] Instead of a "hermeneutical circle," there is a hermeneutical "spiral" that enables the careful interpreter to hone in progressively on what is actually there. This may involve hard work, thoughtful "self-distancing" from one's own biases and predilections, courageous attempts to understand the other's terminology and points of view and idioms and values. Exhaustive understanding of another is doubtless impossible for all save the Omniscience, but that does not mean all real and substantial understanding is impossible.

In much the same way, few today would see the traffic

between biblical exegesis and systematic theology as a one-way system. Indeed, long before the new hermeneutic arrived on the scene, systematicians with a high view of Scripture debated the proper place of the *analogia fidei* (the "analogy of the faith") in the interpretive process. Passages that could, at the merely grammatical level, yield two or three mutally contradictory meanings, would be interpreted according to the "analogy of the faith"—i.e., they would be interpreted in line with the structure of Christian systematic theology ("the faith") developed on the basis of (what was judged to be) the clear and certain teaching of Scripture elsewhere. There are many potential difficulties with this sort of appeal,[29] most of which can be handled responsibly; but the point at this juncture is that an element of circularity in the theological task has always been recognized.

Of course, someone might argue that the very idea of "the faith" is hermeneutically primitive. "The faith" is always the faith of an individual or group. It is "the faith" of the ecumenical creeds, or of historic Protestantism, or of Tridentine Catholicism, or of the Anabaptists. Recognition of this point has helped to foster "Asian theology," "feminist theology," sub-Saharan black "African theology," and so forth. Nor is it that these are all "adjective-theologies," while what I do is just theology: it is immediately pointed out that what I do is white, male, North Atlantic, Protestant, and evangelical theology. And this reasoning has substantially contributed to the push for "contextualization," for properly contextualized theology.

Once again both the truth and the confusion that lie behind this train of argument largely turn on definition and on prior givens. At the risk of reductionism, we may say that two quite different approaches use the same terminology. If by, say, feminist theology one refers to a self-conscious attempt to overcome demonstrable biases in earlier male-dominated theology, so that what Scripture actually says becomes clearer than it has been, and if by, say, African theology one refers to the kind of theological emphases that arise when an informed African studies the Scripture (e.g., he or she will almost certainly see more family and corporate emphases than would be discerned by the Western counterpart steeped in rugged individualism), then the benefits from these adjective-theologies (including my own) are considerable, and the church as a whole should be enriched. Systematicians with comparable training but from highly diverse backgrounds can come together and check one another *against the standard of the Scripture that all sides agree is authoritative.* Protestations notwithstanding,[30] such communication, though certainly not easy, is possible and productive.[31] But if by, say, feminist theology one refers to a structure of theological thought whose essential shape is determined or controlled not by Scripture but by the agenda of some form of modern feminism, prompting feminist theologians to read Scripture in such a way that hermeneutically inappropriate questions are addressed to the text, while the answers provided by the text are heeded only selectively; or if African theology has so focused on family solidarity that suddenly ancestor worship and traditional animism are both consecrated by an ostensible appeal to Scripture, while Scripture itself sanctions neither and condemns both, then the complexities of the new hermeneutic are being deployed not to foster better understanding but to undermine the possibility of unique, normative revelation.

When various exegeses ("readings") of Scripture are proposed, the most probing question, then, is always this: What authority status does the Scripture have for the exegete concerned? It is exceedingly important that this question not be permitted to impede reflection on the enormously complex hermeneutical questions. It is equally important to recognize that fruitful reflection on individual texts in Scripture can be undertaken by those who do not believe them to be authoritative. But if we are attempting a theoretical construction of the relation between biblical exegesis and systematic theology, the status of Scripture must be central to the debate. To word the problem more generically, no systematician has the luxury to avoid identifying what elements may and what elements may not be admitted into one's dogmatics and specifying the grounds for these choices. When the Hanson brothers, for instance, tell us that for them the Bible is a witness to the activity and character of God, a witness of greatly varying worth,[32] they set out with some care what they judge to be a "reasonable" faith. Whether what is reasonable to them will be perceived as reasonable by others cannot be probed here. I cannot altogether escape the feeling that what they do not like they find reasons to dismiss, sometimes caustically, and what they like they find reasons to approve. But what is immediately clear is that the relation between biblical exegesis and systematic theology is in their case fundamentally different from that which obtains where the Scripture is viewed as authoritative.

If it is true that both the systematician who espouses a high view of Scripture and the systematician who denies such a view alike insist that the traffic between biblical exegesis and systematic theology is not one-way, it is important to see that the hermeneutical dangers each confronts are rather different. The former is in danger of minimizing the complexity of the hermeneutical task and of illicitly transferring the authority of the text to the interpretation of the text. The latter is in danger of being ensnared by the shifting sands of the present age. While warning everyone of the hermeneutical myopia of previous generations, such an exegete (and systematician) is unlikely to notice the almost unparalleled contemporary pressures toward relativism and pluralism so profoundly antithetical to the revelation of Scripture—or worse, he or she will notice them and delight in them at the expense of the exclusive claims of God himself in his gracious self-disclosure. Nominally they will admit that solipsism is not a responsible position; practically, the pressures administered by the great god Pluralism will strengthen whatever bias the new hermeneutic has toward subjectivism until all too few will be able to declare the immutables, the nonnegotiables, in the Christian revelation. They will constantly remain uncomfortable with the unyielding disjunctives of Scripture. If it is the duty of the Christian theologian in every age to identify the contemporary manifestation of the Antichrist (cf. 1 John 2:18), i.e., to expose the pretensions of every power that opposes Christ or seeks to usurp his place, these theologians will likely fail in their duty.[33]

Sometimes the more conservative exegete is daunted by the criticism of less conservative colleagues who argue that conservative exegesis is boring. It never thinks up fresh questions and therefore never hears fresh answers. It spends its time responding, rather late, to agendas generated in other parts of the theological spectrum. There are two grains of truth in the charge. The first is that some conservative exegetes, right or wrong in their exegesis, *are* boring—though in my experience that trait is not the sole prerogative of conservatives. The second is that, owing precisely to their allegiance to the authority of Scripture, they are less likely than others to think of reconstructions and interpretations that question that authority. To engage in the mainstream of contemporary debate, they must of course respond to such developments, but they are unlikely to initiate them. Yet it is the new hermeneutic that should reassure them. If it is true that they are unlikely to think up the sorts of questions that generate scholarly excitement (however ephemeral that excitement turns out to be), it is equally true that their more liberal colleagues are unlikely to ask questions that only the interpreter who is committed to the authority of the text is likely to put forward. In other words, provided it is remembered that the line of authority/control must run from the text to the systematic construction, the systematic construction can be an ennobling, fertilizing, enriching element in the exegetical process. The Christian who is convinced that God's revelation coheres, even though we may not have enough of the parts to show how it coheres in every instance, is in a position to see analogies, conceptual similarities, theological links, and organic ties where others are still trying to plot out a debatable trajectory of a hypothetical community. This means that the evangelical exegete and theologian, however much he or she must engage in passing debates, must not devote all mental energy to what is faddish, but must accept the responsibility to ask and answer questions that only those with a high view of Scripture are likely to generate. The resulting theology will not only be creative but also, granted that it is competently done and gracefully articulated, is likely to endure much longer than its competitors.

EXEGESIS AND HISTORICAL THEOLOGY

The contribution of historical theology is weighed elsewhere in this volume and must not unduly detain us here. But because biblical exegesis, historical theology, and systematic theology have a bearing *on each other*, the relevance of historical theology to the way that exegesis contributes to dogmatics must be introduced.

It is possible to think of historical theology as the written record of exegetical and theological opinions in periods earlier than our own, a kind of historical parallel to the diversity of exegetical and theological opinions that are actually current. So construed, historical theology serves exegesis—and thus systematic theology—in several ways. First, it opens up options and configurations that the contemporary exegete might not have thought of, and similarly it may quickly close down what might otherwise appear to be avenues for profitable exploration. It is not only in technology that there is little point in constantly reinventing the wheel. Second, properly studied, historical theology demands that we recognize how many exegetical and theological opinions are powerfully shaped, indeed sometimes determined, by the larger matrix of thought in their own day. Negatively, these become cautionary tales that warn us against forms of Christian thought too captive to passing concepts; positively, they may help us think through how best to articulate the Gospel afresh to our own generation. Third, historical theology often displays remarkable uniformity of belief across quite different paradigms of understanding,[34] even if such uniform beliefs are cast in very dissimilar molds. Thus historical theology may contribute to (though not utterly determine) the *boundaries* of systematic theology, which in turn, as we have seen, contribute to one's exegesis.

In fact, the lines of influence are more tangled. At the level of interpretation, historical theology can no more be said to be a neutral and independent discipline than can exegesis. Both are bound up with the reading, the interpretation, of texts. As it is possible, wittingly or unwittingly, to domesticate Scripture by superficial and culture-bound interpretations whose entire agenda is determined by extrabiblical considerations, so it is possible to read the texts of historical theology with a mind less committed to understanding them on their own terms than to fitting them into some pattern or thesis constructed on other grounds. Thus it is not simply the *fruits* of historical theology that have a bearing on exegesis (insofar as historical theology records earlier readings of the biblical texts) and on systematic theology (insofar as historical theology records attempts at synthesizing interpretation of biblical materials into structures whose coherence is atemporal), but *the discipline itself* provides countless analogies to the work of biblical exegesis and of systematic theology. To put the matter another way, there is no historical theology without the exegesis of historical texts.

In the same way, the "threefold cord" (Scripture, reason, and tradition) so important to Anglican life and thought is beginning to undergo a metamorphosis. Richard Hooker is usually taken as the fountainhead of this approach (although almost certainly he is building on earlier work):

> What Scripture doth plainly deliver, to that the first place both of credit and obedience is due; the next whereunto, is what any man can necessarily conclude by force of Reason; after these, the voice of the Church succeedeth.[35]

Undoubtedly the balance of this threefold cord has been handled in highly diverse ways. But in a thoughtful treatment, Bauckham suggests replacing it by Scripture, tradition, and context (i.e., the context of the interpreter or the interpreting community),[36] where "context" is used "in the broadest sense of every aspect of a society in which the church exists"[37]— much as others speak of "culture." In the light of recent developments on the new hermeneutic and on contextualization, it is easy to see what he is after. What is hard to understand is why he does not go farther and reduce the threefold cord to two: Scripture and context. For tradition itself, once the church escaped the first generations in which oral tradition doubtless enjoyed a status that was sometimes quite independent of Scripture, is nothing other than the accumulated interpretations of, applications from, and reflections on Scripture, whether on Scripture directly or derivatively (e.g., third- and fourth-order deductions might have only the most tenuous connection with Scripture).

All this suggests that the line of *thought* from biblical exegesis to systematic theology is neither straight nor simple, even though the line of *authority*, once the exegete is responsibly satisfied that the meaning of the text has largely if not exhaustively been perceived, must extend in only one direction. And a person who possesses such responsible satisfaction is less likely to be self-deluded in proportion as he or she becomes familiar with the heritage of historical theology.

EXEGESIS AND BIBLICAL THEOLOGY

Biblical theology, because it is bound up with the reading of texts, is as irrevocably tied to hermeneutical complexities as are biblical exegesis and historical theology. There is little point in rehearsing those complexities again and showing how they work out with respect to this discipline. But following the definition of biblical theology advanced in the first section of this chapter, its peculiar emphasis on the individual document or the discrete corpus as the boundary for analysis generates several complex problems that have a bearing on the relation between exegesis and systematic theology. Three may be mentioned:

1. There is little agreement as to how to delineate the biblical corpora. How many epistles constitute "the Pauline corpus"? Should we think of the Pentateuch or the Hexateuch?

Was the Apocalypse written by the same John as the one whose name has traditionally been attached to the Fourth Gospel and to the Johannine Epistles?

Although disagreements among biblical scholars over such matters might well shut down the entire discipline of biblical theology or, rather, ensure that biblical theology would be practiced in separate enclaves shaped by agreement on these critical matters, in practice there is less disagreement occasioned by such matters than is sometimes supposed. Thus the large number of "New Testament theologies" and the several "Old Testament theologies" by and large break down their respective corpora more or less the same way: the differences between, say, Vriezen and Von Rad on Old Testament theology, or between Bultmann and Stauffer or Ladd on New Testament theology, have far less to do with the division of the corpora than with fundamental approaches to the Bible— including the reconstructions of historical development with which the various theologians are operating. The chief reason for this show of agreement is that even where there is a deep division of opinion as to where one corpus ends and another begins *from the perspective of the author*, there are usually agreed historical reasons for grouping them together in something like the traditional configuration. For instance, those who think the author of the Fourth Gospel is someone other than the author of the Johannine Epistles are usually quick to concede that there are notable similarities between the Gospel of John and the Epistles of John and may hypothesize that all of these documents emerged from the same community or school, even if from different authors. On the other hand, even very conservative critics who hold that there was one John who wrote not only the Gospel and the Epistles associated with his name, but also the Apocalypse, are usually quick to point out that there is such a large difference in genre between the Apocalypse and, say, 1 John that they are best treated separately.[38] Thus, corpus distinctions turn on more criteria than mere authorship. If the boundaries are disputed, there is usually sufficient agreement at some other level, perhaps thematic, to ensure that at points where scholars do not agree they are not simply talking past one another.

2. Far more troubling is the widespread view that the differences among the biblical corpora are not differences in emphasis, vocabulary, focus, perspective, development, pastoral situation, and the like, but mutually incompatible differ-

ences in theological structure. In an influential book, Dunn, for instance, has argued that the only Christological cohesion in the New Testament is the common conviction that the resurrected Lord is none other than the historical Jesus.[39] Beyond this point, New Testament Christologies prove to be mutually incompatible. Therefore the most that the New Testament canon can provide is a boundary of acceptable (if mutually exclusive) Christologies—a boundary within which the modern Christian is free to pick and choose.

As I have elsewhere discussed Dunn's book and the problem it represents,[40] it would be invidious to go over the same ground again here. Among the more troubling features of his treatment, however, are two: (1) He repeatedly deploys disjunctive modes of thought and rarely wrestles with the possibility that divergent emphases may reflect profound complementarity. (2) After so strongly insisting on the mutual incompatibility of the New Testament Christological strands, he nevertheless insists that modern readers should feel free to pick and choose among them. This is, quite frankly, astonishing. It reflects how far much contemporary biblical scholarship feels free to explore the discrete biblical corpora (however disjunctive) at the level of mere description, *without asking any thoughtful questions about the truthfulness of the material!* For surely it is axiomatic that if the New Testament Christological descriptions are mutually incompatible, they cannot all be truthful; perhaps none is. Even so, Dunn assures us we are justified in picking and choosing from among (what he perceives to be) the New Testament options. He thinks he thereby sanctions each believer to create his or her own "canon within the canon"; he has failed to see that his own logic requires that he conclude there can be no canon, none at all.

In practice, however sophisticated the attempt may be, the pursuit of a "canon within the canon" despoliates the possibility of biblical exegesis having any controlling voice in the construction of systematic theology. One could wish that Barrett were right not only when he asserts that "canonical texts are used to establish doctrine and the dogmatician requires a canon defined as precisely as possible" but also when he adds that a dogmatician "is likely to be impatient with a hazy canon within a canon which each man defines for himself."[41] The fact of the matter is that when Dunn and Mackey set out to present a test case for the proper relation between New Testament theology and dogmatics,[42] it is not long before they conclude that the evidence that Jesus was born in Bethlehem is too slight to be relied on, that John 14:6 is a credal confession *about* Jesus rather than a claim made *by* Jesus, and that in any case it is not as exclusive as it appears, and that "internecine warfare" between orthodoxy and heterodoxy is to be abominated (contrast Paul, Gal. 1:8–9). When Humphreys writes on the atonement,[43] he soon tells us that notions of sacrifice and penal substitution are utterly alien to us and must be abandoned in favor of new models that moderns can comprehend—even though the metamorphosis does not preserve biblical emphases, and Humphreys himself does not thoughtfully engage with the substance of modern treatments that articulate to the twentieth-century reader the very truths he denies.[44]

All of us, of course, gravitate toward a "canon within the canon," in the sense that at any given time we may feel that the truths of some particular corpus or surrounding some particular theme are especially precious to us or to the Christian community to which we belong. The difficulty arises when this focus becomes a grid that screens out other biblical truth. Genuine Christianity, however biased, culture-bound, faulty, or weak it may be in any specific expression, must embrace some kind of commitment that desires to be "re-formed" by Scripture whenever such reductionism is pointed out. Otherwise, not only Scripture, but Jesus himself, soon becomes domesticated, devoid of a cutting edge that has the potential for reshaping us. We fall into the danger of bouncing the current shibboleths off the Bible and trumpeting them to the world as if they were prophecies, when in fact we have merely christened the current climate of opinion with biblical jargon. I am quite sure that all of us fall into this trap sometimes; I am equally sure that genuine Christian commitment requires that we all attempt to correct ourselves when our own particular failings in this respect begin to surface. This is important not only so that our biblical exegesis may retain its integrity but also so that our systematic theology may retain its proportion. For it has been shown repeatedly that Christian theology is so intertwined that no Christian doctrine can be "abandoned, or subject to radical re-interpretation, without implications for other aspects of the Christian faith. That is part of the problem with the piecemeal approach to the revision of Christian doctrine with which much of the Christian church has been occupied for too long."[45] This is most definitely *not* a surreptitious defense of the status quo, but a frank recognition of the fact that biblical exegesis, generating biblical theology, has immensely serious consequences for systematic theology, some of them quite unforeseen.

The degree of confusion over the way biblical theology is to be done has generated numerous proposals about the way forward. Stendahl, for instance, wants biblical theology to be a purely historical and descriptive discipline, without any normative status whatsoever until we proceed to the level of considering the *application* of our findings.[46] In theory, at least, that would facilitate discussion; in practice, it tends to degenerate into a stream of technical articles and books on the theology of Q and other putative sources. Partly because of the impasse, various forms of "canonical theology" have come to the fore. Best known is the work of Brevard Childs.[47] So widely influential is this approach that fundamental shifts in definition are beginning to take place. Scalise, for instance, suggests redefining *sensus literalis* to mean authoritative teaching of "canonical" Scripture as that teaching develops in the dialectic between Scripture and communities of faith.[48]

But unless I have misunderstood it, at the heart of most forms of canonical theology lies an epistemological problem still largely unaddressed. In the hands of most practitioners, the move from biblical exegesis to biblical theology is a largely arbitrary affair. The "exegesis" tends to proceed along modern critical, historicist lines. The alleged sources are sorted out, considerable skepticism about a variety of ostensible historical claims is administered, ill-controlled conjectures regarding the *Sitz im Leben* of the community are pondered, various interpretive options are weighed. And then, precisely because the new hermeneutic in its more extreme forms is very close to insisting that no interpretation has more intrinsic value than any other (since on this model meaning resides in the interpreter and not in the text), canon criticism decides, somewhat fideistically, that the interpretations of the text *within* the biblical canon should be adopted as the guide to the church's life and thought. Laudably, the result is at many points a biblical theology that is not only insightful but congruent with much of historic Christianity; but the method of arriving at this point seems to be less constrained by the view that this is what the Bible says, that it is true and can be responsibly defended at the exegetical level, than that this is what the Bible says, and the church has traditionally shaped its theology by the canon, and we should do the same, even though our historically informed exegesis cannot in all conscience support the theological interpretations of earlier canonical material provided by later canonical texts. In short, this appears to be a more sophisticated version of the "two storey" spirituality endemic to the more radical strands of Continental biblical scholarship, where "faith" is allegedly made safer by self-consciously distancing all of its objects from any possibility of historical criticism (which was, of course, one of Rudolf Bultmann's primary aims).[49] The resulting "spirituality" is frequently warm, fervent, sincere; it is also epistemologically bankrupt.

To his credit, Morgan understands the problem, but his solution simply returns us to the morass.[50] He rightly wants to begin with the witness of the biblical writers themselves; in this regard he is somewhat parallel to the proponents of canon criticism. But he then proposes that careful distinctions be made between "the good historical information which is true" (by which he means the nexus of historical data and critical judgments that enable the historian to discount certain parts of what the biblical writers say) and "the highly speculative reconstructions of modern historians, which can make no such high claims to truth or knowledge."[51] The latter, he avers, are both legitimate and necessary to historical research but get in the way of constructing biblical theology. His approach, in other words, is to build all the "good historical material into modern Christology and critical interpretations of the evangelists. The conflict is thus no longer between faith and reason but between a reasonable faith and a faithless reason."[52] But as reasonable (and faithful) as this sounds, what it must produce are discrete cadres of New Testament scholars who are largely in agreement about what they feel are the historical-critical fruits strong enough to stand in judgment of the documents, and the historical-critical fruits that must be held in abeyance as unduly speculative. At the level of merely technical scholarship, these cadres of scholars will deploy their training to defend their version of this distinction. But the enormous diversity of opinion as to where the line should actually be drawn will be shaped by the fact that the cadres themselves run the gamut from the most conservative to the most skeptical. In short, Morgan has returned us, by another route, to a canon within the canon.

Of course, these reflections do not themselves constitute a compelling reason for advocating the tighter nexus between exegesis and biblical theology advanced here. At the end of the day, the cogency of such a position turns in large part on one's view of Scripture. But if I am to build a rationale for a particular view of the relationship between biblical exegesis and systematic theology, then the components in that relationship (here, the relationship between exegesis and biblical theology) must be defended against competing models, which have to be assessed in their own light. The widespread disarray in the field is so patent that it would be healthy to return to the fundamental questions, which have to do with *the nature and loci of revelation*: Has God disclosed himself, or not? If so, where, and by what means? Without substantive agreement on such topics, the pursuit of *methods* commonly agreed on will prove largely chimerical.

If we are rightly to assess the contribution of modern historical reconstructions, the advice of Joseph Cardinal Ratzinger will prove salutary:

> What we need now are not new hypotheses on the *Sitz im Leben*, on possible sources or on the subsequent process of handing down the material. What we *do* need is a critical look at the exegetical landscape we now have, so that we may return to the text and distinguish between those hypotheses which are helpful [*sc.* to understanding it] and those which are not. Only under these conditions can a new and fruitful collaboration between exegesis and systematic theology begin. And only in this way will exegesis be of real help in understanding the Bible.[53]

3. The definition of biblical theology given in the first section of this chapter turns on the presentation of the biblical material in a structure that preserves its historical development, its organic growth, not *merely* its corpus distinctions. Better put, granted that the Bible itself is special revelation, its corpus distinctions themselves attest the history of redemption, the progress of salvation history. Evangelical thinkers have long said the same thing:

> Biblical theology occupies a position between Exegesis and Systematic Theology in the encyclopaedia of theological disciplines. It differs from Systematic Theology not in being more Biblical, or adhering more closely to the truths of the Scriptures, but in that its principle of organizing the Biblical material is historical rather than logical. . . .Biblical theology is that branch of Exegetical Theology which deals with the process of the self-revelation of God deposited in the Bible.[54]

It is "nothing else than *the exhibition of the organic progress of supernatural revelation in its historic continuity and multiformity.*"[55] The significance of the discipline of biblical theology for the relation between exegesis and systematic theology is perhaps most strikingly seen when cast negatively. Biblical theology does not allow the systematician to forget that the Incarnation did not take place immediately after the Fall; that the Cross has massive antecedents in the sacrificial system and the Passover rites associated with the Mosaic covenant; that the "new" covenant presupposes an "old" covenant; that the dawning of the kingdom is modeled on and anticipated by the outworking of the theme of theocracy; that Melchizedek appears in Genesis 14 and Psalm 110, and must be understood in those chapters, before he appears in Hebrews 5 and 7; and much more. Biblical theology forces the theologian to remember that there is before and after, prophecy and fulfillment, type and antitype, development, organic growth, downpayment and consummation.

If a systematician wants to know, say, what is meant by the "call" or the "calling" of God, in order to apply it to Christian experience today, it is inadequate merely to perform a word study on the relevant verbs and their cognates and to systematize the results. It is not simply that the call of God has different emphases in the different corpora: in the Synoptics, for instance, God's call is akin to invitation ("Many are *called*, but few are chosen" [Matt. 22:14 RSV]), while in Paul it is customarily effective ("those he called, he also justified" [Rom. 8:30]). Such distinctions could be discerned even if the biblical corpora were discrete but linked with each other by merely logical or thematic, as opposed to chronological or sequential or historical, connections. The semantic differences in the use of terms must of course be observed. But it will also be necessary to think through the call of Abraham, the call of Israel, the call of God's suffering servant, the call of the church, and to sort out how they are linked thematically, in inner-biblical connections across the progress of redemption. Only then can the careful systematician presume to venture what "the call of God" means in the Scripture, and because he or she is a systematician, as opposed to a biblical theologian, the structuring of the presentation will inevitably be logical, primarily atemporal, and with appropriate reflection as to what it means for us today. Even so, this presentation will be informed by the underlying biblical theology, and the systematician may find it necessary to make reference to the historical and sequential distinctions—in short, to the progress of the history of redemption—as part of the systematizing of the material. Indeed, this salvation-historical sensitivity is nowhere better reflected than in the argument of Paul in Galatians 3 and Romans 4 and in the Epistle to the Hebrews. In the former, Paul is combatting those who interpret Torah as the controlling hermeneutical principle in the understanding of what we call the Old Testament: if Abraham was a good man, they argued, then of course he obeyed Torah—even though Torah was not given until centuries later. They simply assumed that he must have enjoyed some private revelation regarding its contents. But if the Pentateuch is read with salvation-historical finesse, then Torah, as pivotal as it is, no longer assumes the same controlling importance. In short, from a hermeneutical point of view, part of the difference between the early Christian church and the Judaism from which it sprang was over whether the Hebrew Bible was to be read atemporally or salvation-historically—or, to use the categories developed here, whether or not biblical theology was to be permitted to intrude between raw exegesis and systematic theology.

To put it another way, biblical theology, as defined in this chapter, mediates the influence of biblical exegesis on systematic theology. Within the limits already set forth, just as systematic theology partially constrains and ideally enriches exegesis, so also does it serve biblical theology. More importantly, biblical theology more immediately constrains and enriches exegesis than systematic theology can do.

EXEGESIS, SYSTEMATIC THEOLOGY, AND SPIRITUAL EXPERIENCE

The question may be put as to whether the exegete's personal spiritual experience can or does exercise decisive influence on the practice of exegesis and whether the systematician's personal spiritual experience can or does exercise decisive influence on the construction of systematic theology. The question cannot be avoided in this chapter, because what we mean by "biblical exegesis," by the way we read the Bible, is so largely shaped by the answer we give to it.

Under the positivism of the older hermeneutic, it was possible to answer with a firm negative. Exegesis was viewed as neutral, "scientific," objective. The new hermeneutic demands that we respond in a more nuanced way. A frankly atheistic approach to the Bible, for instance, is certainly going to yield a different assessment as to what the Bible is actually talking about than one that is predicated on the existence of a personal/transcendent God who has supremely revealed himself in Christ Jesus. Indeed, the prevalence of frankly atheistic interpretations in the guild of biblical scholars has in recent years generated some mild protests.[56]

In both theory and practice, it is possible for an atheist so to distance her own atheism from her exegesis that she can at least describe what is actually there in the text with some accuracy— in some instances (it must be admitted) with more accuracy than the believer deploys who is swamped with warm, mystical feelings but little exegetical rigor. After all, I have earlier argued that the hermeneutical circle looks more like a spiral, that we are not shut up to solipsism; and if we have argued in this way so as to affirm that the discovery of the meaning of the text of Scripture is possible, we must argue the same way when focusing less on the text than on the people who are studying it. Even so, there may be compelling reasons for thinking that some readers of the text will have a harder job discovering its meaning than others, on the ground that their horizon of understanding is so far removed from those of the biblical authors that the task of "distanciation" (the process of self-consciously recognizing one's biases and "distancing" oneself from them in order to hear the text on its own terms) becomes dangerously great. It appears, then, that the nature of the hermeneutical barriers the unbeliever must confront, from the perspective of a confessing Christian, can usefully be spelled out:

1. The sheer numbers of scholars who share the same popular beliefs, or unbelief, conspire to tilt academic societies, university posts, and peer approval along foreordained lines. Just as it may take a modicum of courage to break away from a fundamentalist heritage, it takes no less courage, indeed, much more, to break away from the juggernaut of an approach to scriptural exegesis that is fundamentally uncommitted.

2. If the Bible is nothing less than God's gracious self-disclosure, then as important as it is to understand it on its own terms it must surely be no less important to respond to God as he has disclosed himself. Can the exegesis that is formally "correct" on this or that point but is not cast in terms of adoration, faith, obedience be at heart sound? I do not mean that scholars must wear their faith on their sleeves or parade

their piety each time they take up their pen. On all kinds of technical and disputed points the most dispassionate weighing of evidence is necessary. But is such work cast in the matrix of a scholarship devoted in thought (and therefore in form) to serve the God whose revelation is being studied? To put the matter rather crudely, is there not an important responsibility to ask, each time I put pen to paper, whether what I write pleases the God of Scripture, the God of all truth, rather than worry about how my academic colleagues will react? Is exegesis perennially devoid of such flavor genuinely *faithful* exegesis? Now if such exegetical work is possible, it will flow out of lives that have *experienced* God, that have been struck with the awesomeness of his holiness, melted with the depth of his love, moved by the condescension of his compassion, thrilled by the prospect of knowing him better.

This, after all, is no more than what one should expect. The psalmist can write, "Whom have I in heaven but you? And being with you, I desire nothing on earth. My flesh and my heart may fail, but God is the strength of my heart and my portion forever" (Ps. 73:25–26). Paul has only to refer to Jesus the Son of God, and he spontaneously adds, "who loved me and gave himself for me" (Gal. 2:20). When a contrast is drawn between getting "drunk on wine, which leads to debauchery," and being "filled with the Spirit" (Eph. 5:18), the assumption is that the Spirit, like wine, generates a "high"—but without the debauchery, the loss of control, the enslavement, the sin associated with the "high" gained from wine. The kingdom of God, which generates endless monographs, is a matter of "righteousness, peace, and joy in the Holy Spirit" (Rom. 4:17). When Peter tells believers that they "have tasted that the Lord is good" (1 Peter 2:3), he means more than that they have found Christianity to be intellectually stimulating and satisfying; he is closer to meaning that they "believe in him and are filled with an inexpressible and glorious joy" (1:8).

The question is, Can responsible systematic theology, *even when it is formally congruent with Scripture*, entirely lose the taste of what is nothing more than the overflow of life in the Spirit? Can responsible biblical exegesis, *even when it rightly unpacks the "meaning" of the text*, entirely lose the flavor of the text? Is "meaning" to be utterly stripped of commitment and devotion, the very stuff of an appropriate response to the God of the Bible? And do not such matters turn, at least in part, on the depth of one's spiritual experience, on personal identification with what some have called "the spirituality of the Word"?

3. Systematic theology, as we have seen, is concerned to put together in coherent form the results of rigorous exegesis of the biblical texts. But this "putting together" is never simply additive. The systematician is constantly making choices as to what is central, what is the organizing principle of some discussion, what links are proper or improper—and, ideally, how to cast all of this in modern guise without losing the objective meaning that is there in the text. In addition to all the dangers of subjectivity to which the exegete must give heed, the systematician opens up boundless new possibilities of serious distortion, owing to the hierarchical choices that attend the discipline. These are not simply intellectual dangers; they may be grounded in spiritual experience (or lack of it) or in moral defection. The systematician who has on several occasions engaged in sexual infidelity is likely to configure the biblical material that treats marriage and divorce a little differently from the monogamous believer whose analysis of trends in the nation's homes is profoundly pessimistic. The systematician who is inordinately proud of honors earned and books written will configure the biblical material a little differently from the systematician who, like the sinful woman who washed Jesus' feet with her tears, is overwhelmed by a sense of sinfulness and of the Savior's forgiveness. At what point do such differences fall under the startling analysis preserved in John 3: 19–21? "This is the verdict: Light has come into the world, but men loved darkness instead of light because their deeds were evil. Everyone who does evil hates the light, and will not come into the light for fear that his deeds will be exposed. But whoever lives by the truth comes into the light, so that it may be seen plainly that what he has done has been done through God."

When it is remembered that one's systematic theology (whether it is called that or not) exerts strong influence on one's exegesis, it becomes clear that spiritual, moral experience may not only shape one's systematic theology but may largely constrain what one actually "hears" in the exegesis of Scripture.

4. All this, I take it, is a kind of unpacking of what Paul teaches: "The man without the Spirit does not accept the things that come from the Spirit of God, for they are foolishness to him, and he cannot understand them, because they are

spiritually discerned" (1 Cor. 2:14). Of course, Paul is not talking about exegesis per se, still less about systematic theology. He is, however, talking about the Gospel, the "word of the cross" (1:18), which is simultaneously "foolishness to those who are perishing" and the "power of God" to those "who are being saved." That Gospel is supremely preserved in Scripture; the reading ("exegesis") of Scripture and the correlative organizing of the results of our reading ("systematic theology") are both bound up with what we perceive the Gospel to be and with our response to it. Although Kaiser is right to warn that this verse does not sanction any pietistic, privatized form of mystical exegesis that assumes only those with the Spirit can do exegesis—detailed study of the text will not allow so narrow an interpretation, and all of experience militates against it[57]—his own suggestion that this verse refers merely to the *application* of the exegesis, the willingness to adopt the message of the Gospel into one's own life, is itself without rigorous exegetical foundation.[58]

To put the matter another way, just as the statement "Men are taller than women" does not mean that every man is taller than every woman, so the insistence that the "natural" person, i.e., the person without the Spirit, does not understand the things of God, does not mean that the exegesis of such a person will in fact always be inferior to that of the person with the Spirit! Quite apart from the jump from "understanding the things of God" to performing "exegesis," what is at stake, surely, is an entire way of looking at reality, and what this does to shape one's ability to listen to God, to hear what he is saying, to find oneself aligned with his mind insofar as he has revealed it to us. To use contemporary categories, Paul has deployed the argument of the new hermeneutic against all who want to domesticate the Gospel, who are more interested in being masters of the Gospel than being mastered by it. Spiritual things are spiritually discerned: the presence and power of the Holy Spirit in the life of the believer so changes values, proportion, perceptions, response to God himself, that the simple polarity Paul sets forth is far from being a distortion, even if it is not cast in twentieth-century categories.[59]

EXEGESIS, SYSTEMATIC THEOLOGY, AND PREACHING

From any decisively Christian perspective, disciplined biblical exegesis and thoughful systematic theology do not exist for themselves. They exist, finally, to serve the people of God. The message that is distilled out of such work must be preachable and preached, or (granted that God has indeed revealed himself in Scripture) the entire exercise is such a distortion of the *purposes* of revelation as to approach profanity. "Theology without proclamation is empty, proclamation without theology is blind," writes Ebeling in a much-quoted statement.[60] Garrett is not wrong when, as the first of seven answers he gives to the question "Why Systematic Theology?" he writes, "*Systematic theology is necessary as a proper extension of the teaching function of the Christian church.* . . . This may be called the *catechetical* root of systematic theology" (*emphasis his*).[61]

But there is a sense in which the best expository preaching ought also to be the best exemplification of the relationship between biblical exegesis and systematic theology. If a Christian preacher is expounding, say, Psalm 23, the first priority is to explain what the text meant when it was written three thousand years ago and to apply it, utilizing sound principles (which cannot here be explored) to contemporary life. But the second priority is not far behind. There must be some understanding of how the shepherd/sheep motif develops in later revelation, with some thoughtful reflection and application on the resulting synthesis. There may be reference, for instance, to the prophetic denunciations and promises of Zechariah 11–13, where the false shepherds are excoriated and the coming of Yahweh's own true shepherd is promised. Ultimately there will be some reference to the good shepherd of John 10, and perhaps to the undershepherds of the Chief Shepherd (1 Peter 5:1–4). It is entirely inappropriate to read all the later material back into Psalm 23. That would not only be anachronistic, it would be a miserable betrayal of the preacher's responsibility to help believers read their Bibles aright. But to tackle Psalm 23 with nothing more than exegetical rigor would be to fail at the same task, if for different reasons. As a general rule, the best expository preaching begins with the text at hand but seeks to establish links not only to the immediate context but also to the canonical context, *as determined by the biblico-theological constraints largely governed by the canon itself.* If these lines are sketched out in the course of regular, expository ministry, believers begin to see how their Bibles cohere. With deft strokes, the preacher is able to provide a *systematic* summary of the teaching to be learned, the ethics to be adopted, the conduct to be pursued, *not* by curtailing either exegesis or biblical theology, but by deploying these disciplines on the way toward systhesis.[62]

Similarly, when the preacher with this view of the expositor's task tackles a passage in the Gospels, the resulting sermon will not only explain the chosen passage within its context and apply it fairly (that is the least that expository preaching must do) but will also ensure that this focus within the ministry of the historical Jesus be properly related both to antecedent revelation and, especially, to subsequent revelation. After all, the Christian to whom the truth is being applied, not to mention the believers for whom it was originally written, live this side of the cross, the resurrection, and Pentecost, and therefore the inner-canonical relationships that tie the ministry of Jesus to this setting must from time to time be set out.

CONCLUSION

All the sections of this chapter, indeed many of its paragraphs, beg for expansion and copious illustration: no one is more aware of its shortcomings than I. In particular, the discussion would benefit from examples of exegesis that illustrate what is discussed in rather abstract form. Yet part of its weakness is endemic to any discussion of the systematician's task: as noted in the opening paragraphs, there are so many conceptual balls to keep in the air at the same time, with the added challenge of the fact that each ball influences all the others, that the range of discussion, even on a narrowly focused topic like that set for this chapter, rapidly extends into many other spheres.

Whatever its shortcomings, this chapter is gratefully dedicated to Kenneth Kantzer, who both in the classroom and in the counsel he offers (whether theological or personal) displays to a superlative degree the balance and poise that ought always to characterize the systematic theologian. *In multos annos!*

NOTES

[1]Maurice Wiles, *What Is Theology?* (Oxford: University Press, 1976), 1–7.

[2]Perhaps it is worth mentioning that at the popular level the word *theology* is patient of several meanings, depending to some extent on the country where the word is used. For many in America it is virtually indistinguishable from systematic theology (defined below); in the United Kingdom it is a catch-all

expression that covers biblical study, historical theology, hermeneutics, even philosophy of religion—any discipline that can fall under the general rubric of the study of Christianity.

[3]Robert T. Voelkel, *The Shape of the Theological Task* (Philadelphia: Westminster, 1968).

[4]Stephen Sykes, *The Identity of Christianity: Theologians and the Essence of Christianity from Schleiermacher to Barth* (London: SPCK, 1984).

[5]Nicholas Lash, *Theology on the Way to Emmaus* (London: SCM, 1986).

[6]Cf. John D. Woodbridge, *Biblical Authority* (Grand Rapids: Zondervan, 1982).

[7]Cf. D. A. Carson, "Three Books on the Bible: A Critical Review," *Journal of the Evangelical Theological Society* 26 (1983):337–67; D. A. Carson and John D. Woodbridge, eds., *Scripture and Truth* (Grand Rapids: Zondervan, 1983); idem, *Hermeneutics, Authority and Canon* (Grand Rapids: Zondervan, 1986).

[8]E. C. Blackman, "The Task of Exegesis," in W. D. Davies and D. Daube, eds., *The Background of the New Testament and Its Eschatology* (Fs. C. H. Dodd; Cambridge: University Press, 1984), 4.

[9]Many now resort to this or some similar definition. See, for example, M. Sternberg, *The Poetics of Biblical Narrative: Ideological Literature and the Drama of Reading* (Bloomington: Indiana University, 1985), esp. 1–57.

[10]For all its vast erudition the fairly recent commentary by Hans Dieter Betz (*Galatians* [Hermeneia, Philadelphia: Fortress, 1979]) is in certain respects a quite spectacular failure for this very reason.

[11]Cf. Kevin J. Vanhoozer, "The Semantics of Biblical Literature: Truth and Scripture's Diverse Literary Forms," in D. A. Carson and John D. Woodbridge, eds., *Hermeneutics, Authority, and Canon* (Grand Rapids: Zondervan, 1986), 49–104, 374–83.

[12]Cf. P. D. Juhl, *Interpretation* (Princeton: University Press, 1980), esp. chaps. 1–5, 8; H. D. Hirsch, *Validity in Interpretation* (New Haven: Yale University Press, 1967), chaps. 1–2.

[13]Milton S. Terry, *Biblical Hermeneutics: A Treatise on the Interpretation of the Old and New Testaments* (reprint, Grand Rapids: Zondervan, 1976).

[14]Bernard Ramm, *Protestant Biblical Interpretation*, 2nd ed. (Boston: W. A. Wilde, 1956). (The third edition becomes more sensitive to modern hermeneutical theory.)

[15]E.g., Gordon D. Fee, *New Testament Exegesis: A Handbook for Students and Pastors* (Philadelphia: Westminster, 1983); Joel B. Green, *How to Read Prophecy* (Downers Grove: InterVarsity, 1984); M.A. Chevallier, *L'Exégèse du Nouveau Testament: Initiation à la méthode* (Genève: Labor et Fides, 1985).

[16]E.g., John H. Hayes and Carl R. Holladay, *Biblical Exegesis: A Beginner's Handbook* (Atlanta: John Knox, 1982).

[17]E.g., Tremper Longman III, *Literary Approaches to Biblical Interpretation*, Foundations of Contemporary Interpretation (Grand Rapids: Zondervan, 1987).

[18]E.g., David Alan Black, *Linguistics for Students of New Testament Greek: A Survey of Basic Concepts and Applications* (Grand Rapids: Baker, 1988).

[19]E.g., Peter Cotterell and Max Turner, *Linguistics and Biblical Interpretation* (Downers Grove: InterVarsity, 1989).

[20]E.g., François Bovon and Grégoire Rouiller, eds., *Exegesis: Problems of Method and Exercises in Reading (Genesis 22 and Luke 15)*, trans. Donald G. Miller (Pittsburgh: Pickwick, 1978).

[21]For a useful introduction, cf. Richard E. Palmer, *Hermeneutics* (Evanston:

Northwestern University Press, 1969); Robert W. Funk, *Language, Hermeneutic and Word of God* (New York: Harper & Row, 1966).

[22]With something of a shudder I report the opinion of one fundamentalist theologian, best left unnamed, who explained why, after completing his Th.D., he no longer read much theology: "Why should I? I already learned it."

[23]E.g., Robert L. Thomas, "1 Thessalonians," in Frank E. Gaebelein, ed., *The Expositor's Bible Commentary*, vol. 11 (Grand Rapids: Zondervan, 1978), 275–80.

[24]Apparently this index was considered of such little value that it was not published in the first English-language edition: Paul Tillich, *Systematic Theology*, 3 vols. (Chicago: University of Chicago Press, 1951–63).

[25]For a recent and sympathetic summary of reception theory, cf. Nigel Watson, "Reception Theory and Biblical Exegesis," *Australian Biblical Review* 36 (1988): 45–56.

[26]William J. Larkin, Jr., *Culture and Biblical Hermeneutics: Interpreting and Applying the Authoritative Word in a Relativistic Age* (Grand Rapids: Baker, 1989).

[27]Michael LaFargue, "Are Texts Determinate? Derrida, Barth, and the Role of the Biblical Scholar," *Harvard Theological Review* 81 (1988): 341–57.

[28]Anthony C. Thiselton, *The Two Horizons: New Testament Hermeneutics and Philosophical Description* (Grand Rapids: Eerdmans, 1980). For a thoughtful assessment of recent hermeneutical developments, cf. J. I. Packer, "Infallible Scripture and the Role of Hermeneutics," in D. A. Carson and John D. Woodbridge, eds., *Scripture and Truth* (Grand Rapids: Zondervan, 1983), 325–56, 412–19.

[29]For a recent and thoughtful assessment, cf. Henri Blocher, "L'analogie de la foi dans l'étude de l'Ecriture Sainte," *Hokhma* 36 (1987): 1–20.

[30]E.g., Daniel von Allmen, "The Birth of Theology: Contextualization as the dynamic element in the formation of New Testament theology," *International Review of Mission* 64 (1975): 37–52.

[31]D. A. Carson, "Church and Mission: Reflections on Contextualization and the Third Horizon," in D. A. Carson, ed., *The Church in the Bible and the World* (Exeter: Paternoster, 1987).

[32]A. T. Hanson and R. P. C. Hanson, *Reasonable Belief: A Survey of the Christian Faith* (Oxford: University Press, 1980).

[33]For instance, although Nicholas Lash tries to sidestep solipsism, the thrust of his writings is always toward the side of relativism; e.g., "What might martyrdom mean?" in William Horbury and Brian McNeil, eds., *Suffering and Martyrdom in the New Testament* (Fs. G. M. Styler; Cambridge: University Press, 1981), 183–98.

[34]Cf. Philip Edgcumbe Hughes, "Some Observations on the History of the Interpretation of Holy Scripture," in James E. Bradly and Richard A. Muller, eds., *Church, Word, and Spirit* (Fs. Geoffrey W. Bromiley; Grand Rapids: Eerdmans, 1987), 93–106.

[35]Richard Hooker, *Laws of Ecclesiastical Polity V* (London, 1597), 8.2.

[36]Richard Bauckham, "Tradition in Relation to Scripture and Reason," in Richard Bauckham and Benjamin Drewery, eds., *Scripture, Tradition and Reason: A Study in the Criteria of Christian Doctrine* (Fs. Richard P. C. Hanson; Edinburgh: T & T Clark, 1988), 117–45.

[37]Ibid., 140.

[38]There are regrettable exceptions: e.g., W. Robert Cook, *A Theology of John* (Chicago: Moody, 1979).

[39]James D. G. Dunn, *Unity and Diversity in the New Testament: An Inquiry into the Character of Earliest Christianity* (London: SCM, 1977).

[40]D. A. Carson, "Unity and Diversity in the New Testament: The Possibility of Systematic Theology," in Carson and Woodbridge, eds., *Scripture and Truth*, 65-95, 368-75.

[41]C. Kingsley Barrett, "The Centre of the New Testament and the Canon," in Ulrich Luz and Hans Weder, eds., *Die Mitte des Neuen Testaments: Einheit und Vielfalt neutestamentlicher Theologie* (Fs. Eduard Schweizer; Göttingen: Vandenhoeck und Ruprechet, 1983), 17.

[42]James D. G. Dunn and James P. Mackey, *New Testament Theology in Dialogue* (London: SPCK, 1987).

[43]F. Humphreys, *The Death of Christ* (Nashville: Broadman, 1978).

[44]E.g., James Denney, *The Atonement and the Modern Mind* (London: Hodder and Stoughton, 1903); John R. W. Stott, *The Cross of Christ* (Downers Grove: InterVarsity, 1986); Leon Morris, *The Apostolic Preaching of the Cross* (Grand Rapids: Eerdmans, 1965); idem, *The Cross of Jesus* (Grand Rapids: Eerdmans, 1988); and perhaps especially J. I. Packer, "What Did the Cross Achieve? The Logic of Penal Substitution," *Tyndale Bulletin* 25 (1974): 3-45.

[45]Nigel M. de S. Cameron, "Universalism and the Logic of Revelation," *Evangelical Review of Theology* 11 (1987): 321.

[46]Krister Stendahl, "Biblical Theology, Contemporary," in *Interpreter's Dictionary of the Bible* (1962), 1:418-32.

[47]Of his many writings, cf. especially Brevard S. Childs, *Old Testament Theology in Canonical Context* (London: SCM, 1985); idem, *The New Testament as Canon: An Introduction* (London: SCM, 1984).

[48]Charles J. Scalise, "The 'Sensus Literalis': A Hermeneutical Key to Biblical Exegesis," *Scottish Journal of Theology* 42 (1989): 45-65.

[49]For a more popular exposition of the approach, cf. Rudolf Pesch, *Neuere Exegese: Verlust oder Gewinn?* (Freiburg: Herder, 1968).

[50]Robert Morgan, "The Historical Jesus and the Theology of the New Testament," in L. D. Hurst and N. T. Wright, eds., *The Glory of Christ in the New Testament: Studies in Christology* (Fs. George Bradford Caird; Oxford: Clarendon, 1987), 187-206.

[51]Ibid., 199.

[52]Ibid.

[53]Joseph Cardinal Ratzinger, *Biblical Interpretation in Crisis: On the Question of the Foundations and Approaches of Exegesis Today*. The 1988 Erasmus Lecture (Rockford: The Rockford Institute, 1988), 18.

[54]Geerhardus Vos, *Biblical Theology* (Grand Rapids: Eerdmans, 1948), 5, 13.

[55]Geerhardus Vos, "The Idea of Biblical Theology as a Science and as a Theological Discipline," in Richard B. Gaffin, Jr., ed., *Redemptive History and Biblical Interpretation: The Shorter Writings of Geerhardus Vos* (Phillipsburg: Presbyterian and Reformed, 1980), 15 (emphasis his).

[56]E.g., Peter Stuhlmacher (*Schriftauslegung auf dem Wege zur biblischen Theologie* [Göttingen: Vandenhoeck und Ruprecht, 1975]; idem, *Vom Verstehen des Neuen Testaments: Eine Hermeneutik* [Göttingen: Vandenhoeck und Ruprecht, 1979]) insists that the interpreter must remain open to "the possibility of transcendence." We may be glad for his courage to swim against the tide, while still observing that his insistence is pretty minimal: Can anyone imagine Paul, while reading the Old Testament, urging his fellow believers to no more than openness to the possibility of transcendence? Cf. rather similarly Donald Evans, "Academic Skepticism, Spiritual Reality and Transfiguration," in L. D. Hurst

and N. T. Wright, *The Glory of Christ in the New Testament: Studies in Christology* (Fs. George B. Caird; Oxford: Clarendon, 1987), 175–86. For a useful discussion of many of the issues, cf. Nigel de S. Cameron, ed., *Christian Experience in Theology and Life* (Edinburgh: Rutherford House, 1988).

[57]Walter C. Kaiser, Jr., "A Neglected Text in Bibliology Discussions: 1 Corinthians 2:6–16," *Westminster Theological Journal* 43 (1980–81): 301–19 (esp. 318–19).

[58]Cf. the excellent discussion of Gordon D. Fee, *The First Epistle to the Corinthians*, NICNT (Grand Rapids: Eerdmans, 1987), 98–120 (esp. 113–17).

[59]For a useful discussion, cf. John M. Frame, "The Spirit and the Scriptures," in Carson and Woodbridge, eds., *Hermeneutics, Authority, and Canon* 213–35, 405–10.

[60]Gerhard Ebeling, *Theology and Proclamation* (London: Collins, 1966), 20.

[61]James Leo Garrett, Jr., "Why Systematic Theology?" *Criswell Theological Review* 3 (1989): 259–81. Cf. also Donald Macleod, "Preaching and Systematic Theology," in Samuel T. Logan, ed., *The Preacher and Preaching* (Phillipsburg: Presbyterian and Reformed, 1986), 246–71.

[62]Rather presumptously, I have tried to develop this approach for the preacher in my *Expository Preaching: Priorities and Pitfalls* (Grand Rapids: Baker, forthcoming).

3

THE ROLE OF CHURCH HISTORY IN THE STUDY OF SYSTEMATIC THEOLOGY

RICHARD A. MULLER
FULLER THEOLOGICAL SEMINARY, PASADENA,
CALIFORNIA

PRELIMINARY CONSIDERATIONS

Christian doctrine, as grounded in the life and faith of the church throughout the whole world, is historical by nature. The church, certainly the church in the West, has traditionally understood itself in the terms provided by Augustine's great meditation on Hebrews 11:1–12:2 and 13:14, the *City of God*. Augustine draws out the theme that "here we have no abiding city, but we seek the one which is to come" into an extended meditation on the historical pilgrimage of the people of God, beginning with Abel and extending not only to Christ and the earliest Christian community (as Hebrews indicates) but on through the life of the believing community into his own present.[1] The historical character of this Christian faith, as constituted by the confessional incorporation of successive generations of believers and of their expressions of the faith into the ongoing community of belief is not, of course, the invention of Augustine. Augustine merely gave new form and new definition to an assumption and a practice that is as old as the faith itself.

In Deuteronomy 26:11, we find a liturgical recitation intended for reptition at the time of the presentation of "first fruits" to the Lord. What is striking about the recitation is not only its historical character but also the way in which the history itself is the vehicle of faith and the means by which the

individual believer becomes a member of the corporate community of belief. "A wandering Aramean was my father; and he
went down into Egypt and sojourned there, few in number;
and there he became a nation, great, mighty, and populous"
(v. 5). Immediately we see in the text the association of the
individual and the corporate community: Jacob, the wandering
Aramean, is identified over centuries as the "father" of the
speaker and the "father" is identified in turn with the mighty
nation that "he" became. With this threefold identification in
place, the text goes on, "And the Egyptians treated us harshly,
and afflicted us . . . and the LORD brought us out of Egypt with a
mighty hand and an outstretched arm . . . and he brought us
into this place and gave us this land" (vv. 6–9). The ancient
people is not called "them" but rather "us" and the "us" is
brought forward into the present in the focusing of the
recitation on "this land." The recitation concludes, "And
behold, now I bring the first fruit of the ground, which thou, O
LORD, hast given me" (v. 10). The individual, in present
possession of the land and presently identified with the
historical people of God, recognizes his possession in the
context of the divine gift to Israel. As in the case of Augustine's
meditation on Hebrews, it is the historical rootedness of the
faith itself that provides a foundation for the faith of the
individual and of the community in which he finds his religious
identity.[2]

These introductory remarks point toward a profoundly
historical formulation of theological system—at least insofar as
the system hopes to serve the needs of the believing community. On the one hand, they can indicate a confessional method
for systematic theology based, not on the typical synthetic or
deductive model that begins with a classical statement of the
doctrine of God, but rather on a historical paradigm that arises
out of the mighty acts of God in the salvation-history of a
particular people and concentrates on the covenant relationship
between the people and God.[3] Or, at the very least, they point
toward the incorporation of a strongly historical and covenantal
dynamic into the structure of a more or less traditionally
constructed theological system.[4]

On the other hand, whatever the organizational model
chosen for theological system, these introductory comments
point toward the character of doctrine itself as lodged in a
historical context and as arising out of a fundamentally
historical meditation. Doctrines represent the attempt of the

believing community to express, in terms suitable to a particular historical context, the fundamental religious insights of the community—like the relation between God and the created order, the reconciliation of God with humanity accomplished in Jesus of Nazareth, and the identity of Jesus as known in and through his work of reconciliation. There are various linguistic forms that have been used to point toward each of these fundamental insights, and each of the forms, such as the doctrines of creation *ex nihilo*, penal substitutionary atonement, and the two natures of Christ, all serve to identify, in and through a statement that is historically and culturally conditioned, a reality that transcends the various kinds of conditioning to which all language is susceptible.[5]

Not only does doctrine necessarily arise in a historical context and take its basic conceptual framework and linguistic forms from that context, it also arrives at contemporary expression only by way of a meditation *on*, and even more importantly a meditation *through*, earlier stages of historical expression. We can grasp the significance and application of a doctrinal statement in the present by reaching back through the history of its use toward the fundamental and therefore limiting meaning set by its original intention and use. As Lindbeck argues, "Faithfulness to such doctrines does not necessarily mean repeating them; rather it requires, in the making of any new formulations, adherence to the same directives that were involved in their first formulation."[6] And these "directives" or theological/religious intentions can only be reached through historical analysis. There can, of course, be contemporary doctrinal statements that arise with little or no consideration of the history of the believing community and its doctrines—but all such statements are in danger of misunderstanding their own language, the range of its usefulness, and the limits of its meaning. If the cultural and linguistic stituation in which we presently live has little in common with the construction of reality typical of a past era, then the way in which we construct our theological statements about the reality of God and God's work will necessarily be different from the way in which that past era constructed its theology. These considerations lead directly to a recognition that church history is foundational to contemporary systematic theology and, in addition, to an understanding of precisely why and how that is so.

Church history, including the history of Christian thought as one of its subdisciplines, is, simply stated, the historical analysis and presentation of social, cultural, institutional, political, and intellectual life of the believing community from its point of inception down to the present time. Although the history of the earliest church as witnessed within the canon of the New Testament is typically treated as a separate area of study (particularly in view of the detail of specialization of New Testament studies), the history of the church cannot rightly be severed from its New Testament beginnings, nor—in view of the history of the establishment of the canon of the New Testament—can the New Testament beginnings be legitimately sectioned off from the history of the early church.[7]

Similarly, although the present life of the church is typically set apart from historical study and addressed either in terms of systematic or pastoral and ministerial study, this present must be regarded as the outcome of the preceding history and in no way severed from it. It ought to be a sobering thought in the mind of each and every systematic theologian that the moment his dogmatics is printed as a book, or at least very shortly thereafter, it ceases to be the latest doctrinal formulation on the "cutting edge" of Christian thought and beomes the property of historians whose task is to examine it as a socially and culturally conditioned document reflecting a particular moment in the ongoing life of the believing community. That particular moment, moreover, is not a purely intellectual moment, but a social, cultural, institutional, political, *and* intellectual moment. Just as the New Testament exegete must ask questions concerning the larger context of the canonical materials, so must the church historian engage in this exegetical task whether in the examination of the recent or of the more distant past. And, of course, the New Testament materials, understood as the primary witness to the beginning of the church, must always be included as part of the context for the understanding of the later history.

From the purely formal point of view, the importance of history to systematic theology can be seen, not merely in the movement just noted of the contemporary theological system into the category of historical document, but also and more importantly in the traces of the past left upon all theological systems—whether those traces are recognized or not. I recall examining a recently published theological system, written for use by one of the younger evangelical denominations and noting to myself how much like Louis Berkhof's *Systematic Theology* it had been organized, despite the fact that the new system was charismatic and Berkhof was hardly supportive of that movement. On further reflection, I became quite convinced that the author had not borrowed Berkhof's outline, but had simply learned his theology from one or more theological works organized in that way. And, as a matter of fact, that particular order of theology, beginning with God and moving through the doctrines of human nature, sin, salvation, and the church not only had its roots in the creeds of the early church but was also the standard form of theological system established by John of Damascus (d. ca. 754) and Peter Lombard (d. 1160). What is significant here is that neither Berkhof, nor our modern charismatic theologian, thought critically about the virtues or the demerits of the Damascene's or the Lombard's way of arranging theological system. Both simply followed the traditional order or a variant of it unquestioningly.

This point is not necessarily negative. There is no reason that the order of theological system established by John of Damascus and Peter Lombard and refined in the thirteenth century by such theologians as Alexander of Hales and Thomas Aquinas should not remain a good and useful order for theological system in the present, growing as it did out of the credal order established by the early church. And there is no reason, granting its continuing usefulness, that twentieth-century theologians, whether Reformed or charismatic, ought not to benefit from it. A problem may occur, however, when an older model, adopted without a careful analysis of the historical, theological, and cultural context out of which it came, fails to mesh with the needs of the present historical context. In other words, the theologian must be able to ask fundamental questions concerning the requirements of system in the present—specifically, whether or not a particular model, term, or definition inherited from the past actually does serve the needs of the present or whether it needs to be changed or adapted somehow to a different historical, theological, or cultural context.

From a linguistic point of view, this study of church history including the history of doctrine provides both the terms necessary to our understanding of Christian doctrine and the historical, cultural context out of which those terms arose and in light of which they must be interpreted. Church history also provides, therefore, the best basis for our correct appropriation of those terms in the present. The right use of theological language always presupposes an understanding of the framework of meaning out of which language arises, the alteration and elaboration of meaning as the language is taken up into the ongoing life of the community and is pressed into service in new and different contexts, and the limits imposed on meaning by that historical framework of meaning and usage.

THE DOCTRINE OF THE TRINITY AS A HISTORICAL PROBLEM

Some concrete illustrations of these comments are surely in order. The doctrine of the Trinity, with its language of one God in three persons, is a perfect example of the way in which historical understanding enlightens contemporary teaching—and of the way in which lack of historical understanding renders contemporary teaching suspect, if not utterly impossible. Earliest Christianity inherited from Judaism a radically monotheistic faith which it posed consistently and pointedly against the polytheism of its pagan environment. It also inherited, however, from the witness of the Apostles, an equally powerful testimony to the union of Jesus Christ with God and to the pre-existence of Christ in the "form of God" and as divine Logos. In addition, the church understood the New Testament witness to imply that the Holy Spirit, the Spirit of God and Spirit of Christ, was more than just an exercise of divine power. This double inheritance of Jewish monotheism and of New Testament witness to the divinity of Christ and the Spirit, embodied for the early church in the language of the baptismal formula, "baptizing them in the name (singular!) of the Father, and of the Son, and of the Holy Spirit" (Matt. 28:19), brought about a linguistic crisis for Christian witness. How might it be possible to do justice to the terms or boundaries of the problem—to the oneness of God and individual divine identity of the Father, Son, and Holy Spirit?

The difficulty of the problem can be measured by the three centuries of doctrinal development and debate necessary to arrive at a solution. We must never be deluded by the simplicity of the standard formula of one essence and three presons into thinking that it was easily devised. We cannot rehearse that history here. Instead, we can look at the formulae proposed as solutions to the problem and discuss the way in which they illustrate our primary point concerning the historical and cultural conditionedness of doctrine and the importance of historical study to contemporary theological understanding.

There are two basic formulae: the Western, Latin formula of one substance (*substantia*) and three persons (*personae*) and the Eastern, Greek formula of one essence (*ousia*) and three hypostases. The Western language of substance and person was developed by Tertullian at the beginning of the third century in response to the problem of Sabellianism or Modalistic Monarchianism. In response to a well-intentioned but problematic insistence on the radical monarchy of God to the exclusion of the genuine, ultimate individuality of the Father, Son, and Spirit, Tertullian proposed a new way of speaking of the unity and plurality of the Godhead. The Sabellian teaching made the biblically sound point that God is one—and in order to safeguard that truth against a notion of plurality of divinities that the Sabellians saw implied in the Logos theology of the second century, they taught that Father, Son, and Spirit are roles or modes of self-presentation used by God in the temporal economy of salvation. Tertullian, in common with the Sabellians, refused to give up language of divine monarchy: the unity of God was fundamental to the teaching of Christianity against the polytheism of Graeco-Roman popular religion. Nonetheless, Tertullian also saw the necessity, set aside by the Sabellians, of recognizing the true divinity of Christ in the most ultimate sense: the revelation of divinity in Christ must be a reflection not merely of the way in which God chooses to reveal himself in the temporal economy but of the way God really is. Tertullian drew on the language of Roman law, the terms substance and person, but reinterpreted and redefined the terms, giving them ontological and theological overtones. In Tertullian's new usage, substance indicated the larger category, the oneness of rule, analogous to the one rule of two emperors over a single imperial substance or of two landlords over an estate. A person, legally one who has substance, can share in the rule of that substance with other persons. By analogy, the three divine "persons" could share in the one divine "substance" without implying a breakdown in the monarchy.

What is important here is that Tertullian did not oppose the Sabellian heresy with a ready-made orthodoxy. What he did was to offer a pair of terms in answer to the issue raised by Sabellianism—terms that had never before, as far as we know, been used by any Christian theologian as a way of dealing with the problem of New Testament God-language. These terms did not come from the New Testament, but rather from the pagan cultural context, from the Roman milieu out of which Tertullian himself had come as a convert. Instead of looking at the terms as old dogmatic friends—which is all too frequently our reaction—we ought to take a moment to appreciate the newness and strangeness that they must have possessed in the early third century.

As was surely the case a century later at the Council of Nicaea, the new words were most probably acceptable to Christians only because they appeared to solve the problem posed by the heresy—in Tertullian's day, Sabellianism, at the time of Nicaea, Arianism. Indeed, as was the case with the language of Nicaea, the new theological terms not only answered the heresy, they moved the discussion of God-language ahead to the point that the alternative, Sabellianism, or Arianism, could be defined as a heresy. Like Tertullian's *substantia* and *persona*, moreover, the Nicene *homousios* had a somewhat checkered past: the term had indeed been used by the impeccably orthodox Irenaeus as well as by Origen, but it has also been used by the Gnostics and by the writers of the Hermetic literature.[8] The term *hypostasis*, moreover, which was—in the aftermath of Nicaea—brought forward as a term for the divine threeness, equivalent to the Latin *persona*, originally was so tied to *ousia* in meaning that it was anathematized at Nicaea as an indication of Arianism.

The study of history tells us, in other words, that the language of Christian doctrine arose out of particular social, cultural, and intellectual contexts, and what is more, arose quite frequently out of non-Christian and even non-theological usage and had to be redefined in order to have a theological value. This is not merely the case at the very beginnings of Christianity, when there was not specifically Christian theology and when all of the words used to express the meaning of the Christian truth had to be taken from a context other than that of the rather restricted "Christian" vocabulary of the earliest community of faith—it is also the case in later centuries of the church when the community had been able to develop its own patterns of speech. Nor is it merely the case that the church used the language of the surrounding pagan culture in order to explain its teachings to the culture: in the case of Tertullian's usage and in the case of the Nicene *homousios* the church appropriated language from the culture around it in order to explain its teachings to its own members.

We are faced today when we use such terms with the

problem of shifting meanings of words. I remember once encountering members of a very small denomination who consistently characterized themselves to me as an "odd," "strange," or "curious folk" and who insisted that it was God's purpose that they be odd, strange, and curious. After some inquiry, I discovered that their religious identity had been shaped by a literal reading of 1 Peter 2:9 in the King James Version—"ye are a chosen generation, a royal priesthood, a holy nation, a *peculiar* people. . . ." The considerable change in meaning of the word "peculiar" had not been registered—with, shall we say, peculiar results.

The problem with trinitarian "person" language is not quite as obvious, but it is in fact, far more troublesome, if only because of the importance of the doctrine to so many Christians. "Person," in contemporary usage indicates not merely "a particular individual" but "the real self of a human being," an "I" capable of standing over against a "Thou," an independent center of consciousness, intellect, and will. If this meaning of the term is placed into the trinitarian context and the persons of the Godhead interpreted as independent centers of consciousness, intellect, and will standing over against one another, then the Christian faith will have to relinquish the God of the Bible and become unabashedly tritheistic.

It is easily arguable, moreover, that several of the smaller denominations and sects that arose around the beginning of this century arose at least in part because of a major misreading of the church's doctrine of the Trinity, a misunderstanding caused in no small measure by conservative Protestantism itself. As fundamental elements in their teaching, both the "Oneness" Pentecostals and the Jehovah's Witnesses insist (correctly!) that God is one and (incorrectly!) that the church has been guilty of teaching a message about three gods. The Jehovah's Witnesses in particular attack the notion of divine three persons on the assumption that it is necessarily a form of tritheism.

The theological and historical issue, that ought to be addressed both by the orthodox Christian and by the heterodox sectarian, is the issue of the meaning and significance of the doctrine in question—the doctrine of the Trinity. If the underlying intention of the doctrine is, as Tertullian put it, to affirm the Trinity while upholding the monarchy and, in so doing, to assert the identity of the eternal Godhead to be precisely what was revealed in the creative and redemptive economy,[9] then the doctrinal issue, beyond the words or terms of the dogma can be identified, historically, as twofold. In the first place, the doctrine of the Trinity intends to affirm, first and foremost, the unity of divine rule and, as Tertullian's development of the meaning of *substantia* indicates, the utter ultimate oneness of the divine being, while at the same time affirming a certain threeness of the Godhead.[10] The threeness—whatever terms may be used to explain it—becomes essential to the understanding of God, granting that God, as such, is transcendent and unknowable, but has become known in the work of creation and redemption as Word and Spirit. It was Tertullian's great predecessor in the early Catholic tradition, Irenaeus of Lyons, who referred to the Word and the Spirit as the "hands" or agencies of God in the creative and redemptive process:[11] it was the burden of this early trinitarianism, in other words, to teach the oneness of God in such a way as to affirm the full divinity of the agencies by which God drew himself into relation with the world.

Like the Gnostics and the Middle Platonists, the church assumed that the Godhead was so transcendent that no relationship between God and world could be established and no knowledge of God by the world could be gained without intermediaries—but unlike the Gnostics and the Middle Platonists, the church insisted that there was only one God and that it was an inward self-differentiation in the Godhead itself that accounted for the relationship between God and world, and not a series of lesser divine or quasi-divine beings. The genius of the doctrine of the Trinity, underlying the terms and —when the terms are rightly understood—mediated by them, is its ability to affirm in a biblical and apostolic manner, both the divine oneness and the divine agency, on the ground that the agency itself is truly divine.

CHRISTIAN ANTHROPOLOGY AND THE PROBLEM OF HISTORICAL CONTEXT

Negatively, it is equally the case that sectarian groups that have the "truth" of the Bible but do not belong to the historical and cultural trajectory of the confessing community typically fail to interpret the Scriptures in a manner that does justice to their context. Without the apparatus of the tradition, particularly without the boundaries and rules for religious discourse offered by the theological tradition, sectarian groups develop out of the Bible some very unbiblical concepts—concepts that take a single point of doctrine and press it as a central concern to the point that other aspects of the biblical witness and the church's tradition are distorted or utterly lost. By way of example, it is an easily established scriptural point, based on multiple attestations, that human beings are sinful and are unable, on the basis of their own efforts, to save themselves out of their predicament and renew either a "right spirit" within themselves or a right relationship with God. When this biblical teaching is, however, transmuted into what some writers have called (with considerable exaggeration) "total depravity" rather than "total inability," it becomes all too easy to redefine the doctrine of original sin and of human inability apart from grace so as to declare all human beings who are outside of a particular understanding of the grace of God in Christ to be utterly without any goodness, incapable of renewal, indeed, in need of a total transformation from an utterly worthless nature to a redeemed nature. According to this view, non-Christians have no genuine morality or ethics but live out their lives in a totally depraved moral condition.

This perspective is not only falsified by the high morality and deep ethical commitment of Buddhists, Confucianists, and various kinds of agnostics—it is also falsified by the biblical language of renewal, by the equally biblical doctrine that human beings retain, albeit in an attenuated form, the image of God according to which they were created, and by the Pauline emphasis on the travail of creation as it awaits the consummation of the age. And it is falsified by the churchly doctrines of general revelation, the first (or civil) use of the law, and common grace as they have been drawn out of Scripture over centuries of meditation. Throughout the history of the church, Christians have wrestled with the problem that, as far as can be discerned from the text of the New Testament, salvation is found only in Jesus Christ, while at the same time, both the breadth of the biblical revelation and our own experience of people of other faiths demonstrates—frequently to our individual ethical embarrassment—that high standards of morality and genuinely ethical acts are not the exclusive property or even the distinguishing mark of Christians.

Far, then, from subjecting the mind and heart to a debilitating relativism, the study of the history of the church holds out a promise of objectivity. This objectivity arises at several levels. First, historical study brings an awareness of one's own presuppositions—of the way in which they differ from the presuppositions and assumptions of past ages, of the way in which they contribute, often unconsciously, to our own formulations of issues, and of the way in which they are brought to bear on the interpretation of issues. At this level, the relativization that occurs is a relativization of one's self and of one's immediate context in the presence of the rather weighty tradition of past interpretation.

At a second level, the study of history offers the ability to understand a text or a doctrinal formulation in its original context of meaning, as distinct from (or perhaps even opposed to) the context into which the text or doctrine has been brought. We saw, in our discussion of patristic trinitarian vocabulary just how important this critical, historical approach can be: if the concept of divine "persons" is read out into the context of the twentieth century language of personhood, the result will be a tritheism that is both theologically and biblically unacceptable. It is easily argued that the only valid approach to the doctrines of the church is by way of this historical path. The present-day significance of a theological concept—whether for its use in theological systems or for its use as a guide or rule in the preaching of the gospel—must be governed by the original meaning of the concept as resident in its terminology. This point is as important for the interpretation of churchly doctrines as it is for the exegesis of the text of Scripture. If authorial intention is ignored and the mind and context of the present day interpreter rule the reading of a doctrinal point, the original reference of that point (usually to an issue raised by the exegesis of Scripture or by the encounter of a scriptual teaching with a particular life-situation in the history of the church) will be lost and, most probably, the long-term usefulness of the concept to the Christian community as well.

This latter point is well-illustrated by our reference to the doctrine of "total depravity." The Reformed confessions of the sixteenth and seventeenth centuries speak very sharply and penetratingly of the uttter lostness of human beings, to the point of arguing that there can be nothing good in human nature and nothing good forthcoming from it.[12] Taken by themselves, without any knowledge either of the context out of which they came or of the larger body of Christian doctrine to which they ultimately have reference, these confessions could easily give the impression that the Reformers understood the entirety of human nature to be sin—in a substantial sense—

and entirely devoid of the goodness of the original creative work of God as indicated in the language of the *imago Dei*. Evidence that even in the sixteenth century some Protestants understood the doctrinal point in this way is provided, on the Lutheran side, by the Flacian Controversy and by its resolution in the *Formula of Concord*, and somewhat less clearly on the Reformed side by the way in which the *Canons of Dort* are carefully worded so as to avoid this exaggerated view of sin.[13]

First, the historical and systematic context of the doctrinal point: the Reformers reacted powerfully against the abuses of late medieval sacramental theology and against the Semi-Pelagian view of human nature that accompanied and underwrote those abuses in the thought of late scholastic thinkers like Gabriel Biel. Biel had argued that, although sinful human beings could not, apart from grace, perform any genuinely good work (*meritum de condigno*), they could perform a half-merit or proportionate merit (*meritum de congruo*) that would result in a divine gift of grace.[14] Quite simply, there was some good that human beings could do, however small, that would merit divine favor. The Reformers, working out of a strongly Augustinian reading of the Pauline doctrine of grace, held that no act of human beings could merit divine grace and favor and that our entry into salvation was entirely an act of divine grace, wrought without consideration of merit. In the context of the Reformers' teachings, any divine consideration of human merit would result only in damnation. No human works could be offered to God in exchange for saving grace—not even acts performed in the sacramental life of the church. In order to emphasize the *sola gratia* of salvation, the Reformers also pointed to the utter lostness of human nature, out of which no works meriting salvation could arise. They did not at all mean to argue that human nature, without saving grace, was either absolutely devoid of the goodness of God's creative work or that human nature, apart from saving grace, was incapable of performing ethically good acts. Rather, the issue was that ethically good acts, performed out of the sinfulness of human nature, could not merit salvation.

After Luther's death, Matthias Flacius Illyricus opposed what he believed to be an excessively synergistic doctrine of grace and the human will held by followers of Philip Melanchthon. In opposition to their teaching that sin was an incidental property of human nature and that the will could, therefore, cooperate with grace, Flacius argued that sin was the very substance of our humanity and that the image of God had been replaced, in the fall, by the image of Satan.[15] In response to both of these departures from the teaching of the Reformers, the theologians of the Lutheran church announced, with great clarity, in the *Formula of Concord*, that "within [man's] corrupted nature we are not able to point out and expose the nature by itself and original sin by itself as two manifestly separate things, nevertheless our corrupted nature or the essence of corrupted man, our body and soul or man himself created by God . . . are not identical with original sin (which dwells in man's nature or essence and corrupts it)."[16] In other words, human nature, as created by God in his image, has not been "totally destroyed" by the fall—and in the work of salvation is not created again *ex nihilo*, but is renewed in Christ.[17]

Similarly, the *Canons of Dort* declare in no uncertain terms that all people "are conceived in sin, and are by nature children of wrath, incapable of any saving good, prone to evil, dead in sin . . . neither able nor willing to return to God." Nonetheless, "there remain . . . in man since the fall, the glimmerings of natural light, whereby he retains some knowledge of God, of natural things, and of the difference between good and evil, and discovers some regard for virtue, good, and order in society, and for maintaining an orderly external deportment."[18]

The issue, noted both by the *Canons of Dort* and by the *Formula of Concord* is that the power of evil is not and cannot be greater than the power of the good—and that, therefore, however great the damage done by the fall, the goodness conferred by God upon his creation in the beginning of things, cannot be entirely obliterated by sin. To make the point from another direction, both the Lutheran and the Reformed standards were written in the context of the Augustinian understanding of sin characteristic of Christian orthodoxy in the West: sin is not a substance created by God, but rather a defect in an otherwise good substance. Any other way of understanding the problem would either make God the author of sin or would make evil into an eternal substance outside of the control of God.[19] The meaning of the language of "total depravity," thus is limited by the historical and theological context out of which it arose.

What is more, the phrases used to describe the sinfulness of human nature—"prone to evil," "dead in sin," "utterly indisposed, disabled, and made opposite to all good," "wholly inclined to evil," and the like—when wrenched out of their historical context and read literally and in isolation from other portions of the confessions can all too easily point in a Flacian direction. In other words, the error in theological anthropology noted above is quite understandable granting that its modern proponents, typically, have had little training or interest in the history of the church beyond the bounds of their own denominational or sectarian past. The history of the church and its doctrines are necessary not only to the process of doctrinal formulation in the present but also to the understanding of the doctrines that one already possesses by reason of the history of the faith and, indeed, necessary to one's own theological self-understanding.

CULTURAL CONDITIONING, OBJECTIVITY, AND NORMATIVE THEOLOGICAL STATEMENT

If the foregoing comments about two basic doctrinal issues—Trinity and human nature—have succeeded in addressing the location and grounds of the meaning of Christian doctrine, we must be prepared to recognize that all expressions of Christian doctrine are rooted in history and are, therefore, historically and culturally conditioned. No individual statement of doctrine can escape this conditioning, nor is such an escape desirable. Of course, the historical and cultural conditionedness of theological statements is, frequently, a reason offered for the rejection of particular doctrines or for all of Christian doctrine, but that rejection is as foolish as it is unnecessary. After all, every statement that we make is conditioned by the social, cultural, political, and religious context out of which we have come and in which we make the statement—but this fundamental fact of our intellectual and spiritual life does not lead us to cease and desist from making statements. It is also true that the lowest level of statement, at which the conditioning is least evident and least likely to be the source of intellectual difficulties—statements about hunger, thirst, and the aches and pains of daily existence—is also intellectually and spiritually the least rewarding level of discourse.

What is more, it is hardly the case that the cultural and historical conditionedness of a statement places a barrier in the way of understanding. Quite to the contrary, it is the historical and cultural location of a particular statement or doctrine or theory that makes it intelligible to a particular culture at a particular time in history. Normative theological statements must be historically and culturally conditioned—indeed, the way in which they belong to and reflect the culture and the time to which they speak accounts for their normative status. To make the point in another way, what is normative cannot be this or that particular theologian's system but rather the ability of a doctrinal statement or set of statements to belong to a historical and cultural context in such a way that they reflect adequately the beliefs of the community of faith. It is not a particular system but the churchly, confessing trajectory in which it is formulated that provides the structures and contexts of intelligibility and normative value.

In the concrete, borrowing on the trinitarian example already given, the mere use of the terms substance and person or *ousia* and *hypostasis* does not bestow authority on a theology—any more than those words themselves stand in an intrinsic relation to the divine reality. The doctrine of the Trinity, as proposed at the council of Nicaea was *not* normative—not immediately, at least. In fact, it was highly innovative by the standards of the early church: the language of *ousia* and *homousios* had never before been used as the basis of a standard or normative statement. The bishops departed from the council and, over the course of the next half century, worked at modifying or replacing the formula.[20] Only after the work of the Cappadocian fathers and the Council of Constantinople did the so-called "Nicene" formula receive general acceptance in the church.[21]

The trinitarian formula thus arose out of a particular historical and linguistic context and was not, in its initial statement, a normative doctrine. Its eventual function as the standard term of reference to the unity and diversity of the Godhead resulted not from the obvious, intrinsic merit of the terms employed but from the church's ability to use the formula as a rule for framing its preaching of the Gospel in such a way as to reflect the New Testament language of Father, Son, and Spirit without falling into tritheism. Our present-day use of the formula must proceed on the same grounds as its original ratification. And our identification of those grounds can only arise out of a careful, historical reconstruction of the intention of the authors and interpreters of the formula as it came into its own as a dogma in the later fourth century.

The point can also be made that recognition of the historical character of theological statements, when it is conjoined with the critical, historical study of those statements in the light of their original context and of the trajectory of interpretation that brings their original meaning into the realm of contemporary significance, does not result in a loss of "objectivity" and in the victory of an entirely "subjective" approach to Christian doctrine. In any field of study or realm of discourse, objectivity and subjectivity are not mutually exclusive opposites or, indeed, distinct and separate options for one's style of discourse. Rather, objectivity and subjectivity are necessary correlates in discourse as any human subject or subjects addresses any object of discussion or analysis. Historians have long recognized that the goal of utterly disinterested objectivity sought by nineteenth-century scholars like Leopold von Ranke, J. B. Bury, Charles V. Langlois, and Charles Seignobos, is utterly unattainable, if only because the historian's own selection and identification of relevant data is itself an interpretive act.[22]

To make the point in relation to the doctrinal issues noted in this chapter: the continuing focus of modern histories of doctrine on Trinity and Christology in their examination of the early church and on soteriology in their examination of the era of the Reformation is as much an indication of the continuing doctrinal interests of the present-day church as it is of the theological emphases of the past. And, by the same token, the recognition on the part of an increasing number of historians that religious and soteriological presuppositions concerning the way in which mediation between the divine and human takes place and the way in which a mediated redemption belongs to the life of the individual and of the community lay at the root of even the most seemingly speculative trinitarian formulations, including those of Arius, represents an insight both into the formulation of doctrine by the early church and into the doctrinal concerns of the present.[23] Both historical approaches to the trinitarian and Christological problems have been fruitful, and both have uncovered important aspects of the meaning and intention of the early church's work of doctrinal formulation. One might argue that the positive relationship of two subjectivities—the subjectivity of the writers of the early church and the subjectivity of the modern interpreters—has led to a more objective presentation of the teaching of the early church, when the objectivity is defined in terms of the clearer, fuller, and more adequate description of the beliefs of the past.

Objectivity does not arise out of an unbiased, utterly disinterested approach to the past. Instead, it arises out of the methodologically controlled analysis of the materials of history with recognition of their historical and cultural condition- edness, our own historical and cultural conditionedness, and the human, traditionary line that draws past meanings into contemporary significance.[24] Conversely, the loss of objectivity is not caused by our own existential involvement in the materials of our hitory. Rather it is caused by the incautious and ahistorical address of our own subjectivity to the past. We live within a community and that community has a past. We live and think in the context of the historical tradition and the present-day context of that community. Our doctrines have arisen within and have been carried along by that tradition. Our objective recounting of those doctrines can only arise out of an understanding of the context that produced the doctrine and of the various interpretations given to the doctrine throughout its history that have extended its significance into the present. Any contemporary systematic use of doctrines drawn from our past must follow this historical route of interpetation.

Contemporary systematic theology, therefore, cannot af- ford simply to repeat the language that it has been given—nor can it afford to ignore the past and attempt to strike out in new and innovative directions and expect to achieve any results or lasting significance. The way in which we formulate our beliefs is bound to our historical context and belongs to the forward movement of our history. Innovation that disregards the materials of the past risks—at best—failure to speak meaning- fully or intelligibly to the community of belief, whereas present- day formulation that continues to speak exactly as previous generations have spoken, without attention to the contempo- rary situation, risks immediate obsolescence. Incomplete or mistaken appropriation of the materials of the past results, as I think the discussion of the doctrine of "total depravity" has demonstrated, in poorly formulated and, indeed, dangerous doctrinal statements that violate the fundamental intention of the original formulators of the doctrine.

The work of systematic theology, then, is not the simple repetition of tried and true formulae. (If, that were the case, no new systems would need to be written!) Instead, the work of systematic theology must be the construction of meaningful theological statement for a particular time and place, based on a close attention to the meaning of doctrines and formulae, not merely to their accumulated significance, but also and primarily to their fundamental intention as dictated by the needs of their original context. Construction must proceed, by way of the contemporary assessment of the doctrinal intentions of the past and of the way in which those intentions have reflected the underlying concerns of the believing community, to the creation of contemporary statments of doctrine that attempt to draw the fundamental insights of the community in its historical meditation on the faith into dialogue with the contemporary situation.

Systematic theology, therefore, must be both a historical and a contemporary discipline, granting that it intends to speak to a community that is both historical and contemporary. Its task is the construction of an expanded meditation on the body of beliefs held by the Christian community that succeeds in addressing those beliefs to the contemporary situation without either losing the normative, historically-determined meaning of those beliefs or their significance to the present-day situation. The success of the systematic venture depends in no small measure on the ability of the theologian to penetrate the historically-determined forms of doctrinal statement and, by means of historical analysis, to discern their doctrinal intention—and then, through a painstaking process of interpretation and contextualization, present that intention, even when it demands the use of new and different terms, to the church of the present-day.

NOTES

[1]This theme was one that Augustine meditated on from the very beginning of his theological work: cf. Augustine, *Of True Religion*, xxii.50 (LCC, vol. VI: *Augustine: Earlier Writings*, ed. J. H. S. Burleigh [Philadelphia: Westminster, 1953], 250) with idem., *The City of God*, XI.1; XV-XVIII (NPNF, series 1, vol. 2, 205, 284–396).

[2]Cf. Gerhard von Rad, *Old Testament Theology*, trans. D. M. G. Stalker, 2 vols. (New York: Harper & Row, 1962–65), vol. 1, 121–28.

[3]Note that this approach was attempted by Johannes Cocceius in the seventeenth century in his *Summa doctrinae de foedere et testamento Dei* (1648) and his *Summa theologiae ex sacris scripturis repetita* (1662). Cocceius' approach had a major impact on the theologies of Franz Burmann, Francis Turretin, and J. H. Heidegger, as well as a clear successor in the great *De oeconomia foederum Dei cum hominibus libri quattuor* (1677) of Hermann Witsius. On the history and development of the Reformed federal theology, see: Gottlob Schrenck, *Gottesreich und Bund im älteren Protestantismus vornehmlich bei Johannes Cocceius: Zugleich ein Beitrag zur Geschichte des Pietismus und der heilsgeschichtlichen Theologie* (Gütersloh: Bertelsmann, 1923). It may also be noted that Jonathan Edwards

projected a historically and federally organized system of theology in his incomplete *History of the Work of Redemption.*

[4]As for example, in Turretin's *Institutio theologiae elencticae* (1679–85) or Johann Heinrich Heidegger's *Corpus theologiae* (1700).

[5]Cf. George A. Lindbeck, *The Nature of Doctrine: Religion and Theology in a Postliberal Age* (Philadelphia: Westminster, 1984), 80–84.

[6]Ibid., 81.

[7]See in particular, Edward Reuss, *History of the Canon of the Holy Scriptures in the Christian Church,* trans. David Hunter (Edinburgh: R. W. Hunter, 1891); and Brooks Foss Westcott, *A General Survey of the History of the Canon of the New Testament,* sixth edition (New York: Macmillan, 1889; reprint, Grand Rapids: Baker, 1980).

[8]See G. L. Prestige, *God in Patristic Thought* (London: SPCK, 1952), 197–201 for a brief history of the term *homousios;* Prestige does not mention the use of the term in the Hermetic literature, but see *Hermetica,* 4 vols., edited and trans., Walter Scott (reprint, Boston: Shambhala, 1985), vol. I, 118 (*Poimandres,* 10).

[9]Tertullian, *Against Praxeas,* iv, xi, xiii, in ANF, vol. III, 599–600, 603–04, 607–08.

[10]Cf. J. N. D. Kelly, *Early Christian Doctrines,* second ed. (New York: Harper & Row, 1960), 114–15.

[11]Irenaeus, *Against Heresies,* IV.pref.4; xx.1; V.vi.1, in ANF, vol. I, 463–88, 531.

[12]See *Belgic Confession,* XV; *Second Helvetic Confession,* VIII; *Westminster Confession,* VI.iii-v, in Philip Schaff, *The Creeds of Christendom: With a History and Critical Notes,* 3 vols., sixth ed. (New York: Harper & Row, 1931; reprint, Grand Rapids: Baker, 1983), III, 400–01, 247–49, 615–16.

[13]*Canons of Dort,* III–IV, i–vi, in Schaff, *Creeds,* III, 587–89.

[14]Cf. Heiko Oberman, *The Harvest of Medieval Theology: Gabriel Biel and Late Medieval Nominalism,* revised edition (Grand Rapids: Eerdmans, 1967), 169–174.

[15]See F. Bente, *Historical Introductions to the Book of Concord* (St. Louis: Concordia, 1921; reprint, 1965), 144–48.

[16]*Formula of Concord, Solid Declaration,* I, in *The Book of Concord: The Confessions of the Evangelical Lutheran Church,* trans. and edited by Theodore G. Tappert (Philadelphia: Fortress, 1959), 514.

[17]Cf. Ibid., 513, 515–16.

[18]*Canons of Dort,* III–IV, iii–iv.

[19]Cf. J. Tixeront, *History of Dogmas,* trans. from the fifth French edition by H. L. B., 3 vols. (St. Louis and London: B. Herder, 1910ff.), II, 365–69.

[20]Cf. Athanasius, *On the Councils* with the discussion in Kelly, *Early Christian Doctrines,* 237–51 and Reinhold Seeberg, *Textbook of the History of Doctrines,* 2 vols., trans. Charles E. Hay (reprint, Grand Rapids: Baker, 1977), I, 218–27.

[21]See Kelly, *Early Christian Doctrines,* 263–69 and Seeberg, *History of Doctrines,* 227–36.

[22]Cf. the discussion in G. J. Renier, *History: Its Purpose and Method* (New York: Harper & Row, 1965), 249–50 with Trygve R. Tholfsen, *Historical Thinking: An Introduction* (New York: Harper & Row, 1967), 216–20. A classic statement of the objectivist position is available in Charles V. Langlois and Charles Seignobos, *Introduction to the Study of History* (New York: Scribner, 1908), 63–70.

[23]Cf. Robert C. Gregg and Denis E. Groh, *Early Arianism—A View of*

Salvation (Philadelphia: Fortress, 1981); and Jaroslav Pelikan, *Jesus Through the Centuries* (New York and San Francisco: Harper & Row, 1988).

[24]N.B., the usage of "meaning" and "significance" is consciously drawn from E. D. Hirsch, Jr., *Validity in Interpretation* (New Haven: Yale University Press, 1967), 6–10, 57, 62–64, 140–44 and intends to indicate both the fundamental limitation placed on all legitimate use of a concept, formula, text, etc., by its original "life-situation" and the development of larger realms of significance as any given concept, formula, or text is used, reused, and interpreted in the ongoing life of a community. Discovery both of the original life-situation and of the trajectory of developing significance is the work of the historian. Also see E. D. Hirsch, *The Aims of Interpretation* (Chicago: University of Chicago Press, 1976), 1–13, 79–81.

4

CHRIST AND CONCEPT: DOING THEOLOGY AND THE "MINISTRY" OF PHILOSOPHY

KEVIN J. VANHOOZER
UNIVERSITY OF EDINBURGH, EDINBURGH,
SCOTLAND

INTRODUCTION: COOPERATION OR COLD WAR?

For almost two thousand years Christians have struggled to define for themselves and others how to be in the world but not of it. To what extent should Christian life and thought be distinct? When does similarity become compromise? When does separation become an abandonment of the Great Commission? Should the church be searching for points of convergence with society at large or waging a Cold War? With regard to the matter of Christian living, H. Richard Niebuhr's theological classic *Christ and Culture*[1] examined five ways that Christians have sought to understand their place and role in civilization. With regard to Christian thought, Tertullian's celebrated query about the incommensurability of faith and philosophy, "What has Jerusalem to do with Athens?" reflects the belief that the things of heaven are both above and beyond terrestrial reach and comprehension. Tertullian's strategy of splendid isolation, Amish rather than Athenian in its intellectual affinities, is only one way of conceiving the relation between faith and reason. In this chapter I propose to apply a fivefold typology, similar in structure though not in substance to that of Niebuhr, to Tertullian's question concerning the relation of theology and philosophy.[2] I will therefore investigate the relation of Christ and concept rather than Christ and culture.

All believers, not simply professional theologians, have a

99

stake in this debate over the relation of faith and reason. Jesus and the apostles encourage believers to "grow" in the faith. Such maturity of faith pertains not only to intensity of conviction but also to a more developed comprehension of faith's subject matter. This aspect of the vital Christian life is perhaps best captured in the phrase "faith seeking understanding." Admonitions to "test" the spirits are particularly relevant in our age, in which ideologies and images compete for the imaginations of individuals and whole societies. The question is whether and to what extent philosophy can contribute to faith's understanding of itself and of the world. If theology involves coming to a better understanding of faith and of the world in light of faith, what is the role of philosophy?

This more general question about the role of philosophy for doing theology gives rise to a number of more specific issues:

1. Why be rational? Does not the apostle Paul warn believers against deceptive philosophy that takes every thought captive (Col. 2:8)? While it is true that some philosophical schemes (e.g., materialism) may be inimical to Christianity, rationality itself is not so easily dismissed. Indeed, I would contend that it is precisely those who refuse to think rationally who are in the most danger of surrendering their minds to "vain" philosophy. For the only alternatives to rational thinking are cognitive anarchy (in which there are no rules for thinking but every individual believes what is right in his own eyes) or cognitive totalitarianism (in which the individual must follow the rules dictated by the reigning powers). In the former case the individual enjoys absolute autonomy, and in the latter case the group enjoys absolute authority. But in neither case is there much hope for arriving at objective knowledge or truth.

2. What is rationality? Is the understanding that faith seeks the special province of the philosopher? Is the philosopher's special role that of the judge who determines what does and does not count as "rational" thinking? Or, to play the angel's advocate, is there a special kind, a theological species, of the genus "rationality"? If so, how does theological rationality relate to its philosophical counterpart? Here it is important to avoid a univocal concept of rationality, where every intellectual endeavor must follow the same formal procedures regardless of the disciplinary context. Verifying every statement by empirical observation may work for the physicist, but not for the theologian (where in the world does one look to verify the doctrine of the Trinity?). Hence "positivism," the attempt to

impose the same scientific method on every discipline, is unwarranted. At the same time, one must avoid an equivocal concept of rationality, by which every intellectual discipline plays by its own rules. What we need is an analogical notion of rationality, which both requires each discipline to follow certain basic rules and allows for differences in how those rules apply to the different disciplinary contexts.

3. Why must faith converse with philosophy and other disciplines? To the extent that the theologian claims that the faith is not merely meaningful but true, the truth claims of theology must be brought into contact with the truth claims of other disciplines. Wolfhart Pannenberg points out that the universality of theology's claims stems from its special theme—God, the Creator of all:

> A theology that remains conscious of the intellectual obliga-
> tions that go along with the use of the word "God" will try in
> every possible way to relate all truth, and therefore not least
> of all the knowledge of the extra-theological sciences, to the
> God of the Bible. . . .[3]

I might hold that the event of Jesus Christ is true only "for me," but private truth claims such as this have little evangelistic or apologetic force and usually fall on deaf public ears. Moreover, sequestering the truth claims of theology from those of other disciplines results in a schizophrenic and impractical way of thinking and living.

4. If philosophy *is* deemed necessary for the health of systematic theology, how is the theologian to decide which of the many philosophical options concerning meaning and truth are open to the believer? How does one's faith stance affect one's approach to and use of philosophical theories about the nature of reality (metaphysics), knowledge (epistemology), and value (ethics)? To what metaphysical, epistemological, and ethical postulates, if any, is the believer already committed by virtue of Christian faith? Are there some directions that faith should not pursue in its search for understanding? Does Plato serve fully as well as Plantinga, Descartes as Derrida, Aristotle as A. J. Ayer?

These are, admittedly, large and complex questions. More-over, it is not a matter of relating two abstract notions— Philosophy and Theology—but scores, perhaps hundreds, of particular philosophies and theologies. Consequently, the number of possible relations between faith and reason increase exponentially. I therefore propose to bring a christological focus to the discussion: How does philosophy contribute to theology's attempt to answer one imposing question, "What think ye of Christ?" (Matt. 22:42). How Christ may be *thought* will thus serve as my touchstone for examining the broader relation of philosophy to theology.

The christological "red thread" is hardly arbitrary, for the philosopher also confesses that in the beginning was the Logos. We might say that the Logos serves as Muse for both the philosopher and the theologian. For the philosopher, the Logos represents the standards that govern rational reflection and discussion.[4] For the theologian, the Logos is the divine revelation, the inscripturated and then incarnate Word of God found in the Bible and preeminently in the person and history of Jesus Christ. In light of this common parentage, which child—philosophy or theology—has better claim to the birthright?

The underlying conviction of this chapter is that the relation between philosophy and theology need not always be antagonistic. Why have they been so often at odds with each other? Two faulty views of rationality are responsible for this unedifying rivalry. "Foundationalists" believe that knowledge must be grounded in something certain or highly probable. On this view, a belief is rational only if it is justified, and philosophy's role is to determine the conditions under which this takes place. As Imre Lakatos, a philosopher of science, puts it: "For centuries knowledge meant proven knowledge— proven either by the power of the intellect or by the evidence of the senses."[5] Austin Farrer notes that this vision of rationality determined the kind of role philosophy would have in theology: "The old method of philosophizing about theology was the endeavor to prove."[6] For the foundationalist, intellectual honesty demands that one believe nothing that is unproven. The theologian is forced either to build on what the philosopher considers sound foundations (to "prove") or to construct his theological system out of thin air. Philosophy on this view is a demanding taskmaster, insisting that the theologian build only with preapproved epistemological bricks.

More recently, "nonfoundationalists" have delivered a good number of the children of theology from this burdensome task of laying foundations. The job of theology according to the nonfoundationalists is to describe the faith on its own terms rather than to "found" it. The nonfoundationalist seeks not to prove but to describe the faith. The role of the philosopher on this view is to discover faith's own peculiar logic and rationality. Whereas the foundationalist sees rationality everywhere and always the same, the nonfoundationalist sees each discipline, community, or tradition operating with and speaking its own language with its own "grammar." This conception of rationality involves a career change for Dame Philosophy, who no longer makes the rules but simply tries to clarify the rules that are already there.

To my mind, neither of these two ways of conceiving rationality nor the concomitant role of philosophy gives rise to a healthy relation between faith and reason. The foundationalist demands too much of the theologian, the nonfoundationalist too little. There is, however, a third way of conceiving rationality that neither compromises the integrity of theology nor results in special pleading or a retreat to commitment. I will suggest that this third way—the way of "fallibilism" rather that foundationalism—allows the theologian to be both biblical and rational.[7]

The quest for understanding is not an external requirement of philosophy, but rather it is inherent to the very task of theology. That is, the search for rational intelligibility, far from crashing head-on into faith, receives its initial impulse from faith. The harmonious relation between theology and philosophy is jeopardized only when one or the other of these disciplines becomes undisciplined and exceeds its rightful limits. Philosophy and theology alike have their respective pathological sides. In the case of philosophy, this happens when the principle of autonomy leads to the exclusion, in principle, of any revelatory logos. Such a reduction is both presumptuous and untrue to the nature of philosophy, whose task it is to reflect on what has already been *given* it ("given" is used here as a secular equivalent of "revealed").[8] The pathology of theology takes the form of a retreat to authority. This too subverts the ultimate intentions of theology itself, whose task it is to *reflect* on the faith revealed once for all to the saints in Jesus Christ. Here, then, is the ground on which commonality between philosophy and theology can be had: both reflect on the given. Philosophy is like theology in receiving the given; theology is like philosophy in having to reflect. Moreover, the logos principle is both the given (Word/text) and the principle of reflection (reason). If each discipline remains conscious of its responsibilities and limits, a relation that frequently resembles a

Cold War might be transformed into one of cooperation. Of course, the crucial question is whether or not such a peaceful coexistence is possible without eventually calling the autonomy and integrity of one or the other into question. Indeed, perhaps the basic issue is whether the philosopher and the theologian can each recognize the other's right to exist.

My "wager" in what follows is, to use the christological focus once more, that the Chalcedonian formula, which established the parameters for discussing the relation of the divine and human natures in Jesus Christ, might, with some adjustments, be "stretched" to account for the similar relation of Christ and concept. I will argue that two kinds of thinking—biblical and rational—may be "united" in one person—the theologian. To use the language of Chalcedon, we are looking for a way to preserve both the distinctness and the relatedness of philosophy and theology, reason and revelation, as it were, "in two natures, without confusion . . . the distinction of the two natures being in no way annulled by their union." In short, the burden of this chapter will be to sketch out a way of doing theology that would at once be fully rational and fully biblical.

To accomplish this mediation of Christ and concept, I propose first of all to define with more care the respective natures and tasks of theology and philosophy. The goal here is to articulate the "specificity" of each discipline, that principle that ensures the integrity, individual identity, and distinguishing traits of one thing from another. I will then go on to describe, by means of a fivefold typology, the various functions philosophy has played over the course of theology's history. The types that are most germane to our discussion are those that neither eliminate philosophy altogether from the doing of theology on the one hand, nor simply capitulate to philosophy's rules and concepts on the other. Next, I will consider whether the current, so-called postmodern challenge to traditional Western philosophy may not inadvertently provide the opportunity for a renewed cooperation between philosophy and theology. I will conclude with a final consideration of the Chalcedonian formula as it applies to the relation of Christ and concept.

TWO WAYS TO STUDY GOD, SELF, AND THE WORLD

To define what philosophy is in a tidy formula is almost as heady and improbable an enterprise as the philosopher's own quest to define the nature of reality. It is safer to speak of diverse philosophies rather than Philosophy. Definitions are, however, inevitable and important. To define terms such as reality, truth, knowledge, goodness, and God is already to begin formulating an entire metaphysic, epistemology, ethics, and theology. If, for instance, one defines knowledge in terms of what we experience, we have the groundwork for a whole theory of knowledge—empiricism. Because definitions serve to orient us to a particular subject matter and create a certain set of expectations, we must proceed cautiously. My goal is to define philosophy in a manner that would elicit the assent and approval of as many philosophers as possible—and this without watering down the definition to the point of being vague and unhelpful.

My proposal is that we define philosophy as the critical and systematic reflection on enduring problems that arise in language and life. Each item in this definition warrants further scrutiny:

1. *Reflection.* Philosophy is not a form of immediate experience or direct engagement. Rather, the philosopher is one who pauses to consider what has been experienced, that is, what has been lived or said. The philosopher purposely disengages himself from an experience or a statement in order to inspect it from the outside.

2. *Critical.* The moment of disengagement when the philosopher steps back to consider life and language from a certain distance allows for a critical moment in reflection. Like the traveler to foreign lands, the philosopher finds that distancing oneself from one's usual experience makes possible a fairer assessment. One comes back from a summer abroad with a new awareness of the strengths and weaknesses of one's own society. The critical attitude is not necessarily a negative one. Rather, it refers to an inquiring habit of mind that no longer accepts the status quo or the everyday without question. The critical mindset seeks to press beyond appearances to what is really the case (e.g., the stick does *not* bend when it is put into the water).

3. *Systematic.* For the philosopher, critical reflection must continue until it is complete, that is, until one has attained a total analysis or a total system. The philosopher is committed to solving problems in a consistent fashion that ultimately leads to coherent and comprehensive answers. Like the physicist, the philosopher presses toward a unified field theory—universal

explanation. Throughout most of philosophy's history, analysis has not been enough; what is conceptually dissected must be put back together in systematic fashion.

4. *Enduring problems.* Critical and systematic reflection on life and language gives rise to enduring problems that are specifically philosophical in nature. Indeed, some philosophers maintain that the various academic disciplines are to be distinguished by the kinds of problems they deal with and by the kinds of methods they use to solve them. Engineers, doctors, mathematicians, psychologists, etc., all have their own particular problems and ways of dealing with them.[9] Philosophical problems differ from those of other disciplines in three ways. First, there is no technique we may follow in looking for an answer. You can look at a watch to figure out how long it takes for sound to travel, but there is no way to observe or calculate the answer to the question, What is time? Second, philosophical problems are *conceptual* in nature. Third, these conceptual problems—e.g., What is knowledge? What is truth? What is goodness? What is beauty?—deal explicitly with concepts that are basic to and often simply assumed by other academic disciplines.

5. *Life.* The philosopher does not begin reflecting empty-handed. Rather, he or she comes to a particular area of life or experience and begins asking critical and fundamental questions. Philosophy begins with problems that are part and parcel of everyday life—e.g., Can I really trust my senses? Questions like this give birth to whole disciplines, such as the philosophy of science. What makes the scientific method rational, and should it be used (because of its obvious practical successes) as a paradigm for thinking and method in other disciplines? Similarly, religion as a form of life is also susceptible to critical reflection. The philosopher of religion is puzzled about the religious dimension in human experience. What is a "religious" experience? Why does religion seem to be a universal phenomenon that spans both cultures and epochs? How is one to evaluate the truth claims of the various religions? Whether in science, history, religion, or any other domain, therefore, the philosopher raises questions about the fundamental concepts of an aspect of life or academic discipline.

The philosopher may also choose to ask questions about life taken as a whole—e.g., Why are we here? What is the meaning of my expected seventy-six years on this terrestrial ball? With these questions the philosopher ceases to look over the shoulders of other disciplines and comes into his own—the realm of what Aristotle called "first questions" and what are today called "worldviews." John Kekes suggests that "it is the task of philosophy to show how to live well by the construction and rational justification of worldviews."[10] But even here the philosopher does not begin with a blank slate but with certain clues to the nature of reality given at the outset.[11]

6. *Language.* If conceptual inquiry is the philosopher's task, the words of ordinary language and the technical terms used to clarify the relations between them are the tools. One is hard pressed to say whether a critical attitude toward language or toward life first gave birth to philosophy. Socrates posed what is perhaps the philosopher's Magna Charta with his maxim "The unexamined life is not worth living." But Plato, Socrates' contemporary (and perhaps creator), was interested in the meaning of words and concepts from the very first. Indeed, many of Plato's writings take the form of transcripts of various dialogues between Socrates and his students over the meaning of key terms, such as *good.* Using a mixture of questions and rebuttals, Socrates deftly shows his interlocuters that they do not really know what the terms they use mean. The lesson from these Socratic dialogues is still apt: we may think we know what words such as *good, true,* and *beautiful* mean, but when we are cross-examined, our account breaks down.

There is at present a resurgence of interest among philosophers in language and its uses. On the one hand, some believe that our everyday language is misleading and so leads us into confusion. Some claim that though God-talk seems to be referring to a divine entity, it really refers only to the speaker's emotional state. Thus the statement "God is love" really means, "I feel that love is divine," or something of this sort. Others contend that ordinary forms of language lead to confusion only if one overlooks their special "grammar" or logic. What is of significance to these philosophers are the rules that govern the use of language in specific contexts. Religious language, they might argue, has its own grammar and its own rules and so cannot be compared with, say, scientific language. The analytic philosopher tries to clear paths through semantic jungles. With sharp, machetelike distinctions, the philosopher cuts through the thickets of language and so achieves greater clarity.

This, then, is the understanding of philosophy that I will assume in this chapter: philosophy is the critical and systematic reflection on enduring problems of life and language. What distinguishes philosophy from other academic disciplines, therefore, is not a particular set of facts but a particular set of problems. Philosophy is a way of thinking that seeks rational solutions to conceptual problems. My definition has the advantage of covering a variety of particular philosophies as well as the two major types: Continental philosophy, which focuses on problems stemming from reflecting on life and different kinds of experience, and Anglo-American or Analytic philosophy, which focuses on problems generated by language and its different uses.

Theology, in turn, involves the critical reflection on enduring problems from the perspective of *biblical* language and the life of *Jesus Christ* to which it bears witness. There are two aspects of theology's task: first, the exegetical task, which involves showing the coherence of biblical language and literature. This is an internal problem for the household of faith: to demonstrate the semantic coherence of Scripture. Theology's second task follows from the first, namely, to show how the "Word-view" (the view from Scripture) continues to be relevant for solving contemporary problems of life and reflection. This is theology's "prophetic" task, which includes raising problems that are no longer felt as problems, such as how to enter into a right relationship with God. Again, what distinguishes theology from philosophy is the nature of its reflection: theology is the critical reflection on the language and life of humanity *from* the vantage point of biblical language and the life of Jesus Christ. The task of the Christian theologian is to bring the Word to bear on the world; hence the dual exegetical-prophetic task.

It follows from this understanding of theology that an appeal to revelation (biblical and christological) is constitutive for the practice of theology. Without Scripture and its witness to the life of Jesus Christ, the theologian would have no unique vantage point from which to reflect critically on the problems of language and life. In other words, without biblical language and the life of Christ to serve as norms for its reflection, theology loses its *specificity*. Without its normative appeal to biblical language and the life of Jesus Christ as the definitive self-revelation of God, theology loses whatever it is that makes it a distinct intellectual enterprise. Once cut off from its home in Logos-revelation, theology loses its disciplinary identity and integrity and is set adrift to float in shifting curricular seas, forever doomed to be confused with psychology, sociology, anthropology, literary criticism, history, and yes—philosophy.

My suggestion is that Logos-revelation (again, this term refers both to biblical language and the manifestation of God in the person and history of Jesus Christ) is the constitutive principle of Christian theology. It would be a misunderstanding of my proposal to confuse it with a fideistic appeal to biblical authority. Scripture, far from being an arbitrary norm, is rather like what Kant called a "transcendental" principle. A transcendental principle answers the question, "What are the necessary conditions for the possibility of such and such a phenomenon?" In this case, the phenomenon under consideration is the doing of theology, and the necessary condition for the very possibility of such an enterprise is, I contend, a Logos-revelation. To repeat once more, without such a distinctive transcendental or a priori principle, theology loses its individual identity and specificity. The bane of theology today is that contemporary theologians have, by and large, succumbed to the pressure of their peers and abandoned the idea of divine speech and Incarnation. Apart from its origin in a Logos-revelation, what the theologian says becomes indistinct from other prescriptions for well-being in the marketplace of ideas. Modern culture offers a number of beguiling solutions to humanity's problems, but once shorn of his special relation to the divine, the theologian becomes "as weak as any other man."

Is it really the case that theology would cease to exist without a Logos-revelation principle? Why must a written text—the Bible—be the transcendental condition of theology rather than some other principle? Why could not one espouse, with Schleiermacher, the phenomenon of God-consciousness as theology's a priori principle? This is an important objection to my proposal and one that many contemporary theologians believe to be a valid one. There are, however, at least two significant problems with this alternate proposal. First, other a priori principles are themselves frequently lacking in specificity. Schleiermacher's feeling of absolute dependence, Paul Tillich's sense of ultimate concern, Rudolf Otto's idea of the "holy," Karl Jasper's ciphers of Transcendence—these are principles that are extremely difficult to apply when trying to evaluate competing theological proposals. As criteria, they lack precise shape or appropriate "definition," in the ocular sense of the term.

Second, and more seriously, abandoning the principle of

Logos-revelation in favor of some other governing principle eventually jeopardizes theology's specificity, and thus whatever autonomy and integrity theology may have. As Hans Frei has shown, this was precisely Barth's fear about Schleiermacher's proposal. According to Frei, Barth worried that Schleiermacher, by making the human feeling of absolute dependence rather than the Word the theologian's touchstone, was in danger of losing what is most distinctive about Christianity. Theology for Schleiermacher becomes the science of faith (i.e., human feeling). It was only a matter of time before such a view of theology would become indistinguishable from the psychology of religion. Barth therefore decided that Schleiermacher's focus on feeling rather than the Word was both a christological and an epistemic deficiency: it would guarantee neither a distinctive identity and method for theology nor the uniqueness and absoluteness of Jesus Christ as the revelation of God.[12]

In sum, the role of an a priori principle is to make a certain kind of inquiry possible. I have argued that systematic theology cannot preserve its unique identity and intellectual integrity if it surrenders this principle or adopts a principle that lacks appropriate specificity. The Bible occupies a special role in Christian theology, not, as James Barr suggests, because of a historical accident (the Old Testament and New Testament canons just happened to have developed in the early stages of church history), but rather because the biblical witness alone guarantees the specificity of Christian thinking about God.[13]

Both theology and philosophy are problem-solving enterprises concerned with fundamental questions about God, the world, and the self. Philosophy's reflective strategy privileges no one text but draws on common human experience; theology's reflection is governed by biblical language and its witness to the life of Jesus Christ. Although both may assume humbler tasks, they often meet and confront one another on the level of worldviews. For both the philosopher and the theologian seek wisdom, which is not only a theoretical but also a practical knowledge that seeks to define, and pursue, the good life. The way of wisdom is the desirable approach to the enduring problems of life and language. But what is the way of wisdom? The philosopher thematizes something in the *saeculum* and constructs a worldview, but for the theologian the way of wisdom consists in a Word-view. Two roads diverge in a narrow world. Given this clear distinction, we now turn to possible relations between the two disciplines.

A FIVEFOLD TYPOLOGY

Both philosophy and theology can have as their subject matter God, self, and the world. I now propose to modify Niebuhr's fivefold typology between Christ and culture in order to plot the various possibilities for interaction between the two disciplines. In so doing, we will try to determine which of the five is best suited to achieve a reconciliation between philosophy and theology along Chalcedonian lines—that is, a reconciliation that would preserve the independence and integrity of each discipline while at the same time showing the compatibility rather than competition of Christ and concept.

Christ Subsumed Under Concept

For some philosophers and professed theologians, Jerusalem has no independent status whatsoever. For these thinkers, all talk about God and religion must either use the language of Athens or abandon any pretense to intelligible cognitive discourse.

Immanuel Kant's well-known reduction of religion to ethics is a case in point. In his *Critique of Pure Reason* Kant argued that we could never have any *knowledge* of God because we lack experiences of God to which we could apply our concepts and categories. If God is beyond the reach of our concepts and categories, it follows that everything we say about God must be speculation. However, Kant also realized that the *idea* of God is necessary to make sense of morality. Given the manifest evil in this life, we can only assume that duty and good will receive their just recompense in an afterlife. God is the factor that allows us to think that the scales of justice will be balanced in the end. The idea of God as keeper of the moral ledger thus functions as a guarantee device for Kant's ethical philosophy.

Kant similarly dispatches the story of Jesus. What interests Kant about the Gospels is not their apparently historical reference to the life of an individual person. No, for Kant the Gospels are meaningful, and true, in *exemplary* fashion only. That is, the truth of the Gospels pertains not to their historical factuality, but rather to their moral teaching. For Kant, the figure of Jesus Christ represents an idea. Kant calls Jesus the "Archetype of the Good Principle," and for Kant the Gospels express the truth that the Good Principle (Reason? Duty?) is stronger than the evil principle in human beings. The Gospel is nothing less than an illustration of Kant's ethical philosophy: Kant's postulate "ought implies can" receives instantiation in the story of Jesus' "overcoming" the world. Jesus' story acts as an encouragement to those seeking to attain moral perfection. Kant, like Pelagius, believes that Jesus can help us by giving us a good example to follow. On Kant's view, Jesus is not a Redeemer but an Idea, the idea of moral perfection overcoming the adversity of evil. The story of Jesus adds little to Kant's philosophical system but a good sermon illustration. Just as religion is only ethics writ large for Kant, so Jesus represents the idea that humans are fundamentally do-gooders. In Kant's philosophy, the actual history of Jesus Christ is of little import.

Philosophy's tendency to subsume Christ under concept reaches its apex in the philosophy of Hegel. Hegel was looking for a single principle that would explain not only the Real, but also the phenomenon of change, which had for so long been the major irritant in rational accounts of the world. Hegel's seminal insight was that reality is in movement, and this movement is to be understood as the unfolding of an Absolute Mind or Spirit (Geist). In combining the notions of Mind and change, Hegel thus provided a rational account of reality that left room for—indeed, called for—the phenomenon of change. The Real is both historical and rational.

Hegel also explained Christianity in terms of his philosophy. He argued that the various states of Mind (God) can develop only through a struggle with their opposites. For instance, happiness is gained only by overcoming unhappiness, good by overcoming evil. This struggle between two poles (Hegel calls them "thesis" and "antithesis") results in a third thing ("synthesis"), which in turn enters into conflict with something else. Hegel believed that there would come a point (the end of history) when all such conflicts would be reconciled and Mind would have fully come to itself. It is just here that Hegel appeals to the story of Jesus. Jesus' incarnation, death, and resurrection represent for Hegel the culmination of the development of Mind that he believes to be the motor of history. Consider the following propositions. The Incarnation means that God (the infinite) identifies with the finite. The Crucifixion shows us the extent of this identification. The Crucifixion is the paramount antithesis: the death of Jesus Christ is the negation of both being (life) and goodness. But the Resurrection represents the final synthesis: the negation is itself overcome. Infinity takes finitude onto itself, and the moment of death is transcended in an eternity of reconciliation. Similarly, evil is a negative that is itself negated. History has a happy ending because Mind takes even the things that seem to contradict it into itself and overcomes them.

Here again we see a philosopher treating the Gospel account as representative of philosophical ideas. Hegel apparently believed that the story of Jesus is dispensable (at least, according to the "left-wing" Hegelians). Once one knows the "true" (viz., philosophical) meaning of the story, the story itself is no longer necessary. It could be that others, not having the advantage of Hegel's training, might need the story in order to attain the truth. The Gospel narratives would then serve as narrative grist for the nonphilosopher's mill. But again, the point is that Christ serves only to illustrate a concept. As Hegel's critics have pointed out, there is a certain breathtaking arrogance to his system, pretending to stand at the end of history and explain its rational development. Paul Ricoeur's epithet to Hegel's philosophy is apt: "the greatest attempt and the greatest temptation."[14] "The greatest attempt": philosophy has never come closer to providing a single conceptual scheme to explain reality. "The greatest temptation": a comprehensive conceptual scheme has explanatory power, but when it is raised to the level of the absolute or final word, it runs the risk, like other totalitarian systems, of overlooking or suppressing facts that do not seem to fit it. A premature closing or absolutizing of a system is thus the philosophical equivalent of pride.

It is not only philosophers who seek to subsume Christ under some conceptual scheme. My last example is that of a theologian, Fritz Buri. Buri believes that Bultmann was not consistent in applying his well-known demythologizing method. Although most of the time Bultmann effectively translated the language of faith into the language of existential philosophy, at one crucial point in his scheme, he falters. Buri cannot understand why Bultmann, having demythologized the accounts of the Resurrection (by saying they speak more of the disciples' faith than of the body of Jesus), continues to speak of "acts of God." Why not translate these into existential philosophy as well? This is certainly Buri's strategy, and he consequently appears to be more consistent than Bultmann in his interpretation of Scripture. For Buri, the Bible is a mythological work whose truth must be understood in an existential framework. Theology is here reduced to anthropology, without remainder. What appear to be statements about God are actually truths concerning the universal human condition. The thought of Kant, Hegel, and Buri provides us with clear examples of how theology can quickly lose its specificity once Christ is subsumed under some conceptual scheme. Once the "truth" of the idea, symbol, or myth of Christ is grasped, one no longer needs the figurative, or historical, representation. These philosophers have no need for revelation. The Gospel does not disclose something new but merely illustrates truths that can be reached through reason alone. Theology—that is, reflection on the stories and symbols in Scripture—does have a place, however, for the masses cannot be expected to reach these truths philosophically. The Gospel story is a painless shortcut to truths more adequately formulated (and justified) by the philosopher. Jerusalem thus turns out to be Athens dressed up for Christmas in order to appeal to the uncritical masses.

Christ in this position is simply a figurative representation of a concept. As such, this way of conceiving the relation of philosophy and theology is akin to the christological heresy promulgated by the Docetics. The Docetic denies the earthly reality, the flesh and bones, of the historical Jesus.[15] Jesus' life, suffering, and death were not real; rather, the Logos merely took on the appearance of the man Jesus. In the same way, this first way of relating theology and philosophy denies the historical significance of Jesus Christ and construes Jesus as the figurative representation of an idea or concept. Indeed, this position takes a Docetic attitude toward theology as a whole: theology only *appears* to depend on a historical revelation. In the end, the only Logos that counts is the ideal Logos of the philosopher. It should be evident that theology, along with the figure of Christ, loses its autonomy and integrity in this tradition. To incorporate philosophy in this manner is already to surrender theology's integrity and independence.

Christ Grounded on Concept

Another approach to the relation of philosophy and theology makes Jerusalem a suburb of Athens. On this view, philosophy serves as a support or foundation for theology's talk about God. Unlike the first position, here theology is not reduced to philosophy but must nevertheless depend on philosophy for its intellectual integrity.

An early, less extreme version of this position may be

represented by the second-century Greek apologists, such as Justin Martyr, and by third-century Alexandrian theologians such as Clement. These early theologians shared an appreciation of Greek philosophy and stressed its continuity with Christianity wherever they could, for instance, between Plato and the apostle Paul. They commended Christianity to their Hellenistic contemporaries by presenting Christianity as the fulfillment of Greek philosophy. Interestingly enough, these early theologians appealed to the idea of the Logos as the principle of the purported continuity. In Justin's celebrated *Apology*, he argues from John 1:9 that Christ is the Logos of whom all humanity has a part, the light of Reason that enlightens everyone: "He (Christ) is the reason (Logos) of whom the whole human race partake."[16] Similarly, Clement of Alexandria views Greek philosophy as affording true knowledge of God. Christ and concept are both inspired by the same Logos. According to Clement, "philosophy was a 'schoolmaster' to bring the Greek mind to Christ, as the Law brought the Hebrews."[17] Appropriately, Alexandria is located between Athens and Jerusalem, a convenient half-way house for the faithful pilgrim in quest of understanding.

Modern theologians have also been quick to build bridges between Christianity and secular philosophies on the theory that such bridges give the theologian more credibility. Indeed, this type of approach to theology tends to insist on a prior philosophical foundation if theology is not to be incredible. As the Greek apologists turned to Plato, so contemporary apologists use today's fashionable conceptual schemes to demonstrate the intelligibility and truth of Christianity. Although Christ is not reduced to a concept as in the first position, a prior conceptual scheme is necessary in order to commend Christ to the contemporary situation. Paul Tillich believes that the theologian must somehow establish a "connection" of sorts between the Gospel message and the contemporary situation if the Bible is to be intelligible to modern ears. Tillich calls this strategy of establishing connecting links between the Bible and the modern world the "method of correlation." For Tillich, the common denominator between the first-century situation of the Gospels and the twentieth-century situation of the world and the church is the fundamental question concerning the meaning of life and the threat of death. The question of being—its meaning and possible cessation—provokes the anxiety that is everywhere apparent in Western societies. Tillich's attempt to correlate modern questions about the meaning of life with the Bible is especially apparent in his *Biblical Religion and the Search for Ultimate Reality*.[18] There he suggests that questions about Being find their answers in the symbols and stories of Scripture. For Tillich, theology is the attempt to correlate contemporary questions about human being with the answers Scripture gives in symbolic form. Tillich clearly describes his theological program: "In using the method of correlation, systematic theology proceeds in the following way: it makes an analysis of the human situation out of which existential questions arise, and it demonstrates that the symbols used in the Christian message are the answers to these questions."[19]

Tillich understood his theology to be "apologetical," in the sense that it is an "answering theology" to contemporary concerns. Tillich also used his method of correlation and theory of symbol to defend the intelligibility and truth of the biblical message. He attempts to preserve the unique integrity of Jesus and the biblical revelation by providing an overarching theory of religious language, meaning, and truth, without which the Bible would be unintelligible.

In the same spirit, David Tracy develops a general theory of language and literature that "makes space" for more properly biblical notions such as revelation. According to Tracy, the truth of religion is like the truth of art: both aesthetic and religious classics are true in the sense that they disclose something essential about the human condition. Indeed, this kernel of essential truth is what makes an art work a "classic," that is, a work of universal and permanent validity. Classic works of art capture a fundamental truth about the nature and meaning of human being and about the scope of human possibilities. Similarly, the Gospels reveal a possible way of living in the world: the way of love "in spite of," the way of unconditional love. This is the possibility represented by the story of Jesus. The story of Jesus also manifests the truth that God loves the world. With Tillich, Tracy insists that the story of Jesus can transform us, insofar as it changes the way we look at ourselves. To see oneself as loved by God is to experience God's grace and salvation. For Tracy, religious classics, like works of art, are true because they manifest something essential in reality and, in so doing, have the power to change human beings. Tracy's hermeneutics therefore constricts the kind of truth claims the Gospel can make. There is no room for the historical Jesus in Tracy's hermeneutic inn. Tracy is quite insistent on this point: "The truth claims of art and religion stand or fall together."[20] Tracy thus stands in the tradition of those theologians who believe that the biblical message must be set in a larger philosophical theory of meaning and truth if it is to be intelligible.

On one level, this manner of relating philosophy and theology appears to be fruitful and to theology's advantage. Why not let theology be supported by a general theory of being or meaning? Why not rely on philosophy to create the ontological, hermeneutical, and conceptual "space" within which theology may witness to Christ? Why eschew philosophy's help if it is willing to be an ally? It is perhaps significant that the theologians who favor this role for philosophy are often those most conscious of their apologetic responsibilities. What better way to defend the faith in the world than by using the world's best intellectual resources?

When it comes to actually doing theology, however, such theologians cause Christ not only to be grounded but also constricted (choked) by concept. This is especially apparent in the work of Tracy and Tillich. For Tillich, the Bible answers contemporary questions—questions that for him are existential. These questions determine what Tillich finds in the Gospel. The direction in Tillich's thought is decidedly from world to Word, for the questions of the contemporary situation decisively shape the whole tenor of his theology. The world's anxieties here set the agenda for what the theologian finds in the Word. Aristotle's maxim is worth pondering in this context: "Those who wish to succeed must ask the right preliminary questions." Is it the case that the question of being and nonbeing are more fundamental and more appropriate for theology than, say, the question of how one can once more be right with a personal, holy God? Philosophy, by posing the questions, thereby controls the subsequent discussion. It may not, therefore, be inappropriate to speak of the Athenian captivity of the church. It is evidently possible both to borrow from the Athenians and be plundered by them.

Unlike in the first position, Christ is not simply reduced to an idea or concept. Rather, Christ is introduced by concept, that is, by means of a general conceptual or hermeneutical scheme *within which* biblical language, and Christ, alone make sense. In Tracy's work, for instance, the Bible is introduced as one of many religious classics. The problem of formulating the uniqueness of Christ, however, is endemic to this second construal of the role of philosophy. This follows from the fact that Christ and Scripture are only instances of some larger phenomenon, such as religious classics or religious language. What first appeared to be a strong defense of the intelligibility of biblical language in the end turns out to relativize Scripture. The Bible is only one member of a larger class. It is no coincidence that both Tracy and Tillich display a lively interest in the question of world religious and interfaith dialogue. "Christ" in this position says more than concept, but what is said can only be understood by virtue of a prior conceptual scheme. The way to the Word is philosophically prepared. The Word has something to say to the world, but it can be heard only in a worldlywise metaphysic.

Christ in Dialogue With Concept

Athens and Jerusalem in this third position are more like West and East Berlin used to be—a divided city where people on both sides of the wall searched for passageways. Neither side enjoyed a privileged status in this communication, however, nor was there a broader general theory that governed their conversation. Proponents of this position insist that philosophy and theology maintain their proper authority relative to their respective spheres, namely, the academy and the church. Like the second type, this position seeks to correlate the language of religion with the language of the academy and the world, but unlike the second this third option does not employ a single philosophical scheme to govern the conversation. Instead, philosophy and theology travel along parallel tracks that, from time to time, coincide.

We may take Thomas Aquinas as representative of this tendency to bring philosophy and theology into dialogue with each other. In Aquinas' thirteenth-century context, the philosophy with which Christianity was in dialogue most often was that of the newly rediscovered Aristotle. Unlike Plato, who was concerned with the spiritual realm of ideas, Aristotle gave a complex and comprehensive account of the natural world. While some theologians rejected Aristotle's philosophy altogether because of residual pagan ideas (e.g., the eternity of the world as opposed to Creation), others tended to accept it in spite of its conflicts with the teachings of faith (e.g., the Averroists). Aquinas, however, took a mediating position. He accepted the basic contours of Aristotle's philosophy but revised and supplemented it in light of the Christian revelation; hence his brilliant "medieval synthesis" between philosophy and theology. Aquinas brings Aristotle's philosophy of nature and Scripture's theology of grace together. Aquinas does not simply place faith into an Aristotelian scheme. While it is true that Aquinas, using reason alone, attempted to demonstrate God's existence, he did not consider the principle of reason alone to be sufficient. Philosophers can think about God, but their thought needs the supplementary information and periodic correction that only biblical revelation can give. It was Aquinas who described philosophy as the "handmaiden" to the queen of the sciences—theology. No amount of conceptual cogitation can reach conclusions concerning the possibility and actuality of divine grace, for instance. By its very nature, grace is contingent—it did not have to be. The philosopher searching for conceptual necessity is necessarily confuted when pondering grace. Revelation here gains a real autonomy that it did not have in the first two positions.

Even in Aquinas, however, one wonders about the extent of theology's autonomy. Although the revealed information may have a divine source, once revealed it is processed with Aristotelian concepts and categories (e.g., substance, accident, form, matter). Although the *matter* is revealed, it is Aristotle who provides the *formal* criteria that govern the understanding of faith. Aquinas is certainly on the side of the angels when it comes to revealed information, but the processing of this information requires the same methods and standards that govern any other scientific discipline.

Friedrich Schleiemacher also tries to give equal time to both church and academy. As did the liberal Protestantism to which he gave birth, Schleiermacher strives to break down the walls that separate religion from modern culture, without doing injustice to either.[21] For Schleiermacher, theology is an activity of the church. Unlike theologians who hold either of the two previous positions, Schleiermacher eschews attempts to establish a foundation for theology on general philosophical principles.[22] Rather, theology for Scheliermacher is critical reflection on the religious affections, particularly the feeling of being dependent on a higher Being.[23] At the same time, Schleiermacher is anxious to commend religion to its "cultured despisers," of whom there were many in the wake of Kant's attack on attempts to know God rationally. While insisting that theology is rooted in the concrete life of the church (that is, the life of faith), Schleiermacher attempted to correlate it with the philosophy of his day—Romanticism. Religion, he argued, is no worse off than art or morality, forms of life that are similarly based on modes of human feeling. The feeling that is constitutive of the church and thus of theology as well is for Schleiermacher that of being dependent on that which transcends the individual self of the believer as well as the corporate society of the church. Theology has an autonomy over against philosophy because of this constitutive religious feeling. Moreover, theology has a specifically Christian character for Schleiermacher insofar as it is Jesus Christ who communicated this feeling of absolute dependence or God-consciousness to his disciples and ultimately to the church as a whole.

Schleiermacher's correlation of religion with philosophy is built on his insight into the resemblance yet distinctness of religious feeling to moral and aesthetic feeling. The concept of the church—and thus theology—is unique, but Schleiermacher says that we understand the concept of the church only if we "borrow" ideas from ethics and philosophy. Schleiermacher takes this Romanticist philosophical notion of the self as consciousness and relates it to the God-consciousness that is constitutive of the church. This is a "coincidental" correlation, however, and not the result of some prior conceptual scheme. That is, the bridge between Christianity, culture, and concept that Schleiermacher forges is not dictated by a larger philosophical system but simply borrowed from philosophy. This is a marriage of convenience, not necessity. Schleiermacher describes self-consciousness much as would a philosopher, but in describing the consciousness of being absolutely dependent on God, Schleiermacher is also doing theology—he is reflecting critically on the piety (life and language) of the church as it is expressed in Scripture and tradition.[24]

A third example of one who seeks a genuine dialogue between philosophy and theology is Rudolf Bultmann. Like Schleiermacher, Bultmann believed that the biblical message had to be translated for modern ears. Religion's twentieth-century cultured despisers could not be expected to accept such improbabilities as a three-decker universe populated with angels above and demons below. Bultmann treats these supernatural features as the husk around the true kernel of the Gospels, namely, the preaching of God's act in the cross of Christ. However, Bultmann relies heavily on the existentialist philosophy of Martin Heidegger to communicate this Gospel message. Bultmann claimed that he found virtually the same message in Heidegger's *Being and Time* as he did in the Gospels. Like Schleiermacher before him, Bultmann does not subsume Christ under Heideggerian concepts but rather borrows them for his own purposes. Specifically, Bultmann correlates Heidegger's notion of "inauthentic existence" with a Lutheran doctrine of works (in both cases, the point is that human beings cannot secure their own existence) on the one hand, and Heidegger's notion of "authentic existence" with a Lutheran doctrine of grace on the other (in both cases, the point is that we find our true selves only in the resoluteness of faith).[25]

For Bultmann, the kernel of the Gospel concerns truths about human existence. Some have accused Bultmann of reducing all God-talk to talk about human existence, that is, of reducing theology to a philosophical anthropology. However, Bultmann's intent is decidedly theological. Unlike some of his more radical disciples (e.g., Buri), Bultmann persists in speaking of God's act in the event of Jesus Christ. Bultmann's critics claim that in refusing to demythologize statements about divine actions, he is both incomplete and inconsistent. While this may indeed be the case, Bultmann himself believed that the theologian had something to say that philosophy could not: philosophy might be able to state the necessary conditions for the possibility of authentic human existence, but theology is concerned with proclaiming their reality. Only this proclamation of an actual rather than merely theoretical possibility keeps Bultmann's reading of the New Testament and his whole theology from sliding headlong into a philosophy of human existence *tout court* and from swallowing up Christ in concept.

This third way of relating Christ and concept, with Athens and Jerusalem as equal partners in the discussion, gives rise to a theology "on the borders" of philosophy. While what the theologian wants to say is never simply subsumed under Aristotle's, Kant's, or Heidegger's conceptual scheme, at many points the difference is borderline. This is particularly the case with Schleiermacher and Bultmann. Granted their primary allegiance to the church, their well-intentioned borrowings from philosophy nevertheless threaten the specificity and autonomy of theology. It may be significant that the purpose of such borrowing is often apologetic—the primary beneficiaries are the cultured despisers of religion, not its faithful adherents. Most importantly, is it really possible to please the academy and express the significance of Christ in a foundational conceptual framework without losing the sheer contingency and graciousness of the event of Jesus Christ? Is it more than a coincidence that both Schleiermacher and Bultmann have difficulty in relating the Jesus of history to the Christ of their conceptual schemes?

Christ in this third way of relating philosophy and theology is proclaimed with the aid of concepts "borrowed" from the philosopher. The theologian does not buy into a whole philosophy but only makes such withdrawals as are deemed expedient. Because the philosopher has often proven to be an exacting lender, however, the question is whether theology can remain an equal partner for the duration of the transaction. The challenge for proponents of this third way would be to produce a theology that would be free from the structural inconsistency that plagues Bultmann's, and to a lesser extent Schleiermacher's, theology.

Christ the Lord of Concept

Yet a fourth approach to the relation of theology and philosophy turns the tables on Athens and makes it a borough of Jerusalem. On this view theology is completely autonomous, independent of the philosopher, and is under no obligation to subscribe to a foundational conceptual scheme. The theologian is free to make use of philosophy here and there, but there is no need to cast one's lot with a single philosophical system. Many philosophical schemes and notions may be pressed into theological service from time to time, provided there is theological warrant. On this view, philosophy is less a handmaiden to theology than its bondservant.

Karl Barth has enshrined Anselm as the patron saint of this position.[26] Anselm, the great medieval theologian, explicitly follows the formula "faith seeking understanding" in his theological program: "I am not seeking to understand in order to believe, but I believe in order to understand."[27] Describing, not defending, doctrine is uppermost in Anselm's mind. Anselm is not as interested in proving faith so much as showing its internal coherence. For Anselm this meant that philosophy had a secondary, elucidating role. Biblical revelation provides the material to be understood, and philosophy contributes the impetus toward conceptual clarity. Taking biblical language as his revealed given, Anselm sought to uncover the inner coherence and necessity (= rationality) of what was said. Accordingly, we might say that Anselm's task as a theologian was to demonstrate the logic of biblical language. Barth's Anselm may well be one of the earliest theological nonfoundationalists.[28] Anselm's classic study of the Incarnation, *Cur Deus Homo*, works out a theory of the atonement by demonstrating the necessity of the Cross. Anselm reaches the level of rational necessity, not by employing philosophical concepts, but rather by analyzing the inner logic of biblical language and literature, that is, by discovering the "logic" of the Bible's overall plot. Given God's honor and holiness and man's total inability to render God his due, the Cross is necessary for salvation. To reach these conclusions Anselm need not appeal to any conceptual schemes or philosophical categories beyond the rudiments of logic. Logic seeks not to put the Word into worldly frameworks, but only to make manifest the order inherent in the biblical account itself.

Similarly, Karl Barth views theology as the task of conceptual elaboration of revelation. One does not need to mount arguments defending the possibility of revelation; rather, the theologian takes revelation as a given and then expounds it. Theology is not apologetics; it does not defend revelation but simply explains it. The theologian does not need a prior conceptual scheme within which biblical language can make sense; rather, one simply begins (unapologetically!) with biblical language. Theology qualifies as a science, Barth insists, because it offers a mode of thinking appropriate to the object under consideration. "Objectivity" refers to the kind of thinking that is appropriate to the object under investigation. The Word of God is not something to be submitted to human probing, nor is it subject to human observation or calculation. No, the Word of God—which for Barth is preeminently Christ—is Lord of all human concepts. God's revelation in Christ must not be fit into an already developed conceptual scheme: only God can explain God. The theologian must not be hindered by preconceived philosophical notions but must rather be prepared to follow God's revelation wherever it leads. Hence the well-known epithet for Barth's method: "theology from above." Theology in Barth's view enjoys a rationality all its own, namely, the Anselmian version where concepts are second-order redescriptions of the language of faith.

Hans Frei applies this Barthian view of the relation of philosophy and theology to the question of narrative interpretation. In his magisterial study of eighteenth- and nineteenth-century hermeneutics, *The Eclipse of Biblical Narrative*, Frei argues that Bible scholars mistakenly began to subsume the truth claims made by the Gospels under philosophical theories of historical reference that were then in vogue. According to Frei, the truth of the Gospels is neither the truth of history nor the truth of myth—the two categories that dominated biblical interpretation during the modern era. Frei refuses to let the modern world define the kind of meaning and truth claims that the Gospels make, in the same way that the Word of God for Barth defies every philosophical conceptual scheme.

Frei's aim is to let the Bible itself define the nature of its meaning and truth. Like Barth, Frei is particularly effective in criticizing theologies that subsume Christ under some conceptual scheme or seek to provide the framework within which to understand Christ (our positions one and two respectively). The Gospel narratives, Frei suggests, have a "logic" all their own. They cannot be fit into some predetermined theory of interpretation. Rather, biblical narrative must be understood on its own terms. In the same way, the life and language of the church must be understood on its own terms, rather than casting it into some other mold, such as Marxism, Freudianism, or existentialism. In describing the workings of biblical language, the theologian functions like a literary critic. In describing the life and faith of the church, the theologian functions more like a social anthropologist. The goal for both is to elucidate the meaning of biblical language and Christian faith by showing how it is used. Philosophy may be used in this endeavor, but only in eclectic fashion. For Barth and Frei, biblical language and the language of faith are privileged languages, with no equal partners. Philosophy will never, on this view, be able to approximate what Scripture and the theologian wish to say.

George Lindbeck has helpfully characterized this position as pursuing an "intratextual" approach to theology, that is, an approach that seeks to understand Scripture and the Christian faith with its own resources and in its own terms.[29] Lindbeck contrasts this with the "extratextual" approach, which seeks to ground Christian theology in some conceptual scheme that is obtained apart from the biblical text. In the case of extratextuality, the Word is subsumed under worldly categories. In the case of intratextuality, the world is understood with categories derived from the Bible itself. Whereas the extratextual approach demythologizes the Bible in order to understand it in contemporary terms, the intratextual approach tends to "demythologize" the myth of modernity in order to understand the present situation in biblical terms.

With this fourth position the Word of God and biblical revelation gain real independence from concept. Theology need not justify Christ's universal relevance in terms of some philosophical scheme, nor is theology accountable to philosophers who, braver than Pilate, seek to define truth. The philosopher on this position is not the grand architect whose systems lay bare the very structure of reality, but rather the humble carpenter whose handiwork is from time to time of service in the house of theology. But if philosophy truly is subordinate, then what is to prevent the theologian from saying and thinking *anything*, like Tertullian who said that he believed in the Incarnation *because* it was contradictory? The question is whether this view of Christ as Lord of concept should entail a situation where the theologian can "lord it over" the philosopher, not to mention logic itself. If the theologian need not worry about the philosopher's traffic rules for intelligible discourse, then what will stop him from ignoring the stop signs of rationality, the yield signs of empirical evidence, and the solid double line of noncontradiction? In Frei's words:

> Without the constant, continuing *practice* of correlation . . .
> do not all criteria for intelligibility except the minimal, formal
> rules of grammar and syntax in fact go out the window for
> Christian theology? Do not principles like that of noncon-
> tradiction become not eschatological but Pickwickian if they
> have no clear theology-independent status in their applica-
> tion to theology?[30]

Neither Barth nor Frei is comfortable with the label "irrationalist." Frei does not renounce talk of reference and truth claims, but he does balk at having to justify his Christian beliefs *in terms of* some other conceptual scheme and language. Frei believes he is justified in his Christian belief (rational), but this is not the same as being able to justify Christian belief to someone else. Barth views the Word of God as "capturing" human language and human concepts—but only for a time. This so-called Anselmian position with regard to the relation of Christ and concept is a bit like the Adoptionist heresy with regard to the person of Jesus Christ. On the Adoptionist view, the Logos did not become Incarnate, but rather joined together with—we might say, "captured"—the man Jesus for a time. Theology from above stresses the transcendence of the Word. Just as the Adoptionists refuse to equate the Logos with the man Jesus, so Frei and Barth refuse to equate revelation with the Bible. They believe that theology should have "no secure earthly resting place," no "secure philosophical, experiential, or cultural home."[31]

Christ the Contradiction of Concept

Proponents of the fifth position contend that Jerusalem has nothing to do with Athens. Unlike in the previous position, philosophy does not even serve as sometime handmaiden. The inhabitants of Athens and Jerusalem lead different kinds of lives and speak different languages. For all intents and purposes, Athens and Jerusalem might as well be on separate planets, so little do they have in common. Strictly speaking, philosophy and theology cannot even be opposed, for they are incommensurable forms of language and life.

Tertullian disagreed with those church fathers who viewed Greek philosophy as preparing the way for the Gospel. Tertullian calls philosophy that "rash interpreter" of things divine and goes on to blame the philosophers for the heresies that plagued the early church.[32] The Incarnation renders these vain philosophies obsolete: "There is no need of curious questioning now that we have Christ Jesus, nor of enquiry now that we have the Gospel."[33] A similar denunciation of philosophy can be found in the writings of Luther, who called philosophy "the devil's whore." Luther, perhaps inconsistently, believed that while the devil should not have all the good tunes, he could keep philosophy for himself. Both Tertullian and Luther saw little need for conceptual schemes, given the preeminence of the living Christ. Near the end of his life Luther said to his students, "I have taught you Christ, pure, simply and without adulteration."

In recent times a more sophisticated separation of Christ and concept has become fashionable among certain theologians who work in the tradition of the philosopher Ludwig Wittgenstein. Wittgenstein worked his whole life on problems concerning language and meaning, and late in his career he came to believe that language is not always meaningful or true in the same way. Words are not only used to refer to things, but are complex tools that perform a number of tasks. Wittgenstein argued that we must attend to the way a piece of language is used in concrete life situations. Speaking a language, said Wittgenstein, is part of an activity of a particular form of life. The meaning of a word or concept changes according to the activity or "language game" in which it is being used. In other words, each particular form of life has its own "grammar" that governs the meaning of the terms used in much the same fashion as the rules of a game govern the activity of playing. It follows from this view that linguistic meaning must be public: games are social activities.

Wittgenstein applied his thinking about language to matters of religion only briefly, in a few lectures.[34] In his well-known example of the Last Judgment, Wittgenstein wonders how he would disagree with someone who believed in the Last Judgment. He finds that he does not believe the opposite of this person, nor does his belief contradict the other person's belief. Rather, Wittgenstein's belief is on another plane altogether, part of another game. The implication is that religious belief is in a game of its own, where the rules of other games (such as history, science, etc.) do not apply: "It is an entirely different kind of reasoning."[35] The implication is that the religious believer is off in his or her own world of discourse. One cannot say just anything, for even the religious language game has rules. But "whether a thing is a blunder or not—it is a blunder in a particular system. Just as something is a blunder in a particular game and not in another."[36]

Theology on this view is a community-specific "game" with its own rules. The church's life and language simply do not intersect with other forms of life and language (i.e., history, physics, philosophy). No man may be an island unto himself, but language games may be. Theology is, consequently, impervious to criticism from other disciplines. Theology is an internal matter only, a matter of mapping out the "grammar" of faith. This involves seeing how the language of faith actually functions in the lives of believers. And the best way to achieve this level of understanding is, of course, to participate in the game.

This position, even more than the previous one, has been attacked for its retreat to commitment and its immunization strategy. It is simply too easy to say that theological truth is a special kind of truth that is incommensurable with any other kind of truth claim. It is not simply that the theologian of this position refuses to justify religious belief by using the other disciplines, but that he denies the very possibility of contact between theology and other language games. Proponents of this position refuse to admit that the meaning and truth of theology is commensurable with other forms of human discourse.

THE ECLIPSE OF LOGOS IN THE POSTMODERN WORLD

At this point, a brief parenthesis is necessary. The traditional antagonism between reason and revelation that has characterized much of the history of theology in the modern era has recently become less of a threat than the direct attack on rationality itself that has recently been mounted by certain "postmodern" thinkers. Postmodern thinkers distinguish themselves from "modern" thinkers by their different stance towards reason: whereas the modern era is by and large characterized by an optimistic confidence in reason's ability to gain knowledge of the world and solve its problems, the postmodern thinkers profess a distrust in reason's abilities and a disbelief in reason's professed objectivity.[37] Reason yields no God's-eye point of view; on the contrary, reason is mired in culture myopia and political power struggles in much the same way as are finite human beings. Reflection is never innocent or objective; rather, one reflects from a particular place in history and culture, with all the biases that are to be found there.

Philosophers in the postmodern tradition are busy "deconstructing" the history of Western philosophy. Instead of formulating theories of meaning and truth, these thinkers are more concerned with exposing the contradictions and shortcomings of traditional philosophy. In particular, deconstructionist philosophers challenge traditional attempts to build a bridge between language and the world. In so doing they shake the very foundations of Western philosophy, insofar as it depends on Aristotle's understanding of truth as the correspondence of language or thought to reality. Jacques Derrida, one of the foremost deconstructionist philosophers, argues that Western philosophy erred in making the phenomenon of speech rather than writing the paradigm of the language-world relation. In the speech situation, the speaker is "present" in his speech to ensure that his words will be related to the world as he intends. In writing, however, no such relation is specified. Derrida claims that in writing, language refers only to itself.

There is no "voice" to tell us how to relate language to the world. Derrida further claims that all reflection is similarly "textual"—never anchored in the real but pulled to and fro by other forms of discourse.

What deconstructionist thinkers such as Derrida find most objectionable about traditional philosophy is its "logocentrism," that is, its reliance on speech as the paradigm for the way language is related to the world.[38] Whereas the traditional picture posits a speaker who is in control of his language, Derrida reverses the situation and claims that what speakers say is as much if not more determined by the language itself rather than their conscious intention. Interestingly enough, Derrida associates this logocentric emphasis with the Christian idea of Incarnation—the Logos become flesh. The point of the Incarnation is that the Word is something present. For Derrida, however, there is neither an Author who gives meaning to the world nor authors who determine the meaning of their texts. More precisely, we have no access to Author or authors. As to their texts, meaning and reference are not present but absent. All we have is the text (the world) itself. In Derrida's words, *"Il n'y a pas hors de texte"* ("There is nothing outside the text"). Because there is no God's-eye point of view and no authoritative voice (Word), we have no means to assess the correspondence of language to the world. For Derrida, language refers only to itself. Bereft of any place outside language from which to evaluate it, the human thinker is at the mercy of the "play" of language. Consequently, the True, the Good, and the Beautiful are *all* in the eyes of their human beholders. There is no privileged or absolute viewpoint, no authoritative voice to end the discussion.

For this chapter, what is significant about the deconstructive turn in philosophy is its low opinion of the philosopher's *logos*. For the deconstructionists, the philosopher's language—the language of concept and conceptual schemes—is of no higher value than any other. No conceptual scheme provides a means to anchor language in the real. Indeed, the deconstructionists like to describe philosophy as a form of literary criticism—all reflection is reflection about texts within texts. A good example of the current situation in philosophy may be found in Alasdair MacIntyre's *After Virtue*. MacIntyre makes the point that while contemporary philosophers continue to use the standard terms of ethics (*good, bad, duty*), it is no longer clear what foundation, if any, such language has. Who is to say what "good" means? Any appeal to an absolute perspective, such as the Word of God, is ruled out. But it is precisely this demise of the *logos* principle that has rendered philosophy vulnerable before the deconstructionist critique. Dostoyevsky foresaw the consequences of abandoning theism long before: "If there is no God, everything is permitted."

The postmodern situation provides an interesting vantage point from which to continue debating the relation of philosophy and theology. Although I cannot argue the point here, I suspect that a purely autonomous philosophy—one that makes no appeal to God or to a divine Logos—may indeed be susceptible to the attack of the deconstructionists. Why should we trust reason and believe that it can achieve knowledge of reality and human values if there is no God to, as it were, "guarantee" it? Why should we believe that human rationality is truth indicative? What if there is some structural flaw that prevents our minds from grasping the true nature of reality? The point of this postmodern parenthesis is simple: the *logos* of the philosopher in some way is ultimately linked, as even the deconstructionists tacitly acknowledge, to a logos principle.[39] Somehow, the fates of philosophy and theology appear to stand or fall together. It is with this thought in mind that we now turn to consider the possibility of a Chalcedonian solution to the problem of Christ and concept.

CHRIST AND CONCEPT—
A CHALCEDONIAN PERSPECTIVE

Unlike Niebuhr's approach to the question of Christ and culture, I favor no one of the five ways of relating Christ and concept. Each of the five ways fails to preserve either the individual integrity of philosophy and theology or their relatedness. The reason for this failure stems from the assumption, shared by philosophers and theologians alike, that rationality must be either foundational (justificatory) or nonfoundational (descriptive). A picture of rationality has held us captive. One must either accept foundationalism and try to "prove" Christ "from below" or reject foundationalism and proclaim Christ "from above."

Few theologians are comfortable with the first and last of the five positions, which represent the extremes of foundationalism and nonfoundationalism respectively. Whereas the first position seems to be both in the world *and* of it by incorporating

Christ wholesale to some conceptual scheme, the last position seems to deny theology's rootedness (and responsibility) in the world. Most theologians wish to answer Tertullian's query with more than a shrug of the shoulders. Indeed, defining the precise relation of Jerusalem and Athens is the major burden for the middle three positions. The second option, however, surrenders too much to Athens from the very start, thus slipping toward the first position. That leaves the third and fourth options, those of Schleiermacher and Barth respectively. Each of these two, I believe, contributes something essential to the discussion. According to Stephen Sykes:

> What Christianity will become for men and women of the future is not decided. Nor will it have a future unless, with Schleiermacher, one is open to the contemporary secular disciplines by which its nature and history are exposed to the public gaze, and with Barth, one is open to the Word at whose gracious invitation it has been brought into existence.[40]

A Chalcedonian formulation of the problem of Christ and concept will attempt to preserve both of these moments: the contribution of the Word (Christ) and the contribution of worldly learning (concept). But how is it possible to bring the theologian's reflection on the Word into harmony with the philosopher's reflection on the world? Such an endeavor is repeatedly frustrated when rationality is defined in terms of justifying or "proving" beliefs. The Chalcedonian perspective I now wish to provide will build on the strengths of the third and fourth positions by offering a different account of what it is to be rational. This account of rationality will, I trust, open up new possibilities for the faith-reason debate. However, just as Chalcedon did not provide a definitive statement on the nature of the relation between the two natures of Christ but only set the parameters for the ensuing discussion, so I will limit myself to suggesting certain implications concerning the role of philosophy in the doing of theology—implications that follow from the revised notion of rationality.

How may a theologian's work be "fully biblical" and "fully rational"? For the foundationalist, this occurs only if the theologian "proves," by argument or evidence, the utter reliability of Scripture. For intellectual honesty means withholding belief unless certain (or highly probable) justification is available. The theologian is consequently forced to choose between believing for no good reason or justifying the hope that is within him. But the latter option would mean abandoning theology's constitutive principle, for the theologian would have first to justify the Word with the world's categories before reflecting on the world with the categories of the Word.

It is precisely this problem that generated the five ways of doing theology I set out above. And it is just here that a "fallibilist" conception of rationality allows the faith-reason debate to go forward once more. For the fallibilist, rationality is not a matter of laying solid foundations that hold up the edifice of knowledge. Rather, rationality concerns the way we solve problems. No one kind of evidence is sacred (foundational), because the kind of evidence to which one appeals must fit the particular problem-situation and disciplinary context. What counts as evidence in the biologist's problem situation may not count as evidence in that of the historian or engineer. In suggesting that rationality pertains to the way we solve problems, then, we reject the positivist's claim that all rational arguments must use the same kind of data or evidence. It does not follow, however, that rationality itself must be different for each problem-situation or discipline. Rather, *rationality pertains to the intellectual standards that govern our discussion about any kind of problem whatsoever*. In other words, rationality is not a matter of a particular kind of starting point but of the rules that regulate reflective discourse. Rational discourse is characterized by clarity, logical consistency, conceptual coherence, comprehensiveness, and criticizability. We may not always be conscious of these five rules in everyday conversation, but they are nevertheless the necessary characteristics of all rational discussion.[41]

Why label this conception of rationality "fallibilist"? Those who first coined the term were attempting to explain the rationality of the natural sciences, and they suggested that what made a theory "scientific" was not that it was certain or fully justified, but rather that it was criticizable. What makes a theory scientific or objective is the fact that it can be tested. Lakatos claims that scientists begin with a "hard core" of basic beliefs. This hard core is treated as though it were virtually certain— not because it has been justified but because of a prior methodological decision to treat it as such.[42] This hard core serves as a control to the subsequent work of the scientist and gives rise to what Lakatos calls a "research program." Newton's gravitational theory, for instance, served as the hard core for physics for some two hundred years. Once a scientist has a hard core, subsequent theories emerge that form a "protective belt" around the core. It is this protective belt and the theories that comprise it that get tested, modified, and perhaps rejected. On the fallibilist model of rationality, what counts is not the starting point (the hard core) but the results of testing. For Lakatos, the question is whether the theories generated by the hard core solve the enduring problems of science. Is the research program that is put into motion by the hard core "progressive" or "degenerating"? That is, does it solve previously intractable problems and advance scientific knowledge, or does it lead to more problems and hopeless contradictions? It is important to note that whether a set of theories is or is not rational is not determined in advance as in foundationalism but only over the course of time as they are evaluated on their ability to solve problems on which they bear. Theories are judged not on the basis of whether they are constructed upon infallible foundations, but as fallible attempts to solve problems.

With our fallibilist conception of rationality in hand, we are now in a position to develop our "Chalcedonian" view of the relation between philosophy and theology. In particular, we should now be able to explain how the theologian may think in a way that is fully biblical and fully rational, without confusion, contradiction, or paradox. A Chalcedonian perspective that is imported into the debate over faith and reason yields a view of philosophy and theology that preserves the individual integrity and relative autonomy of each, and at the same time calls for their mutual accountability.

1. *Individual integrity*. Philosophy and theology each have a right to exist. In the case of philosophy, its constitutive principle is critical reflection on universal human experience. Philosophy builds and evaluates worldviews with concepts derived from human experience and speculation. Theology is distinct because its critical reflection is informed by the biblical text (considered as revelation). But it is important to point out that neither the principle of rationality nor that of textuality is the exclusive domain of one or the other of the two disciplines. On the one hand, theology is a form of rational discourse, a thinking about a specific text. On the other hand, philosophy is reflection on life and language, that is, on something that precedes it that has many of the characteristics of a text (seventeenth-century scientists spoke of the "Book" of Nature).

The theologian's text is the Word of God; the philosopher's text is the world of common human experience. Given our fallibilist model of rationality, there is no compelling reason why one could not take either "text" as one's special point of reference. There is neither epistemic virtue nor epistemic vice in starting points.

2. *Relative autonomy.* The primary "texts" of philosophy and theology are therefore distinct. This gives a relative autonomy to each discipline. The philosopher deals with conceptual problems that arise in the life and language of the world, whereas the theologian deals with problems that arise from and are addressed by the Word. Each undertakes to construct a worldview, but only for one is the worldview shaped by a Word-view. But despite their differences, both philosophy and theology are involved in solving problems by constructing worldviews. They therefore share some important formal features.

As we have seen, both philosopher and theologian pursue "exegetical" and "systematic" tasks. The philosopher's "exegetical" task is to interpret reality. The philosopher does not invent what there is but tries to describe it as clearly as possible, whether it is human experience or human language. The analytic tradition in philosophy excels in clarifying meaning— exegesis. However, the philosopher may also make connections as well as distinctions, relating things to one another in order to attain systematicity. The philosopher strives for a coherent view of the world, for a grasp of the basic principles that unify his text, the Book of Nature.

With regard to theology, its exegetical task carries with it a historical and literary mandate: to explicate and understand the biblical text. The systematic task gives the theologian a prophetic mandate: to make what Scripture says understandable for the church today. The philosopher can be of help in both tasks. In the first, philosophy offers a set of logical and linguistic tools that have been refined over the centuries. The "grammarian" tradition of philosophy has a long and distinguished history, and theologians have made frequent use of it. Aristotle's *Categories* and *On Interpretation*, for instance, provided medieval theologians with the basic rudiments of conceptual analysis (e.g., noun and predicate, individual and kind, particular and universal, matter and form). In the case of theology's systematic-prophetic task, the philosopher offers conceptual schemes that facilitate the move from first to twentieth century. Here the philosopher plays the role of Aaron next to theology's Moses, providing the language with which to communicate the Word of God to a wondering people. For better or for worse, Bultmann and Tillich sanctified the conceptual scheme of existentialist philosophy and used it to proclaim the Gospel to anxious twentieth-century secularists.

To repeat, the theologian and the philosopher enjoy a degree of independence from each other because they critically reflect (utilizing the principles of clarity and systematicity) on problems of life and thought from different vantage points (Word vs. world). But their autonomy is only relative. Not only are they both rational enterprises, but the dimensions in which each lives and moves and has its being overlap. Such overlap is inevitable when both are in the business of constructing worldviews. Philosophy (in its metaphysical mood) and theology both aim at solving problems pertaining to worldviews, that is, problems having to do with the basic nature of reality and the meaning of life. For instance, both the philosopher and the theologian are interested in discovering the conditions for human freedom, the good life, salvation, authentic existence, or whatever else one chooses to call the situation for which we hope in the face of finitude, suffering, and death. Ultimately, we are led to view philosophy and theology themselves as competing research programs working on the problem of life's meaning. And at this stage, it may be more appropriate to speak about "life" rather than "research" programs.

Each discipline enjoys, therefore, only a relative autonomy. The theories of each are open to criticism from within and without. The theologian cannot simply retreat to authority and hide behind ecclesial walls as the philosophers march around and around, trumpeting criticisms. While it is entirely proper to give one's primary allegiance to the biblical text, it is both irrational and irresponsible to ignore what other texts (including the philosopher's text, human experience) have to say. It is less than intellectually honest to pretend that nothing any of the other disciplines may say can criticize one's theological position. Although theologians believe that their text is the Word of God, one's theological system or worldview is only a human, and thus fallible, interpretation. Theologians above all should appreciate a fallibilist conception of rationality. Indeed, exposing one's ideas to criticism should not be an unfamiliar idea to those for whom one of the prime ethical, even theological, virtues is humility. To refuse criticism is to absolutize one's fallible perspective and to ignore the impact of one's particular culture, time frame, and tradition on one's thinking. It is also to abdicate theology's prophetic task.[43] Theologies that seek to insulate themselves from criticism under the cloak of biblical revelation fail to give reasons for the hope within them and so fall short of their calling and commission. A robust theology must enter into the conflict of interpretations about the nature of humanity and reality by permitting its text—and the life and research program it generates—to be tested over against the alternatives.

The philosopher, no less than the theologian, has only a limited autonomy. As we have seen, the philosopher's work is always derivative: reflection always comes after life and language. In other words, the philosopher too is dependent on "texts" that precede critical reflection. The philosopher goes astray when he retreats not to authority but to autonomy. Such a retreat most often takes the form of reductionism. Reductionism is the philosopher's besetting temptation: what better way to attain a coherent worldview than to reduce the rich complexity of reality to a single conceptual scheme?

3. *Mutual accountability.* Perhaps the most controversial consequence that follows from our Chalcedonian metaphor is the idea of the mutual accountability of Christ and concept. This mutual accountability derives in part from the overlapping of enduring problems (God, self, and world) as well as from the common affiliation to the *logos* principle. I believe the key to determining the role of philosophy for doing theology is to be sought in this notion of the mutual accountability of Christ and concept. How then are theology and philosophy mutually accountable?

Like the philosopher, the theologian is responsible for seeking conceptual clarity. Inherent in faith itself is the move toward such understanding. The theologian takes the results of biblical exegesis and demonstrates their coherence and relevance for today, thereby making the biblical Word-view into a viable worldview for the contemporary situation. On the other hand, the philosopher, like the theologian, seeks unifying principles that would account for the coherence of general human experience. Inherent in reason is the move toward comprehensiveness and ultimate coherence—toward systematization. Such an ambitious project of developing a universal conceptual framework has long been the *telos* of the great metaphysical philosophers, but since Kant most philosophers have felt that this task remains incomplete. Kant himself spoke of the regulative Ideas of Reason that guide the philosopher's thinking without ever becoming something the philosopher actually knows or possesses.[44]

The philosopher and theologian thus share each other's ambitions: the theologian shares the philosopher's clarifying ambition, and the philosopher—so long as he is true to his task of making a comprehensive whole out of universal human experience—shares the theologian's systematizing ambition. Reason's demand for totalization creates an epistemic restlessness that, like Augustine's restlessness of heart, finds its rest only in that in which all things finally hold together—"it finds its rest in Thee." Provided that neither philosophers nor theologians succumb to the particular temptations that constantly beset them (viz., the philosopher's overestimation of his autonomy that leads to reductionism and the theologian's overestimation of his authority that leads to myopic separatism), we could even speak of the "mutual indwelling" of these two ambitions.

At this point, it may be helpful to address a nagging suspicion. Is there not a point where the Christian theologian must put a halt to the process of critical testing that is the essence of our fallibilist view of rationality? Surely Scripture, the constitutive principle of theology, must remain beyond criticism, for otherwise the very discipline would be threatened. In other words, even on this new understanding of rationality, does not the theologian have to adopt an irrational stance vis-à-vis his constitutive principle—biblical revelation? This question deserves careful attention.

I have suggested that the "hard core" (the "given") of the theologian's life and research program is the Bible. Theology's task is to reflect on the problems of life, using the Scripture and its witness to Jesus Christ as its special source and norm. But what happens when this hard core is itself the target of criticism? We may recall that for Lakatos the scientist makes a methodological decision to regard the hard core as the "given." However, unlike the foundationalist, the fallibilist is aware that this methodological decision may be questioned. How then does the scientist put the hard core itself to the test if there is no unproblematic foundation of knowledge against which to measure it? Lakatos argues that a hard core comes to be rejected if the theories it generates consistently meet with less problem-solving success than the theories generated by another hard core or set of basic beliefs. Newtonian physics was not disproved by one argument alone, but rather, over a long period Einsteinian physics showed that it was better able to account for new facts and for previously unresolved problems. In other words, one tests the hard core of a system by determining whether its theories are able to deal with new and enduring problems as effectively as the theories associated with another hard core. According to Lakatos, only the fittest research programs will survive the greatest test of all—the test of time.

Lakatos' account of scientific rationality may be applied, I believe, to worldviews. The theologian may indeed allow the hard core of his research program to be tested. This does not mean that the theologian gives up or doubts faith. Rather, for the sake of the discussion, the theologian treats his method-ological decision to take the Bible as norm as a fallible one.[45] The question then becomes, Which core generates a worldview that more effectively deals with enduring problems of life and reflection? Of course, when we deal with worldviews as life paradigms, empirical criteria (e.g., Do these theories explain observable phenomena?) are not enough. For instance, the question of meaning is more important for evaluating world-views than for physics. Accordingly, we could test two competing hard cores, say materialism and Christianity, by asking which one better accounts for the varieties and complex-ities of human experience.

Similarly, the various hard cores that underlie competing theological positions may also be compared. Which life and research program—evangelicalism or liberalism—is more suc-cessful in meeting the enduring individual and communal problems of our day? Judgments may indeed be made on this level. I would argue, for example, that the research and life program of Bultmann's demythologizing is no longer a progres-sive one.[46] As has been widely recognized, existential theology is unable to address problems of a communal rather than an individual nature, and it appears inconsistent in the way it interprets Scripture, reducing everything to an aspect of human existence except the central notion of an "act" of God.

In a fallibilist perspective, no one kind of starting point is more privileged than another, at least to begin with. There is no contradiction between one's initial respect for the given and one's subsequent analysis and conceptualization of it. If the reader allows my stretching of the term *revealed* to cover the sum total of what has been given (i.e., that which precedes philosophizing, that which one decides to accept as the hard core), then we could say that both philosopher and theologian work with some such paradigm as "reason within the limits of revelation alone." On a fallibilist view of rationality, what counts is not the *ground* you play on but *how* you play the game.

Philosophy therefore constitutes a standing challenge to theology to be rational, to submit its worldview for inspection in the open market of ideas rather than cloistering it in authority and tradition. In short, the philosopher holds the theologian accountable to the standards of rational discourse. But as one who specializes in thinking with and about concepts, the philosopher also plays a constructive role in the doing of theology. The philosopher is a conceptual "schemer," one who offers coherent systems or frameworks for interpreting reality. As we have seen, theologians have been quick to baptize these schemes and conscript them for the ministry of the Word. To a great extent, the history of theology is the history of such appropriations: Augustine's of Plato, Aquinas' of Aristotle, Schleiermacher's of Kant, Bultmann's of Heidegger, Hartshorne's of Whitehead, liberation theology's of Marx, and so on.

Ultimately, however, no one conceptual scheme is ever equal to the task. The interpretive frameworks never exhaust the meaning of the biblical text itself, because the Bible is both conceptually "underdetermined" and "overdetermined." Biblical language is underdetermined in the sense that it supports more than one conceptual scheme—witness the number of theories of the atonement that seek to explain the significance of Jesus' death. This proliferation of theories and conceptual schemes is not necessarily a problem, however, for to fulfill its prophetic task theology must speak to new and different audiences and generations. But biblical language is also overdetermined. That is, the biblical text enjoys what Paul Ricoeur calls a "surplus of meaning" that eludes any exhaustive conceptual paraphrase. The story is always richer in meaning than the commentary. Such overdetermination of meaning provides a salutary caution for the theologian—*caveat emptor*: let the buyer beware of conceptual schemes that pretend to be equal in value to the biblical text. Ultimately, the temptation to reduce theology to a philosophical scheme can be resisted only by constant exegesis of the biblical text.

On the one hand, therefore, the Bible calls for conceptual clarification and elaboration. But on the other hand, no such conceptual elaboration will ever completely capture "the" meaning of Scripture. The Bible is too under- and overdetermined for that. Instead of submitting to conceptual domestication, Scripture repeatedly breaks out of our narrow and nearsighted conceptual grids to say something new and to call for continued clarification and commentary.

Philosophy is thus necessary for doing theology. Indeed, if theology would regain her throne and again don the mantle of queen of the sciences, she must consult the philosopher, who in turn must play the dual role of minister of internal ("intratextual") and foreign ("extratextual") affairs. Philosophy has first an internal ministry in the "domestic" affairs of theology by providing analytic tools for the task of clarifying theology's hard core, the language of the Bible. As analyst and logician, the philosopher does not set policy (i.e., tell us which text to believe) but explicates what is already written. To change governmental metaphors, the philospher as conceptual analyst functions in the judicial rather than the legislative branch. Conceptual analysis helps us see what we are (logically) committed to on the basis of our "constitutional" text. Second, philosophy serves theology as minister of "foreign" affairs by mediating between the world of the Bible and the contemporary situation. The object of such shuttle diplomacy is to provide conceptual schemes that serve the pedagogical function of leading unbelievers and believers alike to a deeper understanding of Christ and the implications of a Christian worldview.[47] Here of course the theologian must again recognize the fallible nature of his judgments: one may choose to explore process philosophy or existentialism for their potential fruitfulness, but these bold decisions must be tempered with humility. Conceptual schemes, though necessary, are only fallible human attempts to comprehend reality. Although the Word of God may be perfect, theology's crown is always tarnished. A little lower than the angels, we humans know only indirectly, through interpretation. That we must interpret our text and our world, that we must work to make sense of them, is our common human lot. As a form of human knowing, theology is not born to greatness but has greatness—the privilege and responsibility of bringing the Word of God to bear on the world—thrust upon it. Our fallibilist conception of rationality is thus perfectly fitted to theology: rationality in theology as in any other discipline is not primarily a form of power but of vulnerability, for rationality essentially is intellectual honesty and intellectual humility. The queen must follow the example of her Lord: intellectual pride must tread the *via dolorosa*. Thinking that is fully biblical and fully rational (i.e., "Chalcedonian") must take the way of humility.[48]

Our Chalcedonian perspective on the relation of Christ and concept highlights both the humility (rationality) that should characterize all human thinking and the given (revelation) to which our thinking eventually must give account. Philosophy maintains its double ministry to theology as long as it diligently pursues its task: critically to reflect (*logos*-rationality) on the given (*logos*-revelation). Their respective constitutive principles keep theology and philosophy distinct (the philosopher does not privilege any one text), but their common allegiance to rational standards of discourse and their overlapping subject matter (God, self, the world) keep them related. Both disciplines aim, in different ways, at a comprehensive understanding of human being and its place in the cosmos.

Like the framers of the Chalcedonian formula, however, we are hard pressed to define exactly how the two natures (= disciplines) go together. Our proposal for the role of philosophy in doing theology has the status of a regulative idea: it offers only the parameters and general direction that theology must follow, not a blueprint for a final solution. What analytic tools and conceptual schemes the theologian should use is a matter to be addressed on an ad hoc basis, in another forum. Here hard questions await, for there is no guarantee that the theologian will find a neat philosophical package that would permit an easy translation of the Bible to the contemporary situation. Instead, the theologian may have to explore—in humility, fear, and trembling—any number of philosophies, selecting those frameworks that appear to solve the enduring problem of how to bring the Word to bear on the world in the most rational and biblical manner.

Theology and philosophy, while distinct enterprises, share each other's ambitions. Theology moves toward conceptual understanding, and philosophy, in pursuing the course of reason, moves toward ever higher levels of coherence and totalization—perhaps toward God. Perhaps the secret bond between the philosopher and the theologian is their mutual love of wisdom, their *philo sophia*. Indeed, John Kekes observes that the ultimate purpose of a worldview is wisdom, the ability to live well in the world and solve its problems.[49] The philosopher thus moves toward wisdom as he attempts to solve the enduring problems of life and to seek the *logos* or unifying principle thanks to which reality is coherent. And in this quest for wisdom, the Bible, which claims to reveal this unifying principle as a supreme personal being and names him "the Father of Jesus Christ," should not be overlooked ("in him all things hold together"). Philosophers may follow Pilate's lead in washing their hands of the Gospel's truth claims, but they do so at their own risk. Those who listen to the Word, however, may find that the fear of the Lord is not only the beginning of wisdom but also its end.

Wisdom for the theologian refers to the ability to grasp, and fit into, God's plan of creation and redemption personified in Jesus Christ, the *Logos* made flesh (Prov. 8:22–31; 1 Cor. 1:23–24). In the person and work of Christ the meaning of the whole, of human being and human history, is revealed. The work of the theologian is to analyze and systematize (e.g., construct a rational worldview of) this Christocentric perception of the meaning of the whole complex of God, self, and the world displayed in Scripture.

Kant long ago taught us that concepts without percepts are empty, but percepts without concepts are blind. To take Christ (the light of the world) as one's ultimate "percept" does not abrogate the function of philosophy but calls for it. For the believer, Christ is the *given* that we must *think*, the revelation that must be rationally understood. The theologian begins with the Gospel of Jesus Christ and moves toward conceptual understanding—the philosopher's *logos* and wisdom. This ultimate Christian percept calls for a host of concepts. From this biblical starting point, then, the theologian enters the arena of rational discourse—humbly, but singing. The hard core of Christian theology boils down to a single claim, made by Jesus: "I am the way and the truth and the life. No one comes to the Father except through me" (John 14:6). The Christian life and research program generated by this claim is still progressing after some two thousand years, daily meeting—and passing— the acid tests of human inquiry and existence.

If their purpose or activity is of human origin, it will fail. But if it is from God, you will not be able to stop these men. (Acts 5:38–39)

NOTES

[1](New York: Harper & Brothers, 1951). In consecutive chapters, Niebuhr

describes the possible configurations of Christ and culture as follows: Christ could be against culture, of culture, above culture, in paradox with culture, or the transformer of culture.

[2]It is interesting that Niebuhr acknowledges the influence of Etienne Gilson's *Reason and Revelation in the Middle Ages* on his five main types of relations between Christ and culture. In focusing explicitly on the faith-and-reason question, we are doing no more than returning Niebuhr's typology to its original home. The way I formulate my own fivefold typology has also been influenced by the work of Hans Frei, especially his unpublished Shaffer lectures.

[3]Wolfhart Pannenberg, *Basic Questions in Theology*, 2 vols. (Philadelphia: Westminster, 1970), 1:1–2. Pannenberg is almost severe in his emphasis on the universality of theological claims: to plead that theology is one science among others, each with its own separate data and subject matter, is a virtual "betrayal of the first commandment" (p. 2).

[4]Diogenes Allen credits the Greek's persistent "why" questioning with the beginning of humanity's search into the *logos* or fundamental rational principle that explains a particular aspect of reality (*Philosophy for Theologians* [Atlanta: John Knox, 1985] 4–5).

[5]Imre Lakatos, "Falsification and the Methodology of Scientific Research Programmes," in Imre Lakatos and Alan Musgrave, eds., *Criticism and the Growth of Knowledge* (Cambridge: Cambridge University Press, 1970), 91.

[6]Austin Farrer, "A Starting Point for the Philosophical Examination of Belief," in Basil Mitchell, ed., *Faith and Logic: Oxford Essays in Philosophical Theology* (London: George Allen & Unwin, 1957), 9.

[7]In proposing a "fallibilist" conception of rationality, I am following recent philosophers of science such as Karl Popper and Imre Lakatos. For an excellent study of the way in which the work of these philosophers of science can be extended to theology, see Philip Clayton, *Explanation from Physics to Theology: An Essay in Rationality and Religion* (New Haven: Yale University Press, 1989).

[8]In speaking of the "given," I am not referring to so-called brute facts nor am I appealing to a strict dichotomy between observation and theory. I assume that the given, whether it is the world or a text, is always already interpreted as soon as it is received by humans.

[9]In defining philosophy in terms of the problems it attempts to solve, I am following, among others, Isaiah Berlin, *Concepts and Categories: Philosophical Essays* (New York: Viking, 1979), chap. 1, "The Purpose of Philosophy"; Vincent Brümmer, *Theology and Philosophical Inquiry: An Introduction* (Philadelphia: Westminster, 1982); and especially John Kekes, *A Justification of Rationality* (Albany: State University of New York Press, 1976), chap. 8.

[10]John Kekes, *The Nature of Philosophy*, APQ Library of Philosophy (Totowa, N.J.: Rowman and Littlefield, 1980), xii.

[11]In the twentieth century, for instance, secular existentialist philosophers such as Jean-Paul Sartre and Martin Heidegger focus on the experience of absurdity and death. Anxiety and dread become clues to the meaning of human being. On the other hand, other thinkers such as Gabriel Marcel and Paul Ricoeur (not to mention C. S. Lewis) focus on experiences of faith, hope, and love in their search for the meaning of life.

[12]See Hans Frei, "Barth and Schleiermacher: Divergence and Convergence," in James O. Duke and Robert F. Streetman, eds., *Barth and Schleiermacher: Beyond the Impasse?* (Philadelphia: Fortress, 1988), 65–87, esp. 68–69.

[13]In this respect there is a formal analogy one can draw between what E.

D. Hirsch says about the discipline of literary criticism and what I have said about theology. For Hirsch, the criterion of authorial intent is the indispensable condition for the discipline of literary criticism, for there is no other norm available that allows validity or reasoned consensus in literary interpretation (*Validity in Interpretation* [New Haven: Yale University Press, 1967]). In my view, the Bible guarantees the disciplinary integrity of theology as does authorial intent for literary criticism.

[14]See, for instance, Ricoeur's essays "The Hermeneutics of Symbols and Philosophical Reflection I," in Paul Ricoeur, *The Conflict of Interpretations* (Evanston: Northwestern University Press, 1974), 287–314, esp. 310–13, and "Biblical Interpretation," *Semeia* 4 (1975).

[15]The name "Docetic" comes from the Greek verb *dokein*, "to seem or appear."

[16]Justin Martyr, *Apology* I.xlvi.2-4.

[17]Clement of Alexandria, *Stromateis* I.v.28.

[18](Chicago: University of Chicago Press, 1955).

[19]Paul Tillich, *Systematic Theology* (Chicago: University of Chicago Press, 1951), 1:70.

[20]David Tracy, *The Analogical Imagination* (London: SCM, 1981).

[21]Note that Niebuhr classifies liberalism under the heading "The Christ of Culture" and describes liberalism as accommodating or capitulating to the reigning cultural assumptions of the day.

[22]F. D. E. Schleiermacher, *The Christian Faith* (Edinburgh: T. & T. Clark, 1928), §2.

[23]Schleiermacher states that all of Christian doctrine may be derived through critical reflection on the religious affections (*The Christian Faith* §31).

[24]Cf. Frei, "Barth and Schleiermacher."

[25]Cf. Roger Johnson, *The Origins of Demythologizing: Philosophy and Historiography in the Theology of Rudolf Bultmann* (Leiden: Brill, 1974).

[26]See Karl Barth, *Fides Quaerens Intellectum*.

[27]Anselm, *Proslogion*.

[28]I say "Barth's Anselm" because many philosophers of religion would dispute Barth's interpretation.

[29]George Lindbeck, *The Nature of Christian Doctrine: Religion and Theology in a Postliberal Age* (Philadelphia: Westminster, 1984), 114.

[30]Frei, "Barth and Schleiermacher," 85.

[31]Ibid., 70–71.

[32]Tertullian, *De praescriptionae haeretricorum* vii (cited in Henry Bettenson, ed., *Documents of the Christian Church* [New York: Oxford University Press, 1943], 7–8).

[33]Ibid.

[34]Ludwig Wittgenstein, *Lectures and Conversations on Aesthetics, Psychology, and Religious Belief*, ed. Cyril Barrett (Los Angeles: University of California, n.d.).

[35]Ibid., 58 Cf. Paul L. Holmer's example: the theology game relates everything to God; the history games relate everything to each other in terms of antecedents and consequences. These are two types of understanding (*The Grammar of Faith* [New York: Harper & Row, 1978], 6).

[36]Ibid., 59.

[37]For more on postmodernism, see David Tracy, *Plurality and Ambiguity: Hermeneutics, Religion, Hope* (New Work: Harper & Row, 1987), esp. 69–81.

[38]See Jacques Derrida, *Of Grammatology* (Baltimore: Johns Hopkins University, 1976), 10–18.

[39]As I have already mentioned, Descartes and other philosophers acknowledge this dependence. Perhaps the best example is that of the Scottish thinker Thomas Reid, who argued for the validity of common sense on the basis of the fact that God created the human mind in such a manner that it could gain true knowledge of its world.

[40]Stephen W. Sykes, "Schleiermacher and Barth on the Essence of Christianity—an Instructive Disagreement," in Duke and Streetman, *Barth and Schleiermacher: Beyond the Impasse?* 105.

[41]Those who wish to dispute this are advised to imagine a conversation in which one or more of these rules is not in force. It should be obvious that attempts to communicate would simply break down before long.

[42]The hard core is therefore a methodological a priori, similar to what I have been calling the "constitutive principle" of a discipline. The Bible, for instance, would be the "hard core" of evangelical theology.

[43]I take theology's prophetic task as including apologetics.

[44]Immanuel Kant, *Critique of Pure Reason*, trans. Norman Kemp Smith (London: Macmillan, 1933), B 536–B 543. Paul Ricoeur goes so far as to speak of the truth that philosophy seeks as being "eschatological," an object of hope as much as reason. Given the effects of history and culture on human thinking, Ricoeur argues, the philosopher should be more humble in his interpretations of reality, less willing to make one finite perspective absolute. For Ricoeur, Kant's account of the limits of reason make him the epitome of the humble philosopher.

[45]Under the conditions of what Thomas Kuhn calls "normal science," the hard core is rarely questioned. It is only in "revolutionary" periods, where a program is increasingly beset by anomalies, that one begins to question the hard core itself. The theologian who, for the sake of the discussion, is willing to submit the hard core of theology to the test does so reluctantly, recognizing the signs of his revolutionary times.

[46]What counts as a "progressive" research or life program in theology is an important, though probably disputed, question. On a formal level, success is measured in terms of successful problem solving. But the problems with which the theologian is concerned are not only theoretical but also practical. It may well be that the criteria for a successful theological program would include holiness as well as truth. In the discipline of theology, we may judge a research program by its fruit.

[47]It is the philosopher as minister of foreign affairs who, I believe, is most likely to try to mount a coup against the theologian (see positions 1 and 2 above).

[48]This is not to say that theological thinking is wishy-washy and lacking conviction. On the contrary, I think theologians may have bold convictions, provided they hold them humbly. Although I cannot argue the point here, I believe that humility (which for me is the prime Christian virtue) points to a profound connection between rationality and ethics.

[49]See Kekes, *The Nature of Philosophy*, 199–200.

5

ON METHOD AND MEANS
IN THEOLOGY

HAROLD O. J. BROWN
TRINITY EVANGELICAL DIVINITY SCHOOL,
DEERFIELD, ILLINOIS

INTRODUCTION

During an after-dinner conversation at Harvard in the late 1950s, a student asked Professor Georges Florovsky precisely how he became a believing Christian. Florovsky, a Russian-born Greek Orthodox priest, was one of the only two or three Christians on the Harvard Divinity School faculty who unashamedly professed an orthodox, biblical Christianity and who let himself be called evangelical. In those days, the word *evangelical* had not yet quite become the party label it is today—distinguished from fundamentalism—but it was already a term used only by those who were not ashamed of the Gospel, even if it meant being labeled obscurantist or simple-minded. In fact, Florovsky often remarked, "Around here [at Harvard] they call me a fundamentalist because I actually believe in God."

But let me return to the question. Other members of a highly liturgical and sacramental denomination might have answered, "By being baptized." There were still a few conservative admirers of Karl Barth around, although their numbers were waning even then, who would perhaps have replied, "When you say that you are surest about being a Christian, that is when you may be farthest from it." To them, any objective factor or subjective experience that one might use to gain confidence concerning one's standing before God detracted from the authority of the Word. A person who thinks thus

147

could hardly speak of "becoming" a Christian at any identifiable point in his or her life. Faith must be nothing but
reliance on the Word of God without any subsidiary supports,
whether in outside, objective reality or in internal, subjective
experience. The general run of liberal teachers, on the other
hand, would probably have shrugged the question off as
meaningless or embarrassing or both.

Father Georges knew what the questioner meant. "My
father [also an Orthodox priest]," he said, "initiated me
without compulsion into the mysteries of the faith."

This simple answer contains three positive components
and one negative component. Positively, Florovsky said that
one whom he knew and trusted *initiated* him; that is, his father
did not merely expound doctrine but led his son where he
himself had gone before. A second positive component is
suggested by the term *mysteries*. A mystery in this sense is
something that can be known—indeed, that to some extent
must be known—but cannot be fully or exhaustively understood. A mystery in the Christian sense is neither an enigma
nor a secret but a truth to be proclaimed, a truth that engages
and challenges the human intellect and yet one that requires
humility and submission because it surpasses human comprehension. By speaking not merely of mysteries but of "mysteries
of the faith," Florovsky indicated the third positive component:
what we do know and understand of such mysteries is enough
to warrant our confidence and trust. By saying "mysteries of
faith," we express our commitment to and confidence in a
surpassing wonder, one that will lead us beyond the ordinary
limitations of human finitude, fallibility, and sin.

The negative component of his statement is "without
compulsion." Faith cannot be compelled, and logically the steps
that lead to faith also must be taken without compulsion, or at
least without *human* compulsion: Scripture does speak of a
constraint or control that occurs in the experience of the love of
Christ (2 Cor. 5:14). To say "without compulsion" does not
mean, of course, that there is to be no discipline in teaching and
in learning, but it does mean that the decisive steps of faith
must be freely taken.

FIRST, FAITH

Before approaching our topic, method and means in
theology, it is necessary to speak of faith. Theology *as an*

intellectual discipline, as a science, must begin with faith. What is theology? One writer calls it "the reflective self-understanding of faith" (Trillhaas). The fact that the Christian faith is based on propositional revelation given in history and has major historical components means that it appeals to the intellect and challenges the believer to make decisions and commitments concerning the truthfulness and reliability of its propositions. Such a decision and commitment, however, goes far beyond the type of informed guesses, hypotheses, and dogmatic assertions that are common in other branches of science and scholarship, for such leave the scientist or scholar unchallenged in his authority as the judge and arbiter of his discipline. It is possible for him to make mistakes and to be forced to accept correction, but he retains his autonomy. In the case of Christian faith, the faith brings one into a relationship of submission to a higher authority, an authority that is personal and that is in fact the highest of all authorities.

This requirement, that faith precede theology, deprives the theological scholar or "scientist" of the possibility of being the autonomous judge and arbiter of his material in the same way that a literary critic, a social scientist, or even a historian is. In this respect a theologian must be somewhat more like a physical scientist, a chemist, or a biologist, for each of these must deal with reality as it is, not as he would have it be. The honest natural scientist does not have the possibility of saying with Milton's Satan—or at least not for long:

> *The mind is its own place, and of itself can make*
> *A Heav'n of Hell, a Hell of Heav'n.*

The Epistle to the Hebrews states that without faith it is impossible to please God (11:6). One cannot have *Christian* faith without knowing God, and we can confidently go beyond that and say that one cannot have anything that deserves to be called *knowledge of God*, which has to be the primary stuff of theology, without faith. Faith is a precondition for doing theology properly so called, not only or even primarily because personal faith is a touchstone of one's acceptability or a kind of spiritual union card, but because it is a necessary means to arrive at the kind of knowledge that is theology's object, namely knowledge of God and about God. This is a fundamental truth that, if acknowledged, will transform the enterprise known as theology. True theology cannot be done apart from faith. By this I do not mean merely theology that states truths, but theology as an authentic scholarly discipline.

If theology is the "reflective self-understanding of faith," it cannot exist without and apart from faith on the part of the theologian. There can be a kind of intellectual enterprise on the part of a nonbeliever in which he deals with the topics covered by traditional theology, but this enterprise not only is not *Christian* theology, it is not even *theology* in the sense of a scholarly quest for real knowledge; in other words, it is not *scientific*, because it does not make use of the means appropriate to scientific endeavor. Paradoxically, it is precisely the enterprise that prides itself on being "scientific theology"—*wissenschaftliche Theologie*—which proceeds on a methodological basis that categorically rules out the possibility of ever arriving at true *Wissen*, knowledge, or recognizing it as such if it should happen to chance on it.

AMBIGUOUS TERMINOLOGY

Because of the necessity of faith for a proper understanding of theology we must discuss faith before we can discuss theology and method in theology. But the word *faith* is often used in an ambiguous sense. This ambiguity must be clarified before we proceed. Faith can and often does mean that which is believed—in other words, a content or body of doctrine. When this is what we mean by faith, it is possible to systematize and codify it, to put it down in print, and to make it accessible to all who can read. This enterprise need not involve the decision and commitment mentioned above.

In its second and more fundamental sense, however, faith refers precisely to a personal engagement and a personal relationship. In this sense faith never exists apart from one or more "faithful" people, in other words, apart from believers; indeed, when we are speaking of theology as an enterprise that involves learning and teaching, faith must have a *community*, a company of believers. The etymological meaning of "company" is "those who eat bread together"; in a Christian context, this refers to those who not only are in communion with one another and with their Lord around his Table but also "break bread" in the secular sense of sharing the important things of life with each other.

Faith must be personal in the sense that an individual holds it personally and is committed to it with his person, but it should not be private or unique in the sense that it is different from that of everyone else. Christian faith is a community phenomenon, shared in a community or family of believers, and the same will apply to theology, not only if it is to be *Christian* but also if it is really to be *knowledge* and not mere speculation.

Does not this stress on community downgrade the importance of *faith*? What about Paul's stirring declaration, "We maintain that a man is justified by faith" (Rom. 3:28)? A faith that can justify must indeed be personal; it must be the "property" of the believer in the sense that it is "proper" to him and distinguishes him from the unbeliever, but this does not mean that it isolates him from the community of belief. Faith in this sense cannot be packaged in a book, but only in the human heart. The score of a symphony may be written out in a book, but that is not really the symphony. The symphony is really there only when the orchestra is playing it; each of the violins and the woodwinds and the brass instruments must play its appropriate part, but the obvious intention is that all the instruments should play together. The violinist who has never heard or seen anything but the first-violin part of the symphony may play it quite correctly; nothing more would be expected of him if he were sitting in the orchestra. The individual believer may "believe"—in this sense, "perform"—quite correctly all alone, yet something very important is still lacking if he is not part of the company of faith. If theology is nothing more than the disinterested study of the phenomena of Christian doctrine and experience, detached from personal commitment and out of touch with a company of believers, it is not theology at all in the sense of true knowledge of the true God, but merely a sophisticated and dangerous project in self-deception—and in the deception of others.

We know that it is possible for those without faith in Christ to examine, to discuss, and even to dissect the testimonies and records of Jesus' life, his ministry, and his message, and to write volumes about him, learned or sensational or both, and about the faith others have in him. Indeed, by so doing, countless professional "theologians" have spread doubt and confusion among Christians; thus they have confirmed unbelievers in their refusal to believe the Gospel. Such professional theologizing is essentially a self-deceptive effort. Scripture plainly states that the natural (ψυχικός) person "does not accept the things that come from the Spirit of God, for they are foolishness to him, and he cannot understand them, because they are spiritually discerned" (1 Cor. 2:14). As Johann Albrecht Bengel (1687–1752) emphasized, *cor facit theologum* (the heart makes the theologian). An unconverted heart has no access to the truth of theology.

Before we discuss theological method, we must examine the theological heart. God demands a transformation "by the renewing of your mind" (Rom. 12:2). Apart from minds renewed by the power of the Holy Spirit, there is no confession of Christ and hence no faith (1 Cor. 12:3). Where there is no saving faith, there is nothing to engage in reflective self-awareness, no real world within which theology can live— therefore, no theology.

AN UNNECESSARY OBSTACLE?

From one perspective, to demand faith as the starting point for a theological enterprise might seem to block any truly scholarly or "scientific" approach to theology. Does not true scholarship, like true science, demand impartiality and absolute objectivity from the scholar? Can something be a *science* if it does not proceed in an orderly, verifiable manner, but begins instead with an irrational, nonobjective "leap"? (This question contains a false assumption, namely that the decision of faith is essentially irrational and nonobjective, but this assumption is so common that for the moment we must let it stand and deal with what it says.)

In the English-speaking world, we tend to restrict the term *science* to the natural sciences, which generally proceed on an experimental basis. The "social sciences," for example, are not always acknowledged to be science, nor are academic disciplines such as history always so acknowledged, although they may proceed with great rigor and commitment to truth. Certain natural scientists, such as geologists and paleontologists, make claims as confidently as do physicists and chemists, and their disciplines are granted the status of "science" even though the claims made for them cannot be verified historically or experimentally, for the events they describe lie in the past. Even if the events could be repeated and thus proved *possible* (and generally they cannot be repeated), this would not prove that they *did* happen. At best it would be possible to demonstrate that the events postulated by geology and paleontology can be reproduced in certain ways in the present, but, again, this does not prove that they came about in those ways in actual fact in the unobservable distant past.

A considerable amount of harm has been wrought in the world by taking certain postulates as true and basing policy decisions on them today. The best example was accepting the Darwinian theory of the survival of the fittest as fact and as right and then applying it in "social Darwinism" to robber-baron capitalism and even to war in World War I. Less bloodshed but similarly great spiritual harm has been wrought by taking some of the unproved and unprovable postulates of "historical-critical theological science" and refashioning life as though they were established and dependable truths.

In science, as we generally use the term in English, knowledge is gained by inspection, measurement, calculation, and prediction and then, through verification or falsification of the resulting hypothesis, by experiment. To call only the experimental sciences science is a limitation that does not do full justice to what the word *science* means. This limitation is not rigorously applied in the intellectual world, for, as indicated above, disciplines such as geology and paleontology are accepted as sciences even though they cannot be verified experimentally. This is not wrong, for "science" ought to and does mean more than experimental science only. The Latin word *scientia* (knowledge) is derived from *scire* (to know) and carries the implication of thorough, systematized knowledge. Such knowledge is not confined to the natural or experimental sciences. To limit science to "experimental natural science" is to fall prey to the empiricist fallacy that only that which is experimentally verifiable can be truly known.

If experimental science is what we mean by a science, then theology is not a science. Nevertheless, there is an honored academic tradition that permits us to call it such. When Germans speak of *wissenschaftliche Theologie* (scientific theology), they apply a more general definition of "science." Science, as suggested in the preceding paragraph, refers to "a department of systematized knowledge as an object of study" (*Webster's Ninth New Collegiate Dictionary*, 1987). Defined in this way, theology indeed can and should be a science. The difficulty that arises when we speak of "theological science" in the German sense, *especially* when we contrast it with "practical theology," or, even worse, with "simple faith," is that we thereby give the impression that there are some things that are "known" in theology and others that must be "taken on faith" and therefore may be of doubtful reliability, if indeed they are reliable at all. However, the things that science claims are "reliably known" and are the "assured results of critical science," often are things that have little to do with the true goal of theology, which is knowledge of God, and may even hinder access to the knowledge of God. Often that which "theological science" claims to know is least reliable, and indeed least *scientific*, if by science we mean "systematized *knowledge*" and not merely a system of speculation.

WHAT A SCIENCE IS

A science in the sense in which I use it here is characterized by four things. It has (1) a real object of study, (2) a means of study appropriate to that object, (3) a systematic procedure for carrying out that study, and (4) truth as its goal.

First, by a real object, I mean something that exists in objective reality, outside of the scientist and his subjectivity. That something need not be a "thing" in the sense of a physical object available to physical measurement, chemical analysis, and the like. For example, we can engage in "scientific" study of classical mythology because the myths exist objectively—in written form, outside the observer—and can be examined and studied in a systematic way. By contrast, we cannot have a scientific study of the gods and goddesses portrayed in those myths, because they cannot be found in order to be examined. If such gods and goddesses were real persons, as Homer's heroes believed them to be, then potentially they could communicate with the scientist and make themselves known to him, in which case he could study them scientifically, at least as scientifically as a psychologist or psychiatrist examines a client.

Second, we can create a branch of systematized knowledge when in addition to a real object we have an appropriate means for obtaining information about it. Histology, the study of cells, will be a science if one has access to the appropriate tools; but without a microscope, very little scientific knowledge about cells can be obtained.

Third, a science must proceed in an orderly, systematic manner; simply listing observations in a random manner will not create a systematized body of knowledge. However, not everything that is systematic and presented in an orderly fashion is a science. A catechism, such as the Westminster Larger Catechism, can be very systematic indeed, yet we would not call it scientific. (Ideally, such a catechetical or confessional statement should be in harmony with the best theological science, but it is not itself scientific.)

Fourth, scientific inquiry must seek truth; an inquiry that is intended to prove a preconceived idea is not scientific *unless* the inquirer is prepared to abandon his preconceptions when and if evidence against them accumulates. Most (natural) scientific experiments originate in an hypothesis, the validity of which the experimenter wants to test. It sometimes happens that an experimenter is emotionally committed not merely to *testing* the validity of his hypothesis but also to attempting to *prove* it. This does not in itself make his procedure unscientific, provided he is ready and able to subordinate his desire to prove a theory to his will to know the truth. Sometimes an ambitious and unscrupulous natural scientist will "cook" his data, in order to be able to claim to have proved something that in fact he has not proved. This deception is dangerous enough in the "hard" natural sciences, where discovery and correction are usually possible because the experiments are repeatable, but it is far more dangerous in the "softer" social sciences and humanities and in theology, where an erroneous presupposition can cause great damage before it is identified as such.

Let one example serve. It is possible to make a comparative study of the races of mankind, identify and classify characteristics, and make a statistical survey of differences, but what Hitler's academic lackeys called "Aryan racial science" was not a science at all, since it did not seek the truth and was quite ready to ignore evidence and "cook" data in order to "prove" Hitler's doctrines of the superiority of the Nordic peoples and the baseness of the Jews. Observations that supported those doctrines were recorded, accepted, and disseminated; those that ran counter to them were suppressed.

The Real "Object" of Theology

Theology can be a science if and only if it has a real object. The term *theology* and the discipline of theology as a science developed first and foremost within Christianity, because for Christianity God is real, self-existent, and personal, and has communicated much about himself in the accessible, understandable, propositional revelation we call Holy Scripture. Learning about the God of Christian theology through the study of the Bible differs significantly from attempting to learn about Zeus, Athena, and the other gods and goddesses of Greek mythology through the study of the myths because the God of the Bible, being real and personal, can and does interact with the believer to demonstrate his reality and his presence and to make his will known, a phenomenon that is commonly called the internal testimony of the Holy Spirit (cf. Rom. 8:16). One can know *about* Zeus, or at least what certain ancient Greeks believed about him, but one cannot know *him*, because—as we will presumably concede—he does not exist as an objective, personal reality.

Just as it would be foolish to burden our desires to know *about* Zeus with the quest to know personally a being that does not exist as a person, it is foolish to seek to know *about* the living God without taking his personal self-manifestation into account. It would be silly to want to know all about an accessible, living person without ever trying to converse with him, or to know all about a figure of history simply by looking at portraits and statues but not at his personal letters or published writings. The most important data for the knowledge of persons are furnished by their self-disclosure in communication, primarily in verbal communication (oral and/or written).

In Christian thought the theologian is one who learns, speaks, and teaches about God as the "object" of his scientific study and who does so in an ordered and systematic matter. To refer to God as the "object" of study is somewhat unsatisfactory, for God is the ultimate personal reality who called the physical universe into existence out of nothingness and is not an "object" in that universe at all in the normal sense of the term. He certainly is not the type of "object" that is at the disposal of whoever wants to study it. God *is* accessible to those who seek to know him, and he really is there, outside of their individual subjectivity. In this sense, God is objective. However, he is accessible and knowable only on his own terms—in somewhat the same way that we can get to know another human person only on his terms, i.e., only if he is willing enough to be known to enter into a meaningful encounter with us.

Under such circumstances, the theological "scientist" is not the master of his "object" in the same sense as the physical scientist is the master of the objects in his laboratory. Even the physical scientist, of course, must interact with his objects on *their* terms, not according to his own whims—one cannot measure voltage with a thermometer, for example. But there is a difference: the objects that an experimental scientist studies have certain attributes and are governed by laws that he must observe in order to have access to them, but they do not have a personal will to which he must subject himself and in some respects conform if he wishes to know them, as other human persons have in some degree and of course as God himself has absolutely. Thus the necessity to accommodate himself to the nature of the object of his study does not require the same kind of submission from the physical scientist as a similar necessity does of the theologian. And this leads to a peculiar problem of theological science. It is not possible to be a theologian without being willing to submit. This is precisely what is difficult for the highly placed academic professional. Adolf Schlatter (1852–1938) put it well when he was asked, "Professor Schlatter, do you stand on the Holy Scripture?" he answered, "No! I stand *under* the Holy Scripture." Submission is placing oneself "under," and this is a vital decision that is very hard for the unreconstructed human heart, not least for the unreconstructed academic heart.

In order to be objective, and thus scientific, many professional theologians in effect agree to confine themselves only to the accessible "objects" that place no such personal demand of submission on them. In other words, they concentrate their attention on the documents that purport to tell of God and of God's dealings with humans, as well as on the human phenomena of religious literature and experience and of church and institutional politics. They hear Jesus' words "Unless you repent, you too will all perish" (Luke 13:5) and ask whether they represent an authentic saying, from what document they may have been extracted, what their *Sitz im Leben* in the primitive community may have been, but they do not read them as an urgent warning to repent personally, themselves, lest they also perish.

Things of this kind can indeed be made into an orderly study, a sort of science, inasmuch as the documents and other data do exist in the objective world and can be handled and studied. However, any "theologian" who does only this is really not a theologian but a kind of mythologian, handling the biblical documents that purport to be the Word of the living God with the same indifference and unbelief with which classical scholars deal with Homer's gods and Sophocles' furies. If one insists on studying the Bible "as one would any other literary document," he is virtually certain to misunderstand it, as the Bible is precisely *not* just like any other literary document; and if one closes his mind to this possibility, he will inevitably entangle himself in gross errors. As R. L. Bruckberger writes, "The most miserable among us are those who expect nothing from God, and who proclaim it in a loud voice, with a sort of arrogant satisfaction."[1]

The scientific study of early Greek literature, its epics, and its dramas causes no great confusion among either the learned or the general public, for no one—or virtually no one—fails to recognize that the real objects of such study are simply written texts, not gods and goddesses. We may be interested to learn what Homer's heroes, or Homer himself, Sophocles' King Oedipus, or Sophocles himself, believed about the gods, goddesses, and furies, but we are not apt to follow them in seeking the help of Zeus or Athena or in fleeing the vengeance of the furies. To study the Bible "scientifically"—if by that we mean with a similar detachment, studying it either as literature or as a witness to what an earlier community of faith believed—*is* confusing, because most of those who listen to Christian theologians are precisely not trying to learn about the beliefs of an earlier community but about what they can and should believe and rely on for their own life and their own salvation.

We would approach the study of Greek myths quite differently if we thought that being aided by Apollo or hounded by the furies were a real possibility to reckon with. The study of Scripture takes on one meaning for those who expect the return of the Lord Jesus in person and who therefore anticipate being required to stand before his judgment seat and quite another meaning for those who view the Second Coming as a mythical event with only literary significance, the product of intertestamental Jewish apocalyptic imagination.

Appropriate Means

As noted earlier, the second requirement of a science is that it must have a means of study appropriate to its object. One cannot pursue astronomy with a microscope nor histology with a telescope. It is this consideration that raises the serious question whether what is called "scientific theology" is scientific at all. How do we know the God about whom theology purports to speak? The God of the Bible and of Christian faith is not some impersonal First Cause or Cosmic Force, but is intensely personal.[2]

Because God is personal, we must seek to know him in ways that are appropriate for persons. Things can be studied by observation, measurement, and computation. Persons can be known only when two conditions are fulfilled: first, the person must communicate, generally in understandable language, and, second, the one receiving the communication must respond with a measure of *trust*. At this point, it is most important to emphasize that trust is not a substitute for personal knowledge, as though we have to trust because we do not know. Trust is the appropriate *means* for attaining a knowledge of persons; without it, we cannot know another person in any intimate way, and without the theological equivalent, which we usually call faith—simply another word for the same thing—we cannot know God.

In the realm of persons, trust is not unscientific. *It is the refusal to employ trust* that is unscientific. When dealing with another human being, if we place trust in him, such trust, we know, may be confirmed but can also be disappointed. In either case, however, we increase our knowledge of the person as a person—as opposed to the merely observational knowledge of his or her physical characteristics such as sex, height, weight, hair color, etc. If one treats all of a speaker's words with systematic disbelief, the way to personal knowledge is blocked. It is for this reason that we correctly say with Karl Heim that when dealing with persons, trust is not a substitute for knowledge but a means to gain knowledge.

If trust is necessary in dealing with human persons, a similar engagement is necessary when dealing with the divine Persons. If the scientific theologian brings no trust or faith to his work, he is proceeding unscientifically, because he has deprived himself of the necessary and appropriate means to obtain knowledge, and for that reason he has nothing to systematize.

The Third and Fourth Criteria

The application of the third criterion of a science—a systematic procedure—to the study of theology becomes relevant only when one has reliable data to systematize, in other words, when the first and second criteria have been met. But these three criteria—real object, appropriate means, and systematic procedure—are not enough without the fourth characteristic of a true science—the seeking of truth as one's goal. If the "science" has as its goal the support of some preconceived position, it may become fraudulent and unreliable, even though it may still succeed in uncovering individual truths from time to time. A great danger in academic theology is that other goals—such as academic advancement or peer recognition, or perhaps the tranquilizing of one's conscience when confronted with the threat of God's judgment—may take precedence over the search for truth.

In a celebrated poem Rainer Maria Rilke reacts to the sight of an archaic torso of Apollo as to the challenge, "You must change your life." The reality and the beauty of the Word of God far exceed that of any archaic statue, and when a theologian refuses to react to them, he is being anything but authentic. He is not seeking truth, but something else.

MEANS

Although my goal in this chapter is to make some suggestions about an appropriate method for doing theology, it is evident that the best *method* will produce no worthwhile results unless the appropriate *means* is available and is put to use. The appropriate means for knowing God, as I have said, is trust—i.e., faith. Practically, what this means is that in order to be a trustworthy guide in the study of theology, a theologian must trust Christ personally.

Twenty-odd years ago, during the last decade of Rudolf Bultmann's life, his disciples dominated most of the strongholds of academic theology. One of them, Ernst Käsemann, was labeled by the conservative "No Other Gospel" movement as "not a teacher of the church." Käsemann reacted indignantly with an *ad hominem* defense, pointing to his years spent in a mining-town parish, his opposition to Hitler, and the like. Not one of these things, commendable thought it was, was an appropriate means to do what a theologian must do, namely, to know God. Käsemann, who shared his mentor Bultmann's programmatic skepticism about the authenticity of Jesus' reported words and deeds, would not publicly commit himself to personal faith in Jesus as his Lord and Savior but only spoke in terms of an "encounter" and "authentic existence."

At the beginning of one's theological enterprise there must be a firm personal commitment to Christ and a clear public confession of faith. In addition, there must be evidence that this commitment is more than a mere *postulate* but that it has a formative influence on the life of the theologian. There is no standard scale by which one can evaluate private devotional life and public worship, but surely such things will be present and evident if the faith commitment is real. The theologian who does not make a clear profession of faith, does not participate in the life of the church with its sacraments, and is not submissive to its discipline does not appear prepared to do Christian theology. Theology can be done only within a community of faith.

METHOD IN THEOLOGY

The fundamental starting point for the systematized knowledge of and about God that is theology must be God's self-disclosure. Three fundamental principles about God's self-disclosure must be observed: *First*, it took place *in human space and time*. As a consequence, it is historically and geographically situated. With respect to any particular doctrine, there was a time when it was not yet known, because it had not yet been revealed, and there were and still are places where it is not known and people who do not know it, because the message has not crossed all barriers of distance and culture.

God's self-disclosure, both in the general textbook of nature, bearing as it does the traces of the handiwork of its almighty Creator (Rom. 1:19–20), and in the incomparably more explicit sovereign intervention in acts and in verbal communication (Heb. 1:1–2), is a self-disclosure into the realm we inhabit, that of real geographical space and real historic time. From the very nature of human beings, it is self-evident that whatever is to be perceived by them must be presented to them in the context of their historic, geographic, time-space real existence. Just as the world is a place that has a history and just as humanity has a location and a history, so God's self-disclosure to us is in a historical setting and an *arbitrary* form. Like the act of creation itself, God's self-disclosure is the expression of his free and sovereign will and displays specificity. Just as it is inconceivable that God—or any power—could create in general, without creating some specific things and without refraining from creating other conceivable and potentially creatable realities, it is inconceivable that God could disclose himself in any comprehensible manner to human beings without doing so with specificity and particularity. Obviously this means that the very particularity and specificity of God's works of creation, revelation, and redemption to which so many object as being "arbitrary," "selective," and "exclusive," are necessary if we particular and specific human beings are to be able to perceive them and to make sense of them. Why did God do this and not that? Why did he speak thus and not otherwise? Why did he choose Hebrew and not Egyptian, Israel and not Ireland? Even more generally, why did he create his intelligent "offspring" (as Paul, citing pagan authors, also calls us in Acts 17:28) as mammals and not as fish, nor as birds, nor as giant insects? It is not for us to know why God did as he did and not otherwise and said what he said and not something else, but we are to *recognize* what he has done and said and to frame our own acts and attitudes accordingly. There is a specific content and a specific act or series of acts of transmission, so that it is proper to speak, with Jude, of the "faith that was once for all entrusted to the saints" (Jude 3). If we recognize and accept the *specificity* of God's outward works, his *opera ad extra*, then the second and third principles become not merely plausible but necessary.

Second, God's self-disclosure was given in specific, understandable human words in particular human languages, and as such has been reliably transmitted to us in written form, namely, in the canonical Scriptures of the Old and New Testaments. Some aspects of this revelation were disclosed and known before being inscripturated. Presentation in written form is not a necessary condition of God's self-disclosure, but a definitive presentation in fixed—i.e., written—form is altogether consistent with the nature of God's revelatory acts. (Additionally, some things revealed by God at various times and to various people have not been fixed and transmitted in Scripture, and as a result they are no longer generally available to all nor generally binding on all human beings.)

The most fundamental, reliable, generally available, and generally binding component of God's direct revelation thus came into being and has been presented to us in a verbal, propositional form, and as such it has been handed down, intact, through millenia. The historic preservation and transmission of scriptural revelation were as much an act of God's sovereign and providential will as was its original inspiration. The resulting inspired text represents a fixed, unchanging deposit. There is a *content* to the revelation and there is also, hardly less important, the fact of a divine *conveying* to the "saints," the community of those separated from the world to God by his call, heard and accepted.

Third, the mighty deeds of God were done and the verbal communication given in a life situation, in part to a community already formed, in part to cause the formation of a community. The verbal, propositional communication never existed *in vitro* but was *in vivo* from the very beginning. In an evangelical, Reformation context, this statement may well be the most controversial of the three made here, and yet it is hardly less self-evident and undeniable than the others.

From the outset, even before it was complete in its present canonical form, the self-disclosure of God that we now have in Scripture was embedded in the life of the community of faith. Both before and after its inscripturation, it was transmitted by believers in the context of faith. This process of transmission is properly called tradition, i.e., "handing over," or "handing down."

At no time in the history of God's people has the Scripture been transmitted, as it were, by a kind of Ancient or Medieval Parcel Service, all wrapped and sealed. It has always been carried from place to place, group to group, and person to person by messengers who themselves had been transformed by its message, whose lives were being refashioned by it. The mere handing on of the text of Scripture, whether in the original languages or in more or less faithful, more or less readily understandable vernacular translations, is not sufficient to give shape and solidity to a community of faith and life. The content will inevitably be "fleshed out"—to borrow Clark Pinnock's expression—from the existential situation of those who are called to faith and obedience by the Word of God. Without such a fleshing out within a community of faith, the Word of God in Scripture is little more than the record of God's past deeds and of the faith of peoples long vanished. While tradition as the bearer of the scriptural message must never *dominate* the message, it can never be inactive, any more than a human messenger can carry a vital dispatch to its intended destination apart from his own personal qualities of strength, energy, commitment, and fidelity.

Tradition is a valid and important concept and a necessary means to be consulted and employed in doing theology, provided it is consulted and heard as *context* and not as *content*. No individual Christian or community of Christians has ever lived nor could ever live solely from the content of written

Scripture or any other fixed and limited body of information and instruction. (*A fortiori*, it would be impossible for either to live solely from the vague and general information communicated by God's general revelation in nature.)

The transmission of the inspired writings from generation to generation is itself a process of tradition. The Scriptures are handed down literally, from hand to hand, and in addition the way in which they are understood and applied is communicated from person to person by acts, attitudes, and customs.

Here we can draw a lesson from the experience of general society. No human community can live solely out of its written constitution, laws, and regulations. A vast amount of the information that is necessary for people to relate to one another in effective and harmonious ways in secular society is transmitted in unwritten forms—forms of politeness, formalities, customs, rituals, forms of address, linguistic patterns—all of these things communicate information that permits a community to exist, a society to function.

In the increasingly pluralistic environment of the United States, the juxtaposing and mixing of differing cultures with differing expectations and differing values—sometimes widely different ones—is causing social disorientation that cannot be compensated for by increasingly detailed legislation, judicial decisions, and bureaucratic regulations at any level—federal, state, or local.[3]

In the context of the Christian community, "ecumenical" pluralism, even "evangelical" pluralism, is leading to spiritual disorientation as various traditions that have heretofore transmitted much of the context of Christian faith from person to person and from generation to generation intermingle and blend, thereby losing not only their distinctiveness but also the capability of handing on a clear, comprehensive, meaningful, and livable Christian message.

The great service of Christian tradition has been the faithful handing down of God's inerrant revelation in the context of worship and lived-out faith. In this sense the tradition is like a living human runner who hastens to his destination and either literally hands over an intact manuscript or orally reports accurately memorized words.

The great disservice of tradition to the Christian faith has been to add to or even to distort revelation by introducing adventitious elements drawn from the ambient culture, other religious and philosophical sources, or elsewhere. In this sense, tradition is like the human messenger who lingers along the way, gossips with others in taverns, and hands over at last a wrinkled, stained, and blotted manuscript or orally gives an expanded and altered version of the original message. When tradition does either or both of these things, it is no longer fulfilling the original, God-given task of faithful transmission. Nevertheless, even though tradition can and sometimes does distort what has been "once delivered," it remains true that without tradition there is no transmission of the message.

From these three principles of God's self-disclosure we may draw three conclusions. First, God's revelation is particular and peculiar—historically, geographically, and culturally. Potentially offered to all mankind, the message has been received and handed on by a minority. Others were passed over, or, hardening themselves, let the message slip by unheeded.

Second, because the revelation is now fixed in a permanent, written form, it has a universal validity and accessibility that transcend the limits of time and space. Indeed it did come at a particular time and in a particular place; now people of other times and other places must adjust, mould, and adapt themselves and their understanding to the unchanging truths of Scripture. This means that care must be exercised to make the unchanging truths of Scripture intelligible in the context of changing times and cultures without adapting them to the times or the cultures, letting Scripture transform them, not permitting them to deform it.

Third, because the message has always been embedded in a living tradition, because it was entrusted to human hearts and to human hands—to a living community of faith—it should not be considered in the abstract, away from the people of God who draw their life from it and in the midst of whom it lives, but it should be received in its living context, namely, within tradition.

PRACTICAL SUGGESTIONS

Against this background, let us consider some practical suggestions for method in theology. We begin with a spiritual and a conceptual presupposition. The spiritual presupposition is that the student himself will be personally committed to Jesus Christ, and that he will take as his *teachers* those who are also committed. The conceptual presupposition is that God's historic self-disclosure was given to specific people at specific times and in specific contexts—all of which are relevant for our understanding of his communication. The Scripture was not handed over in packaged form; there was more than a millennium between the inscripturation of the first inspired texts of the Old Testament and the closing of the canon of the New Testament. People were able to serve and worship the Lord before the Old Testament was compiled, and people learned to trust and follow Christ before the New Testament was complete. God's Old Testament people and the first Christians had to grow as they learned and to learn as they grew. Their life situations and life experiences not only are important to an understanding of the message, they also were instrumental in its formation.

With these two presuppositions behind us, we can go on to the next step, which is to read, to learn, and to understand the fixed content of scriptural revelation. A "due use of the ordinary means" is essential here: a study of the ancient languages in which the revelation was given and has been transmitted and an attentive study of the texts themselves. These texts must be studied in the context of the thought world and the culture into which they were given, so that their original meaning and original intent can be discerned.

It is essential not merely to *ingest* the message of the texts but also to *digest* it and thus begin to receive life and strength from it. At this point it is important to share as much as possible in the life of the community that lives out of the message it communicates. This means that we must be attentive to the voice and the life of the church from the very first centuries onward. The fellowship of the church, participation in a community of faith and Christian service, is essential for the enterprise of Christian theology as a whole. This reinforces my point that the church is vitally important for theology and that Christian fellowship and service are vital for the community of theologians, though an individual theologian may arguably get away with neglecting them for a considerable period of time.

Everyone needs to hear the message of the Bible, but not everyone is able to devote the time, energy, and mental effort necessary to explore the whole literary, linguistic, cultural, and historical background of Scripture. Indeed, only a few will. This makes it all the more important to recognize the role of the community of faith, in which scholarly insights are exchanged, compared with one another, and tested in the crucible of the life of faith by a community of believers seeking to follow Christ and to live in ways that are pleasing to him. Protestantism, especially the evangelicalism of recent days, has carried the good principle *"ad fontes!"* ("to the sources!") to absurd lengths when it acts as if we can forget nineteen centuries of collective Christian pilgrimage and, armed with the Bible alone, ignore the help and the warnings that it could give us.

THE VITAL MEANING OF TRADITION

The study of theology has its proper life situation within the community of faith. What we call tradition can be and has been both exaggerated and deformed and has often come to hamper the knowledge and service of God rather than enhance them. This danger is especially great when the written Word in Scripture is not readily available to the believing community or when through ignorance or poor instruction the community neglects it. During the Protestant Reformation *"Sola Scriptura!"* became a war-cry of the evangelical movement. Systematic application of the Scripture principle, which had been all but forgotten in twelve centuries of established religion, permitted the segment of the church that was willing to apply it to recognize and excavate, as it were, the renewing and saving Gospel from the mass of accretions, distortions, and actual contradictions that had been piled upon it through centuries of expansion and of stagnation. This work of recognition and excavation was necessary largely because the long-term custodian of scriptural revelation, the Latin-speaking Western Catholic church, carried on tradition in the bad sense of the laggard runner turning in at taverns and amusement halls on the way to his destination.

Any evangelical Protestant who wishes to defend the essential importance of tradition will find himself forced to protest against the Roman Catholic understanding of tradition. He will judge the Eastern Orthodox concept more acceptable, at least in theory, although there too he will find that practice has often overrun the strict safeguards the theory is supposed to provide and has created a Christian life and practice that has been adulterated rather than enhanced. Nevertheless, it is neither scientific nor possible to ignore tradition and to attempt to understand theology anew every year or every day.

When Roman Catholic polemicists claimed that it was the church that had preserved the Scripture and handed it on, they were correct. But when they said that the authority of the church established the authority of Scripture, they were wrong. Protestants were correct to counter this contention with the doctrine of the autopisty, the self-authentication of Scripture. But when they said or implied that it was the Scripture that produced the church, they were involved in the error of anachronism. It was indeed the *message* of Scripture that produced the church, but the actual written *texts* of Scripture are younger than the early Christian community and hence cannot have produced it.

The authority of tradition in Roman Catholicism differed from that in Eastern Orthodoxy largely in that in medieval Catholicism, tradition and Scripture were placed side by side, or even in opposition to each other, with tradition being seen as the final authority, whereas in Orthodoxy Scripture was presented as the primary and normative treasure preserved, handed down, and interpreted, but never altered or supplanted, by tradition. Indeed, to be explicit about what has already been implied, in Orthodoxy tradition was presented essentially as an interpretation of Scripture, not as an amplification of it. Even though from an evangelical perspective we may question whether this is what the Orthodox always *did* with Scripture in their tradition(s), the concept itself is far less misleading than the contention that tradition stands alongside Scripture as a second source of revelation, as declared during the anti-Protestant Council of Trent.

But this is not all that we need to say. If the church erred by smothering Scripture in tradition, much contemporary scholarship, especially evangelical scholarship, errs by dissecting the Scripture out of the body of believers and the body of belief, by cutting it out of and away from its place in the life—i.e., the tradition—of the company of believers. The value, indeed the necessity, of tradition for the life of the people of God and the enterprise of theology has been unrecognized and often denied in Protestant circles. This was in large measure an understandable reaction, a necessary corrective, to the excesses of medieval Christianity, particularly of medieval Catholicism. Wherever tradition added to Scripture, becoming a kind of second source of spiritual truth, it overstepped its proper bounds and called for correction.

It is important to recognize that historically there has never been a Scripture existing *in vacuo*. Communities of disciples existed for twenty years or so before the first books of the New

Testament were written, and the church was a century old before the New Testament itself even began to take on final form. Even as we assert the plenary inspiration of Scripture and the controlling authorship and oversight of the Holy Spirit in its formation, we recognize that there was never a time when a single book of the New Testament existed totally apart from a fellowship of believers seeking to live out in practice what it would proclaim in inspired words.

CONCLUSION

What, then, is the conclusion of the matter? One cannot be a theologian without faith, nor a really knowledgeable one unless that faith is biblical and orthodox, in conformity to the inerrantly inspired Scripture. One cannot, or can hardly, learn, nourish, or even maintain such a faith without a surrounding and supporting community of belief, and such a community of belief never exists without a community of practice; together these form a living Christian tradition, apart from which and outside of which the individual Christian's life will be impoverished and this theology, if such it should be called such, pale and weak. Within it, both the individual believer and the believing community can be vital, active, fruitful, and—most important of all—faithful to the Lord they love.

NOTES

[1]R. L. Bruckberger La révélation de Jésus-Christ (Paris, 1981), 140ff.

[2]In fact, God is not a person, but a Trinity eternally subsisting in the three Persons—the Father, the Son, and the Holy Spirit. Contemporary tendencies toward "inclusive language," whatever their merits in other contexts may be, are fraudulent and drastically out of place when applied to the Holy Trinity. The doctrine of the Trinity is a "mystery of faith" as described above, a mystery known only through God's special, propositional revelation given in human language. Although some of the terminology proposed by advocates of inclusive language is biblical, to substitute "Creator, Redeemer, and Sanctifier" for "Father, Son, and Holy Spirit" is both insipid and wrong. The Father is not Creator in distinction from the Son, nor is the Son Redeemer in distinction from the Father. Creation, redemption, and sanctification are so-called "external works" of God, and traditional theology rightly says, "The external works are undivided."

[3]This phenomenon is discussed by Christof Gaspari and Hans Millendorfer in Konturen einer Wende. Strategien für die Zukunft (Graz-Vienna-Cologne: Styria, 1978), esp. 217–45.

6

THE THEOLOGIAN'S CRAFT

DAVID WELLS
GORDON-CONWELL THEOLOGICAL SEMINARY,
SOUTH HAMILTON, MASSACHUSETTS

INTRODUCTION

There are few lines quite so poignantly applicable to the theologian's craft as those of the medieval poet Geoffrey Chaucer, who wrote of "The lyf so short, the craft so long to lerne. Th' assay so hard, so sharp the conquering."[1] It is, in fact, surprising that the thought should ever cross our minds that the theological undertaking could be otherwise, for understanding—understanding of God, of ourselves, of the world—comes so slowly, so painfully slowly, that "lyf's" summer passes and the winter arrives long before this fruit is ripe to be picked. Or so it seems. And that, perhaps, is why we are so fiercely tempted to turn theology into a technique that we can use to produce a more efficiently gained and bountiful knowledge of God! God, however, is not like the periodical table. He is not a quantity that can be "mastered" even though he can be known; and though he has revealed himself with clarity, the depth of our understanding of him is measured, not by the speed with which theological knowledge is processed, but by the quality of our determination to own his ownership of us through Christ in thought, word, and deed. This is an inescapable part of "th' assay so hard," the "craft so long to lerne."

Already, then, I am tipping my hand as to how the word *theology* is being used. It is not being used simply as a synonym for a skill or an activity. It does require professional skills and it does issue in moral activities, but theology itself transcends both. For theology is the sustained effort to know the character, will, and acts of the triune God as he has disclosed and interpreted these for his people in Scripture, to formulate these in a systematic way in order that we might know him, learn to think our thoughts after him, live our lives in his world on his terms, and by thought and action project his truth into our own time and culture.[2] It is therefore a synthetic activity whose center is the understanding of God, whose horizon is as wide as life itself, and whose mission echoes the mission of God himself, which is to gather together in Christ a progeny as numerous as the stars above (Gen. 15:1–6; Gal. 3:6–16). Linguistic, historical, and philosophical skills often contribute to this work, but it is evident that linguists, historians, and philosophers do not function as theologians *per se* simply on account of their skill, however finely developed that may be. And, in the same way, we can say that a theological vision should produce a love of all that is good in life, however we qualify that word *good*; outrage over what is wrong; compassion for those to whom wrong is done; and an indefatigable care for this poor, battered, and fragmenting world in which we live. Yet, those who are cultured, moral, benevolent, and caring are not in and by those actions "doing" theology as the liberal Protestants thought earlier in this century in America and as the proponents of liberation theology do today. To reduce what is known about God to a small manageable domain over which a small, human manager presides is to reverse the proper roles of creature and Creator. For what is known is subjugated to the knower and what can be known to what the knower wants to know. Truth is reduced merely to technique or action. Christianity thus becomes simply a twig, rather than a branch, of knowledge, or one program amidst a myriad of competitors beneath whose collective and acculumated weight the world seems ready to disappear.

It is important to see that systematic theology so conceived will find little comfort in our Western world. In an age that is naturalistic, it must speak from a self-consciously supernaturalistic viewpoint; in a world whose only "revelation" is what the human process throws up, it must continue to insist that it is God alone who can accurately interpret this process and that the vagaries of human experience are no more to be depended on than Plato's tale about Atlantis; in a world that is increasingly enamored of its pluralism, it must speak of the one true God and the uniqueness of his Son and of the Son's work on the Cross; in a world illumined by technological brilliance and redolent with human self-confidence, it must continue to point, as the prophets of old did, to the vacuity beneath the glittering appearance; in a world where the highest good is what can be bought and traded, it must go on patiently insisting that men and women have been made for a far greater end, to know God, which is their glory or their damnation; and in a time of specialization with its inevitable fragmentation, it must continue to unite what our age tears apart, seeing the whole complex enterprise of work and civilization from the single perspective of God's Word and thus bringing it all into the light of Christ's work on the Cross, which will eventually be seen in its full cosmic significance. In this task, then, systematic theologians can expect little aid from a civilization now hurrying on into the late twilight of its existence and whose memories of its Judeo-Christian parentage have long since faded and whose *Geist* is now thoroughly alien to the body of Christian thought.

It is this fact, of course, that is rendering inescapable the missionary nature of theology, at least of the kind of theology that is being played in a biblical key, for, like it or not, we are in a cross-cultural situation. Ours is a culture often as alien to Christian conviction as many of those that, today, are under the dominance of Marxism, Islam, or Hinduism and within which missionaries labor to make known the truth of God and his Christ. The difference, and it is no small difference, is that the Constitution in the United States disallows repression and secures the right of this type of theology to be thought and practiced, a freedom that is not enjoyed by many of these other countries. Only the naïve could imagine, however, that we today are living in a context hospitable to this undertaking.

When compared with other kinds of knowledge, Christian theology, as Herman Bavinck has noted,[3] differs in terms of its origin, object, and effects. With respect to origin, first we should note that other kinds of knowledge such as history, psychology, or biology are gained by hard work. One becomes proficient in these spheres by diligence, application, and insight. Although there is a technical side to theology that requires the same kind of dedication, its "mastery" is by no means simply a matter of human dedication, for then, as Karl Barth rightly insisted, the knowledge of God would be awarded to the fastest runner, and that we know does not happen. This knowledge is a gift of grace and has to be received, not as a reward, but for what it is, an undeserved gift. Second, this knowledge has God as its object, and it seeks to understand the world as God sees it. To that extent its knowledge is theocentric. By contrast, all other knowledge is anthropocentric and hence is relative and fallible. To say this is not necessarily to speak ill of the human quest for understanding. It merely seeks to recognize the nature of that quest, which is one undertaken from within the flux of human experience employing the tools available to human experimenters. And certainly, when it comes to matters of meaning, these tools never yield any certainty beyond that of an interim report offered from within the fallibilities of the fragile, human psyche, and this needs to be seen as quite different from the kind of knowledge given by revelation. Third, the effects of theological knowledge should be humility and a deepened desire to serve and honor God in all of our commerce with created reality. The truly profound thinkers in life are often brought to humility, too, but perhaps for different reasons. They are humbled out of a sense of their own smallness; theology should humble us through a sense of the greatness and grandeur of God. It is what we know, not what we do not know, that subdues our pride and causes us to render to God the worship that is his due.

From this sketch it will be evident that there are really three major factors that bear on the theologian's craft as conceived in this chapter. These are, first, the functioning of Scripture, which provides both the norm and the substance of theology; second, the role of the theologian, who is the interpreter of Scripture and a knower of God; and third, the significance of the church, for whom theology is initially and most immediately constructed. So this chapter, like Wittgenstein's *Philosophical Remarks*, is intended "for those who are in sympathy with the spirit in which it is written." "This is not," Wittgenstein went on to say, "the spirit of the main current of European and American civilization. . . . I have no sympathy for the current of European civilization and do not understand its goals, if it has any. So I am really writing for friends who are scattered throughout the corners of the globe."[4] And so am I.

THE OBJECTIVE NORM

Sources for Theology

The sources customarily used in theological construction—Scripture, tradition, reason, and experience—need to be thought about carefully before we will be able to see how to proceed. There is no question that in some form this quadrilateral will be present in every theology. After all, every theologian has had at least a brush with Scripture, brings with him or her some sense of past formulations, attempts to reason about the meaning of all of this, and does so from the standpoint of someone who sees the world in a particular way. The questions to be decided, though, are those of primacy and divine access. By which of these means do we understand the mind of God, and is this understanding of such clarity as to constitute a functioning authority?

In considering these questions, contemporary theology has effectively reduced the traditional four sources to two: Scripture and experience. This is, to be sure, an assessment that will not attract universal consent, for, among other things, it effectively reduces the theological options to variations on historic Protestant orthodoxy, on the one side, and variations on classical Protestant liberalism, on the other.[5] A good case can be made, however, for thinking that this is indeed the case.

Of the four sources, reason was the first to cease functioning, and here it might be helpful to distinguish reason, which is our tool for understanding the sensory world around us, from Reason, which some, especially in the idealist tradition, have seen as the eye of the human spirit. As such it was seen to gain for us access to the invisible world and thus to ultimate reality. It is Reason about which I am speaking here, for every human being continues to analyze, think about, and make inferences from the natural world through reason. To borrow from Coleridge, we apprehend through reason, but we comprehend ultimate reality through Reason. The point, then, is that apprehension from reason is seen simply as the way we organize our experiences; it cannot be our access to ultimate reality, thereby giving us theological comprehension. And that is why reason cannot function as a source for theology in the absence of Reason.

The disappearance of Reason is probably to be attributed to three main causes. First, it would be difficult to overemphasize the effect of Kant's *Critique of Pure Reason*. He simply lopped off Reason and proposed that reason was always tied to, and worked only in conjunction with, sensory perception. Furthermore, what we know is not the external world in itself but merely how our minds have collated and organized our experiences of that external world. About the inner relations of things in this world as well as what lies beyond it, we have to remain agnostic.[6] Second, the basic assumptions of Freud and Adler continue to be accepted in contemporary psychology,[7] the upshot of which is that the conscious life is seen as being determined by the unconscious, and this means, at least in its hard form, that reason simply dances to the tune that is piped by deep subterranean instinct. To follow the thread of reason, therefore, would not lead us out of the labyrinth of our confusing experiences and into the presence of God but, rather, into their source, which is in our own internal conflicts. Third, modernization, with its twin products of secularism and secularization,[8] has inclined us to believe that there is no overarching order, moral or supernatural, that is revelant to, or intersects with, the stuff of everyday life. There is nothing there to which Reason, even if it exists, can have access. Not a few contemporary theologians simply begin on this premise and then ask what it now means, given the fact of modernization, to have "faith." So Reason has more or less disappeared as a source for theological construction.

Tradition has not disappeared as Reason has, but its real nature has undergone a startling transformation in the post-Vatican II period. The argument for tradition historically has been an argument for authority in the church and specifically in the Catholic magisterium. After all, the church's thinking about itself, its life, its role in the world, its faith, and its hope has been as diverse and as wracked with conflict as one would expect would be the case when the body in question is as large and as culturally diverse as the Roman Catholic church is. Where, then, is the Spirit's presence in all of this? And what should the church believe has been revealed through the passing of the years? The answers to these questions have never been self-evident. Indeed, in the Middle Ages Abelard argued this point in his *Sic et Non* on the grounds that in the patristic period there were at least one hundred and fifty subjects on which the fathers were in substantial disagreement. This is partly why, with the passing of the years, the church saw fit to invest the magisterium with the authority to say finally and definitively what was to be considered of faith and what was not. And it was this development that was contested at the time of the Reformation. The Reformers were not opposed to tradition *per se*, but they did repudiate magisterial authority in the church, for it presumed to have the right to incorporate beliefs from the past into the substance of the faith to be believed (and this authoritative and interpreted tradition, following current convention, is what is here meant by tradition). This, the Reformers believed, was a relocation of authority from Scripture, where it belonged, to the church where it did not.[9]

At the Second Vatican Council, however, two extraordinary changes occurred. First, the Holy Spirit, who had formerly been seen to be the exclusive preserve of the magisterium, given for their role of defining the faith, was now said to be given to all the people of God.[10] What this meant, in effect, was that the whole people of God was in a position to define for itself what should be believed, and the current defiance of Rome on the question of artificial contraception shows that the laity is taking its responsibility seriously! This decision regarding the Holy Spirit may seem like a move toward a more biblical understanding, but, given the Catholic teaching of the development of doctrine, it was also a move laden with mischief. It is no surprise to note that the Catholic modernists had earnestly contended for this position, seeing in it not only the means of liberation from the Vatican, but also the means of creating a synthesis between faith and modern experience.[11]

This move, as it turned out, coincided with a second change, which was the redefinition of authority. In the traditional model, which was hierarchical, authority moved from the top downward. This was counterbalanced at the Council by a new model in which authority, understood as the aggregate of spiritual perception, began among the laity and moved upward.[12] The role of the magisterium now became that simply of recognizing what the Spirit was revealing to the people. The practical import of this has been that the magisterium has been hamstrung and so the argument for tradition is no longer an argument for church authority. Today, it is an argument for experience, for the experience of the Holy Spirit within the people of God, who include, by the Council's reckoning, not only Catholics but also Protestants, the Orthodox, and possibly even those in non-Christian religions. It is an argument for allowing modernity to define what faith is and what can and cannot be believed.

By a circuitous and strange route, then, a substantial part of the Catholic world now finds itself reiterating ideas for which the modernists were excommunicated at the turn of the century. And this changed direction has brought Catholic theologians into close proximity to many Protestants for whom the formulations of classical liberalism, after disappearing for a while under the avalanche of neoorthodox criticism, are once again dominant. In combination, these two streams are powerfully asserting the role of experience in providing us with the materials out of which a theology is to be built.

The forerunner of this methodology was Schleiermacher. His conception of theology was remarkably simple. Like the early Greek thinkers, he assumed that God is to be found by, with, and under all human personality, and this presence produces a "feeling of absolute dependence," which, he said, is "in itself a co-existence of God in the self-consciousness."[13] The entire reality of God, he said, is contained within and explicated by this sense of dependence and therefore the task of theology is simply that of crystallizing out of this inner sense propositions that adequately describe and explain it. This approach has come to characterize much of the contemporary theological construction, both Protestant and Catholic, and Schleiermacher's title as the father of modern theology looks increasingly apt.

All theology is an interpretation of the reality and meaning of God. The question, then, is where and how one encounters this "given" and what the experience is that either yields this "given" or is related to it. The answers today spill out in all directions, but the link to Schleiermacher's liberalism is everywhere present.

This lineage, for example, is specifically owned by John Cobb,[14] who then goes on to develop a model of theological construction based on a common human experience of divine reality. Nature is the medium through which God is experienced. This divine presence yields a "prereflective knowledge" that is always in flux and movement because the being of God is. It is this experience that gives theology its substance.[15] Cobb also notes the relationship between his approach and that of the political theologians.[16] This relationship holds true, however, not only in relation to Johannes Metz, Jürgen Moltmann, and Dorothee Sölle, but also to the liberation theologies. Juan

Segundo, for example, begins his theology with the experience of political injustice and alienation.[17] This then leads him to question prevailing ideologies and biblical interpretations, and this, in turn, leads to a new theology. The encounter with social and political reality, he believes, is one in which he is also encountering the reality of God. It is to this extent an experiential theology because it is the experience of God in society that is determinative of the way that the subsequent theology is put together. James Cone makes the same assumption and follows the same procedure.[18]

So heavy is the pall of liberalism today that even when theologians are trying to escape from it, they often end up reaffirming it. An interesting example of this is the so-called new Yale theology. George Lindbeck's *Nature of Doctrine* has the interesting subtitle, *Religion and Theology in a Postliberal Age*. Undoubtedly he, and for that matter Hans Frei, have been deeply influenced by the Barthian interest in the Word as something that ought to replace the old liberal interest in experience as the source for theology. The bloom, however, fast fades from this rose when their interest in Scripture is seen in the light of David Kelsey's work. For what Kelsey argues is that Scripture lends itself to the interpretation of reality in a variety of ways and what determines the interpretation is the existential orientation of the interpreter. Thus a marriage occurs between the older Protestant interest in *sola Scriptura* and a cognitive relativism, which was the hallmark of liberalism.[19] Thus Lindbeck can argue for the propriety of the biblical Word as a foundation for theology and then go on to say that the meaning of that Word is not self-contained but must be ascertained from the community of faith! This actually brings him into very close proximity to the new Catholic thinking on tradition. In both cases, revelation is foundational to theology. Revelation, however, is found in its ancient form in the biblical Word and in its contemporary extension in the church and it is the latter that is the key to the meaning of the former.

The liberal approach sees experience—whether of ourselves, of the natural world, of political reality, or of society or within the church—as providing the stuff out of which theology is made. It therefore always incorporates modernity into its theology, not simply as an external pole of reference for that theology, but as its internal substance. It imagines, as Barth noted earlier in the century, that we can call God by shouting man in a loud voice!

Specifically, this approach must operate with a view of divine immanence that assumes that the being of God is washed ashore on the edges of our mind by the ebbing and flowing of our experience. This further assumes that our experience does not seriously refract what we see of the divine in the depths of our world or ourselves. And it also makes the assumption that there is no radical alienation from God within ourselves that would undercut experience as a trustworthy bearer of the divine revelation. The arguments against these perversions of Protestantism's formal and material principles have been made many times. Gresham Machen was surely right in declaring that this represents, not a variation on the biblical faith, but another religion altogether.[20]

Scripture

The Protestant insistence that Scripture alone secures us access to the character, will, and acts of God was based on the realization that what we know of him cannot result from human discovery but must come from divine disclosure, that God is his only infallible interpreter, that as made in his image we have the capacity for receiving his self-revelation and disclosure but that as rebels we distort this unless the Holy Spirit renews and strengthens us, and that without this constant divine intervention, the natural human tendency is to make God in our own image, which is idolatry. Scripture, therefore, provides the substance and the norm of theology. It is our access to the mind of God, the rule by which we live, the external and unchanging authority in accordance with which our theology has to be constructed.

It is entirely possible, however, for those with an equal commitment to the centrality and primacy of Scripture to reach quite different theological conclusions on large as well as small points. Indeed, Robert Johnston's recent book *The Use of Scripture in Theology: Evangelical Options* demonstrated the potential for this because it showed an extraordinary array of theological methodologies now in operation among evangelical theologians. So how can we account for a diversity so broad and, at times, so argumentative as to threaten evangelical unity?

There are, it would seem, at least four main factors. First, it is clear that theologians use reason, tradition, and experience in different ways and in different proportions in their work, but all within their commitment to the functioning authority of Scripture. The result is a family of theologies whose family resemblance is not always easy to see. This, however, is treated elsewhere in the volume and so will not be explored further here.

Second, and more or less unnoticed, has been the disappearance of biblical theology, and the consequences of this loss are hard to overstate for systematic theology. The term *biblical theology* is here used not of content—for all theology should be biblical in this sense—but of method. Biblical theology seeks to understand the progressive unfolding of the revelation, locating each phase within its specific historical circumstances and within the wider epoch within which it was given. It does so with the intention of clarifying what the relations are between the testaments and of the material within them. Since this approach is concerned especially with tracing out the development in God's dealings with his people, its understanding of the coherence in that dealing is undertaken primarily chronologically rather than thematically as would be the case with systematic theology. This is, however, a vital link between exegesis and systematizing, as Geerhardus Vos demonstrated so well earlier in the century, and its disappearance in recent decades is most significant.

There are many issues in theology that are determined by how the testaments are related to each other. This is true not only of how the law is seen to function, or how baptism and the millennium are understood, but also what future Israel has and even in extreme cases whether salvation for Jews today must occur through the Christian Gospel. It is also true of some of the larger proposals before us for the restructuring of the faith emanating from the theonomists and the (evangelical) liberationists. Neither could sustain their interests without assuming that the Old Testament paradigms for national and spiritual life are operative in an unchanged form today. Bernhard Anderson was not exaggerating when he wrote that on the relation between the testaments "hangs the meaning of the Christian faith": it is, he said, "a question which confronts every Christian in the Church, whether he be a professional theologian, a pastor of a congregation, or a layman."[21] And the fact that we are without the discipline that could be of most help in sorting out these issues means that we will probably continue stumbling over them with predictable regularity in the future.

It is to the remaining two factors, though, that fuller

attention will be given. These are the questions, third, of presuppositions, and, fourth, of the recipients. How should theologians understand their roles as interpreters and for whom are they primarily interpreting? The answers given to these questions, however implicitly or unselfconsciously, will affect the shape and spirit of the theology as well as its criteria for truthfulness and usefulness. It is, then, to these issues that we must now turn.

THE INTERPRETER

In a recent study, Brian Hebblethwaite posed the question as to whether theology actually exists.[22] He was not unaware of the fact, of course, that there are people who understand themselves to be theologians, that each year theological books are written, and that among their readers are theological students. His question, though, was whether this activity is different from what goes on in a religion department. Is "doing" theology different from "doing" religion? And how would a person who "does" theology be different from one who "does" religion?

If theology is merely "rational thought or talk about God," as Hebblethwaite says, or, in Maurice Wiles' words, "reasoned discourse about God,"[23] then it is hard to see what the difference would be. And if there really is no difference, then the practitioners of theology should surrender their pretensions to being something other than philosophers of religion.

It may seem from this opening salvo that what is being discussed is how theology is to be defined. That is in part correct but the reason it has been raised at all is that theology's right to function in anything like its traditional form has been put in jeopardy by the assumptions and the functioning of modern academic life.

The roots of this modern academic attitude reach down at least into Descartes who proposed that it is in the knowing subject alone that certainty is found and this subject can stand outside himself or herself and dispassionately strip away all ideas for which there is no rational support. No belief, therefore, is viewed as credible if that credibility rests on external authority. "If there is any characteristic of the modern critical spirit readily identifiable," says Van Harvey, "it is the insistence on the right to think for oneself, to be free from any authority that would circumscribe research and inquiry. . .to think without direction from another."[24] This has produced the twin assumptions that the modern scholar can expect credence only for what is "rational" and that he or she must be personally disengaged from the process of discovery. The academic must suspend whatever beliefs he or she has and become a neutral observer in order to preserve the objective criteria without which the work done cannot hope for any serious consideration. And if this academic is also a theologian, that means he or she must function as an unbeliever while in the academy.

If a theologian is expected to be both a believer and an unbeliever, then plainly a fissure is appearing between that person's "work and vocation,"[25] as Gerhard Ebeling notes. If a theologian approaches his or her work in terms of the knowledge of God through Christ, and on the basis of a God-breathed and God-given revelation, then that work runs the risk of being judged academically unacceptable because, as Helmut Thielicke notes, "Since Kant discovered man's autonomy one can no longer accept a truth-claim or an imperative unless it has passed the censor of theoretical and practical reason."[26] This kind of work does not pass that kind of test. In order to become acceptable, then, the theologian working in academia must be stripped of obedience to Christ, of faithfulness to the expressed truth of God, and of any desire to serve the people of God. Or, at least, these attitudes must be held in abeyance as long as the academic work is being done. Once this person assumes his or her vocation in the church, then these attitudes are not only permissible but indispensable! One is reminded of Alfred Loisy's disparaging remark about Harnack, that unfortunately a remnant of traditional piety was spoiling his scholarship; and one is reminded also of Harnack's own advice to one of his students who was headed for an academic career, that he would be wise to stay clear of the church if he wanted to be considered a serious scholar. Think also of Philip Schaff's efforts to interpret America to his German friends and how he noted the extraordinary habit of ecclesiastical academics here to be involved in the life of the church! Given this fissure between work and vocation, it is no surprise that Germany, which has pursued it with more vengeance than anyone else in the modern period, has also become the seedbed of most academic heresy, for we are surely courting disaster to imagine that truth can be found only by the unbeliever and that the functioning believer becomes a cripple in its pursuit on account of his or her belief!

With this discussion in the background, it is almost startling to read a book like B. B. Warfield's *Right of Systematic Theology*. It is true that he was not addressing the question of theological method directly, but what is so striking is the innocence of his conception. What he seems to assume is that if the Bible is treated as divinely inspired, as it should be, it will naturally and without difficulty deliver its doctrinal cargo. Once the matter of inspiration is settled, the question of what doctrine the Bible teaches will resolve itself more or less automatically.

Warfield, of course, was writing in a context in which it was still widely accepted that the natural world would yield its meaning to those who would simply apply their powers of observation and deduction to it. And in the same way it was assumed that the meanings and values of our actions are as self-evident as those of the natural world, that they, too, simply needed to be observed and pondered and they would unlock to the observer their secrets.

It is no surprise, then, that most nineteenth- and early twentieth-century theologians spoke of theology as a science. As the scientist has to find, explain, and organize the facts of the world, so the theologian has to find, explain, and organize the facts of biblical revelation. And the one is as apparent, as self-evident, as the other. Theology, Charles Hodge said, is "the science of the facts of divine revelation"; it is "the scientific arranging" of the "facts" about God and his world, said Lewis Sperry Chafer; it is "the science of God and of the relations between God and the universe," said E. H. Bancroft; it is a construction built from the "facts" of biblical revelation, said H. O. Wiley.[27] Whether this kind of talk was simply part of an unconscious style or whether it represented the adoption of the principles of Baconian science in general and of Scottish common sense realism in particular by these theologians has been explored with considerable interest in recent years. At the very least there was a linguistic alliance in effect, even if it did not produce a marriage of content, an alliance that I believe made it difficult for evangelical theology to take with sufficient seriousness the substantial epistemological challenge that was slowly being mounted against this way of thinking.

It is certainly curious that in the nineteenth century and the early part of the twentieth century any alliance should have been struck with a philosophy that arose in the Enlightenment and assumed that the observer was in fact neutral, especially when one notes that evangelical theology has generally been committed to the view of the radical insufficiency of human reason and has been quite mindful of the power of reason to recreate "reality." The neutrality of the thinker follows most naturally from the Enlightenment's assumed autonomy of the individual, but it follows most unnaturally from the notion of our bondage to our sinful egos about which Scripture speaks. If there were benefits to be had from this linguistic alliance, then, they were also accompanied by some perils.

At about the same time that Warfield wrote his little book, Abraham Kuyper in Holland was also giving some thought to this matter. He noted that theologies are different because the objects under investigation are different. The reason for this is that "the object of theology lies closely interwoven with our subjectivity."[28] There is no escape, he said, from the "refraction of subjectivity." On the one side this means that it is no more possible for a person to put together a satisfactory theology if that person's "organ for the world of the divine is inactive" than it is for a person who is blind to speak of the colors of the world. And, on the other side, it means that even where the knowledge of God is present, the subjective still has the power to distort or even "eliminate" the objective, in this case, God and truth about God. Kuyper's perspective is helpful as a way into the modern discussions.

Current hermeneutical thinking, in fact, reveals just how troublesome and difficult it is to set text and interpreter, objective and subjective, in right relationship. There are at least three key issues that need to be clarified for the purposes of fruitful theological function.

First, the notion that the interpreter can be uninvolved in the process of interpretation and that the meaning of the Bible can be unlocked simply by the application of a set of antiseptic and objective rules is extraordinarily naïve philosophically. Every interpreter brings with him or her a whole skein of experience, experience through which the text is read and that inclines him or her to see some things and not to see other things. Furthermore, everyone brings to the text the inclination to rebel against the God who demands as a condition for our knowing him a spirit of glad submission to him and to his truth.

For many years Van Til waged a lonely battle for these points but it is interesting to note how his arguments are being strengthened from some unexpected quarters. Paul Ricoeur has spoken of the ineradicable preunderstanding that every interpreter brings to the text, and Michael Polanyi has spoken of the way he has had to disentangle himself from the notion that interpreters are uninvolved and that the meanings of the words in the text can be deciphered by objective, antiseptic rules. He counters by saying that words by themselves do not mean; speakers meant to say something and employed certain words to do so.[29] The interpreter, therefore, must find out what the speaker intended and that is an exercise far more subtle and intricate than simply finding out the lexical use of the words that were used. It requires the ability to stand inside the words with the speaker, to know the speaker's intentions. To be sure, there always have been generally observed conventions about what words mean and how they should be used, but, at the same time, it has also been recognized that words have ranges of meaning and that over a period of time those meanings sometimes change. There are no assurances of fixed values to words as there are to mathematical digits, or that words will always and only have one meaning. And when this kind of consideration is applied to the interpretation of Scripture, to the knowledge that is required of both the human and the divine authors, it distinguishes theology quite sharply from a study that is simply an academic and literary exercise. One has to know the Bible, the circumstances in which it was written, the outlook of the author, how he used words; and one has to know God, his character, his intentions, and acts as they have been revealed.

Second, the notion that there is an inescapable interaction between text and interpreter does not mean that the interpreter should dominate the text. It is this fear, or the recoil from the fact that this breach occurs every day in the theological world, that makes the nineteenth-century supposition that the interpreter is uninvolved seem so appealing. Those seem like the good old days when texts said what they meant and meant what they said, and readers could receive their cargo of meaning simply by opening the book! So, if one had to choose on which side of the pendulum's swing one wanted to be located, with those of former days who overlooked the subjective but had a firm grasp on the objective, or with those today who are enamored of the subjective and lose in it the objective, this is not the time in which one should want to live!

A good illustration of how close at hand the quagmire can

be today is seen in the work of Hans-Georg Gadamer. He argues in *Truth and Method* that there is a constant interchange between text and interpreter, objective and subjective, such that the meaning of the text becomes merged into the meaning that the self brings to the text. The cognitive horizon of the interpreter and that of the text become fused. Out of this emerges a synthesis, whose Hegelian form Gadamer recognizes,[30] in which the reader *contributes* as much meaning to the text as he or she draws from it. Here is the "unearthly ballet of bloodless categories," the pirouette of thesis and antithesis out of which, in the theologian's study, emerges the long-sought-for synthesis in which the text is accommodated to the interpreter! This, as far as theology is concerned, means that the interpreter must breach the distinction between creature and Creator in order to participate in the divine order from which is derived the divine meaning that is brought to the text. This is, in other words, simply another variation on the old liberal, experiential theology. It is an attempt to transform the self into an organ of inspired revelation, an attempt that becomes possible only to the extent to which we imagine ourselves to be uninvolved in a rebellion against God and no longer creatures in their Creator's world.

By contrast this leads, third, to the recognition of the importance of soteriology in establishing the right relationship between text and interpreter. The place of the subjective cannot be ignored, but then neither may it be allowed to run rampant. Biblical revelation itself denies that it is objective data that can be analyzed by thinkers neutral to its content, but then so, too, one should deny that theology is an "interpretation" if by that one means random fantasy, an excursion into imaginative reconstruction that can be undertaken in disregard of the "given" of biblical revelation. And the key to the proper functioning of the interpreter in relation to the text is not some sort of psychological negotiation to see how the territory between the poles, objective and subjective, might be divided up. It is, rather, to establish the proper functions of each, and the key to this is soteriology.

The Word of God is God's truth, his own disclosure of his character, will, and acts, whether or not we acknowledge it as such. And our acknowledgment adds nothing to that disclosure any more than our denial of it removes something from it. It is, nevertheless, a disclosure to *sinners*—"to sinners," Paul Holmer says, "not the curious; to the ill who need a physician, not to those who are well and self-assured; to those who want to redeem their lives, not to idlers who are looking for exciting ways to spend them."[31] This suggests the terms on which the interpreting work must be done. It means that it is vital that we do not attempt to approach as uninvolved, neutral observers but that we come in a spirit that is in accord with the nature of the work to be interpreted. If we are to understand it aright, in addition to observing the conventions of language and grammar, we also need to be the kind of people who love righteousness, care for what is right, and hate what is wrong. God is like that, and those who are most like him morally are in the best position to know him most deeply cognitively. It is these and the other Christian virtues that are an essential part of the theologian's "equipment" without which profound theology will not be done.

In the academy, theology is required to denude itself of the knowledge of God, the knowledge that is founded in the death of Christ, structured by the Word of God, and mediated by the Spirit of God; in reality, theology cannot properly be done without this knowledge. The theologian must first and foremost be a man or woman of God and know what it is to be in Christ; he or she must be determined to learn to think God's thoughts after him and, as a creature unworthy of redemption, to bring to God, even in the work of theology, the love and worship that are his due. In the academy, it is judged that the presence of these sentiments vitiates the whole enterprise; in reality, if they are not there, the whole enterprise is vitiated.

Theology arises from and is disciplined by the biblical Word, but it is nurtured in worship. The theologian works in the sheer wonder that God in his grace has deigned to make himself known and has called fallen, broken sinners to declare his praise even in theology. "To become and be a theologian," says Barth, "is not a natural process but an incomparably concrete fact of grace,"[32] the kind of grace that elicits adoration, gratitude, commitment, and service. The theologian's work is his or her vocation, and the vocation is his or her work. Unless this is seen, then theology is simply religion, the theologian but a philosopher, and the work of understanding God but a human enterprise caught up in the passage that time makes through all things human.

THE RECIPIENTS

The modern period has seen a double estrangement between church and academy, on the one hand, and between theology and Chrisitan life, on the other. The former has been brought about, as we have noted, by the Enlightenment mentality that sees faith as an impediment to knowledge, as well as by the growing professionalization of theology.[33] The latter has probably occurred through a baleful combination of modernization, anti-intellectualism, and illiteracy. Together these developments powerfully raise the question as to who is the audience whom theologians should seek to address. For whom is theology to be written? Is it for the professional academics, most of whom see it as an invalid enterprise, or for the church, much of which sees it as a useless undertaking? Or is it for those in the wider culture, most of whom will not have the faintest idea what it is all about? The importance of answering these questions lies in the fact that the purpose that one has in constructing a theology will significantly affect its shape and function.

Until the nineteenth century, theology was seen as a churchly activity, done by those in the church for those in the church; hence the early connection with dogma on the Catholic side and with dogmatics (which Brunner defines as "the critical examination of the 'given' doctrine")[34] on the Protestant side. But in many countries in Europe and in America the assumption was that those outside in the culture were also included in the circle of discussion even if some were further from the center than others. The picture has, however, become complicated with the disengagement of most educational institutions from the church's aegis and the growing cleavage between Christian understanding and the accepted norms of Western culture. Does this change the objective?

The purpose in thinking theologically, we must remember, arises from the nature of the enterprise itself and is not prescribed or proscribed by cultural considerations. If theology is about God, his character, his will, and his acts, then the most obvious audience is still those who, through Christ and their knowledge of his Word, know him. But since theology's mission also echoes the very mission of God, that Christ's progeny should be as numerous as the stars above, then it also has to look beyond the people of God to those who are outside the circle of faith. Thus we might say that proximately theology is for God's people, mediately it is for those who are not his people, and ultimately it is for God himself as all of our service returns to him in praise and adoration. This threefold objective, then, prescribes for theology a threefold and basic means of evaluation. Is this theology a faithful repristination of the revelation of God? Does it give the believer a cogent and constructive view of the world and, in the process, does it project Christian norms and values into the society?[35] And does it nurture the life of God in his people, strengthening Christian understanding, nurturing Christian virtues, and undergirding Christian worship?

It is in thinking about the people of God, the church, that we encounter a perplexing reality. Theology is to be written for them but it now seems quite evident that the church is no longer the audience it once was. Indeed, it would be true to say that the level of receptivity in the church is often no higher than it is in the culture, although the reasons are quite different. Theology does not fare well in the culture because it is not believed; it does not fare well in the church because it is not wanted.

In recent years two studies have addressed this reality from different angles but with a common perceptiveness. James Smart has lamented the growing silence of the Bible in the more liberally oriented churches. Lip service is given to the importance of the Bible, but then unobtrusively and unconsciously it is undermined by being ignored. "We could awaken one day," he says, "to find ourselves a church almost totally alienated from the Scriptures."[36] He sees the problem to lie in the fact that in a postcritical age the Bible is exceedingly difficult to preach; so congregations, whose mental processes are thoroughly modern, are left with a view of the Bible that is really thoroughly medieval. They cannot put the two together and their pastors are not helping them to do it. The result, of course, is that these congregations have been cast loose upon the high seas of modernity and as they drift they find few Christian (or, for that matter, theological) ports they can enter.

What is more surprising is to see much the same process at work within the evangelical world, and this has been charted by James Hunter. In his most recent study, he surveyed representative groups of students from both evangelical seminaries and evangelical colleges. These are an educational elite among whom we would certainly expect to find people who are learning to think theologically about life. This is espeically the çase when one remembers, as Hunter notes, that theology has always defined what evangelicalism is, that it has had a central role in evangelical faith that is perhaps unmatched in any other Christian group. What Hunter found, however, was a substantial erosion of theological substance among these students. "There is less sharpness," he wrote, "less boldness, and, accordingly, a measure of opaqueness in their theological vision which did not exist in previous generations (at least to the present extent). A dynamic would appear to be operating that strikes at the very heart of evangelical self-identity."[37] That dynamic is produced by the intrusion of the culture's norms.

Hunter finds evidence of this in the way the Bible's teaching is often rationalized so that its substance is eviscerated. What was once a matter of certain knowledge is now only a loosely held belief or a "feeling." In matters of salvation, the uniqueness of Christian faith is often lost in the "normative ethic of civility," which judges "tolerance and tolerability" in our pluralistic culture more important than matters of truth. And the growing interest in a social gospel among evangelicals is not always all that it seems to be, for Hunter has found that it also represents a shift from other-worldly concerns to those of this world, which, as it happens, are the only matters our secular culture feels comfortable with. Given these changes, it is no surprise to learn what the evangelical publishers are producing for people in the churches. In an earlier study Hunter analyzed this and found that only 12.2 percent deal with understanding Christian faith in a way that required thinking doctrinally. The rest of what is published is devoted either to the issues raised by psychology and the need for inner wholeness and balance (59.9 percent) or to the issues raised by hedonism and narcissism (27.9 percent) with some obvious overlap between these categories.[38]

Evangelical theology therefore finds itself alienated from the academy with whose Enlightenment assumptions it must be at odds, from the wider culture to whom it is understandably a stranger and an alien, and from the life of the church whose habits of mind and interests now lie substantially elsewhere. It is this third alienation that is most unexpected, most grievous, and most damaging. A church that neither is interested in theology nor has the capacity to think theologically is a church that will be rapidly submerged beneath the waves of modernity. It is a church for whom Christian faith will rapidly lose its point, and this is already well underway within evangelicalism. And a church whose interests are thus adrift is one that no longer is an audience for whom theologians can think. They are on the point of becoming artists whose work no one bothers to view. As a new generation of evangelical theologians emerges and begins to learn the craft, this will be the most urgent and pressing of problems to which a solution will have to be found. And may God help them to do it!

NOTES

¹Geoffrey Chaucer, *The Complete Works of Geoffrey Chaucer*, ed. Walter W. Skeat, 6 vols., (Oxford: Clarendon Press, 1899), I, 335.

²"Theology is the doctrine of God; systematic theology is the presentation in a systematic form of that doctrine. But the doctrine of God, in the very nature of the case, is related to everything that enters into our knowledge: all of our world depends on Him; and hence it follows that a systematic presentation of the doctrine of God involves a general view of the world through God. It must contain the ideas and the principles which enable us to look at our life and our world as a whole, and to take them into our religion, instead of leaving them outside." (James Denney, *Studies in Theology* [Grand Rapids: Baker, 1976]).

³Herman Bavinck, *Our Reasonable Faith*, trans. Henry Zlystra (Grand Rapids: Eerdmans, 1956), 24–31.

⁴These words are taken from the initial draft of Ludwig Wittgenstein's foreword in his *Culture and Value*, trans. Peter Winch, ed. G. H. Von Wright (Chicago: University of Chicago Press, 1984), 6e.

⁵Excluded from consideration in this chapter on methodology are the Greek and Russian Orthodox. Although their representatives have participated in World Council of Churches dialogues, their theologians have not shown large interest in this topic and in many of the countries where Orthodoxy is strong, books and journal articles written even within the last three decades are often hard to find.

⁶Cf. Nicholas Wolterstorff, *Reason Within the Bounds of Religion* (Grand Rapids: Eerdmans, 1976).

⁷Ruth Monroe, *Schools of Psychoanalytical Thought* (New York: Holt, Rinehart and Winston, 1955).

⁸Secularism is here understood to be the set of values that has emerged within our culture and assumes there is no supernatural or moral order that impinges meaningfully on the decisions and activities of everyday life. Secularization is understood to be the social organization that we now have that gives life and validation to the secular values. This organization derives principally from industrialization and urbanization. Thus, secularism and secularization are related as the hand is to the glove.

⁹David F. Wells, "Tradition: A Meeting Place for Catholic and Evangelical Theology?" *Christian Scholar's Review* 5,1 (1975): 50–61.

¹⁰See Hans Küng, "The Charismatic Structure of the Church," *Concilium* 4,1 (April 1965): 23–33.

¹¹See, for example, George Tyrrell, "Medievalism and Modernism," *Harvard Theological Review* 1,3 (July 1908): 308–24.

[12]The original draft of the Dogmatic Constitution on the Church opened with what became, in the final arrangement, the third chapter, which is entitled, "The Hierarchical Structure of the Church, with Special Reference to the Episcopate." In the debate that ensued, it was decided to add two chapters, which were inserted before the discussion on the hierarchy. These chapters deal with the mysterious presence of God among his people. This concept significantly affected how authority in the church could be conceived, and it opened up the possibility of a new role for the laity. See E. Schillebeeckx, "Un Nouveau Type de Laic," *La Nouvelle Image de L'Eglise*, ed. Bernard Lambert (Paris: Editions Maine, 1967). 177.

[13]Friedrich Schleiermacher, *The Christian Faith*, ed. H. R. Mackintosh and J. S. Stewart, 2 vols. (New York: Harper & Row, 1963),1:126.

[14]John B. Cobb, *Liberal Christianity at the Crossroads* (Philadelphia: Westminster, 1973).

[15]John B. Cobb and David Ray Griffin, *Process Theology: An Introductory Exposition* (Philadelphia: Westminster, 1976), 30–40.

[16]John B. Cobb, *Process Theology as Political Theology* (Manchester: Manchester University Press, 1982).

[17]Juan Luis Segundo, *Liberation of Theology*, trans. John Drury (New York: Orbis, 1975), 7–38.

[18]James Cone, *A Black Theology of Liberation* (Philadelphia: Lippincott, 1970), 32–33.

[19]See Mark I. Wallace, "The New Yale Theology," *Christian's Scholar's Review* 17,2 (December 1987), 154–70.

[20]J. Gresham Machen, *Christianity and Liberalism* (New York: Macmillan, 1923).

[21]Bernhard W. Anderson, *The Old Testament and Christian Faith: A Theological Discussion* (New York: Harper & Row, 1963), 1.

[22]Brian Hebblethwaite, *The Problems of Theology* (Cambridge: Cambridge University, 1980), 1.

[23]Maurice Wiles, *What Is Theology?* (Oxford: Oxford University Press, 1976), 1.

[24]Van Austin Harvey, *The Historian and the Believer: The Morality of Historical Knowledge and Christian Belief* (New York: Macmillan, 1966), 39.

[25]Gerhard Ebeling, *The Study of Theology*, trans. Duane A. Priebe (Philadelphia: Fortress, 1975), 2–3.

[26]Helmut Thielicke, *Evangelical Faith*, trans. Geoffrey Bromiley, 3 vols. (Grand Rapids: Eerdmans, 1974), 1:38.

[27]David F. Wells, "An American Theology: The Painful Transition from Theoria to Praxis," in George Marsden, ed., *Evangelicalism and Modern America* (Grand Rapids: Eerdmans, 1984), 86.

[28]Abraham Kuyper, *Principles of Sacred Theology*, trans. J. Hendrik De Vries (Grand Rapids: Eerdmans, 1954), 14.

[29]Michael Polanyi, *Personal Knowledge: Towards a Post-Critical Philosophy* (Chicago: University of Chicago Press, 1960), 252.

[30]Hans-Georg Gadamer, *Hegel's Dialectic: Five Hermeneutical Studies*, trans. Christopher P. Smith (New Haven: Yale University Press, 1976).

[31]Paul Holmer, *The Grammar of Faith* (San Francisco: Harper & Row, 1978), 10–11.

[32]Karl Barth, *Evangelical Theology*, trans. Grover Foley (New York: Doubleday, 1964), 71.

[33]The professionalization of theology is not unique to it as a discipline;

194 I David Wells

mainly in the nineteenth century all academic life became professionalized. In two of these professions, however, the tensions that arose between the way the subject was thought about in the academy and how it was practiced were deep and have not been resolved. Those fields are theology and law. On this development as it relates to the study of Scripture see the fine study by Mark Noll, *Between Faith and Criticism: Evangelicals, Scholarship and the Bible* (San Francisco: Harper & Row, 1986), 32–61.

[34]Emil Brunner, *Dogmatics, Vol. I: The Christian Doctrine of God*, trans. Olive Wyon (Philadelphia: Westminster Press, 1950), 57. On the history, see Charles Augustus Briggs, *History of the Study of Theology* 2 vols. (New York: Scribner's, 1916).

[35]I have sought to avoid repeating myself in this chapter when I have already written on some question elsewhere, but this has left some gaps in this discussion. The question of method in contextualization I have addressed in my essay "The Nature and Function of Theology" in Robert K. Johnston, ed.*The Use of The Bible in Theology: Evangelical Options* (Atlanta: John Knox, 1985), 175–99.

[36]James D. Smart, *The Strange Silence of the Bible in the Church* (Philadelphia: Westminster, 1970), 15.

[37]James Davison Hunter, *Evangelicalism: The Coming Generation* (Chicago: University of Chicago Press, 1987), 46.

[38]James Davison Hunter, *American Evangelicalism: Conservative Religion and the Quandary of Modernity* (New Brunswick: Rutgers University Press, 1983), 93–99.

Part II

DOING THEOLOGY: CONTEMPORARY EVANGELICAL PROTESTANT PERSPECTIVES

7

HOW DO LUTHERAN THEOLOGIANS APPROACH THE DOING OF THEOLOGY TODAY?

DAVID P. SCAER
CONCORDIA THEOLOGICAL SEMINARY, FORT
WAYNE, INDIANA

Lutheran theology is derived from Holy Scripture, but it is also normed or regulated by the ancient, catholic creeds and the Lutheran Confessions from the sixteenth century. The ancient creeds that are normative for Lutheran theology are the Apostles', the Nicene, and the Athanasian creeds. The sixteenth-century documents normative for Lutheran theology were collected into the Book of Concord of 1580 with the Augsburg Confession serving as the primary Lutheran Confession of faith.[1] Lutheran theology has historical referents outside of the Scripture, and these referents are normative for the way Lutherans do theology. If Lutheran theology is biblical, it is also confessional. The church is not only able to, but also must, set forth its theology according to the Confessions, which, after examination, are recognized as doctrinally binding statements. The first task of the Lutheran theologian is to test the Confessions and to accept them as his confession of faith after comparing them to the biblical documents. Then he forms and tests his own theological formulations against both the Scriptures and the Lutheran Confessions. Different Lutheran churches do not produce their own confessional documents to meet particular needs associated with time and place. All are bound to these sixteenth-century documents, even if not all are able to work with these Confessions in their original German or Latin.[2] Because these Confessions do not differ from church to church or from country to country,[3] and are recognized by all churches that call themselves Lutheran, they, at least hypothetically, serve to prevent Lutheran theology from being splintered.[4] However, the authority of these Confessions in the actual performance of theology is not uniform, as I will indicate. Thus doctrinal unity, which is the purpose of these Confessions, has rarely been achieved since the beginning of the eighteenth century.

In the creation of these Confessions and in the theology derived from them, the Holy Spirit is not working apart or independent from the Scriptures to reveal something new. The Spirit works through these Confessions of Scripture's teaching to address changing situations of the church. So confident of their Confessions' biblical basis were the first subscribers to the Luthern Confessions that they were willing to die for the sake of their Confessions.[5] While the Confessions remain fixed, the church's theology addresses the questions raised in particular situations. Thus Lutheran theology does not simply restate what the Lutherans of the sixteenth century believed, though the temptation to do only that exists. The Lutheran Confessions add still another dimension to the theological task: they assert that when the interpretation of the Confessions is disputed, the writings of Martin Luther should be consulted for the proper understanding and intent of the Confessions.[6] This does not mean that Luther may be cited in place of the Confessions or the Scriptures. Rather, his writings may be brought into the discussion where these Confessions do not speak or where they need clarification. This approach does not negate but rather requires that all theology be derived from the Scriptures, with the understanding that the Confessions themselves and the theology derived from them be continually tested against them.[7] Reference to the writings of Luther as a factor in Lutheran theology should not be overstressed, even though it may appear to non-Lutherans that the Reformer has become an authority in his own right.[8] With the exception of the Formula of Concord, the Lutheran Confessions were written by Luther and his close associate at Wittenberg, Philip Melanchthon, but even the Formula defers to Luther. And even the Augsburg Confession is regarded by the Formula as Luther's theology, even though Melanchthon was the author.

Blind submission to the creeds and confessions is not required of the theologian before he begins his task; rather, he submits them to the same scrutiny to which he submits his theology. Only when he has arrived at the juncture of commitment to these confessions is he permitted to begin his own theological task of reflecting on the contemporary church situation and responding to it with the word of God. This doing of biblical and confessional theology is not done in a historic vacuum set in the sixteenth century, but in the lively application of the binding word of God within the church's contemporary situation. Thus Lutheran theology is biblical, because it recognizes the Scriptures as the ultimate authority.[9] It is confessional, because its conclusions are measured against the confessions. Because it does not speak to past issues but to contemporary ones, it is proper theology and not simply historical theology or history of dogma. This approach does not ignore or condemn the church's past, but affirms it and projects it into the present as normative for the church's theology. Such a theological approach is "catholic," because it conscientiously desires to derive its life from the church and to perpetuate that life.[10] Confessional theology is also apostolic because it recognizes and depends on the unique and unrepeatable role of the apostles as infallible witnesses to the death and resurrection of Jesus Christ and on their role as the foundation of the church. The stress is on continuity from the apostles, through the history of the church, to the present.[11]

This approach to theology, which provides definite points of historical reference in the creedal and confessional documents in addition to the biblical ones, presupposes the unity of the Bible and its doctrine and the possibility of doctrinal consensus among Christians even before the theological task begins. The content of the church's doctrine is a given, and not a goal. Theology may be discovered in what is already present, but it is not created nor can it result from new revelations. The Holy Spirit works only through the biblical witness. The experience of theologians is not a factor for theology. Theology does not go beyond this biblical and confessional core to produce new doctrines but strives to explicate this core in new and different situations. The confessions do not possess an independent theological authority apart from the Scriptures; their authority springs from their faithfulness to the Scriptures.

Ideally, theological disputes and questions within the community of Lutheran churches may be resolved simply by demonstrating in a cogent way that a certain position set forth now either is or is not the natural conclusion of principles set forth by the confessions. Because Lutherans often disagree on the confessional doctrines, doctrinal unity derived from and based on the confessions has been difficult to achieve.[12] More and more Lutheran theology is done within an ecumenical context, where even agreement on the ancient creeds can hardly be presupposed.[13] Thus it is not uncommon, even among Lutherans, to view Chalcedonian Christology, with its endorsements of the councils of Nicea and Constantinople, as only one step in the development of doctrine, not necessarily as binding reflections of the New Testament.[14]

Quite clearly any unanimity in Lutheran theology that might have been evident in the sixteenth-century confessions, and then in the classical dogmatics of sixteenth and the seventeenth centuries, is lacking today.[15] Pietism in the late seventeenth and early eighteenth centuries, the Rationalism of the eighteenth-century Enlightenment, and Schleiermacher's influential idea of religious self-consciousness with the feeling of absolute dependence as a source of theology, all devastated the classical Reformation Lutheran understanding of theology as the church's response in its confessions to the authoritative word of God. The supernatural origin of the Bible as the inspired word of God (a basic presupposition of the Lutheran Confessions,[16] fundamental to Lutheran theology)[17] was no longer uncontested after the Enlightenment. A partial recovery of the genius of Lutheran theology followed in the mid-nineteenth century.[18] In practice the reality of doctrinal unity presupposed in the people's submission to the Lutheran Confessions is now frequently lacking and has been replaced by a confessional subscription that in most cases is more formal than real.[19] Contributing to this lack of Lutheran theological consensus is disagreement not only over the nature of the Bible as the word of God[20] but also over the precise definition of confessional principles and the validity of their judgment in the current situation. Many theologians wishing to be identified as Lutheran regard the Confessions as having been binding for Lutheran theology only at the time of their writing. They are now regarded only as part of the Lutheran heritage without any real normative function for theology. In spite of the wide divergence among Lutheran theologians, these confessions serve as doctrinal boundaries and encourage a more conservative theological position on the church and its theology. The confessional approach has not resulted in theological uniformity, but it does require that whatever purports to be Lutheran theology must be measured continually not only against Scriptures but also against these historic confessions.[21] Even

Rudolph Bultmann's insertion of the gospel principle in interpreting the New Testament could be understood as superifcially Lutheran, though his definition of the Gospel as discovering the authentic self does not even begin to approach the confessional or scriptural definition. Where church practice— and subsequently theology—go beyond the confessional bounds, the confessional principle is made inoperative for theology and it is questionable whether this kind of theology should any longer be understood as Lutheran, at least according to its classical definition.

The violation of the confessional principle can happen in several ways. The confessions may be regarded merely as part of the church's historical heritage without any normative function for theology today, as is the case in the established churches of Scandinavia and Germany. Lutheran theology can be written without any clear indication that it wants to be Lutheran.[22] In some cases the number of the binding confessional documents may be reduced. For example, the Augsburg Confession may be retained, but not the Smalkald Articles and Formula of Concord—with their references to the pope and Reformed theology, they may be embarrassing in an ecumenical context.[23] Submission to the confessions may be reduced from a binding commitment to a conditional one.[24] Thus the confessions have a function in theology, not because they are the correct statements of the biblical truths, but only insofar as they do this.[25]

While strictly adhering to the Bible as norm and source for theology, the confessional approach in Lutheran theology adds two dimensions that are prior to or part of the theological task. First, the doctrinal positions of these confessions must be presented and defended in the courtroom of other opinions claiming to be authentically Lutheran. Just as most Christian theology must enter into the hermeneutical question to ascertain the meaning of a certain biblical pericope, Lutheran theology must also address the hermeneutical question of its confessions. "What do the confessions say and mean?" is the first question.[26] It should be stated clearly that Lutherans do not substitute their confessions for the Scriptures as the basis for authority. Determining what is intended by the confessions does not relieve the theologian of the task of biblical research and defense of his position. The Lutheran theologian has the double burden of determining and agreeing on the intention not only of the Scriptures but also of the confessions. Matters are made more complex when Luther is cited. Thus studies of Luther do not play an insignificant role in Lutheran theology.[27] A debate at the 1989 convention of the Lutheran Church–Missouri Synod centered around Luther's position on the ministry.

Second, Lutheran theology does not claim that the historic creeds and confessions are necessarily able to address completely every theological problem that has arisen since the sixteenth century. Lutheran theology must demonstrate that newer theological formulations, especially in disputed matters, are logically acceptable conclusions of the confessions and are in harmony with them. An example of this approach is the way Lutherans approach unitarian theologies that deny the deity of Christ. The refutation of the Arian heresy by the Council of Nicea provided the basis for rejecting certain unitarian elements among the Anabaptists by Augsburg Confession I. In turn Lutheran theology today repudiates certain unitarian elements not only in churches that are called unitarian or have a similar teaching, such as Jehovah's Witnesses, but also among theologians, whether or not they may call themselves Lutheran. This repudiation is made on the basis not only of the Scriptures but also of the Nicene Creed and the Augsburg Confession. The use of the creeds and confessions in this way introduces into the theological discussion the concept of the unity of the church and its doctrine.

In regard to the esteem and veneration given the creeds and confessions, the older ones are given the place of honor. This honor is shown in the part they play in the Lutheran liturgy. The regular church services with the Holy Communion generally use the Nicene Creed, and other services, especially the baptismal service, have the Apostles' Creed. On the First Sunday after Pentecost (Trinity Sunday), the Athanasian Creed is commonly confessed. The creedal foundation of Lutheran theology flows out of and is part of the worship life of the people. The Lutheran theologian studies the creeds because of their historical significance, but he uses them in his theology because, first and foremost, they are part of his life of faith. Only that which is part of the worship life of the congregation has a place in theology. Among the sixteenth-century confessions, the place of honor is given to the Augsburg Confession and then to the Small Catechism. Cornerstones for Lutheran church buildings frequently are marked with the letters "U.A.C," which stand for the Unaltered Augsburg Confession.

This shows, first, the Lutherans' high regard for their confessions, but the word "unaltered" is added to distinguish it from later versions, especially Melanchthon's *Variata*, which were amended to accommodate Reformed churches. Luther's Small Catechism, after more than 460 years, remains the basic educational instrument in preparing children and adults for full communicant participation in the church. Thus the creeds and confessions, which are determinative for Lutheran theology, are first formative for Lutheran church piety.

In doing theology, the order of honor of the confessions is reversed so that the later ones serve as interpretations of the first. The most fundamental confession remains the Apostles' Creed, but the much more detailed Nicene and Athanasian Creeds provide the interpretation for it. For example, in the Apostles' Creed, the word "only" in "his only Son our Lord" speaks to the deity and the pre-existence of Christ. This is more clearly explicated in the Nicene Creed: "God from God, Light from Light, true God from true God, begotten not made, being of one substance with the Father, through whom [Christ] all things were made." The Nicene Creed cannot replace the Apostles' Creed as the foundational document of Christianity, but in the matters of Christ's pre-existence, deity, and creation of the world, the Nicene Creed is not only more explicit, it also establishes the correct interpretation. The Augsburg Confession stands as the interpreter of the ancient creeds, especially in the matter of justification, but in turn it is interpreted by the later confessions. The Apology of the Augsburg Confession and the Treatise on the Power and Primacy of the Pope were written by Melanchthon as appendices to the Augsburg Confession. Luther intended the same with the Smalcald Articles. The Formula of Concord, as the last, is the authoritative interpretation for the other confessions.[28] As the churches associated with the Lutheran World Federation move into closer relationship with other churches, e.g., Anglican churches, the confessions other than the Augsburg Confession have lost their normative value for Lutheran theology. The Formula of Concord (Solid Declaration) VII condemns the Reformed errors in regard to the Holy Supper, which were adopted by the English church. Ecumenical alliances have the effect of limiting the normative function of the confessions in Lutheran theology. Although all the confessions should inform Lutheran theology, in practice only the more elastic and less abrasive Augsburg Confession performs this function.

Another nuance in confessional Lutheran theology has to do with the bilingual character of the confessional documents. One case in point is Augsburg Confession X, the article on the Lord's Supper, whose Latin may possibly be read in a Reformed way to suggest that the body of Christ is "distributed to those who eat in the Supper of the Lord," but it does not say in so many words that it is received. The German version clarifies this by affirming that Christ's body "is distributed and received."[29] If the Latin version was written first, as for example in the case of the Apology written by Philip Melanchthon, then the German translation provided by Justus Jonas serves as the correct interpretation in disputed matters.[30] It should be added that the German translation of Jonas is such an expansion of the original Latin by Melanchthon that it virtually constitutes its own confession.[31] These creeds and confessions stand in an organic relationship with one another, the later ones affirming the earlier. The later creeds and confessions claim to derive their authority from the earlier ones. In this order of hierarchial ascendancy, all the creeds and confessions are seen as ultimately derived from the New Testament. The Apostles' Creed, along with the closely related Nicene Creed, is the link to the New Testament. The creeds and confessions are not something in addition to the apostolic Scriptures, but rather natural consequences of them.

The use of the confessional principle in Lutheran theology is a postapostolic custom, foreign to the New Testament but actually derived from it. The church, in continuing the theological task in a confessional mode after the apostolic era, is engaging in a practice with which the first Christians, including the apostles and the New Testament writers themselves, were involved. Confession is a necessary and vital part of Christian faith (Matt. 10:32; Rom. 10:9–10), and theology serves only to explicate the basic Christian confession that Jesus is Lord or Christ, who died for sins and rose for justification. Since the affirmation that Jesus is the Christ constitutes the substance of the church's confession in both apostolic and ancient church periods, the form of this confession and the theology derived from it, is thoroughly Christological, a point that will be elaborated below. On this point, perhaps more than any other, Lutherans are in agreement, at least in a formal way.

Post-apostolic creeds and confessions can hardly qualify as the word of God in the original sense, as that word was preserved in the canonical apostolic writings of the New

Testament. By definition theology claims to be a word of God. Like preaching, theology must be addressed to the situation in which the church and her theologians find themselves. Lutheran theology is a deliberate continuation of the apostolic heritage into the present, a heritage that must continue if the church really wants to be the church. Lutheranism endorses certain periods of the church's history by making their statements of faith normative for the present and future life of the church.

The New Testament documents are the written Word of God but are also confessional statements reflecting the faith of the writers themselves. Certain confessional statements—e.g., "Jesus is Lord," "Jesus is the Christ, the Son of the living God"—serve in the New Testament as standard and norm for baptism and inclusion of others into the church. Creeds that serve as boundaries for participation in the church through baptism continue to regulate the church's theology. These confessions give confessional character to the New Testament documents in which they are found. As diverse as these creeds may have been in the New Testament times, a certain uniformity can easily be detected. Jesus of Nazareth had a supernatural origin as the Son of God. He was put to death for sins, and by his resurrection he was declared Lord and Christ. As short and simple as this understanding of Jesus is, it still serves as the substance of ancient creeds and the Lutheran Confessions. The New Testament documents are confessional statements of what the writers and the apostles themselves believed and, in this confessional sense and not only as authoritative word of God, they belong to the confessional corpus of the church.[32] The confessions of the church begin with the apostolic era and its documents and not first in the postapostolic period with the creeds. The New Testament still serves as a confession very much in the sense that ancient creeds and sixteenth-century confessions do now.

The sixteenth-century confessions and writings of Luther are never regarded as equal to or more authoritative than the catholic creeds, not to mention the Scriptures themselves. No later period, whether it be the fourth century with Athanasius or the sixteenth century with Luther, can replace the first century. Only the apostles were infallible in their writing of Scripture and, more importantly, they were witnesses of the death and resurrection of Jesus Christ, the events comprising the substance of the Gospel. Lutheran theology desires to be first apostolic and then, only in a secondary and historical sense, Lutheran. Or put another way, to be "Lutheran" is simply to be one who adheres to the ancient faith of the catholic and apostolic church, revived and restored at the time of the Lutheran Reformation. Again, it must be pointed out that some Lutheran theologians recognize little or no binding function in the confessions for theology and go no further than recognizing them as historical and cultural documents reflecting the belief of the church at a particular time and place. This approach allows for theological expression that may be at variance with the confessions themselves.[33] Since in the actual practice of Lutheran theology, the subscription or submission to the confessions may range from theologically binding to only formalistic assent to a past religious history and culture, their use in Lutheran theology since the eighteenth-century Enlightenment is not uniform. Thus it is quite possible for a Lutheran theologian to put forth a view that is admittedly at variance with these confessions or that may completely ignore the confessions as being in any way part of the theological task.[34]

Even in those cases—and they indeed may be the majority—where the older confessions and creeds are not normative for the theological task, these documents are not without meaning. Any theology claiming to be Lutheran cannot ignore this heritage, even if in the strictest sense the documents no longer perform their original function as confessions, statements of what the church believes. For example, even though some Lutheran theologians may have doubts about the biblical basis for infant baptism, they are more likely to provide theological, historical, and cultural reasons in place of the exegetical ones to preserve the confessionally mandated practice.[35] Such a procedure is hardly the intent of the authors and first subscribers of the confessions, including Luther, who said that if he had been convinced of the absence of biblical proof, he would have not baptized infants.[36] A theology that is at variance with the accepted confessions no longer deserves to be called Lutheran theology, at least in the classical sense. However, it is necessary to recognize that valuable contributions are made by those Lutheran theologians who admittedly do not follow precisely in the paths of Luther and the confessions. Any definition of Lutheran theology must take into account those who want to belong to this tradition, even if the confessional commitment does not fit the classical understanding of this commitment. With a broader definition,

Lutheran theology may include those who may not accept the principle of biblical authority for theology but are sill committed to the principle of justification as the essential ingredient for this theology. Defining a theology as Lutheran according to its use of the principle of justification is not without its problems, since Lutherans today are not agreed what is meant by it.[37] If some Lutheran theologies ignore and in fact deny the doctrinal relevancy of these confessions, other approaches treat these confessions as having taken on a life of their own. While formally affirming the *sola scriptura* principle, they may ignore it in practice. This approach is really not Lutheran according to the classical understanding, since the scriptural principle is not correctly used. For Lutheran theology the creeds and confessions were established as living reflections of biblical truth. They do not serve their intended purpose when they become autonomous authorities for theology or are referred to only as legal code books.[38] To use the confessions in this way results only in historicism, not theology. While such historicism may be preferred to other kinds that depend on other times in church history, it remains mere historicism and not confessional theology.[39]

Although not possessing a Lutheran understanding of confessions as documents reflecting and deriving their doctrinal content from the Scriptures, Schleiermacher followed an almost Lutheran approach in his theology by incorporating the major confessional documents of the Protestant churches—i.e., Lutheran, Reformed, and Anglican—into his *The Christian Faith*. His approach was hardly confessional in the traditional sense, but it did reflect an understanding that the documents produced by the Christian community, even from more recent times, are not inconsequential for the faith of the contemporary church and thus should be taken into account in its theology. Schleiermacher recognized that historical continuity is part of the historical task.[40] While Lutherans see their confessions as part of their historical heritage, they include and go beyond this to see that the doctrinal unity of the creeds and confessions of their church reflect the deeper and more profound consensus of the biblical writings themselves. Creeds and confessions are hardly mere matters of the ethnic, cultural, national, and linguistic heritage, a role they played for some Lutheran theologians during nineteenth-century German Romanticism,[41] but they necessarily flow out of the biblical faith. The Lutheran theologian is not relieved of the burden of measuring his

208 | David P. Scaer

theology and that of others whom he is addressing against the
biblical norm. Then he measures these conclusions against the
creeds and the confessions. Thus theological thought must be
shown to be both derived from the Scriptures and in accord
with the historic creeds and confessions. The argument does
not involve only the question of what the Scriptures teach and
allow but also what can be demonstrated from the confessions.
This approach may have the unintended disadvantage of
making the sixteenth century determinative for theology in a
sense that was never intended by the Reformation theologians.
In their confrontation with the Church of Rome, the Lutherans
in their confessions were determined to set forth their position
as that of the Scriptures, because ultimately, for theological
truth to be valid in the church, it must be scripturally
demonstrable. In doing so, they were convinced that the
Lutheran position was that of the ancient church at Rome.[42]

The authority that Lutherans give to their confessions not
only distinguishes them from Reformed and Arminian
branches of Protestantism (whose historical confessions may in
fact number many more than those produced by the Lutherans)
but strangely also from Roman Catholicism, which, in spite of
the plethora of its decrees and councils, requires in some cases
little more than submission to the church authorities, the
ordinary [bishop] and the pope, and the ancient creeds. Doing
theology within a completely Lutheran context, the church's
confessions, and to a certain extent its subsequent history of
interpreting these confessions, may seem to non-Lutherans to
take on a life all of their own. This is never intended and must
explicitly be repudiated.

When Lutherans do theology in a non-Lutheran setting,
they must pursue the theological task on the basis of Scripture
as the word of God and the sole source of their theology,
without reference to their confessions. Such an approach is
mandated by any ecumenical context. While recognizing their
confessions as correctly reflecting the biblical revelation, Lutheran theology does not insist on a prior acceptance of the
Lutheran Confessions by others as a precondition for theological debate and reflection. The creeds may play a role in
theological debate, since there is wide acceptance of them
among Christians, but this is not necessary. In this situation
Lutheran theology may adopt a polemical tone, since in stating
the biblical truth, it is obligated to renounce opposing viewpoints.[43] This is precisely how the Augsburg Confession and

the Formula of Concord proceed. The Preface to the Book of Concord is quite clear in stating that positions in opposition to the word of God cannot coexist with true teaching in the church. This was especially true of any suggestion that the elements of the Lord's Supper were not Christ's actual and real body and blood.[44]

Lutherans happily recognize that correct "Lutheran" theology can be and is being done by others outside of the context of its confessions and readily introduces their methods and conclusions into the theological task. Such is the approach of the confessional documents themselves whose authors not only knew the early church fathers but also cited them as authoritative in their theology. In seeking to reach a doctrinal consensus for the unity of the church, Lutherans also recognize the positive aspects of the theologies of those who are not committed to the same confessions. The Apology of the Augsburg Confession notes with appreciation those parts of the Augsburg Confession that the Roman Catholics accept in their Confutation. In Apology X the epiclesis of the Greek liturgy (the priest's eucharistic prayer of consecration during the mass) is cited to show that the bread is turned into the body of Christ.[45] Lutheran theology, rather than being a parochial or sectarian enterprise, is catholic and ecumenical by drawing on the broadest possible expanse of church tradition. In this way confessional Lutheran theology gives a positive endorsement to the historical life of the church, even if it is not directly part of its own tradition, as in the case of Greek liturgy. The Lutherans approach the Scriptures through the broad spectrum of church history, of which the confessions are a normative part.

Lutherans insist that even with the confessional principle there is one source of theology, not two, as both the Scriptures and the confessions are recognized as normative for theology, though in different senses. While Lutheran theology may be said to be derived from "the Scriptures and the confessions," the statement may in fact be untrue if it in any way suggests that the confessions are set up as an independent norm alongside the Scriptures. Such an approach would be liable to the same kind of censure leveled, perhaps unfairly, against Roman Catholic or Eastern Orthodox theologies for their establishing tradition as a norm independent of the biblical documents. Regardless of the high role that their confessions play in their theology, confessional Lutheran theology must show that it is ultimately drawn from the Scriptures.[46] Lutheran theology insists that being confessional is being biblical.

For Lutheran theology, the Scriptures possess their authority in themselves by virtue of their being God's authoritative prophetic and apostolic word for salvation. The confessions have biblical authority because they correctly reflect this authority. They do not possess it in themselves. The unified doctrinal content of the confessions presupposes and is derived from the unified doctrinal content of the Scriptures, which possess a divine authority that the confessions never claim for themselves. The *sola scriptura* principle means that in approaching Scriptures the experience of the interpreter and the use of reason cannot be used against its plain meaning or sense. The theologian must make his reason and experience captive as servants to the Scriptures. While historical precedents—e.g., the confessions, early church fathers, Luther, the theologians of sixteenth and seventeenth Lutheran Orthodoxy—may confirm or supplement the Scriptures as the sole source of theology, the reason, experience, and even the common sense of the theologian are simply unacceptable as sources. Even the confessional commitment required of Lutheran theologians demands that the confessions be subjected to the normative authority of the Scriptures.

The Scriptures do not serve as the source of theology in a vacuum but as part of the living faith of the church, passed on through the creeds from one generation to another. This living faith, which the New Testament identifies as tradition, stands under the judgment of the same Scriptures as the written form of the tradition. The sixteenth-century Lutheran Confessions, along with the earlier creeds, are now also normative written traditions reflecting scriptural teachings. In one sense, theology may be described as the continued conversation between the Scriptures and living tradition, permanently reflected in written confessions. In making Scripture the final doctrinal arbiter, it, like the confessions themselves, may not be handled as a legal handbook, without consideration of the historical context in which it was written and, more importantly, apart from the Gospel. The application of "biblical principles" to life, apart from the Gospel is characteristic of Reformed theology and is not Lutheran. This does not mean that Lutheran theology at times does not succumb to Reformed influences. The central role of the gospel, particularly Christology, in theology is a distinctively Lutheran emphasis and must be developed.

As the confessions derive their life from the Scriptures, so in turn the Scriptures derive their life and authority from the early church's confessional response to the preached gospel. The Scriptures are the final accessible source for the church's theology today, but they were not the church's first authority. Prior to the Scriptures were the apostles and the earliest Christian communities, which, by apostolic preaching, responded in faith and confessed that Jesus was Lord and Christ. Even earlier than the apostles was the preaching of Jesus, who evoked the confession from the apostles that he was the Christ, the Son of the living God. From this confession, that Jesus was the Christ, evolved the fuller understanding that he died for sins, rose from the dead, and would return to judge the world. This primitive Gospel, whose content centered in the crucified, resurrected, and returning Lord, was the apostolic message that came to expression in the creeds of the apostolic church and has been perpetuated since then through confessions.[47]

For theology, the Scriptures are not only the word of God but also confessions preserving the human writers' own faith in Jesus' death. Thus underlying the authority of the Scriptures and confessions as the basis of theology is the Gospel, centering on the historical death of Jesus as the occasion for the atonement. Thus the Scriptures, and subsequently the confessions, are normative for Lutheran theology in the application not of abstract and disconnected doctrinal truths, but of the Gospel. The Gospel, the teaching that God accepts the sinner as righteous for Christ's sake, provides organic unity to both the Scriptures and the confessions. Because it is the adhesive giving them unity, it plays a functional role in theology.

When Lutherans make the Gospel the functional principle of operation for theology, they are not in any way substituting it for the inspired Scriptures or the Lutheran Confessions as the basis for theology. Rather, the operative and functioning authority of the Scriptures is the Gospel, which is their heart and content. The Gospel is the form and substance of the Scriptures and the confessions. This Gospel, preached by the apostles and given by Jesus, originates from the incarnation of God in Jesus and is brought to full expression by his atonement. The Gospel, defined in terms of the incarnation, atonement, and resurrection of Jesus Christ, becomes the theological standard for judging doctrine. Thus theology is not only a matter of "what hath God said?" but "what preaches Christ?" In actual practice a contradiction between these two principles of Scripture and Gospel is rare, but it may happen. Luther's rejection of Hebrews, James, and Revelation from the New Testament canon was an application of this principle. For Luther the Christological norm superseded the biblical one. The Reformer's approach to the New Testament was no different from his approach to the theological task in general. Theology throughout was to glorify Christ. Without Christ there was no true theology, even where it claimed to be apostolic or a word of God or based on these. Luther was not introducing an outside norm into theology. The God who revealed himself in Jesus, reflecting the prior reality that he was Father and Son, was necessarily bound to a Christological revelation of himself in all points. While acknowledging without any reservation the supernatural nature of the Scriptures, when Lutherans do theology they apply the touchstone of the Gospel, i.e., that God justifies the sinner freely for Christ's sake. In Lutheran theology every doctrine has to be Christological. Because of this Christological principle, Lutherans speak not in the plural, of "doctrines," but in the singular, of "doctrine"—the one about Christ. For example not only do Lutherans fail to find any biblical support for millennialism and the Evangelical enthusiasm for the State of Israel, but they reject these notions out of hand because they depend on non-Christological understandings of both the Old Testament and the New. Since Christ is the content of both the Old and the New Testaments, any understanding that the modern State of Israel has biblical support for its existence is a priori rejected.[48] Infant baptism and infant faith are biblically demonstrable for Lutheran theology, but they are also necessary correlations of the universality of sin and of Christ's atonement. Those who have been condemned in Adam are justified in Christ. The denial of baptism and faith for infants is quite simply the de facto denial of the Christological principle in theology. If the doctrine of Christ and the subsequent justification of the sinner cannot be involved in the theological task, then that theology is simply not Lutheran. Lutherans, like other conservative Protestants in general, see the Holy Scripture, the inspired and inerrant word of God, as the basis for their doctrine; however, the inspiration of the Scriptures is not seen as an autonomous act of a sovereign God through the Holy Spirit, but as an extension of the Incarnation in the life of the apostolic church, confirmed and endorsed by the Spirit. Stated in these terms, a scripturally based theology whose authority is derived from the Holy Spirit is throughout and thoroughly Christological, because the Spirit comes from Christ and testifies to him. If theology must ask the question about the divine origin of the doctrine, it must also make sure that it is organically related to Christology in all its parts. Scriptures are given, not for the purpose of setting down codes and rules for living, but for revealing Jesus Christ. Thus the Scriptures serve theology, not as separate, autonomous passages, without one being related to the other, but in their witness to Christ. Where, for example, Melanchthon could have argued the case for total human depravity on the basis of Psalm 51, he chose to do so on the Christological principle. Condemned are ancient and modern Pelagians who with their denial of original sin "obscure the glory of Christ's merit and benefits by contending that man can be justified before God by his own strength and reason."[49]

As the foremost document among the sixteenth-century Lutheran Confessions, the Augsburg Confession sets forth the articles of faith around the central theme of the justification of the sinner by faith for Christ's sake. Thus Lutheran theology operates with a bifurcated method. It seeks not only to demonstrate the biblical support for its positions, but asks first and last how a certain doctrine may impinge on justification, i.e., the application of the forgiveness earned by Christ to the sinner. In fact the Augsburg Confession relies more frequently on the Christological principle than it does on the citation of biblical passages. Thus infants are to be baptized, because denying them baptism would restrict the universality of God's grace in Christ.[50] A denial of the identification of bread and wine with the body and blood of the exalted Lord is an affront to the person of Christ and his salvation (Formula of Concord VII and VIII). This is not to say that exegetical arguments have no part in the theological task. They absolutely do! Yet biblical exegesis may produce inconclusive results in certain cases and perhaps even contradictory ones in others. The Gospel or Christological principle with the justification of the sinner provides direction for theology even before the theological task is begun. Derived from the Scriptures, it provides a compass to the exegetical task so that the reader knows that Christ is the center and content of the Scriptures, their origin and their goal.

How Lutheran theology is done today on the basis of the Scriptures and the Gospel principle can be seen in the case of the ordination of women as pastors, a practice that most Lutherans accept, but which under careful examination contradicts both the scriptural and the Christological principle in Lutheran theology. Paul's prohibitions against women's preaching should logically bring one to the conclusion that women should not be ordained as pastors. The argument could go something like this: (1) Since women may not preach, only men may. (2) Ordination is reserved for those who preach. (3) Therefore, only men, and not women, should be ordained as preachers. This argument is clearly valid, but Lutherans know that the Christological principle is the necessary foundation on which such argumentation must be constructed. Without it, theology remains biblicistic, i.e., citing passages without reference to the Gospel, and not necessarily Lutheran. A woman who preaches the word and distributes the sacraments in Christ's stead distorts the image of the Incarnation for the congregation and thus misrepresents him, even if her message should in all points be doctrinally correct. A woman standing in the place of Christ distorts the image of him as God's Son and in turn of God as the Father. Her appropriating the office to herself gives a false impression of Christ to the congregation and contradicts her message—assuming that it is a correct preaching of the Gospel. When the Gospel is damaged (perhaps fundamentally), it no longer functions as the norm of theology. The Gospel does not allow her, if we dare speak like this, to be a pastor. A woman functioning in the role of a pastor conflicts with the truth of the Gospel that the Son of the Father became incarnate in the man Jesus.[51] Where the Incarnation is denied by a visible contradiction (a woman as pastor), the Gospel is also denied.

It is difficult to speak of the Gospel as the touchstone for theology, when there are different and even contradictory definitions of the Gospel put forward by those who wish to be Lutheran. If Bultmann's existential definition of confronting one's authentic self is allowed to stand as an adequate definition of theology, an entirely different theology will result than if we see the Gospel as the atonement based on the prior supposition of the Incarnation. Only this latter definition is adequate for the theological task and does justice to the biblical documents.

The centrality and primacy of the Gospel in the practice of theology has been traditionally expressed by asserting that justification is the doctrine by which the church stands or falls.[52] This statement cannot mean that the doctrine of justification of the sinner by grace through faith is the only doctrine that God reveals to man. On the surface this would be absurd, as the scope of biblical revelation leads up to and goes beyond this. The law, for example, belongs to God's revelation, but without the Gospel it is, by itself, not part of the biblical understanding of justification. But this is precisely the point! The law has no independent, autonomous existence in revelation, but is given for the very purpose of God's justifying the sinner for Christ's sake. The doctrine of justification (the Gospel principle) in Lutheran theology does not depend on the ability to articulate it. It cannot mean that without the proper intellectual comprehension and definition of what this doctrine entails, there is no theological truth at all. It does mean that theology in all of its parts or articles must be Christological for God's purpose of justifying the sinner.

Christology is the key not only for doing theology but also for developing biblical hermeneutics. Without Christology the Scriptures remain a closed book. Since they are derived from Christ and he is their content, any reading of them without primary and sole reference to Christ necessarily involves a misreading of them.[53] The tasks of biblical hermeneutics and dogmatics are similar in that both require the application of the Christological principle. The Christological content of the Scriptures becomes the functioning norm in theology. It may appear that the Christological principle, while not false, is inadequate for interpreting the Scriptures. If this is really so, then its use as a functional tool in doing theology is questionable. Thus, for example, the Christological principle may not be appropriate in studying the Synoptic Gospels, which may not at first reading appear to address the doctrine of justification as forthrightly as first Paul and then Luther did. We would have to conclude that the Gospel principle, at least as hermeneutical principle, is inadequate. If it is an inadequate method for biblical interpretation, can it really serve as a theological principle? However, it is incorrect to assume that the Christological principle does not serve as the hermeneutical key in understanding the Synoptic Gospels. The centrality of justification (the Gospel principle), applied first to the Bible as a hermeneutical key and then to all of theology, providing it with a functional unity, means only that God intends in his every address to human beings to count them righteous, that is, to forgive them for the sake of Christ. The justification of the sinner is the content and goal of all the biblical documents. What the fourth Evangelist says about his gospel being written so that the readers (hearers) may believe that Jesus is the Christ, the Son of the living God, and have life in him (John 20:30–31) is true of all the Gospels and the other Scriptures. In Israel's history God was not acting merely to preserve a political state; he was preparing the world for the advent of the Christ, promised to the people of the Old Testament through prophecies and hidden under the external forms of the sacrificial cultus. Thus by prophecy and types the coming of Christ was made more plain from one generation to the next. The Old Testament is inadequately explained as only the history and faith of an ancient people, even if they are God's people, but it must be understood as the account of God's action in history to prepare a people for the coming Christ. The history and events of the Old Testament served to portray the work of the Messiah. The New Testament is the account of God's accomplishment of what he promised. This promise fulfilled in Christ is the Gospel that now saves. If Christology together with the article of juctification, does not serve as the primary principle of biblical interpretation, then it is a foreign principle to introduce when doing theology. But if the article of justification, or the Christological Gospel principle, is the heart and content of the biblical revelation, then it must be the heart of the theological task as well.

I must point out that in accomplishing the theological task, Lutherans do not come at it from several levels. They do not use their historic confessions, the creeds, the Bible, and then the Gospel as a kind of court of last resort so that the criteria for the truth is multiple and varied. Such an appearance is false. If a variety of authorities were competing with each other, theology would not be unified and would eventually become confused. The proverbial "no man can serve two masters without hating or loving one or the other" applies also to theology. With several competing sources or methods of theology, doctrinal unity on any issue would be an elusive goal and never the reality that the confessions claim for themselves as their content and purpose. The problem of multiple levels of authority is resolved when it is understood that the Gospel of man's redemption is the content first of the Scriptures, then the creeds, and finally the confessions. It will simply not do in setting forth any locus in theology simply to accumulate biblical or confessional citations without reference to the Gospel. Unless the theologian understands that the biblical references have to do in some way with God's redemption of the sinner for Christ's sake, he is not a biblical and confessional theologian. Again, it must be stated that this Lutheran reliance on the Gospel in theology presupposes and is built on the greater reality of the Incarnation and the Atonement.

Lutheran theology, done in light of the Incarnation and the Atonement, does not go beneath or around the Gospel and the biblical documents to a prior historical or theological [philosophical] reality that can be approached apart from the Scriptures. Lutherans approach these realities through the Scriptures. It is evident that an extra-Scriptural approach to locate the divine truth would be a denial of the Scriptures, not only as the inspired word of God but also as the authoritative depository of the Gospel. It would in effect be putting in place as authorities for the theological task sources that were in some sense accessible to human reason. The theological significance of history cannot be known without the Scriptures and the Gospel. It would be a synergism of the reason and the intellect to assert the opposite, and thus would contradict the doctrine of divine grace by which God alone, through the revelation of the Gospel, saves the sinner. Although the Incarnation and the Atonement are realities anchored in history, i.e., the virgin birth and the death of Christ, and are obviously in the mind of God prior to any divine revelation in and through the Gospel and subsequently in the Scriptures, they are not accessible to human beings apart from this revelation in the Gospel. The Incarnation serves in history as the anchor of the revealed Gospel, but the part of biblical history that may be properly called salvation history remains inaccessible for the theological task apart from the Bible. On this account apologetics and any historical method that confidently claims to go beyond and above the biblical texts to establish a firmer or further basis of authority for theology is repudiated not merely for epistemological reasons but for the sake of the Gospel principle that must maintain its position of centrality. Apologetics provides a service to theology when it demonstrates that certain alleged historical inaccuracies in the biblical messages are simply unfounded. Historical critical methods may be useful in reconstructing the original situation of the Gospel events and of the biblical writers, but such approaches may not arrive at conclusions contrary to the texts themselves or more importantly, to the Gospel. Certain parts of the biblical history may be accessible apart from the biblical documents, but these extrabiblical researches cannot become normative for the message itself.

Lutherans in America have not equaled the dogmatic productions of their predecessors in the sixteenth and seventeenth centuries. What is available in English are translations from German,[54] Danish,[55] and Swedish.[56] Those who follow the Braaten-Jensen *Christian Dogmatics* do not want to be bound by the Lutheran Confessions. Presently, two works are coming to completion under the editorship of two men formerly associated with Concordia Seminary, Saint Louis. Both projects, like Braaten-Jensen, have a multiple authorship. Ralph Bohlmann is the general editor of *International Lutheran Dogmatics*, a production of the Lutheran Church–Missouri Synod in which as many as twenty writers are involved. It follows an encyclopedic approach, not unlike the one used in *Religion in Geschichte und Gegenwart*, with each topic divided into parts: Old Testament, New Testament, Lutheran Confessions, Systematics, History, and Practical Theology. Robert Preus is editing the *Confessional Lutheran Dogmatics*, for which all but two of the six authors are on the faculty of Concordia Theological Seminary, Fort Wayne, where he has served as president. The Preus dogmatics follows the traditional systematic approach to theology and is available now in two volumes.[57] The Bohlmann dogmatics is scheduled for publication in 1992. The publication of these two dogmatics is a milestone. They will be the first Lutheran dogmatics, (in the classical confessional sense), written originally in English, published in the twentieth century that are committed to the Scriptures as the inspired and inerrant word of God. Whether this is the end of the confessional revival begun in the nineteenth century or the beginning of a new golden age in Lutheran dogmatics will only be known by the next generation.

NOTES

[1]The critical edition of these confessions is *Die Bekennensschriften der evangelisch-lutherischen Kirche*, 6th ed. (Gottingen: Vandenhoeck & Ruprecht, 1967). The specific Lutheran Confessions are three by Philip Melanchthon: the Augsburg Confession (1530), the Apology of the Augsburg Confession (1531), the Treatise on Power and Primacy of the Pope (1537); three by Martin Luther: his Small and Large Catechisms (1529) and the Smalkald Articles (1537); and the Formula of Concord (1577). Sometimes the Introduction to the Book of Concord is considered a separate confession. Appended to the original edition of the

Book of Concord (Dresden, 1580) was the *Catalog of Testimonies*. This is a listing of pertinent quotations from the early church fathers demonstrating that Lutheran Christology is not a deviation from, but a faithful exposition of, the Christology of the early church. A remarkable new took for students of the Lutheran Confessions is the *Concordance to the Book of Concord*, ed. Kenneth Larson (Milwaukee, Wis.: Northwestern, 199).

²Two English translations. The *Concordia Triglotta* (Saint Louis: Concordia, 1921) is now published by Northwestern Publishing Company, Milwaukee, Wisconsin. The most frequently cited is *The Book of Concord*, trans. and ed. Theodore G. Tappert (Philadelphia: Fortress, 1959). The Saint Louis edition is commonly called the Triglot because it appears in three languages—the original German and Latin and the English translation. The Fortress edition is commonly referred to as Tappert. The Triglot edition is a translation based on older texts of the Book of Concord, often relying on previous translations of the Book of Concord. The Tappert edition is based on the more accurate critical edition of the *Bekenntsschriften*. However, the Triglotta is sometimes more accurate than Tappert. Tappert often offers more of a free translation that tends, at times, to skew the meaning of the text. The Triglot, while at times more wooden in style, often offers a more literal rendering of the Latin or German. Another advantage of the Triglot is its inclusion of the Catalog of Testimonies. It is prefaced by the now old, but still very valuable, historical introduction by F. Bente.

³The Reformed churches, unlike the Lutheran churches, adopt confessions for individual churches in particular places. Thus, for example, while the Heidelberg Catechism has authority in the Reformed and Union churches in Germany, it has little in the Presbyterian church in Scotland.

⁴Historically, the Scandinavian Lutheran churches and their daughter churches in the United States held to only the Augsburg Confession and Luther's Small Catechism. This was done for historical reasons and not because the theology of the other Lutheran Confessions was repudiated. The Evangelical Lutheran Church, formed in 1917 of smaller Norwegian groups, held to only these two confessions along with the ancient creeds. (Eugene L. Fevold, "The Place of the Confessions in American Lutheran Churches of Scandinavian Background," in Vilmos Vajta and Hans Weissgerber, eds., *The Church and the Confessions* [Philadelphia: Fortress, 1963], 84–105.) The Formula of Concord is often viewed as applicable only in the German situation. In some cases, however, subscription to less than the entire Book of Concord is done for theological reasons. This is the case with some third world churches who understand themselves as Lutheran but were established by union churches of Germany, where Lutheran and Reformed confessions exist side by side. (Andar M. Lumbantobing, "The Confession of the Batak Church," in Vajta and Weissgerber, eds., *The Church and the Confessions*, 119–38.

⁵"By the help of God's grace we, too, intend to persist in this confession until our blessed end and to appear before the judgment seat of our Lord Jesus Christ with joyful and fearless hearts and consciences." Preface to the Book of Concords (Tappert), 9.

⁶"Luther is rightly to be regarded as the most eminent teacher of the churches which adhere to the Augsburg Confession and as the person whose entire doctrine in sum and content was comprehended in the articles of the Augsburg Confession and delivered to Emperor Charles V, therefore the true meaning and intention of the Augsburg Confession cannot be derived more correctly or better from any other source than from Dr. Luther's doctrinal and

polemical writings." Formula of Concord, Solid Declaration, VII.41 (Tappert), 576.

[7]"Here [Luther] expressly asserts by way of distinction that the Word of God is and should remain the sole rule and norm of all doctrine, and that no human being's writings dare be put on a par with it, but that everything must be subjected to it." Formula of Concord, Solid Declaration, Rule and Norm.9 (Tappert), 505.

[8]To see the importance of Luther in Lutheran theology, one has only to refer to two works by the respected theologian Werner Elert. *Der Christliche Glaube: Grundlinien der lutherische Dogmatik*, 5th ed., ed. Ernst Kinder (Hamburg: Furche Verlag, 1960), 567, and *The Structure of Lutheranism*, trans. Walter A. Hansen (Saint Louis: Concordia, 1962), 534–35. In the latter, there are approximately eighty topics from anxiety to worship with some having multiple references. In the *Index to Christian Dogmatics* by Francis Pieper, an index prepared by Walter W. F. Albrecht, nineteen double-column pages are used to locate Luther citations (Saint Luouis: Concordia, 1957), 951–69.

[9]The Preface to the Book of Concord speaks of the Augsburg Confession as "the witness of the unalterable truth of the Word of God" Tappert, 5.

[10]The following sentence is found in the Preface to the Book of Concord: "They [the signers of the Augsburg Confession] have held fast and loyally to the doctrine that is contained in it, that is based solidly on the divine Scriptures, and that is also briefly summarized in the approved ancient symbols, recognizing the doctrine as the ancient consensus which the universal and orthodox church of Christ has believed, fought for against many heresies and errors, and repeatedly affirmed" (Tappert), 3. The appendix to the Book of Concord is the Catalog of Testimonies in which are listed citations from such early church fathers as Athanasius, Cyril, Theodoret, Basil, Ambrose, Chrysostom, Nicephore, Hilary, Augustine, and even Pope Leo the Great. *Bekennisschriften*, 1103–35; Triglot, 1106–49.

[11]The doctrinal portion of the Augsburg confession concludes with this afirmation: "As can be seen, there is nothing here that departs from the Scriptures or the catholic church or the church of Rome, in so far as the ancient church is known to us from its writers," Tappert, 47.

[12]The 1963 Helsinki convention of the Lutheran World Federation could not come to agreement on a definition of justification, even though this is the characteristic Lutheran doctrine. *Messages of the Helsinki Assembly of the Lutheran World Federation: Christ Today* (Minneapolis: Augsburg, 1963).

[13]The late confessional Lutheran theologian Edmund Schlink attempted to set forth a theology within the context of Lutheranism, Eastern Orthodoxy, and Roman Catholicism. *Okumenische Dogmatic*, 2nd ed. (Gottingen: Vandenhoeck & Ruprect, 1985). As valuable as this contribution is, it is difficult to see how it fits into the tradition of the classical Lutheran dogmatics, as it ignores the historical sixteenth century to work out a consensus on a previous and earlier level. It does, however, develop the Lutheran theme of agreement with the consensus of the early church.

[14]Cf. Carl E. Braaten and Robert W. Jensen, eds., *Christian Dogmatics* (Philadelphia: Fortress, m.d.) 83–192. Barthian and process theology definitions of God are accepted in this work.

[15]For an analysis of those centuries see Robert D. Preus, *The Theology of Post-Reformation Lutheranism: A Study of Prolegomena* (Saint Louis, Mo.: Concordia, 1970).

[16]"We pledge ourselves to the prophetic and apostolic writings of the Old

and New Testament as the pure and clear fountain of Israel, which is the only true norm according to which all teachers and teachings are to be judged and evaluated." Formula of Concord, Solid Declaration, Rule and Norm.3 (Tappert), 503–04.

[17]See Preus, *Theology of Post-Reformation Lutheranism* I. Preus covers in some detail the theology of Lutheran orthodoxy in the late sixteenth and seventeenth centuries, a period for Lutheran theology that has remained unmatched. The hallmarks of this period were doctrinal unity as the basis for church fellowship; a polemical stance against Calvinism, Arminianism, and Roman Catholicism; and commitment to the Bible as the inspired and inerrant word of God.

[18]In 1879, more than two hundred years after the period of Lutheran orthodoxy, a dogmatics book from that period (1685) was edited and republished for use in the seminaries of the Lutheran Church–Missouri Synod. (John William Baier, *Compendium Theologicae Positivae* 3 vols., ed. C. F. W. Walther [Saint Louis: Concordia Verlag, 1879]). Until the 1920s, American-born theological students, whose primary language was English, were hearing theological lectures in German and reading a textbook in Latin! Works that contributed to the revival of confessional Lutheranism include A. F. C. Vilmar, *Die Theologie der Tatsachen wider die Theologie der Rhetorik*, 3rd ed., 1857; F. A. Philippi, *Kirchlich Glaubenslehre*, 3rd ed., 1883; and Francis Pieper, *Christliche Dogmatik*, 1917. Pieper's volume was translated into English and remains the standard dogmatics textbook in the seminaries of the Lutheran Church–Missouri Synod. (*Christian Dogmatics*, 3 vols. [Saint Louis, Mo.: Concordia, 1950]). An abridged version in English of Pieper's German work was prepared by his student John Theodore Mueller (*Christian Dogmatics* [Saint Louis, Mo.: Concordia, 1934]. This abridged version, translated into Spanish and Finnish, carried this confessional theology back to Europe, ironically the continent of its origin three centuries before. The first and perhaps only native American confessional Lutheran dogmatics from the nineteenth century was Charles Porterfield Krauth, *The Conservative Reformation and Its Theology* (Philadelphia: Lippincott, 1871). Its style is not easily recognized as that of dogmatics. Michael Reu, of the Iowa Synod, produced his own dogmatics text, *Lutheran Dogmatics*, which was never published but is available in typescript form in the holdings of Concordia Theological Seminary and other Lutheran seminary libraries.

[19]A meditating school grew up around the University of Erlangen in which Lutheran theological substance was built on the presuppositions of the Enlightenment and Schleiermacher. Though not all who were involved in this movement were at Erlangen, the university gave its name to the movement known as the Erlangen school. Among those associated with the movement were Gustaf Thomasius (*Christi Person und Werk*, 1852–1888) and Ludwig Ihmels (*Die christliche Wahrheitsgewiszheit, ihr Grund and ihre Entstehung*, 1901). Characteristic of the movement was a repudiation of the Bible as the infallible source of theology and the acceptance of a modified form of Schleiermacher's Christian consciousness as the basis of theology.

[20]The confessional subscription is abrogated when the Bible is not acknowledged as God's word. That the Bible is God's word is not only the basic presupposition of confessional subscription but is a belief required by the Lutheran Confessions themselves. For example, the Preface to the Book of Concord speaks of "the unalterable truth of the divine Word" and warns "against doctrine that is impure, false, and contrary to the Word of God," Tappert, 5.

[21]Regin Prenter wants to be considered a Lutheran theologian but defines inspiration as applying to the message and not the letter of the Scriptures, a position characteristic of the Erlangen school in the nineteenth century. Regin Prenter, *Creation and Redemption*, trans. Theodor I. Jensen (Philadelphia: Fortress, 1967), 88.

[22]This is the stated approach of Braaten and Jensen, *Christian Dogmatics*, 1:xvii-xix. References to the Lutheran Confessions in the body of the dogmatics put together by six Lutheran theologians is simply lacking. In the introduction the editors state that such labels as theologians of hope, theologians of process, etc., would be appropriate, but hardly exhaustive in describing them. They do admit to a Lutheran bias in places.

[23]This is the case with the Evangelical Lutheran Church in America, in which the later confessions are not put on par with the earlier ones. Thus the Augsburg Confession is accepted, and other confessions are accepted "as further valid interpretations of the faith of the Church." *ELCA Constitution*, ch. 2.

[24]The Danish Lutheran theologian Regin Prenter is clearly confessional in his approach to theology, but he is unwilling to give an uncondidtional subscription to the creeds and confessions. Prenter, *Creation and Redemption*, 115.

[25]The best example of this is the Union Church of Germany, where in some states since the Prussian Union of 1817, Lutheran Confessions have been placed on par with the Reformed ones. Hans Weissgerber, "The Lutheran Confession in the Union Church," in Vajta and Weissgerber, *Church and Confessions*, 39–59.

[26]For a good discussion of basic principles for interpreting the Lutheran Confessions see Arthur Piepkorn, *Suggested Principles for a Hermeneutics of the Lutheran Symbols* (Fort Wayne: Concordia Theological Seminary Press, 1984; reprinted from *Concordia Theological Monthly* 29,1 [January 1958]).

[27]The best critical edition of Luther's works is contained in the enormous collection known as the Weimar edition. It has been in production since before the turn of the century as is still not complete. Work is presently underway on compiling an index to this set of Luther. It may not be complete until the end of the century. For the English-speaking student of Luther there is the excellent series of translations available in *Luther's Works: American Edition*. There are also excellent study helps to assist the theologian in his study of Luther. Kurt Aland, *Hilfsbuch zum Lutherstudium* (Witten: Luther-Verlag, 1970), is an indispensable guide to Luther's works and editions of Luther's works, providing topical and chronological indices. An important work for locating the critical edition of works contained in the American edition is provided by Vogel's *Cross Reference and Index to the Contents of Luther's Works: A Cross Reference between the American Edition and the St. Louis, Weimar, and Erlangen Editions of Luther's Works* (Milwaukee, Wis.: Northwestern, 1983). Another resource that should not be overlooked when studying Luther is the footnotes in the BKS edition of the Book of Concord. Often the footnotes will indicate where one may find a discussion in Luther pertinent to the Confessions' discussion. Many, but not all, of these footnotes were included in Tappert's translation, which depends almost entirely on the BKS for its footnotes as well as its index.

[28]The Evangelical Lutheran Church in America (ELCA) reverses this process. Whereas the confessional principle, practices for example by the Lutheran Church–Missouri Synod, understands the Formula of Concord as the correct interpretation of the earlier confessions, the ELCA regards the Formula

only as providing "valid interpretations" but not exclusively correct ones. The position of the Lutheran Confessions explains, however, that the later confessions are the correct expositions of the earlier ones. (Tappert), 503–06.

[29]The German and Latin versions of the Augsburg Confession came into existence at the same time, but the place of honor is given to the German one, as it was read before the Emperor Charles V in Augsburg on June 25, 1530. Melanchthon, its author, regarded the Latin version as the primary document.

[30]This does not mean that the Latin and German versions of the same confessions were ever understood by their writers to be at variance with one another. In a letter to Wilhaelm Reiffenstein in Stolberg (September 26, 1531), Melanchthon says that he "has no trouble with the emendations" made by Jonas. *Corpus Reformation*, 2:541–42.

[31]It is strange that the German translation is not available in English. Tappert provides a translation only of the Latin, and the Triglot provides (within brackets) only Jonas' emendations. The results are often confusing. It is unfortunate that a complete translation of the Jonas translation of the Apology has never been done.

[32]For a further elaboration of this approach see Prenter, *Creation and Redemption*, 115–40, the chapter entitled "The Bible and the Confession of Faith."

[33]E.g., Prenter, *Creation and Redemption*; Braaten and Jensen, *Christian Dogmatics*.

[34]While the Augsburg Confession (II and IX) sees original sin as the basis for infant baptism, this argumentation does not enter into the dogmatics of Braaten and Jensen. *Christian Dogmatics*, 2:315–36.

[35]Robert W. Jensen takes this approach in Braaten and Jensen, eds., 2:318. See also Kurt Aland, *Did the Early Church Baptize Infants?* trans. G. R. Beasley-Murray (Philadelphia: Westminster, 1963). Aland, though disputing infant baptism on his biblical grounds, was quite willing to accept it for theological grounds easily recognizable as Lutheran.

[36]*The Adoration of the Sacrament, Luther's Works: American Edition* (Philadelphia: Fortress, 1975), 36:300–01.

[37]Braaten and Jensen define justification as the answer to this question: "Does this particular act of ministry lead people to find their life's justification, their reason to be, in the fact that crucified Jesus lives, or are people left on their own to depend on themselves for the ultimate meaning of life?" *Christian Dogmatics*, xix. We are clearly operating with a definition of justification other than the confessional Lutheran one, which speaks of the justification or the vindication of the sinner before God (*coram deo*) for Christ's sake. Confessional Lutheran theology does ask the question of the personal meaning of life, but of the relationship of the sinner to God, *coram deo!* Augsburg Confession IV.

[38]Robert Preus, a respected Lutheran theologian, makes this valid point: "The Lutheran Confessions themselves never claim to be final work on the understanding and exegesis of the Scripture." David P. Scaer, *Christology*, Volume VI in *Confessional Lutheran Dogmatics*, ed. Robert D. Preus, with a general introduction by Robert D. Preus (Fort Wayne, Ind.: International Foundation for Lutheran Confessional Research, 1990), VI

[39]Another work that contributed to the confessional Lutheran revival in the nineteenth century was Heinrich Schmid, *Die Dogmatik der Evangelisch-lutherischen Kirche* (Erlangen: Carl Heyder, 1843). A compilation of citations from the sixteenth and seventeenth century Lutheran Confessions and dogmaticians listed according to doctrinal topics, it was translated into English and was an

influence on Lutheran theology in America. *The Doctrinal Theology of the Evangelical Lutheran Church*, trans. Henry E. Jacobs and Charles A. Hay (Minneapolis: Augsburg, 1961). As valuable as this compilation is, it can not be substituted for biblical theology.

[40]Friedrich Schleiermacher, *The Christian Faith*, 2 vols., edited by H. R. MacKintosh and J. S. Stewart (New York: Harper & Row, 1963). The English translation index lists the confessional documents cited by Schleiermacher: Apostles', Constantinopolitan (Nicene), and Athanasian Creeds; all of the Lutheran Confessions; The Thirty-Nine Articles, and certain Reformed confessions such as the Belgic, Second Helvetic, and Scottish.

[41]The union of Lutheran and Reformed churches in the Prussian Union begun in 1817 and completed in 1831 placed the confessions of both churches on a par and was as much a national event for Prussia as it was religious. Walter H. Conser, Jr., *Church and Confession: Conservative Theologians in German, England, and America 1851–1866* (Mercer, Ga.: Mercer Univ. Press, 1984), 13–27.

[42]Augsburg Confession XXI (Tappert), 47.

[43]Nearly all of the doctrinal articles in the *Formula of Concord* are divided into two parts with the first affirming a specific doctrine and the second condemning the opposing position. The Latin is *damnamus*, literally "we condemn." For a detailed study of this see Hans-Werner Gensichen, *We Condemn: How Luther and 16th Century Lutheranism Condemned False Doctrine*, trans. Herbert J. A. Bouman (Saint Louis: Concordia, 1967).

[44]Tappert, 3–14.

[45]"We know that not only the Roman Church affirms the bodily presence of Christ, but that the Greek Church has taken and still takes that position. Evidence for this is their canon of the Mass, in which the priest clearly prays that the bread may be changed and become the very body of Christ." *Apology* X.2 (Tappert), 179.

[46]"Other symbols and other writings are not judges like Holy Scripture, but merely witnesses and exposition of the faith, setting how at various times the Holy Scriptures were understood in the church of God by contemporaries with reference to controverted articles, and how contrary teaching were rejected and condemned." *Formula of Concord* (Epitome) (Tappert), 465.

[47]The centrality of the Gospel in Lutheran theology is evident in Werner Elert, *The Structure of Lutheranism*, 59–176, and idem, *Der Christliche Glaube*, 113–98.

[48]Augsburg Confession XVIII specifically condemns millennialism.

[49]Augsburg Confession II (Tappert), 29.

[50]Ibid., IX (Tappert), 33.

[51]See Alvin Kimel's excellent article, "The Holy Trinity Meets Ashtoreth: A Critique of 'Inclusive' Liturgies." *Anglican Theological Review* 71:11. Kimel writes, "The naming of God as Father and Jesus as Son is more than figurative speech. God truly is the Father. He is the Father of Jesus, and Jesus is his Son. . . . The divine paternity is not an arbitrary metaphor chosen by humanity and then projected onto the deity: God is self-revealed as Father in and by his Son Jesus Christ."

[52]For an up-to-date historical and theological evaluation of the use of the principle of justification in Lutheran theology, see Carl E. Braaten, *Justification: The Article by Which the Church Stands or Falls* (Philadelphia: Fortress, 1990).

[53]The Lutheran approach in understanding and applying all the Scriptures Christologically must be distinguished from that of the Reformed. A case study could be made of Martin Bucer, the German Reformation theologian, who,

though allied with and influenced by Luther, saw the Scriptures, including the Old Testament, as having directives for the Christian life. For his influence on English Reformation theology and Puritan thought in England and America, see Henning Graf Reventlow, *The Authority of the Bible and the Rise of the Modern World*, trans. John Bowden (Philadelphia: Fortress, 1985), esp. 73–87.

[54]I should mention the excellent dogmatics by Adolf Hoenecke, *Evangelical-Lutheran Dogmatik*, 4 vols., ed. Walther and Otto Hoenecke (Milwaukee, Wis.: Northwestern, 1909). In a way it is superior to Pieper's *Christian Dogmatics* in regard to style, exegetical treatment, and handling of the early church sources. It has been translated into English, and Northwestern Publishing House is making plans to publish the translation. After it appeared shortly before World War I, its original German-speaking readers soon were speaking only English.

[55]Prenter, *Creation and Redemption*.

[56]Available in English translation from the Swedish is Gustaf Aulen, *The Faith of the Christian Church*, trans. Eric H. Wahlstrom and G. Everett Arden (Philadelphia: Muhlenberg, 1948). From the outset it makes no attempt to be a specifically Lutheran dogmatics (p. 3), even though Aulen was a bishop in the Lutheran Church of Sweden. His approach revolves around the opposition of good and evil, and this develops into his central theme of *Christus Victor*. The Lutheran principle of Gospel and justification simply do not play a role in this dogmatics.

[57]Scaer, *Christology* (vol. 6) and Marquart, *Church and Ministry* (vol. II) in *Confessional Lutheran Dogmatics*, gen. ed. Robert D. Preus (Fort Wayne: The International Foundation for Lutheran Confessional Research, 1990).

8

HOW REFORMED THEOLOGIANS "DO THEOLOGY" IN TODAY'S WORLD

FRED H. KLOOSTER
CALVIN THEOLOGICAL SEMINARY, GRAND RAPIDS, MICHIGAN

The words *Reformed* and *Reformation* belong to the same family. The Reformation of the sixteenth century rejected or modified several Roman Catholic doctrines and practices. Acknowledging the sole authority of Scripture, the Reformers reached back over the Middle Ages to the convictions of the early church to establish Protestant churches, compose new confessions, and develop new theologies. According to Webster, the adjective "reformed" simply means "changed for the better."[1] When capitalized, "Reformed" was originally a synonym for "Protestant," so that it covered the Lutheran, Zwinglian, and Calvinian branches of the Reformation. Gradually the term was restricted to the Calvinist churches on the European continent, while in British lands such churches were generally called "Presbyterian."

When applied to churches, the terms *Reformed* and *Presbyterian* are often used interchangeably. The names of three ecumenical organizations that include both types illustrate the point. The oldest international body of such churches is known as the "World Alliance of Reformed Churches" (WARC). A smaller international organization of confessionally Reformed and Presbyterian churches now calls itself the "Reformed Ecumenical Council" (REC). In the United States an organization of such churches is called the "National Association of Presbyterian and Reformed Churches" (NAPaRC). Strictly speaking, "Reformed" refers to a type of doctrine, confession, or theology, whereas "Presbyterian"designates a certain kind of church government. That usage is reflected in WARC's full designation, which was originally "Alliance of the Reformed Churches throughout the world holding the Presbyterian system." Therefore this chapter aims to describe how Reformed theologians in such Reformed and Presbyterian traditions do theology.[2]

Most theologians do not make a habit of explaining how they go about doing theology; they simply do it. What one is doing and how one does it are difficult questions to answer when what one is doing seems obvious. A little neighbor boy used to amuse me when I was mowing the lawn, washing the car, or painting the house. He would amble by and inevitably ask, "What are you doing, Mr. Klooster?" I usually gave him a silly answer, to which he would reply, "No, you aren't." That approach is hardly appropriate here. Hence I must attempt to answer the question that Reformed theologians generally ignore or to which they give only passing notice. I am therefore compelled to attempt to describe what I think I see them doing. As a result, I will be indicating how I as a Reformed theologian do theology and how I think it ought to be done. Not all Reformed theologians will agree, but I hope my description will have general validity.

Since Reformed theology is one species within the genus of "theology," it shares basic theological characteristics with other types of theology. I will be concentrating on what is usually designated systematic theology but is also called dogmatic theology or simply theology. However my description will have some bearing on the other main branches of theology as well. The main thrust of this chapter will be on the adjective "Reformed."[3] What is unique about Reformed theology? How do Reformed theologians pursue their craft? Do they do theology differently from other theologians? What accounts for the varied results of such theological activity? These are some of the difficult questions that must be addressed.

Doing any kind of science requires patience, because a slow, meticulous process is involved. Theology is no exception. Addressing a methodological question about "doing theology" may prove tedious as well. Yet some awareness of what one is getting into is useful and, if one approaches the task self-consciously, one will increasingly become aware of what one is doing when actually engaged in it. In fact, this may well be one of those instances where the proof of the pudding is only in the eating.

My description of how Reformed theologians do theology in today's world follows these seven steps: (1) survey the history and literature of systematic theology; (2) distinguish the main types of theology and note their chief characteristics; (3) become aware of the two main options for beginning theology within the Reformed camp; (4) examine the nature of scientific activity to understand the nature of theology as a science; (5) identify theology's field of investigation and its norm; (6) recognize Scripture as the final norm, seek to understand the entire Scripture in light of biblical history, biblical theology, careful exegesis, and attention to hermeneutical questions; finally, (7) draw out the implications of Reformed theology for both personal and communal faith and life.

SURVEYING THE HISTORY OF THEOLOGY

Reformed theologians recognize that they stand on the shoulders of previous generations and build on foundations laid earlier. No one can do theology in a vacuum. A theologian must understand past history as well as the contemporary situation. One does theology in communion with theologians of all ages, including those with whom one disagrees. Hence one should get to know the major theologians who have left their mark on history and learn about their main writings. What were the key issues faced by these theologians? To what were they reacting and what did they attempt to accomplish? What contributions did they make and why are they important for a Reformed theologian today? What can I learn from them, both positively and negatively? Facing such questions by way of an initial survey of the history of theology will prove fruitful as one begins to do theology today. Generally a short book will provide good orientation.[4]

Dividing past history into periods is always somewhat arbitrary. From the perspective of systematic theology the following six periods can be distinguished: the ancient or patristic period (90–800), the Middle Ages (800–1500), the Reformation era (1500–1650), the Enlightenment period (1650–1800), the post-Enlightenment period (1800–1920), the period between the two World Wars (1920–1939), and finally the contemporary period (1939 to the present). What happened in each of these periods is important for a Reformed theologian, and detailed knowledge will facilitate doing theology responsibly. Of course the entire Reformation period is of special interest to every Protestant theologian. Knowledge of the Middle Ages will enable the theologian to understand Roman Catholic developments during that period—developments the Reformers largely rejected.

The theological history of the early church is also of great significance. As early as the second century the church faced a life-and-death struggle against Gnosticism, the massive liberalism of the time. Contrary to popular opinion, theology did not begin in ivory-towered academic isolation; it arose in the context of the church's mission of bringing the gospel of salvation through Jesus Christ to the pagan world.[5] Some of the most profound theological questions were faced as a result—questions concerning the Trinity, the person of Jesus Christ, human sin, and God's grace. The decisions of the first six great Ecumenical Councils (325–680) provided perspectives and formulations that are still basic to Reformed theology and demand consideration by all types of theologians.

Even a brief survey of the entire history of theology and its literature may overwhelm a beginning student. Yet a beginning must be made so that one gradually feels at home in the arena of theology. Hands-on acquaintance in the library of the main writings of the major theologians will help, and a growing personal library of choice selections is indispensable.[6] Good maps, theological dictionaries, and encyclopedias should always be within arm's length when one engages in theological study, especially as one begins doing theology. Soon Irenaeus and Tertullian, Athanasius and Augustine, Anselm and Aquinas, and a host of others will become acquaintances with whom today's theologian is in regular dialogue.

DISTINGUISHING THEOLOGICAL TYPES

A survey of the history and literature of theology reveals a few distinct types of theology. These should now be made a specific concern so that one may engage in Reformed theology with awareness of its competing types. The patristic period displays emerging emphases but no clear-cut types. The Western and Eastern tendencies reached a climax in Augustine and John of Damascus respectively.

The first major distinct type of theology is the Roman Catholic, which emerged during the Middle Ages. Building heavily on the *Summa* of Thomas Aquinas, Roman Catholicism reflects a "both-and" approach. Christianity was combined with Aristotle to produce a basic dualism of the natural and the supernatural, reason and faith, natural theology and supernatural theology. Within this both-and dualism, Scripture and tradition were both considered authoritative, faith and works together contributed to one's salvation, and other similar combinations resulted. The challenge from the Reformation led Rome to reaffirm these positions at the Council of Trent (1545–63) and to clarify and expand some of its dogmas at Vatican I (1869–70). In spite of a new spirit that greeted Vatican II (1962–65), this both-and approach remains the official Roman Catholic position.

The Latin slogans of the Reformation reflect the fundamental contrast between the both/and of Rome and the *sola* (only or alone) of Protestant theology. *Sola Scriptura* emphasized the sole authority and normativity of Scripture in contrast to Scripture and tradition. Obedience to Scripture's message led to *sola fide* and *sola gratia*, since salvation comes only from Christ by grace alone through faith, not by faith and works. Lutheran, Zwinglian, and Calvinian branches were agreed on those Reformational basics, but they differed especially on the sacraments and aspects of Christology. The merging of the Zwinglian and Calvinian sectors in the Zurich Agreement of 1549 resulted in two main Protestant branches of theology, the Lutheran and Calvinistic. Anyone who desires to do Reformed theology today will be working within the Calvinistic tradition while always paying careful attention to the Lutheran as well as the Anabaptist types.

In the wake of Immanuel Kant's philosophy and the Enlightenment a new type of theology developed—namely, liberalism, or modernism. It arose out of the bosom of the Reformed (F. Schleiermacher) and Lutheran (A. Ritschl) churches of Germany, but it rejected the teaching of the Protestant confessions as well as the patristic doctrinal decisions. Several early Trinitarian, Christological, and anthropological heresies were combined into its systematic constructions. Taking their starting point in human autonomy, liberal theologians rationally rejected the authority of the Bible and focused theological attention on human religious experience in the phenomenal realm open to rational description. Scripture was considered simply the record of the religious experiences of an ancient Semitic tribe. Questions of true or false in religion

232 I Fred H. Klooster

and theology were replaced by evolutionary categories of higher or lower. Protestant churches throughout the world were deeply affected by this radically new type of theology. Orthodox Lutheranism and Calvinism lived on in small pockets within the established churches, but, especially in the Netherlands and North America, ecclesiastical separation was considered necessary.

Under the impetus of Karl Barth another new theology, neo-orthodoxy, arose out of the ashes of liberalism in the context of the First World War. Seeing the optimistic, Pelagian doctrines of liberalism shattered by the war, neo-orthodox theologians claim to return to Scripture, the Reformers, and the patristic theologians. Especially within American circles debate continues as to whether neo-orthodoxy is actually a new type of theology or really a genuine return to Reformation principles.[7] Because neo-orthodox theologians regard Scripture as only a witness to revelation and not itself revelation and because of the new doctrinal positions involved, I am convinced neo-orthodoxy is a new, distinct type of theology. In its reaction to liberalism and in contrast with classic Reformed theology, neo-orthodoxy is historically docetic. Revelation is not rooted in real historical events but involves a mysterious, transcendent event that occurs today in the context of preaching. Neo-orthodoxy is an extremely complex type of theology reflecting the philosophical influences of existentialism.

The contemporary scene is varied and extremely complex as well. Old types of theology are often modified and combined with newer types. This is especially true of recent developments within Roman Catholicism. Theological faddism, such as the "death-of-God" theology, was the style of the 1960s. Varieties of neo-liberalism are also on the rise. But W. Pannenberg and J. Moltmann reacted to the docetic theologies of Barth and Bultmann and developed more enduring theologies rooted in history. Process theology finds several representatives in North America. Since the 1970s several varieties of liberation theology, including black and feminine types, have become a world-wide phenomenon. Beginning theologians should be alert to all the theological variety in the contemporary world, but they should first attempt to understand the four main types—Roman Catholic, Protestant (Reformed and Lutheran), liberal, and neo-orthodoxy—and then move on to understand the more recent types of theology.

BECOMING AWARE OF OPTIONS FOR BEGINNING

After completing the two stages of historical survey, one is probably itching to begin doing theology. But immediately a crucial question arises: How should one begin? Within the Reformed tradition two quite different approaches have appeared, and the budding theologian is forced to make a very important decision. Must he begin by rationally establishing his presuppositions or should these presuppositions simply be acknowledged in faith?

The names of the two positions reflect their place of origin. The Old Princeton position developed within Presbyterian churches of British rootage and is best represented by B. B. Warfield (1851–1921). The Old Amsterdam position was developed on the continent, especially in the Netherlands, and was most clearly enunciated by A. Kuyper (1837–1920). The dates indicate that these alternative Reformed positions were developed during the period in which liberalism was dominant and modern science had emerged. C. Hodge was a contemporary of Schleiermacher, and both Warfield and Kuyper were contemporaries of Ritschl and especially Harnack, Herrmann, and Troeltsch. Both Kuyper and Warfield appealed to Calvin, but they interpreted the relevant sections differently.[8] Within evangelical circles debates about these two approaches, especially as they relate to apologetics, are often intense.

The Old Princeton approach was heavily influenced by Scottish Common Sense philosophy and the empirical tradition. Warfield argued that a science reduces a section of our knowledge to order and harmony and always presupposes three basic things. The science of theology presupposes the existence of God, the religious nature of human beings capable of knowing God, and a revelation by which God is made known. Responsible science, Warfield argued, requires that these presuppositions be rationally established before one can responsibly engage in the science of theology. Apologetics, according to Warfield, is the discipline that rationally establishes these presuppositions, and therefore apologetics is the place to begin. Solely on the basis of rational arguments and without any appeal to Scripture or faith these presuppositions are to be established. In this way apologetics places in our hands the great facts of God, religion (Christianity), and revelation (the Bible). Only after these presuppositions have been rationally established by apologetics can one begin doing theology in all four main branches.

Representing the Old Amsterdam position, A. Kuyper recognized the same three basic presuppositions involved in his theological activity. However, he argued that these presuppositions are Scripture-given and embraced in faith; they are to be recognized and frankly acknowleged. The attempt to establish them rationally is not only impossible; it is also in conflict with the very perspectives of the Reformed faith. One can never take a position above God or above the Scriptures or outside of faith. Adam's fall affected human reason and the noetic effects of the fall make it impossible to rationally establish one's presuppositions. Evidence for the Christian position is clear and abundant, but the human mind, corrupted by sin, is incapable of a proper response without appealing to Scripture in faith. The spectacles of Scripture are needed to perceive general revelation correctly. According to Kuyper, apologetics has a legitimate place as a subdivision of systematic theology aimed at defending the latter against attacks from non-Christian philosophy, heretical positions, and other religions. But apologetics had to operate with the same faith-presuppositions needed for every theological science. Kuyper did not operate from a clearly defined philosophical position, but a Christian philosophy "in Kuyper's line" was developed later by the Dutch philosophers H. Dooyeweerd and D. H. Vollenhoven; C. Van Til also followed Kuyper's lead in further developing an apologetics in sharp distinction from that of Warfield and the Old Princeton approach.

The choice one makes between these two main options in Reformed theology will undoubtedly be influenced by his or her ecclesiastical roots and previous training. The choice will be a fundamental one, however, since key biblical passages are involved, such as Psalm 19; Romans 1:18ff.; Acts 14 and 17; 1 Corinthians 2; and Hebrews 11. Such basic issues as general revelation, the noetic effects of sin, and the possibility of a valid natural theology are at stake. Even more than natural theology is at issue, since Warfield contends that the whole of Christianity is established by means of these three presuppositions. His main objection to what he called "vulgar rationalism" was not really its rationalism but its attempt to establish Christianity piecemeal by way of a long series of arguments.

My personal understanding of the passages mentioned and the issues enumerated leads me to embrace the Old Amsterdam position as I begin theology. The student who is beginning to do theology should not make this choice until adequate attention has been given to the biblical passages mentioned. Even before one has made a personal choice, it is important to know about these options so that a more intelligent reading of theological works may occur. Yet a personal choice cannot be avoided, and that choice should be made as soon as it can be done responsibly.

EXAMINING THE NATURE OF THEOLOGY AS A SCIENCE

Whether one begins doing Reformed theology along the lines of Old Princeton or Old Amsterdam, crucial questions concerning the nature of theology and science require consideration. Before the Enlightenment such questions were not given much attention. Today they cannot be avoided, even though there is no common agreement on the answers. Both Warfield and Kuyper considered theology a science and agreed on the presuppositions involved in spite of their important personal differences.

It is clear that science involves a distinct, unique activity that must be distinguished from common, everyday experience. In everyday life we experience things in their wholeness and interrelatedness. In autumn, for example, we walk through the woods to enjoy the fall colors and smells. We marvel at the varied scenes and may wonder why some leaves are red or yellow and others still green. Everyday experience involves some reflection or analysis for such questions to arise.

When we deliberately set out on our own to discover why leaves turn color in the fall, why some turn one color and others another, and why some color earlier than others, we will have to engage in scientific activity. In distinction from everyday experience, science requires a secondary analysis and deeper scrutiny and examination. We must pull specimen leaves from the tree and bring them to a laboratory. Using microscopes and other specialized equipment, we must conduct tests and experiments. How, when, and why questions pursued with rigor and thorough analysis involve science.

Analogous activity is required in doing theology. Sometimes the term theology is used in a popular way to refer to any talk about God, Scripture, or religious subjects, but that is a superficial use of the term. Something different from everyday religious activity or talk is involved in doing theology. Individually Christians read the Bible and pray to God. Communally they worship, read Scripture, confess their faith, and discuss the sermon. To be personally engaged in those activities requires attentiveness, reflection, and first-level analysis. Science, however, as a disciplined, scholarly activity, requires a secondary analysis. In the doing of theology, laboratories and specialized equipment are not usually used, but the analysis of the subject should be microscopic in nature and telescopic when scrutinized in the light of history. The nature of the Bible, the characteristics of prayer, the qualities of a church's confession, and the precise meaning of a specific text are topics that may be made objects of theological investigation. Theology must therefore be seen as a science, for it shares those general characteristics present in all particular or specific sciences.

Whether presuppositions are present in every science remains in some dispute today. Their presence is more widely recognized in recent decades with the demise of positivism. I am personally convinced that science is impossible without presuppositions, but that need not be discussed here. The presence of presuppositions in theology can hardly be in dispute, however. Schleiermacher may have thought his science of religion met Enlightenment requirements of objectivity, but we can readily recognize his presuppositions today. Barth openly admitted that his concern for revelation meant that he could not meet the criteria of positivism as outlined by H. Scholz.[9] Bultmann declared that there could be no presuppositionless exegesis. Recently Pannenberg challenged the presuppositions of the principle of analogy in historical science that led some Bultmannian theologians to declare that resurrections cannot happen. One can even say that the Reformation took place when Luther was forced to alter his theological presuppositions. His careful analysis of the text of Romans 1 led him to reject the dualistic presupposition of faith and works and thus to discover and to believe that salvation comes by faith alone through grace alone.

In summary, then, we must say that science, also theological science, involves a person—a knower, who always operates from certain religious presuppositions, whether they be acknowledged or not. Positively or negatively those presuppositions relate to God, Scripture, and some confession. They will be Christian presuppositions or some non-Christian type of presuppositions. For Christians they may be Roman Catholic, Lutheran, or Reformed presuppositions. Working from such presuppositions, the knower as a scientist directs his analytical capacity at some narrow aspect in order to subject it to detailed scrutiny and careful study. The knower puts that aspect under the "microscope" for secondary analysis. Those are the common features of all the sciences, including theology. One should be aware of such characteristics of science when one begins to do theology because there are unique temptations involved as well as wonderful opportunities.

What constitutes the difference between the sciences then? That question leads to our next consideration, the particular field of investigation for theology and specifically for a Reformed theologian. The following diagram illustrates what has been said in this section and leads us on to the next.

Knower { religious presuppositions } → secondary analysis { field of investigation } = science

IDENTIFYING THE FIELD OF INVESTIGATION

What really distinguishes one science from another is its field of investigation. What is that field for theology? Some have identified it as God, revelation, Scripture, or religious experience. Contemporary answers refer to multiple sources of, or formative factors in systematic theology. If we want to avoid superficial answers, it seems more difficult to answer this question for theology than for the other sciences.

God's created universe displays a variety of distinct aspects so that similar kinds of basic science are engaged in throughout the world. Biology, for example, investigates the biotic aspect, the life (*bios*) aspect, and concentrates its secondary analysis on plant, animal, and human life. Historical science seems to have a clear field of investigation, as do sociology and economics. The nature of the field being investigated accounts for differences between so-called natural science and the humanities in terms of testing, experimentation, and apparent "objectivity." Yet each of these scholarly, academic disciplines displays the characteristics of "science," or what the Germans call *Wissenschaft*. Involved in scientific study is the secondary analysis of an aspect of reality theoretically abstracted from its total context for scrutiny in depth. Furthermore, the person engaged in scientific activity does so from the perspective of personal presuppositions or convictions. What distinguishes one science from another is its specific area of investigation.

What then is theology's field of investigation? The most common definition of theology is that it is "the science of God." A. Kuyper challenged that definition, arguing that God cannot be put under a microscope; God can be known only to the extent that he has revealed himself. In that light a more common description of theology came to be the "science of revelation" or the "science of Scripture."[10] Under Schleiermacher's impetus this was replaced by the "science of religion."[11] Barth's new view of revelation led him to consider "Sunday's sermon as the raw material of dogmatics."[12] Paul Tillich considered "neo-orthodox biblicism" too narrow and identified the "sources of systematic theology" as the Bible, church history, history of religion, and culture.[13] John Macquarrie identifies the "formative factors in theology" as experience, revelation, Scripture, tradition, culture, and reason.[14] A black theologian, James Cone,[15] adjusts the above to his perspective, identifying black experience, black history, black culture, revelation, Scripture, and tradition. Although liberation theologians represent several ecclesiastical backgrounds, they uniformly highlight the "experience of oppression" as the crucial source and adapt it to the items just mentioned.

Reformed theological textbooks that appeared before the rise of neoorthodoxy provided a standard answer to the question of theology's field of investigation. For Roman Catholic theology the field of investigation was said to be both Scripture and tradition. For Protestant theology, specifically for Reformed theology, it was Scripture alone. And for liberal theology the field of investigation was human religious experience. That is what I was taught and those were also my preliminary answers when I began teaching systematic theology in the early 1950s.[16]

After teaching theology for several years, I discovered that all the elements mentioned above come into my field of investigation as a Reformed theologian. Scripture has priority, of course, but I must also subject the confessions of the church, including those which I personally endorse, to secondary analysis. In fact, the entire Reformed tradition, as well as the tradition of the whole Christian church, is part of my field of investigation. I must also examine other types of theology and scrutinize their sources and formative factors, including anything relevant from philosophy, psychology, sociology, and other prespectives. Also "experience," so hard to define and always suspect since Schleiermacher, plays its role in some way, even when black experience or the experience of oppression are not part of my personal history. For me as a Reformed theologian all these factors call for consideration and can be subjected to scientific secondary analysis.

What is crucial, however, is that in all this diversity within the theological field of investigation there is some norm or criterion by which final decisions are made. What functions as the theologian's norm in investigating this diverse field of study? That may well be what the older Reformed textbooks were actually identifying when they focused on Scripture and tradition, Scripture alone, or human religious experience. A Reformed theologian attempts to judge all his sources by the final authority of Scripture. Tradition, religious experience, other theologies, and everything else in the field of investigation must be subjected to biblical norms. A single term to identify the field of investigation may be difficult to find. H. Dooyeweerd has called it the "pistic aspect," or "faith aspect," with Scripture as its norm and the church as primary subject or agent within that pistic aspect.[17] That may be a promising way of identifying the field of investigation, but the preceding discussion is needed to concretize any summary term. The primacy of Scripture as the Reformed theologian's norm thus calls for further discussion.

RECOGNIZING THE PRIMACY OF SCRIPTURE

A Reformed theologian should be deeply concerned with everything that is part of theology's field of investigation, thus with that which concerns all types of theology. In all facets of theological investigation, however, Scripture must have priority for a genuinely Reformed theologian. Scripture is the primary source and the final authority for judging whatever else comes under consideration. What are popularly called "proof texts" for systematic theology (dogmatics) are more accurately called key "source texts." Space allows only a cursory consideration here of what is most basic for a Reformed theologian—the priority and normativity of Scripture in doing theology. I will briefly consider the following subpoints: concern for the entire Scripture (tota Scriptura), biblical history, biblical theology, careful exegesis, and the hermeneutic question.

SOLA AND TOTA SCRIPTURA

As noted earlier, Protestant theologians agreed that Scripture alone (*sola Scriptura*) was authoritative for all theological activity. This conviction remains basic for Reformed and other evangelical theologians today. Scripture is the absolute norm and final authority by which to judge whatever else comes under a theologian's purview, whether that be the church's confessions, dogmas or traditions, human religious experience, experience of oppression, or the work of other theologians— including those in one's own tradition. Scripture alone is the inspired, authoritative Word of God. All human activity, theology included, is fallible and is to be judged by the infallible rule of faith and practice.

Yet there were significant differences among the Reformers, and such differences are still present today among representatives of the classical Protestant theologies. Until rather recently, for example, covenant doctrine was almost exclusively the concern of Reformed theologians even though Scripture bristles with covenant references. The biblical covenants have received so much attention from Reformed theologians that "covenant theology" has become a common label that many theologians use, especially dispensational theologians. Another example is Reformed theology's emphasis on the kingdom of God as the redemptive-historical means by which God exercises his sovereignty in history. Rooted in Augustine's *City of God* and in Calvin's writings and Genevan practice and developed especially by A. Kuyper and Dutch Reformed theologians, this kingdom perspective has become the hallmark of Reformed theology. I am convinced that the various biblical covenants are themselves instruments or agencies of God's kingdom adminstration in history. The kingdom of God is intimately linked to the sovereignty of God and the world-and-life view that have characterized historic Calvinism.

What accounts for such differences within classic types of Protestant theology, not to mention other types? What explanation is there for this almost unique Reformed attention to covenant and kingdom? These subjects are certainly prominent throughout the Old and the New Testaments and should have received attention from all who confess *sola Scriptura*. I am convinced that this Reformed emphasis resulted from its balanced concern for *sola Scriptura* along with *tota Scriptura*. Even though *tota Scriptura* never became a popular slogan,

concern for the total message of Scripture uniquely characterized Reformed theology.[18] Not simply its view of the sacraments or its emphasis on the sovereignty of God or its vigorous
defense of sovereign predestination or the "five points of
Calvinism" highlight the uniqueness of Reformed theology.
Rather, the uniqueness of Reformed theology must be seen in
its goal to be faithful to the whole of Scripture. At the heart of
Calvin's theology was the compulsion to speak where the
Scriptures speak and to be silent where they are silent. That
demanding goal should be the goal of every Reformed theologian today. One should aim at a theology of the entire canon of
Scripture and avoid any temptation to restrict oneself to a canon
within the canon. Of course, Reformed theology has not yet
reached (and may never reach) that goal. No Reformed
theologian has ever plumbed the full depths and riches of
Scripture's gold mine. There remains plenty of work for anyone
who contemplates doing Reformed theology today!

Bible History

The Bible does not provide a collection of "proof texts" that
can be cited when thought to be appropriate as one may select
illustrations from Bartlett's *Familiar Quotations*. Biblical revelation comes to us in distinct historical contexts over a long
period of history. The Old Testament was composed over a
period of more than a thousand years and it covers an even
longer span of history. The New Testament covers less than a
hundred years and was written within a single generation. That
long period of history must always be reckoned with when
interpreting a given passage of Scripture.

Biblical history falls into several distinct epochs, and when
one is working on a specific passage, one must always consider
the book of which it is a part and the time frame to which it
belongs. This should be no less a concern for the systematic
theologian than it is for Old or New Testament scholars. The
main periods begin with each of the following events or names:
Creation, the Fall, the Flood, Babel, Abraham, Moses, Joshua,
Judges, the monarchy, the divided kingdom, Judah alone
(intertestamentary period), Jesus' incarnation, his public ministry, his ascension, and Pentecost. In this connection it is
especially important to recognize the historical context of the
many prophetic books within the five centuries from the
divided kingdom to the end of the Old Testment canon.

Understanding specific passages and appealing to them for systematic theology requires that one recognize when and to whom the words were spoken and when the book was composed. Understanding the entire sweep of biblical history and the specific historical circumstances of a given passage is essential if one is to do justice to the whole of Scripture, *tota Scriptura*.

Biblical Theology

Systematic theology or dogmatics aims at a comprehensive summary or compendium of what the Bible teaches. The most common way of organizing the material is to deal successively with the doctrines of revelation (prolegomena), God (theology proper), humanity (anthropology), Christ (Christology), salvation (soteriology), church (ecclesiology), and the future (eschatology). (See the previous diagram.) In understanding and presenting the final and total message of Scripture, systematic theologians find that another theological discipline called biblical theology can prove extremely helpful. Biblical theology did not appear as a distinct discipline until the end of the eighteenth century. Initially a product of the Enlightenment's rationalistic rejection of the inspired and authoritative Scripture and recently appearing in various theological types, biblical theology along Reformed lines was developed by Geerhardus Vos (1862–1949).[19]

Biblical theology follows the redemptive-historical approach and is primarily concerned with the various stages in the history of special revelation. Vos stated that biblical theology draws a line, whereas systematic theology draws a circle. In its concern with historical progress in drawing that line, however, biblical theology also engages in correlation and systematization within the time frame of its particular concern. Thus biblical theology might limit itself to the Pentateuch and describe the doctrinal development set forth within that period. Similarly it could deal with one of the prophets or with several contemporaneous ones. Biblical theology could restrict itself to the entire Old Testament or to the New alone. Again biblical theology might restrict itself to the covenants in the Pentateuch or to the kingdom in the Synoptic Gospels.

By concentrating on the historical structure of the revelational process, biblical theology becomes indispensable for doing Reformed systematic theology. Not only does giving

THE INTERRELATIONS
OF THE TOPICS
IN SYSTEMATIC THEOLOGY

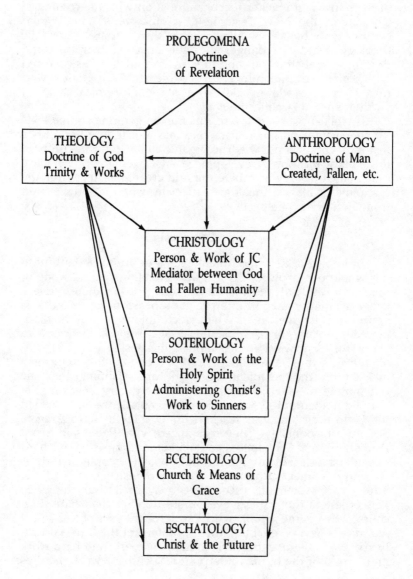

one's attention to the restricted revelation on a given subject in a particular historical period sharpen one's attention to what is new in later stages but it also aids in grasping the total message of Scripture as it reaches its consummation with the coming of Christ and the New Testament. At the same time regular contact with biblical theology helps those doing systematic theology avoid the danger of dehistoricizing Scripture and dealing with abstractions and timeless formulations as occurred with some seventeenth-century Protestant scholastics who turned to Aristotle or Descartes for philosophical help in writing their dogmatic theologies.

If biblical passages are to function as genuine source texts for the systematic theologian, one may not ignore Scripture's historical contexts nor the true organic character of the unity of the biblical message. Developing a vital and vibrantly biblical systematic theology will therefore find great assistance from the discipline of biblical theology, especially when it is developed from Reformed perspectives.

Biblical Exegesis

In light of a Reformed theologian's desire to be faithful to the whole of Scripture, biblical interpretation becomes one of the most difficult responsibilities one must pursue. Every believer must engage in interpretation of Scripture in order to apprehend its message. When such interpretation is disciplined, scholarly, or scientific, it is called exegesis. There are no simple or easy ways to accomplish this task.

Over against the Roman Catholic church the Reformers insisted on the perspicuity of Scripture, claiming that the redemptive message is clear for every ordinary believer. Yet that did not tempt them to neglect the scholarly training needed for their ministers and teachers to enable them to exegete Scripture responsibly. They recognized what Peter said about Paul's writings: "His letters contain some things that are hard to understand, which ignorant and unstable people distort, as they do the other Scriptures, to their own destruction" (2 Peter 3:16). And systematic theologians may well find things in Peter's letters that appear even more difficult than Paul's! Of course, the same Spirit who inspired the Scriptures must illumine believers, enabling them to interpret the Bible correctly. Yet we may not expect this to happen apart from hard work on the part of the human interpreter. Such hard work requires careful attention to the original Hebrew or Greek of the biblical passage in the light of the message of the whole Bible.

The exegetical method of the Reformers, especially of Calvin and his successors, has been called the grammatical-historical-theological method of interpretation. Simply put, this means that the analysis of the biblical text must take account of biblical history as well as biblical theology, as already noted above. Today it may be helpful to add two more terms to that label and call it the grammatical-literary-historical-theological-canonical method of exegesis. A very brief explanation of this complex but basic exegetical task must suffice here.

The Bible is God's Word written; biblical revelation comes to us in a verbal, lingual form. Hence exegesis must seek to interpret and understand words in their sentences, and sentences in their contexts. And these sentences are parts of a literary composition. There are a variety of literary types or genres in the Bible and one must take that genre's characteristics into account in interpreting a specific text. Hence grammatical-literary exegesis is required of one doing Reformed theology. And, it really goes without saying, that involves knowledge of the original languages in which Scripture was written.

The words of Scripture report, interpret, reveal, and proclaim what God has done in history. Scripture presents the revealed account of creation and redemption, involving both God's actions and his words. Scripture reveals good news, news about things that really happened in history—real historical events. Furthermore, the biblical accounts of these redemptive-historical events are themselves set in a historical context. Correct interpretation of these historical events and words therefore requires understanding Scripture in its historical context. Hence historical exegesis of Scripture is required in doing Reformed theology.

Scripture presents a message, a message from God and about God and his redemptive work in history. Exegesis must seek to understand this "theological" message of Scripture. All the lingual expressions of revelation are partial and occasional. But the interpreter must aim at understanding the entire message in its wholeness through all its parts. The message of the entire canon must be gained from the contributions of each of the individual books. Hence the theological-canonical exegesis of Scripture is required in doing Reformed theology. While these are distinct facets of exegesis, the Reformed interpreter must aim at grasping the unified message that comes through

246 Fred H. Klooster

the distinct but interrelated facets of grammatical-literary-historical-theological-canonical exegesis.

In thus engaging in microscopic analysis of the biblical text, one should also pursue the telescopic view by examining specimens from the history of interpretation. Examination of interpretations by one's contemporaries from other theological traditions may challenge one to see perspectives in the text that might otherwise be missed. All valid results of such exegesis must then be incorporated into a Reformed systematic theology that truly reflects the whole message of Scripture.

Hermeneutics

Before Schleiermacher, hermeneutics was generally thought of simply as rules for exegesis. Schleiermacher recognized that his new theology required a new hermeneutic. Since then, hermeneutical questions have become much broader in scope and increasingly important. Some followers of R. Bultmann actually claim that hermeneutics includes the whole of theology. Although that is probably an exaggeration, hermeneutic questions deserve careful attention today.

Differences between exegetical results cannot always be explained by the competence of the scholar or by errors committed by one or more of the exegetes. Interpretation aiming at real understanding of a biblical passage is a very complex matter as hermeneutic studies make clear. Issues like those mentioned above—the nature of theological science and the role of one's presuppositions or preunderstanding—are now recognized as hermeneutic questions. Differences between Lutheran and Reformed theologians on the sacraments may simply concern the question whether the verb "is" in Jesus' statement "This is my body" is to be taken in a literal or in a figurative, spiritualistic sense. But other differences in Lutheran theology arise from the law-gospel distinction that functions hermeneutically in Lutheran exegetical work.[20] Even greater hermeneutical differences distinguish Reformed theology from Roman Catholic, liberal, neoorthodox, and post-Bultmann theology.

The dimensions of the hermeneutic question cannot be considered here, but reflection on issues raised earlier will lead one increasingly into this complex area of concern. The more self-consciously one engages in biblical interpretation as one does theology, the more one will be impressed with hermeneutic questions. And one who engages in the study of and the doing of Reformed theology will grow in the awareness of its importance, even where the issues have not been explicitly raised.[21]

DRAWING OUT IMPLICATIONS FOR FAITH AND LIFE

The pursuit of theology has consequences for faith and life. Indeed, the issues concern life and death! Doing Reformed theology can and should be a delightful experience in itself. By means of secondary analysis and reflection on key biblical passages one can grow personally in both faith and life. Doing Reformed theology is an enriching experience because, unlike all the other sciences, Reformed theology offers an intimate relation between one's religious presuppositions and the field of investigation. When the sound results of theological activity are poured back into one's total experience, surprising personal growth can occur.

When one aims at genuine understanding of Scripture and the whole field of investigation, something more than intellectual gratification is involved. Understanding is really a matter of the heart; it affects the whole person, intellect, will, and emotions. Heart-understanding concerns faith and life: believing God and doing what He requires. Such theological activity aims, not at domination, but at service—the service of God and of one's fellow human beings through the building of Christ's church and the advance of God's kingdom. The ongoing process of listening to God's Word, of interpreting it in the doing of theological science as well, should contribute to a believer's increasing personal conformity to God and his Word so that life is lived today according to God's directives as revealed in Scripture. God's gift (*Gabe*) calls for our task (*Aufgabe*) in today's world for his glory.

I conclude with this doxological description of the nobility of that task as expressed by a dedicated Reformed theologian:

When we properly weigh the proposition
    that the Scriptures are the deposit of special revelation,
    that they are the oracles of God,
    that in them God encounters and addresses us,
      discloses to us his incomprehensible majesty,
      summons us to the knowledge and fulfillment of his will,

unveils to us the mystery of his counsel,
and unfolds the purposes of his grace,
then systematic theology, of all sciences and disciplines,
is seen to be the most noble,
not one of cold, impassioned reflection,
but one that stirs adoring wonder
and claims the most consecrated exercise of all our powers.

It is the most noble of all studies
because its province is the whole counsel of God
and seeks, as no other discipline,
to set forth the riches of God's revelation
in the orderly and embracive manner
which is its peculiar method and function.

All other departments of theological discipline
contribute their findings to systematic theology
and it brings all the wealth of knowledge
derived from these disciplines
to bear upon the more inclusive systematization
which it undertakes.[22]

NOTES

[1]*Webster's Ninth New Collegiate Dictionary* (Springfield, Mass.: Merriam-Webster, 1986).

[2]Reformed theologians are also present in some other churches today, especially in evangelical churches.

[3]In my inaugural lecture I discussed "The Adjective in 'Systematic Theology' " (Grand Rapids: Calvin Theological Seminary, 1963), 26.

[4]Many options are available. A recent one is *The Science of Theology*, by G. R. Evans, A. E. McGrath, and A. D. Galloway (Grand Rapids: Eerdmans, 1986). This is volume 1 in the series *The History of Christian Theology*, edited by P. Avis. The older works of L. Berkhof, *The History of Christian Doctrine*, and J. Orr, *The Progress of Dogma*, remain useful for beginners.

[5]L. Newbegin, *Trinitarian Faith and Today's Mission* (Richmond, Va.: John Knox, 1964), 31–34.

[6]The Library of Christian Classics from Westminster Press in 22 volumes provides a good selection of original sources in English translation.

[7]D. Bloesch and B. Ramm are examples of those who consider Barth Evangelical or Reformed. A Dutch writer who relfects Barth's influence is H. Berkhof, *Introduction to the Study of Dogmatics* (Grand Rapids: Eerdmans, 1985), 114.

[8]*Institutes* 1.7 & 8. See A. Kuyper, *Principles of Sacred Theology* (Grand

Rapids: Eerdmans, 1954); B. B. Warfield, "Apologetics," in *Studies in Theology* (New York: Oxford University Press, 1932), 3–21; idem, "Introduction to F. R. Beattie's *Apologetics*: or *The Rational Vindication of Christianity*" (Richmond, Va.: John Knox, 1903), 19–32. The second is reprinted in *Selected Shorter Writings of B. B. Warfield*, 2 vols. (Phillipsburg, N.J.: Presbyterian and Reformed, 1973), 2:93–105.

[9]K. Barth, *Church Dogmatics: The Doctrine of the Word of God*, 13 vols., trans. G. W. Bromiley (Edinburgh: T. & T. Clark, 1975), I.1.8–9.

[10]Prior to Abelard's use of the term "theology" in the twelfth century, the designation of this discipline as "the sacred page" (*sacra pagina*) served the same purpose. "Sacred doctrine" (*sacra doctrina*) was another early designation of "theology."

[11]His systematic work is entitled *The Christian Faith*.

[12]Barth, *Church Docmatics*, I.1, 77–79.

[13]P. Tillich, *Systematic Theology* (Chicago: University of Chicago, 1951), 1:40.

[14]John Macquarrie, *Principles of Christian Theology*, 2nd ed. (New York: Scribner, 1977), 4–18.

[15]James Cone, *A Black Theology of Liberation* (Philadelphia: Lippincott, 1970), 50ff.

[16]See L. Berkhof, *Introductory Volume to Systematic Theology* (Grand Rapids: Eerdmans, 1932), 21ff., 59ff. Cf. also A. Lecerf, *An Introduction to Reformed Dogmatics* (London: Lutterworth, 1949). In spite of his many books in the series Dogmatic Studies, G. C. Berkouwer has given very little attention to prolegomena questions.

[17]See J. M. Spier, *What Is Calvinistic Philosophy?* (Grand Rapids: Eerdmans, 1953); idem, *An Introduction to Christian Philosophy* (Philadelphia: Presbyterian and Reformed Pub. Co., 1954); also L. Kalsbeek, *Contours of a Christian Philosophy* (Toronto: Wedge Pub. Foundation, 1975).

[18]Cf. "The Uniqueness of Reformed Theology: A Preliminary Attempt at Description," F. H. Klooster, *Calvin Theological Journal*, 14,1 (April 1979): 32–52.

[19]See R. B. Gaffin, Jr., "Systematic Theology and Biblical Theology" in J. Skilton, ed., *The New Testament Student and Theology* 4 vol. (Philadelphia: Presbyterian and Reformed, 1976), 3:32–50.

[20]The Lutheran edition of the NIV Study Bible, *Concordia Self-Study Bible* (St. Louis: Concordia, 1986), includes a section entitled "Law and Gospel" in its introductory section.

[21]In the light of hermeneutics from Schleiermacher to Pannenberg, I wrote "Toward a Reformed Hermeneutic" in *Theological Bulletin* of the Reformed Ecumenical Synod, 2,1 (May 1974): 1–12.

[22]John Murray, *Collected Writings of John Murray* 4 vol. (Carlisle, Pa.: Banner of Truth Trust, 1982), 4:4. I have introduced the line arrangement to highlight the main emphases.

9

THINKING THEOLOGICALLY FROM A FREE-CHURCH PERSPECTIVE

JOHN H. YODER
NOTRE DAME UNIVERSTIY, NOTRE DAME, INDIANA

LOCATING THE "FREE CHURCH" STANCE

The spiritual family whose mode of theologizing I am assigned to interpret differs from the others represented in this book, not first of all in content, but in form. The stance known as "believers' church,"[1] "free church,"[2] or "radical reformation,"[3] differs from the other streams of evangelicalism represented in this symposium in that it has no one founder, no one classical place or generation of origins, no foundational corpus of normative writings, no primary institutional bearer of its theological identity, and no accredited body of teachers and writers whose way of working we could observe.[4]

What gives this stream of confession and witness its specific character then, is not one theological notion or one Reformer but a set of shared experiences of grace and a common *stance*, which we may well describe by returning to take a closer look at the three phrasings just cited. To speak of "reformation" means standing in judgment on what has come of Christianity over time. That wrongness is not only a fading of vigor or clarity or unity or depth but also the intrusion of wrong "forms," whether they be the lifestyle of Christians, the organization of the visible churchly institutions, or doctrinal formulations. To say that that reformation should be "radical," i.e., should go to the root, means not being satisfied with

251

superifical corrections that fail to take account of why things had gone wrong in the first place.

To say "believers' church" is to have discerned that the root mistake was at the point of the "Constantinian"[5] commitment to inclusivism in the composition of the visible church. Thus renewal demands the formation of communities based on a common adult confession of faith.

To say "free church" is to discern that since it was "establishment" that caused and sustained an apostate state of affairs, the renewed community must refuse to be governed by any worldly authority or even to accept any informal subservience to or identification with the powers that be.

In the sixteenth century, the three marks of "radicality" that turned out to matter most, because they made the difference between an insufficient Reformation and going to the root, were (1) voluntary membership, as implemented by believers' baptism, (2) the rejection of the civil authorities' control of the form and pace of the reformation of the church, and (3) the rejection of war. On the first two of these, most "evangelicals" today would agree; but Luther and Zwingli, Calvin, Knox, Erastus, and Cranmer did not, as the civil authorities to whom they entrusted the implementation of reformation did not.

It should, then, not be surprising that the specificity we are looking for in the "free church" tradition will often not center on particular doctrinal themes stated in a scholastic mode (e.g., Atonement, Creation, Incarnation). Often renewal leaders, even in the foundational generation, make do with the formulations of the common tradition they are critiquing. They are too busy with missionary, pastoral, and polemic tasks to ask whether there might be better alternatives to the language already in use. Even more so is this the case in later generations. Apologetic interests lead to the adoption by free-church thinkers of "mainstream" patterns of theologizing.[6]

Specificity should, then, be expected first at points of stance and setting. Thus in this chapter I will attend especially to those points, not to the many other ways in which the accents of free-church thought would not be distinctive from those represented by much of the work of Kenneth Kantzer or by many books from Zondervan. My assignment is to characterize the specific while not denying the common.

WHY AND HOW SHOULD SOME THEOLOGY BE "SYSTEMATIC"?

"System" means simply that things—in this case statements, ideas—stand together and are seen and treated in their connectedness. There are varied reasons for attending to connections. The teacher may be concerned for a pedagogical sequence in which learners may best enter into their material, or he or she may want to be sure not to leave anything out. The polemist may be interested in lifting up the specific point of erroneous belief that explains why the views held by someone else, within or beyond one's own group, can be held. The historical theologian will be concerned to gather especially the classical formulae; then the discipline may be called "dogmatics." The apologete may be describing a step-by-step path leading from unbelief to affirmation. The advocate of reconciliation or unity will seek for the commonalities that are more important than the differences that divide. The philosopher may consider it a mark of either truth or beauty that the way things all hang together exhibits a certain architectonic elegance[7] around some master theme (e.g., Trinity, nature and grace, justification, sanctification, dispensationalism). The rationalist, convinced that consistency is a mark of truth, will argue in such a way that any hint of contradiction, paradox, or flux condemns positions less rigorously "logical" than his own. Each of these systems can be useful; each may, if wrongly accented, became unfaithful.

The free-church thinker will not hesitate to affirm respect for system (in these various, not identical, modes) as one of the contributions of those members of the body who bear the charisma of *didaskalos*.[8] Yet the urge to impose one particular pattern of utter consistency on all of one's own thoughts, or on other persons, may become an oppressive power in any of the following ways:

1. It may be wrongly assumed that the concepts used in one's system can be timeless. This assumption does violence to the organic historical flexibility that marked the people of God in the course of history, that therefore marks the Bible itself, and that should continue to mark the missionary church entering ever new arenas and language worlds. In the past experience of evangelicalism, this notion of timelessness has sometimes protected from criticism certain systems that were neither biblical nor eternal. It has made teachers and even

ecclesiastics tributary to some older or contemporary philosophical school, whether the neo-Platonism of Augustine, the Aristotelianism of Thomas, the rationalism of the Protestant scholastics, or the Lockeanism of Campbell.

2. The notion of what counts as "consistent" may be tilted in favor of certain models of communication specific to one class, gender, or culture more than another. Today non-Caucasians from one angle and women from another are having to remind us that there are other models of coherence besides rationalistic noncontradictoriness.

3. It may be wrongly assumed that all the reasons for being systematic cited above (pedagogical, polemic, irenic, apologetic, esthetic, etc.) will call for the same system, or that one of those modes must reign over the others.

4. The system builder may be unclear about how to validate the choice of the foundational concepts that give order to the rest. Does Jesus represent the climax of Yahweh's mighty deeds, so that salvation's being historical is the root image?[9] Does Jesus as God incarnate represent the divinization of creation, so that not history but nature is epistemologically basic?[10] Do we believe Jesus because of the Bible or vice versa? Do we trust the Bible as God's Word because we can first make a rational case for revelation, or is the sequence the reverse? People who call themselves "evangelical" can be as divided as others on these matters, and some of them take those differences very seriously.

5. It may be wrongly thought that the maker of the system should also be the ruler of the church. Sometimes this calls for the sanctions of nonecclesiastical powers (e.g., universities, civil governments), sometimes for nondialogical governing entities within the "church."

6. "System" may, like Saul's armor of old, hamper the flexibility that the Gospel communicator needs. Heresy hunting may undercut evangelistic or apologetic flexibility, or it may hobble scholarly honesty. Our system building needs to be leaner in hard times and more mobile in mission settings. The greatest theological minds—e.g., Paul, Augustine, and Luther—have been occasional rather than systematic[11] thinkers.

The above survey of the ways and reasons to be "systematic" has left one of the models for special attention. When Paul Tillich wrote his *Systematic Theology*, he was doing none of the above. His concern was to demonstrate how his own frame of reference could master and encompass everyone else's, whereby the internal coherence of his system, he claimed, validated itself, standing above communities, Scriptures, and histories. Some call such an approach "constructive"; some Catholics call it "fundamental." Each theologian who takes on such a task must of course do it as a personal *tour de force*, since its criteria are internal to the thinker's own system, or derived, in a way that may not be self-critical enough, from the regnant mentality in his own secular setting. By definition such a system cannot claim to govern a community. Therefore its evaluation must be done from case to case.

There is no reason a free-church person *could not* in principle take on such a "constructive" enterprise, but the criteria it would need to meet would differ from those of the ivy-league settings where it is usually done. The claim that the constructive enterprise is foundational, either that it tests the validity of all other views or that it (finally!) makes belief rationally credible, must be denied, or even laughed at. The fundamentalist or Protestant scholastic will be concerned about the traditional formulations that the "constructive" theologian dares to question. The free-church thinker, while sharing respect for the past, will be more worried about elitism, faddism (i.e., subservience to the regnant cultural *Zeitgeist*), or the stewardship of creative energies.

WHO SHOULD DO THEOLOGY SYSTEMATICALLY?

It is the theologian, above all others amid the manifold charismata in the people of God, whose calling it is to think carefully about language. That must mean not only using language confidently, expertly, and properly. It calls also for suspicion. The role of teacher is strategic, James writes, because of the unruly nature of language (i.e., "the tongue").[12]

Language often, in fact usually, leads us astray. Reification leads us to think that to every word there corresponds a real entity. Homonymy leads us to think that all usages of the same term say the same thing. Monolingual culture encourages both of the above logical errors[13] even while the world in which we have our mission is more and more polyglot. The magnification of the mass media heightens the ability of demagogues to lead people astray by the sparkle of their rhetoric.

We therefore need in the body of Christ a few (but only a few)[14] persons whose sensitivity to the fragility of language and its susceptibility to abuse enables them to watch defensively over the usefulness of our words. Language is, like the Gospel it bears, nonviolent and vulnerable. "System" should aid the servant of language to catch the most frequent and damaging abuses.

The free-church theologian's answer to the question "Why system?" is that clarifying the coherence of method and message serves the unity of the believing body. The people of God are called to serve their Lord in a hostile world, and this demands countercultural prophetic polemic. They are called to bring Good News to a waiting world, and to do so demands creative appropriation and transformation of their neighbors' words and values. For all of this to be done "faithfully" demands attention to the pitfalls—past, present, and predictable—that can undercut Christ's primacy. For all of this to be done *together* demands the care for completeness and unity that characterize the scribe (Matt. 13:52) and the teacher.

But the task will never be done. Responding to the question "Which system?" the free-church *didaskalos* will pay more attention than some others to the unity of faith and life.[15] He or she will be more suspicious than others of the value of one overarching key concept.[16] There would be reason for some relative preference for the dominant organizing concepts to be Hebraic/biblical, not on obscurantist grounds (as if there were a premium on thinking only in old categories) but on ecumenical ones. We should expect the task to have to be done over in every other time and place.

SOLA SCRIPTURA

"No creed but the Bible" has been a frequent slogan, especially within the Baptist and Disciples branches of the free-church family. The slogan is deceptive if it is thought to mean that we can get along without postapostolic formulations. Baptists have numerous confessions,[17] and Mennonites have several.[18] Parachurch agencies often write their own. The polemic point is not that such formulations should not exist. It is probably better that there should be more of them. Neither the ancient ones of Nicea, Athanasius, and Chalcedon nor the modern ones of Augsburg, Thirty-nine Articles, or the Westminster Confession should be a last word or a filter between us and the Scriptures.

The slogan is deceptive also if it is thought that in our own reading of the Bible we can avoid having any grid, any internal canon, of our own. Fundamentalists deny that; the refusal to acknowledge the hermeneutic problem is in fact perhaps the most useful functional definition of fundamentalism. The free church seeks rather, acknowledging the temporality and finitude of every such grid, to keep testing all of them, including one's own, both by the entirety of the canonical texts and by the criterion of pertinence to the world of her mission, in an unending spiral of new learnings and self-correction.

When John Robinson said to the "pilgrims" leaving Plymouth, "The Lord has yet much more light and truth to break forth from His holy Word," he meant that such a spiral could be the instrument of God the Spirit to let the ancient text speak in every age in tones not heard before. That is happening today in some of the free-churches with regard to concerns of peace and justice, always there in the Scriptures but hitherto often filtered out, or with regard to charismatic patterns of ministry or the priority of narrative over rationalist communication.

The positive value of the slogan "No creed but the Bible" is the leverage the Bible as a whole gives us to surmount our local limits. Wesley had his reasons for centering on holiness, and Luther had his reasons for centering on justification. Edwards and Finney had theirs for experience. But the Bible is bigger than all that. When we read the law first, canonical accountability reminds us of the prophets and of wisdom. If we read Paul first, it reminds us of the Gospels and of apocalypse. When we read of the church, it points us to the world and to the person, and vice versa.

The Bible, then, is not best taken as a repository of infallible propositions, better understood when lifted from their particular settings, which God would have been better advised to give us in a less narrative, more "systematic" mode. The Bible is the document produced by the formative and thereby normative generations of God's working with us. I say "with us" and not only "with our fathers and mothers," because my brothers and sisters and I own our belonging by grace to that story. It is historically conditioned like all human reality and thereby demands that it be read as history. It is written demanding to be read like any other text. It is the record, then, of God's calling men and women into obedience and praise and will be most aptly read as calling us now into the same obedience and praise. A mode of systematizing that takes account of this narrative quality will be more likely to encompass and situate our task than would a more timeless or concept-centered mode.[19] Principles of organization that some would not call "systematic"—e.g., narrative forms, poetic parallelisms—might be equally useful.

OTHER KEY CONCEPTS

Missionary Daring

One of the reasons the Bible is not a systematic book is that it records a constant movement of the story from one setting to another. The New Testament account leads in two generations from Aramaic-speaking Palestine to Greek-speaking Mediterranean cities. Establishment Christianity may sometimes be content to settle into just one nation and language world, but the free-church rejects that, being by nature missionary. For that reason theology should always be ready to learn new languages, to use new sets of concepts.[20] That does not mean a mandate to uncritical assimilation, for that would be a new form of establishment. It rather poses new challenges to critical sensitivity. It does, however, decrease the utility of traditional systems.

Ecumenical Etiquette

Even if I should be convinced, at some point, that another Christian or a given group or tradition is quite wrong, I cannot know until there has been conversation that their holding to that belief (however wrong I think it) is accountable, unless and until I have seriously sought to inform them more correctly. I can't do that if I insist that they come to me and learn my language. I must be open to the possibility that our different views are not contradictory but rather complementary.

The risk of ecumenical openness must be renewed in every generation. I know that John Calvin was quite wrong when he really believed that the heretic Servetus should be punished by death at the hands of the state; but I should not assume that someone who today calls herself a Calvinist believes that heresy should be considered a capital crime. Not all Lutherans believe in massacring peasants or in baptizing babies. Not many Catholics today approve of the Inquisition or the Crusades. . . .

KNOWN MISTAKES

The main difference in mood that distinguishes the "free-church" stance from those claiming "orthodoxy," as a virtue that one can securely possess, is the awareness that traditions claiming the power of establishment have been wrong. Since things have regularly gone seriously wrong in the history of Christendom, it would be a mistake to think one can take off "from scratch" or from the Bible without taking account of the errors known to have beset believers for centuries. Explaining mistakes will often be a more fruitful avenue toward clarity than seeking simply to spell out what one is sure of. A list of past mistakes likely to be perennial may be of some help, though it offers no guarantee. The next mistake to trip up the churches may be unprecedented.

Government of Church by State

The wrongness of having the church (or its reformation) be governed by the state has already been mentioned. On this matter the mainstream of "official" Reformers of the sixteenth century were wrong. Why were they wrong? What could it have been that kept sincere churchmen from seeing this error?

Imposition of Belief

The notion that either faith or correctness of belief can be imposed or guaranteed by authority has reasserted itself repeatedly, especially in settings of change and stress. The official Reformers knew full well that neither personal believingness nor right beliefs could be forced, yet they resorted to state-backed agencies to attempt to do just that. Others who can no longer appeal to governmental sanctions use other modes of "informal establishment" to try to reach the same goals. Shall we call the root cause "patriarchalism"? lack of trust in the Holy Spirit? unwillingness to risk rejection and suffering?

Use of Dichotomous Reasoning

The notion that fidelity can be served by dichotomous reasoning, ascribing greater importance in God's eyes (and therefore the churches' and the theologians') to the "upper" realm, can be of great use in analysis and description of certain issues, but it soon becomes apostate. That evangelism cares for souls but not bodies, that justification is independent of sanctification, that the people of God come before the world, that the spirit takes precedence over the letter, the inward over the outward, are partial truths, necessary in some settings and false in others. Sometimes proper theological wisdom will consist in making such distinctions.[21] In some more critical areas it will call for overcoming them.[22]

Misuse of Analogy

All communication about God must use analogies from the human world. Yet every analogy has limits. That "Yahweh is King" is the central Hebrew doxology; that "Jesus Christ is Lord" is its Christian counterpart. Jesus taught his followers to call God "Father." Yet there are meanings of "King," "Lord," and "Father" that are inappropriate, because they connote oppression. The perspective of the cross, of the victim, of the outsider, of the slave or the child or the woman is a necessary corrective to wrong uses of analogy, especially to such usages as might support power gradients instead of undoing them as the Gospel does.

Undervaluation of the Middle Ages

Once the mainline Protestant Reformation had succeeded in creating an establishment culture from which Roman Catholicism had been banned, it was easy to fall into the notion that Christian history had leapt from the first century (or from the fifth) to the sixteenth, with the "middle" ages having been only "dark." This not only wrongly conceded to the Roman Catholics the ownership of that period; it also wiped off the board the values of the Eastern Orthodox communions[23] and of the critical traditions banished by the early Christian Caesars.[24]

Overreactions to the Experiential Focus

The experiential focus represented by the Ranters and the Quakers of the seventeenth century, the Shakers of the eighteenth, the camp meetings of the nineteenth, and the Pentecostals of the twentieth has been open to disorder, to personality cults, and to other abuses. The criticism of past apostasies and the anticlericalist retrieval of lay culture has been open to anti-intellectualism. This has led regularly to corrective overreactions both from those whose dullness they challenged and from people in the respective second or third generations of their own organizations. Some of these overreactions have been intellectual,[25] some institutional.[26] A more "radical" or "free" theological strategy like that of Paul's Corinthian pastoral correspondence will see order, both intellectual and institutional, as one of the works of the Spirit rather than as their negation. It will reject the sociological determinism according to which an inexorable "sect cycle" dictates a choice between vitality and stability, or between diversity and unity.

Compromise of Theological Principles

The best political solution we democratic moderns have found to the church-state problem is institutional pluralism— i.e., prohibiting government intervention in church matters and demanding civility in competition and comity cooperation between church structures, with the "client" choosing "the church of her choice" as if in a free market of services. This development has, however, led to compromise phenomena that are not theologically acceptable:
1. epistemological pluralism, as if all positions were equally true,
2. ecumenical pluralism, as if visible unity were unimportant,
3. the informal establishment of chaplaincy arrangements, whereby individual "clergymen" do their work on behalf of the state or of other "rulers" (hospitals, schools, factories).
4. reductionism, whereby in order to build a coalition or a caucus, one selects a minimal list of criteria. The five "fundamentals" of the 1920s and the eight points of the National Association of Evangelicals represent such misleading efforts. Both in what they exclude and in what they include, they short-circuit theological accountability.
5. demagoguery, in which a strong preacher reaches electronically into the home and the mind of the defenseless viewer, bypassing critical accountability.

Unnecessary Denominational Separation

The separate groups most easily listed as representative free-churches are those whose origins were in times of crisis and schism, so that they had to take the form of independent fellowships. The same concerns can, however, bring about renewal more gradually, if they are not excluded by the leadership of the established churches. Wesley and Zinzendorf both intended to keep their renewal groups within "the church," being pushed against their will into denominational separation.

All the churches that migrated into the United States accepted becoming in one sense free-churches, whether their European experience or their theology called for it or not.

Franklin Littell has long argued that the communions that, although pedobaptist, make adult membership meaningful through a substantive and binding practice of confirmation (conservative Wesleyans, Missouri Lutherans, Christian Reformed) could be counted as functionally free churches.

The currently most interesting specimen of gradual renewal of a free church type without schism is the profound rethinking of the issue of infant baptism that has been going on for a generation in some originally pedobaptist churches. This began in French and Swiss Reformed churches under the impact of Karl Barth and in East German churches in response to the socialist takeover of their government; and it is happening now in Roman Catholicism around the recently authorized "Ritual for the Christian Initiation of Adults." It arises from pastoral realism about the loss of the "established" control by the church of the culture in which the young person will grow up, more than from arguments about biblical warrants for baptism or from hearing the witness of the free churches.[27]

THE UNENDING TASK

Many of our contemporaries, reacting to the mental or cultural rigidity they have perceived in historic Christianity's ideas or institutions, honor a kind of noncommittal "openness" in principle. This cure is worse than the disease; yet the alternative is not to seek to rehabilitate the discredited authoritarian forms they reject. It is to rediscover the meld of charismatic flexibility, canonical accountability, and prophetic perception that in the apostolic vision was called forth by a waiting world, enabled by the Spirit, heightened by rootage in the doxological life of the community, and humbly served by the *didaskalos*, who in the fear of God is very careful about his words.[28]

NOTES

[1]Donald Durnbaugh, *The Believers' Church* (New York: Macmillan, 1968; Scottdale: Herald, 1985). The term comes from the German father of the sociology of religion, Max Weber.

[2]Franklin Hamlin Littell, *The Free Church* (Boston: Starr King, 1957). The origin of the term in British church history refers to a broader spectrum of denominations. Presbyterians are a free church in England, Anglicans a free church in Scotland. Cf. Gunnar Westin, *The Free Church Through the Ages* (Nashville: Broadman, 1958).

[3]George Huntston Williams, *The Radical Reformation* (Philadelphia: Westminster, 1962).

[4]By virtue of the same formal considerations, there can be no one correct list regarding which movements should be counted as belonging in the "free church" category. Moving on from the Durnbaugh and Westin listings, we should include the Waldensians of the twelfth century; the Czech Brethren of the fifteenth; the "Anabaptists" of the sixteenth; the Baptists and the Friends of the seventeenth; the Brethren (and perhaps the Moravians and the Methodists) of the eighteenth; the Plymouth Brethren, Churches of God, and Churches of Christ (as well as the Wesleyans and perhaps the Millerites and the communitarian utopians) of the nineteenth; and, of the twentieth century, Pentecostals, Bible Churches, Japan's MuKyoKai, Asia's "Jesus Families" and Bakht Singh, community churches, "parachurch" group movements like Faith at Work and Yokefellows, "faith missions," the "underground churches" of the 1960s, the "base communities" of Latin America, and others. The shortcoming of this list is that it describes movements that have come into independent existence by arising in a time of crisis. Below, under the heading "Unnecessary Denominational Separation" I also indicate that a free-church dynamic can also be at work without schism being imposed on its bearers. I am a Mennonite. The Mennonite denomination is neither the earliest nor the latest of the "free churches," neither the biggest nor the best. In formal matters Mennonites represent a less radical reformation than do the Friends. In various ways, notably in its acceptance of ethnic encapsulation at the expense of missionary vision, Mennonitism has denied the free-church vision. In this sense as in others, this chapter is not cognate with the others in this book. I am not an apologist for my own denomination, but rather for one of the visions to which that denomination looks for its legitimacy and its renewal.

[5]What the Constantinian shift meant for ethics has been surveyed in my book *The Priestly Kingdom* (South Bend, Ind.: University of Notre Dame Press, 1985), 135ff. There were, however, equally far-reaching changes in the meaning of ministry, sacraments, and spirituality, from which flowed yet other differences in the role of theology.

[6]As examples we may note three generations' works: John Christian Wenger, *Introduction to Theology* (Scottdale: Herald, 1954); Edmund G. Kaufman, *Basic Christian Convictions* (Newton, Kans.: Bethel College, 1972 [but written much earlier]); and Gordon Kaufman, *Systematic Theology: An Historicist Perspective* (New York: Scribner, 1968). Each author is Mennonite, yet each work takes its frame of reference from what the author took to be the main stream of Christian thought in his time. Each assumed that no explanation was necessary to justify his replicating "mainstream" theology (borrowed from a different mainstream each time) within a denominational frame of reference.

[7]Some theologians think with a concern for "system" that is so thought-

through, so "elegant" in the formal sense, that it is possible to study their work by analyzing only the table of contents, without going into the text; cf. John Godsey, "The Architecture of Karl Barth's *Church Dogmatics,* in *Karl Barth Table Talk* (Richmond: John Knox, 1963).

[8]For the logic of the Pauline vision of the place of the "teacher" among the bearers of gifts, see my book *The Fullness of Christ* (Elgin: Brethren Press, 1986), and my chapter "The One or the Many? The Pauline Vision and the Rest of the Reformation" in Melanie May and David Eller, eds., *Servants of the Word* (Elgin: Brethren Press, 1990). How the gifts interlock in moral discernment is the theme of my "Hermeneutics of Peoplehood," in *The Priestly Kingdom,* 15ff.

[9]Bellwether of the focus on divine acts was G. Ernest Wright, *God Who Acts: Biblical Theology as Recital* (London: SCM, 1952). Since then various foci on biography, or on narrative as the preferred form, have claimed attention. Some of them are ways to take the Bible seriously, and some are new forms of modern conformism.

[10]This view has been especially possible among Eastern Orthodox and high Anglican theologians.

[11]Karl Barth in his *Church Dogmatics,* (Edinburgh: T. & T. Clark, 1936) I.1. 316ff. makes this same distinction: his terms are "regular" and "irregular" dogmatics.

[12]The warning in James 3:18 against the temptations of "the tongue" refers to language as a power, not merely to impulsive chattiness.

[13]Platonic idealism, what the medievals called "realism," i.e., the notion that to a given word there corresponds an unchanging ultimate reality in the mind of God, is possible only for monolingual persons. Any bilingual person, any linguist, has to be "nominalist," i.e., aware that the naming process is a human and historical work (Gen. 2:19–20), with the correspondence between words and reality constantly shifting.

[14]James 3:18; this is the only charisma of which this is said.

[15]Cf. James Wm. McClendon, Jr., whose *Ethics: Systematic Theology* (Nashville: Abingdon, 1986), vol. 1, demonstrates that beginning with ethics is one way to do systematic theology.

[16]Many of the early Protestant systematic theologies were organized almost completely around the polemic against Rome. Lutheran Francis Pieper devoted one-eighth of his entire work to unfolding one point of controversy between Lutheranism and Calvinism on the doctrine of the Eucharist. Some contemporary evangelicals center on the clash with modernity or secularism. There need be no apology for a polemic edge, but if it dictates the structure of the whole argument, the heretics have begun to have their way.

[17]William L. Lumpkin, *Baptist Confessions of Faith* (Philadelphia: Judson, 1959).

[18]John Christian Wenger, *Doctrines of the Mennonites* (Scottdale: Herald, 1954), includes as appendices three confessions and three catechisms. Howard John Loewen, *One Lord, One Church, One Hope, and One God: Mennonite Confessions of Faith in North America* (Elkhart, Ind.: Institute of Mennonite Studies, 1985), lists at least twenty-seven (some in more than one edition).

[19]Cf. my chapter "The Use of the Bible in Theology" in Robert K. Johnston, ed., *The Use of the Bible in Theology: Evangelical Options* (Atlanta: John Knox, 1985), 103ff.

[20]Yoder, *The Priestly Kingdom,* 49–54, describes striking apostolic models of this kind of missionary appropriation of a host culture's forms.

[21]Martin Luther notoriously said that the ability to distinguish "Law" from

"Gospel" is the heart of theology. Sometimes he used this dualism to make very right points about the gratuitousness of grace, and sometimes to defend very wrong decisions about social ethics.

[22]Gustavo Gutièrrez in his *Theology of Liberation* properly denounces socially defensive uses of various kinds of dualistic analysis, which he groups together as "the distinction of planes." It was once my role to correct the notion that politics is a realm alien to Jesus. Establishment social thought often makes much of a distinction between the orders of creation and redemption, tending not to distinguish carefully between creation "as such," which is revelatory of God's will, and its present fallen state.

[23]Such as the sense of historical continuity, the sense of doxology and of beauty in worship, and the priority of worship over hierarchy and dogma.

[24]The "Donatism" against which Augustine mobilized Caesar's constraints; the Arianism to the north, which Nicea anathematized; the "Nestorianism" to the East; and the "monophysitism" to the south, condemned by later imperial councils, were all more spiritually alive, culturally creative, and missionary than was imperial catholicism. Without arguing that the distinctive doctrinal stances for which they were condemned (fairly?) were right, we must cast doubt on the way the clashes with them were handled.

[25]A prime example was the polemic of Benjamin Breckenridge Warfield, *Perfectionism* (1931; reprint, Philadelphia: Presbyterian and Reformed, 1958), against Charles H. Finney. Donald W. Dayton, *Discovering an Evangelical Heritage* (New York: Harper & Row, 1976), 128ff., describes how scholastic theology displaced "Wesleyan" piety beginning in the late nineteenth century.

[26]Ronald A. Knox, *Enthusiasm* (New York: Oxford, 1950), is directed against the dissenters of the seventeenth and eighteenth centuries.

[27]Cf. John H. Yoder, "Adjusting to the Changing Debate on Infant Baptism," in A. Lambo (ed.), *Oecumennisme*, Amsterdam, Algemene Doopsgezinde Sociëteit, 1989, 201–14.

[28]A further theological concern, which the other modes of system-building do not help with, is to think about the phenomenon of reformation itself as a theological topic: cf. mg "The Free Church Syndrome" in: Terry L. Breusinger and E. Morris Soder, eds., *Within the Perfection of Christ*, Nappariee, Ind.: Evangel Press, 1989), 169–76.

10

HOW WESLEYANS
DO THEOLOGY

ALLAN COPPEDGE
ASBURY THEOLOGICAL SEMINARY,
WILMORE, KENTUCKY

There is no understanding of Wesleyan theology without a
clear picture of how John Wesley did theology. Not only is
Wesley's work the standard for the content by which all
subsequent Wesleyan theology must be judged, but it is also
the standard with regard to the method by which theology is
done. Accordingly, we will focus our primary attention on
Wesley's theological method, with only secondary indications
as to variations from that standard.

One primary factor about the way Wesley did theology is
that he did it, like Paul, within the context of the life and
ministry of the church. This has led to Wesley's being known in
church history as a "practical theologian." Wesley's concern
that God's truth actually be applied in everyday life led to his
writing theology differently from the classic systematic model
of a *Summa* (Aquinas), *Institutes* (Calvin), or *Encyclopeida*
(Hegel). More like the writings of the early church, his pattern
was developed in documents designed to meet the needs of the
life of the church. Thus we find Wesley's theology in his
"Standards of Doctrine," which appeared in creedal form in
Articles of Religion, in preaching form in his *Standard Sermons*,
and in study form in his *Notes on the New Testament*. In addition,
Wesley wrote certain practical treatises on key theological
issues, while other parts of his theology appear in *Minutes*,
which were hammered out in conference with his preachers; in
his *Journal*, which he kept as a record of the revival movement;

and in the hymns he and his brother Charles produced for worship in the Methodist societies. The vehicles for Wesley's theologizing were not scholastic but practical in nature.[1]

The fact that Wesley was vitally concerned about "practical divinity" might easily mislead one into thinking that Wesley was not a systematic theologian.[2] As a matter of fact, however, behind Wesley's practice of ministry is a very clearly identifiable whole system of Christian theology. Failure to recognize this fact could easily cause some to miss the significant contribution of Wesleyan theology to Christian thought.[3]

The advantage of Wesley's approach to doing theology is that there is always an eye for the practical application of truth to life and thus the value of theology is highlighted for the practical life and ministry of the church. The disadvantage of Wesley's approach is that there was no quick standard reference work—i.e., no easily accessible "authority," as the *Institutes* provided for Calvin's theology. This meant that those following in Wesley's tradition sometimes could focus too heavily on one facet of his theology or practice of ministry to the neglect or even distortion of the whole.[4] The corrective to any such distortions must be continual reference to the standard Wesley set both for content and method in theology.[5]

SOURCES FOR THEOLOGY

Scripture

Early in his ministry John Wesley decided that the Bible was central for his theology. "In the year 1729," he wrote, "I began to not only read, but to study the Bible as the one, and the only standard of truth, and the only model of pure religion."[6] Wesley's comment indicates two major roles the Scripture played in his theology. One had to do with his reading and studying of Scripture to know its content. The year 1729 was also the year that the Oxford Methodists began a serious study of certain key books from the Greek New Testament. From then until 1738 Wesley made it his business to become a master of the content of Scripture both in English and in the original languages. The result was a very holistic grasp of biblical truth, which formed the heart of his theology.

Wesley described his convictions at the beginning of the revival: "Any one who asketh me concerning myself or those whom I rejoice to call my brethren, what our principles are, I answer clearly, We have no principles but those revealed in the Word of God."[7] The Bible served not only as the basis of his understanding of the faith but also as the basis for his ministry. "If by catholic principles you mean any other than scriptural they weigh nothing with me. I allow no other rule, whether of faith or practice, than the Holy Scriptures. But on scriptural principles I do not think it hard to justify whatever I do."[8] It was his living with the data of Scripture until it became a part of his thinking and life that led Wesley to describe himself as *homo unius libri*, a man of one book.

But Wesley also in 1729 began to make Scripture his master, as he determined the Bible to be "the one, the only standard of truth." Between 1729 and 1738 Wesley fully settled the question of Scripture as the final authority in all religious matters.[9] How the Scriptures served as final authority for Wesley is illustrated in the way he dealt with theological questions in his personal quest for salvation. From March to May 1738 Wesley wrestled with the challenge from Moravian Peter Bohler regarding a new definition of faith and justification. Although Bohler was convincing, Wesley was not to be won over to a new position by reason alone but began to test Bohler's views against the Scripture. He wrote, "The next morning, I began the Greek Testament again, resolving to abide by 'the law and the testimony' and being confident that God would hereby show me whether this doctrine was of God."[10]

Some weeks later Wesley struggled to comprehend Bohler's assertion that conversion was an instantaneous experience, so again he turned to the Bible.

> I could not comprehend what he spoke of an instantaneous work. I could not understand how this faith should be given in a moment. I searched the scriptures again touching this very thing, particularly the Acts of the Apostles: but, to my utter astonishment, I found scarce any so slow as that of St. Paul, who was three days in the pangs of the New Birth.[11]

It was because of Wesley's commitment to the final authority of Scripture that he was willing for his own theology to be corrected in the light of the Word of God. "I trust wherein so ever I have mistaken, my mind is open to conviction. I sincerely desire to be better informed. Point out a better way than I have known. Show me it is so, by plain proof of scripture."[12]

Very early in the eighteenth-century revival a major doctrinal dispute arose between Wesley and his co-laborers, the

Moravians, that provided a test for Wesley's own commitment to Scripture as final authority. The issue arose over the Moravian doctrine of "stillness" in which people were enjoined to avoid the danger of a belief in salvation of works by not attending church, partaking of the sacrament, using private or corporate prayer, reading Scripture, or using any other "means of grace." Rather, they were told to be "still" until they were given faith. Wesley recognized the problem as a form of antinomianism and saw that the basic problem was that the Moravian position was contrary to Scripture.

Because of his commitment to the Word of God as the basis of truth Wesley decided to separate from the Moravians, even though that meant dividing the forces of the revival. He believed this was necessary because of the theological errors into which they had fallen.

> I believe these assertions to be flatly contrary to the Word of God. I have warned you hereof again and again, and besought you to turn back to the "law and the testimony." I have borne with you long, hoping you would return. But as I find you more and more confirmed in the error of your ways, nothing now remains, but that I should give you up to God.[13]

Wesley knew that the practice of ministry would be undermined for the future if this crucial doctrinal issue was ignored. Accordingly, he separated himself from those who refused to recognize the ultimate authority of the Word of God in doctrine and practice.[14]

Wesley did not see Scripture as only the first in a line of several equal or coordinate criteria for doing theology, but rather as the final authority in all matters. As Howard Snyder describes it, Wesley had "scripture as the 'norming norm' to be placed above all other authority."[15] In the light of this, Wesley must certainly be classified within the classical Protestant tradition on the matter of religious authority. Wesley not only began his ministry with this view but continued to maintain this commitment all of his life. Nearly fifty years after the Methodists "began to preach that grand scriptural doctrine, salvation by faith," Wesley could reiterate his own identification with the Reformers' position.

> The faith of the Protestants, in general, embraces only those truths as necessary to salvation, which are clearly revealed in the oracles of God. Whatever is plainly declared in the Old and New Testaments is the object of their faith. They believe

neither more nor less than what is manifestly contained in, and approved by, the Holy Scriptures. The Word of God is "a lantern unto their feet and a light in all their paths." They dare not, on any pretense, go from it, to the right hand or to the left. The written word is the whole and sole rule of their faith, as well as practice.[16]

It is significant for those who stand in the Wesleyan tradition that this position was not only Wesley's personal one but that it characterized the Methodists as a whole. In 1742 Wesley wrote in the "Character of a Methodist":

> We believe, indeed, that "all scripture is given by the inspiration of God": and herein, we are distinguished from Jews, Turks, and Infidels. We believe the written Word of God to be the only and sufficient rule both of Christian faith and practice; and herein we are fundamentally distinguished from those of the Roman Church.[17]

It is clear that for Wesley the Bible was the final norm for all of his theology as well as his practice of ministry. "My ground is the Bible," he declared. "Yea, I am a Bible bigot. I follow it in all things, both great and small."[18] Thus with regard to God's truth Wesley could affirm, "The scriptures are the touchstone whereby Christians examine all, real or supposed, revelations. In all cases, they appeal 'to the law and the testimony' to try every spirit thereby."[19]

Wesley's conviction about the final authority of Scripture rested on his presupposition that the whole of Scripture was given by the inspiration of God and is therefore entirely accurate. For Wesley the concept of inspiration extended not only to the general content of revelation but also to the precise wording of the text. Thus he declares the actual terminology of Scripture must be taken very seriously. "We should observe the emphasis which lies on every word."[20] Along with Wesley's strong view of inspiration was his equally strong position on the accuracy of the biblical text. "All scripture is given by inspiration of God," avowed Wesley, "consequently, all scripture is infallibly true."[21] The infallibility of Scripture extended not only to doctrine for Wesley but to factual matters as well. "If there be any mistakes in the Bible, there may as well be a thousand. If there be one falsehood in that book, it did not come from the God of truth."[22] It is clear that by the use of the term *infallible* Wesley meant that the Bible was inerrant. Since Scripture is wholly reliable in every way, "nothing which is written therein can be censored or rejected."[23] Nor can it be ignored: "We may not, therefore, lay these expressions aside, seeing they are the words of God and not of man."[24] Frank Baker has accurately concluded, "Wesley was one with the Reformers in the tendency to substitute an infallible Book for an infallible Church."[25]

Scripture provided not only the norm for Wesley's theology but the content of it as well:

> The scripture, therefore, of the Old and New Testament is a most solid and precious system of divine truth. Every part thereof is worthy of God; and altogether are one entire body, wherein is no defect, no excess. It is the fountain of heavenly wisdom, which they who are able to taste prefer to all the writings of men, however wise or learned or holy.[26]

Certain basic principles guided Wesley in his building theology from the Bible and here Wesley's debt to the Protestant Reformation is evident. His hermeneutical presuppositions are the same as those of Luther and Calvin in their basic insistence that the literal sense of the text is to be the primary one. This is one of the major gains of Reformation exegesis as opposed to the allegorical method of medieval catholicism. For Wesley "the general rule of interpreting scripture is this: the literal sense of every text is to be taken, if it be not contrary to some other text; but in that case the obscure text is to be interpreted by those which speak more plainly."[27] By the "literal sense" Wesley meant the text must be read as the authors intended it to be read. He is not ruling out the figurative or analogical use of language in Scripture. "It is a stated rule in interpreting scripture, never to depart from the plain, literal sense, unless it implies an absurdity."[28] Obviously for Wesley it would be an absurdity to take an intended figurative portion of Scripture and interpret it with a wooden literalness. What he was after was the plain sense of the text.

The safeguard for the literal sense was the importance of interpreting a text within its context. Wesley warns that "any passage is easily perverted, by being recited singly, without any of the preceding or following verses. By this means it may often seem to have one sense, when it will be plain, by observing what goes before and what follows after it, that it really has the direct contrary."[29] Wesley's method, then, is to observe "the plain, literal meaning of any text, taken in connection with the context."[30]

The third of Wesley's principles of interpretation has already been alluded to in reference to obscure texts, which must "be interpreted by those which speak more plainly." Wesley was constantly comparing Scripture with Scripture in an attempt to get a holistic view of its total theological perspective. "I then search after and consider parallel passages of scripture, 'comparing spiritual things with spiritual.' "[31] For Wesley it was not the church that was the best interpreter of the Bible but rather the Bible itself: "Scripture is the best expounder of scripture. The best way, therefore, to understand it, is to carefully compare scripture with scripture, and thereby learn the true meaning of it."[32]

Finally, Wesley's hermeneutic requires that Scripture also be understood in the light of reason, tradition, and experience. All of these may help clarify and confirm Scripture, while at the same time never superseding it. Since each of these provides an important source for doing theology for Wesley, we will now turn to each for more extended discussion.[33]

Secondary Sources

Within the parameters of biblical truth there are some things the Scripture does not make clear or address in detail. This was the place, i.e., under the primary commitment to Scripture as the first source of theology, that Wesley saw a proper role for reason, tradition, and experience.

Reason

Wesley saw reason as something based in the personality of God and that reflected a part of the image of God in man. It was a gift from God and although it had been adversely affected by the Fall, because of prevenient grace it was still operative. Since reason comes from God himself, Wesley felt that all true religion will be reasonable in essence. If God is the source of reason, then true religion will reflect that. When accused of renouncing reason, Wesley responded, "It is a fundamental principle with us that to renounce reason is to renounce religion, that religion and reason go hand in hand, and that all irrational religion is false religion."[34]

Wesley understood that it was the reason of God that stood behind the wholeness and unity of God's revelation in Scripture. The reason of man was that which made possible the reception of revelation.

> The foundation of true religion stands upon the oracles of God. Now, of what excellent use is reason, if we would either understand ourselves, or explain to others, those living oracles! And how is it possible without it to understand the essential truths contained therein?[35]

For Wesley reason was first given by God so man could understand what God was saying to him through his Word. In addition it had two secondary uses. One was to work out the implications of scriptural data. Not all theological truth is explicit in Scripture; much of it is implied by materials included therein. Wesley felt that reason was necessary to put together the materials from Scripture and see their implications, e.g., in the doctrine of the Trinity. Further, the role of reason was necessary for the application of biblical truth to life. Since not all applications were immediately apparent in Scripture, it is necessary to exercise careful reasoned judgment about how the theology of the Word is applied in the everyday circumstances of life.

Although Wesley felt that reason was extremely valuable in explicating Christian doctrine, he was careful to make clear that every doctrine must in turn be judged by Scripture: "I try every doctrine by the Bible. This is the Word by which we are judged in that day."[36] No doctrine, he wrote, "is anything to me unless it be the doctrine of Christ and His apostles."[37]

Wesley's use of reason in theology is an attempt to distinguish himself both from those who undervalued reason and from those who overvalued it. To the mystics and others who slighted its use, Wesley was quite strong in his commitment to reason as God's method for explaining truth. To the rationalist of his day who believed reason was the final authority in religious matters Wesley pointed out the dangers of overvaluing it. He described it rather as the "handmaiden of faith" that makes possible the reception of revelation, but its limitation was that it could never produce the vital content of the Christian faith. As a result, reason could never serve as a coordinate source of theology with Scripture. Wesley wanted reason to do everything it could, but he recognized that there were clearly limits to its contribution to the theological enterprise: "Let reason do all that it can: employ it as far as it will go. But at the same time, acknowledge it is utterly incapable of giving either faith, or hope, or love; and consequently, of producing either real virtue, or substantial happiness."[38]

For Wesley reason means both induction by inference from other materials (chiefly that of Scripture) and then a careful consistent deduction from the premises he derived from the Bible. It does not have primary reference to discursive or philosophical reasoning. Very often it is for Wesley almost the equivalent of "common sense." It is this that Wesley is appealing to when he writes to "men of reason and religion."[39] This understanding of reason made Wesleyan theology particularly compatible in the nineteenth-century with the Scottish realism of Thomas Reid. So for Wesley the primary use of reason is not in terms of philosophy but in terms of explicating biblical truth. Robert Cushman argues that because the Wesleyan revival was rooted in the rediscovery of the Bible it implied "a most emphatic protest, from within the church, against the substitution of philosophy and ethics for the faith and doctrine of the Bible."[40] *HC Tradition

For Wesley tradition does not mean church law or customs. It is not the pronouncements of the church, speaking *ex cathedra*, nor the practices of the church; rather, tradition was a history of (1) the church's understanding of Scripture, (2) its use of reason in formulating doctrine, and (3) its models for the application of truth in experience. Tradition was never to be taken lightly, and Wesley had a special appreciation for the tradition of the early church, the Ecumenical Councils, and the Anglican church. These segments of church tradition he found particularly helpful because he saw them as the best interpreters of Scripture. Wesley was aware he was not the first person to interpret the Bible and was quite unsympathetic to those who did not take the history of biblical interpretation seriously. When he was accused of rejecting ancient and modern authorities, Wesley responded:

> Sir, who told you so? I never did; it never entered my thoughts. Who was it who gave you that rule I know not; but my father gave it to me thirty years ago (I mean concerning reverence to the ancient church and to our own), and I have endeavored to walk by it to this day. But I try every doctrine by the Bible. This is the Word by which we are to be judged in that day.[41]

Thus while Wesley was willing to consult the great expositors of the church to assist him in his own interpretation of Scripture, it is clear he was not willing for them to become final authority in theological matters. He recognized that for a period early in his life he had given too much weight to the early church tradition, but then he rejoiced that he had been delivered from the error of "making antiquity a coordinate rather than a subordinate rule with scripture."[42] To the Roman Catholic practice of placing the traditions of the church on an equal footing with that of Scripture, Wesley responded, "The scripture, therefore, being delivered by divinely-inspired men, is rule sufficient of itself: so it never needs, nor is capable, of any other further addition."[43] Wesley not only insisted that the theology of the church come under the authority of Scripture, but the organization as well. "In all cases, the Church is to be judged by the scripture, and not the scripture by the Church."[44]

For theological descendants of Wesley certain theological positions have been set forth as secondary standards for the "Wesleyan tradition." These have come primarily in the "Standards of Doctrine" that Wesley established for his followers in America. They include Twenty-five Articles of Religion, Wesley's *Standard Sermons*, and his *Notes on the New Testament*. The Articles of Religion were an adaptation of the Anglican Thirty-nine Articles and thus were a part of Wesley's attempt to tie Methodism to Protestant orthodoxy. The *Notes on the New Testament* and *Standard Sermons* contained Wesley's understanding of Scripture and his particularly "Wesleyan" distinctives. These secondary standards have served as a part of the normative tradition for Wesleyans since Wesley's day.[45] *HC

Experience

Wesley's use of Scripture as final authority along with tradition and reason as subordinate criteria for doing theology placed him squarely within the pattern set by the Church of England in his day. To this Anglican use of Scripture, tradition, and reason Wesley adds the component of experience. He was vitally concerned about the application of biblical truth to life and would not be content to view truth only in the objective sense. It must become subjectively experienced if it is to do what God intended.

Care must be taken to understand what Wesley means by experience. General experience was only of minor interest to him. Since he was especially concerned with the appropriation of biblical truth in everyday life, in one sense experience for Wesley may be understood to mean "evangelical experience."[46] Wesley was certainly not providing a basis for the emphasis on experience that came later with Schleiermacher, who focused on a religion of feeling. Wesley repeatedly warned people not to be overly concerned about moods or feelings but to focus on the promises of God.[47] God has objectively revealed himself to mankind through his Word, and his revelation was in no sense produced by man's feelings, desires, or experience. There is an objective reality about God and his revelation apart from any experience of it, and therefore experience is not to be understood as that which produces revelation.

To the accusation that Wesley placed experience over the norm of Scripture, he replied, "I have declared again and again that I make the word of God the rule of all my actions, and that I no more follow any secret impulse instead thereof than I follow Mohammet or Confucius."[48] If Wesley was afraid of any approach to Christianity that slighted personal appropriation, he was also aware of the problem of making experience a final norm. Thus for him "experience is not the test of truth, but truth the test of experience."[49] Accordingly, he warned Christians against "that daughter of pride, enthusiasm," and the danger of "hastily ascribing things to God" such as "dreams, voices, impressions, visions, or revelations." His standard rule was:

> Try all things by the written word, and let all bow down before it. You're in danger of enthusiasm every hour, if you depart ever so little from the scripture: yea, from that plain, literal meaning of any text, taken with the context.[50]

Wesley carried a deep conviction that biblical truth actually works in practical life, and if it does not, then something is wrong. He was afraid of the formalism of the Church of England in which many had a proper understanding of Christianity but no vital experience of it. Concerning one friend he wrote, "The theory of religion he certainly has. May God give him the living experience."[51]

If Scripture is not actually working in life, one possible problem may be with the application. So Wesley constantly had an eye for people's experience to determine how truth could be best applied to life. But the other possibility, if truth is not working in practical experience, is that one's biblical understanding of that truth is incomplete. Therefore, Wesley was willing for experience to drive him back to Scripture to be sure he had understood all it said on any given matter. This was certainly true in Wesley's own life when his experience of failure to receive salvation led him to reconsider the scriptural data on both the nature of faith and the instantaneous character of conversion.

A further use of experience for Wesley was that it provided a means for clarifying and confirming Scripture. "Whereas it is objected that experience is not sufficient to prove a doctrine unsupported by scripture . . . we answer, Experience is sufficient to *confirm* a doctrine which is grounded on scripture."[52] Experience then was never a primary source for theology that judges Scripture but rather it functioned to confirm scriptural truth.

The role of the Holy Spirit is particularly significant for anyone vitally interested in experience. Wesley clarified the relationship that the Spirit has to Scripture in his evaluation of the Quaker practice of his day of making the Scriptures "a secondary rule, subordinate to the Spirit." Wesley responded, "The Spirit is our principle leader, yet he is not our rule at all; the scriptures are the rule whereby he leads us into all truth."[53] Wesley was certainly convinced that the Spirit of God never led in personal experience to anything contrary to the principles laid down in the Word of God.

WESLEY'S THEOLOGICAL METHOD

The fact that in addition to Scripture as the foundation of all theology Wesley also uses the subordinate criteria of reason, tradition, and experience arose out of his awareness of two things. First, he was aware that Scripture needs to be interpreted and that there are divinely ordered tools for that theological task. Thus he was convinced that Scripture properly understood would be confirmed in experience. It was obvious to him that understanding the Scripture and seeing its implications were possible only through the use of reason. Further, he did not wish to isolate himself from all other interpreters of the Bible throughout the history of the church. So Wesley was willing that all three of these tools be used to correctly interpret Scripture. If any one of them should be in conflict with Scripture, he was ready to reexamine the Bible again to see if it had been properly understood. But when Scripture was rightly interpreted and there still was a conflict with one of the other criteria, for Wesley it was the Scripture that continued to serve as the final authority.

Second, Wesley was aware that on many subjects Scripture

does not give specific guidance but only general principles. It was in these situations that Wesley was willing to use secondary criteria for truth; it was not a matter of reason, tradition, and experience contradicting Scripture then, but complementing it. These criteria were not for undermining biblical authority but for assisting in its application. Where Scripture is not precise, reason, tradition, and experience are the best means for understanding truth and determining its application in life. Colin Williams succinctly puts Wesley's view when he writes:

> Wesley must be placed with the Reformers in his principle of *sola scriptura*, in the sense that scripture is the final authority in matters of faith and practice: not in the sense that tradition and experience have no value, but in the sense that these further sources of insight must be congruous with the revelation recorded in scripture.[54]

Thus when these insights were in harmony with Scripture, Wesley made use of them. Their authoritative status was clearly more tentative than if they had been clearly stated scriptural principles, and accordingly were not to be used in the same absolute sense as biblical truth. Nevertheless, they could be used within their limitations.[55]

The fact that Wesley used four major norms in forming theology has led parts of twentieth-century Methodism into mistakenly equating these four as coordinate sources of authority. It has been quite common for some to speak of a "Wesleyan quadrilateral" that seemed to imply that Scripture was on an equal footing with the other three sources of theology.[56] The largest denominational descendant of Wesley even adopted this position as an official theological statement for a period of years. This has now been recognized as inconsistent with Wesley's theological method and the spirit with which he did theology. As a result this error has recently been corrected by the same denomination to make it clear that, as it was with Wesley, Scripture must continue to be the final norm in all theological questions.[57]

THE ROLE OF NATURAL THEOLOGY

In the light of an understanding of Wesley's commitment to Scripture and the role of the three other subordinate criteria for doing theology, it is now possible to evaluate the place of natural theology for Wesley. Natural theology has its roots primarily in the areas of the use of reason and general experience. Wesley edited *A Survey of the Wisdom of God and the Creation: or, A Compendium of Natural Philosophy*, and this with a few other references contains some elements of a natural theology.[58]

That which provides the key to any "natural" theology in Wesley is his understanding of prevenient grace. This grace, given by God to all people has restored to them the faculty of reason that allows them to understand many things about the world of creation and their own experience. Yet fallen humanity does not have the capacity to either reason his way to God or discover him in creation or experience apart from revelation. Thus Wesley makes almost no use of the arguments for the existence of God and bases his ethics entirely on revelation.[59] For Wesley reason and experience may indicate something about the existence of God but without any real description of what he is like. Thus, while there is some knowledge available by general revelation, it is not adequate revelation to bring man to an experience of saving grace. So, while there may be a limited awareness of God, in practice it is not possible to know him by natural understanding only.[60] In accord with what we have seen earlier, natural theology plays a very minor role and subordinate role for Wesley in the building of Christian theology.

For Wesley general revelation that might lead to a natural theology may be seen as that which confirms and supports special revelation in Scripture but is wholly inadequate without it. Thus Wesleyans sometimes tend to see things revealed in creation or understood by reason and general experience as confirming principles established in Scripture, yet they may not be used to build a theology apart from the principles of God's Word.[61]

THE WHOLENESS OF SCRIPTURE

One of Wesley's advantages was that he lived two centuries after the beginning of the Protestant Reformation's rediscovery of the Bible. While Reformers like Luther and Calvin were able to use much newly discovered biblical truth, Wesley was able to build on their insights and continue to ask where Scripture has other things to say about the same subjects.[62] For example, Scripture uses a number of major metaphors to describe God, humanity, and their relationship to each other, and these language categories are spread throughout the entire Bible. These analogies that describe God are multiple, but some are more widely used than others. The Reformers leaned heavily on the language categories that describe creation, sovereign majesty, the legal world of the law court, and to some degree the language of redemption from slavery. This meant that in their understanding of God they tended to focus on his roles as creator, king, judge, and redeemer.

Wesley uses all these but also adds to them categories of person-to-person relationships, the sanctuary, the pastoral scene, and most often the home. This meant that Wesley understood more clearly the roles of God as teacher/friend, priest, shepherd, and father. The effect of Wesley's adding these biblical analogies to those emphasized by the Reformers was a modifying of the severity of the earlier categories. The roles of God as creator, king, judge, and redeemer carry with them a built-in factor of psychological distance. The focus is on God's objective relationship to the world and his distance from it. Whereas the categories of God as teacher/friend, priest, shepherd, and father are much more intimate and personal in nature. God is not just an objective distant reality, he is one who desires to relate intimately to people. Thus Wesley's holistic perspective brings a biblical balance between the transcendence and the immanence of God that had a very profound effect on his theology.

This multiple use of biblical roles and language categories also makes it possible for Wesley to have a very holistic approach to other doctrines in each of the language categories. For example, Wesley felt free to preach on salvation from the two major categories used by the Reformation that saw God as sovereign king and as righteous judge. Accordingly, he proclaimed saving grace in terms of "entering the kingdom of God" and "justification by faith." Wesley also preached from the lesser-used Reformed categories of God as creator and as redeemer, and thus preached salvation in terms of re-creation (or regeneration) and redemption from the power of sin. To these categories he added the focus of God's priestly role and God as Father, and so he spoke about salvation in terms of an initial cleansing and the experience of a new birth. The effect of accenting the role of God as creator (regeneration) and adding the roles of God as priest (cleansing) and as father (new birth) mean that Wesley was able to focus on the subjective side of salvation as well as its objective dimensions. In other words he was concerned for the actual internal change within the heart of the individual, as well as the relational change between man and God. Further, his emphasis on God as teacher/friend and God as shepeherd made it imperative that he also give attention to growing and developing relationships with God after salvation as well as the biblical mandate about following Jesus. While no one category fully describes all that happens in salvation, the use of multiple biblical metaphors to describe salvation insures a much fuller and therefore much more accurate picture of all the dimensions of God's saving grace.

THEOLOGICAL NORMS

Within Wesley's commitment to Scripture certain key biblical themes continue to appear as dominant emphases in his thought. Wesley saw three themes as central throughout Scripture and all three affect the way he interprets the rest of the Bible and builds both his theology and his practice of ministry. In effect these become overarching themes that shape the rest of his theology and may be properly understood as the hermeneutical norms by which he interprets biblical truth.

1. The first of these is the role of God as a *Father*. Because this picture of God was so dominant for Jesus and such a controlling concept for the New Testament church, Wesley understood it to be the most important picture of God for Christians. Looking at all the biblical data, Wesley felt this role was the most dominant in Scripture and that many of the activities of the other figures that describe God are also performed in some measure by a Father. While this role is the most prominent, Wesley does not ignore the other descriptions of who God is and how he relates to mankind. However, when any one of the other roles is understood in connection with God as a loving Father, it is clearly modified significantly. For example, it is one thing to see God as sovereign King, but when the King is also your Father, the whole relationship is changed.

The picture of God as Father means the accent of his relating to mankind focuses on love.[63] Our Father wants people to become his children, to relate to each other as brothers and sisters in Christ, with salvation as a part of their inheritance from him. It involves the use of the language of the home and the family, which becomes very pervasive in all of Wesleyan theology.

The concept of God as a loving Father stands behind several key distinctives within Wesley's theology. One has to do with the distinction Wesley makes between sin as a voluntary transgression of the law and as an involuntary transgression of the law. Wesley classified the latter as "infirmities"—those failings in which the will was not involved in deliberate disobedience. Behind Wesley's perspective is the concept of God as a father, concerned about the motivation of his children (rather than as a Judge or a King concerned about an absolute standard of law). Further, not only was the concept of salvation understood in terms of a new relationahip to God but also the figure of the new birth meant for Wesley a genuine internal transformation of the nature of the individual. This accounts for his strong focus on a real subjective change within a person as well as a new relative change in one's relationship with God at conversion.

It is the picture of God as a Father that accounts for Wesley's strong focus on the concept of assurance. As a Father God desires that his children know how they stand in relationship to him. Further, the concept of a Father who wants to raise his children from babes, to children, to young men and women, to fathers and mothers in the faith stands behind Wesley's understanding of spiritual growth. The Father begets children, but he also raises them to maturity, and much of Wesley's pastoral theology is designed to provide a family context in which that growth and nurture could take place.

One of the ways Wesley's distinctive doctrine of entire sanctification was described was in terms of perfect love. Wesley understood this perfectness to deal with the motivation of the heart and the intent of the will, and this relative perfection is possible only if God is understood as evaluating the heart as a Father would.

In addition, the role of God as Father led to Wesley's rejection of unconditional reprobation; it stood behind his commitment to an unlimited atonement (God so loved the world he provided provisional salvation for everyone); and it undergirded his view of God's provision of grace that made it possible for a person to love him but also made it possible for him or her to resist God's grace and reject his offer of salvation. Thus his whole understanding of predestination was influenced by this emphasis. Indeed, almost every distinctive part of Wesley's theology was significantly affected by his feeling that the dominant picture of God in Scripture is that of a loving Father.

2. The second overarching theme that had a controlling effect on other scriptural data for Wesley was the concept of *holiness*. He began with God's appearance to Moses on Mount Sinai, where God revealed that the essence of his character is holiness (Lev. 11:45) and that he wants people to be like him, i.e., holy as he is holy (1 Peter 1:15–16; 2:9). This understanding of a holy God looking for a holy people clarified not only something of the nature of God for Wesley, but also the purpose of God throughout the order of salvation; i.e., he was remaking mankind like himself, that they should be holy as he is holy. This is why Wesley was not content with any understanding of salvation that did not produce an actual change in people's lives—a change that made them holy and moved them toward greater degrees of holiness throughout their lifetime.[64]

In addition to the concept of holiness having an impact on Wesley's view of the moral nature of God and on his understanding of the order of salvation, it also had an effect on a number of other distinctives in his theology. Thus he understood sin basically as that which is unholiness. Salvation had to include an element of imparted holiness as well as imputed holiness. Further, Wesley was concerned that all believers continue to grow in holiness of heart and life and finally come to an experience of entire sanctification where God does a deeper work of purifying their lives from sinfulness. One of Wesley's reactions to unconditional election was his feeling that this had a tendency to undercut a strong motivation for holiness of heart and life. Because Wesley had a vital concern for the practice of the Christian life, holiness became a very central focus for him in his preaching and practical ministry.

3. The third overarching theme Wesley sees running through Scripture is the concept of *grace*.[65] Grace particularly has to do with the way God works in relationship to men and women. Accordingly, Wesley's whole understanding of the order of salvation is dominated by this concept, beginning with prevenient grace and going all the way through to glorification. For him there is grace that comes before salvation (prevenient grace), grace that leads to repentence, grace that is the basis of justification by faith,[66] grace that is behind assurance of

salvation, grace that makes possible growth in Christian experience, grace that works entire sanctification as well as its assurance, and grace that leads to further growth after sanctification until God graciously glorifies the saint.[67]

The concept of prevenient grace was particularly significant for Wesley's theology in providing a basis for human responsibility. Because God has provided a measure of grace for all people (including non-Christians), all had some measure of free will to respond to God's commandments as well as to his offer of salvation, and therefore they could be held responsible for their decisions. This prevenient grace also meant that saving grace for Wesley was resistible. God, who provided the capacity by prevenient grace for people to say yes to his offer of salvation, also provided the freedom to resist the offer.

Wesley's understanding of growth in the Christian life is also dominated by the concept of grace. It is particularly connected with what he referred to as the "means of grace"— i.e., the spiritual disciplines necessary to allow grace to continue to work in one's life. It was the disciplining of the spiritual life around certain regular habit patterns that led to the name "Methodists." These were those who had chosen certain regular methods or means by which God's grace could continue to work in their lives. The whole of Wesley's pastoral theology is intimately bound up with encouraging believers to go on in God's grace through the use of the "means."

The combination of these three central themes in Wesley's theology may be summarized in terms of a holy Father working by grace to produce a holy people. These themes are clearly interwoven, and sometimes it is difficult to tell which of the three is most central. From Wesley's writings the concept of holiness appears dominant, or at least the most visible. It is from that perspective that Wesley sees God as a holy Father, who expresses his love by coming to people through grace and making possible their salvation by restoring them into his own image, i.e., making them holy as he is holy. Thus for Wesleyans the means a holy Father uses to make people holy is grace.[68]

In conclusion, we must note again that Wesley's theological method has set the standard for all subsequent Wesleyans. His approach to theology is firmly based on Scripture for content and as final authority. Here Wesley stands solidly within the Reformation tradition and with evangelicals today in their commitment to the Bible as the basis of their theology and as the final norm for all theological questions. Other sources for doing theology—such as reason, tradition, and experience—had a clearly restricted role in building theology for Wesley, in that they were always secondary criteria and subordinate to the Word of God. Wesley's distinctive contribution to the church has come with his understanding that the whole of Scripture is best understood in light of three of its dominant themes: God as Father, holiness, and grace. Wesley felt that because these three were so pervasive in Scripture, they were the best means to interpret other scriptural data and build a truly Bible-centered theology. Accordingly, the scriptural truth that dominated both his theology and his practice of ministry was the picture of a holy Father seeking to make people holy by grace.

NOTES

[1]This is not to say that subsequent Wesleyans have not used the systematic model for presenting a holistic Wesleyan theology. Classical examples of systematic theology in the Wesleyan tradition include Richard Watson, *Theological Institutes*, 4 vols., (London: John Mason, 1829); W. B. Pope, *A Compendium of Christian Theology* (London: Wesleyan-Methodist Book-Room, 1880); John Miley, *Systematic Theology*, 3 vols., (New York: Methodist Book Concern, 1892); H. Orton Wiley, *Christian Theology*, 2 vols., (Kansas City: Beacon Hill, 1941); H. Ray Dunning, *Grace, Faith and Holiness* (Kansas City: Beacon Hill, 1988).

[2]See Randy L. Maddox, "John Wesley: Practical Theologian?" An unpublished paper.

[3]Cf. Albert Outler for the misleading reference to Wesley as a "folk theologian," *The Place of Wesley in the Christian Tradition* (Metuchen, N.J.: Scarecrow Press, 1976), 13.

[4]Cf. the use of Wesley for support and/or justification for liberation theology in Theodore Runyon, ed., *Sanctification and Liberation* (Nashville: Abingdon, 1981); Elsa Tamez, "Wesley as Read by the Poor," *The Future of the Methodist Theological Tradition* (Nashville: Abingdon, 1985), 65–84; N. Durwood Foster, "Wesleyan Theology: Heritage at Task," and M. Douglas Meeks, "John Wesley's Heritage and the Future of Systematic Theology," in Theodore Runyon, ed., *Wesleyan Theology Today* (Nashville: Kingswood, 1985).

[5]For discussion of transitions and deveopments within Wesleyan theology since Wesley see Timothy L. Smith, "Historical and Contemporary Appraisal of Wesleyan Theology," in Charles W. Carter, ed., *A Contemporary Wesleyan Theology* (Grand Rapids: Zondervan, Asbury , 1983), 72–102; Robert E. Childs, *Theological Transition in American Methodism: 1790–1935* (New York: Abingdon, 1965); Thomas A. Langford, *Practical Divinity* (Nashville: Abingdon, 1983).

[6]John Wesley, *A Plain Account of Christian Perfection* (London: Epworth, 1952), 6.

[7]John Wesley, *The Works of John Wesley*, 3 vols., (Oxford: Clarendon, 1980), 25:533. Hereafter referred to as *Works* (Oxford).

[8]Wesley, *Works* (Oxford), 25:615.

[9]Further discussion of the development of Wesley's views on Scripture, particularly the years 1729–1738, see Allan Coppedge, "John Wesley and the Issue of Authority in Theological Pluralism," *Wesleyan Theological Journal* 19, 2 (Fall 1984): 62–66.

[10]John Wesley, *The Journal of John Wesley*, ed. Nehemiah Curnock, 8 vols., (London: Robert Culley, 1909), 1:447. Hereafter referred to as *Journal*.

[11]Wesley, *Journal*, 1:454.

[12]John Wesley, *The Standard Sermons of John Wesley*, ed. E. H. Sugden, 2 vols., (London: Epworth, 1921), 1:32–33. Hereafter referred to as *Standard Sermons*.

[13]Wesley, *Journal*, 2:369–70.

[14]For further discussion of Wesley's separation from the Moravians over these theological issues see Allan Coppedge, *John Wesley and Theological Debate* (Wilmore, Ky.: Wesley Heritage Press, 1987), 57–62.

[15]Howard Snyder, *The Radical Wesley* (Downer's Grove, Ill.: InterVarsity, 1980), 69.

[16]Wesley, *The Works of the Rev. John Wesley*, 3rd edition, ed. Thomas Jackson, 14 vols., (London: Wesleyan-Methodist Book-Room, 1831), 8:198–99. Hereafter referred to as *Works*; to be distinguished from the newer *Works* (Oxford).

[17]Wesley, *Works*, 8:340. Subsequent classical Wesleyans have continued to maintain Wesley's commitment to Scripture as the standard for theology as well as the primary source for theology: Watson, *Theological Institutes*,1:289 (cf. Childs, *Theological Transition*, 87–92); Pope, *Christian Theology*,1:35, 41, 156, 193, 206–13; John Miley, *Systematic Theology*, 1:12, 22; Wiley, *Christian Theology*, 1:33, 37, 167, 185; Ray Dunning, *Grace, Faith and Holiness*, 55–58.

[18]Wesley, *Journal*, 5:169.

[19]Wesley, *The Letters of The Reverend John Wesley, A.M.*, ed. John Telford, 8 vols., (London: Epworth, 1931), 2:117. Hereafter referred to as *Letters*.

[20]John Wesley, *Explanatory Notes on the New Testament*, (London: Epworth, 1966), preface, paragraph 12.

[21]Wesley, *Standard Sermons*, 1:249–50.

[22]Wesley, *Journal*, 6:117.

[23]Wesley, *Notes on the New Testament*, John 10:35.

[24]Wesley, *Standard Sermons*, 2:151.

[25]Frank Baker, "John Wesley's Churchmanship," *London Quarterly and Holborn Review* (October 1960), 270.

[26]Wesley, *Notes on the New Testament*, preface, paragraph 10. For further discussion of Scripture and Wesley's theology see A. S. Wood, *The Burning Heart*, (Grand Rapids: Eerdmans, 1967), 209–19.

[27]Wesley, *Letters*, 2:129.

[28]Wesley, *Works*, 7:395.

[29]Ibid., 470.

[30]Ibid., 11:429.

[31]Wesley, *Standard Sermons*, 1:32.

[32]Wesley, *Works*, 10:142.

[33]For further discussion of Wesley's principles of biblical interpretation see William Arnett, "John Wesley—Man of One Book," Ph.D. thesis (Madison, N.J.: Drew University Press, 1954), 98ff.

[34]Wesley, *Letters*, 35:364.

[35]Wesley, *Works*, 4:354.

[36]Wesley, *Letters*, 3:172. Cf. Pope, *Christian Theology*, 1:209–11.

[37]Wesley, *Works*, 2:149. For other examples of Wesley's judging doctrine by Scripture see *Works*, 10:225, 242, 254.

[38]Ibid., 4:360.

[39]Ibid., 8:266, 466. See also Childs, *Theological Transition*, 82–84.

[40]Robert Cushman, "Theological Landmarks in the Revival Under Wesley," *Religion in Life* 27 (1957–58):106ff.

[41]Wesley, *Letters*, 3:172.

[42]Wesley, *Journal*, 1:419. For the Wesleyan position that makes Scripture final authority over tradition see Pope, *Christian Theology*, 1:211-13.

[43]Wesley, *Works*, 10:141.

[44]Ibid., 142.

[45]For more discussion on how authoritative doctrinal standards were to be for Wesleyans, see Albert Outler and Robert E. Cushman in *Wesleyan Theology*, ed., Thomas A. Langford (Durham, N.C.: Labyrinth, 1984), 273–90; Richard Heitzenrater, "At Full Liberty: Doctrinal Standards in Early Methodism," *Quarterly Review* 5, 3 (1985); Thomas Oden, "What Are 'Established Standards of Doctrine?' A Response to Richard Heitzenrater," *Quarterly Review* 7, 1 (1987). See also Thomas Oden, *Doctrinal Standards in the Wesleyan Tradition* (Grand Rapids: Zondervan, Asbury, 1988).

[46]Childs, *Theological Transition*, 80.

[47]Wesley, *Letters*, 8:190.

[48]Ibid., 2:205; idem, *Standard Sermons*, 1:202ff. For an additional example of a Wesleyan position that makes experience a secondary source of theology subordinate to Scripture see Wiley, *Christian Theology*, 1:37–39.

[49]Colin Williams, *John Wesley's Theology Today* (Nashville, New York: Abingdon, 1960), 34.

[50]Wesley, *Works*, 2:429.

[51]Wesley, *Letters*, 7:47.

[52]Wesley, *Standard Sermons*, 2:357ff.

[53]Wesley, *Letters*, 2:117.

[54]Williams, *John Wesley's Theology Today*, 25–26.

[55]For more on the hierarchy of Scripture over reason, tradition, and experience within the Wesleyan tradition see Pope, *Christian Theology*, 1:208.

[56]*The Book of Discipline of the United Methodist Church, 1972* (Nashville: United Methodist, 1973), 75–82.

[57]*Doctrinal Standards in Our Theological Tasks*: Part II of *The Book of Discipline of the United Methodist Church, 1988* (Nashville: United Methodist, 1988), 15, 37–39.

[58]Wesley, *Natural Philosophy*,1:313; 2:184, 447–49; idem, *Letters*, 2:71, 379; 4:90ff. idem, *Works*, 6:325–27; 7:271; 8:197.

[59]Williams, *John Wesley's Theology Today*, 330–31.

[60]Wesley, *Standard Sermons*, 2:216.

[61]See Dennis F. Kinlaw, *Preaching in the Spirit* (Grand Rapids: Zondervan, Asbury, 1985), 81–91.

[62]For further discussion of Wesley's holistic view of Scripture see Timothy L. Smith, "John Wesley and the Wholeness of Scripture," *Interpretation* (July 1985), 246–62.

[63]This emphasis in Wesley has led some Wesleyans to feel that the major theological emphasis of Wesley was on love. See Mildred Bangs Wynkoop, *A*

Theology of Love: The Dynamic of Wesleyanism (Kansas City: Beacon Hill, 1972), 15–20.

[64]For a discussion of holiness as the dominant theme in Wesley's theology see Harold Lindstrom, *Wesley and Sanctification* (Wilmore, Ky.: Francis Asbury, 1980), 15–16.

[65]Because Wesley is very concerned about the way people experience God, and grace is the chief means by which God works in people's lives, a number have concluded that grace was *the* dominant theological motif for Wesley. See Randy Maddox, "Responsible Grace: The Systematic Perspective of Wesleyan Theology," *Wesleyan Theological Journal* 19, 2 (Fall 1984):12–14; Robert L. Wilson and Steve Harper, *Faith and Form* (Grand Rapids: Zondervan, Asbury, 1988), 52–56; Thomas A. Langford, *Practical Divinity* (Nashville: Abingdon, 1983), 262; Albert Outler, in M. Douglas Meeks, ed., *The Future of the Methodist Theological Traditions* (Nashville: Abingdon, 1985), 44, 48–49.

[66]Because of the practical focus on preaching justification by faith, some have felt this was the hermeneutical norm for Wesley's theology. See William R. Cannon, *The Theology of John Wesley* (New York: Abingdon, 1946), 14; A. Skevington Wood, *The Burning Heart* (Grand Rapids: Eerdmans, 1967), 220–22. See Ray Dunning's choice for a norm for Wesleyan systematic theology as justification by faith/sanctification by faith in the context of prevenient grace, in his book *Grace, Faith and Holiness*, (Kansas City: Beacon Hill, 1941), 747.

[67]Because grace is so closely connected with the order of salvation for Wesley, some have seen the *ordo salutis* as the dominant motif for understanding Wesley's theology. See Williams, *John Wesley's Theology Today*, 39–40.

[68]For further discussion on the present and future states of Wesleyan theology see Richard S. Taylor, "Historical and Modern Significance of Wesleyan Theology," in Carter, *A Contemporary Wesleyan Theology*, 51–71; Wilson and Harper, *Faith and Form*, 24–27; Langford, *Practical Divinity*, 197–272; Runyon, *Wesleyan Theology Today*; Outler, *The Place of Wesley in the Christian Tradition*; M. Douglas Meeks, "The Future of the Methodist Theological Traditions," and Albert C. Outler, "The New Future for Wesley Studies: Agenda for Phase 3," in Meeks, *The Future of the Methodist Theological Tradition*.

11

THEOLOGICAL STYLE AMONG PENTECOSTALS AND CHARISMATICS

RUSSELL P. SPITTLER
FULLER THEOLOGICAL SEMINARY,
PASADENA, CALIFORNIA

We hope and trust that no person or body of people will ever use these minutes, or any part of them, as articles of faith upon which to establish a sect or denomination.

Minutes of the Annual Assembly of the Churches of East Tennessee, North Georgia, and Western North Carolina, held January 26 & 27, 1906, at Camp Creek, N.C.

Twenty years after the traditional date of the origin of the Church of God (Cleveland, Tennessee), early conferees expressed in the above statement the creedal hesitance that regularly marks churches of the Spirit. In less than five years the beliefs of the group were "codified." Such doctrinal modesty does not mark only the oldest of the established American Pentecostal denominations; similar declarations surrounded, for example, the origin of the Assemblies of God in 1914—only to be superseded two years later by a page-long "Statement of Fundamental Truths" necessitated by the rise of the non-Trinitarian "Jesus Name" teaching, the Statement quite lopsidedly addressing that issue.

Such a history makes clear, then, the first thing to be said when thinking about how Pentecostals and their kin theologize: *The writing of theological books and articles does not rise naturally among classical Pentecostals.* Doing evangelism, on the other hand, is their great strength. Doing theology, if that means publishing monographs and densely reasoned articles, is not native to the tradition. Charismatics, in contrast, quite easily and productively theologize.

NUANCING PENTECOSTALS AND CHARISMATICS

But how do charismatics differ from Pentecostals? Global Pentecostalism, largely a twentieth-century phenomenon, has become "arguably . . . the most influential Christian tradition of our time" in the view of Donald W. Dayton.[1]

Religious statistical researcher David B. Barrett defines three distinguishable waves in the rise of the comprehensive Pentecostal-charismatic movement. The *first* began about 1901 and led to the formation of classical Pentecostal churches like the Church of God (Cleveland, Tennessee), the International Pentecostal Holiness Church, the International Church of the Foursquare Gospel, the Church of God in Christ, and the Assemblies of God. The *second* wave brought about the charismatic movement (at times called the New Pentecostalism), beginning among mainline Protestants about 1960 and within the Roman Catholic church in 1967. The *third* wave emerged around 1980 and describes evangelicals who are not at all inclined to leave their churches nor to describe themselves as either "Pentecostal" or "charismatic," but who nevertheless have adopted Pentecostal supernaturalism and such practices as prophecy, exorcism, prayer for the sick, "words of knowledge," and speaking in tongues.

On Barrett's mid-1988 worldwide count, 351 million persons—one in every five church members—reflects a Pentecostal or charismatic persuasion.

The Pentecostals of the early 1900s left their original churches, found each other, in various ways and degrees banded together, and—more or less—have lived happily together ever since. For that reason they form a more or less predictable doctrinal profile: conservative and orthodox belief in the Trinity (with an important exception being the "Jesus Name" sector of Pentecostalism), the sinfulness of humankind, personal salvation through a distinct conversion experience, expectation of an imminent premillennial return of Christ. To this quite standard evangelical cluster was added, although nuanced by various interpretations of sanctification, the distinctive belief in the baptism of the Holy Spirit—a second (or in some cases, a third) crisis experience marked by an individual replication of speaking in tongues of the sort mentioned in

Acts. To this day, the family of classical Pentecostal churches feels deeply that God has placed them in the world for such a time as this; and bearing witness to the baptism in the Spirit with glossolaic consequence is their *raison d'être*.

On the other hand, charismatics for the most part stayed put in their churches and thus showed no need to define their identity by the preservation of a "distinctive." Charismatic spirituality for them resulted in individual and group renewal, and that often included the rediscovery and deepened appreciation of their own churchly heritages.

In those cases where the charismatic impulse resulted in fractious schisms, the independent charismatic churches that ensued, detached and often hostile to their ecclesial mothers, took on considerably greater likeness to the classical Pentecostals from whom they had learned the new spirituality.

Some of these severed, pentecostalized local congregations have found each other and, often catalyzed by the personal magic of a doubly charismatic leader, new charismatic denominations are being formed these days before our eyes. Occasionally, disavowals of doctrinal exclusivity are heard and these disavowals faithfully echo the 1906 *Minutes* of the Camp Creek Assembly. The emergence of the new charismatic denominations from the 1970s onward in one respect resembles the onset of an economic recession: the trend becomes clear only after it has begun.

To speak about Pentecostal or charismatic theological style therefore risks the peril of unmanageable breadth. As a whole, the world's Pentecostals generally can be described and nuanced. Not so charismatics. That is true because Pentecostals have become far more institutionalized and have existed for nearly a century as distinguishable ecclesiastical entities. Charismatics, to the contrary, are all over the place, and that is true doctrinally as well as demographically. Pentecostals, you could say, are nouns whereas charismatics are adjectives: "*charismatic* Presbyterians," "*charismatic* Mennonites," "*charismatic* Greek Orthodox," and so on.

Because of this difference—because Pentecostals make up a distinct ecclesiastical species, while charismatics don a pentecostalized spiritual lifestyle within their mainstream Christian churches—it is considerably easier to speak about the theological style of Pentecostals than to do the same for charismatics. Thus arises a second generalization: *Global Pentecostalism presents a predictable set of theological beliefs, but charis-*

*matic theology results from the mix of Pentecostal supernaturalism
with one or other of the mainstream Christian traditions.*
The theological products are bound to reflect the foundational
values of those who produce them. In other places[2] I have
suggested five core values among Pentecostals (still true, but
less so, among charismatics). These are (1) religious experience, (2) orality, (3) spontaneity, (4) otherworldliness, and
(5) biblical authority. It can be instructive to reflect on how
these bedrock foundations control both the content and the
form of theology among Pentecostals and their charismatic
offspring. I will try to show here how that happens in the
theological expressions of these twin traditions.

Theological style in the Pentecostal-charismatic tradition
can be illuminated by dividing that group into four historically
distinct parts, surveying the nature and extent of each sector
and reviewing in greater detail one or two representatives of
each strand. What follows therefore considers first the classical
Pentecostalism, which began at the dawn of this century. The
second phase appears in Protestant neo-Pentecostalism that
emerged within mainline churches in the 1950s. Third to appear
were the considerable theological outcomes of the charismatic
movement within the Roman Catholic church, where charismatic matters began in 1967. Fourth and latest to appear is the
"Third Wave," an outburst of a pentecostalized evangelicalism
stemming from the early 1980s. (The "Second Wave" includes
both Protestant and Roman Catholic neo-Pentecostalism, here
numbered separately.)

"THEOLOGY" IN THE
CLASSICAL PENTECOSTAL MOVEMENT

It cannot be overemphasized that any successful analysis of
classical Pentecostalism cannot be based solely on printed
materials.[3] We deal, in this still growing movement, with a
culture that is profoundly oral in its style.

Swiss missiologist Walter Hollenweger, one of the world's
leading analysts of global Pentecostalism, has emphasized
insistently the role of orality in that Christian family—specially
among its growing representation in the two-thirds world. His
ten-volume *Handbuch der Pfingstbewegung* (Handbook of the
Pentecostal Movement)—presented as his 1966 doctoral thesis
to the theological faculty of the University of Zürich—made
very clear, through the abundance of bibliographic items which

were typewritten and without date, the paucity of publication among the world's Pentecostals. The *Handbook* was a collection of virtually everything published and obtainable in world Pentecostalism's first half century.

The Pentecostals of the 1900s, 1910s, and 1920s were not unaware of the potential of print. But their presses churned out tracts, handbills of coming revivals and camp meetings, first-person testimonial accounts of "My Baptism in the Holy Ghost," and similar materials not usually reckoned within the genre of serious academic theology.

There was theology in such materials, of course. But as was true also of the earliest Christian writings, theology would have to be extracted and systematized from what were really everyday situational letters, reports, descriptions of physical healings and exorcisms, and stories about Jesus that outsiders would quickly label propaganda.

The earliest Pentecostal theologizing can now be traced in considerable detail, thanks to a major analysis of the movement in *Theological Roots of Pentecostalism*,[4] which began life as the doctoral thesis (University of Chicago) of Donald W. Dayton. This study fixes on Aimee Semple McPherson's "Foursquare" motif as a useful key to the basic beliefs of classical Pentecostalism. Rumored to have originated in a colorful sermon given by the pioneer Pentecostal evangelist that made use of boxing-ring imagery, the Foursquare quartet embraced (1) salvation by grace, (2) divine healing, (3) baptism in the Holy Spirit, and (4) the second coming of Christ. These basic doctrinal beliefs have long characterized all varieties of classical Pentecostalism—even the so-called "oneness," or "Jesus Name," non-Trinitarian species regularly shunned by the more orthodox sectors of the movement.

These four themes, of course, were not the only things believed by Pentecostals. Nineteenth-century wellsprings within the broad Holiness movement, for example, yielded a variety of views about "entire sanctification." On the sanctification issue, in fact, modern Pentecostalism exhibits widely diverse viewpoints. Some coalesce sanctification into the baptism in the Holy Spirit. Others mark it as a second distinct personal religious experience with the separate and distinct baptism in the Spirit as a third crisis experience.

Professor Dayton's important study gives all the historical fine points, citing and connecting the plethora of Holiness themes and publications that ripened the times for the birth of modern Pentecostalism. "Indeed," he asserts, "one might argue that the whole network of popular 'higher Christian life' institutions and movements constituted at the turn of the century a sort of pre-Pentecostal tinderbox awaiting the spark that would set it off."[5]

One of the highly illuminating examples of these nineteenth-century stirrings lay in the evolution of terminology. Dayton shows how John Wesley's phrase "pure love" was transformed—among his followers—into "entire sanctification." Then that phrase itself, which abounded in Holiness, Wesleyan, and revivalist circles in the decades surrounding the 1840s, was gradually replaced by the term "baptism with the Holy Ghost"—although no connections with speaking in tongues were made till that linkage became the theological birthmark of twentieth-century Pentecostalism.

The terminological shift, Dayton observes,[6] was epitomized in the writings of Holiness leader Asa Mahan (1799–1889), a colleague of Charles Finney and a member of the Oberlin perfectionist school. In 1839, Mahan published a book entitled *Scripture Doctrine of Christian Perfection*. A generation later, the same author published a book with the title *Baptism of the Holy Ghost* (1870). This shift, so helpful in understanding the rise of modern Pentecostalism, is but a strand in the thick cable that ties the movement to its nineteenth-century origins.

Here, then, is a third generalization about Pentecostal theology: *Early classical Pentecostal theology grew out of nineteenth-century Holiness and (for at least some parts of the movement) Keswickian themes. For this reason, Pentecostal theology in the first decades, say deep into the 1930s, had no reason to develop its own full-orbed doctrinal handbooks.* The central belief, the baptism in the Holy Spirit, was set on top of the commonly accepted conservative Christian orthodoxy. Only about the time of the second World War did a literature of comprehensive doctrinal handbooks arise, along with the first titles describing themselves as "systematic theologies."

In Pentecostal circles no work has matched the circulation or longevity of Myer Pearlman's doctrinal summary entitled *Knowing the Doctrines of the Bible*.[7] Published at first in three parts in 1938, the work appeared in a single volume of less than three hundred pages in 1948. It has been in print continuously for over a half century. More than 125,000 copies have been sold in English alone—6,500 copies in 1988. Translated into French, Portuguese, and Spanish, Pearlman's work to this day serves as the doctrinal textbook of choice in many of the overseas Bible schools conducted under the auspices of the Assemblies of God. It was used in earlier stages of the domestic colleges and Bible institutes of that denomination and is still used in some of them.

Born in Scotland, the son of Jewish parents, Myer Pearlman (1898–1943) came to faith after arrival in the United States, which he served as an Army medic in World War I. He knew Hebrew, French, and Italian, and he read the Old Testament in the readily available and inexpensive King James Version. (The New Testament pages had been torn out of his copy.) A scholarly youth, he read much. Eventually, he enrolled in what was then called Central Bible Institute in Springfield, Missouri, widely known in the Assemblies of God as "CBI." His obvious intellectual abilities led to an invitation to teach at CBI—a role he filled from about 1925 till his untimely death in 1943.

Myer Pearlman never held any academic degrees, earned or honorary. As a convinced Pentecostal, he undertook in 1937 to write *Knowing the Doctrines of the Bible* to provide his classes with what till then did not exist. Salaries were meagre for CBI faculty, and faculty members with families had to find additional income. Pearlman wrote Sunday-school curriculum material.

He also wrote other works related to the Bible. *Seeing the Bible*, his first publication (1930), guided many Pentecostal Sunday-school teachers and ministers, most of whom had very little formal training. Through the later 1930s and into the 1950s—much longer in many places—Pearlman's *Knowing the Doctrines* and a well-marked copy of the Scofield Reference Bible in the King James Version were the twin staples for serious Pentecostal students, lay or clergy.

There is not a single footnote in Pearlman's book. Neither is there any bibliography. The lack of these features was common in that day—and characteristic of the Pentecostal style of theologizing. *For classical Pentecostals, "systematic theology" is an elegant name for doctrine. And doctrine consists of a concise statement of biblical truth presented in a logical order and marked by gathered scriptural support.* That description exactly fits *Knowing the Doctrines.*

What theology on this level does not do is to address social issues or cultural situations, to interact with the Western philosophical tradition or even with the history of Christian thought and doctrine, and above all to criticize prevailing social themes.

Theology, in such a mode, is simply an organized summary of the teaching of the Bible set down in plain language. No more is needed, it would be thought. It is not unfair to say that to the present day such a conception of the task of theology would rank as the majority opinion throughout global classical Pentecostalism—where the matter got any attention at all.

Pearlman's little work is a deserving classic in its own right. He avoids technical language, speaking for example of the "doctrine of sin" rather than "hamartiology." His work is balanced, mediating, irenic, nontechnical, a model of clear writing, easily followed. Yet it reflects the careful thinking of its gifted author, only a fraction of whose thoroughly digested sources show up formally quoted. Pearlman knew and read other systematic theologies, but *Knowing the Doctrines* is no mere digest of its ancestors. The book is the theological jewel of classical Pentecostalism's middle period—written after the era of tracts, at the throes of self-conscious polemic, and before the "evangelicalization" of Pentecostalism led to the training of its teachers in places like Wheaton College and the interdenominational theological seminaries. Pearlman belonged to an era when a master's degree on the faculty of a Pentecostal Bible school was a rarity and doctorates were unknown. The wide dissemination of his book and its long life earn it top honors and senior status in the scantily populated ranks of Pentecostal theological writings.

A much briefer work still used in the Assemblies of God is Nelson's small book *Bible Doctrines*.[8] This work could be described as a sort of primitive dogmatics. Each of its chapters reproduces at the beginning one of the sixteen points of the "Statement of Fundamental Truths" of the Assemblies of God.[9] Each chapter then summarizes the doctrines treated in the quoted part of the Statement. Nelson was the president of Southwestern Bible Institute near Dallas (now known as Southwestern College of the Assemblies of God). Today, candidates for ministerial credentials in the Assemblies of God who are unable to attend Bible college are expected to pursue a specified course of reading that includes Nelson's *Bible Doctrines*.

The only Pentecostal work known to me that actually bears the title *Systematic Theology* is the three-volume work by Ernest Williams (1885–1981).[10] This work, as its editor, Frank Boyd, says in the preface, was compiled by Boyd from notes Williams had used when presenting lectures on theology at CBI, where he taught for some years following his twenty-year tenure (1929–1949) as general superintendent. Compared with Pearlman's works, William's volumes will show a far higher number of quotations from outside sources. The "doctrine of sin" becomes "hamartiology." But the work does not match Pearlman in consistency and coherence. More accurately it might have been entitled *Notes on Systematic Theology*.

The tradition survives, however, in classical Pentecostal circles of esteemed pastors and church leaders producing doctrinal expositions. Foursquare pastors and administrators Guy Duffield and Nathaniel Van Cleve jointly wrote a six-hundred-page volume entitled *Foundations of Pentecostal Theology*.[11] Published in 1983 and originally commissioned by Foursquare megachurch pastor Jack Hayford when he was president of LIFE Bible College, the work is the first comprehensive theology to have arisen among the churches founded by the talented evangelist Aimee Semple McPherson.

In level of technicality, the work of Duffield and Van Cleve rises a notch or two above Pearlman's volume. They have footnotes; he did not. It is clear that these authors draw upon earlier systematics by Lewis S. Chafer, Charles Hodge, A. H. Strong, Henry C. Thiessen, and even Myer Pearlman himself. The sources consulted are chiefly books, very few articles are cited. No bibliography is given, but a thirty-nine-page index of biblical references shows the high role of biblical citation in this recent example of classical Pentecostal theology. The Church of God of Prophecy about the same time published *Fundamentals of the Faith*, by Raymond Pruitt—a pastor and bishop of the church.[12] Bishop Pruitt's opening line in his preface reads: "Worship, evangelism, and Christian service have generally taken precedence over theology in our tradition, and that is as it should be."[13] He is right.

These recent theologies by classical Pentecostals show the secondary role of theology in communities of simple faith and mission zeal. Theology as engagement with societal or ecumenical issues is given little value. Drawing from two millennia of church history risks embarassment to restorationist devaluation of most things ecclessiastical between the first and the twentieth centuries. Doctrine, a word that comes more easily in the tradition than theology, serves the pragmatic function of edification of believers.

Such a theological style may not be appreciated by large sectors of the church, but it should not for that reason be misunderstood. There are millions of believers who think that way. Professor Lederle makes a telling point about the state of the charismatic renewal in West Germany:

> One finds the anomalous situation that where the goundwork has been most thoroughly and reflectively done by theologians (such as [Arnold] Bittlinger and [Heribert] Mühlen) the harvest of renewal as far as the number of renewed lives is concerned seems disproportionately smaller than in places where the theological basis for renewal is an inadequate tottering edifice. The causes for this state of affairs would be diverse and are not the focus of this study.[14]

Pretheological Pentecostals would have little difficulty in suggesting the "causes" on which the professor demurs.

It is instructive for understanding Pentecostal theological style that Duffield and Van Cleve in their work argue much like Pearlman and Williams, though their work was published decades later. Their book, in fact, followed Harold Lindsell's *Battle for the Bible*[15] and the inerrancy controversy that surrounded it. But the authors did not engage the literature of that controversy, never referred to Lindsell, nor did they engage specific authors or present alternative exegeses of specific texts. In other words, even down to the latest available classical Pentecostal doctrinal handbook (the nearest thing in the movement to systematic theologies) quotation from previous writers is done chiefly to support or illustrate the doctrinal topic under discussion. Classical Pentecostal theology, though at times apologetic, is nevertheless precritical. *The aim of Pentecostal theologizing is edification and not criticism or controversy.*[16]

The character of classical Pentecostal theological style shifted somewhat with the emergence of Stanley M. Horton, now nearing the end of a distinguished career as the successor, more or less, to Myer Pearlman as the house theologian for the Assemblies of God. Professor Horton, who teaches at the Assemblies of God Theological Seminary, holds a Th.M. from Harvard Divinity School and a Th.D. from Central Baptist Theological Seminary in Kansas City.

Like Myer Pearlman before him, Horton supplemented a thin teachers' salary (at the same institution—CBI) by moonlighting at the Gospel Publishing House. For decades, Sunday-school literature flowed from his pen. Although he never produced a comprehensive systematic theology, he did write a full treatment entitled *What the Bible Teaches About the Holy Spirit.*[17]

Horton's seminary training acquainted him with the continental critical tradition in biblical scholarship. But his ministry positioned him amid a people who knew little of that world and cared less. Consequently, Horton's considerable abilities found no call in his context for detailed critical engagement. Aiming nevertheless to reassure his Pentecostal readers of the trustworthiness of the Bible, Horton often wrote of the "biblical critics" as an undiversified class of generic enemies. It is not easy to locate in his writings any citing of such critics or even any partial appreciation of their work.

Throughout his writings, where the issue comes up, Horton readily affirms verbal inspiration and sides with biblical inerrancy—even though he understands the complicated implications of "apparent discrepancies." Given Horton's context, his long and substantial service among the classical Pentecostals, it would be unreasonable to expect from him any other theological posture.

In the period following the evangelicalization of Pentecostalism, another variety of classical Pentecostal scholar has arisen. It was in 1970 that the Society for Pentecostal Studies was established.[18] There emerged Pentecostal ministers indelibly formed within the Pentecostal tradition but educationally trained beyond it. (To this day, no Pentecostal schools offer a research doctorate.) As a group, they more readily earned university doctorates in the biblical field rather than in systematic theology.[19] Many of them hold teaching posts in schools outside those operated by the movement's member churches,[20] though most had also earlier taught in Pentecostal schools or served in pastoral roles in Pentecostal churches. They understand themselves as classical Pentecostals. But they function as evangelical biblical scholars in evangelical seminaries or in major universities, as well as within the newer graduate theological schools emerging within Pentecostalism.

The rise of university-trained Pentecostal scholars within and without the Pentecostal movement has not yet resulted in the publication of a systematic theology or even a doctrinal handbook that reflects the brand of evangelical scholarship now fully discernible among Pentecostal evangelical biblical scholars. *No full-fledged classical Pentecostal systematic theology has yet appeared.* Systematics lags behind exegesis. The exegetes have arrived, the systematicians are on the horizon.[21] What do exist and have long served the Pentecostal movement are the unadorned doctrinal handbooks exemplified in Myer Pearlman's *Knowing the Doctrines of the Bible.*

SYSTEMATIC THEOLOGY IN PROTESTANT NEW PENTECOSTALISM

What distinguishes classical Pentecostalism from all her children in the renewal—Protestant charismatics, Roman Catholic charismatics, "Third Wavers"—lies in the character and longevity of the ecclesiastical traditions involved, and especially in the very different valuations of the academic enterprise.

The pneumatological penchant of Pentecostals is well known: their constant reliance on the Holy Spirit, who would teach them all things in Jesus' absence, who would facilitate "greater works" than Jesus himself performed, who would grant a "word of knowledge" understood as divinely originated disclosures of hidden information, and whose empowerment would result in accompanying signs (Mark 16:17). The Johannine reminder (1 John 2:27) "you do not need anyone to teach you" is often cited among Pentecostals to obviate academic study.

Given such an anti-intellectualism, the disinterest of Pentecostals in academic enterprises is understandable. Only in 1970 did the first graduate Pentecostal seminary appear, and that among black Pentecostals.[22] (Seminaries were opened by the Assemblies of God in 1970 and by the Church of God/Cleveland, Tennessee, in 1976.) The same scholarly disinterest accounted for the minimal Bible school training long held to be sufficient for ordination to ministry. This anti-intellectual mood prevails to this day and renders surprising the large and growing number of Pentecostal seminary students in both Pentecostal and evangelical theological seminaries, for no Pentecostal denomination requires seminary graduation for ordination. Most denominations require students to go to seminary in order to be ordained; many Pentecostals voluntarily attend seminary because they are already ordained.

Outside the Pentecostal movement, education and study gain greater value. The Reformation traditions for example— Lutheran, Reformed, Anglican, and "right wing" (Mennonite or otherwise)—have been at the theological business for over four hundred years. By contrast, the Pentecostal tradition is less than a century old. And the Reformers themselves were no mean scholars: the works of Calvin and Luther are still read in seminaries of every stripe. The first edition of Calvin's *Institutes*—a classic systematic theology, to be sure—was written by the Reformer at age twenty-six. Luther's peppery tractates, and maybe his blue-language personality, did not lend themselves to a tranquil systematic theology. But his voluminous theological output is still read by many persons well beyond Lutheran boundaries.

The ecclesiastical maturity of the major Protestant traditions, coupled with their positive valuation and support of academic inquiry, insure that theological outcomes stemming from the charismaticized mainline churches will outrank in technicality the modest and pragmatic doctrinal products of the much younger classical Pentecostal tradition.

There is more. Over nearly half a millennium, Protestantism's bent to split has yielded countless[23] varieties of Protestants. Systematic theologies, of course, have appeared only in the major varieties of these. But the differences among varieties of Protestants far exceed those among types of Pentecostals. To speak therefore of Protestant charismatic theologies involves considerable diversification: the many varieties of Protestantism, when they are charismaticized, yield still the familiar motifs of each tradition. *Therefore Protestant charismatic theology, when compared with classical Pentecostal theology, comes out more academically substantial, capable of much greater variety because of prior centuries of diversification, likely to reach print far sooner after the arrival of the charismatic impulse, and (due to the maturity of the Reformation churches and the existence of long-standing catechetical resources) more likely to move beyond edification to critical and societal engagement.*

Just as Donald Dayton's book *Theological Roots of Pentecostalism* gives useful guidance for tracking intellectual connections, a recent work by a professor of theology formerly at the University of South Africa, Henry I. Lederle, provides a useful navigational aid among the varieties of contemporary charismatic theology.

In his volume entitled *Treasures Old and New: Interpretations of "Spirit Baptism" in the Charismatic Renewal Movement*, Lederle describes the charismatic theologies of some forty different writers—Protestant, Roman Catholic, and Eastern Orthodox.[24]

These he broadly classifies into three (not air-tight) groups. The first are "neo-Pentecostal interpretations" of spirit-baptism, those that adopt the classical Pentecostal idea of subsequence and—often but not always—make the same insistence upon glossolalia as necessary initial evidence (e.g., Don Basham, Larry Christenson, Stephen Clark, Everett Fullam, Peter Hocken, and J. Rodman Williams). A second group he calls "sacramental interpretations," found predictably among Anglican, Roman Catholic, and Lutheran thinkers (e.g., Arnold Bittlinger, J. M. Ford, Donald Gelpi, John Gunstone, Theodore Jungkuntz, Kilian McDonnell, Heribert Mühlen, and Eusebius Stephanou). The third cluster groups "integrative interpretations," which more strongly reflect denominational allegiances and vary considerably among themselves (e.g., Tormond Engelsviken, Siegfried Grossmann, Michael Harper, Morton Kelsey, Thomas Small).

Professor Lederle's work provides an indispensable guide to the varieties of charismatic theology. The book also makes clear that the first generation of charismatic theology was spent, like the first efforts of the early Pentecostals but on a notably higher academic level, in both contextual apologetics and in-house exposition. The academic level is clearly higher. But the fundamental sociology is the same: the believers interpret their enthusiasm to their communities and pass it on to the open-minded and the open-hearted. The significant difference is that the charismatics as a rule, unlike the earlier Pentecostals, were not required to leave their churches.

But did these newer charismatics with their abundant literary production, produce systematic theologies incorporating a thoroughgoing theological viewpoint? Not till 1988. In that year, charismatic Presbyterian systematic theologian J. Rodman Williams published, *Renewal Theology: God, the World, and Redemption*. Given the tag line "Systematic Theology From a Charismatic Perspective,"[25] Williams' *Renewal Theology* was conceived as a comprehensive systematic theology. It can be described as the first comprehensive systematic and openly charismatic theology to emerge from any sector of the Pentecostal or charismatic movements.

Professor Williams was a natural for the task. Educated at Davidson College, Union Theological Seminary in Virginia, and Columbia University, he served as a pastor and military chaplain before undertaking the teaching of theology at Austin Presbyterian Seminary. Earlier a member of the southern

Presbyterian Church (Presbyterian Church of the United States), he continues as a clergyman of the merged Presbyterian Church (U.S.A.). Today, he teaches theology at Regent University in Virginia Beach (formerly CBN University). Earlier he served as president of the Melodyland School of Theology in Anaheim, California. "In *Renewal Theology*," Williams writes in his preface, "my concern is . . . to deal with the full range of Christian truth. It will nevertheless be 'renewal theology,' because I write as one positioned within the renewal context."[26] Williams sees his work as not unlike similar works, except in three regards. First, he consciously preserves a style close to conversational, in order to communicate well. Second, he writes unabashedly with the enthusiasm he reports as an outcome of his personal renewal experience in 1965. Third, primarily in volume 2, he redresses a neglect of charismatic dimensions of the doctrine of the Holy Spirit.

For his analysis of Williams, Professor Lederle in *Treasures* had access only to writings published before *Renewal Theology*.[27] The fullest pneumatology among Williams' prior writings appears in his book *The Gift of the Holy Spirit Today*.[28] In this book Williams distinguished the gift of eternal life from the gift of the Spirit, and he thus approaches the classical Pentecostal distinction expressed more typically with the lanugage "conversion" followed by the "baptism in the Holy Spirit."

On Lederle's analysis, Williams unsuccessfully tries to blend classical Pentecostal separation and subsequence with sacramental initiation: "With remarkable tenacity he tried to bridge the gap by accepting the validity of both portions. In my opinion," Lederle continues, "he could not maintain this dichotomy."[29] That gloomy assessment may rise in part from chronological misplacement: some of Williams' pieces were written much earlier than the date of their publication.

At any rate, it is clear from volume 2 of *Renewal Theology*, that Williams has moved away from a sacramentalist view and much closer to classical Pentecostal notions (but not their language, exactly). His thought now shows the benefit of mature reflection and articulated balance. Volume 2 is a major contribution to the doctrine of the Holy Spirit in a systematic context—a treatment that boldly and extensively develops topics like spiritual gifts and the "coming of the Spirit." A penchant for one-word headings prevails. It may be a sign of the times that the three-volume work is being published by an aggressive Grand Rapids evangelical publisher (Zondervan) compared with the now-defunct prior publisher of charismatic titles (Logos International).

Williams does not hesitate to let his personal renewal show through in his writing, not offensively but as a means of engagement with his material. "What I hope the reader will catch," he writes, "is the underlying excitement and enthusiasm about the reality of the matters discussed. The old being renewed *is* something to get excited about."[30] An illuminating section entitled "The Method of Doing Theology"[31] starts with "seeking the guidance of the Holy Spirit." But theological method, Williams feels, must also show "reliance on the Scriptures," "familiarity with church history," "awareness of the contemporary scene," and "growth in Christian experience."

Williams produces theology much like Pearlman's: thoughtful, organized, respectful of Scripture, readable, giving place to the Spirit, valuing personal experience. But there are differences. Williams' work shows deeper appreciation of the church's past; Pentecostals often belittle the past, interpreting the Pentecostal movement along restorationist lines as the "latter rain" following a long, medieval drought. Wider ecumenical openness as well characterizes *Renewal Theology*; unlike the early Pentecostals, Williams never left his denomination. He writes into his own tradition.

Williams' style in the use of Scripture more closely parallels the nontechnical approach common to classical Pentecostalism, and this feature separates his approach from that of the Roman Catholic charismatic theologians to be described later. For example, when treating creation in Genesis, he offers no discussions about the genre or possible diverse sources of the passage; Pentecostals would do likewise. On the other hand, he refuses to endorse the recent emphasis on "scientific creationism" found in right-wing evangelicalism, which many Pentecostals (but far fewer charismatics) would incline to accept. Something of Williams' charismatic creativity appears when he begins the treatment of creation with the categories of "blessing and praise . . . marvel and wonder," focusing not "on *how* God created but *that* he did."[32] His is a theology marked by expressed joy.

The sole available systematic theology by a Protestant charismatic thus shares with Pentecostals a high value placed on experience and allows this to show up in the very design of theological topics (joy over creation and for the benefits of atonement). But *Renewal Theology* shows wider knowledge of theological literature and deeper acquaintance with (as well as greater ecumenical openness toward) the broad church. At the same time, it can be observed that Williams uses the Bible precritically. In addition, he does not engage the broad range of European theology and exegesis—James Dunn being a happy exception.

Protestant charismatics, as a whole, reflect a theological style that is more sophisticated than that found in classical Pentecostals but less technical than that of certain Roman Catholic charismatic theologians. These Protestant neo-Pentecostals do not rigidly press the identity-related "distinctive doctrines" of classical Pentecostalism. They openly and positively affirm the total range of the church and work hard at loyalty to their own mainline denominations (rather than vest suspicion in "other" denominations). They more easily affirm the global glory and variety of the church than the restrictive ecclesiology of the Roman Catholic tradition. This cluster of features prompts much hope for the future of theology among Protestant charismatics. As a whole, their style is more sophisticated than that in Pentecostalism, less ecclesiastically exclusive than the Roman tradition, and simply older and hence more mature than the newborn "Third Wave."

SYSTEMATIC THEOLOGY AMONG ROMAN CATHOLIC CHARISMATICS

Whatever is made of it, happy coincidence or inspired prophecy, Pope John XXIII in 1959 taught the church to pray for God to renew his wonders in our time "as by a new Pentecost." Eight years later, in 1967, in the chapel of the Roman Catholic Duquesne University in Pittsburgh, the Catholic charismatic movement began, the third phase of this century's far-reaching Pentecostal-charismatic movement. And with the emergence of the Roman Catholic charismatic movement has quietly come a large volume of high-quality theology.

Roman Catholicism has a lengthy and positive regard for academic tradition. Tenaciously, it never relinquished spirituality as a theological discipline, though Protestant liberalism, pressed by scientific historicism and in large sectors by skeptical positivism, abandoned seminary courses in prayer to noncredit fireside talks by esteemed pastors emeritus. *More and better charismatic theology (of the written sort!) has come from Roman Catholic quarters than from elsewhere in the movement—and in briefer time.* "More and better" here includes greater attention paid to past writers, wider use of resources in European languages, the support of an ecclesial tradition accustomed to the production of academic theology.

Once again, Professor Lederle's *Treasures Old and New* provides an illuminating guide to the varieties of Roman Catholic Pentecostal ideas. It is interesting that he finds Roman representatives in all three of his major categories—Neo-Pentecostals, who closely echo classical Pentecostal theology (Stephen Clark, Peter Hocken); sacramentalist charismatics (J. M. Ford, Donald Gelpi, Kilian McDonnell, Edward O'Connor, the Ranaghans, Simon Tugwell); and the more peculiar "integrative interpretations of Spirit-baptism" (Heribert Mühlen, Francis Sullivan).

All Roman theologians show profound allegiance to Roman Catholic presuppositions. I cannot name a charismatic theologian who is a *former* Roman Catholic: among either classicals or "neos" it would be much easier to list former ecclesiastical affiliations. *The Roman Catholic church, three times the size of all Protestant churches together, is large enough, to date, to embrace charismatic theologians within it, and, for that matter, to absorb the charismatic impulse without conspicuous schism* (a generalization not vitiated by the occasional conversion of individual Catholics, including some priests, to other branches of Christendom).[33]

Two features of certain Roman Catholic charismatic thinkers so far not apparent in classical Pentecostal or Protestant charismatic writing are (1) the ready use of sophisticated critical methodologies (such as form- and redaction-criticism) in biblical interpretation and (2) interaction with philosophical schools in order to craft a theological framework.

Francis Martin, for example, has written a brief work entitled *Baptism in the Holy Spirit: A Scriptural Foundation*.[34] A reader accustomed to the nontechnical approaches found in classial Pentecostal and nearly all Protestant charismatic treatments of Spirit-baptism will be not a little surprised to find references to the "synoptic tradition," to parallels at Qumran and Nag Hammadi, and to Luke's Pentecost narrative in Acts 2 as a "composite event . . . a theologico-literary procedure . . . described as the construction of a 'paradigm event.' "[35] And this all from an undoubted charismatic. *The positive use of biblical critical methodologies, assumptions, and results (without the negative consequences often accompanying that enterprise) occurs most readily among Roman Catholics within the total span of Pentecostal and charismatic scholarship.*

Only two Catholic charismatic works, to my knowledge, could in any sense be taken to reflect a systematic theological intent. Heribert Mühlen, who teaches systematic theology at the Universtiy of Paderborn in West Germany, published in 1978 *A Charismatic Theology*.[36] This volume is a "coursebook" consisting of two seven-week series—one of lectures for understanding, the other of guidance for prayer. The work is intended as a course of study for charismatic parish renewal. It is reminiscent of Ignatius Loyola's *Spiritual Exercises*, a written-to-be-read plan for renewal. The work is not really a systematic theology at all.[37] Yet the work parallels Myer Pearlman's *Knowing the Doctrines* in a certain sense: it is readable and free of jargon, it builds upon basic Christian experience. But the differences between Mühlen and Pearlman greatly exceed their similarities.

Both parts of Professor Mühlen's course start with "meaning" (meaning invigorates life and must withstand death), move through God, preparation (sin, fear, confession), Jesus Christ, the church, spiritual gifts, to conclude with discernment (charismatic balance). All this is a sort of systematic theology of renewed Christian experience, and for that reason, Mühlen's work should not be judged as something for which it was not intended.[38]

In fact, there may well never be a comprehensive systematic theology from a Roman Catholic charismatic perspective. That church enjoys a long-standing systematic tradition, one highly informed by the Roman location of ultimate religious authority in tradition rather than Scripture. And the regard for emerging tradition yields an accumulative corpus of community theology that needs no updates from any perspective beyond Rome itself.

What *is* feasible in Roman Catholic charismatic theology is typified in the work of Jesuit scholar Donald Gelpi, especially his major work entitled *Experiencing God: A Theology of Human Emergence*.[39] This volume is difficult but rewarding to read. In the author's words in a later book, *Experiencing God* explores "in some detail the psychodynamics of Christian conversion."[40]

In his book Fr. Gelpi crafts a decidedly charismatic theology for a specific religious group in a defined geographic region, which reflects his concept of the task of theology as derived from Bernard Lonergan. A student of the American philosophical tradition, he knows well the Yankee intellectual tradition from Franklin, Paine, and Edwards to William James, Dewey, Santayana, and Whitehead. In these he finds *experience* to be a sort of American intellectual theme, accounting as well for the individualism of the region.

By linking this American philosophic tradition with the ideas of the Canadian Catholic Bernard Lonergan, Fr. Gelpi constructs a theology that is decidedly Roman Catholic, North American, and charismatic. In truth, we have here a sort of heavyweight theological probe—not a systematic theology, nor even one solely biblical in method.

As a sample of his creativity, Gelpi defines conversion quite differently from the way other Pentecostal or charismatic theologians do. He allows that one may be converted morally, but not yet intellectually—or esthetically or affectively. Bizarre and immature actions of Christians might be explained by such "partial conversions."

Thus, theological style reaches its most technical, abstract, philosophical level in the Roman Catholic charismatic sector. There, sophisticated critical models of biblical interpretation are blended with very learned philosophic theology—still with a fundamental recognition of individual glossolalic experience.

CHARISMATIC THEOLOGY IN THE "THIRD WAVE"

C. Peter Wagner of Fuller Seminary applied the phrase "Third Wave" to describe what I have come to call the Pentecostalization of evangelicalism. Evangelicals—the last major sector of the church at large to be affected by the charismatic movement—as a whole keep a careful distance from younger sibling Pentecostals. The "Third Wave" terminology, now also adopted by church statistician David B. Barrett, describes evangelicals who see themselves as neither Pentecostal nor charismatic but who believe and act like them.

The Third Wave is too young as a movement to come near to producing anything like a systematic theology. But it has produced a literature that in genre—namely, personal testimony—repeats the first publications of the classical Pentecostals, the Protestant neo-Pentecostals, and the Roman Catholic charismatics. In the beginning come testimonies.

Several personal stories from these charismaticized evangelicals have emerged. C. Peter Wagner, who is a sort of anchor to the movement, maps its growth in his book *The Third Wave of the Holy Spirit: Encountering the Power of Signs and Wonders To-day.*[41] John Wimber's *Power Evangelism*[42] followed by *Power Healing*[43] mingle testimony of a former rock musician and sometime Quaker with popular exposition and rationale. Wimber leads the rapidly growing Vineyard church movement. Kevin Springer's volume *Power Encounters Among Christians in the Western World*[44] gathers testimonies from a variety of persons who have been affected by John Wimber's beliefs, which include a plea to regularize front and center in Christian assemblies the supernatural aspects, "signs and wonders," so markedly characteristic of the Gospels.

In rapid order have come committed and supportive expositions of the new evangelical supernaturalism from such academic professionals as psychiatrist John White (*When the Spirit Comes With Power: Signs and Wonders Among God's People*),[45] anthropologist Charles Kraft—whose conversion to the Third Wave has been profound (*Christianity With Power: Your World-view and Your Experience of the Supernatural*),[46] and pastor-theologian Don Williams (*Signs, Wonders, and the Kingdom of God: A Biblical Guide for the Reluctant Skeptic*).[47] Of these works, Williams proposes a completed theology of the Kingdom of God to warrant the realization of signs and wonders. Kraft speaks from a global worldview, talks of a needed paradigm shift, and worries about the sufficiency and myopia of the Western cultural outlook.

As for the theological style of this late-breaking Third Wave, the Bible is taken very seriously and at face value—just as in classical Pentecostalism and among most Protestant charismatics. Buoyant, life-changing, paradigm-shifting individual experience figures promi-nently. Third-wavers, as a whole, are better trained than classical Pentecostals and at least equally as competent as the declared Protestant charismatics.

The high incidence of the word power in these third-wave titles declares another round in the politics of theological adjectives. (Are "*turbo*-Christians " next?) "Power" expresses the heart of the third-wave mission—to recapture and to cause to resurface within the evangelical tradition the visibility of the miraculous in everyday Christianity. "Power" was, for classical Pentecostals, the consequence of the baptism in the Holy Spirit. In the emerging charismaticized evangelicalism, however, "power" serves to sum up the whole impact of renewal Christian life. Moreover, the prime movers in the third wave have been persons of global cross-cultural experience, who have had their packaged American theologies tested by the realities of third-world cultures that never did give up beliefs in spirits, ancestors, and the unseen world.[48]

Thus, theological style across the Pentecostal and charismatic movements shows a breadth of variety that may well exceed that in any other family of Christians. Although Pentecostals have become institutionalized (and, in rare instances, charismatics as well), developments since the late 1970s argue that Pentecostalism has become a widespread Christian lifestyle nurtured not least by religious television and has become increasingly apparent across the entire range of the church. David Barrett's figures, in fact, disclose that the number of Pentecostals and charismatics, embracing both the established Pentecostal churches worldwide and those in other denominations committed to charismatic values and practices, actually exceeds the total number in the whole of Protestantism.[49]

The conclusions reached in this sketch of theological style can be summarized as follows:[50]

1. *Classical Pentecostals* are reluctant theologians. They express their truest theology in oral features of their spirituality—singing, testimonies, lively preaching. When they have done written theology, the products are often *imitative* and *isolationist*. Themes and approaches often reflect, in North American examples at least, the contexts of Scofieldian dispensationalism and American fundamentalism. Cues and catchphrases are at times absorbed from intra-evangelical theological debate, though Pentecostals as a whole are not fluent and facile in theological controversy.

That the doctrinal works come more often from esteemed pastors who have been denominational administrators (Ernest Williams, Duffield and Van Cleve, Pruitt, Brewster) than from Bible college professors (Pearlman, Horton) is a sociological comment on the role of pastoral authority in classical Pentecostalism.

Classical Pentecostals, at least among those in North America, make a nontechnical face-value use of Scripture. That the exact words "baptism in the Holy Spirit" (using the *noun* form "baptism") do not occur in Scripture seems to have been unnoticed and unimportant to Pentecostals, even though they so highly value the Bible. Often, a simple apologetic based on historical precedent is presented to communicate the fresh personal encounter with the Holy Spirit.

As the Pentecostal movement approaches its fourth generation, its scholarly efforts are moving beyond simple Bible exposition and denominational histories (we are now seeing regional and even local histories of Pentecostal churches as well as major critical biographies). A few more technical biblical studies are emerging and, especially in Europe, the first throughgoing theological dissertations have appeared.

2. *Protestant charismatics*, as Professor Lederle clearly shows, range from transplanted Pentecostalists to denominationally contextualized and sacramentally conceived charismatic overlays. The range and style of theologizing here is broader than that characteristic of any of the other three sectors.

3. *Roman Catholic charismatics* leave undisturbed the intricate and highly developed theological texture of Scripture and tradition that marks that body of Christians. Unlike the other phases of the movements here examined, Roman Catholic scholars doing charismatic theology easily move within the loftiest levels of critical biblical scholarship. Speaking in tongues, in the Roman tradition, does not wipe out form criticism. The highly developed body of traditional Catholic doctrine makes it unnecessary to rush to press with a systematic theology that bears a charismatic accent. At the same time, the ample theological resources of the Roman tradition, coupled with the high value put on theological inquiry there, have yielded the most insightful and thoroughgoing charismatic theological writings so far published.

4. *Third-wave neosupernatural evangelicals*, whose recent origin sharply contrasts with Roman Catholic antiquity, are at the initial stage of personal testimony of renewed individual spirituality. Since for the most part the representatives are professional academics, their testimonies put scholarship to the service of renewal by springing from revitalized personal experience to exploratory theological essays incorporating the vantage point of their several professional fields.

It seems safe to conclude that Pentecostal theology, with its many faces and varied accents, is here to stay and to grow. It will be intriguing to see the environmental impact of these new and vigorous theologies of the Holy Spirit on the changing ecclesiastical landscape of the third millennium about to dawn.

NOTES

[1]From the publisher's blurb on the book jacket of the *Dictionary of Pentecostal and Charismatic Movements*, ed. Stanley M. Burgess and Gary B. McGee (Grand Rapids: Zondervan, 1988). This volume, hereafter abbreviated *DPCM*, is indispensable for the study of these movements.

[2]"Implicit Values in Pentecostal Missions," *Missiology: An International Review* 16 (October 1988): 409–24; "Spirituality, Pentecostal and Charismatic," *DPCM*, 804–9.

[3]Reliance only on published materials seriously flaws Frederick D. Bruner's critique, *A Theology of the Holy Spirit: The Pentecostal Experience and the New Testament Witness* (Grand Rapids: Eerdmans, 1970). From such sources he concludes a "doctrine of conditions for the baptism in the Holy Spirit" (pp. 87–117). Such a "doctrine" is more his own construction than that of the Pentecostals, for whom any listing of "conditions" is far more homiletic and hortatory than creedal or doctrinal. I have seen published reports about the Assemblies of God as a church of conscientious objectors, which was true in the main until World War II. But the official constitution and by-laws were not changed until 1967. Analysts therefore who limited themselves to official printed documents could thank only their neglect of the oral tradition for a flawed statement of reality. Times change. And they and the oral tradition change often long before official documents catch up.

[4]Donald W. Dayton, *Theological Roots of Pentecostalism*, "Studies in Evangelicalism, No. 5" (Metuchen, N.J.: Scarecrow; Grand Rapids: Zondervan, 1987).

[5]Ibid., 174.

[6]"From 'Christian Perfection' to the 'Baptism of the Holy Ghost,' " in Vinson Synan, ed., *Aspects of Pentecostal Origins* (Plainfield, N.J.: Logos International, 1975), 48.

[7]Myer Pearlman, *Knowing the Doctrines of the Bible* (Springfield, Mo.: Gospel Publishing House, 1937). Some details on Pearlman's life are given by his widow, Irene P. Pearlman, *Myer Pearlman and His Friends* (Springfield, Mo.: Privately published by Irene Pearlman, 1953).

[8]P. C. Nelson, *Bible Doctrines* (1934; rev. ed., Springfield, Mo.: Gospel Publishing House, 1948). A new revision was made in 1971 by J. Roswell Flower and Anthony D. Palma to adjust to changes in the doctrinal statement made in 1961.

[9]It is not widely known that the original "Statement of Fundamental Truths" adopted in 1916 contained seventeen, not the present sixteen, numbered points. The seventeenth point was an elaborate reaffirmation of the doctrine of the Trinity; it was written to counter the "Jesus' Name" belief that led to the drafting of a doctrinal statement. By 1920, this point had been absorbed, without other substantial change, under the third point (doctrine of God) where it has since remained. There were also over the years slight but substantial (and some inadvertent) changes in the language of the Statement.

[10]Ernest Williams, *Systematic Theology* (Springfield, Mo.: Gospel Publishing House, 1953). Few figures are so highly revered in the Assemblies of God as the saintly Ernest S. Williams. Not theologically trained, Williams came from poor origins and served as a pastor in Philadelphia. Always respected as a gentle, humble, and unassuming person, Williams preferred a simple lifestyle that spun off its own set of stories. He would take trains, not flights, to save denominational money. When he was in his 90s, living as a resident in a

denominational home for aged ministers, a group of concerned patients, staff, and friends noticed that he always wore the same trousers. They decided to buy him some new clothes. Greeted with the announced intent, the story goes, Williams replied, "Now what would an old man like me do with two pairs of trousers?" Quite a contrast with stories about Assemblies of God leaders who emerged from the television ministry scandals of 1987–88.

[11]Guy P. Duffield and Nathan M. Van Cleve, *Foundations of Pentecostal Theology* (Los Angeles: L.I.F.E. Bible College, 1983).

[12]Raymond M. Pruitt, *Fundamentals of the Faith* (Cleveland, Tenn.: White Wing, 1981). In the name genre lies *Pentecostal Doctrine* (Chaltenham, UK: Grenehurst Press, 1976), edited by Percy S. Brewster, former secretary-general of the British body known as the Elim Pentecostal Church.

[13]Ibid., 2.

[14]Henry I. Lederle, *Treasures Old and New: Interpretations of "Spirit Baptism"* in the Charismatic Renewal Movement (Peabody, Mass.: Hendrickson, 1988), 185.

[15]Harold Lindsell, *The Battle for the Bible* (Grand Rapids: Zondervan, 1976).

[16]A recent book that futher illustrates Pentecostal theological style is Donald Lee Barnett and Jeffrey P. MacGregor, *Speaking in Other Tongues: A Scholarly Defense* (Seattle: Community Chapel Publications, 1980). The dust cover of this work of 840 pages describes it as "the most comprehensive work ever produced on the baptism in the Holy Spirit and speaking in tongues." But it was possible to complete such a work without attention to James Dunn's monograph, *Baptism in the Holy Spirit: A Re-examination of the New Testament Teaching on the Gift of the Spirit in Relation to Pentecostalism Today* (London: SCM, 1975). We have to call this theological isolation, whatever else it may be.

[17]Stanley M. Horton, *What the Bible Teaches About the Holy Spirit* (Springfield, Mo.: Gospel Publishing House, 1976). Someone should write a history of book titles that surprised their authors. Horton told me he was not consulted about this wording. Similarly, F. F. Bruce reported that the title *Paul the Apostle of the Heart Set Free* (Grand Rapids: Eerdmans, 1977) was not his own choice, and, worse, a reviewer cited use of the word *heart* in a non-Pauline sense (Laurel and Ward Gasque, "Saint Paul, Apostle of Freedom for Women and Men: An Interview with F. F. Bruce," *Priscilla Papers* 3, 2 [Spring 1988]:3). Two books written by the late William Sanford LaSor, were published with rather sensational titles other than those submitted by the author: *Amazing Dead Sea Scrolls and the Christian Faith* (Chicago: Moody, 1956) and *The Truth About Armageddon* (Grand Rapids: Baker, 1987).

[18]For more information on this society, see *DPCM*, 793–94.

[19]The first scholars to rise in a maturing sectarian tradition, it seems, are historians. Then come exegetes. Finally, I would guess, the systematicians and the ethicists appear.

[20]At the risk of omission, I name Gordon Fee at Regent College, Vancouver; Larry Hurtado at the University of Manitoba; and Gerald Sheppard at Immanuel College in Toronto. These, I think it fair to say, are to date the most technically published Pentecostal scholars in the biblical field. What should be concluded from the fact that they are all expatriated Americans teaching in Canada?

[21]Again with risk (and apologies where due) I name Harold Hunter, whose Fuller Seminary Ph.D. thesis sought to engage the contemporary exegetical field. Yugoslav Pentecostal Miroslav Volf completed, in 1986, a thesis at Tübingen under Jürgen Moltmann on the concept of work in Marx. I continue to believe that Third World sources may yield a Pentecostal systematic

theology unencumbered with the fundamentalist and evangelical preoccupations of American Pentecostalism. But a systematic for the North American scene is still needed, too.

[22]This seminary (the Charles H. Mason Theological Seminary, which was established by the Church of God in Christ) shares in the umbrella accreditation of the Interdenominational Theological Center by the Association of Theological Schools.

[23]Maybe not countless. Statistician David B. Barrett counted nearly 21,000 separate Christian denominations, or the equivalent, around the world. See his *World Christian Encyclopedia* (New York: Oxford University Press, 1982), 3, with annual updates in the January issues of the *International Bulletin for Missionary Research*.

[24]Lederle knowingly reverses the order of "old" and "new," from the textual order at Matthew 13:52 in order to make the point that the charismatic renewal adds to the old traditions (orthodox doctrines) new affirmations (charisms, renewed piety). That he so easily reverses a biblical text lets me try for a point of my own: mainline charismatic Protestant theologians show more interest in systematic coherence than in minute exegesis. Later, I will venture the point that Roman Catholic charismatic theologians tend to be multicompetent: they bring highly developed technical exegtical skills to the service of focused systematization. A Roman Catholic theologian, I think, would be less likely to use for a book title a biblical phrase in reversed order. *Treasures* is based on a doctoral thesis completed by Lederle at the University of South Africa. In 1990 Prof. Lederle joined the faculty of Oral Roberts University in Tulsa, Oklahoma.

[25](Grand Rapids: Zondervan, 1988). I am grateful to the author, who provided me with a draft copy of a portion of the second volume of this work. Williams' *Renewal Theology* was not available to Lederle when he wrote *Treasures*, which included (pp. 90–94) an analysis of Williams' views on Spirit-baptism. Both works were published in 1988. The second volume of Williams' work appeared in early 1990. It will cover, as the subtitle indicates, "Salvation, the Holy Spirit, and Christian Living." A third and final volume—treating the church, the kingdom, and last things—is in preparation.

[26]Ibid., 11–12.

[27]These are not inconsiderable. Apart from published articles in journals and encyclopedias and papers prepared for use in ecumenical dialogue, Williams published in the year of his personal renewal *Contemporary Existentialism and Christian Faith* (Englewood Cliffs, N.J.: Prentice-Hall, 1965). His systematic interests were even earlier apparent in a privately published volume entitled *Ten Major Doctrines of Christianity* (Rockford, Ill.: Privately published, 1959; reprinted as *10 Teachings* [Carol Stream: Creation House, 1974]). Williams' charismatic theology began with the *Era of the Spirit* (Plainfield, N.J.: Logos International, 1971), which reviews the role of the Holy Spirit in Barth, Brunner, Bultmann, and Tillich. The next year previously published articles were gathered as *The Pentecostal Reality* (Plainfield, N.J.: Logos International, 1972).

[28]J. Rodman Williams, *The Gift of the Holy Spirit Today* (Plainfield, N.J.: Logos International, 1980).

[29]Lederle, *Treasures*, 94.

[30]Williams, *Renewal Theology*, 1:12.

[31]Ibid., 21–28.

[32]Ibid., 98.

[33]Among topics for the next six-year segment of the International Roman

Catholic-Pentecostal Dialogue (1990–1995) will be missions and evangelization, including mutual proselytism.

[34]Francis Martin, *Baptism in the Holy Spirit: A Scriptural Foundation* (Stubenville, Oh.: Fransiscan University Press, 1986). This work is a "revised English version" of "Le baptême dans l'Esprit: tradition du Nouveau Testament et vie de l'Eglise," *Nouvelle revue théologique* 106 (1984): 23–58.

[35]Ibid., 18–19.

[36]Heribert Mühlen, *A Charismatic Theology: Initiation in the Spirit* (London: Burns and Oates; New York: Paulist Press, 1978).

[37]Lederle (p. 181) approvingly refers to Simon Tugwell's surprise that the title of the book, originally *Einübung in die Christliche Grunderfahrung*, ever got translated as *Charismatic Theology*, since Mühlen is at pains to make a churchwide reference to renewal and to avoid the sectarian implications of a distinctively "charismatic" theology; Simon Tugwell, "Faith and Experience I: The Problems of Catholic Pentecostalism," *New Blackfriars* 59 (August 1978): 360.

[38]Mühlen, in the assessment of Lederle (p. 180), has provided "the most advanced form yet of the integration of charismatic theology into the structures of established Christianity." It is a pity that Mühlen's major theological works have not been put into English from German (for a partial list, see Lederle, *Treasures*, 254–55).

[39]Donald Gelpi, *Experiencing God: A Theology of Human Emergence* (New York: Paulist Press, 1978). This book has been reviewed by R. Spittler, *Agora* 3 (Winter 1980): 21–28. An easier entry to Gelpi's writings is his *Charisma and Sacrament: A Theology of Christian Conversion* (New York: Paulist Press, 1976). *The Divine Mother: A Trinitarian Theology of the Holy Spirit* (Lanham, MD: University Press of America, 1984), along with *Experiencing God* and *Charisma and Sacrament* made a sort of esoteric trilogy; but, in the author's own view, the three illumine each other and were conceived together but need not be read in any particular sequence. Two earlier works are readable presentations of his thought, coupled with characteristic pastoral concerns: *Pentecostalism: A Theological Viewpoint* (New York: Paulist Press, 1971) and *Pentecostal Piety* (New York: Paulist Press, 1972).

[40]*The Divine Mother*, viii.

[41]C. Peter Wagner, *The Third Wave of the Holy Spirit: Encountering the Power of Signs and Wonders Today* (Ann Arbor: Servant Publications, 1988).

[42]John Wimber, *Power Evangelism* (San Francisco: Harper & Row, 1986).

[43]John Wimber, *Power Healing* (San Francisco: Harper & Row, 1987).

[44]Kevin Springer, *Power Encounters Among Christians in the Western World* (San Francisco: Harper & Row, 1988).

[45]John White, *When the Spirit Comes with Power: Signs and Wonders Among God's People* (Downers Grove, Ill.: InterVarsity, 1988).

[46]Charles Kraft, *Christianity with Power: Your Worldview and Your Experience of the Supernatural* (Ann Arbor: Servant Publications, 1989).

[47]Don Williams, *Signs, Wonders, and the Kingdom of God: A Biblical Guide for the Reluctant Skeptic* (Ann Arbor: Servant Publications, 1989).

[48]Paul Hiebert gives an eminently sensible description of Western cultural shortsightedness in his analysis in "The Flaw of the Excluded Middle," *Missiology: An International Review* 10 (January 1982): 35–47.

[49]"Annual Statistical Table on Global Mission: 1989," *International Bulletin of Missionary Research* 13 (January 1989): 20–21. He reports, for mid-1988, about 351 million Pentecostals and charismatics and about 318 million Protestants (not including 53 million Anglicans, who officially eschew the term "Protestant").

[50]This chapter has focused on theological work of the "systematic" sort. An expense of that limitation has been the omission of theologians whose work did not aim at comprehensive systematic statement. Not treated here, for example, has been the impact of classical Pentecostal writer Donald Gee and Roman Catholic theologian Kilian McDonnell. Though neither has attempted a systematic theology, both show a profound allegiance to their heritages coupled with a keen realization of the larger church. Both do a pragmatic ecumenical theology that links the conservative cores of their traditions with the larger work of God in the world. Both are highly competent within the ethos of their own churches. Both make of theology an instrument, not an aim. Both are preeminently ecumenical pastoral theologians. On the Protestant charismatic side, I also have left untreated Howard M. Ervin, of Baptist heritage. In his writing, he has forthrightly engaged the work of James Dunn. I am wistful about the omission of these writers, among others, in a review of theological style.

Part III

DOING THEOLOGY TODAY: OTHER SIGNIFICANT APPROACHES

12

REACHING FOR FIDELITY: ROMAN CATHOLIC THEOLOGY TODAY

STEPHEN BEVANS
CATHOLIC THEOLOGICAL UNION,
CHICAGO, ILLINOIS

THE VISION OF CATHOLICISM

"I regard the *analogia entis* as the intention of Antichrist, and I think that because of it one cannot become Catholic. Whereupon I at the same time allow myself to regard all other possible reasons for not becoming Catholic, as shortsighted and lacking in seriousness."[1] These are the famous words of Karl Barth written in 1932 in the Foreword to Volume I of *Church Dogmatics*. Barth mitigated this judgment somewhat toward the end of his life in the essay "The Humanity of God" and in his message of reconciliation to Emil Brunner;[2] and Catholic theologians would certainly deny that they work on a principle devised by the Antichrist. But in his basic intuition Barth was correct: the essence of Catholicism is the *analogia entis*, the analogy of being.

As important as the Petrine ministry is for Catholics, as important as is tradition and reason, as important as is the role of Mary in Catholic and devotional life, none of these really hold the key to what being a Catholic means; they are all derivative. The principle on which Catholicism stands or falls is rather the conviction that the world, the human person, and human experience in the world is a plus and not a minus, that finite reality of any kind has a capacity to be diaphanous of infinite meaning and a bearer of God's revelation. And this is why, to do Catholic theology, one must first of all be possessed of an "analogical imagination." One's basic worldview, in other words, must be one that can perceive "the profound similarities-in-difference in all reality," and can see in the individual and the particular the "disclosure of radical, all pervasive grace."[3]

Sacramentality

What is perhaps a less cumbersome and more accessible way of describing the genius of Catholicism is to speak in terms of its basic *sacramental* principle. The Catholic vision, writes Richard McBrien in the conclusion to his *Catholicism*, is one that discovers God in and through the things of this world. "The visible, the tangible, the finite, the historical—all these are actual or potential carriers of the divine presence. Indeed, it is only in and through these material realities that we can even encounter the invisible God."[4] A sacramental perspective is one in which the secular can reveal the sacred, the immanent can reveal the transcendent, the particular and partial can reveal the unity of the whole. A person, an event, or an object is clearly not to be identified with the divine—identification is a danger of the sacramental perspective and, as Protestants (Barth!) have pointed out, it can end in an un-Christian and unbiblical idolatry. But at certain graced times and in certain graced circumstances these created realities can manifest the power and glory of their creator. Julian of Norwich's conviction of God's universal love in her vision of "something smaller, no bigger than a hazelnut," Oliver Plunkett's ability to see Christ's blood on the rose, and Gerard Manley Hopkins' sense that "the world is charged with the grandeur of God" are all eloquent expressions of a perspective that regards creation as a mystery, and so "imbued with the hidden presence of God."[5]

If one understands this fundamental sacramental principle, one has come a long way in understanding Catholicism both as a social phenomenon and as a point of departure for doing theology. It is because of sacramentality that Catholicism values worship that appeals to every sense; and it is because of the same sacramental worldview that Catholics can profit from devotion to Mary as well as from activism for world peace or the right to life. Naturally, ceremony can become an end in itself, Mariology can become "Mariolatry," and social activism can become mere humanism; but Catholics accept such a risk because they are convinced of the truth of the underlying principle that "transcendence can be, and most appropriately is, symbolized in and mediated through sensible realities."[6]

This chapter will address in more detail below how the sacramental worldview provides the key for Roman Catholic theological method, but we might anticipate a bit of that development here. Because of Catholicism's belief that God's saving presence is mediated through the ordinary, the material, the human, Catholics can place great emphasis not only on the book of the church, the Bible (the Word of God in words of women and men) but also on the church itself as a sacramental reality, visible and invisible, both human and divine.[7] In a real sense, Schleiermacher's twenty-fourth thesis in *The Christian Faith* is right. Catholics do believe that one's relationship to Christ does depend on one's relation to the church.[8] But this is not because of any idolatry; it is because the church is believed in as a sacrament, "a sign and instrument of communion with God and of unity among all" (LG#1). From the understanding of the sacramental nature of the church it is a small but logical step for Catholics to understand that the church's tradition, particularly as articulated in the papal and espicopal ministry of teaching (Magisterium), must be taken with utmost seriousness both as a source and a judge of theology. And with the same sacramental point of view one can see why Catholic theology places such a premium on the role of reason in theological expression[9] and why it is concerned, especially today, with the construction of a theology that takes seriously history, culture, and the need for social justice.[10]

Catholicity

The perception of the sacramental nature of created reality is also the key to understanding the word Catholic. To be a Catholic (from the Greek *kata holos*, "according to the whole") means to be radically open to "all truth and value."[11] Nothing that is truly good and really valuable can be excluded, for everything that is genuine can be a manifestation of the divine, and the divine reaches out to embrace all that is genuine. What this means is that every person, every nation, every culture, every race is included in the church because each has not only something to gain, but something to give as well.

It is because of this catholicity in all its richness of meaning that there exists a tolerance in the church, both in terms of quality of membership and plurality of theological expression.

Catholicism is all-embracing, as inclusive as Jesus himself. The opposite of "catholic" is not really "Protestant"; it is rather a sectarianism that insists on only one way of being Christian or doing theology. As Rosemary Haughton writes, catholicity means being open "not only to the highest but to the lowest, the repulsive, the self-hating; it can never be the cult of the beautiful, which is why it is not for the religious connoisseurs or the seekers after fulfillment."[12]

There have always been a number of "schools" of theology within the Catholic tradition, and sometimes they have been in rather bitter opposition to each other: witness the Molinist-Thomist controversy over the question of grace and freedom. Of equal significance is the existence in the Roman communion of a number of "rites" (Roman, Milanese, Ukranian, Melchite, Maronite, and most recently Zairean—to name a few). Within these groups not only the style of worship differs; the style of theologizing differs as well. Today, as the church begins critically to appropriate modernity's discovery of subjectivity and history, the plurality of theological expression has become even more evident. There have emerged African and Asian theologies, Latin American, feminist, African American, and Hispanic theologies of liberation, and theologies based on philosophies that represent a genuine departure from the Aristotelianism that had become (but only from the twelfth century!) the traditional basis for Catholic theologizing. The tolerance demanded by catholicity has not always been put into practice, and Catholicism cannot deny a history of Inquisitions, cultural insensitivity, and active cooperation with European colonial designs. But these moments of intolerance must be looked upon as moments of betrayal of catholicity rather than as expressions of it. As Rosemary Haughton writes, Catholicism is "the attempt to integrate the whole of human life in the search for the kingdom of God";[13] and, as Stephen Happel and David Tracy point out, when this attempt has failed, "Catholicism has cheated itself of its own universality."[14]

Catholicity has been characterized as having a "both-and" character, in contrast to Protestantism's "either-or."[15] While a key word in Protestantism is the intensive *solus* (alone), Catholicism's word is the comprehensive *et* (and). Catholicism emphasizes therefore faith *and* works, Scripture *and* tradition, Christ *and* Mary, the human *and* the divine, God *and* humanity, the sacred *and* the secular, spiritual *and* material, nature *and* grace. It is not a question of authority *or* freedom, but authority nurturing freedom. It is not a question of past *tradita* opposed to and preventing contemporary expression, but the present against the background of the past, giving the present more depth. Unity is not opposed to diversity, and it is not achieved by uniformity. Rather, true unity flourishes when diversity can be expressed. It is the tensive character of this "both-and," as we will see below, that provides the ideal and the challenge to Catholics as they do theology today.

Critical Realism

In his keynote address to the 1974 convention of the Catholic Theological Society of America, John J. Connelley tried to answer the question "Is there a Catholic theology?" by laying down several principles that shape theological reflection in a Catholic context.[16] Besides a sacramental principle that emphasizes the way the invisible is represented by the visible, and a dogmatic principle that emphasizes the role of authority in Catholic theology, Connelley proposes a third, *philosophical* principle. This philosophical principle is not the mere observation that one needs philosophy in order to do theology; rather, Connelley insists that the Catholic vision, rooted as it is in a sacramental worldview that takes the whole of reality with utmost seriousness, needs a philosophy to underpin and undergird what it articulates theologically. Connelley speaks of this philosophical principle in terms of a Catholic realism, but it is perhaps better known in philosophical terms as *critical* realism.

As Connelley expresses it, Catholic theology is based on the underlying philosophical conviction that our theological expressions, as much as they are products of various cultural and historical influences, express nevertheless what is objectively true; they are not just objectifications of mere subjective affections. Richard McBrien has explained this principle under the rubric of *Christian* realism, and says that this critical realism is a position that avoids both the extremes of naïve realism or raw empircism on the one hand and idealism on the other. Precisely because of its foundational principle of sacramentality, Catholicism holds that all knowledge, including the knowledge of God in revelational encounter, is an experience mediated by one's individual and cultural/historical context, but one also that is objective, and empirically and rationally verifiable.[17]

While the position of critical realism is the *foundation* of the sacramental principle, the comprehensiveness of catholicity and the "both-and" character of the Catholic worldview, it also functions to bring to light several important aspects of Catholic theological method. Since critical realism avoids any näive notion that reality is wholly "out there already," any idea of a ready-made revelation or system of doctrines can find no real home within the Catholic vision. A fundamentalism, therefore, that believes only because "it's written in the Bible" or "taught by the church" is radically unacceptable to Catholic thinking or theological reflection. Similarly, a dogmatism that reads the tradition uncritically or obeys authority unthinkingly is—contrary to wide popular conception—profoundly un-Catholic. On the other hand, however, since the Catholic vision eschews idealism, even in its critical form, any thinking and theology that do not grapple with the concrete biblical word, with particular teaching and traditions of the past and with the legitimate claims of church authority, is thinking and theological reflection that cannot be called Catholic either. Critical realism is a philosophical position that takes seriously all of reality, the human *and* divine, the material *and* the spiritual. And it is convinced that our partial and always inadequate knowledge is still real knowledge. Critical realism knows that our knowledge does not provide a photograph of reality, but it does provide real insight into reality. And so, rather than a photograph, our knowledge provides a map. And although maps are not the reality itself, they do get us where we want to go.[18]

Incarnation

The philosophical principle of critical realism is the foundation for the principles of sacramentality and catholicity, and it gives shape to the way Catholics approach their life in general and the doing of theology in particular. Undergirding this philosophical principle, however, is a further, properly *theological* principle of Incarnation. Jesus Christ, Word made flesh (John 1:14), truly God and truly human (DS 301), is ultimately the reason for the sacramental and catholic worldview. It is through Jesus' particularity—this person, of a specific height and weight, of a specific hair color and blood type, an Aramaic-speaking Jewish male in Roman-occupied Palestine during the reign of Tiberius—that believers have, from the very beginning, experienced as the full revelation of God. Because Jesus' humanity has revealed to us the fullness of divinity, theologians speak of Jesus as the sacrament. "There is no other sacrament of God than Christ," wrote Augustine.[19] Jesus is the primoridal sacrament, the "sacrament of the encounter with God" (Edward Schillebeeckx).

The whole history of the development of classical Christology, from Nicea through the Councils of Constantinople and Ephesus to the Council of Chalcedon, is not simply a game of "getting the facts straight" or getting the doctrine right. Rather, Christology developed as a struggle to maintain the balance that Incarnation demands: Jesus is truly God, not merely a creature, and so in Jesus we have truly met God; Jesus is not two separate identities, and so humanity (wondrously) has a real role to play in its own salvation (this is symbolized by the doctrine that Mary is truly *theotokos*); Jesus has a fully human soul, and so God really has emptied Godself, and has entered fully into human history. Jesus is both human and divine: the human is the vehicle for the expression of divinity, and the divinity has shown in the body and humanity of Jesus both the depth of God's love and the holiness and goodness of all that is created.

Catholicism claims nothing more than to take the Incarnation with utmost seriousness. It is, as Thomas F. O'Meara puts it, an intense form of faith in the Incarnation:

> Carthusian abbesses in mitre and stole, mischievous Peruvian acolytes in red cassocks carrying silver reliquaries with saints' bones and hair (none of which is older than the ninth century), . . . the novels of Graham Green or the short stories of Flannery O'Connor—these are figures in a procession whose source and goal are the one incarnation in many incarnations.[20]

And like the philosophical principle of critical realism, this theological principle of Incarnation has profound implications for Catholic theological method. Because God is manifested fully in the flesh of Jesus, nothing material and, a fortiori, truly human, can be incapable of leading men and women into relationship with God. Objects, events, or persons can become metaphors, analogies, or symbols of God's saving activity, and so can become partial but real tools for theological discourse. Persons and institutions can be invested with—if not total, then nevertheless real—holiness, and so must be respected and listened to. Human activity and human cultures can have real, if not ultimate, meaning, and so are able not only to be used as raw material for theological reflection, but also in themselves to reflect a ray of God's luminous truth. The Incarnation is more than a way of explaining who Jesus is—or a crude expression to be explained away. It is a symbol of the meaningfulness of human life in God's world and a cardinal principle of Catholic theologizing.

TENSIONS IN THE VISION

What has been presented so far in this chapter is what I have called the vision of Catholicism—Catholicism's ideal, the "idea" of what it means to be Catholic and do Catholic theology. It is to this vision, I believe, that the best of Catholicism and of Catholic theology attempts to be faithful, and it is because of these continued attempts at fidelity that Catholic theology has developed as such a rich tradition.

Real fidelity is a difficult enterprise, however, because the Catholic vision is one that contains an inbuilt tension. The Catholic "both-and," the analogical imagination of being able to see similarity in difference, is not something that is easily maintained, and history is witness to constant compromises and betrayals for the sake of clarity and simplicity—or for the maintenance of power. The Catholic vision is one that demands the constant work of integration, and it does not promise a success that is easily achieved.

In her study of the idea ("thing") of Catholicism, Rosemary Haughton often has recourse to the interplay between two allegorical figures, which she sketches at the beginning of her book,[21] and the tension in this interplay, Haughton maintains, is the tension that is built into the Catholic vision itself.

The first figure in the allegory Haughton names "Mother Church," and she is a figure who stands for all that is institutional, traditional, and visible in the church. Mother Church is deeply dedicated to her children and concerned about every detail of their welfare. She is a woman of long and deep experience, shocked no more by human wickedness, wise and full of many time-tested stories and proverbs. She is a wonderful housekeeper, and has made her home beautiful and her life rich with the art and music of the centuries. However, says Haughton, Mother Church has a shadow side. She sometimes—and rather often—is inclined to confuse her wisdom with God's will, and she cares so much for her children and knows them so well that she tends to make decisions "for their own good." She knows the past so well and has been nourished so much by it that she is suspicious of anything new, and often simply supresses it.

But Mother Church has a twin sister. Her name is "Sophia," the word for "wisdom" in Greek, but she is called many other names besides: Romantic Love, Mysticism, Superstition, Inspiration, Adventure, Imprudence, Sanctity, Folly. As these names imply, Sophia, like her sister, has both good and bad sides. She is a free spirit and wants everyone to be free; she prefers the new to the old, the risky to the tried and true, and the individual to the institution; but she is completely unpredictable and often irresponsible. "She also wrote and illustrated books which the children read instead of learning their lessons, and played the piano to them when they were supposed to be doing the dishes."

In many ways Mother Church and Sophia are opposites and often Mother Church in her pushy way would like to get Sophia out of the picture so that she could get on with providing what she knows is best. The truth is, though, and every once in a while even Mother Church acknowledges it, the two cannot get along without each other. Mother Church needs Sophia's freedom so she does not end up smothering her children; and Sophia needs Mother Church's discipline and experience so she will not make people totally confused and disordered. Strange as it may seem, the two sisters are really quite devoted to each other. The sad thing, says Haughton, is that their respective admirers do not always know this, and so they are always claiming one against the other instead of seeing the richness of the relationship that is beneath the surface.

The Catholic vision is one that emerges out of this "strange, yet essential" relationship between Mother Church and her twin sister Sophia: between institution and charism, authority and freedon, nature and grace, etc. It is a vision that bears within it an inherent tension, and the tension has often failed to be maintained. The Catholic church's respect for authority on the basis of its deep conviction that the visible and institutional can "re-present" the authority of Jesus can and has become an authoritarianism that takes no account of the shared dignity and responsibilities of the People of God (cf. LG#32). The need to be faithful to the past, based on the conviction of the need to provide an understanding of its unity has often been perverted into a positivism that cannot provide a "cogent understanding of the contemporary."[22] The sacramental world-view of the sensible and tactile can degenerate into an attitude of magic and superstition, the significance of culture for Christianity can become a "culture Christianity," and the value Catholicism places on human partnership with God can fall into an almost Pelagian "good works" mentality.

Despite all its tension, however, and despite all the failures, Catholics still believe that the vision is worth reaching for. After all, God did manifest Godself fully in and through a particular person, and so present, material, and human reality must have a meaning. The vision might be difficult to maintain, but in trying to be faithful to it Catholics can—and in some uncanny way do—manifest the true face of God.

It is this tension , this failure, and this continual reaching for fidelity that can explain the main characteristics of Roman Catholic theology and that can provide as well the key to understanding the diversity of theological opinion among Roman Catholic theologians today. The following section, therefore, will explore these characteristics and this diversity.

ROMAN CATHOLIC THEOLOGY TODAY: CHARACTERISTICS AND DIVERSITY

Rooted in the philosophical principle of critical realism and the theological principle of Incarnation, the sacramental, comprehensive, and "both-and" quality of the Catholic vision provides distinctive elements in Catholic theological method. As the Catholic does theology, therefore, she or he is attentive to the scriptural witness but is also in contact with its interpretation by the wisdom of tradition. Her or his guide to such wisdom will be the teaching of the church, in particular the teaching articulated in what has come to be called the papal and episcopal Magisterium. But as she or he listens to the church, the theologian must listen with a critical ear, aware of the cultural, historical, and even ideological conditionedness of doctrinal expression and of the contribution that can be made from her or his own historical and cultural situation and from the way that God is speaking in her or his contemporary experience. Only in this way, the contemporary Catholic theologian is convinced, one can do theology that is both appropriate to the Christian tradition and adequate to late twentieth-century experience.[23] In true Catholic form, Catholic theological method is one that attempts constantly to integrate Scripture and tradition, past and present, reason and faith, flesh and spirit, personal and communal experience.

Were space sufficient, a whole constellation of distinct Catholic theological characteristics could be singled out and reflected upon: the Catholic approach to Scripture, to tradition, to reason, to authority, to the person, to culture. In this necessarily introductory chapter, however, space allows me to focus on only one or two of them, hoping that a narrower focus that is a bit more in depth will be more useful than a more superficial general overview. Consequently, from among many possibilities I have singled out two elements characteristic of Catholic theology, both of which are under great discussion in Catholic theology today. I will treat first the question of the Catholic need to be faithful to what claims to be an infallible ecclesiastical Magisterium, and then I will speak of the need for Catholic theology today to be conscious of the historical, cultural, and ideological conditionedness of all theological expression.

As I discuss these two important characteristics of Catholic theology today, however, I want also to point out that the Catholic vision out of which these characteristics emerge is a vision that is in constant tension. It is because of this tension that we can distinguish various theological points of view, all of which vie with one another for ascendancy, but none of which really should ever have the claim of embodying the Catholic theology. And so in all areas of Catholic theology today, but I believe especially in the areas of Magisterial authority and historical/cultural diversity and ideological critique, Catholic theology today is possessed of an immense and basically healthy plurality. As long as these theological positions remain truly Catholic, they contribute to the overall theological effort of the church.

Magisterium

If there is a distinctive element of Catholic belief and theological method that immediately springs to mind, it would doubtlessly be the element of loyalty to the teaching office (Magisterium) of the church and, in particular, loyalty to the claim to the infallibility of the Roman Pontiff. To understand how this element actually functions in Catholic theological method, however, is often quite wrongly or naïvely understood.

One must read carefully the First Vatican Council's definition of papal infallibility.[24] When one does, one will see that, in the first place, the exercise of infallibility by the pope is highly restricted: it must be a solemn exercise as head of all Christians and articulator of the church's faith, restricted to matters that pertain directly to the Gospel. The negative form of the word further restricts papal exercise: the meaning is that a particular formula is "not wrong" or "immune from error."[25] In the second place, the careful reader will realize that "papal infallibility" is really an inaccurate way of phrasing the matter. If the pope meets all the conditions for defining a particular dogmatic matter, he is then endowed with the infallibility that Christ willed for the church. In other words, it is not really the pope who is infallible as such; rather, in solemn definitions the pope *articulates* the infallibility of the community of believers.

> It is the Church as a community which has been given the Spirit of truth which cannot fundamentally err in its understanding of the heart of the gospel. The Pope is infallible only insofar as he enunciates and proclaims the infallible faith of the whole Church, Catholic and non-Catholic. He is not infallible unto himself, in complete independence from the Church.[26]

It is this second observation in regard to papal infallibility that can serve as a point of departure for understanding the role of the teaching office of the church in Catholic theological method. It is the church that is infallible; infallibility is a gift given exclusively to the people of God as a whole.[27]

The church's claim to infallibility, in turn, rests on the Catholic principles of Incarnation, critical realism, and sacramentality: the church is not Christ, but the church is the body of Christ, a sacrament of God's continued incarnate presence in the world, among men and women (cf. LG#7–8). As Happel and Tracy put it, in the church "the unique saving action of Jesus is disclosed anew in the authentic actions of the past and present, the official authorities and ministries whithin the Church, and the worship of believers. In these social expressions, the incarnation of divinity has been extended until the end of history."[28]

Because of this infallibility with which the church is endowed, the church has the duty to preserve its original apostolic message by faithful teaching, occasional clarification, and, although rarely, solemn definition.[29] And in the Magisterium the bishops of the church united with the pope, or the pope in the name of the bishops of the church, articulate this duty of teaching, which is the duty, most properly, of the whole church.

Catholics, to put all of this another way, do not believe first in church authority or even in the church, and only then in the God of Jesus Christ. They believe first and foremost in the God revealed in Jesus—but they do this, they are convinced, not in a direct or unmediated way, but through the church, and even more concretely, through authorities in the church. The visible, the finite, the human is the vehicle of the invisible, the infinite, the divine.

But in regard to *how much* weight the visible, finite, and human should have, there is at present among Catholics much disagreement. What we might call the "right wing" position was articulated by Pope Pius XII in his 1950 encyclical *Humani Generis*, which held that the role of the Catholic theologian was to "show how what is taught by the living magisterium is found, whether explicitly or implicitly, in Sacred Scripture and divine Tradition" (DS 3886). While few Roman Catholic theologians would subscribe to this position today, it seems to be the underlying attitude to the Magisterium in groups like Catholics United for the Faith (C.U.F.F.), in newspapers like *The Wanderer* and *Twin Circle*, and even in some papal and curial attitudes. The opposite extreme would hold that the Magisterium has little right to say anything definitive. As I write this, however, I must say that I can think of no credible Catholic theologian who embodies this position. Hans Küng might be styled a "magisterial minimalist," and Charles Curran, like Küng, has gotten into trouble for what he considers responsible and faithful dissent from teachings that he considers noninfallible, but neither of these theologians, nor several others that could be mentioned, would deny in principle the need for papal and episcopal magisterial teaching. Both Rosemary Radford Ruether and Leonardo Boff can be highly critical of the Magisterium's teaching, but, again, neither would deny, I think, its right to teach.

The great majority of Catholic theologians can be spotted in the middle of the continuum that I have suggested. Some, like Edward Schillebeeckx or Karl Rahner, might be located a bit to the left; others, like Francis Sullivan or Gerald O'Collins, might locate themselves slightly to the right. But most Catholic theologians view the Magisterium with utmost seriousness and deep respect, and would subscribe wholeheartedly to the twelve theses on the relationship between the Magisterium and theologians proposed by the Vatican's International Theological Commission in 1976.[30]

The question of magisterial authority is certainly an aspect of Roman Catholic theology that reveals both what is distinctive in Catholic theological method and in what ways Catholic theologians differ among themselves. It is a question that is getting much attention today, both inside and outside the Catholic church. What is important to understand about it, however, is that it is a question of how to balance the various elements involved in the sacramental, comprehensive, incarnational worldview.

History and Culture

As Catholicism has begun to appropriate the turn to subjectivity demanded by modernity (and even by "postmodernity"), it is becoming more explicitly conscious of something that has always been present implicitly in its tradition but has not until recently been so clearly understood or appreciated. This new consciousness is of the role of historically conditioned culture and cultural change in the articulation of theology. From the fact of the various theologies present in the Bible, through the earliest theologians' move toward a theology in dialogue with Hellenistic culture and philosophical categories, to the highly culturally and historically conditioned emergence of the modern papacy, Catholic theology has come to see itself as a "history of local theologies."[31]

This discovery of the importance of culture and historical circumstances in the construction of theology is a discovery of another facet of Catholicism's vision of the analogical, sacramental nature of the world. It is because Catholic theology takes the human so seriously that it has been an expression of Christian faith that has changed and developed through the ages. As this has come into more explicit consciousness, Catholic theology has become more willing to acknowledge the cries of dissatisfaction with traditional theology from the churches in Asia, Africa, and Latin America and has begun to do theology by taking account not only of the witness of Scripture and tradition but also of culture and social change (brought on either by technological growth or by struggles of liberation—or by both simultaneously) within a culture. As a result, theologies have begun to emerge that are truly Filipino, authentically Zairean, genuinely Indian or U.S. American, or that reflect the conditions of men and women who struggle for justice within Latin America, feminist, or racist contexts.

A spectrum of positions, however, can be seen to develop according to how a particular theologian understands the relationship among the four elements mentioned above (Scripture, tradition, culture, and social change). An approach that emphasizes the Christian message in Scripture and tradition a bit more than the importance of culture tends to conceive theology as a *translation* of a "naked gospel" (Vincent Donovan) into the language and worldview of other cultures. Pope Paul VI is of this mind when he speaks about the need to "evangelize culture" (EN # 20). On the opposite side of the spectrum would be theologians who put emphasis on the revelatory value of culture itself and speak of a "Hidden Christ" (Raimundo Panikkar) in particular cultures. Still others stress the fact that God is in a culture as one calling women and men to be partners in working for social change, especially in terms of equality and justice, and in this group one can locate the various theologians of liberation, Latin American (Gustavo Gutièrrez, Leonardo Boff, Jon Sobrino), and otherwise (the feminist theologian Rosemary Radford Ruether). These theologians call for a "hermeneutic of suspicion" regarding previous doctrinal expressions, for often doctrinal formulations are not only conditioned culturally and historically, but also ideologically.[32] In the middle of the spectrum would be found a number of theologians to keep an even balance among all four elements. Such is the theology of Aylward Shorter in Africa, Robert Schreiter in the U.S.A., and Jose de Mesa in the Philippines.[33]

Despite the variety of possible approaches to or models of contextual theology, all have one basic thing in common: all are trying to be faithful to the Catholic vision of a world that is fundamentally good, a world that serves as a sacrament of God's marvelous love. Because of the new-found consciousness of the historical and cultural conditionedness of theology, Catholics are realizing that Scripture and tradition must take into account the wealth of culture and the opportunitites of social change, and so, for Catholics, this process of what is called "contextualization" is becoming less of an option and more of what might be styled a theological imperative.

CONCLUSION

The vision of Catholicism that forms the parameters of Roman Catholic theological method is not in any way a vision that is confined to the Roman church. Roman Catholicism has been both maintained and challenged in its vision by men and women loosely or even not at all associated with the Catholic church (e.g., T. S. Eliot; C. S. Lewis; Gandhi; Martin Luther King, Jr.), and has contributed to the vision of many who never felt moved to become official members (e.g., Thomas Carlyle and John Ruskin) or who have (in Catholic jargon) "fallen away" (e.g., James Joyce or Bruce Springsteen). The whole church—Catholic, Orthodox, Protestant, evangelical—is endowed with catholicity; it is not something that is Roman Catholicism's exclusive possession.

Catholicism is a wider notion than Roman Catholicism, but it is also a distinct form of Christianity and provides a distinct veiwpoint from which one does theology. As Richard McBrien puts it, while there is no one particular feature, apart from Catholicism's conviction of the importance of the Petrine ministry, that makes Catholicism different from all other churches, "a case can be made that nowhere else except in the Catholic Church are all of Catholicism's characteristics present in the precise *configuration* in which they are found within Catholicism."[34]

This chapter has been an attempt to sketch out the Catholic vision and to see how it—and the tensions and inevitable failures that go with it—provide both what is distinctive about Catholic theology and the range of theological opinions among Catholic theologians. It has been an introduction; much more could be said. I hope, however, that this chapter has contributed toward a better understanding of the complex but exciting task of doing theology in today's world.

NOTES

[1]K. Barth, "Foreword" to *Church Dogmatics*, I.1, *The Doctrine of the Word of God*, trans., G. T. Thomson (Edinburgh: T. & T. Clark, 1936, 1960), x.

[2]K. Barth, "The Humanity of God," J. N. Thomas, trans., in *The Humanity of God*(Richmond: John Knox, 1960), 37–65; cf. E. Busch, *Karl Barth: His Life from Letters and Autobiographical Texts*, trans., J. Bowden (Philadelphia: Fortress, 1976), 476–77.

[3]D. Tracy, *The Analogical Imagination: Christian Theology and the Culture of Pluralism* (New York: Crossroad, 1981), 410.

[4]R. McBrien, *Catholicism*, (Minneapolis: Winston, 1980), 2:1180.

[5]Pope Paul VI, the opening speech at the Second Session of the Second Vatican Council, September 29, 1963, in *Il Concilio Vaticano*, 7th ed. (Bologna: Edizioni Dehoniane, 1968), 96. The pope was referring to the mystery that is the church, but Richard McBrien takes this phrase in a wider sense as a way of describing a sacrament. Cf. R. McBrien, "Roman Catholicism," in *The Encylclopedia of Religion*, ed., M. Eliade, (New York: Macmillan, 1987), 12:437.

[6]L. Cunningham, *The Catholic Experience* (New York: Crossroad, 1985), 115.

[7]Dogmatic Constitution on the Church (Lumen Gentium [LG]), # 8, in A. Flannery, ed., *Vatican II* (Collegeville, Mich.: Liturgical Press, 1981).

[8]F. Schleiermacher, *The Christian Faith*, trans. and ed., H. R. Macintosh and J. S. Steward (1928 reprint, Philadelphia: Fortress, 1976), 103.

[9]The classic text in which this relationship between faith and reason in theology is expressed is the decree *Dei Filius* of the First Vatican Council (1870). Cf. H. Denzinger and A. Schoenmetzer, eds., *Enchiridion Symbolorum Definitionum et Declarationum de Rebus Fidei et Morum*, 34th ed., # 3015–20. Catholic theologians refer to this as "Denzinger," and it is abbreviated "DS," followed by a number that is found in the margin of the text.

[10]A recent magisterial document that includes all these concerns is Paul VI, *On Evangelization in the Modern World* (EN) (Washington, D.C.: U.S. Catholic Conference, 1976). Cf. also R. Schreiter, *Constructing Local Theologies* (Maryknoll, N.Y.: Orbis, 1985).

[11]McBrien, *Catholicism*, 1173.

[12]R. Haughton, *The Catholic Thing* (Springfield, Ill.: Templegate, 1979), 59.

[13]Ibid., 15–16.

[14]S. Happel and D. Tracy, *A Catholic Vision* (Philadelphia: Fortress, 1984), 14.

[15]McBrien, *Catholicism*, 1174–75; A. Dulles, *The Reshaping of Catholicism: Current Changes in the Theology of the Church* (New York: Harper & Row, 1988), 72.

[16]J. J. Connelley, "The Task of Theology," *Proceedings of the Convention of the Catholic Theological Society of America*, (1974), 1–58. The three principles referred to in the text are laid out on pages 42–53.

[17]McBrien, *Catholicism*, 1176–80.

[18]Cf. Paul Hiebert, "Epistemological Foundations for Science and Theology," *TSF Bulletin* (March-April 1985), 7.

[19]Augustine, Ep. 187 (PL 83, 845). Quoted in R. Kress, *The Church: Communion, Sacrament, Communication* (Mahwah, N.J.: Paulist Press, 1985), 138.

[20]T. F. O'Meara, "The Future of Catholicism," Inaugural Lecture as William K. Warren Professor of Theology at the University of Notre Dame (October 15, 1986), 3.

[21]Cf. Haughton, *The Catholic Thing*, 9–11. All the quotations in the following paragraphs (before the next note) are from these pages.

[22]Happel and Tracy, *A Catholic Vision*, 31.

[23]Cf. D. Tracy, *Blessed Rage for Order* (New York: Seabury, 1975), 29 and passim. In this quite Catholic formulation, Tracy is indebted to S. Ogden. Cf. Ogden's essay "What Is Theology?" in *On Theology* (New York: Harper & Row, 1986), 1–21.

[24]"The Roman Pontiff, when he speaks solemnly in his capacity as pastor and teacher of all Christians by virtue of his supreme apostolic authority,

defines a doctrine concerning faith and morals to be held by the whole Church, by the divine assistance promised to blessed Peter, is endowed with that infallibility which the divine Redeemer willed for his Church. . . ." (DS 3074). Vatican Council II basically repeated this doctrine in LG #25.

[25]Cf. K. Rahner, Commentary on LG #25 in *Commentary on the Documents of Vatican II*, ed., H. Vorgrimler (Montreal: Palm Publishers, n.d.), 1:213.

[26]R. P. McBrien, "Church," in J. Dyer, ed., *An American Catholic Catechism* (New York: Seabury, 1975), #12, p. 22.

[27]F. A. Sullivan, "The Infallibility of the People of God," in *Magisterium: Teaching Authority in the Catholic Church* (Ramsey, N.J.: Paulist Press, 1983), 4–23.

[28]Happel and Tracy, *A Catholic Vision*, 181.

[29]These are the three basic functions of the church's teaching office as commonly expressed in Catholic theology. Cf. R. Latourelle, *Theology: Science of Salvation* (New York: Alba, 1969), 44–51.

[30]International Theological Commission, *Theses on the Relationship Between the Ecclesiastical Magisterium and Theology* (Washington, D.C.: U.S. Catholic Conference, 1977). For further reading in this area one would do well to consult L. Orsy, *The Church: Learning and Teaching* (Wilmington, Del.: Michael Glazier, 1987); A. Dulles, "Authority and Conscience: Two Needed Voices," in Dulles, *The Reshaping of Catholicism*, 93–109; and F. A. Sullivan, "Magisterium and Theology," in *Proceedings of the Convention of the Catholic Theological Society of America* (1988), 65–75.

[31]Schreiter, *Constructing Local Theologies*, 75–94.

[32]Cf., for example, R. R. Ruether, *Sexism and God-talk: Toward a Feminist Theology* (Boston: Beacon, 1983).

[33]For a more detailed and comprehensive presentation of this spectrum, cf. S. Bevans, "Models of Contextual Theology," *Missiology* 13, 2 (April 1985): 185–202.

[34]McBrien, *Catholicism*, 1172.

13

LIGHT FROM THE EAST? "DOING THEOLOGY" IN AN EASTERN ORTHODOX PERSPECTIVE

JOHN MEYENDORFF
SAINT VLADIMIR ORTHODOX THEOLOGICAL
SEMINARY, CRESTWOOD, NEW YORK

Following a lecture I recently gave on the campus of an American University, a student—obviously interested in the content—asked, "Does your denomination have communities in California?" I was taken aback by his question, and it took me a moment to realize that I had been introduced as an "Eastern" Orthodox and that, to average North American ears, this evoked facts of American geography and the history of American religious denominationalism. Was I "Eastern" Orthodox in the same sense as there are "Southern" Baptists?

As I pondered how I could answer the question best, I realized that a purely historical answer—something like "We are Eastern Orthodox because we come from Eastern Europe"—would be insufficient and unfair to the questioner. Of course, his puzzlement clearly showed some lack of historical and geographical information. There was indeed a schism within Christendom, sometime in the high Middle Ages, that opposed the Latin-speaking West to the Greek-speaking East,[1] but the theological issues involved in the schism greatly transcended historical circumstances. When one refers to "Eastern" or "Greek" Orthodoxy, one has in mind a Christian tradition that claims to have preserved the integrity of the apostolic faith (this is implied in the term orthodoxy) and the reality of "catholicity," in spite of obvious historical and cultural limitations, defined by history and geographics. To North America, this tradition came originally, not from the East with the later waves of immigrants, but from the West, when in the late eighteenth century, monks from the Russian monastery of Valaam (or Valamo) preached Christianity to the indigenous population of Alaska.

Today Orthodox communities are a presence throughout a society that is fundamentally Western in its religious traditions. Some of these communities are still immigrant communities, others are utterly American in language and mentality. Traditions of the Orthodox church are being challenged by the inherent religious pluralism of America, by modern secularism, by the task of preserving an ancient liturgical tradition in an environment accustomed to puritan and individualistic forms of worship. Such are at least some of the conditions under which an Orthodox theologian is "doing theology," with the additional awareness that the great mass of Orthodox faithful in today's world are living in Eastern Europe and the Middle East,[2] struggling—often quite successfully—against various forms of hostile environments.

THE SOURCES OF THEOLOGY

Since Christian theology acquired, in the medieval Western universities, the status of a "science," to be taught and learned with the use of appropriate scientific methodology, it was inevitable that one began also to list the "sources" of theological discourse. Just as natural sciences begin, according to Aristotle, with an experience of reality reached through the use of senses, so theology began with data found in "Scripture" and "tradition." Besides, there was also a "natural theology," based on the observation of the created world, with human reason—sometimes enlightened by the Holy Spirit—discovering God in created nature.

There is nothing plainly wrong in categorizing the sources of theology in such a neat way, except that the categorization raises more questions than it solves.

What is Scripture? What is tradition? What are the guidelines of "natural" theology, if one exists?

Orthodox theology takes for granted the divine inspiration of Scriptures. Even a casual acquaintance with the Orthodox liturgical ethos shows the biblical character of the Orthodox religious experience. The office, almost entirely, is made up of scriptural texts, particularly Psalms, which are sung or read in the context of the various celebrations. However, if one takes the liturgy as a guide, the Bible is not read as a uniform collection of equally holy texts. There is a certain hierarchy within it: the New Testament, read during the Eucharistic liturgy, is the fulfillment of the Old, and within the New Testament itself, the book containing the four Gospels is the object of special and direct veneration not accorded the rest of the New Testament. It is interesting that the book of Revelation—although it is accepted as part of the scriptural canon—is never read during public worship. It is more likely that this omission is rooted in the fact that the church of Antioch—which is the origin of the lectionary of Constantinople, adopted by the church universally—did not include Revelation in the canon until the fifth century, i.e., until after the lectionary was formed.

This system of internal priorities *within* the canon of Scriptures is further shown in two facts in the history of the scriptural canon in the Eastern half of the Christian world. The first fact is that the final settlement of the canon did not take place until 692 (council in Trullo, canon 2),[3] and that uncertainty as to the boundaries of written revelation was not, for many centuries, considered a major problem in "doing theology." The second fact is that, when the settlement took place, a measure of uncertainty remained as to the exact status of the "longer canon" of the Old Testament: books like Wisdom and Ecclesiasticus—which were not a part of the Hebrew canon, but only of the Septuagint, and are called Apocrypha in the West—were still recognized by some in the eighth century only as "admissible," but were not included in the canon.[4] Even today, Orthodox theologians refer to them as "deuterocanonical books." They are considered part of "Scripture" and read in church liturgically but occupy something of a marginal place in the canon.

This rather detached Orthodox attitude toward the problem of the scriptural canon shows clearly that for them the Christian faith and experience can in no way be compatible with the notion of *Scriptura sola*. The issue of tradition arises inevitably, but certainly not in terms of a "second source" of revelation (fortunately, no one would defend such terms today). Of course, there is a famous text by St. Basil the Great of Ceasarea (d. 379), which might at first reading be interpreted as affirming a kind of parallelism between Scripture and oral tradition:

Among the doctrines and teachings preserved by the Church, we hold some from written sources, and we have collected others transmitted in an inexplicit form (μυστικῶς) from apostolic tradition. They have all the same value. For if we were to try to put aside the unwritten customs as having no great force, we should, unknown to ourselves, be weakening the Gospel in its very essence; furthermore, we should be transforming the *kerygma* into mere words.[5]

What this text in fact implies is that God speaks to humans, as living God to living persons; that he manifested himself in Jesus Christ, who chose a group of *people*—his "apostles"—to be his witnesses, and that his unique manifestation, death, and resurrection have indeed been witnessed by them and announced to later generations as *apostolic tradition*; that the essence of this *kerygma* is indeed contained in the books of the New Testament, but that this *kerygma* would be mere human words if it is not delivered in the full context of the living tradition, particularly the sacraments and the ligurgy of the church.

In this sense, tradition becomes the initial and fundamental source of Christian theology—not in competition with Scripture, but as Scripture's spiritual context. The ultimate truth was "delivered to the saints" when Jesus taught them and when the Spirit descended upon them as a community at Pentecost. The church, as eucharistic community, existed before the New Testament books were written, and these books were themselves composed in and for concrete local churches. Their written text is meant to be read and understood by baptized, committed people, gathered in the name of the Lord. Theology, therefore, is not simply a science, using Scripture as initial data; it also presupposes living in communion with God and people, in Christ and the Spirit, within the community of the church. Biblical theology is, of course, the best theology, but being truly biblical implies living communion in Christ without which the Bible is a dead letter.

This approach in no way implies that biblical science does not possess its own proper integrity and methodology, but it implies a certain understanding of what the Bible is: a collection of writings, composed on various historical occasions, in and for a community. This point is has direct implications for a doctrine of "inspiration," particularly in its relation to the "election" of Israel. In the Bible, God speaks to Israel, through the mouth of some writers, but he also speaks through Israel, as a people, to the world. So inspiration does not concern only a given individual writer—whose name is often either unknown or conventional—but Israel, chosen as people, whose literature and history are in their entirety the vehicles of divine revelation. Critical historical problems concerning particular books or authors must therefore be solved with proper scientific methodology, because these texts and these authors appeared indeed within the concrete human history of Israel, using various literary genres: history, poetry, parables, and ethical discourse.

Those whom Orthodox theologians call "the fathers of the church"—essentially those who in the past have become the recognized defenders of Truth against heretical distortions and have therefore become the privileged spokesmen of the authentic Christian tradition—had no difficulty with a purely symbolic interpretation of some Old Testament accounts (cf. Alexandrian allegorism; cf. also the concept of ἀλληγορούμενα in Gal. 4:24) or with understanding the creation accounts of Genesis in the light of the scientific knowledge of their time (cf. the homilies on the *Hexaemeron* by Basil of Caesarea).[6] Difficulties with the modern critical approach arise only when it denies the *sacred* character of Israel's history or when *any* form of divine intervention in created reality is deemed to be a myth.

If the collection of books known as the Old Testament reflect the continuous history of a people, directed toward the *future*—the messianic kingdom—the New Testament is entirely concerned with one particular *point* of history: the passion and resurrection of Jesus, in which the fullness of God's love and wisdom was manifested and to which there is nothing to add. The apostles witnessed the event, and the "apostolic tradition" preserves its meaning and interprets its significance within the realities of later human history. New writings continued to be added to the Old Testament collection until the time of Christ, but the New Testament was closed with the death of the last "witness" of the Resurrection. There was a continuous revelation to the Old Israel, but nothing of the sort is possible in the new dispensation, because salvation has been accomplished once and for all in Christ. The church can only define the *limits* of the authentic witness but cannot add anything to it.

This last point is, of course, crucial for our understanding of what "tradition" is. If, indeed, it is not a series of new revelations, what is the content of the yet "unexplicit" or "mystical" teachings, which according to the text of Basil quoted above, are transmitted in the church from generation to generation, as the very "essence " of the Gospel, but are not contained in Scripture? Basil himself gives several examples (baptismal immersions, meaning of the Lord's day, etc.),[7] all of which refer to sacraments, worship, and the spiritual experience of the Christian community. His point is, therefore, that the Christian faith does not consist only in the rational acceptance of certain propositional truths that can be spelled out in writing, but that it implies a continuous, living communion with God in Christ, through the Holy Spirit, an experience of "new life," which is not individual or subjective, but sacramental and "common" to all the baptized.

It is probably impossible to fully grasp what Eastern Christians have understood by "theology" without giving full credit to such sayings as one uttered by a major leader of Egyptian monasticism, Evagrius Ponticus, in the fourth century: "If you are a theologian, you truly pray. If you truly pray you are a theologian."[8] Although Evagrius himself—and other monastic writers—may have occasionally fallen into some exaggerated "charismatic" individualism, it is unquestionable that the whole tradition of the Christian East has attributed to the saints, the spiritual leaders, the *startsi* (as such people are called in modern times by Russians and Romanians) a certain particular authority in preserving the truth and guiding the Christian community.[9] It is interesting to note that this particular aspect of the Eastern Christian tradition has attracted the attention and admiration of John Wesley, who even translated the writings attributed to St. Macarius of Egypt into English.[10] However, it was inevitable that, in a Protestant ecclesiological context—which is the one Wesley adopted in his opposition to the polity of established Anglicanism—his reading of the Eastern tradition would lead to a somewhat emotional "prophetic" subjectivism. The ecclesial and theologically "realistic" context of the Orthodox tradition—which was certainly also that of the Greek Fathers, who fought against Arianism and other heresies—does not allow the reduction of Truth to subjective, personal experience.[11] In the fourteenth century, there was even a famous doctrinal dispute, which ended with the formal endorsement by the church of the theology of St. Gregory Palamas, whose main point consisted in affirming a real, "uncreated" divine presence in the experience of the saints, accessible to all the baptized, and not to a few select mystics only.[12]

I have mentioned earlier the *ecclesial* context of tradition. Indeed, the church, as eucharistic assembly, was the proper *locus of teaching* in the local church. It is also the eucharistic assembly that provided the setting and the models for the exercise of teaching ministries, particularly that of the bishop and the presbyter. What today we call apostolic succession was preserved—as is clearly shown in the writings of the early fathers like Ignatius of Antioch (d. c. A.D. 100) and Irenaeus of Lyons (d. c. 202)—*within* (not above!) the eucharistic assembly of each local church. The teaching ministry of the apostles, who were chosen personally by Jesus, consisted in witnessing to the Resurrection to the entire world. Theirs was a unique traveling ministry, unattached to any local church and intransmissible to others, because it was limited to the "eyewitnesses" of the Lord. When the apostles disappeared, it was within the framework of the local, eschatological, and sacramental communion of the eucharistic assembly that the apostolic tradition was preserved. The bishop, as occupying the Lord's own place at the assembly, possessed a certain "charisma of truth."[13] Without claiming any personal infallibility, he was the guardian of the tradition coming down without interruption from the apostles—a tradition that also had to be witnessed by the unity of faith, which was maintained by all the members of each church and which bound together all the local churches.[14] The clearest sign of this ecclesial function of the episcopate is the requirement, normal in the early church, for a new bishop to be elected by the clergy and people of a local church and to be solemnly ordained through laying-on-of-hands by neighboring bishops, who represented the entire episcopate of the world church.

Thus, in "doing theology" today, an Orthodox theologian is answerable to Scripture and to tradition, as expressed in the reality of "communion," which I tried to describe above.[15] But his responsibility is that of a fully free person, entrusted by God to learn the truth and to communicate it to others. This freedom could be restricted only by the truth itself, but divine truth does not restrict human freedom but "makes us free" (John 8:32). The early church did not know—and the Orthodox does not know today—any automatic, formal, or authoritarian way of discerning truth from falsehood. To quote St. Irenaeus again: "Where the Church is, there is the Spirit of God; and where the Spirit of God is, there is the Church, and every kind of grace; but the Spirit is Truth."[16]

DOCTRINAL DEFINITIONS, THEOLOGICAL
DEVELOPMENT, AND LEGITIMATE PLURALISM

One of the most difficult challenges for Orthodox theologians engaged in ecumenical dialogue consists in explaining what is the permanent criterion of truth in Orthodox theology. Their embarrassment before the challenge makes them look like subjectivists, or liberals. But on the other hand, their basic concern for truth and their unwillingness to surrender anything to fashionable doctrinal relativism associates them with extreme conservatism. They themselves, however, refuse to be identified with either.

There are also times and places when the Orthodox take the offensive and question the usual Western concern for criteria and authority. The very influential nineteenth-century Russian lay theologian, A. S. Khomyakov, expresses the question in a very vivid way:

> The Church is not an authority, just as God is not an authority, and Christ is not an authority, since authority is something external to us. The Church is not authority, I say, but the Truth—and at the same time the inner life of the Christian, since God, Christ, the Church live in him with a life more real than the heart which is beating in his breast and the blood flowing in his veins. But they are alive in him only insofar as he himself is living by the ecumenical life of love and unity; i.e., by the life of the Church.

Khomyakov continues by giving a critique of Western Christianity, where, according to him, "authority became external power" and "knowledge of religious truths [was] cut off from religious life." Obedience to authority became the content of church life in Roman Catholicism, whereas Scripture as a compendium of written propositional truths, replaced church authority in Protestantism. "The premises are identical," Khomyakov concludes.[17]

Unfair as it is, as all sweeping generalizations are, A. S. Khomyakov's view is nevertheless illustrative of the way the Orthodox view theology—as *internal* vision, which requires personal, ascetic effort. It does not require an individual effort only, however, but a communal effort: an effort made within the "community of saints." The character of knowledge, bestowed by the Spirit, is indeed a personal knowledge, but one that is accessible in communion of love with the apostles, the fathers, the saints. The nature of God himself, who is love, is Triune, and it can be known only within the categories of loving communion.[18]

This "mystical" and experiential approach to theology does not mean, however, that the Orthodox church does not possess dogmas that are considered as final, and therefore authoritative, expressions of tradition. Church history is a history of doctrinal controversies, which usually end with guiding doctrinal definitions and aiming at excluding error. Theologians are called to accept such definitions as essential references.

Doctrinal definitions, or dogmas, always result from conciliar agreement. Truth can, indeed, be expressed by an individual, or a group, or a local church, but such an individual expression by itself does not create a dogma. A dogma always reflects ecclesial consensus along the lines we find expressed by St. Irenaeus. At the time of the Christian Roman Empire, the most normal way to register a consensus was for the emperor to call an "ecumenical" council. The Orthodox church recognizes seven of such councils as fully expressing the tradition of the church: Nicea I (325), Constantinople I (381), Ephesus (431), Chalcedon (451), Constantinople II (553), Constantinople III (680), and Nicea II (787). The councils define basic Trinitarian and Christological issues. But the recognition of those seven councils as "ecumenical" in no way precludes the existence of an Orthodox consensus, reached through other means than an "ecumenical" council. Local councils have received universal recognition (1341, 1351, 1675, 1872), and, at present, commissions are preparing another "great council" without being sure whether the adjective "ecumenical" should be used in advance to designate it. Indeed, this adjective has had such a variety of meaning (e.g., in the past it pointed to imperial convocation, and today it is associated with either Roman Catholic universalism or "inter-Christian" activity) that one wonders whether it remains useful at all in the context of Orthodox ecclesiology.

Be that as it may, for the Orthodox it is the consensus that matters as a sign of truth and unity from God. It remains, however, that the knowledge of truth does not depend on consensus either: consensus is not external authority, but a helpful sign, which might be temporarily lacking, leaving the responsibility for the truth to only a few. Historical examples are many: St. Paul, in his conflict with Judeo-Christians; St. Athanasius, struggling alone for the Nicene faith in the fourth century, as the episcopates of both East and West seemed to have surrendered to Arianism; St. Maximus the Confessor, a lonely monk (but also the greatest theologian of the late patristic period), refusing in the seventh century to surrender to "Monothelitism," which—as he was told—had been accepted universally; St. Mark of Ephesus, an equally lonely dissenter, as union with Rome was signed in 1439 at Florence.

These and other historical examples stand before the theologian, making him *personally responsible* for the truth, aware of his obligation to follow Scripture and tradition, but also conscious of the fact that—at the limit—he might have to stand alone—but with God—on the right side of the fence between orthodoxy and heresy.

One of the consequences of the absence in the Orthodox church of permanently infallible *magisterium* is that universally accepted formal definitions of faith are brief and rare. The ancient ecumenical councils themselves entered quite reluctantly on the path of issuing doctrinal statements. At the time of the Council of Chalcedon (451) the predominant Eastern opinion was that the common baptismal creed adopted at Nicea (325) and Constantinople (381) was a sufficient guarantee against recurring heresies. The famous definition of Chalcedon (451) begins, therefore, with an apologetic preamble:

> The wise and salutary formula of divine grace [i.e., the Creed of Nicea-Constantinople] *sufficed* for the perfect knowledge and confirmation of religion. . . . But, for as much as persons undertaking to make void the preaching of the Truth have through their individual heresies given rise to empty babblings. . .this present holy, great and ecumenical council, desiring to exclude every device against the Truth, and teaching that which is unchanged from the beginning, had decreed. . . .[19]

What this text indicates is that doctrinal definitions have a primarily negative role—that of preventing the spread of error—and that, in any case, their aim is not to exhaust the truth or freeze the teachings of the church into verbal formulae or systems, but only to indicate the "boundaries" of truth (this is the meaning of the Greek term *horos*, used to designate conciliar decrees on doctrine). There is no doubt that, once accepted by the church, such ecumenical decrees have a final doctrinal authority, but—by their very nature—they are not to be considered "new revelations," but interpretations of the fullness of truth revealed once and for all in Christ. In no way are they to be understood as "additions" to Scripture. Their very nature is different. The dogma of Chalcedon about the two natures of Christ may have a central and permanent theological importance for understanding Scripture as a whole—it might perhaps be more important than some particular New Testament epistle taken by itself, but still it represents the voice of the apostolic church, guided by the Spirit, and not the witness of the apostles themselves.

These limitations, which are inherent to the Orthodox understanding of the meaning and role of doctrinal definitions, have a direct impact on our topic: What is "doing theology"?

Within present-day Orthodoxy there are polarities in the answer given to this question. There exists a "liberal" trend: the definitions are few and brief, some say, therefore theologians have the freedom to say anything that does not contradict the conciliar definitions. Others—conventionally called "conservatives"—would define theology as an exercise in repeating what has been said by the fathers when they prepared and explained the existing definitions by the ancient councils. However, there is also a large consensus among modern Orthodox theologians to avoid such artificial polarizations. They would also be reluctant to accept unreservedly the predominant Roman Catholic view about "doctrinal development," as found, for instance, in Newman, and practically implying "continuous revelation" on issues such as the papal power or the Marian dogmas, which were "defined" by Rome only in the nineteenth and twentieth centuries. I think I would be faithful to the Orthodox general feeling on the matter if I said that in the Orthodox church formal doctrinal definitions can only concern *essentials*, without which the whole New Testament vision of salvation would not stand. This was certainly the case for the dogmas of the seven ecumenical councils, including the decree of Nicea II (787) on the veneration of icons, which in fact was not so much a decree on religious art as an affirmation of the reality of the Incarnation, which implied that Christ was a historical person—visible, depictable, and representable. But particular signs, such as the bodily glorification of the Virgin Mary after her death (the dogma of the "Assumption")—alluded to in some patristic writings and liturgical hymnology, and reflecting a belief in an eschatological anticipation of the general resurrection in her case—are simply not a matter for formal definition, but for reverence and pious respect.

Here one clearly touches on a point that is essential for

doing theology in an Orthodox context: the necessary distinction between "Holy Tradition" itself and human traditions, which may well carry on precious truths but are not absolute in themselves, and which may furthermore easily become spiritual obstacles for true theology, as were those human "traditions" that Jesus himself condemned (Matt. 7:8–13).[20] The Orthodox often lack the ability to make the necessary distinctions in practice. Probably because they lack a formal permanent *magisterium*, responsible for the whole life of the church universal, the Orthodox often feel *themselves* responsible for the integrity of the faith. They tend to identify their Orthodoxy as an integral whole, where doctrinal beliefs are inseparable from worship, customs, language, and cultural attitudes, some of which are fairly recent and quite independent from holy tradition itself. This "holistic" perception of the faith goes back to the times when, early in the Middle Ages, nations of Eastern Europe were converted to Christianity by Greek missionaries whose policy was to translate Scripture and liturgy into the vernacular and thus indigenize Christianity at the very start. The fact that the Orthodox faith has become very much "their own" explains the remarkable survival of Orthodox communities in the Middle East and in the Balkans during centuries of Muslim rule and of the Church of Russia under the assault of totalitarian secularism. But the price of this identification of faith and culture is the frequent inability of masses of the faithful to distinguish between tradition and traditions, especially when theological information is lacking. This even leads to schisms, like that of the "Old Believers" in Russia in the seventeenth century[21] and the present-day "Old Calendarists" in Greece.

Clearly, only a living theological tradition can provide the church with adequate definitions of priorities and issues to solve.

More than in other Christian traditions, the *patristic* period is accepted by the Orthodox as a preferred model of theological creativity—a model that has not been historically superseded, as it was in the Latin West, by the great medieval scholastic systems, or rejected as a "Hellenization" of authentic biblical Christianity, as liberal Protestants of the nineteenth century thought it to be. The task pursued and accomplished by the Fathers was to make the Gospel acceptable and understandable to a world accustomed to the categories of Greek philosophy. They used Greek philosophical terms to express the teachings of the church about the Trinity and the divine-human being of Christ. Characteristically, however, those trends within patristic thought that surrendered to the metaphysical categories of Platonism, at the expense of the biblical idea of God and creation, were deliberately eliminated by the church, as was the case with Origenism.[22] In spite of this critical attitude to the Greco-Roman civilization, to which they culturally belonged and to which they had to announce the Gospel, the Fathers did succeed in their task: Christianity was accepted by the intellectual elite of their time, and the doctrinal controversies of the day were solved not only by condemnations and anathemas, but also through a constructive and creative theological synthesis, which is most adequately enshrined not in intellectual systems, but rather in an overall perception of the Gospel, in the liturgy, the hymnography, the sacramental actions, and the festal cycles.

The primary task of theology was, at the time, primarily "apologetic." Theological speculation often went wrong when it was used as an end in itself and not as a creative tool to answer the questions posed to the church by the surrounding world. Today, this world is no more the world of Plato or Aristotle: it is a post-Reformation, post-Enlightenment, post-industrial, and sometimes revolutionary *secularized Western world*. Historically, Eastern Christianity was spared the crises that shaped this modern Western world, but, as if coming straight from the Byzantine Middle Ages, it is confronting this modern world head-on today.

The encounter was late in coming. In the seventeenth century, Roman Catholics and Protestants were looking to the East for support in their struggle against each other. They solicited from the Orthodox to send them their "Confessions of Faith." The results were not very successful: the Orthodox, basically ignoring the implications of the questions they received from their Western colleagues, produced rather unsatisfactory "Confessions." Some were fundamentally Calvinistic (e.g., the *Confession* of Cyril Loukaris, 1629); others were basically Latin and Tridentine in spirit (e.g., the *Confession* of Peter Moghila, 1640). These episodes only showed that the Orthodox tradition could not be adequately expressed in the "confessional" forms of post-Reformation Europe (neither could Roman Catholicism, for that matter).

Russia encountered the West brutally in the eighteenth century, with social and educational reforms imposed by Peter I

(1672–1725) and Catherine II (1762–1796). However, by the nineteenth century, the period referred to by G. Florovsky as the period of "Western captivity," ended. Solid scientific and creative schools of theology resulted from the encounter with the West and became more adequately equipped to answer issues of the day.

As I tried to show earlier, an Orthodox theologian, although he necessarily defines himself as a consistent follower of the patristic and conciliar tradition of the early church and although he is inevitably respectful of the present positions of his church as they are expressed in the consensus of the episcopate, is fundamentally free in his expressing the faith. Of course, he is also responsible, since freedom entails the risk of error. Most often he or she belongs to the laity. Lay professors are a majority in the theological faculties in Greece, and they represent a sizeable minority in the theological schools of Russia, or Serbia. This lack of professional clericalism might, in some cases, denote a certain lack of commitment by academic teachers to the practical and pastoral tasks of the church. On the other hand, men like A. S. Khomyakov (1804–1860), quoted earlier, were *lay* theologians in a real sense. Their dedication to the church was entirely spontaneous, and they contributed much to establishing links between Orthodox theology and the world of secular *intelligentsia*.[23]

If one looks at the world of Orthodox theology in the twentieth century, one can measure a rather wide spectrum of styles, approaches, and schools. Men like I. N. Kamires, from Athens, are exponents of the tradition of dogmatic systems, exposing the coherence of Greek patristic theology, vis-à-vis the Western confessional approach. The Russian school of "sophiologists," inspired originally by V. S. Soloviev (1853–1900) and his vision of the "wisdom of God," seen as the *Uhrgrund* of creation, includes big names like P. Florensky[24] and S. N. Bulgakov.[25] Their goal is basically a synthesis of Christianity, with the tradition of German philosophical idealism, not very dissimilar to the methodology and the "philosophical theology" of Tillich. Highly critical of the sophiologists, G. V. Florovsky,[26] V. N. Lossky, and Justin Popovich initiated a return to the Fathers. Their work is often referred to as a "Neo-Patristic" synthesis. The truly great Romanian theologian, D. Staniloae, also belongs to the "patristic" school, but with deliberate openness toward modern existential philosophy. A very creative and challenging trend, particularly in the fields of ecclesiology and ecumenism, is the one usually referred to as "eucharistic." It includes authors like A. Afanasieff, A. Schmemann, and J. Zizioulas. In our century a number of Orthodox theologians were drawn to Western Europe and America by political events in their own countries. Others became actively involved in ecumenism. As a result, Orthodox theology began to contribute more actively to Western problematics, and the particular Orthodox way of "doing theology" became better known within the international theological community.

The observations that I have presented earlier, particularly in reference to the Orthodox attitude toward the "sources" of theology, have clearly shown, I believe, that Orthodox theology does not fit in the categories of liberalism or conservatism as they have developed in Western Christendom. Direct communion with God rather than external authority, "sanctification" rather than "justification," personal experience rather than intellectual proof, consensus rather than passive obedience—these are some important Orthodox intuitions about the nature of the Christian faith. In stressing such contrasts, I do not mean at all that the Orthodox church does not believe in authority, that it rejects the Pauline doctrine of justification by faith, that it does not respect the power of reason, or that dogmas are accepted through democratic referendums. But I do want to emphasize the point that the mystery of the Holy Spirit, present in the church, is the fundamental reality of Christian experience, that this experience is a personal and free one,[27] and that authority, reason, and formal hierarchical and conciliar criteria are meant to protect it, not to replace it. In any case, the Spirit guiding the faithful is also the creator of church order, the bestower of the *charismata* of teaching and governing, as well as the inspirer of the prophets. Thus the personalism of the faith does not result in charismatic subjectivism, or individualism: it initiates each person to think and to act as a responsible member of the body, seeking the truth within the communion of the saints.

CONCLUSION: "DOING THEOLOGY" IN AMERICA

At the beginning of this century, Christian East and Christian West still lived in practical isolation from each other. It is true that even then—and already in the previous century—Orthodox theologians were generally informed of Western theological trends and used Western theological literature profusely. But their Western colleagues—with the exception of a few specialists—had practically no access to Orthodox theological thought and hardly considered it a potential challenge at all. Today an Orthodox presence in ecumenical dialogues is considered a must, and Orthodox theological literature becomes more and more available. This gives a historically unprecedented responsibility to those Orthodox who are "doing theology": how to be understood, but also how to remain faithful to the authentic tradition, whose spokesmen they pretend to be.

It seems to me that their greatest challenge is to preserve the "ecclesial" character of their theology.

The American religious scene is quite familiar with "sectarian" theological thinking—that of a relatively small religious group claiming to possess the truth, affirming that "salvation" has reached its members (and not that of other groups), and rejoicing in its exclusivity and uniqueness. There are Orthodox people who would gladly adopt the psychological attitude of a sect: it would give them a certain (false) security and justify the exotic and unfamiliar sides of historical Eastern Orthodoxy, which frequently seem strange to native Americans. It would free them from the obligation to listen to others and from the effort needed to look at themselves as others look at them. It would make it unnecessary to draw the line between holy tradition and the human traditions inherited from history, and it would reduce theology to straight affirmations, repeating that which was supposedly "always said." Such an attitude, in fact, would not only exclude real theology and renounce the true tradition of the Fathers, whose main achievement was to express and explain the truth to their *neighbors and contemporaries*, necessarily using their language, but it would align the Orthodox psychologically with the most extreme forms of Protestant fundamentalism. In both cases, there would be a denial of history, a temptation that, unfortunately, is familiar to large segments of American religious mentality.

But the American religious scene is equally familiar with what is called "denominationalism"—a belief that doctrinal issues have little to do with the "church of my choice," or simply of my neighborhood, and that all (or most) Christian "denominations" have equal rights within the church universal. As a matter of fact, the mainstream American denominations have indeed been formed within the social framework of immigration history.[28] The Orthodox could fit nicely in the scheme, especially if—as is sometimes the case—they identify their ecclesiastical allegiance in purely ethnic terms. The Orthodox church is the church of the Greeks, or of the Russians, and its elaborate rituals have no other significance than the preservation of a cultural heritage. In the perspective of "denominationalism," doctrine is largely relativized and theology easily becomes an interdenominational reflection on social, anthropological, or political issues.

I would like to submit emphatically that authentic Orthodox theology can be neither sectarian nor denominational, but only "ecclesial." It presupposes the existence of a "catholic" church, which receives the fullness of divine revelation for the sake of the salvation of all people. This church has existed since Pentecost, preserving the apostolic message and interpreting it in all languages for the sake of all human societies. Therefore the theologian who belongs to it must make sure that his theology is consistent with that of the apostles and the fathers, but also—precisely because the church is "catholic"—he is called to rejoice in everything that is true, beautiful, and holy, even beyond the visible limits of the church, because all true and beautiful realities truly belong to the one church of Christ—the eschatological anticipation of the "New Jerusalem." Only that which is false and sinful must be rejected. Thus the Cappadocian Greek fathers of the fourth century admired Origen; St. Maximus the Confessor was inspired by Evagrius in his spirituality; St. Nicodemus the Hagiorite (18th c.) paraphrased the *Invisible Warfare* of Scupoli and the *Spiritual Exercises* of Ignatius Loyola; St. Tikhon of Zadonsk (18th c.) was fond of German pietism. . . .

So today there is clearly no way of "doing Orthodox theology" in America, except the "catholic" way, hating error and skeptical relativism, but always seeking the best way to be faithful—in agreement with others. The "others" include the apostles and the fathers, the living witnesses of tradition, but also those with whose commitments and allegiances one may disagree, but with whom a constant and intelligent dialogue is necessary if the Orthodox witness *today* is to have any significance.

NOTES

[1]Historians agree today that the schism began as a gradual estrangement

between East and West and led to a different perception of church authority. The estrangement was a reality as early as the fourth century, without entailing at that time a permanent break of communion. The usual date of 1054, which appears in encyclopedias and textbooks as the date of the schism, corresponds to a relatively minor incident between the churches of Constantinople and Rome. A more permanent state of schism prevailed in the thirteenth century following the Crusades. For good historical information concerning the issue, see, for instance, F. Dvornik, *Byzantium and the Roman Primacy* (New York: Fordham University Press, 1966).

²There are today fifteen "autocephalous" Orthodox churches, administratively independent of one another, but united in faith, sacraments, and canonical discipline, aware of their being together one church. The "ecumenical patriarch" of Constantinople (modern Istanbul, Turkey) traditionally enjoys first honorary rank among them. The Church of Russia is the largest in numbers. The Orthodox church in America was the last to graduate into "autocephaly" in 1970, although most Orthodox churches in the "old countries" also maintain jurisdiction over groups of American communities, parallel to the autocephalous American church. The largest of these—predominantly ethnic—jurisdictions is the Greek archdiocese of America; on the contemporary structure of world Orthodoxy, see J. Meyendorff, *The Orthodox Church*, 2nd ed. (Crestwood, N.Y.: SVS, 1981).

³An English text can be found in *Nicene and Post-Nicene Fathers*, 14 (Grand Rapids: Eerdmans, n.d.), 361. The council in Trullo confirms the validity of the so-called "Apostolic canon" 85, which admits some books of the "longer canon."

⁴John of Damascus, *On the Orthodox Faith*, IV, 17; J. P. Migne, *Patrologia graeca* (later quoted as PG) 94: 1180 B.C.

⁵St. Basil, *On the Holy Spirit*, 27, PG 32, col. 188A; Eng. trans., *Nicene and Post-Nicene Fathers*, VIII:41.

⁶Original Greek in PG 29, cols. 4-208; Eng. trans., 52–107.

⁷Basil, *On the Holy Spirit*, 27, PG 32, col. 188A.

⁸Evagrius Ponticus, *Chapters on Prayer*, 60, trans. J. E. Bamberger (Spencer, Mass.: Cistercian Publications, 1970), 65.

⁹I have discussed this issue more in detail in my book *The Byzantine Legacy in the Orthodox Church* (Crestwood, N.Y.: SVS, 1982), particularly in the chapter entitled "St. Basil, the Church and Charismatic Leadership," 197–215.

¹⁰In his *Christian Library*, I (1749; reprint, London, 1819).

¹¹This is well shown in the classical work of Vladimir Lossky, *The Mystical Theology of the Eastern Church*. The last, most accessible edition is by SVS Press (Crestwood, N.Y.: SVS, 1986).

¹²Cf. J. Meyendorff, *A Study of Gregory Palamas*, 2nd ed. (Crestwood, N.Y.: SVS, 1969).

¹³*Charisma veritatis certum*, Irenaeus *Against the Heresies*, 4, 26, 2; Rousseau-Doutreleau, ed., *Sources chrétiennes*, 100 (Paris: Cerf, 1965), 718.

¹⁴The entire book 3 of the work by St. Irenaeus *Against the Heresies* is important for the understanding of tradition in the early church. The *publicly known* succession of bishops in each church is opposed by the author to "secret" spiritual genealogies, allegedly supporting the teachings of the Gnostics. He cites particularly the known successions in the churches of Rome, Ephesus, and Smyrna. But the truth of authentic Christianity is also upheld, according to Irenaeus, by the universal consensus of local churches. On modern discussion by Orthodox theologians of what is commonly called "eucharistic ecclesiology,"

see N. Afanasieff, *L'Eglise de Saint-Esprit* (Paris: Cerf, 1975), and particularly John Zizioulas (now metropolitan of Pergamos) in "Apostolic Continuity and Orthodox Theology: Towards a Synthesis of Two Perspectives," *St. Vladimir's Theological Quarterly* 19, 2, 1975): 75–108; several articles by this author are now gathered in the volume *Being as Communion* (Crestwood, N.Y.: SVS, 1985); cf. also J. Meyendorff, *Catholicity and the Church* (Crestwood, N.Y.: SVS, 1983), 49–64.

[15]More detailed discussion of connected problems in J. Meyendorff, *Living Tradition* (Crestwood, N.Y.: SVS, 1978).

[16]*Against the Heresies*, 3, 24, 1; ed. cit., 472.

[17]A. S. Khomyakov initially published his writings in French, including the pamphlet entitled *Quelques mots d'un chrétien orthodoxe sur les confessions occidentales* (Paris: 1853); this text is available in an English translation by A. E. Morehouse in A. Schmemann, ed., *Ultimate Questions* (1965; reprint, Crestwood, N.Y.: SVS, 1975); see 50–51.

[18]This approach to theology as "internal" knowledge and as communion is very well established in Orthodox theology, though it takes a variety of forms and expressions; cf. particularly Sergy (Stragorodksy, future patriarch of Moscow 1943–44), *Pravoslavnoe uchenie o spasenii* ("Orthodox doctrine of salvation"), (Sergeiv Posad, 1894), and in recent years, the work of the Greek theologian John Zizioulas, "Apostolic Continuity," and of the Romanian Dumitru Staniloae; cf. Engl. trans., *Theology and the Church* (Crestwood, N.Y.: SVS, 1980).

[19]English text in *Nicene and Post-Nicene Fathers*, 2nd series, 14:203.

[20]On the issue of "Tradition and traditions" in Orthodoxy, see V. Lossky, *In the Image and Likeness of God* (Crestwood, N.Y.: SVS, 1974), 141–68; cf. also my own remarks in "Tradition and traditions," *St. Vladimir's Theological Quarterly* 6, (1962): 118–27 and in *Living Tradition, 13–26*.

[21]For a summary history, see F. C. Conybeare, *Russian Dissenters* (New York: Russell and Russell, 1962).

[22]For more detailed discussion of this problem see my article on "Greek Philosophy and Christian Theology in the Early Church" in Meyendorff, *Catholicity and the Church*, 31–47. In general, modern historians of Christian thought like Florovsky and Pelikan are inclined to reject the nineteenth-century idea of a "surrender" of the patristic tradition to Hellenism.

[23]On A. S. Khomyakov and other "older Slavophiles," see the successive volumes by Peter K. Christoff on A. S. Khomyakov, I. V. Kireevsky, and K. S. Aksakov. The last (third) volume was published by Princeton University Press, 1982. The preceding volumes and other literature are referred to there.

[24]On Florensky, see R. Slesinsky, *Pavel Florensky: A Metaphysics of Love* (Crestwood, N.Y.: SVS, 1984).

[25]Cf. J. Pain and N. Zernov, eds., *A Bulgakov Anthology* (Philadelphia: Westminster, 1976).

[26]Cf. G. V. Florovsky, *Ways of Russian Theology* (in Russian) (reprint Paris: YMCA Press, 1981).

[27]Perhaps the greatest witness in the Orthodox tradition to the personal and conscious nature of the Christian experience is the great Byzantine mystic of the eleventh century, St. Symeon the New Theologian; on Symeon, see Abp. Basil Krivocheine, *St. Symeon the New Theologian: Life, Spirituality, Doctrine* (Crestwood, N.Y.: SVS, 1986).

[28]Cf. the classical and brilliant book of R. H. Niebuhr, *The Social Sources of Denominationalism* (New York: Meridian, 1957). It is interesting that the

Orthodox church is not mentioned in the survy at all—in Niebuhr's mind, its existence within American society was of negligible impact to his scheme.

[29]These are well-known examples, taken from the history of Orthodox theology and spirituality; for a brief survey, cf. J. Meyendorff, *St. Gregory Palamas and Orthodox Spirituality* (Crestwood, N.Y.: SVS, 1974).

14

THE TASK OF FEMINIST THEOLOGY

ROSEMARY RADFORD RUETHER
GARRETT-EVANGELICAL DIVINITY SCHOOL,
EVANSTON, ILLINOIS

In theory the task of theology for a woman in the Christian church should be the same as for a man. However, in practice, at this time in the history of the church one must speak of a specific task and vocation of feminist theology for the Christian church. This is because, for most of its two-thousand-year history, the Christian church has not only kept women from the ordained ministry but has also kept women from the study of theology and from the public role of theologian in the church. In fact, proscriptions against women teaching publicly in the church are earlier and continue to be more vociferous than proscriptions against their ordination. Ordination was usually thought to be out of the question, while the possibility that the religious and intellectual gifts of women might be perceived as giving them the status of teachers was continually seen as a threat to be averted.

One finds already in the post-Pauline strata of the New Testament the proscription against women as teachers:

> I do not permit a woman to teach or to have authority over a
> man; she must be silent. (1 Tim. 2:12)

This ban against women as teachers or preachers reflected the fact that the earliest model of Christian leadership was drawn from the rabbinic role of teacher. Only gradually (by the fourth century) was this redefined as priesthood. The ban against women as teachers is repeated in the early church orders, such

359

as the *Didascalia* (early third century) and the *Apostolic Constitutions* (late fourth century). The *Constitutions* declare that Jesus chose to commission men, not women, and also that the male is the head of the woman. It concludes that, for these reasons, women my not teach.[1]

This repression of women as teachers is reiterated in the Middle Ages and is renewed in the Reformation in the mainline Protestant traditions. It continued to be asserted in nineteenth- and twentieth-century arguments about women's right to preach. This repression shows that women preachers were continually appearing and finding a favorable hearing among Christian communities. One does not ban things that are not happening. Some marginal groups, such as the Waldensians in the twelfth century and the Society of Friends in the seventeenth century, supported women's right to teach and preach and even developed scriptural arguments to justify it.[2]

A few theological schools, such as Oberlin College, were open to women in the mid-nineteenth century. Antionette Brown, a graduate from the Oberlin theological program, was also the first woman to be ordained (1853). The struggle over women's ordination raged in much of American Protestantism in the 1880s.[3] By the end of the nineteenth century a number of smaller denominations, such as the Unitarians, Universalists, Congregationalists, and Methodist Protestants, had begun to ordain women. Small numbers of women were present at many theological schools, though most were preparing for home or foreign missionary work, not for the ordained ministry

The key turning point for women's ordination was 1956, the year that both the Methodist church and the Presbyterian Church, USA, decided to ordain women. The Lutheran churches of Scandanavia also accepted women's ordination in the years 1956–58. However, it was not until the late sixties that women began to enter American theological schools in growing numbers, reaching the 50 percent mark by the late 1970s in many seminaries.

With growing numbers of women students, women faculty members also began to appear. A body of critical reflection on the antifemale bias in Christian theology began to be developed and to be taught in seminaries. Thus for the first time it became possible, not only for women's theological teaching to be publicly accepted in the Christian churches but also for the theological tradition that had silenced women to be critically examined and revised.

Christian feminists are only beginning to glimpse the extent of the distortion of the understanding of the Gospel that has resulted from this long history of the exclusion of women as teachers and preachers. What this means, first of all, is that women's experience has been mostly eliminated from the shaping of the official theological culture. A few female saints, prophetesses, and local leaders may have been influential behind the scenes for some male theologians. But their influence was seldom acknowledged, and, even when it was recognized, their thought was edited to make it acceptable to the patriarchal church. Women, half of the human race, with their distinct psycho-physical and social vantage points, have not been able, openly and fully, to enter into the conversation about God and humanity, good and evil, from their own experience. Thus Christian theology has been enormously impoverished by drawing on the experience of only one half of humanity—men.

Not only were women prevented from becoming theological learners and teachers but also the theological tradition itself was biased against them. Christian theology has been distorted both by women's absence and by the need to justify and reinforce their absence. Christian theological tradition is pervaded by dictates that rationalize and justify the women's exclusion by defining her as an irrational and morally inferior expression of the human species, unfit to learn, teach, or minister. Males and male experience have been assumed to be the generic and normative expression of humanity as such. The female has usually been noticed only to define her as "other," as confined to limited roles and excluded from the larger roles of public leadership monopolized by men.

Feminist theology begins with a recognition of this profound distortion of Christian theology, both in its scriptural roots and in its ongoing development, by the absence and silencing of women. The first moment of feminist theology develops from this "hermeneutic of suspicion." This means that its first task is the unmasking and naming of the sexist bias of biblical and theological tradition. Examples of such critical works are Mary Daly's first book, *The Church and the Second Sex* (New York: Harper & Row, 1968) or a book that I edited, *Religion and Sexism: Images of Women in the Jewish and Christian Traditions* (New York: Simon and Schuster, 1974). These works trace the male bias against women from the Scriptures, the Talmud, and writings of the church fathers, medieval and

Reformation theologians into contemporary theology. The
intention is to demonstrate that this male bias is not accidental
or marginal. It is not the expression of an ideosyncratic,
personal view of a few writers. Rather, it runs through the
whole tradition. It shapes, in conscious and unconscious ways,
the whole symbolic universe of Christian thought.

This documentation of male bias in the tradition has greatly
developed, both in depth and sublety, in the last twenty years.
The first works tended to be generalist, an attempt by one
author to survey the whole tradition, bringing out the more
egregious statements of misogyny (woman-hating) in theological history.[4] Examples of this are Tertullian's infamous statement that women are "the Devil's gateway";[5] Augustine's
denial that women possess the image of God in themselves;[6]
Thomas Aquinas's definition of women as "misbegotten
males";[7] Luther's statement that because of her greatest fault
for the Fall, women are in a state of subjugation: "The woman
is like a nail driven into the wall, she sits at home";[8] or Karl
Barth's definition of the relation of male and female as an order
of priority and posteriority, of "A and B."[9]

From this more general stage, feminist critique moves both
to more indepth studies of particular theologians or theological
eras and to the larger issues of androcentrism that surround the
more occasional outbursts of open misogyny. Androcentrism is
the unconscious assumption of both past theologians and their
modern interpreters that males are the normative humans and
normal actors in Christian history. This androcentric bias
screens out the actual presence of women in Scripture and
theological tradition when it does occur. Through this androcentric bias, the memory of alternative traditions is repressed.
This repressive tradition is, in turn, received by the later church
as if it were the normative situation of the Christian past.

The critical feminist examination of Christian tradition has
led to a recognition that overt misogyny occurs in the tradition,
not because women are absent or passive, but because women
are present and active. There is no need to assert that women
should "keep silence," if women are silent. So those moments
when theologians and church leaders are overtly defining
women as inferior or in a status of punishment or, for some
other reason, justifying the negation of their leadership must
also be examined as a time when female leadership was actually
happening. Misogyny is a signal of the actual presence of
female leadership.

An example of this principle can be found in recent feminist study of the statement in 1 Timothy 2:12. This statement is shown not to reflect the universal practice of the Christian church at that time but rather to be one side of an argument. Other Pauline churches took a different view. They believed that the difference between male and female had been transcended in Christ. Particularly the celibate woman, who transcends her sexual role, is freed from these traditional patriarchal restrictions, and is called to preach and teach. This view is found in the apocryphal "Acts of Paul and Thecla." New Testament scholar Dennis R. MacDonald has argued that this alternative Pauline view was developed among churches of the subapostolic or second-generation period. Thus 1 Timothy must be seen as a reaction against and an effort to refute among Pauline churches this alternative understanding of women's equality in Christ.[10]

The documents that expressed this view were not declared heretical and repressed, but they were preserved as legitimate, although noncanonical, tradition. But, by being excluded from the canon, they were not taken seriously. One side of the argument, that which sought to repress women's leadership and restore the patriarchal model of family and society, was received by the later church as the normative teaching and universal practice.

Thus the seeming passivity and absence of women does not accurately reflect the real Christian past. It is the product of the erasure of the memory of women's actual participation and the reediting of that past. The problem for women in Christian tradition is not so much that they have been absent, as that they have lacked legitimating power. They have lacked the power to preserve the memory of their own participation and to see that that memory is taught as part of the tradition. What makes the present situation of women in the church somewhat different from the past is that, for the first time, there is a chance that what women are doing today, and also what they have done in the past, might be reclaimed as part of Christian tradition.

This recognition that outbursts of misogyny do not occur in a vacuum but are reactions against women's activity and that women in the Christian past have not so much been silent as silenced leads to the second moment of feminist theology. This is the reclaiming of alternative tradition, alternative history that supports the full personhood and participation of women.

This search for alternative tradition takes a plurality of

forms at the present time. It takes the form of feminist biblical exegesis of Hebrew Scripture and of the New Testament to show that there are overlooked recollections in the Scriptures of women participating in prophecy, in teaching, and in ministry and of this participation as accepted and affirmed.[11] Such a quest does not deny patriarchal bias, but it shows that, even amid this bias, there are many glimpses of other realities. Women are there in the biblical drama, not just as objects, but as subjects. Women are there, acting as spokespersons of God and are being affirmed as images of God and as vehicles of the Spirit.

Such a quest for alternative tradition takes the form of new research into the histories of the church fathers, the Middle Ages, the Reformation, and more recent Christian history, discovering and chronicling the stories of the church mothers who were there, but whose existence has been overlooked or covered up. Such a quest for alternative tradition is not confined to those women who remain within the "orthodox" tradition of the dominant church of the time, the Paulas and Melanias of the fourth-century ascetic movement, the medieval abbess, or the Reformation pastor's wife. These stories of more mainline Christian women are an important starting point in the recovery of the memory of Christian women's history. But the quest also moves into other regions of traditions that have been more deeply buried, rejected, and repressed by orthodox leadership. It looks at the Montanists and Gnostics of the early church; the Beguines, Joachites, and Waldensians of Medieval sectarianism; the radical Baptists, Levelers, Diggers, and Quakers of the explosive period of the English Civil War; and the Shakers, mystics, utopians, and transcendentalists of American Christianity.[12]

In searching out these by-ways of the tradition, feminist theology discounts the judgment of the various exponents of "orthodoxy" against them, which have defined such figures as out of bounds for the discussion of theological truth. It reads these traditions with an open mind, receptive to their insights and struggles for authentic understanding on their own terms. But feminist theology is not just engaged in a campaign to reverse orthodoxy, judging all that is traditionally accepted as corrupt and all that has been marginalized as impeccable. Rather, it applies its hermeneutics of suspicion to these marginal traditions as well and finds them inadequate at best. The very effort to assert an alternative in the face of dominant tradition, often backed up by persecutory power, generally took its toll on such persons and movements. Many times they could express their alternative insights only in a fanatical way, setting up their own antithetical dualisms.[13]

The search for useable tradition also looks at the cultural and social worlds in which Christian thought is operating in any period. What are the presuppositions of that culture that remain unquestioned? There is a hermeneutical circle in this quest for useable tradition. The searcher begins to shape a working hypothesis of what a holistic and adequate perspective would look like, one that would be affirmative of women's humanity in mutality with that of men. One seeks to find reflections of this holistic vision in both the recognized and the buried parts of the Christian past. In this process one is continually forced to expand and revise one's hypotheses, as possibilities for understanding the fullness of humanity in relation to creation and to God emerge in unexpected ways from recovered communities of experience and reflection. One may not be satisfied that one has found the whole of what one seeks anywhere in past tradition, either in orthodoxy or in heterodoxy, either in scholastics or in mystics, but one finds some touchstones of authentic life in all of them in different ways. Out of this quest one is assembling a vision of the Gospel that can be articulated for today.

The third moment of feminist theology, then, consists in the tentative effort to state a feminist constructive theology to articulate the redemptive Good News in a way that would be truly inclusive of women. A feminist constructive theology begins to work through the basic keys to theological reflection: What are one's sources and norms? What is the nature and action of the divine in relation to creation? How is human nature, male and female defined? What is evil, and how does it come about? What does redemption mean? How do conversion and transformation come about? What does redemptive community mean? What is the nature of the ministry and mission of this redemptive community? What can we hope for, both within and beyond history?[14] Even this use of the traditional structure of systematic theology is tentative. Are the presuppositions of this systematic framework themselves androcentric? One cannot know what is down the road except by walking it and seeing the new vistas that appear in the process.

The feminist Christian theologian is standing within, reevaluating and reconstructing a tradition that has been profoundly biased against her very gender-humanity. This is possible only through a fundamental act of faith. This act of faith is not, first of all, in the infallibility of the church, of its tradition or its Scriptures. It is an act of faith in God. It is an act of trust in authentic reality. It is an affirmation of the ultimate truthfulness, goodness, and reliability of the divine One who created us, as women, and of the ultimate goodness of that which God created.

The foundational faith of feminist theology is that God created women fully human and intends to affirm and promote the realization of her fullness of humanity. Therefore whatever denies, diminishes, and distorts the full humanity of women must be evaluated as nonredemptive and not as a reflection of the authentic intention of our Creator. Such denial or diminishment of our humanity does not express either our true nature or true relation to our Creator. It is not the authentic message or work of our true Redeemer or of a true community of redemption.

This negative principle implies a positive principle. What does promote the full humanity of women, in mutual affirmation of the full humanity of men, is of the Holy, does reflect true relation to God, is the authentic message of Christ, and is the true mission of the church. Yet we do not know what this fullness of women's and men's humanity means. We live in a distorted reality and gain only fragmentary glimpses of our true nature and potential. To affirm it is a fundamental act of faith in the true ground of our being, over against all that has alienated us from God and distorted us from our authentic humanness, in relation to ourselves, to one another, and to the created world around us.

I have said that male bias against women in Christian theological tradition is not marginal or occasional. It pervades the entire symbolic system of theology. What I wish to do is to summarize the way this bias pervades Christian theology as a system. I will then discuss the basis for rethinking this bias. I will look at the way in which male bias interconnects five major categories of theological doctrine: (1) anthropology, (2) the interpretation of sin and salvation, (3) Christology, (4) God-language, and (5) ministry.

In anthropology, the male is defined traditionally as the normative human person. In the Genesis 2 account of the creation of "man," the male is described as having been created first, with the female taken from his "rib." This mythic account

reverses the actual relation of males to females in birth. All men
(and women) obviously are born from women. The myth of
Eve's birth from Adam's "side" serves to locate the male as the
primary expression of humanity. The female is defined as
secondary and auxiliary to the male.

The Genesis 1 account of human creation defines Adam
generically, male and female, as made in the image of God.
This text has been read in modern times as an egalitarian text.
Both males and females are made in the image of God. This
establishes a relationship of equality and mutuality between the
sexes in relation to God and as God's corporate representatives
in ruling over creation.[15]

However, this text was not read as establishing equality
between men and women in classical Christian tradition.
Rather, the term *Adam* was understood to mean the male as the
normative representative of humanity. The term *image of God*
was understood to mean rationality and authority. The male
alone possessed these qualities. Therefore he alone possesses
the image of God. As St. Augustine interpreted this text, in his
treatise on the Trinity, women do not possess the image of God
in themselves, but only when taken together with the male,
who is their head. In herself woman was seen as "imaging" the
body and those passionate parts of the psyche that must be
subjugated to male rationality and sovereignty.[16]

The Christian doctrines of sin and salvation reinforce,
through overt misogyny, the androcentrism inherent in these
definitions of humanity. In Genesis 3 the woman is said to have
initiated the sin of disobedience to God that caused the
explusion of the primal human pair from Paradise. This story,
which is not accorded any other mention in the rest of Hebrew
Scripture, took on a new meaning and authority in Jewish
exegesis during the Hellenistic era.[17] It was picked up and used
in the 1 Timothy text mentioned earlier as the key text to prove
that women are both secondary in the order of creation and
doubly subjugated because of their priority in sin.

This interpretation of Genesis 3 in 1 Timothy becomes key
for the understanding of original sin in subsequent Christian
theology. Women are seen as having a special guilt in causing
original sin. This special role of women in causing original sin
comes about because woman got out of her proper "place,"
as secondary and auxiliary to the male, by questioning God's
orders and acting on her own initiative. Pain in childbirth and
subjugation to her husband's will has been imposed on her by

God as punishment for this primal sin of woman—the sin that lost to humanity original blessedness and imposed on them the troubles of harsh toil in a hostile world.

Thus Christianity establishes what can be called an anti-female "scapegoating" understanding of the origins and cause of sin. Women are to be redeemed, according to this line of theological thought, by voluntary submission to their subjugation to male domination and acceptance of painful childbearing. Her female nature is defined through these sexual and social roles. Women are to accept the abusive use of these roles, not only as their nature, but also as expression of their guilt for a primal sin that is the source of all human troubles. This suggests that any male physical and social abuse she receives is her just deserts. If a man rapes her, she probably has caused it by being sexually provocative. If her husband beats her, she must deserve it because she has been insufficiently docile in response to his demands. This Christian victim-blaming ideology justifies male domination over women and even the abuse of this domination and directs women to accept both as her means of salvation.

In the patriarchal construct of theology, God-language and Christology provide the divine counterparts to this androcentric and misogynist anthropology. Athough God is defined as "Spirit" who is beyond human words and metaphors, nevertheless God is to be referred to as "he," to be described by exclusively male physical and social metaphors. Because only males, not females, possess the image of God and represent divine reason and sovereignty, only male metaphors are seen as appropriate for God. This further denies that women are theomorphic, or possess the image of God, since female images and female persons cannot represent God.

Maleness also is seen as characterizing the divine Word or "Son" of God manifest in Christ. The maleness of the historical Jesus, then, can be seen as doubly necessary, both because this represents the masculinity of God and God's Son or divine Word and because only the male possesses full and normative human nature.

This masculinist Christology was accentuated in scholastic theology of the medieval and Reformation periods by the appropriation of the false biological view of gestation derived from Aristotle. According to Aristotle, the male semen is the embryo or entire genetic potency in gestation. The mother provides only the "matter" that "fleshes out" the male seed.

Every male seed should normatively result in a male. A female is born only through a defect in gestation in which the male potency fails to fully master the female matter. Females are defined as defective or "misbegotten" humans, lacking full human nature, physically, mentally, and morally.[18] It followed from this use of Aristotle in Christian theology that Christ must be a male to incarnate the fullness of human nature. Only a male, in turn, can represent Christ. Although women are redeemed by Christ, they cannot represent Christ.[19]

This masculinist Christology, then, finds expression in a denial of the possibility of priesthood to women. This argument is found in the 1976 Vatican Declaration against the ordination of women; it says that "there must be a natural resemblance between the priest and Christ."[20] The incapacity of women to "image" or represent Christ has been central to the denial of women's ordination among priestly or sacramental churches, while those churches that stress the minister as preacher focus more on the Pauline texts that define women as being under male headship and the command found there to be "silent" in church.

The hierarchy of male over female, reduplicated in the hierarchy of patriarchal clericalism over women as laity, is further underscored by the use of the imagery of bridegroom and bride as symbols of Christ and the church. This metaphorical image of Christ and the church as husband and wife is not based on a companionate model of marriage but on a patriarchal concept of the husband as sovereign over the wife. He is seen as her "head," while she is defined as the extension of his "body" or as his possession.[21] In the same way the church is defined as Christ's body and Christ as her "head."

Although this imagery in Ephesians 5 has nothing to do with a hierarchy of clergy and laity, it soon comes to be used for this relationship. For priestly churches especially, this image of the bridegroom-bride as Christ and the church, and as clergy and laity, becomes another favorite argument against women's ordination. Since women cannot be "husbands" or "bridegrooms," it follows that they cannot represent Christ as bridegroom in relationship to the church. This argument was key in the recent declaration by Pope John Paul II that reiterated the incapacity of women to be ordained because they cannot represent Christ.[22]

Interestingly enough, this same bridegroom-bride imagery is never used to argue that men cannot be members of the laity.

Indeed the pope explicitly claims that males also, in relation to Christ, are symbolically "brides." The underlying assumption here is that men can represent divine sovereignty and authority in relation to those under them and can also be in the status of subjugation in relation to God and to those men who represent God, but women can symbolize only the status of subjugation. The importation of patriarchal hierarchy into the definition of the relation of clergy and laity also defined this relationship paternalistically. The ordained ministry is defined as monopolizing all active ministry, while the laity become the passive consumers of the ministry of the clergy.

This brief summary shows how pervasively androcentric assumptions shape the whole system of Christian theology. By itself such a summary can easily lead to dispair of any significant possibility of liberation of Christianity from patriarchy. Many feminists of Protestant and Catholic background, who have studied Christian theology, have come to this conclusion. They have decided that this patriarchal bias is not accidental but essential to Christianity. It cannot be significantly changed. Therefore Christianity cannot be a religion that affirms women's full humanity. Women (and men) should leave the Christian churches, they say, and seek out or create alternative spiritualities, perhaps from ancient nature religions, that are most conducive to real gender equality nd mutuality.[23]

Such a judgment would be just if this dominant patriarchal tradition were the sole Christian tradition and if there were not significant countercultural trends in both the Bible and in the Christian tradition of thought and practice that provide different options. The alternative options have been developed in modern times by liberal and liberationist theologies that have effected a significant transformation of women's roles in the churches. Christian churches today demonstrate features, not of univocal patriarchalism, but rather of sharp conflict between liberalizing trends that promote equality of women in society and in the church, and of reactionary efforts to shore up patriarchal patterns.

What are the roots of this alternative, egalitarian tradition? I regard this tradition as rooted in the prophetic understanding of Hebrew faith, which experiences God as located, not on the side of the wealthy and powerful in society, but on the side of the poor and victimized. This message was renewed by the Jesus movement within first-century Judaism with its good news to the poor and its criticism of the oppressive power of the ruling social and clerical classes.

The prophet speaks as an advocate of the marginalized and despised people who have no hope within the existing religious and social systems of power and righteousness. The prophet denounces social injustice and also the religious ideologies that justify this injustice. The prophet holds up the cultic and legal proscriptions of the clerical establishment to the standards of divine justice and mercy and finds them wanting. The prophet announces God's judgment on this unjust society and also envisions a transformed world where justice and peace will prevail—where, as Jesus puts it in the Lord's Prayer, God's will is done on earth, as it is in heaven.

In Hebrew Scripture this prophetic denunciation and annunciation focused on the exploited peasantry, the widow and orphan, *vis à vis* the urban elite. The New Testament extends this vision to those dominated within the patriarchal household, women and slaves. It also universalizes the vision, moving it beyond the ethnocentric limits of Israel to a new community that makes redemption available to those of all nations. The Christian church held out a vision of a new humanity in which the divisions of Jew and Greek, slave and free, male and female had been overcome in Christ.

However, this egalitarian vision conflicted with the deep-seated assumption that patriarchy—the control of the male head of family over women, young people, and slaves—was intrinsic to all social order. Patriarchy was seen as foundational to the natural or cosmic order itself. The emancipation of women from patriarchy was unimaginable except through some transformation of the cosmos that would transcend death and hence the need for reproduction. So the radical egalitarian groups of the early Christian movement envisioned women's equality and freedom from the patriarchal family as an anticipation of that heavenly order when there would be "no more marriage or giving in marriage," when death and birth would no longer be necessary. Their conservative opponents, who opposed women's equality, also opposed the ascetic denial of marriage and reproduction.[24]

This conflict between patriarchalists and eschatological egalitarians defined the major options for classical Christianity. Patristic and medieval Christianity combined a patriarchal church and family order with an instituionalized asceticism in monastic orders. Egalitarian radicals were marginalized and declared heretical, although this option continually reappeared in both mystical and apocalyptic forms; i.e., Gnosticism and Montanism and their heirs.

Only in the late eighteenth and nineteenth centuries did it begin to become possible to imagine an alternative reading of the Christian egalitarian tradition. Liberalism naturalized the biblical vision of original equality in God's image. This original equality, and not patriarchy, was understood to be the primal "order of Nature." Class hierarchy, slavery, racism, and, finally, sexism, came to be seen, not as divinely ordained "orders of creation," but as unjust, humanly created social systems. It became possible to imagine changing these systems, and establishing civil equality between classes and races of men and between men and women. This no longer was understood to mean transcendence of creation but renewal of creation within history on its original foundations.

Feminism and feminist theology are rooted in this Enlightenment reinterpretation of the biblical prophetic tradition. Feminism reinterprets the biblical and Christian egalitarian tradition in terms of the modern consciousness of social systems as human artifacts, not divine orders of nature. It takes original equality to be the foundational truth of human nature in the light of which patriarchy can and must be transformed. It recontextualizes this tradition in terms of the problematic of female subjugation and emancipation.

What would it mean to reconstruct the Christian symbolic system from its androcentric, misogynist form detailed earlier to egalitarian inclusivity? This would imply a clear repudiation of still lingering assumptions that patriarchy is a divinely ordained order of creation. It would mean naming patriarchy as sin, as unjust, distorted relationality that corrupts the humanity of women and men. It would also mean the rejection of any gynecentric reversal of gender relationships and symbolisms that would make women the primary exemplars of true humanity and primary bearers of the divine image.

Feminist theology calls for a comprehensive effort to express the whole system of theology as mutual interrelation. I will briefly summarize what such a theology would look like in terms of the major symbols of anthropology, sin and redemption, Christology, God-language, and ecclesiology.

In terms of anthropology this would mean affirming that both men and women possess the fullness of human nature. They do not relate to each other as superior to inferior or as complimentary parts of a human nature in which each has the half that the other lacks. Rather, woman as woman and man as man each possess the fullness of human nature. Their relationship should be that of mutually transforming love that nurtures and enables the full and equivalent human personhood of each.

The understanding of sin would name sexism as sin and patriarchy as a sinful social system. Sexism and patriarchy express sin as a distortion of human relationality into domination and subordination, corrupting the humanity of both men and women. Grace gives the critical consciousness that will enable us to recognize such distortions as sinful, to be converted from them, and to struggle against them in order to overcome patriarchy both in personal relationships and in social systems. Redemption means building new human relationships, personally and systemically, based on mutual co-humanity.

Our experience of Christ as the presence of God reveals the nature of God as the power of co-humanity. Christ is our revealed paradigm of the Logos-Sophia, or Word and Wisdom of God. God's Wisdom-and-Word is beyond male and female and at the same time is personified in both women and men. The maleness of the human person of Jesus of Nazareth in no way limits God representation to one gender. Rather Jesus' male gender is simply one of the forms of his historical particularity as an individual person, in the same sense as his Jewishness and the fact that he was born in a particular place and time and had particular physical features.

Jesus is both fully an individual person and also the Representative of all persons. The fact that he was a male no more limits those who speak in his name to males than the fact that he was a Jew limits those who speak in his name to Jews. We are the Christian community who know Christ, not after the flesh, but after the Spirit; that is, no longer limited by particularities of place, time, race, or gender. In the ongoing community of faith we are called to encounter Christ in one another, particularly in our sisters and brothers who suffer for justice and are victims of injustice.

Our God-language must also reflect this understanding of Christ and ourselves. If all persons, female and male, are fully human, mutually interrelated, then God cannot be imaged in terms of only one gender. God is both beyond gender, neither male nor female, and the ground of mutual personhood of both men and women. All language of God is metaphorical, not literal. If women are as fully the image of God as men, then God must be imaged in metaphors drawn from female being and activity as much as from that of males. But this female imaging of God should not reinforce unjust gender stereotyping. Rather, it should point us to the redeemed fullness of personhood of both women and men.

Finally, in our understanding ministry we should begin by understanding church as both a nurturing and a prophetic community of liberation from evil, including evil as patriarchy. As church we seek to enter into just and loving co-humanity. Ministry is the enabling of the community of faith to develop its life together as mutual birthing of our full humanity and as witness to the world of its exodus from patriarchy and its entrance into co-humanity in Christ.

This means a fundamental transformation of the clerical model of ordained ministry that has been modeled after patriarchal hierarchy. Patriarchal clericalism monopolizes the powers of teaching, sacramental acts, and administration for an ordained caste and reduces the laity to dependency on this caste. Christian ministry as mutual service, on the other hand, draws forth the gifts of the whole community to enable one another to grow and to build up their life together. This does not do away with the need for organization, designation of leaders, and testing of gifts and skills. But it means that these gifts and powers are used in a fundamentally different way, to empower others and bring forth their gifts in service, rather than to disempower others and reduce them to consumers of the ministry of the ordained.

Many women and men today have caught this vision of co-humanity and redemptive community, but they find it increasingly problematic to try to experience and live out this vision in the Christian churches. Most local churches of established denominations either reject the legitimacy of such critique and revisioning of the Gospel altogether or else allow it only in token and minimal ways. Attendance at church becomes an increasingly enraging and demoralizing experience for those who have glimpsed this redemptive vision.

Some women and men are leaving the Christian churches altogether, convinced that patriarchy is much too intrinsic to at least the historical reality, if not the essence, of these bodies. Feminist Christians, however, are clear that only through an egalitarian revisioning can Christianity be recovered as a viable good news for today. But many are at a loss to find communities that are in sincere struggle to live out this vision. Many women have turned to the creation of women-church or feminist Christian base communities as a way of creating the new culture and spirituality of co-humanity that expressess what it might mean to be redeemed from patriarchy.

I believe that this feminist recovery of the "free church" is probably essential to the renewal of the church and its theology and spirituality today. But I believe that it will have its most effective power by remaining dialectically interactive with historical churches rather than withdrawing into self-enclosed sectarianism. The free-church strategy of autonomous women-church base communities needs to be related to places within established historic churches that can receive the gifts of these free communities and mediate them through their wider netowrks of communication. Only by holding on to both sides of this dialectic is there the possibility that the new vision can both develop freely and become a leaven for the larger Christian community.

Feminist theology must see itself as called to do theology both within and for the church by also doing theology against its millennia-old heresy of sexism. To take this calling seriously will transform and redefine all the traditional symbols of theology. But it will also call this theological task out of intellectual and academic abstraction into being the practical means of conversion of the church from sin and alienation into fullness of life in Christ. It is for this process, and not as an end in itself, that theology exists.

NOTES

[1]James Donaldson, ed., *The Apostolic Constitutions* (Edinburgh: T. & T. Clark, 1890).

[2]Margaret Fell, *Women's Speaking Justified, Proved and Allowed of by the Scriptures* (1667; reprint, London: n.d.).

[3]Barbara Brown Zikmund, "The Struggle for the Right to Preach," in Rosemary R. Ruether and Rosemary S. Keller, eds. *Women and Religion in America: The Nineteenth Century* (San Francisco: Harper & Row, 1981), 193–240.

[4]Mary Daly, *The Church and the Second Sex* (New York: Harper & Row, 1968).

[5]Tertullian, *On the Dress of Women*, 1, 1 in *Ante-Nicene Fathers*, 55 vols., ed., James Donaldson and Alexander Roberts (New York: Scribners, 1890), 4:14.

[6]Augustine, *On the Trinity* 7, 7, 10; in *Later Works*, ed., John Burnaby (Philadelphia: Westminster, 1955).

[7]Thomas Aquinas, *Summa Theologica*, pt. 1, q. 92, art. 1; ed., Anton Pegis (New York: Random House, 1945).

[8]Martin Luther, *Lectures on Genesis*, Gen. 2:18, in *Luther's Works*, ed. Jaroslav Pelikan (St. Louis: Concordia, 1958), 1:115.

[9]Karl Barth, *Church Dogmatics*, 3 vols. (Edinburgh: T. & T. Clark, 1975), 3.4, 158–72.

[10]Dennis R. MacDonald *The Legend and the Apostle: The Battle for Paul in Story and Canon* (Philadelphia: Westminster, 1983).

[11]For feminist New Testament hermeneutics, see particularly the work of Elizabeth S. Fiorenza, *In Memory of Me* (New York: Crossroad, 1983).

[12]Rosemary Radford Ruether, *Women of Spirit: Female Leadership in the Jewish and Christian Traditions* (New York: Simon and Schuster, 1979).

[13]For an example of the precarious line between insanity and prophetism, see Joyce L. Irwin, *Womanhood in Radical Protestantism, 1525–1675* (New York: Edwin Mellen, 1979).

[14]See Rosemary Ruether, *Sexism and God-talk; Toward a Feminist Theology* (Boston: Beacon, 1983).

[15]For a modern egalitarian interpretation of the concept of the *imago dei*, see Phyllis Bird, "Male and Female, He Created Them: Gen. 1:27b in the Context of the Priestly Account of Creation," *Harvard Theological Review* 74, 2 (1981): 129–59.

[16]For a careful analysis of the Augustinian anthropology, see Kari Borresen, *Subordination and Equivalence: The Nature and Role of Women in Augustine and Thomas Aquinas* (1968; Eng. translation, Washington: University Press of America, 1981).

[17]The first reference to this theme in Genesis 3 is the apocryphal work *Ecclesiasticus* or *The Wisdom of Ben Sirach*, 25:24, written about 180 B.C.

[18]Aristotle, *Generation of Animals*, 729, 737–38, 775.

[19]See note 7 above, also Borresen, *Subordination and Equivalence*.

[20]*Declaration on the Question of the Admission of Women to the Ministerial Priesthood* (October 15, 1976), 5, 27, (37).

[21]In Roman law the patriarch or head of the family was not seen as a member of the family. Rather, the term *familia* was understood to refer to the persons and property owned and ruled over by him; see David Herlihy, *Medieval Households* (Cambridge, Mass.: Harvard University Press, 1985), chap. 1.

[22]See the document by Pope John Paul II, "The Dignity and Vocation of Women" (September 30, 1988), Vatican City, Libreria Editrice Vaticana.

[23]This is the position taken by Mary Daly in *Pure Lust: Elemental Feminist Philosophy* (Boston: Beacon, 1984).

[24]Rosemary Ruether, "Asceticism and Feminism: Strange Bedmates?" in Linda Hurcombe, ed., *Sex and God: Some Varieties of Women's Religious Experience* (London: Routledge and Kegan Paul, 1987), 229–50.

15

THE SUBVERSIVENESS OF FAITH: A PARADIGM FOR DOING LIBERATION THEOLOGY

ORLANDO E. COSTAS
LATE PROFESSOR AT ANDOVER NEWTON
THEOLOGICAL SCHOOL, NEWTON, MASSACHUSETTS

In an essay published several years ago, the Asian-American theologian Roy Sano posited the use of stories as a common method of doing ethnic liberation theologies.* Stories, he argued, help ethnic minorities recover their social, cultural, and historical identity and shape their consciousness as a people. He went on to suggest that the Biblical story of Esther has the potential of enabling ethnic minorities to make better sense of their oppressive past and present in a society that has been programmed to by-pass, ignore, marginalize, and repress those communities that refuse to conform to the Euro-American melting pot.[1]

This is especially applicable to the four large racial minorities in the United States (Afro-American, Asian-American, Hispanic-American, and Native-American). Curiously enough, these minorities have not only been given color labels (black, yellow, brown, and red), but for more than two centuries they have also experienced, at different intervals and in varying degrees, the brunt of economic poverty, political powerlessness, and socio-cultural oppression. As a Christian theologian from Puerto Rico working in the continental United States and fully identified with the struggle of North American racial

*This chapter is the text of a public lecture delivered at the TANTUR Ecumenical Institute for Theological Research, March 19, 1987, Jerusalem, Israel.

minorities for economic justice, political empowerment, and socio-cultural fulfillment, I have taken up Sano's suggestion.

I see in Esther, however, not just a narrative that has the potential of enabling oppressed minorities to reappropriate their past and present and reshape their historical consciousness, but a paradigm for any theological discourse that seeks to be liberating. While I readily acknowledge that the story of Esther is couched in language that can lend itself to a purely secular and ideological interpretation, its place in the Hebrew canon and its appropriation by Christians as part of their Holy Scripture give it the character of a narrative of faith. It is my contention that the faith the book of Esther portrays is one of commitment to a providential and liberating God. Such a faith is capable of subverting the status quo, for it empowers the weak and downtrodden by energizing their spirit and setting them free to struggle for the transformation of their historical conditions.

A liberating theology is a critical reflection on the praxis of faith in light of the Word of God. *Praxis* is the creative and transforming action of God's people in history, accompanied by a critical reflection and prophetic process that seeks to make the obedience of faith ever more efficacious. Thus Gustavo Gutièrrez states in his seminal work *A Theology of Liberation* that a liberating theology is

> a theology of liberating transformation of the history of (humankind) and also therefore that part of (humankind)— gathered into *ecclesia*—which openly confesses Christ. This is a theology which does not stop with reflecting on the world, but rather tries to be part of the process through which the world is transformed. It is a theology which is open—in the protest against trampled human dignity, in the struggle against the plunder of the vast majority of people, in liberating love, and in the building of a new, just, and fraternal society—to the gift of the Kingdom of God[2]

A liberating theology constitutes both a protest against oppression and injustice and a struggle for emancipation and justice. It emerges from a context of "powerlessness in society and voicelessness in the church."[3] It is a theology of liberating engagement. As such, it is not divorced from the foundational source of knowledge of the Christian faith: the Hebrew Scriptures and the New Testament. On the contrary, it is

characterized by a critical dialogue with biblical faith, bringing
to the written Word of God the questions that rise out of reality.
In his book *The Liberation of Theology* Juan Luis Segundo has
noted that a liberation theologian starts with the questioning of
the customary way of interpreting the Scriptures, a questioning
that arises out of a new experience of reality in the praxis of
faith. Such a hermeneutical suspicion, applied to culture in
general and exegesis in particular, is accompanied by a
simultaneous search for a new understanding of the Word of
God that will set free the community where the theologian
serves and to whom he or she is accountable; thus the
theologian becomes an agent of transformation in that socio-
historical situation.[4] This critical hermeneutic of suspicion and
hope enables the community of faith to discover in the Bible
certain stories and texts that pose new questions and enable it
to come up with new answers to the questions that emerge out
of its historical praxis.

The story of Esther offers a paradigm for doing liberation
theology. Its central episode represents a radical questioning of
the status quo. It does not accept a negative event as fate or an
accident of history. Rather, it identifies it as a wicked historical
deed and challenges it in the name of justice. It sees history as
open to change for the better because it is led by a providential
and liberating God who is veiled behind the powerless and
oppressed.

In this chapter I want to demonstrate a way of doing
liberation theology. I will do so by examining Esther as a
paradigm of a liberating theology. This will require an exploration of Esther's prophetic praxis, leading to a statement on the
challenge of the story for Jews and Christians in our time and in
our respective situations. It should be clear that my purpose is
to engage in neither a scientific exegesis nor a literary analysis
of the biblical text, but rather to reflect theologically on the
central episode of the book of Esther as a story that demonstrates the subversiveness of faith, invites us to critically reflect
on our faith from the underside of history, and summons us to
a liberating praxis in our respective historical situations. In so
doing I will illustrate how I approach the theological task in a
liberation perspective.

THE EPIC OF ESTHER[5]

The story of Esther is the rationale for the annual Jewish feast of Purim. This feast commemorates the irony (or tragic humor) of that event. The date for the proposed massacre of the Jews had been fixed by the Persian method of casting *pur*, or the lot (3:7; 9:24). As it turned out, however, the lot fell upon Haman, the very person who had devised the wicked plot to exterminate the Jews, thanks to God's providential intervention through Esther's faithful endeavors.

The story, according to the biblical text, takes place during the reign of Ahasuerus, emperor of the Persian Empire from 485 to 465 B.C. He has been identified as Xerxes I. Susa, capital of the empire, was witnessing a great feast that Ahasuerus was holding for the most important functionaries of the empire. He wanted to present Queen Vashti to the public so that all his guests could admire her beauty. According to the custom of the time and culture, women covered themselves with a veil. Therefore, because showing herself to the guests of the king (all male) would lower her dignity and publicly humiliate her, Vashti refused to obey the king's command. For this reason, "the king became furious and burned with anger" (1:12).

According to the king's advisors and ministers, what Vashti had done was embarrassing not only for the king but also for the entire empire. Besides, they feared that the queen's deed would become known by the women of the empire, causing them to "despise their husbands" (1:17). Therefore they advised the king to depose and get rid of Vashti and search for a better woman to serve as queen. Vashti was punished; her dethronement was intended to serve as an example for all the women of the empire. Several days later, the king ordered a "contest" featuring the most beautiful young women of the empire in order to choose a new queen.

Esther was a beautiful young woman whose father and mother had died early in her life; she had been reared by her cousin and adopted father, Mordecai, one of many Jews "who had been carried into exile from Jerusalem by Nebuchadnezzar, king of Babylon" (2:6). Conscious of what it could mean for the Jews to have one of their own near to the king, he encouraged Esther to enter the contest and trained her for it. He advised her, however, to conceal her ethnicity. In the divine providence, Esther was selected from among hundreds of contestants to be the queen of the Median-Persian Empire.

One day the future of the Jews was suddenly endangered. The king had commanded that all the royal officials at the king's gate kneel down and pay honor to Haman, prime minister of the king. "But Mordecai would not kneel down or pay him honor" (3:2). In revenge, "Haman sought to destroy, kill and annihilate all the Jews—young and old, women and little children" throughout the empire (3:13). He managed to get the king to sign a decree condemning all the Jews to destruction.

As soon as Mordecai heard of the decree, he "tore his clothes" and "put on sackcloth and ashes" (4:1). He went all over the city "wailing loudly and bitterly" (4:1).

Esther learned of Mordecai's odd behavior and sent him clean clothes so that he could enter the palace and explain to her what was wrong. Mordecai refused the clothes. Then Esther sent her chief personal guard to inquire of Mordecai what had happened. Mordecai relayed the news of the decree and asked that the queen intercede before the king on behalf of her people. Esther hesitated at first because of a law that forbade anyone to approach the king unsummoned under the penalty of death—unless the king graciously held out "the gold scepter" allowing him or her to live (4:11). When Mordecai heard of her hesitation,

> he sent back this answer: "Do not think that because you are in the king's house you alone of all the Jews will escape. For if you remain silent at this time, relief and deliverance for the Jews will arise from another place, but you and your father's family will perish. And who knows but that you have come to royal position for such a time as this?" (4:13–14).

Then Esther agreed to appear before the king. Before doing so, however, she ordered Mordecai to gather all the Jews in Susa and to fast for three days on her behalf. She and her maids would participate in the fast. After the three days of fast, she would go to see the king, even though it was against the law; and if she should perish, so be it (4:16).

God responded favorably to the fast of Esther and her maids and of Mordecai and all the Jews of Susa. Not only did the king receive her and make it possible for Jews to be spared, but he brought Haman to judgment and rewarded Mordecai's faithfulness by making him his prime minister.

> Mordecai left the king's presence wearing royal garments of blue and white, a large crown of gold and a purple robe of

fine linen. And the city of Susa held a joyous celebration. For the Jews it was a time of happiness and joy, gladness and honor. In every province and in every city, wherever the edict of the king went, there was joy and gladness among the Jews, with feasting and celebrating. And many people of other nationalities became Jews because fear of the Jews had seized them. (8:15–17).

The epic of Esther is meaningful for Jews as well as for oppressed people everywhere. Esther (and we should also add the other hero of the story, Mordecai) represents what J. B. Metz has called a "subversive memory." Her example (and that of Mordecai) lives in the memory of oppressed and powerless people in every society in which they are threatened with annihilation by the wicked machination of unscrupulous, idolatrous, and unjust power brokers.

The high place that has been given to the story of Esther in the collective history of the Jews (as symbolized by the Feast of Purim and the canonical place given to the book at the Council of Jamnia)[6] and the natural sympathy that such a story expresses for any oppressed people are superseded only by Esther's obedient character. Even though she rose to the throne on account of an event that could be described as alienating and opportunistic, she managed to put her resources at the service of the oppressed. While the courageous Vashti disobeyed as an act of protest without any other consequence than opening the way for Esther (a contribution that from the "providentialist" perspective of the narrative is to be viewed as rather significant), Esther distinguished herself by her submission and subversion. Esther is remembered, therefore, as a strong, courageous woman, who disobeyed the law of the empire in order to obey God. In such a context, obedience cannot be understood simply as blind acceptance of an order imposed from above, but rather as the grace to hear sensitively the liberating word of God implicit in the unfolding of the story, the wisdom to understand it, and the strength to fulfill it, leaving one to do what is right and just in God's sight.

THE PROPHETIC PRAXIS OF ESTHER

What was the secret of Esther's daring and courageous obedience? A close scrutiny of her prophetic action will reveal that her secret lay in her ability to remember several foundational aspects in her life—aspects that are common to all beings.

She Remembered Her Roots

First, Esther did not forget her roots. She remembered that before she was the king's wife, she was the daughter of Mordecai's uncle, the girl he adopted as his own daughter when her father died (2:7; 4:4–6). That is why when she learned that he had put on "sackcloth and ashes" and had gone throughout the city "wailing loudly and bitterly" (4:1–2), she "was deeply distressed" and sought to help him (4:4). To be sure, she acted out of family love, but interestingly enough, she did so in a manner that was more proper of a queen than of a relative. Perhaps she was embarrassed by his attire and behavior. She sent her servant with proper clothing for Mordecai "to put on instead of his sackcloth" (4:4). Mordecai refused the clothes. Esther then sent her chief servant, Hathach, to find out what was happening and why (4:5). Mordecai informed him what had happened and appealed to Esther "to go into the king's presence to beg for mercy and to plead with him for her people" (4:8). For a while Esther was hesitant on account of the law of the land. Besides, it had been thirty days since she had been called to the king's presence. She acted, therefore, in accordance with her royal role. She did what any politician would do—she thought of the consequences of her action. She acted as a realist. Mordecai was asking her to commit political suicide!

Mordecai reminded her, however, that she was a Jew *before* she was queen, and that she would not escape suffering and death if she remained silent. When he added the punch line— "Who knows but that you have come to royal position for such a time as this?" (4:14) it was *then*, according to the narrative, that she remembered that the liberation of her people took precedence over *her* individual well-being or her political office. In such a time as this, she needed to remember that it was not her individual attributes as a beautiful woman or even her political sense as the queen that mattered. What was important was that she was a Jew, that her people were condemned to death, and that she was in a position to do something about it! She *remembered* her roots and thus realized that the life of others, and especially the salvation of her people, took precedence over her personal survival and well-being.

How difficult it is indeed for us to remember who we really are and where we come from when the waters get rough! It is such a great temptation to deny ourselves, our roots, our families, our collective self in order "to make it" big, particularly if we happen to be members of an ethnic minority where there is always the pressure to forget who we really are in order to win the acceptance of the dominant sectors of society and be free from bigotry and prejudice.

There is no shame in proceeding from a humble origin, in being the son or daughter of an immigrant, in being black or white, yellow or brown, a Yankee or a Southerner, Easterner or Westerner, Arab or Jew, Ashkenazi or Sephardi. But there is shame and tragedy in forgetting where we come from—for sooner or later it will all catch up with us. Those we deny will manage to live without us, but we will not be able to live with ourselves. Remembering who we are and where we come from is, therefore, essential to living at peace with ourselves and with our posterity.

She Remembered Her Calling

Second, Esther remembered the nature of her calling. Her vocation was not simply to be a queen and thus enjoy the privileges of royal life. Her training for and participation in the "beauty contest " that won her the crown was not meant to be an opportunity offered to her to succeed financially, socially, or politically; it was rather an opportunity given to her to serve her people in a moment of crisis. Indeed, Esther's vocation was to represent her people in the royal court when the need and opportunity arrived. For "such a time as this " she had come to the kingdom. That is, she had not reached the crown so that when the crunch came she and her father and mother's house might survive. Instead, she had been brought to the kingdom as a sign of hope and an instrument for life among her people.

There are people who came from the "under and outer side" of life and yet manage to make it in the centers of power only to forget the plight of those they have left behind. They see their success as a private affair. They develop a deformed vocation—a selfish, individualistic inclination for survival and success.

Jesus taught that people who think only of surviving end up losing their lives. "Whoever wants to save his [or her] life

will lose it. . . . What good is it for [a person] to gain the whole
world, yet forfeit his [or her] soul? " (Mark 8:35–36).

The fact of the matter is that the life calling of the people of
God is to be one of service rather than of survival or achieving
personal success. We are not called to be trouble-free and enjoy
the good life, but rather to represent the cause of the oppressed
and be a sign of hope among them. God has indeed shown us
what is good and acceptable: "to act justly and to love mercy
and to walk humbly with . . . God " (Micah 6:8).

We need, therefore, to keep our priorities straight. It is too
easy in consumer-oriented societies to set our goals on wealth
and power rather than on justice and righteousness. It is too
tempting, especially in times such as ours, to want to forget
about the plight of others and think only about ourselves.

In the fall of 1984, Mortimer and Esther Arias learned that
Esther did not have long to live. They decided to leave
immediately the School of Theology at Claremont, California,
where Mortimer had been teaching, and return to their
homeland in Bolivia to await Esther's death. Late in December
1984 she finally rested from her labors. A poem entitled "Gastar
la Vida " (Spending Life) by the Bolivian martyr of human
rights, Father Luis Espinal, was read at the funeral. It is a poem
inspired by the teachings and example of Jesus; the words
express quite vividly the point I have been trying to make. It is
presented here in its English translation in prose form:

> Jesus Christ has said "whoever does not want to spend life
> will lose it." . . . But we are afraid to spend our life, to give it
> away without reserve. To spend life is to work for others,
> even without pay, to make a favor without expecting return.
> To spend life is to throw yourself ahead, even to fail, without
> false prudence. It is to burn your bridges for the sake of the
> neighbor. We are torches that have no meaning except
> burning out [for others].

Such was the case with Esther Arias, who for years gave all
she could for the dispossessed children of Bolivia. And such
was also the example of Queen Esther, who remembered her
call to service and put her future on the line for the cause of her
condemned people. "I will go to the king," she said, "even
though it is against the law. And if I perish, I perish" (4:16).
That was her final answer to Mordecai. Both of these women
kept their priorities straight. They were faithful to their calling.
They were willing to spend their lives in the service of others.

She Remembered God

Third, Queen Esther remembered to whom she really belonged. The fact of the matter is that ultimately she did not belong to herself, to her husband-king, to her adopted father, or even to her own people. She belonged to God.

It was out of this deep conviction that she called for a fast and opted to go before the king. She demonstrated her loyalty to God, not in words or in religious actions, but in an almost suicidal political deed.

Interestingly enough, the book of Esther has no direct reference to God. Nowhere does it mention God explicitly. Esther's call for a fast and Mordecai's claim that "deliverance will rise for the Jews from another quarter" should Esther refuse to help, are the only indirect references to God to be found in the original story.[7] This is congruent with a basic conviction of the Hebrew Scriptures: commitment and loyalty to God is best demonstrated not with our lips and outward functions, but by following the path of justice. "Your father . . . did what was right and just. . . . Is that not what it means to know me?" asks the Lord (Jer. 22:15–16).

In many contemporary situations we run the risk of confusing a "pious" vocabulary and a "religious" lifestyle with faith and spiritual commitment. The real crisis of faith in societies with a religious tradition is not secular humanism but rather the lack of a radical obedience among those who profess commitment to the living God. "Anyone who does not do what is right [and just] is not a child of God," says the apostle John (1 John 3:10).

Tomas Borge, Minister of the Interior of Nicaragua and the lone surviving member of the original Sandinistas, was leaving his office one day shortly after the overthrow of Somoza's regime (July 1979). A former member of Somoza's guard had been captured and was being brought to trial. Borge recognized him immediately as the man who had tortured him. Borge looked the guard member straight in his eyes and asked him, "Do you recognize me?" The man answered, "No." Borge insisted, "Look at me! I was one of those you tortured! And now you will see what the Revolution will do with people like you. Shake my hands! *I forgive you!*"

Here is an avowed Marxist who makes no pretense of being a believer in God. Yet he was the Sandinista who immediately, upon the triumph of the Revolution, began to speak of "generosity in victory." Here is someone who, while not professing to be religious, can demonstrate the most profound expression of what faith in the living God is in reality all about. "I forgive you!" Without professing to believe, he demonstrated what true faith is all about. He showed mercy and did what was right and just in God's sight. Like Esther, he demonstrated what the apostle Paul called the "obedience that comes from faith" (Rom. 1:5).

True faith means obedience, and obedience means doing what is right and just in God's sight. By remembering her roots and thus accepting her Jewish identity at a time when it was very dangerous to do so, by being faithful to her vocation of service and thereby risking her own well-being, and by expressing her loyalty to God in an act of unlawful disobedience for the cause of justice, Esther demonstrated an obedient—indeed, a subversive—faith, a relationship of trust in God's liberating power and commitment to God's justice that went beyond words and religious deeds. Such a faith transcends traditional categories and makes concrete the providential and liberating presence of the living God whom ancient Israel worshiped, the prophets proclaimed, and Jesus embodied—the God who is confessed today by Jews, Christians, and Moslems.

THE THEOLOGICAL CHALLENGE OF ESTHER

It remains for us to consider the challenge of the story of Esther as a liberating theological paradigm. I will pinpoint three issues of fundamental importance in doing liberation theology.

The Importance of Race and Sex in Theology

First, the story of Esther challenges theology to take seriously the dual issue of racism and sexism. Liberation theologies, particularly in the Third World, usually stem from situations where the predominant concern is socio-economic. Class, rather than race or sex, is the issue they address. Gustavo Gutièrrez's statement at the conclusion of his *Theology of Liberation* is typical of at least the Latin American model (which is generally recognized as one of the most representative types of liberation theologies):

The theology of liberation attempts to reflect on the experience and meaning of the faith based on the commitment to abolish injustice and to build a new society; this theology must be verified by the practice of that commitment, by active, effective participation in the struggle which the exploited social classes have undertaken against their oppressors.[8]

I agree that socio-economic exploitation, or classism, is a fundamental issue in the Third World and the poverty-stricken pockets of Western Europe and North America. But in the particular context in which I live and work, class oppression passes through the racist and sexist line, as James Cone, Virgilio Elizondo, Letty Russell, and Rosemary Radford Ruether, among others, have shown in their respective liberation theologies.[9] Therefore, I disagree with Gutièrrez's conclusion that

> liberation from every form of exploitation, the possibility of a more human and more dignified life, the creation of a new man [sic!]—all pass through [the struggle which the exploited social classes have undertaken against their oppressors]![10]

Rather, I hold, with Letty Russell, that

> liberation theologies . . . try to express the gospel in the light of the experience of oppression out of which they are written, whether that be racial or sexual, social or economic, psychological or physical.[11]

The story of Esther contains a strong note on liberation from ethnic (and therefore racist) and sexist oppression. The central concern of the story is not economic in nature. In fact, we may assume that during the time in which the book was written, the Jewish community in the Eastern Diaspora was economically well-off. There is, however, a racial issue at stake. Jews were condemned to death because they are ethnically different. They refused to assimilate. Haman complained to the king, "[Their] customs are different from those of all other people and [they] do not obey the king's laws; it is not in the king's best interest to tolerate them" (3:8). He said this because Mordecai had refused to "kneel down or pay him honor" (v. 2). For the original readers of the story, the message was clear: Be firm on your ethnic identity! Resist assimilation! God will deliver you from those who try to take away your peoplehood!

The story also highlights the dignity and strength of women. Vashti's protest, as I stated earlier, should not be taken lightly. She demands respect from a male-dominated court, and her story stands as a sign of the "subversive memory" of all women who would rather lose prestige and comfort defending their dignity than enjoy a position of privilege and luxury at the expense of their self-worth. It is Esther, however, who shows the full liberating potential of women. She was observant and graceful, politically astute and prophetically courageous. Notwithstanding her respect for and devotion to Mordecai, and his prophetic role, she was ultimately the one who unmasked Haman before the king, achieved the liberation of the Jews, and made it possible for Mordecai to rise to a position of honor.

The story portrayed by the book of Esther is a challenge to all who consider offensive the particularity of ethnic and feminist struggles as part and parcel of the story of faith. Indeed, it is significant that one reason why the canonical status of Esther was questioned in both the Jewish and Christian traditions was its ethnic particularity. The particularity of Esther has been especially offensive to those Christian scholars, theologians, and preachers who have so reconstructed the Biblical drama of salvation that they have highlighted the universalism of the Bible and rejected its particularistic moments. In the words of Roy Sano,

> They [have] used Ruth and overlooked the ethnicity that Esther espoused. They [have] preached about Jonah's conversion to preach grace to the hated Ninevites, but they failed to preach about the glee Nahum felt when he saw the doom that threatened the oppressive Assyrians centered in Nineveh. They [have] gravitated toward the universalism of Isaiah and Amos and the historians who wrote from their viewpoints, but they found no use for Chronicles, Ezra and Nehemiah . . . [who] sought fortifications around Jerusalem, restoration of the Temple within which the divine would manifest itself, and refinement of rituals that celebrated their ethnic histories.[12]

Equally striking is the way in which the feminist line of the book of Esther has been traditionally minimized in scholarly and homiletical circles. No small number of exegetes and preachers have consistently highlighted Mordecai's role in the story and downgraded Esther's making Mordecai the real hero. In fact, this tendency may go all the way back to Hasmonean times when the feast of Purim was know as the "Day of

Mordecai" according to 2 Maccabees 15:36. One contemporary exegete states quite bluntly that "between Mordecai and Esther the greater hero in the Hebrew is Mordecai, who supplied the brain while Esther simply followed his direction."[13] Yet it was Esther who called for a fast on her own initiative, who risked her life and political future to intercede for the Jews, and who set up the trap for Haman. This reflects leadership and cleverness rather than passiveness and dependence. At the very least, it should be acknowledged that the story portrays two equally important heroes, and this constitutes a challenge to male exclusiveness in both the Jewish and Christian traditions.

A Warning to Victims and Oppressors

A second theological challenge I see in the story of Esther is a warning to Jews and Christians alike and by inference, to victims and oppressors. I have argued that the story of Esther is meaningful for Jews (and by inference, for Christians as well) and for all oppressed people everywhere. Esther, Mordecai, and the Jews of Susa represent a victimized community. In this respect they are symbols of the victims of all times and places. To read the book of Esther is to remember the History of Jewish oppression throughout the Diaspora and in the land of Israel, but it should be no less to remember the plight of other innocent victims all over the world. For on the Feast of Purim Jews are mandated to do more than celebrate the days in which they got "relief from their enemies," when their sorrow was turned into joy. They are not just to "give presents of food to one another" but also to give "gifts to the poor" (9:22). This latter requirement stands in the tradition of the Torah, which warns every Jew to be kind to the poor and needy, to the widow and the orphan, to the stranger and sojourner, remembering that they were once "aliens in Egypt" (Exod. 22:21; 23:9; Lev. 19:9–13, 33–34; Deut. 24:14–18: 27:19) and "the Lord . . . God redeemed" them from bondage (Deut. 24:18).

What happens, however, when the situation changes and Jews are no longer victims, as is true today in the land of Israel? Then Purim, like the Passover, is to be a reminder of the justice God expects toward the oppressed. And if perchance Jews are preventing the cause of justice, God will hear the cry of the oppressed and turn a deaf ear to the celebration of these holy days.

Jews (and by inference, Christians) do not have an absolute franchise on the memory of Esther. Her memory also belongs to other oppressed people. In situations such as in the land of Israel and in the so-called Christian nations of the world, where there are many people suffering economic exploitation and political repression, racial discrimination, social marginalization, and sexist harassment and degradation, it is *their* cry and *their* struggle for liberation that has the legitimate claim to the memory of Esther. In such circumstances, Jews and Christians are challenged to critically search their conscience and evaluate their actions, for God may have indeed changed sides!

There are few Jews better equipped to undertake a moral evaluation of the shifting role of the victim in the land of Israel and the so-called Christian nations of the Americas than Jacobo Timerman, who suffered imprisonment and torture at the hands of a ruthless Argentine military government for his courageous denunciation of human rights violations in a state that has long claimed to be Christian, and who several years after his release from prison and subsequent nationalization as an Israeli citizen was horrified by the destruction brought to Tyre, Sidon, Damar, and Beirut by the Israeli army in 1982. "With painstaking honesty" he writes in his book *The Longest War*:

> The Israelis have worked out the role of victims that the Jews fulfilled and continue to fulfill to this day in certain regions of the Diaspora. By necessity, this led to vindications and justifications. . . .
> Yet . . . the Israelis never traded on the Jewish blood spilled in Europe. Strict moral limits were kept because, as popular saying puts it, "We cannot do to others what was done to us."[14]

But in regard to Lebanon in 1982, he states that "the moral and institutional foundations of the state" were affected, and he adds:

> The long list of firsts . . . has many of us jumping from one argument to the next . . . trying to preserve something of our credibility, of our moral tradition, of our justifications, which were accepted from us because of our condition as victims of [humanity], of nations, and of the world for an extended stretch of history. We are uneasy because . . . we cannot continue to deceive ourselves, and . . . we begin to feel the shame—a strange and unreal sensation for a Jew this conception of oneself as a victimizer.[15]

Quoting Abba Eban, he states that Israel's war in Lebanon has been "a dark age in the moral history of the Jewish people" (p. 157). "In these past two months," he writes in his journal, "I have left behind many illusions, some fantasies, several obsessions. But none of my convictions."[16] With prophetic courage, he addresses the future of the Palestinians:

> Survival is the most imperative problem of the Palestinians. I don't know how they will achieve it . . . they will have to survive without resorting to terrorism or violence. They will have to survive by using the huge moral capital yielded by their suffering in Lebanon at the hands of Israel. They will have to survive on the basis of dignity and honor, on the message of the tragedy, on the morality of the victim—all of them attributes that before belonged to the Jews and now belong to the Palestinians.[17]

Timerman goes on to recall how during the second and third presidential terms of Juan Domingo Peron, he saw Argentina "seized by a collective madness, sometimes violent, sometimes peaceful; living in a mystical state, translating hallucinations into daily routine." He "witnessed such transports" in other Latin American countries during the past two decades and noted how they allowed "a government to manipulate collective terrors and impose an escape from reality through hallucination or messianism." "This happened," he says, "in Chile and Uruguay after 1972, and in Argentina after the military dictatorship took over in 1976."[18] He asserted that Israel's war in Lebanon has led him to relive that experience. In his adopted country, he has

> watched a repetition of the devices of complicity, involving presumably civilized people, just as in Argentina [he] saw politicians, lawyers, and journalists become accomplices in the greatest mass crime in Argentine history: the kidnapping, torture, murder, and disappearance of more than fifteen thousand people. . . . [Similarly] in Israel [he] witnessed a complicity which is not portrayed as participation in a crime, but presented instead as sober analysis, as an explanation of a painful reality. An inclination to madness accomplished through the rationalization of a lesser evil.[19]

After the massacre in Beirut and the Israeli news blackout that followed for twenty-four hours, he asked, "Why are the Israelis incapable of recognizing the high degree of criminality in their army's campaign against the Palestinian people?" But there was no answer. Then his oldest son, Daniel, who had been called to serve at the Lebanese front after having served already the first forty days of the war, counseled with him about the price of desertion. The "thought of military prison repels him," says the elder Timerman. "He is still traumatized by the memory of his visits to the jail in which I was imprisoned in Argentina."[20] But he told him:

> Son, you can't compare an Argentine jail to an Israeli jail. In our jails, only Arabs are maltreated, and you are a member of the superior race. It's true that once we were the people chosen by God to be witnesses in his truth, but now that we have girded ourselves for the murder of another people, we are a superior race since, as our government says, nobody can defeat us. They won't torture you in jail. Once you arrange your daily routine, thirty or sixty days pass quickly. But if you don't go now to your base, it will be merely an individualistic act. Perhaps others in your regiment think as you do, and together you can organize a collective protest. In any case, all of you must refuse to go to Lebanon. One can't be an accomplice in a crime and justify oneself by citing orders from above. It's time to rebel. [21]

Daniel Timerman refused to return to the Lebanese front and on October 4, 1982, was sentenced to twenty-eight days of confinement in a military prison.

Jacobo and Daniel Timerman's moral indignation, protest, and prophetic courage is representative of a significant minority of Jews in Israel and throughout the Diaspora. They are conscious of the fact that the memory of Esther (and Mordecai) can be claimed only in faithfulness to the cause of justice, in solidarity with the victims of injustice, and in daring obedience to the God who stands on the side of the poor, the powerless, and the oppressed.

God As Verb As Well As Noun

A third theological challenge posed by the story of Esther is in connection with the lack of a direct reference to God. This was one of the major objections of some of the rabbis for refusing to admit the book of Esther into the Jewish canon.[22] But, according to Albert I. Baumgartner, in the kabbalistic and hasidic literature there is a great deal of emphasis on Purim as "the celebration of God at work, as it were, behind the scenes,

unlike Passover which celebrates God's more direct intervention."[23]

The story of Esther challenges us to think of God as a verb
and not just as a noun, or as the one who is known in and
through historical events as well as in the revelation of the holy
name. As important and sacred as the name of God may be,
God's mighty deeds are just as crucial for the people of faith.
For God's ultimate name, as Moses discovered, is "I AM WHO I
AM" or "I WILL BE WHAT I WILL BE" (Exod. 3:14). Learning to discern
God at work in liberation and judgment is as crucial as learning
to call upon God's name in prayer. Doing God's will is even
more important than praying to God.

In countless places and in various times and circumstances,
many pray to God, yet many fail to do the will of God; therefore
it is often necessary to point to God's deeds rather than to
God's name. This is why liberation theologies in the Americas
put more emphasis on the priority of right action (orthopraxis)
than on correct doctrine (orthodoxy). It is not that doctrine is
not important for liberation theologies, but surely without a
correct practice there is not much that one can say about sound
doctrine.

I conclude with a poem quoted by Hugo Assmann in the
preface of his book *Teologia desde la praxis de la liberacion*. It is a
challenging statement to Christians and Christian theologians,
but it could very well be applicable to Jews and perhaps to
Moslems as well. Indeed it is another way of posing the third
theological challenge of the story of Esther from someone
deeply committed to the liberation of his fellow human beings
and who is not particularly religious:

> *When you succeed in changing*
> *all your abstract nouns*
> *for a few concrete ones*
> *whose meaning can be felt,*
> *perhaps it will make sense again*
> *for you to talk to us of Christ and God.*
> *When it is seen to be true,*
> *in a way that can be genuinely proclaimed,*
> *that Justice has "dwelt amongst us,"*
> *then perhaps what your Bible calls*
> *the "name of God" can make itself known.*[24]

The story of Esther represents a "word of action" rather than an "action of the word." Therefore it is an excellent paradigm of doing liberation theology in the land of Israel, Palestine, and the Americas.

NOTES

[1]Roy Sano, "Ethnic Liberation Theology: Neo-Orthodoxy Reshaped or Replaced?" in *Mission Trends No. 4: Liberation Theologies*, ed. Gerald H. Anderson and Thomas F. Stransky, C.S.P. (New York: Paulist Press/Grand Rapids: Eerdmans, 1979), 248, 251–52.

[2]Gustavo Gutièrrez, *A Theology of Liberation*, trans. and ed. Sister Caridad Inda and John Eagleson (London: SCM, 1974), 15.

[3]Justo L. Gonzalez and Catherine G. Gonzalez, *Liberation Preaching: The Pulpit and the Oppressed* (Nashville: Abingdon, 1980), 11.

[4]Juan Luis Segundo, *The Liberation of Theology*, trans. John Drury (Maryknoll: Orbis, 1976), 8ff.

[5]This section and the next are adapted from chapter 2 of my book *Evangelizacion contextual: Fundamentos teologicos y pastorales* (San Jose, C.R.: Editorial SEBILA, 1986).

[6]Cf. Carey A. Moore, *Esther: A New Translation with Introduction and Commentary*, The Anchor Bible (Garden City, N.Y.: Doubleday, 1984), xxi-xxv; Albert I. Baumgartner, "The Scroll of Esther," *Encyclopaedia Judaica* (Jerusalem: Keter, 1971), 14:1048-58; Brevard Child, *Introduction to the Old Testament as Scripture* (Philadelphia: Fortress, 1979), 598-607; Alberto J. Soggin, *Introduction to the Old Testament*, trans. John Bowden (Philadelphia: Westminster, 1980), 401-5, 439-41; Bernhard W. Anderson, "Esther: Introduction," *The Interpreter's Bible* (New York and Nashville: Abingdon, 1954), 3:823-32; idem, "The Place of the Book of Esther in the Christian Bible," *Journal of Religion* 30 (1950): 32-43.

[7]There are 107 additional verses (four and one half chapters) in Greek versions, including the Septuagint (LXX), which do not appear in the Hebrew text. This additional material is located before 1:1; after 3:13; 4:17; 8:12; 10:3; and at the end of the book. For Saint Jerome, the canonical authority of these verses was controversial; therefore, he placed them in an appendix in the Vulgate. Contemporary Catholic versions tend to follow the order of the Septuagint and the numbering of the Masoretic Text. (See, for example, La neuva Biblia Espannola, 771-85; The New Jerusalem Bible, 659-73; and La nueva Biblia Latinoamericana, 839-50 for three samples of contemporary Catholic translations.) The Protestant Spanish version, Casiodoro de Reina (1569; revised 1960) follows the Hebrew text and leaves out the additional verses in the Greek versions. (The same thing applies to the King James Version and the Revised Standard Version.) The additions give the book a greater theological justification and supply elements that are not found in the main text. For example, they speak of God directly, include prayers, and give a direct theological focus to particular problems. Without this material, argue several scholars, the book lacks theological content and its canonical justification would be endangered. Soggin observes, very perceptively, that the additional material, notwithstanding its theological explicitation, makes the book a sort of anti-gentile manifesto

on account of its excessive nationalistic language. For my part, it seems that the main text may be justified theologically by itself, given the twofold references to fasting and providence. These two references point indirectly to God, coinciding with the tradition of avoiding pronouncing God's name. The additional material demonstrates, however, an excessive zeal to conserve the identity of a sector of the Diaspora in light of the gentile threat and takes to the extreme the festival of Purim as a symbol of nationalist authenticity. Moreover, it takes away the universal value of the original story. (Cf. also Moore, *Esther*, lxi-lxiv, 103–13.)

[8]Gutièrrez, *Theology*, 307.

[9]Cf. James Cone, *A Black Theology of Liberation* (Philadelphia: Lippincott, 1970); idem, *God of the Oppressed* (New York: Seabury, 1975); Virgilio Elizondo, *Mestizaje: The Dialectic of Cultural Birth and the Gospel* (San Antonio: Mexican American Cultural Center, 1978); idem, *Galilean Journey: The Mexican American Promise* (Maryknoll: Orbis, 1983); Rosemary Radford Ruether, *Liberation Theology* (New York: Paulist Press, 1973); Letty M. Russell, *Human Liberation in a Feminist Perspective: A Theology* (Philadelphia: Westminster, 1974).

[10]Gutìerrez, *Theology*, 307.

[11]Russell, *Liberation*, 54.

[12]Sano, "Ethnic Liberation," 252–53.

[13]Moore, *Esther*, lii.

[14]Jacobo Timerman, *The Longest War: Israel in Lebanon*, trans Miguel Acoca (New York: Random House, Vintage, 1982), 15.

[15]Ibid., 23.

[16]Ibid., 158.

[17]Ibid.

[18]Ibid., 159.

[19]Ibid., 159–60.

[20]Ibid., 165.

[21]Ibid., 166.

[22]Baumgartner, "The Scroll of Esther," 1056..

[23]Louis Jacobs, "Purim," *Encyclopaedia Judaica* (Jerusalem: Keter, 1971), 13: 1396. See also Andre Hajdu and Yaocov Mazor, "Hasidism," *Encyclopaedia Judaica* (Jerusalem: Keter, 1971), 7:1404–20.

[24]Hugo Assmann, *Practical Theology of Liberation*, trans. Paul Burns (London: Search, 1975), 25.

16

DOING THEOLOGY FROM A LIBERAL CHRISTIAN POINT OF VIEW

GORDON D. KAUFMAN
THE DIVINITY SCHOOL, HARVARD UNIVERSITY,
CAMBRIDGE, MASSACHUSETTS

For freedom Christ has set us free; stand fast therefore, and do not submit again to a yoke of slavery (Gal. 5:1 RSV)

This volume has been organized in such a way as to suggest that a rather sharp contrast is to be made between what is called "evangelical theology" and other approaches such as "liberal theology." There are, of course, significant differences between these points of view; and I want to explore some of these. However, I would like to make clear at the outset that in my view there are also important shared assumptions and intentions. I have been asked to write here as a "liberal Christian theologian," and I am quite happy to accept this label. But it must be understood that it is the word *Christian* in this phrase that most directly specifies my central concerns as a theologian: to struggle with, to seek understanding of, to give an appropriate contemporary interpretation of Christian faith and the Christian gospel. The word liberal is used to indicate something about the particular understanding of Christian faith and the Christian gospel that seems to me both true and of central importance for human life today.

I use the word "liberal" (which means literally "befitting the free")[1] to characterize the kind of theology I do because I believe that at its very heart the Christian gospel is concerned with human liberty, human liberation, human freedom. It is the good news about how the various kinds of human bondage are overcome—*all* bondage, including bondage to religious institutions and religious traditions. Liberal theology emphasizes the importance of freedom for human existence, especially the freedom to construct and reconstruct our institutions, our styles of life, and our beliefs; and it emphasizes also, therefore, as a kind of corollary, the importance of criticism, of carefully examining and assessing all claims to truth and value. Ongoing critical assessment is indispensable if we are to become and remain free from bondage to ignorance, to prejudice of various sorts, to oppressive and unjust traditions and institutions. Such criticism must include, of course, self-criticism—attempting to get sufficient distance on our own beliefs and values, commitments and practices, to enable us to assess them and, when appropriate, to reconstruct them so they will better meet the needs of contemporary life. This liberal emphasis on freedom and criticism and self-criticism I understand to be a direct expression of the heart of the Christian gospel.

As the motto put at the heading of this chapter makes clear, the proclamation of radical freedom is central to St. Paul's understanding of Christian faith. But what is this "slavery" from which Christ sets us free? Paul gives his answer in the next verses: he apparently understands "slavery" here to be the sort of bondage into which men and women are put by rigid or legalistic interpretations of religious traditions. (He had in mind on this occasion the tradition that required circumcision of Gentile Christians, Gal. 5:2ff.). Paul, of course, had no doubt that religious traditions are important; indeed, a little earlier in his letter to the Galatians he had suggested that religious tradition can be a "custodian" (RSV) or "schoolmaster" (KJV) that leads humans to Christ (Gal. 4:24–25). But the central point about salvation through Christ is that it frees women and men from understanding religious tradition as presenting a set of *requirements* that they must carry out, a set of rites that must be performed or beliefs that must be accepted. The only requirement to be carried out by those in Christ is, as he says a little later in this chapter, to love their neighbors as themselves (5:14). Thus, the liberty that Paul teaches is quite radical. It is the kind of freedom that expresses itself in an ongoing assessment and criticism of traditional values and beliefs and institutions, rejecting those that no longer conduce to loving relationships between human beings, and reconstructing the others so they will help to foster communities of reconciliation and justice and peace. Precisely this sort of liberty is what the word "liberal," as I use it, is intended to highlight.

A similar point about Christian liberty can be drawn from some of Jesus' teachings, especially as epitomized in his well-known saying reported in Mark 2:27, that "the sabbath was made for man, not man for the sabbath." We might state the principle expressed in these words in this way: all religious institutions, all religious practices, all religious creeds, religious beliefs, religious ideas, have meaning and validity only to the extent that they contribute to human well-being, human fulfillment; they should never, therefore, be given unquestioned or unqualified authority over human life.

One can also approach this emphasis on Christian freedom from the side of the central Judeo-Christian claim that God alone is to be served, that to worship or devote oneself without qualification to anything other than God is idolatry. From this perspective every human belief, every human practice, every human institution, must be sharply distinguished from God; and devotion to any of these—including devotion to Christian creeds or practices or beliefs, or to the Bible—should always be provisional, always subject to reexamination and continuing criticism. What the Christian gospel promises is liberation from all such idolatries, all such bondages, so that we can exist as fully human before God.

These remarks have been quite brief, but I hope they make my principal point clear: liberal theology is concerned with central emphases of the Christian gospel. Both "liberals" and "evangelicals" should be able to agree that at the very heart of the Christian evangel is the good news that we were created for freedom and that that freedom is available to us: freedom from every form of bondage, physical and social and spiritual.

Modern liberal theology is often said to have had its beginnings in the nineteenth century, and that is not an incorrect understanding. Not until the time of the Enlightenment was it clearly perceived that emphasis on the centrality of human liberation and freedom has radical implications for Christian belief itself; and during and after the Enlightenment the insight gradually developed that Christian institutions and theological ideas can enslave and oppress humans, just as surely as pagan beliefs or the sinful corruption of the human heart. Much significant theological reflection in the eighteenth and especially the nineteenth centuries became, therefore, a form of Christian self-criticism, undertaken by theologians and philosophers and biblical scholars in behalf of Christian faith and the Christian community. In the name of human freedom it had become necessary to reexamine Christian institutions and beliefs in order to see in what respects they might be contributing to human bondage.

Descartes' proposal of the method of radical doubt suggested a procedure for examining theological beliefs critically; and Kant's later development of the so-called critical philosophy made it clear that all domains of human life and culture and tradition must be continually subjected to criticism if humanity is to become truly free. Kant expressed in a famous sentence this central demand of the liberating movement of enlightenment: "Have courage to use your own reason!"[2] Much theology since Kant—certainly what has been called "liberal theology"—has taken this imperative very seriously. An important expression of this self-critical movement has been the careful historical examination of the Christian Scriptures. It is one of the glories of Protestantism that its sense of the freedom promised by the gospel was powerful enough to encourage radically critical reinterpretations of the Scriptures during the nineteenth and twentieth centuries.

The self-critical theological spirit was not addressed only to investigation of the Bible. In F. D. E. Schleiermacher's work the traditional authoritarian understanding of theology was itself subjected to trenchant criticism, and a more experientially grounded approach was proposed. Later on, in the work of Ernst Troeltsch, the relativistic implications of the historical particularity of Christianity in a religiously and culturally pluralistic world were worked through carefully for the first time. In the twentieth century the radical critique of all human religiousness (including Christian faith) that was offered by men like Feuerbach, Marx, Nietzshe, Freud, and Dewey has been taken up by liberal (and liberation) theologians conscious of the many sorts of prejudice, ignorance, superstition, false consciousness, and special pleadng that have in many ways crippled and corrupted Christian faith, reflection, and institutions. And most recently, theological critiques of the sexism and gender bias in traditional Christian language, practice, and institutions have opened the eyes of many to yet another form of idolatry and oppression that the Christian tradition has everywhere encouraged. As liberal theologians see things, the "freedom (with which) Christ has set us free" calls Christians to work toward the overthrow of all these kinds of bondage.

Modern liberal theology thus has an important root in the Enlightenment and in the critical movements it spawned during subsequent centuries. Liberal theologians came to see that the central Christian claims about human freedom demand a willingness to use modern methods of radical criticism within theology itself; for the God who is known in and through Christ is that ultimate Power or Resource—our Creator and Liberator—which is working to set humans free from every form of bondage. The relationship to God that was made possible through Jesus Christ, therefore, was a relationship to the Reality that brings true human freedom, genuine human fulfillment. Thus liberal Christian theology understands itself as evangelical through and through—particularly in its convictions about the critical and creative spirit that frees women and men from the many bondages into which they continually fall, thus bringing about their salvation.

Given this emphasis on Christian freedom and openness, creativity and self-criticism, it should come as no surprise that liberal theologians have always sought to incorporate into their understanding of Christian faith whatever could be learned about humanity and the world from scientific and historical research and from philosophical reflection. Since the world (and all that is in it) is God's creation, what we come to know (or believe) about the world and what we believe (or know) about God must cohere with each other. This implies that our understanding of God will be illuminated (and may need to be corrected) by what is learned in the sciences, history, and philosophy, just as our understandings of ourselves and the world around us must be kept consistent with our conception of God. Since in the modern world all these matters have been in rather continuous change and expansion, a fixed canon of liberal theological doctrines or dogmas is never to be expected: all beliefs must be kept open to critical examination and reformulation, as modern knowledges about the world, humanity, and history develop in quite unexpected ways. The Copernican displacement of humanity from the physical center of the universe, the Newtonian vision of a scientifically ordered world of unvarying cause and effect, the Darwinian discovery of the mutual interconnectedness and evolution of all life on earth, the radical reinterpretation of the course of human history (including the history of Israel and of the Christian movement) made possible by the emergence of critical historical methods, Marxist insights into socio-historical dynamics and Freudian probing of the "unconscious," the growing appreciation of the meaning and significance of non-Western cultures and non-Christian religions—all these (and more) have had decisive impact on liberal theological understanding.

This necessity continually to absorb new and unexpected insights and understandings from many different sources has led liberal theology to see itself more as an ongoing *process* of thinking and rethinking the Christian faith and its meaning than as a particular body of beliefs. That is, liberal theologians have come to understand theology as essentially *historical* in character—always in process of development, never having arrived at a definitive statement or position, always subject to new criticism and thus demanding new and creative reformulation. It is hardly surprising, therefore, that those who expect Christian faith to supply life with a secure and unchanging foundation of absolute certainties find liberal theologies profoundly disturbing and dissatisfying. But, conversely, for those who understand that our creatureliness implies that we must learn to live with the vicissitudes and transience of continual change and with the relativities and contingencies of history, the openness of liberal theology to transformation and reformulation may appear both refreshing and profoundly true to the human condition.

This self-understanding of liberal theology is rooted in the "historical consciousness" that today underlies much reflection on human existence. Historians and anthropologists have shown that the patterns of life of every society—the customs, values, institutions, ideas, worldviews, practices—have all grown up and developed within the course of the history of that society. As women and men responded to various contingencies and problems and crises that confronted them, they found it necessary to adapt and adjust their ways of living and acting. Thus they created and shaped the social and institutional, cultural, and ideational patterns that gradually came to characterize their various societies. Quite different patterns of living and quite different structures of roles and institutions have developed in different parts of the world and different historical periods; and this has meant that the men and women who grew up in those societies and historical periods were formed in different ways, came to have different skills, different needs, and different sorts of relationships to other humans. In short, they became quite different human beings than they would had they grown up in some other period or some other place. Each of us would be a very different person had we grown to maturity as, say, a low-caste Hindu in an Indian village, or as a member of a commune in central China, or as a child in a Roman emperor's family.

Historical understanding of this sort enables us to see that what seems important in life—indeed, what *is* important to us—is largely a function of the context in which we live and of the roles we are called on to play in our world. The conception of what a *good* human life is develops in the history of a culture (or subculture) in connection with experienced needs; and each person emerging in that cultural matrix comes to think of himself or herself, and molds herself or himself, in these terms. Thus, what virtues are stressed and vices avoided is a culturally relative matter; what sorts of human activities and arts are valued as important, to be cherished and cultivated, are shaped by the culture; the sorts of claims to truth that are regarded as credible, the patterns of social organization taken to be just or proper, the ways to treat fellow human beings that are believed to be right and good—all such values and ideals that orient and guide human life and serve as standards for evaluating the various alternatives confronting women and men, take different forms in different historical and cultural settings. All humans eat; they must eat to survive. But no humans simply consume food, as do other animals: humans eat with chopsticks or with knives or forks, or they may eat with no utensils at all but with the right hand only and never the left; they may cook some or all of their food; they may prepare it with special spices and condiments; they may eat regularly three meals a day—or two, or one—and fast in certain culturally prescribed periods and ways; they may accept as edible only certain vegetables or meats that other cultures regard as revolting or poisonous; and so forth. Although our behavior is doubtless always in response to biological need, in almost every detail it is culturally formed—and that means it is historically relative. It is the business of historians, anthropologists, psychologists, and others to uncover, describe, interpret, and explain all of these complex relativities in their interconnection with each other.

In the course of history men and women have developed

many significantly different worldviews; and quite diverse conceptions of human life, of the central human problems and the solutions to those problems, have been worked out, as various metaphors for grasping human existence were developed and explored in different cultures. Human life might be seen, for example, as a journey through hazardous territory where one encounters wild beasts and evil monsters as one seeks the safety of home; or it might be understood as participation in a great warfare between forces of light and forces of darkness; or it might be grasped as citizenship in a cosmic political order, as the life of a subject in the kingdom of God. The individual self might be seen as a soul fallen out of its proper home in heaven above and become trapped in a physical body from which it must find some way of escape; or, in sharp contrast, the very sense of self or soul might be taken to be an illusion—the product of ignorance, the veil of *maya*—that right insight can dispel; or human existence might be understood as a product of the accidental collocation of material atoms, or of blind evolutionary processes that could just as well have gone in other directions and formed other patterns. Every great civilization, indeed every isolated tribe, has worked out one or more such conceptual or imagistic frames for understanding and interpreting and orienting human life; and humans have shaped and reshaped their lives and institutions and values and practices in accord with these various visions of Reality and the human.

Human existence, thus, is historical through and through; and this is above all true of the religious dimensions of human life. It was in their religious practices and institutions and rituals that humans found a kind of fundamental orientation for life, found an interpretation of what human existence is all about and how it is to be lived. Or rather, to put the matter more accurately, in their search for orientation in life as they gradually came to awareness of themselves and their world, in their attempt to come to some understanding of what human existence is all about and how it is to be lived, humans created and developed the great religious traditions; and thus they found life to have—and, gave to life—such variant meanings as it has come to possess.

Such a basically historical conception of human existence and human religion—taken for granted by most educated people today—is presupposed in the work of most contemporary liberal theologians. We are a part of the evolutionary web of life that has gradually evolved here on planet Earth over many millions of years; but we have gained our own peculiar and unique character as humans, and have created the enormous diversity of forms of humanity, as the biological substructure of our existence has become increasingly open to historical modes of shaping and development.

Given this understanding of human being and human religion, what is Christian theology, and how should it be done? Although there would doubtless be many disagreements about details, most contemporary liberal theologians would concur, I think, with the substance of what I have said thus far about the liberal understanding of the meaning of Christian faith and the modern biohistorical understanding of human existence. In what follows, however, with respect to the way theology should be done in light of these commonly accepted presuppositions, no such wide agreement is to be found. Some liberal Christians think of themselves as essentially theologians of (religious) experience (e.g., Langdon Gilkey, Edward Farley, H. R. Niebuhr, many feminist theologians); others work with a "method of correlation" between experience and tradition (e.g., Paul Tillich, Schubert Ogden, David Tracy); some work out of a modern metaphysical framework (e.g., Whiteheadian theologians like John Cobb and Hegelians like Wolfhart Pannenberg). It is impossible to set out here all the various liberal approaches to constructive theological work that are presently being explored. I will confine myself in the remainder of this chapter, therefore, to my own interpretation of Christian theology as essentially "imaginative construction" of a picture or conception of humanity, the world, and God.

Let us begin with the fact that in many respects life confronts all humans as profound Mystery.[3] Although this deep awareness is often softened, and sometimes significantly obscured, by religious symbolisms that seem to offer answers to our most difficult questions, we must admit, I think, that we really do not know, and we can see no way in which we will ever be able to plumb, the true meaning of human life—or whether there even is such a thing. The ultimate meaning and context of our existence are inscrutable mysteries. From the earliest period of self-conscious human life, so far as we can see, women and men have grappled with this fact, and in the great systems of religious symbolism and ritual, which they have created in consequence, they have found such partial answers as they could. However, none of these pictures or conceptions or stories of the world—these frames of orientation—are able to interpret all dimensions of experience satisfactorily; and in consequence there have always been persons like Job and the writer of Ecclesiastes, Camus and Sartre, who have cried out against the unintelligibility of what they were living through.

In Western religious traditions this ultimate mystery of and behind all human existence has usually been identified as "God"; and in their affirmations that God is "infinite" or "absolute," "transcendent" or "ineffable," believers have reminded themselves regularly that this One whom they worship is ultimately beyond human comprehension, is ultimately mystery. This point, however, is a highly dialectical one, and it is important, as we consider how we are to do theology, that we recognize its implications for our talk about God. On the one hand, the image/concept "God" is intended to symbolize that—whatever it might be—which brings true human fulfillment, salvation; that is, when we speak of the ultimate mystery as *God*, we are attempting to attend to it from a point of view that emphasizes the respects in which it is the source and ground of our being and our well-being, as that on which, therefore, we must finally rely absolutely. But on the other hand, even in this move of faith we cannot help but recognize that this God on whom we call remains beyond our knowledge and understanding. This fact, that God is always a mystery to us, requires continual acknowledgment in our theological work—continual recognition, that is to say, of our profound *unknowing* with respect to God, acknowledgment that we really do not know how the images and metaphors in terms of which we attempt to conceive God actually apply, since they are always our own metaphors and images, infected with our limitations and biases, our interests and desires. (For just this reason we dare not claim, as theologians all too often have done, that what we are saying in our theology has been directly "revealed" by God.) Only in and with the acknowledgment of our profound unknowing can the symbol "God" turn us—by a kind of indirection—toward its intended referent: the ultimate source and context of our humanity, the ultimate mystery of life.

The complex dialectic to which I am pointing here is not

merely of intellectual interest: it is a direct expression of something that has always been regarded by Christian piety as of great importance, namely, repentance. Repentance is certainly a human act (or attitude), but it has the peculiar dialectical character of being an act of self-renouncing, an act of giving up our own claims. Although not often acknowledged by theologians, this self-renouncing must extend also to our theological claims, particularly any claims to certainty of knowledge. For whenever we try to overcome, and thus control, the ultimate mystery that is God—through, for example, confident affirmation of theological or philosophical ideas that we think we *know* are true, or through religious rituals or practices or beliefs that promise us a secure place in the ultimate scheme of things—we are actually attempting to make *ourselves* the ultimate disposers of our lives and destiny; and thus we sin against God. Genuine faith involves a "letting go" (as Kierkegaard put it) of all attachments, including specifically and especially our religious and theological attachments; for it is just these idolatries that shield us from—and thus close us off from—that divine mystery in which both our being and our fulfillment are grounded. We must, then, repent: we must turn around from this posture, which we all too often take in our theological interpretations of the ultimate mystery of life, and move toward a recognition that our desitny is ultimately in *God's* hands, not ours; that is, toward recognition that even in faith life remains a mystery to us.

This emphasis that our faith must always be in, and our dependence must always be on, that which is ultimately *mystery* does not mean, however, that there is no place for careful and sustained theological work. Perhaps it is only in and through the activities of theological reflection and imaginative construction (to which I will turn in a moment) that we are enabled to perceive clearly this dialectic in the symbol "God," this dialectic that necessarily involves a certain agnosticism within and about our own work. This is not a cynical agnosticism, of course, that is destructive of everything we believe in and need, but the agnosticism that indirectly opens us to what is beyond our present understanding, opens us to that which we do not yet know but which can be creative of our future.

Certain aspects of human life, however, can (and should) largely be controlled by humans, and it is important for us also to recognize this; the doing of theology is among these. For it is *we* who decide that we will do theology: we decide what methods we will pursue in our work; we decide what sources we will use as we try to come to grips with our theological subject-matter and what criteria will govern our judgments; it is we who finally reach the theological conclusions to which we come and who then decide what will be written on the page before us. Theology is in every respect a human work, and we must take full responsibility for everything we do or say theologically. Liberal Christian theologians have recognized this clearly; and they have often, therefore, denounced the claims of traditional theologians to be speaking with divine authorization (that is, on the basis of what they were certain was "divine revelation") as a presumptuous and insidious form of self-idolatry, a failure to acknowledge that "God is in heaven, and we are on earth." Only as we cease to make transcendental claims of this sort for our work and forthrightly admit that it is *we ourselves*—we quite ordinary human beings with our particular frailties, faults, and other limitations—who are doing and saying what we say and do theologically, does our work actually begin—indirectly—to become open to that which we do *not* control, that which we do not and cannot understand, analyze, explore, prove: the ultimate mystery, the mystery that we (in faith) call God.

This understanding, that we theologians must take full responsibility for all our affirmations and claims, means that the principle of *authority* that was taken for granted by most traditional theologians must be rejected. According to this principle, theological truth is not something we humans create or discover in our work; it is, rather, something already present and available in *tradition* (especially the Bible), simply awaiting our appropriation. The task of theologians, then, is essentially one of extracting this truth from the traditional writings in which it is contained and setting forth its meaning for the present time and situation. What the truth is, is already determined and directly accessible; the theologian is simply to believe what has been handed down and seek to understand and interpret it. It was, of course, the belief that the principle contentions of the Bible (and other central traditional documents) had been divinely revealed that grounded this special authority of tradition.

Most liberal theologians have taken the position that theology can no longer justifiably be done in this authoritarian way.[4] For with such an approach, instead of taking full responsibility for all of his or her major claims, the theologian assumes, from the beginning, that a number of the most crucial theological issues have already been resolved and that it is unnecessary, therefore, to raise serious questions about them. These include such central and highly problematic contentions as (1) who or what God is; (2) that God is self-revealing and trustworthy (i.e., a being to which personal attributes can properly be ascribed); (3) that God has revealed Godself in the Bible and especially through Jesus Christ; and (4) that the proper method of interpretation of the Bible and tradition, enabling us to apprehend without serious error or distortion the divine revelation given in them, is available and known to us. If, however, we reformulate these assumptions of traditional theologies into *questions*—a form that highlights their problematic character—we can see immediately that it is unjustifiable to take any of them for granted: each needs to be carefully investigated and argued in the course of our theological work itself. (1) Are we justified in holding that, prior to all theological reflection, we already know who or what God is, or is this something that can be decided (if at all) only in the course of our theological inquiries? (2) Can we simply take it for granted that God is a personal being of the sort who reveals Godself to humanity, or is that a point to be investigated? (3) Is it justifiable any longer today, in light of the great variety of religious claims and traditions of which we are aware, simply to assume that God has fully and definitively deposited this self-revelation in the Bible, or is that a claim that must be explored? (4) Can we assume that we know, without careful investigation and argument, what is *the* correct and adequate way to interpret Scripture and tradition?

None of these questions admit of easy answers, but to take the authoritarian approach to theology is to presume certain definite answers to them all. Although this may have appeared justifiable to earlier generations of theologians, it is so no longer. We are too well aware that religious ideas and beliefs have appeared in great variety, not only in the course of human history generally but within Christian history as well; and it is difficult to see on what grounds it can be held that one particular selection out of this immense assortment is to be regarded as in some special and definitive way the result of direct divine revelation. It would seem, rather, that all are largely products of the creativity of the human spirit, attempting to find its way in the face of ever new problems and crises and opportunities arising in life. Theology (reflection on the language and ideas of faith)—as much as any other aspect of human activity or praxis—has always been done for specific human purposes and to serve human needs; it has always been addressed to the problems troubling a particular generation of Christians. In practice, theologians have recognized this: despite their reverence toward tradition, they have often been quite critical of the way Christian faith was understood and interpreted by earlier writers, and have called, in the light of their own insights and understandings, for new conceptions in response to new perceived needs. What we call the history of theology has been largely the story of these cumulating insights into, and thus creative transformations of, the understanding and interpretation of Christian faith.

We can see, then, that theology has never been simply the translation and handing on of tradition: it has always been a newly creative imaginative work of the theologian as well. Theologians have examined and reexamined received ideas of God, humanity, and the world, and they have criticized these in light of new experience and conceptions that were becoming persuasive in their own time, so that they would more adequately express, and thus could become more effective vehicles of, human salvation, genuine human fulfillment— more effective vehicles of what we today might wish to call true *humanization*. Theology has always been essentially a creative activity of the human imagination, seeking to provide more adequate orientation for human life in face of the new problems confronting each new generation. Since, however, we are now more aware of this creative dimension of theological work than ever before, it is important that we acknowledge its real place in our own theologizing, so that we can take full responsibility for it.

If theology is no longer understood to be essentially translation or interpretation of an authoritative Scripture or tradition but is conceived as essentially imaginative construction of a picture or understanding of God, humanity, and the world, how is it to be done? Religious reflection has always worked with the great symbols and concepts that have provided meaning and significance for a particular historical community (or civilization), as that community has attempted to understand life and give it some order in institutions, customs, and practices. In the case of Christian faith, two symbols above all have been fundamental for the orientation of life: *God* and *Christ*. These have provided resources of meaning in terms of which human-life-in-the-world could be understood, and thus they have helped to give it a basic order and significance. The other principal terms of the Christian vocabulary—sin, salvation, church, sacraments, trinity, gospel, and so on—all helped to elaborate and fill out the articulation of human existence in the world under God. It was not the case, of course, that the traffic here was only in one direction, that God and Christ were inexhaustible symbolic fountains pouring meaning into all the other concepts and symbols that gave Christian life and faith their distinctive character and content. On the contrary, the creation and use of terms like "sin" and "faith," "Trinity" and "Son of God," "sacraments," and "love of neighbor" each in its own way enriched and deepened the meanings that God and Christ came to have within the devotion and lives of Christian men and women. Thus exceedingly complex webs of meaning developed—in various quite distinct ways within the different Christian subtraditions—providing orientation, moral and religious guidance, and patterns of interpretation within which ongoing experience and life could be grasped, and its preplexities and problems faced.

Christian theology today (as understood from the liberal Protestant point of view that I am explicating here) works within and upon this complex web of meaning inherited from the Christian past: it attempts to grasp as fully as possible all the richness and variety of this network of meaning; it analyzes carefully its strengths and weaknesses, as these have shown themselves in the course of history; it critically examines this complex of meanings in the light of evils for which they have been partially responsible (e.g., Western imperialism and the oppression, indeed enslavement, of some classes and peoples; sexism; racism; the exploitation of the earth; even genocide); finally, it attempts to reconstruct the Christian network of meaning in whatever ways are required to enable it to serve more effectively as a frame of orientation for life today, a frame that will help to identify, and will suggest ways of addressing, the most fundamental problems women and men now face.

How is this critical appropriation and imaginative elaboration and reconstruction of the Christian web of meaning to be carried out? The Christian understanding of human life and the world, like all other frames of orientation for life (religious or secular), is given its basic form and character by what I call its categorial structure. When human existence in its context (the world) is grasped and interpreted in terms of the two fundamental orienting symbols of Christian faith—God and Christ—a pattern of meaning is established governed by the interrelations of four principle terms or categories: God, the world, humanity, Christ. (The first three of these, it may be noted, are not uniquely Christian; they have figured importantly in Jewish and Muslim perspectives as well.) These four categories provide the principle reference points in terms of which Christian maps of reality are drawn. Although I cannot take them up in detail here, let me say just a few words about each so that it is possible to get some sense of how the Christian categorial structure functions.[5]

For Christian faith "God," the mystery behind and underlying all life, is, of course, the ultimate point of reference in terms of which all else is to be understood. This point has ordinarily been expressed by speaking of God as the source of all that is, as the ultimate ground of all reality, as the creator of the world and the Lord of history. In the biblical documents God is portrayed as a quasi-personal or agential reality—that is, the model in terms of which the notion of God was constructed was the human self or agent. (This was greatly complicated in classical Christian theology by the development of the doctrine of "three persons" in the one God.) Just how this "ultimate point of reference" for all life and thought should be conceived today is (as we have noted) a major issue that theological reflection and construction must address.

The second principal category that has given structure to Christian perspectives—the "world"—designates the overall context within which human life falls. In the earlier mythopoeic versions of Christian faith this context was thought of as simply "the heavens and the earth"; but in our time modern concepts like "world" or "universe" have come to seem more adequate for this purpose. We are obliged today to think of human life as falling within an almost unimaginably immense universe, hundreds of light years across and billions of years old. Within this universe are millions of galaxies, and within one of these is to be found the solar system, which includes planet Earth. Earth in turn is a complex eco-system apart from which human life would not be possible. For Christian theology all of this is ordinarily understood as in some sense God's "creation."

"Humanity," the third major category, refers to those creatures here on earth who have sufficient self-consciousness and knowledge of the world around them (having been "created in God's image") to be capable of taking significant responsibility for themselves, their lives, and their futures. They do this in part by imaginatively creating world-pictures and interpretations of human life that show forth its possibilities, problems, and parameters; it is to this task, of course, of setting out and interpreting human-existence-in-the-world that Christian theological reflection and construction make their own distinctive contribution.

The fourth fundamental category is "Christ," that figure from human history who is believed by Christians to reveal or define, on the one hand, who or what God really is, and, on the other hand, what true humanity consists in. The historical figure of Jesus Christ thus gives concreteness and specificity to the understandng of both God and humanity, in this way providing significant shape and content to these other central terms that structure the Christian web of meaning.

There is not space here to spell out in detail the way(s) in which critical analysis and appropriation of the Christian network of meaning can be effectively carried out, and then its imaginative reconstruction undertaken.[6] There are obviously many dimensions to this task, and different persons will each find their own distinctive vocation within it. Liberal Christian theology as a whole is the ongoing conversation of these various voices seeking to understand and interpret and reconstruct the network of Christian meanings so it can contribute more effectively to the humanization—the salvation—of our world.

Every theology in every generation has been a constructive and creative activity of this sort, as theologians have attempted to address the problems and possibilities of their times with the resources made available to them by Christian (and other) webs of meaning. Theologies have always thus been essentially works of the human imagination, bringing into being new meaning as they continually transformed what had been inherited from the past. The distinctive feature of liberal theological method, in my view, is that it recognizes clearly this creative moment in the theological task; and in doing so it is led to carry on its imaginative work as self-consciously, and thus as responsibly, as possible.

Given their understanding of theology as a human activity through and through, it is, of course, not possible for liberal theologians to claim their assertions to be directly and uniquely authorized by divine revelation (as theologians have so often done in the past). To make such claims would, as we have seen, idolatrously violate the integrity of the ultimate mystery that in faith we name "God." (This does not mean, of course, that there is *no* significant sense in which theological reflection and construction should be regarded as grounded in God—that would be an absurd, even self-contradictory, view; nor does it mean that there is no way in which the concept of revelation could properly be used to articulate that grounding.) But surely this modesty has enormous advantages over the more traditional authoritarian pomposity. The belief of theologians that their views were authorized by divine revelation has all too often led them to forget the thoroughly human character of their work; and after that but a few short steps sometimes led to the torture and burning of supposed heretics, those who were unwilling to acknowledge what God had so distinctly revealed and what this or that theologian or church official knew with such certainty. Admitting forthrightly that all our theological claims are simply *ours*—the product of our own human study and reflection and of the spontaneity and creativity of our own human powers imaginatively to envision a world and our human place within that world—frees us from these false moves toward the demonic authoritarianism that has so tarnished much Christian theology in the past. And simultaneously it opens us to the serious consideration of other quite different interpretations of Christian faith—indeed, of quite different perspectives on human life generally—than those to which we are presently committed.

Once we recognize clearly its thoroughly human character, we are enabled to see that theology as a whole today should be regarded as essentially an ongoing *conversation*. It is a creative conversation among a variety of speakers, each contributing new insight to the others and to the Christian community as a whole—not, as it may so often seem, a cacophony of monologues with each voice loudly claiming it alone properly represents significant truth. Liberal Christian theologians see themselves as free and open participants in this conversation, addressing themselves especially to the tasks of the present and the future, though recognizing that they always draw on resources from the past. They believe that it is this *freedom* ("the glorious liberty of the children of God" (Rom. 8:21 RSV)—to live in the world as we find it today, attempting to take responsibility for the world of tomorrow, which we are helping to create—for which Christ has set us free. Because we are enabled to live out of this gift of freedom we refuse to submit again to any yoke of slavery—even a yoke proffered under seemingly impeccable Christian auspices.

NOTES

[1]See *The Random House Dictionary of the English Language*, ed., Jess Stein and Laurence Urdang (New York: Random House, 1967), 826.

[2]"What Is Enlightenment?" in L. W. Beck, ed., *Critique of Practical Reason and Other Writings in Moral Philosophy* (Chicago: University of Chicago Press, 1949), 286.

[3]In what follows I have borrowed freely (without indicating direct quotations) from my article "Mystery, Critical Consciousness, and Faith" (published in the *Festschrift* for Basil Mitchell, *The Rationality of Religious Belief*, ed., W. J. Abraham and S. W. Holtzer [Oxford: Clarendon, 1987], 53–69), and from ch. 2 of my book *Theology for a Nuclear Age* (Manchester: Manchester University Press, and Philadelphia: Westminster, 1985).

[4]My reasons for taking this position have been most fully spelled out in my *Essay on Theological Method* (Missoula, Mont.: Scholars Press, 1975; rev. ed., 1979). The most thorough historical analysis and deconstruction of the traditional authoritarian approach to theology is to be found in Edward Farley, *Ecclesial Reflection* (Philadelphia: Fortress, 1982).

[5]For further elaboration of the "Christian categorial scheme," see my *Theological Imagination: Constructing the Concept of God*, (Philadelphia: Westminster, 1981), ch. 4.

[6]For fuller discussion of these matters, see my *Essay on Theological Method* and *The Theological Imagination*; for an example of the kind of theological reconstruction to which this approach may lead when a contemporary problem like the nuclear crisis is confronted, see my *Theology for a Nuclear Age*.

17

DOING THEOLOGY TODAY

SCHUBERT M. OGDEN
PERKINS SCHOOL OF THEOLOGY, SOUTHERN
METHODIST UNIVERSITY, DALLAS, TEXAS

THE QUESTION

What is it to do Christian systematic theology today? This, as I understand it, is the more precise formulation of the question to be addressed in this chapter. The theology into the doing of which we are to inquire is not theology in general, but Christian theology in particular; moreover, the doing of Christian theology that is the object of our inquiry is not the doing of it in any or all of the ways in which it may be done, but that specific way of doing it that is properly distinguished as systematic theology. But if this makes clear how the term "theology" and its cognates are henceforth to be understood, in the absence of explicit indication to the contrary, just how we are to understand our question is still far from obvious and in need of further clarification.

We should note, first of all, that while we could well ask the question from the standpoint of a number of different inquiries, we are to ask it here from the standpoint of theology, and thus as itself a properly theological question. Clearly, doing theology is one of the many things that human beings do, and so it might very well be asked about in one way or another by any of the special sciences concerned with human praxis, as well as by history and philosophy, which in their somewhat different ways share this same concern. Our way of asking about it, however, is supposed to be theological, and this has some implications that we need to keep in mind. It implies, for one thing, that just what it means to ask the question can be made clear only by answering it. But it also implies that we can answer the question only by doing the very thing it asks about doing. We have to do theology ourselves if we are to ask theologically what it is to do theology today.

More precisely, we have to do systematic theology, since the second thing to note is that this is not only a question *about* systematic theology but also a question *of* it. We are asking what it is to do systematic theology today as itself a properly systematic theological question. Here again, just what it means to say this can be made clear only by answering the question. For the present, suffice it to say that systematic theology is a properly systematic inquiry and that systematic inquiries in general are distinguished from properly historical inquiries, on the one hand, and properly practical inquiries, on the other. Whereas historical inquiries have to do with what human beings have thought, said, and done in any situation already past, and whereas practical inquiries have to do with what human beings are to think, say, and do in some situation still future, systematic inquiries have to do with what human beings would be justified in thinking, saying, and doing in this or any other situation now present, whatever may have happened in the past or ought to happen in the future. To say, then, that this question is a systematic theological question is to distinguish it both from a historical question such as might well be asked by historical theology and from a practical question of the sort that practical theology might very well want to ask.

Of course, the question is not just about theology but about doing it, and doing it today; and it is clear from the whole character of this volume that this chapter, like all the others, should serve in its way to advance the actual praxis of theology in today's world. But as true and important as this is, our inquiry is nonetheless a systematic, rather than a practical, theological inquiry. Although we are indeed concerned with what it is to do theology today, ours is not the properly practical question about what ought still to be thought, said, and done about theology in the upcoming future but rather the properly systematic question about what it would be right to think, say, and do about theology in this or any other present in which such thinking, speaking, and doing might be required.

The difference of our inquiry also from that proper to historical theology can be made clear by distinguishing two ways of construing our question, What is it to do theology today? Construed in one way, this question asks for a *prescription* of what by right ought to be done today in order to do theology. This is how we are construing the question in asking it as a systematic theological question. But it can also be construed in another way as asking for a *description* of what in fact is being done in doing theology today. And this is how historical theology would ask and answer it in describing one or more of the approaches currently being made to the doing of theology.

To be sure, any approach to doing it, including the approach being made in this chapter, is itself thoroughly historical even as systematic theology. Like everything else that we think, say, and do as human beings, theology is historically conditioned and situationally located relative to some particular society and culture with their distinctive links to the past and their peculiar possibilities for the future. This means, among other things, that any approach to doing theology has to be made within the limits and by means of the resources of its particular situation. But it also means that each such approach is only one among many others, past and present, with some of which it is more closely, with yet others of which it is more distantly, related. Even so, it is the task of historical theology, rather than the systematic theology that we are concerned with here, to undertake the description of any of the various approaches to the doing of theology. And this is so even when the approach described happens to be one's own or one with which one's own is closely related. Because the question we are seeking to answer is a systematic theological one, I need not describe any approach to the doing of systematic theology, not even my own, but may go ahead and do it by prescribing as simply as possible what it is to do so.

So much by way of clarifying the question. We may now proceed to answer it by considering in turn two more specific questions having to do respectively with the *what* and the *how* of doing theology today. In conclusion, then, we may reflect briefly on the validity of the answer.

WHAT IS THERE TO DO?

Literally defined, "theology" means *logos* about *theos*, or, as we may translate, thought and speech about God. This seems to indicate that doing theology today, just as in any other day, is to think and speak about God. But while this may well serve as an initial answer to our question, there are certain points at which it must be developed if it is to be an adequate answer.

In the first place, we need to recall that speech is one thing, while using language to say something is another. Although the various speech acts that we perform are typically performed by uttering certain words, and thus by saying something, we can also speak, and speak quite eloquently, without saying anything at all. Hence the familiar adage, "Actions speak louder than words." This means that the speech proper to theology may very well comprise *doing* along with *saying* and that theology must be understood accordingly as not only what is thought and said about God but what is done about God as well.

This leads to another point where the initial answer is in need of development. Granted that theology is thinking, saying, and doing about God, there is more than one way in which God can be the object of what is thought, said, and done. This is so because there is more than one kind of question about God that human beings may be concerned to ask and answer by what they think, say, and do. Of course, any way of asking about God is a way of asking about something real beyond ourselves and the other persons and things that make up the world around us. In fact, in radically monotheistic religions such as Judaism, Christianity, and Islam, the term "God" refers to the strictly ultimate reality that is the necessary condition of the possibility not only of ourselves and the world but of anything whatever that is so much as conceivable. But characteristic of these religions precisely as religions is that they ask about this strictly ultimate reality not merely abstractly, in its structure in itself, but rather concretely, in its meaning for us. In other words, in asserting that God is the strictly ultimate reality, these religions not only answer the question of who God is, but also, at one and the same time, address the question of who we ourselves are supposed to be in relation to this strictly ultimate reality. By contrast, metaphysics asks about God, insofar as it does so, in pursuit of its rather different, if by no means unrelated, kind of question. While it, too, asks about the strictly ultimate reality that theistic religions understand as God, it does so nonexistentially by abstracting from the meaning of this reality for us so as to inquire simply into its structure in itself. In this respect, metaphysics is much more like science than religion, although the reality about whose structure it inquires abstractly is the same reality about which religion asks concretely—namely, the ultimate reality of our own existence in relation to others and the strictly ultimate.

Because their questions are of different kinds, what religion and metaphysics respectively have to think, say, and do about God are also different. And this naturally raises a question about theology, itself understood as thinking, saying, and doing about God. Does it ask and answer yet a third kind of question, or does its question belong to one of the other two kinds? Pending a more nuanced answer that can be given in due course, let us say simply that the question of theology is existential in kind and, therefore, more like the concrete question of religion than the abstract question of metaphysics. This means that what theology thinks, says, and does about God all has to do with the meaning of God for us, not merely with the structure of God in itself. In the nature of the case, however, theology and metaphysics are closely related; for while theology goes beyond metaphysics as the concrete exceeds the abstract, it nonetheless includes or implies metaphysics as an abstract aspect of itself.

But with even this much development, the initial answer to our question is still wanting at a crucial point. We noted at the outset that the theology, the doing of which we are inquiring about is not theology in general but Christian theology in particular. Up to now, however, nothing said in developing the initial answer accounts for theology's having this particular scope. That its question about God is existential rather than merely metaphysical, and that it includes what is done about God as well as what is thought and said, still does not explain what makes it *Christian* theology. To explain this, we must take account of what alone makes anything properly Christian—namely, that particular experience of Jesus as of decisive significance for human existence which somehow comes to expression in all that Christians think, say, and do. To be a Christian is to have experienced Jesus as thus significant, because it is decisively through him that our own existential question about the meaning of ultimate reality for us receives its answer. If what it is to do theology, then, is so to think and speak about God, by what one does as well as what one says, as to address this same existential question, what it is to do Christian theology in particular is to do exactly this as a Christian—out of one's own Christian experience and in such a way as to be appropriate to Jesus as Christians experience him.

The question now, however, is whether even this developed understanding of what it is to do theology allows us to see what there is to do. Is all there is to do already done simply by whatever one thinks, says, and does about God existentially on the basis of one's Christian experience? I do not believe so, and, in point of fact, I question whether what we have so far understood theology to be ought still to be called "theology" at all in the proper sense of the word.

One reason for questioning this is that the word has long since come to be used by both Christians in general and Christian theologians in a much stricter sense. Far from referring to *all* that Christians think, say, and do about God, "theology" is commonly taken to refer to only *some* of it— namely, to such as is involved in reflecting more or less critically on the validity of all of it. Thus, on this common use of the word, what it is to do theology properly so-called is not done at all unless and until one engages in just such critical reflection. It is not surprising, then, that Christians today typically disclaim doing theology simply by what they think, say, and do about God in expressing their Christian experience.

The other and deeper reason for my question is what finally lies behind this typical disclaimer and the much stricter sense of "theology" that it reflects. I refer to the fact that in all that Christians think, say, and do about God on the basis of their experience of Jesus they necessarily make or imply certain distinctive claims to validity. Specifically, they express or imply the two claims that what they think, say, and do is adequate to its content and that their thinking, saying, and doing it is fitting to its situation. Actually, they make or imply three claims, since the claim to be adequate itself involves two further claims: first, that what is thought, said, and done is appropriate to Jesus as Christians experience him, and, second, that it is credible to human existence as any man or woman experiences it. In most cases, no doubt, these claims to validity are not made explicitly but are merely implied. Even so, there is no alternative to at least implying them, insofar as they are necessarily involved in anything that Christians think, say, and do about God in expressing their Christian experience. The proof of this is that no Christian ever intends to think, say, or do anything that is either inadequate to its content, because inappropriate to Jesus or incredible to human existence, or else not fitting to its situation.

But what Christians intend to do is one question, what

they succeed in doing, another. And by the same token, it is one thing to make or imply claims to validity, another and clearly different thing to critically validate them. Because of this difference, there are the best of reasons why "theology" should have come to have the much stricter sense in which it is now commonly used. Instead of referring to all that Christians think, say, and do about God on the basis of their experience of Jesus, it is quite reasonably used to refer to either the process or the product of a certain kind of critical reflection—namely, the kind that is required to validate the claims to validity that Christians either make or imply in expressing their experience.

Recognizing this, I take the stricter sense of "theology" to be its proper sense, and it is in this sense alone that I will henceforth use the word. For what is called "theology" in the broader sense of all that Christians think, say, and do about God I prefer and will use the term "witness." Thus, in my terms, what it is to do theology proper is adequately understood, not simply as bearing witness, but only as critically reflecting on witness with a view to validating its claims to validity.

What there is for theology to do, then, is just such critical reflection. And it is clear enough that there must always be plenty for theology to do. In the nature of the case, the claims made or implied in bearing witness either are or become more or less problematic. The claims of any witness can be invalid insofar as it fails in some way to be either adequate to its content or fitting to its situation. Moreover, the claims of any one witness to be valid must be immediately contradicted by every other witness that is sufficiently different that the claims of the witnesses cannot logically both be valid claims. But a pluralism of witnesses, obviously, is just the condition in which Christians have typically found themselves from the earliest days of their history as a community. There has never been simply one Christian witness; there have always been only many Christian witnesses. And as often as not, the differences between them have been such that their claims to validity could not all be equally valid. There is no question, then, that Christian witness itself makes critical reflection on its validity not only possible but necessary and, in many cases, urgent.

But if this kind of critical reflection is what there is for theology as such to do, what is there for specifically systematic theology to do? My answer is that the specific task of systematic theology is to reflect critically on the claim of Christian witness to be adequate to its content. Remember that, on the analysis offered above, this is one of two claims that are expressed or implied in bearing Christian witness, the other being that witness is fitting to its situation. In my view, the difference between these two claims allows for the self-differentiation of theology into the two ways of doing it that I distinguish respectively as systematic and practical theology. Thus, while the specific task of practical theology is to validate the claim of witness to be fitting to the situation in and for which it is borne, the object of systematic theology's reflection is the other claim of witness to be adequate to its own content as Christian witness.

To validate this claim, systematic theology must validate the two further claims that, as we have seen, it itself involves. There is, first of all, the claim that witness is appropriate to Jesus Christ, in the sense that what is thought, said, and done in bearing witness suitably expresses the experience of Jesus that is properly Christian. Secondly, then, there is the claim that witness is credible to human existence, in the sense that what Christians think, say, and do in bearing it is worthy of belief, practically as well as theoretically, by any man or woman simply as a human being. Of course, for any Christian, to validate the first claim is tantamount to validating the second, this being the very meaning of the assertion that constitutes Christian witness explicitly as such—namely, the Christological assertion that Jesus is of decisive significance for human existence. If this assertion is true, any witness that is appropriate could not fail to be credible as well. But although this explains why both claims must be valid if Christian witness is to be adequate to its content, it in no way allows for a confusion of the two claims or for the reduction of either claim to the other. On the contrary, the claims are so related that they are logically independent and mutually irreducible. Thus, notwithstanding the christological assertion, which might, after all, be false, a witness that is appropriate to Jesus Christ need not for all that also be credible to human existence.

Because this is so, the specific task of systematic theology is really always two tasks—namely, the two tasks of validating both of these claims, neither of which can be validated merely by validating the other. This is recognized to some extent by the traditional division of theology into dogmatics, on the one hand, and apologetics, on the other—the one serving to validate the claim of witness to be appropriate, the other, its claim to be credible. My own preference is to distinguish the two tasks themselves, dogmatic and apologetic, as both being included in the one task of systematic theology to reflect critically on the claim of witness to be adequate to its content. But however we take account of it, what there is for systematic theology to do is not only one thing but two, and that simply because the one claim it has to validate comprises two other distinct claims.

There is a final point to be made before proceeding to ask how systematic theology is to accomplish its tasks. I said earlier that the question theology asks and answers is existential in kind and, therefore, more like the concrete question of religion than the abstract question of metaphysics. Meanwhile, we have seen good reason to distinguish clearly between the witness that may be called "theology" in a broad sense of the word and the critical reflection on witness to which the word properly refers. Given this distinction, however, it becomes clear that there must also be a difference between the way in which the existential question is asked and answered by witness and the way in which theology proper asks and answers it. Whereas witness addresses the question at the primary level of self-understanding and praxis, theology addresses it at the secondary level of critical reflection, the only place where the claims to validity that are expressed or implied on the primary level can be critically validated. Thus, while the question of theology is indeed the same in kind as the existential question of religion, theology's way of addressing its question is *indirect* as compared with the direct way of witness.

To understand this, however, is to realize something very important about what there is for theology to do. What there is to do, I have argued, is so to reflect critically on the claims to validity that witness makes or implies as to validate them. But to do this is obviously to be of service both to witness itself and to all who ask the existential question that witness addresses. On the other hand, because to do theology is not to bear witness but to critically reflect on its validity, the only service that theology is ever in a position to perform for either witness or existence is the *indirect* service of just such critical reflection.

HOW IS IT TO BE DONE?

If we now have some idea of what there is for theology to do, our next question is how, exactly, to do it. To approach an answer to this question—so far, at least, as we can hope to answer it here—I want to start with a point that could have been made perhaps equally well at the end of the preceding section as at the beginning of this one.

As I understand it, to do theology is not simply to bear witness but to reflect critically on the claims to validity that bearing witness expresses or implies. But this understanding of theology as being in essence critical reflection may seem to suggest that the only way to do it is critically, in the sense of passing critical judgment on particular witnesses that have already been borne. In point of fact, however, the critical reflection of theology can also be done constructively, in the sense of making a constructive statement of what must be thought, said, and done in order still to bear a witness that is adequate as well as fitting and, therefore, both appropriate and credible. At first glance, perhaps, making such a constructive statement may seem to be indistinguishable from actually bearing witness; and this impression may be reinforced by the observation that the constructive statements of theology once made have usually been integrated into the later witness of Christians and the church. But upon more careful consideration, it is clear that the difference remains between even a constructive theological statement of what a valid witness would be and the act or process of actually bearing a witness that claims to be valid. In fact, there is still this difference even when the concepts and terms in which theology and witness are formulated are not different but the same.

The first thing to say, then, about how theology is to be done is that it is to be done constructively as well as critically, with a prospective view to bearing witness as well as a retrospective view of witness borne.

To say this, however, scarcely goes beyond saying in different words what there is for theology to do. We do not speak to the real question about the *how* of doing theology until we address the question of theological method—of the way or procedure that theology has to follow to accomplish its tasks, whether it does so critically or constructively. These tasks, we have seen, are, first of all, the dogmatic task of validating the claim of witness to be appropriate to Jesus Christ and, then, second, the apologetic task of validating witness's claim to be credible to human existence. The question of theological method, then, is just how theology is to perform these successive validations.

For our purposes here, I propose to answer this question by distinguishing three phases in the single process of theological reflection. These phases can be clearly distinguished because each of them involves theology's following a specifically different method. Thus, in my view, the method of theology is in the nature of the case complex, being in effect a method-encompassing method. Moreover, none of the different methods it encompasses is peculiarly "theological," but is otherwise followed in human reflection generally in one or more of the so-called secular fields or disciplines. What makes any of them theological, insofar as it is so, is the encompassing method of theological reflection of which it is a part and, in particular, the distinctive claims to validity that following it somehow helps to validate. Naturally, each of the methods specific to one or the other of the three phases may itself be complex, in that it encompasses other still more specific methods. Thus historical method, for instance, is commonly reckoned to include, among others, the more specific methods of text criticism, source criticism, form criticism, and tradition criticism. But to pursue our question down to this level of detail is not necessary for our purposes, and so I will speak simply of the three methods specific to the three phases of theological reflection without going into the complexity that each of them may in turn involve.

The first phase of theology is the *historical* phase, and the method specific to it, historical method. In this phase, the objective of theological reflection is to meet the first of the two conditions that are necessary to validating the claim of witness to be appropriate to Jesus Christ. To validate this claim, theology must first determine both in principle and in fact what is to count as formally normative witness. By "normative witness" I mean any witness that, being itself appropriate, properly functions as a norm for validating the appropriateness of some or all other witnesses. If it properly functions to validate *some* other witnesses, I distinguish it as "substantially normative," because it thereby agrees in substance with all other appropriate witnesses. If, on the other hand, it properly functions to validate the appropriateness of *all* other witnesses, I speak of it as "formally normative," because it is the witness with which any other has to agree in substance in order to be appropriate. Theology's first objective, then, is to identify what properly functions in this sense as formally normative witness in fact as well as in principle. This it can do only by determining the conditions that any witness must satisfy to function properly as formally normative and then identifying the particular witness that satisfies these conditions.

The method it must follow to do this can only be historical method. For what is to count as formally normative witness both in principle and in fact is what witness itself asserts or implies to be so; and this, like witness, is given only through particular historical experience and can therefore be determined only by following a properly historical method of reflection. This explaims why, in its first phase, in which it has to follow such a method, systematic theology properly relies not only on its sister theological discipline, historical theology, including biblical theology, but also on the secular discipline of history.

The specific task of historical theology, in performing which it is continuous at every point with secular history, is to identify and understand the whole history of witness, beginning with the earliest traditions lying behind, and now accessible only through, the writings of the New Testament. In performing this task, historical theology naturally comes to understand, among other things, what has in fact counted as formally normative witness in all the situations now past in which one witness or another has been borne. But it is just this that systematic theology evidently has to know in order to perform its specific tasks by first determining what is to count as formally normative witness. There is every reason, therefore, why the systematic theologian should learn as much as possible from all who do historical theology, including biblical theologians, as well as from secular historians. This does not mean, of course, that any of these fellow inquirers can be expected to do the systematic theologian's job or that he or she is obliged to accept the results of their inquiries without criticism. Although what witness is to count as formally normative can be determined only by historical inquiry, determining it is no part of any historical theologian's job, much less that of a secular historian. This remains the inalienable responsibility of the systematic theologian, and in discharging it he or she may by all means be critical of the results achieved by historical theologians and historians, provided only that the grounds for any criticism are themselves results of historical inquiry.

But if how theology is to proceed in this first phase is clear enough, how it is actually to be done is anything but easy, especially today. This is because there has never been complete consensus in witness and theology about what is to count as formally normative, either in principle or in fact. To be sure, from at least the second century there has been widespread agreement about the basic principle: that witness is to count as formally normative which is apostolic, in the sense of being the original and originating, and, therefore, constitutive, witness of the church. But aside from the fact, evidenced by the history of the canon, that there has always been disagreement about just what witness or witnesses can be validated as apostolic, exactly what apostolicity itself is to mean has been profoundly controversial. Thus, while Protestants, Roman Catholics, and Orthodox have all traditionally accepted the same apostolic principle, they have understood it in sharply different ways— Protestants appealing to "Scripture alone" as apostolic, Roman Catholics and Orthodox invoking alternative understandings of "Scripture and tradition" as the real meaning of apostolicity. And as if this were not enough, the revisionary forms of witness and theology that have emerged in the course of modern Christian history have challenged the very principle of apostolicity, replacing it with an appeal to "the historical Jesus" as the real principle of formally normative witness.

There is little question, then, that any determination a theologian today can make of what is to count as formally normative witness will be even more controversial than ever before. The range of options has never been as great; and none of them is so free from objections as to make it the only reasonable choice. This does not imply, in my judgment, that no option is sufficiently better than all of the others to be at least relatively preferable. But it certainly does mean that validating the appropriateness of witness today can never be easy and that doing theology responsibly requires one to reckon with its difficulties.

Much the same can be said about the second, *hermeneutical* phase of theology, where it follows a specifically hermeneutical method. Here there are two objectives of theological reflection, even though both are accomplished by doing one and the same thing. The one objective is to meet the second of the two conditions that are necessary to validating the claim of witness to be appropriate to Jesus Christ. To validate this claim, theology not only has to determine what witness is in fact to count as formally normative but must also understand and, therefore, interpret this witness so that it can actually perform its proper function as formal norm. But the interpretation of the norm that is thus required to validate the appropriateness of witness is exactly what is also required to accomplish the other objective of theological reflection in its second phase—namely, to meet the first of the two conditions that are necessary to validate the claim of witness to be credible to human existence. Before the credibility of witness can be validated by the truth about human existence, what it does and does not claim concerning such truth has to be understood, and this, too, requires interpretation of formally normative witness.

The method that such interpretation calls for is what I mean by "hermeneutical method," though it could perhaps also be called "exegetical method." By either name, it is the procedure one has to follow in order to understand and interpret formally normative witness in relation to the kind of human question to which it is addressed as an answer. Assuming, as I have argued, that the question addressed by witness (and, therefore, formally normative witness) is the existential question of the meaning of ultimate reality for us, we may say that the proper hermeneutical method for theology is existentialist interpretation. But whether we call it this or not, if witness is addressed to the existential question, it must be understood and interpreted accordingly; and this means that it must be interpreted in concepts and terms in which this question today can be rightly asked and answered and human existence itself rightly thought and spoken about. This is the reason why, in this second hermeneutical phase, in which systematic theology must work out just such an interpretation, it properly looks for help not only to historical theology and secular history but also to the secular field of philosophy and its discipline of philosophical theology in particular.

That systematic theology should rely here, too, on historical theology and, indirectly, on secular history will be obvious. As understanding of the whole history of witness, historical theology, and, in particular, biblical theology, includes understanding of formally normative witness as well. But because understanding witness also requires interpreting it, historical theology itself is already dependent on philosophy and philosophical theology. This is so because to interpret what is thought and spoken in one set of concepts and terms always requires another set in which to interpret it. And it is precisely the business of philosophy and, in the case of the existential question addressed by witness, of philosophical theology to provide the requisite set of concepts and terms. Consequently, systematic theologians have every reason to learn whatever they can not only from historical theologians and secular historians but also from all who do secular philosophy in general and philosophical theology in particular. Again, this does not imply that the systematic theologian can abdicate his or her own responsibility either to historians or to philosophers or that he or she must accept uncritically whatever they happen to say. Interpretation of the witness that is to count as formally normative as being precisely that ever remains the systematic theologian's responsibility. And this means that he or she is also responsible for criticizing the work of philosophers as well as historians, provided only that the method followed in doing so is the same hermeneutical method that they in their ways must play a role in developing.

But, as I have already indicated, how theology is actually to be done in this second phase is also problematic, especially for anyone doing it today. In this phase, the source of the difficulties is the extensive pluralism of both theologies and philosophies, a pluralism that has continued only to grow with the passage of time. I remarked earlier that there has never been simply one witness, but always only many witnesses, through which Christians have expressed their experience of the decisive significance of Jesus. This pluralism at the primary level of self-understanding and praxis, however, is scarcely reduced even at the secondary level of critical reflection, where there has never been simply one interpretation of formally normative witness, but always only many. A principal reason for this, of course, is that there have also always been many philosophies, in the sense of secular interpretations of human culture and religion generally. Depending on which of these philosophies have provided their concepts and terms, there have also been many theologies. This means that the new philosophies that have continued to be developed have allowed for yet other theological interpretations beyond those already represented by traditional theologies.

The upshot of this is that no interpretation of formally normative witness today can expect to surmount this ever-growing pluralism of other theologies and philosophies. At best, it will be but one interpretation among many; and if this need not preclude its being at least relatively more appropriate than other interpretations, the odds against its actually being so have never been greater.

This brings us to the third and last phase of theology, which is its *philosophical* phase and the method specific to which is philosophical method. In this phase, the objective of reflection is to meet the second condition that is necessary for validating the claim of witness to be credible to human existence. To validate this claim, theology not only must interpret the witness that is to count as formally normative but also has to determine both in principle and in fact what is to count as the truth about human existence. Here again, I am assuming that the human question to which witness is addressed is the existential question about the meaning of ultimate reality for us. If this is correct, the claim to credibility that witness makes or implies is a claim to existential credibility. It claims to be worthy of belief because it expresses existential truth. But, then, to validate its claim, theology has to determine what is to count as such truth, and that in fact as well as in principle. It can do this only by determining the criteria that any assertion must satisfy to be existentially true and then formulating an understanding of ultimate reality that satisfies these criteria.

The method required to do this has to be philosophical method. For what is to count as existential truth both in principle and in fact is what human existence itself discloses to be so; and this, like existence, is given only through common human experience and can therefore be determined only by following a properly philosophical method of reflection. Because this is so, theology in its third phase, in which it must follow such a method, also properly relies on the assistance of the secular field of philosophy and of its particular discipline, philosophical theology.

I already indicated that, in my sense of the word, philosophy is the secular interpretation of human culture and religion in general. This is the reason, indeed, that theology properly looks for philosophy's help, and especially for philosophical theology's help in working out its own interpretation of witness in particular. But if philosophy, too, thus has a hermeneutical phase, the objective in its final phase, or, at any rate, in the final phase of philosophical theology, is a reflective understanding of the truth about human existence, and thus of the criteria proper for validating all formulations of this truth. Just such an understanding, however, is what theology clearly has to have in order to carry out its specific tasks by finally determining what is to count as existential truth. Therefore, in this phase, also, theologians have the best of reasons for learning everything they can from secular philosophers and philosophical theologians. Once again, this in no way implies either that they can leave their job to these others or that they must accept without question anything that the others have to say. They remain fully responsible for validating the credibility of witness; and in exercising this responsibility, they not only may but also must ask questions about the others' claims to existential truth, provided only that their reasons for doing so arise out of their own pursuit of a philosophical method of reflection.

In this phase, too, however, how theology is actually to be done involves serious difficulties, especially for anyone attempting it today. The reason for this, of course, is the same ever-growing pluralism of theologies and philosophies as well as of religions and cultures already referred to. Not only have human beings always had many different and often conflicting understandings of existential truth, but they have also never been able to agree on the criteria proper for adjudicating their differences. In fact, some of the bitterest and most intractable human conflicts have arisen from irresolvable differences over just these criteria. Nor has the extent of such pluralism at the primary level of self-understanding and praxis ever been significantly reduced at the secondary level of critical reflection. There, also, at the secondary level, the one truth about existence has been present only in the many claims to truth, not all of which can be valid.

But if this has always been the case in any situation in which theology could have been done, it is still more strikingly the case in our situation today. With the emergence of a truly global human community, the pluralism of claims to truth with which theology somehow has to reckon has become practically limitless. It now comprises not only all the classical expressions of world cultures and religions but also all the more or less radical revisions of these expressions, including the modern secularistic humanisms, both evolutionary and revolutionary. And of particular importance for theology are the significant challenges to traditional understandings of truth that are now coming from groups and individuals hitherto marginalized and unheard from for reasons of class, race, gender, or culture. These challenges converge in insisting that the truth about existence is not only to be believed but also done and that, therefore, any claims to tell it must be credible practically as well as theoretically.

The import of all this is that theology today has an all but

434 | Schubert M. Ogden

impossible job in determining what is to count as the truth about human existence. My own belief is that the job can still be done, or, at any rate, reasonably attempted, insofar as some understandings of the truth are at least relatively more credible than others. But if there ever was a time when theologians could have been excused for looking to some one theology or philosophy to provide such an understanding, it has long since passed. We today are without excuse for all of our traditional provincialisms, and we must scrupulously avoid even a hint of dogmatism in our attempts to formulate existential truth.

This, then, is my answer to the question of theological method, and thus of how theology is to be done today. There are certain dangers, admittedly, in distinguishing, as I have done, between its three different phases, insofar as they may be falsely separated or the order between them may be too simply construed. Even so, the phases, like their methods, are as distinct as they are inseparable, and their order is preserved even though it is evident that the first in a way presupposes the second, just as the second in a way presupposes the third.

THE ANSWER

Having now answered the question of what it is to do theology today, I want to add a few concluding reflections on the validity of my answer. We noted at the outset that the question itself is a properly theological, more precisely, systematic theological, question; and this implies that any answer to it must be validated as a properly systematic theological answer. But how, exactly, is such an answer to be validated?

It is evident that the criteria proper for validating it must be the same criteria by which the adequacy of witness itself has to be validated. Thus an answer to the question is valid if, and only if, it is at its own level adequate to its content and, therefore, both appropriate to Jesus Christ and credible to human existence. The question, then, is whether the answer for which I have argued can be validated in this sense.

That this is certainly not an academic question is evident from the very different understanding of theology that continues to be widely represented by theologians even today. According to this understanding, the apologetic task of validating witness as credible either is not acknowledged at all as a proper theological task or else is held to be reducible to the properly dogmatic task of validating witness as appropriate.

Thus even though theology is understood to be critical reflection on witness, it is regarded as involving only the first and second of the three phases into which I have distinguished it. Consistent with this, then, the credibility of at least formally normative witness is assumed to be already accepted by the theologian as a necessary condition of the possibility of his or her doing theology at all. Clearly, the differences between this common understanding of theology and my own are sufficiently great to render the validity of my answer problematic. Nevertheless, the reasons that can be given for it seem to me to be weighty enough that it cannot be easily dismissed as invalid.

This strikes me as particularly obvious in the matter of its appropriateness. The test of this, it will be recalled, is agreement in substance with formally normative witness. But there seems little question that this test can be met, since the understanding of theology as including critical reflection on the claim of witness to be credible exactly corresponds to the logical structure of witness as such and, therefore, to any and all witnesses, including formally normative witness. Any witness at all makes or implies the claim to be adequate, and hence makes or implies the further claims to be credible as well as appropriate. But, then, any witness simply as such makes critical reflection on both claims alike at once possible and necessary—as soon, at least, as they are in any way problematic. Consequently, to understand theology as I have, as just such reflection, is only to take witness at its word and to make fully explicit the understanding of theology that any witness itself already implies.

As for the credibility of this understanding, the case for it, too, appears to me to be strong, even if in this matter any case is bound to be more controversial. The test here is whether the understanding of theology is validated as credible by the truth about human existence. The problem, of course, is that there is nothing like a consensus about what is to count as such truth. But precisely in a situation all but overwhelmed by pluralism in understandings of the truth, no claims to truth are likely to be regarded as exempt from the requirement of validation. By the same token, no theology is likely to be accepted as critical reflection in the full sense of the words that excludes validating the credibility of the witness on which it reflects. On the contrary, any understanding of theology that insists on its including such validation is bound to seem more credible than any understanding that precludes it.

So far as I can see, then, the answer for which I have argued can be theologically validated—in the sense that it can at least claim the relative adequacy that is also the most that any theology today can responsibly claim.

18

HOW DO NEOORTHODOX AND POST-NEOORTHODOX THEOLOGIANS APPROACH THE "DOING OF THEOLOGY" TODAY?

GERALD T. SHEPPARD
EMMANUEL COLLEGE, VICTORIA UNIVERSITY,
UNIVERSITY OF TORONTO, ONTARIO

The question of how neoorthodox and post-neoorthodox theologians approach the doing of theology immediately raises a plethora of other questions about terminology, and answering it is not made any easier when the experts differ greatly among themselves. The *Westminster Dictionary of Christian Theology* illustrates the problem well. On the one hand, under "Method, Theological" Yale theologian David Kelsey provides one of the best single presentations of how contemporary theologians do their work.[1] Besides the commonly accepted figures from the 1930s, 40s, and 50s, Kelsey regards most recent theologians as either conservative or liberal "neoorthodox." On the other hand, under the entry "Neoorthodoxy" in the same dictionary of theology, James Richmond offers the following:

> This term refers to the deplorable imposition of an outdated synthesis of theology and secular thought in an altered contemporary situation. It is also used of theologians of the schools of Karl Barth and Emil Brunner in the sense of their reassertion of the principles of the Reformation in a post-liberal form.[2]

If Kelsy is inclined to use the term "neoorthodoxy" in a very generous fashion, Richmond uses it only in its most narrow and pejorative sense. In any case, Kelsey's understanding is more widely accepted today than that of Richmond.

The roots of this conflict lie deep in the historical process behind the origin, application, and adoption of the term. In the early part of this century theologians who originally labeled their own work Christian realism, theology of crisis, dialectical theology, kerygmatic theology, or neo-supernaturalism all attracted the label, created by their opponents, of neoorthodoxy. Over time this term, despite its pejorative, oxymoronic connotations, came to be accepted even by many of those who, at first, felt libeled by it.[3] This irony in the label underscores the first challenge of this chapter: to appraise the social-historical context in the United States of what could be called neoorthodox theology. In that effort, I will make some observations about the range of theological methods used within neoorthodoxy. My emphasis will be on how neoorthodox theologians have interpreted Scripture and the role of historical criticism in that activity. Within this framework, I will attempt to provide a historical reexamination of the relation between neoorthodox and "evangelical" theology. Finally, I will offer some comments about what might be described as post-neoorthodox, postliberal, or postmodern theology, highlighting proposals that currently define theology in seminaries that had formerly been considered centers of neoorthodoxy.

SOCIAL-HISTORICAL OBSERVATIONS ABOUT NEOORTHODOXY

Neoorthodoxy covers at most a loose consortium of theological approaches sharing in common a critical response to certain key elements within "old liberalism" as it was known prior to World War I. The rallying cry of neoorthodoxy was "realism," in contrast to an old liberal confidence in rationalistic idealism, what Reinhold Niebuhr liked to deride as "utopian idealism." In the stark light of the experience of World War I that idealism appeared unsupportable, resting, as it were, on a fragile foundation of remarkably naïve assumptions, such as the intrinsic goodness of humanity, the sufficiency of science and reason, and the inevitability of social progress.

The resulting criticism, which became the "neoorthodox" response, attempted to wed modern discoveries and methods to a recovered Reformation heritage. Neoorthodox approaches could be considered "new" because they entailed an overhaul of some accepted tenets of liberalism and because they supported the still relatively new insights of historical criticism along with controversial conclusions of modern science. At the same time, these theological interpretations could be considered "orthodox" insofar as they revived traditional affirmations of faith, especially orthodox doctrines that had been rejected or neglected by liberals, including belief in the sinfulness of human nature and God's revelation within the events of human history. This new drive within theology even went so far as to take a strong stand against natural theology, denying it any place in the Christian spectrum of doctrine. The very concept of "Christianity" often was distinguished by the neoorthodox camp from "religion" and this dichotomy stood in opposition to the earlier tendency of liberalism to leave room for immanentalist or even pantheistic possibilities. Many other doctrines characteristic of the Reformation, such as justification by faith, also gained new attention and by virtue of their neglect provided further evidence of the dangerous complacency of old liberalism. Harry Emerson Fosdick dramatically illustrated the radical nature of the shift from old liberalism to neoorthodoxy when he announced in 1935, "The watchword will not be, Accommodate yourself to the prevailing culture! but, Stand out from it and challenge it!—we cannot harmonize Christ himself with modern culture."[4]

In his enthusiastic review of progress among theologians associated with neoorthodoxy, William Hordern in 1951 properly observes that their proposals did not simply reject liberalism but in many respects confirmed the vitality of the older liberal tradition.[5] Neoorthodoxy retained liberalism's emphasis on social justice and on a positive appropriation of the results of a modern consensus on science, philosophy, and historical criticism. In other words, neoorthodoxy maintained full continuity with old liberalism's preference for wrestling with the problems and possibilities raised by the left wing of modernity, including the triumph of historical criticism over premodern assumptions about the origins of the Bible. However, the old liberal heritage of neoorthodoxy can be easily misunderstood. In his *Blessed Rage for Order*, David Tracy sought to distinguish five models—orthodox, liberal, neoorthodox, radical, and revisionist—that disclose basic features of contemporary theology. I agree with Tracy's goal that each model "will, in some way, attempt to interpret the Christian tradition in the context of modernity."[6] My objection to his work is that he locates reactionary groups—fundamentalists and some pre-Vatican II Roman Catholics—as representative of the "orthodox" camp. I would argue that this inclusion is inaccurate both because it allows those who take a reactionary stance to claim to be the true inheritors of orthodoxy and because it ignores or is blind to the modernist impulse in a movement such as fundamentalism.

Tracy quotes with approval the axiom of Wilhelm Pauck that "orthodox theologies give rise to more orthdoxies; liberal theologies give rise to neoorthodoxy."[7] A conservative evangelical such as Harold Lindsell in his *Battle for the Bible* presumes exactly the opposite for trends among conservatives! Lindsell's assessment suggests that liberal theologies lead to more liberal theologies, orthodox theologies give rise (by a dangerous compromise to liberalism) to neoorthodoxies.[8] In my view, both of these approaches identify "orthodoxy" too readily with the extreme right wing of the theological spectrum. This assumption twists our perception of both fundamentalism and neoorthodoxy by portraying "orthodoxy" only as a set of beliefs inherently resistant to modern ideas or alien to an authentic and critical engagement with modern consciousness.

It is my thesis that fundamentalism is itself a form of modernism. Liberalism and fundamentalism are two sides of the same coin. At their worst, old liberalism and fundamentalism appear as extreme representatives of the left and right wings of modernism. Each thinks it is transforming whatever are the persistent truths of an earlier orthodoxy into the grammar and syntax of modernity. In the United States at least, one can find remarkable agreement between them on most modern ideas concerning the nature of history, revelation, the semantics of biblical interpretation (a strict intentionality theory of meaning), and the primacy of reason in matters of faith. Despite contrary liberal claims, educated fundamentalists were rarely self-consciously anti-intellectual.[9] Fundamentalists certainly invested heavily in the right wing of modernity as shown by their rationalist rejection of evolution, psychoanalysis, secular philosophy, socialism, and historical criticism. Only intensely intellectual, even fastidiously scholastic, precision can account for either the dispensationalist scheme of prophecy championed by many fundamentalists or their subtle theories of what within a biblical author's intent might be recognized as infallible but still nonrevelatory.[10] The fundamentalist proposal that Scripture should be interpreted by means of "historico-grammatical" exegesis further betrays a thoroughly modern system, strongly invested in linguistics and archaeology, one that sought to rival their opponents' proposals of "historical-critical" exegesis. Based on their own adamant acceptance of modern conceptions of history, fundamentalists could charge liberals with reaching destructive historical conclusions solely due to biased "presuppositions" that determined the results beforehand.[11] Fundamentalists themselves were as critical of "fideism," any approach that requires belief prior to rational evidence, as were the old liberals they opposed. Moreover, liberals were often as pious and as avidly "evangelical" in their confessions as were fundamentalists.

According to this description, neoorthodoxy as a theological movement represents a self-corrective impulse within the left wing of modernity rather than a result of liberal acquiescence to the arguments for orthodoxy from fundamentalists or conservatives. The fundamentalist alternative to liberalism was based both on its own particular, peculiarly modern way of reading Scripture and on its own modern scientific, historical, and philosophical sources, drawing heavily, for example, on a modern application of Scottish realism.[12] The common disposition to think of a modern outlook as inherently liberal derives in part from modernity's most optimistic interpreters, such as, for example, Ernst Troeltsch. Nonetheless, while he praises the "progress" incumbent on a burgeoning modern society, Troeltsch recognized very well that the issues were not clear-cut. In 1906 he stated, "The present-day world does not live by logical consistency, any more than any other; spiritual forces can exercise a dominant influence even where they are avowedly opposed."[13] In the spirit of Troeltsch's grasp of the unexamined presuppositions behind the surface motions of social change, we might apply his statement to the right wing of modern religious groups by saying, "Modern ideas can exercise a dominant influence even where they are avowedly opposed." Even fundamentalists who stand against "modernism" have been thoroughly changed by the assumptions of modernity and often unwittingly prove themselves to be among its more uncritical devotees. Therefore, fundamentalism should never be identified uncritically with a defense of premodern orthodoxy against modern views.

There is no way to escape the fact that change has been introduced by modernity into how we try to articulate for ourselves the past confessions. The onslaught of modernity has introduced new elements of continuity and discontinuity into how we can express orthodox belief. In my view, those who want to be orthodox, whatever they think that may mean, can justify the inevitable discontinuities in their modern expression of faith only by laying claim to a new precision, and they must do so at the risk of introducing a new distortion or heterodoxy into their hearing of both the biblical witness itself and the Gospel, which is its subject matter.

I would propose that for historical reasons we should use the term orthodoxy in two distinct senses. On the one hand, orthodoxy can be used to encompass a past, premodern set of expressions that are treasured by the church and that each modern theology, whether conservative or liberal, inherits, if it is Christian theology at all. On the other hand, orthodoxy as it finds expression in Christian theology in the modern period can be at most a reinterpretation of that older set of beliefs into a modern consciousness. This endeavor is always subject to the discernment within the churches regarding whether such an interpretation has been true to the Gospel and, therefore, to the heritage of orthodoxy that precedes it. One may conclude that some liberal theologies offered a more accurate retention of orthodoxy within modernity than did fundamentalist theology. As a crude instance of right-wing modernism, fundamentalism may appear by comparison to be less indicative of orthodoxy. Therefore, my proposal is that neoorthodoxy, as a critical response from within old liberalism, sought to reassess truths of orthodoxy in terms of the left wing of modernity. The contemporary counterpart to neoorthodoxy was "neo-evangelicalism," which offered a critical response within fundamentalism, seeking further to revise the expression of the truths of orthodoxy through the right wing of modernity.

If we think in terms of fundamentalism as being on the right wing of modernity and liberalism on the left, instead of the choices of orthodoxy and liberalism as Tracy suggests, then we can also more accurately recognize a wide range of other contemporary theological proposals that arose with equal energy. These include many movements within the Roman Catholic church, Afro-American and Hispanic Protestants, holiness, Pentecostal, and many other so-called sectarian Christian groups and denominations. We might consider many of these massive representatives of contemporary theology as "submodern," marginalized from the major public forums of the modern debate by reason of classism, racism, and, in some cases, educational deprivation.[14] Because these groups and their theological work often responded to a different perception of modern social, economic, political, and theological issues, they cannot be circumscribed as either simply fundamentalist or premodern. We might say they fed off the crumbs that fell beneath the table of privileged, primarily white and wealthy, American culture.

Neoorthodoxy belongs, therefore, to a particular social stratum within the history of contemporary theology. Regarding the role of Scripture, neoorthodox approaches clearly sought to reclaim in various ways the authority of the Bible as a guide to God's revelation about the nature of reality that could not be known by reason alone. In the United States, major theologians who became widely popular as pioneers of neoorthodoxy included Karl Barth, Emil Brunner, Rudolf Bultmann, H. Goldwitzer, Reinhold Niebuhr, H. Richard Niebuhr, and Paul Tillich. David Kelsey has shown that in their use of Scripture these theologians used a very wide range of different theological methods so that there is no single neoorthodox method of appealing to biblical authority.[15] Nevertheless, common among these theologians there was a sense of the rediscovery of "the strange new world of the Bible" (Barth). Indicative of this new climate of opinion is a set of terms relevant to the neoorthodox interpretation of Scripture—terms that include "realism," "revelation," "kerygma," "authenticity," "actualization" (and/or "radical reinterpretation"), "salvation history," "the biblical witness," and "the Word of God" in contrast to "the word of man." Of course, this change in vocabulary away from that typical of liberalism denoted far more than a minor adjustment in the language of theology; it was a highly significant shift in the entire theological perspective.

A HISTORICAL SCENARIO OF NEOORTHODOXY

In order to understand better how and why neoorthodox theologians do their work, we might begin by considering more carefully the historical boundaries of this approach to theology. In brief, neoorthodoxy developed differently in the United States than in England and in Europe, forged out of an increasingly heated conflict in the 1910s and 1920s between "old liberalism" and "fundamentalism." Not until 1929 did

Princeton Seminary reorganize, signaling the full triumph of modern historical criticism in the major denominational seminaries. If the events of World War I helped destroy liberal optimism about human nature, it also fueled popular beliefs in fundamentalist ideas about biblical prophecy. The breakup of the Ottoman Empire could be cited by them as a sign of historical fulfillment in line with dispensationalist views and evidence in support of their version of literal interpretation of the Bible. By 1920 the word fundamentalism became accepted as a popular label for large groups of opponents to liberalism (often called modernism) and historical criticism.[16] Neoorthodoxy finds its origins in the liberal camp, where, between 1925 and 1935, a dramatic change of mind took place, many called it a conversion. Remaining firmly opposed to fundamentalism, many theologians who had been associated with liberalism began to have misgivings about how adequately modern idealism could address the human situation. Integral to their criticism was a fresh appeal to realism and biblical revelation. This new approach continued to value humanistic goals but tried to view them from God's perspective above the gloom and disillusionment of the present moment. Yale historian Sydney Ahlstrom argues that, just as Barth's *Commentary on Romans* created a sensation in Europe over a decade and a half earlier, H. Richard Niebuhr's *Church Against the World* (1935) comes "as close as any single book to being a manifesto of the neoorthodox movement."[17] For the period that follows, Ahlstrom concludes that the major figures in neoorthodoxy all became prominent by the mid-1930s and that they had no equally original successors despite impressive contributions by some of their students.

On these historical grounds neoorthodoxy, as a lively theological movement, belongs to a period roughly from the mid-1920s until the 1960s when the consensus that it represented almost entirely collapsed. By the 1950s divisions among systematic theologians had already begun to increase so that Walter Horton discerned "three strong parties, neoorthodox, neo-liberal, and neo-naturalist, all related to the realistic movement of 1930–35."[18] Concomitantly, the so-called Biblical Theology Movement reflected work done almost exclusively by Bible scholars who in the United States were usually considered neoorthodox in their theological orientation. By the mid-fifties it too began to show similar signs of a loss of consensus. These two theological movements in the United

States, distinct from Europe, were interdependent and very closely related. A major problem for both of them concerned how well they actually handled the implications of modern historical criticism. For example, G. E. Wright's effort to develop a biblical theology based on "the acts of God in history" illustrated an American attempt to refine the popular European model of viewing the Bible as a record of "salvation history." In the face of criticisms that the Bible itself often gave preference to the Word of God over the Act of God, Wright tried to include the role of God's speaking alongside his acts.[19] Other biblical theologians faced more severe criticism. James Robinson threw into question the validity of all talk about salvation history in both Old Testament and New Testament theology. Langdon Gilkey exposed an array of difficulties in the conventional neoorthodox synthesis of Bible and theology when he wrote,

> The trans-natural reality that neo-orthodoxy proclaimed— the transcendent God, his mighty acts and his Word of revelation—became more and more unreal and incredible to those who had learned to speak this language. Younger enthusiasts began to wonder if they were talking about anything they themselves knew about when they spoke of God, of encounter, of the eschatological event and of faith.[20]

Ahlstrom has argued with some justification that H. Richard Niebuhr's *Radical Monotheism and Western Culture* (1960) provides a "requiem for the neoorthodox period, and an opening into the secular theology and non-religious interpretation of Christianity for which the 1960s would be remembered."[21]

Before commenting on what has transpired theologically since the 1960s in the old centers of neoorthodoxy, I want to argue that the group of scholars most resembling the older conservative neoorthodox theologians of the past can be found today within the progressive "evangelical" seminaries. The scenario for this development has already gained scholarly attention.[22] In brief, when neoorthodoxy was gaining momentum in liberal circles, a quite different movement among predominantly Reformed theologians identified with fundamentalism, often including other Anglo-American subcultures of Protestantism loosely affiliated with those outside the "mainstream" of churches in the Federal Council of Christian Churches (later, the National Council of Christian Churches). In association with the success of *Christianity Today*, the

founding of Fuller Seminary, the national public acceptance of
the Billy Graham crusades, and the establishment of the
National Association of Evangelicals, all in the 1940s, postfun-
damentalist, "new evangelicals" or "neo-evangelicals" appeared massively on the scene. These biblical scholars and
theologians, including Kenneth Kantzer, arose parallel to
neoorthodoxy and often drew selectively upon its resources,
particularly from Barth, Brunner, and Reinhold Niebuhr. Many
of the younger scholars at Fuller Seminary by the early 1960s
had studied with Barth or other prominent neoorthodox
theologians. While neo-evangelical scholars often sought to
expose errors or limitations in neoorthodoxy, they also drew
criticism from other evangelicals for becoming too liberal in
their own views. Harold Lindsell, a leader among the early neo-
evangelicals and at that time an editor of *Christianity Today*,
eventually sought to attack publicly various evangelical scholars
and Fuller Seminary more generally for compromises to what
he considered neoorthodox and liberal views.[23]

Neo-evangelicals in the United States, so different from
their counterparts in Europe and England, allowed for certain
advances in modern biblical criticism but sought to minimize
the consequences in two ways. First, they relentlessly questioned the presuppositions implicit in what they regarded to be
an improper application of modern historical criticism. Second,
they usually retained from fundamentalism and old liberalism a
fairly rigid historical conception of the author's intent as the
criterion for how a biblical text has meaning.[24] What causes
these theologians to be so close to neoorthodoxy in the United
States is their predominantly Reformed doctrinal tradition and
their preference for a "liberal" rather than "radical" view of
social justice.[25] Finally, neo-evangelical theologians differ from
older neoorthodox theologians by their defense of the "infallibility" of Scripture, at times in contrast to its "inerrancy," as
they find it expressed in the Westminster Confession. In this
last feature, neo-evangelicals again betray the peculiarly American heritage of fundamentalism and usually focus on "the
author's" or, as a refinement, the last redactor's "intent" as
authoritative in matters of faith and practice. Consequently,
evangelicals, generally more than neoorthodox theologians, try
to distinguish the revelatory content of a biblical writer's intent
from any "accommodations" that writer may have made to
antiquated views of the world, science, or so forth.

Neoorthodox theologians themselves were far less preoccupied with the infallibility of the author's intent and far more concerned with how the biblical text offered a trustworthy testimony or witness to God's revelation; the relation between the witness and the content of revelation remained dialectical, often highly theological in character or even somewhat mystical or philosophical, as in reference to a "word event." Despite these differences, the issues and approaches of many neo-evangelical scholars in the United States today resemble the work of the earlier conservative neoorthodox scholars far more than do many of the current movements within seminaries that might be considered the cradles of neoorthodoxy. It is especially in the decades of the 1970s and 1980s that many of the evangelical seminaries seem to have become centers of approaches typical of conservative neoorthodoxy in the American theological scene. At the same time, the term *evangelical* or *neo-evangelical* has become increasingly ambiguous as a label to describe any particular kind of theological work.

Seminaries that were once centers of neoorthodoxy, such as Union Theological Seminary in New York City and Yale Divinity School, might best now be considered post-neoorthodox. They are no longer focused on a recovery of "realism" in contrast to the "utopian idealism" of liberals. Furthermore, they are less devoted solely to the Reformed tradition of the so-called magisterial Reformation. Renewed attention is being given to the Radical Reformation that came into conflict with Luther, Calvin, and Zwingli. From this perspective, the older neoorthodox positions on issues of social justice were in their tactics liberal, supportive of gradual change in the status quo, rather than radical. Instead of assuming that the older types of historical criticism provide the only proper modern way to interpret biblical texts, the more recent theologians may emphasize new literary (e.g., narrative and metaphorical), rhetorical, socio-anthropological, or canonical approaches that inevitably reopen the most basic issues of how the Bible should be read. At times these proposals seem to set traditional historical criticism in the background as only remotely relevant. Conversely, new socio-anthropological investigations stress the larger socio-political realities implicit in a text as being more important than whatever may have been the authors' or editors' original intents. Bible scholars, in what I would call post-neoorthodox seminaries, now tend to allow for a multiplicity of "readings" and show more interest than did their predecessors in modern literary criticism, comparative literature, philosophy of language, and what Tracy calls radical theology.

HOW NEOORTHODOX THEOLOGIANS USE HISTORICAL CRITICISM OF THE BIBLE

In order to describe how neoorthodox theologians interpret Scripture it will be helpful to consider separately the contributions of systematic or dogmatic theologians from the proponents of biblical theology. Krister Stendahl provided one of the most widely accepted explanations for why a distinction should be made between biblical theology and systematic or dogmatic theology.[26] The former was primarily the concern of the biblical scholar who sought to ascertain what the biblical text originally "meant." This information, it was argued, should lend itself to an ordered presentation that could be called biblical theology. By contrast, the systematic or dogmatic theologians aimed at discerning what the biblical text "means" in a contemporary sense; they could draw on the results of biblical theology, but their work required additional interpretation according to extrabiblical disciplines, resources, and authorities in the life of the church. Giving separate attention to the systematic theologians and then to the biblical theologians, we can perhaps see more clearly some of the variety found within a neoorthodox orientation.

Systematic or Dogmatic Theologians

This large group of neoorthodox theologians approached their work from differing perspectives. David Kelsey has stressed that the distinctions among these theologians can be drawn along the lines of how they viewed the Bible in relation to "modern consciousness." Kelsey identifies as liberal neoorthodox theologians such figures as R. Bultmann, S. Ogden, K. Rahner, P. Tillich, D. Tracy, and G. Gutièrrez. He observes that these theologians agree that "the biblical message calls for a way of being human, a mode of human existence that is genuinely modern and hence compatible with modern consciousness, but truly authentic, and hence a decisive transformation of modern consciousness."[27]

Conversely, another large group of confessionally more conservative neoorthodox theologians (e.g., K. Barth, D. Bonhoeffer, J. Moltmann, R. Niebuhr) rejected the view of modernity as a unified and true conception of reality to which the truth of Scripture must correspond. These theologians in the course of their interpretation tended to draw upon the resources of modern study in an *ad hoc* manner, in ways that supported a search for a divine revelation concerning reality. Although their theological work showed substantial indebtedness to modern consciousness, it equally sought to respond to a biblical revelation that could not be confused with any alleged truth claims of modernity. In this respect, Karl Barth would not make allowance for natural theology and, in so doing, stood firmly against many Roman Catholic views and some other neoorthodox theologians, including Emil Brunner.

Likewise, there were remarkably different stances among systematic theologians on the nature of the biblical text as an authoritative "witness" to revelation and how it conveys truth.[28] Many of the more liberal neoorthodox theologians viewed the Bible as composed essentially of premodern symbolism or mythology that required some form of translation in order to disclose its real theological significance for a modern world. In this way, the Bible could use expressive language to convey abiding interior truths of human experience and/or divine revelation about the nature of existence. Nonetheless, Rudolph Bultmann is a prime example of a neoorthodox biblical theologian who strongly influenced work done in dogmatic theology. Daniel Fuller recalls that, during his oral examination at Basel for his doctoral degree, Karl Barth wanted him "to tell the several reasons why even Bultmann had no taint of Liberalism."[29] Among the reasons is Bultmann's consistently Lutheran insistence that Christ alone is the fully efficacious symbol of God's grace, the cause of our justification by faith, and the possibility of our living according to a full measure of authenticity.

Other theologians viewed the Bible as a witness primarily by means of its reference to divine revelation in ancient history. This approach, nuanced in various ways, was common among some major neoorthodox theologians who were most attractive to American evangelicals (e.g., H. Thielicke). W. Pannenberg represented the extreme of this position, speaking of "history as revelation." Other neoorthodox theologians affirmed the witness of the Bible to revelation in history but put weight on holding the biblical witness together with its revelatory subject matter. Consequently, the Bible read biblically depended less on its reference to the ancient past than on its capacity as human words to bear witness dialectically and immediately to that reality revealed by the Word of God (e.g., K. Barth, J. Moltmann). Even if one might grant the presence of errors in the Bible's form as a human witness, this mode of interpretation still presumed the possibility of a true hearing of the Word of God that stood apart from and in judgment on human error.

The Biblical Theology Movement

Although the concept of biblical theology as distinct from dogmatic or systematic theology was long familiar to European scholarship, it was not until after World War II that the climate was favorable for such a full-blown effort on this side of the Atlantic. The Biblical Theology Movement in America was strongly influenced by the robust strength of neoorthodox dogmatic and systematic theologians who encouraged biblical scholars to contribute to the contemporary theological scene. Various detailed accounts of this movement are readily available.[30] My aim is to point out that many biblical theologians in the United States took up the same key issues that belonged to the arena of neoorthodox systematic or dogmatic theologians and tried to demonstrate a degree of convergence with them within the Bible itself.

The variety of ways in which the Bible has been used by these neoorthodox theologians reflects a peculiarly American crisis in modern biblical and theological studies. In the period prior to World War I, historical criticism in the United States mainly consisted of source criticism and, to a lesser extent, form criticism. Bible scholars sought to recover, in a highly nuanced and complicated manner, ancient written sources—e.g., J, E, D, P in the Pentateuch, Q from Matthew and Luke, some "genuine" sayings of Jesus from the four Gospels, and the "genuine" as distinguished from the deutero-Pauline epistles. These were regarded as the most "original" traditions preserved in the Bible and, therefore, superior in historical worth to the later text of the Bible itself. Systematic theologians were not required to master all the linguistic tools and critical methods involved in the recovery of these sources, because the results of biblical scholarship seemed sufficiently assured. A liberal systematic theologian could defend historical criticism in principle, making use of its conclusions as a resource for doing theology. In a similar manner, Bible scholars, keeping abreast of the recent trends in theological studies, pursued their own investigations with a fervent awareness of how their work might have a bearing on theology and contribute to the life of the church.

However, after World War I Bible scholars began to use more diverse critical methodologies that relativized basic assumptions of source criticism. Moreover, an avalanche of unforseen linguistic resources (e.g., Ugaritic texts in 1929) generated tremendous excitement, as did vast, new archaeological discoveries. This wealth of esoteric knowledge about the ancient Near East fueled the tendency of biblical scholars in the postwar period to view themselves as objective specialists engaged in historical sciences distinct from the faith biases required of theologians. In his review of these circumstances, Harvard Old Testament scholar G. E. Wright lamented that in the United States the "productive Old Testament scholar had become for the most part an orientalist and a technical philologian," a colleague in the seminary who could be easily avoided by theologians and regarded with disdain philosophically and even pastorally as a harmless but irrelevant antiquarian.[31]

Similarly, form criticism, practiced earlier in Europe, now displaced source criticism by recovering the form and function of a much more ancient "oral" tradition. Within just a few decades, form criticism radically changed some historical views of the Bible. For example, the older liberal assumption that almost all of the Psalms were written in the postexilic period was replaced with the confident assertion that most of the Psalms faithfully preserved oral discourse from the earlier preexilic periods, in some cases going back to the time of David. Although reversals in the dating of New Testament traditions might have appeared less dramatic, the same historical complexity dominated. Such changes in the dates of certain traditions offered little comfort to fundamentalists, but the furor they caused illustrated just how volatile modern historical criticism could be. Ministers and theologians, if not thoroughly confused about the entire hierarchy of methods required of proper "exegesis," now became vulnerable to the charge of being outdated in their use of criticism. In the midst of this proliferation of methods and conflicting conclusions, including the sterility and sublety of the results, Bible scholars still chided their systematic colleagues in the 1950s: "Theologians must deal with that Biblical history more directly and seriously than many theologians have done in the last half century."[32] Under the banner of "biblical theology," at least, we find a more vigorous interaction between Bible scholars and theologians in the 1940s and 50s than had been common in the 1920s and 30s.

The problem of how to organize the theological content of the Bible constituted a major issue for biblical theology, which was usually divided into Old Testament theology and New Testament theology. Neoorthodox biblical theologians, particularly in the United States, saw the issue as almost forcing a choice between finding either a central theme to the Bible (e.g., covenant or the kingdom of God) or some scheme within the Bible of transhistorical development (e.g., "salvation history").[33] Suspicions were regularly voiced about whether this effort imposed an order on the biblical materials from without, a charge that threatened to undermine the objectivity of biblical theology and its distinctiveness from other types of theological interpretation. Another major concern was how the past tense of the biblical text could be heard in the present tense of the contemporary church. A number of biblical theologians in the United States popularized the view that preaching and theological commentary were dialectical forms of "radical reinterpretation" of biblical texts. This method of holding together what a text once "meant" and what it now "means" for the life of the church is vividly illustrated by a commentary series called *The Interpreter's Bible*, which has two levels of commentary, one from a biblical scholar, the other from a pastor or theologian.

In summary, the Biblical Theology Movement in the United States served predominantly as a neoorthodox response from the side of biblical scholarship separate from systematic or dogmatic theology. These biblical theologians sought to determine by means of modern historical-critical exegesis the theological content of the Bible itself apart from later Jewish and Christian interpretation. This model of interpretation began to face a growing uncertainty over the proper relationship between various critical methods—text, source, form, traditio-historical, redaction, and, later, rhetorical criticism—as well as whether each method contributed to the same hermeneutical conception of a biblical "text."

POST-NEOORTHODOX APPROACHES

From these descriptions of the work of various neoorthodox theologians I have argued that neoorthodoxy, as an energetic theological approach, collapsed in the 1960s. Ahlstrom has already argued this position for neoorthodox systematic and dogmatic theologians, as has Childs for the Biblical Theology Movement.[34] We can now ask what characterizes the work of post-neoorthodox theologians. Even the term post-neoorthodox is perhaps too linear and constructive in tone. After all, not every theologian builds on the past in the same way, and even those who inherit much from it may assume that only the dead should bury the dead. A better way to frame the question might be to ask what highly confessional types of theology we currently find in seminaries that were considered the centers of neoorthodoxy. The following examples are *ad hoc* but, I think, significantly representative.

One indication of the trend away from the older neoorthodox formulations of theology can be seen in the recent work by liberation theologians. Liberation theology is treated elsewhere in this volume, including especially the work of feminist and Third World theologians. For the purpose of illustrating a movement beyond neoorthodoxy in the United States I have chosen James Cone at Union Theological Seminary in New York City. When Cone wrote his formative contribution to black theology, under the title *Black Theology and Black Power* (1969), he sensed "a conversion experience . . . like experiencing the death of white theology and being born again into the theology of black experience."[35] Nevertheless, in that book he showed considerable dependence on key terminology and basic positions of neoorthodoxy. This aspect of his work drew sharp criticism from some black theologians whose views he most respected. As a response to this criticism and a sign of his theological maturity he wrote *The Spirituals and the Blues* (1972) and *God of the Oppressed* (1975), which demonstrate greater independence and include an increasingly refined criticism of neoorthodoxy.[36] Just as neoorthodox theologians challenged and changed their minds about old liberalism, Cone's theological work provides much more than a slight corrective within a neoorthodox theological perspective. Cone questions the dominant role of historical criticism, disputes misconceptions regarding the relation of revelation to political and social analysis, and launches a sustained attack on neoorthodoxy's wrong priorities and racist investments.

At a minimum, Cone advocates a radical shift in our perception of church tradition so as to give privileged status to the experience of black Christians as a necessary resource and corrective to Christian theology. The history and culture of black people in Cone's proposal are no less relevant than the history of Nicea, no less anguished and articulate than the sixteenth-century Protestant response to the Roman Catholic church. Cone breaks completely from the liberal view of social justice that characterized both neoorthodoxy and the magisterial Reformation. While he, in my view, affirms an orthodox confession of Christian faith, he does so without disparaging the insights of modernity. Unlike neoorthodox theologians, his nemesis is not theological "liberalism" but all theology, whether to the left or right, that is consciously or unconsciously invested in its own elitist, predominantly white sources of history and visions of the church. A key feature of Cone's contribution to theology and its post-neoorthodox future is his insistence that a Christian exegete cannot adequately hold the biblical text together with its subject matter without ascertaining how and for whom that subject matter is indeed Good News. Cone insists that the Bible must be read as a public text shared with black and poor people. Concerning future theology, Cone calls for a wedding of "that 'good old-time religion' " and "a Marxist critique of society."[37] In this respect, his theological use of Scripture cannot properly be labeled fundamentalist, liberal, or even neoorthodox.

Quite different post-neoorthodox approaches can be found among Yale theologians Hans Frei and George Lindbeck.[38] Frei's *Eclipse of Biblical Narrative* (1974) endeavors to describe the nature and interpretive implications of realistic narrative in the Bible. In this respect, Frei's study is seen by some theologians as providing a justification for K. Barth's approach to biblical interpretation. However, Frei's work belongs more clearly to a large group of literary interpreters who seek to identify formal elements of biblical texts that can explain the capacity of a text to make a reality claim on the reader.[39] Similarly, George Lindbeck's *Nature of Doctrine* introduces a "cultural-linguistic" approach that regards religious language neither as expressive symbolism for some interior reality nor as language that makes a truth claim that is valid for everyone else in the world. Rather, Lindbeck proposes that the eccumenical language of church doctrine is primarily regulative or corresponding to "rule theory."[40] In sharp contrast to neoorthodoxy with its bold endeavor to challenge the modern world in terms of biblical revelation, Lindbeck's strategy attempts to give priority to linguistic competence, minimizing the possibility of first-order truth claims, which, in any case, would be defensible only by an agnostic appeal to such extrabiblical resources as history.[41] For both Frei and Lindbeck "realism" is no longer an antidote to liberal "idealism" but is now the result of a proper use of Scripture based on an accurate construal of the socio-linguistic nexus of Christian interpretation. Although Frei and Lindbeck value the classical confessions of the church, they differ from neoorthodoxy in their treatment of history in biblical interpretation and in how Christians can make first-order truth claims about God's revelation in history and in the world.

Finally, in biblical studies we might observe, as an example, that the commonplace neoorthodox defense of historical criticism has been altered by the emergence of new approaches that run the gamut from synchronic literary to socio-anthropological investigations of the biblical text. Suffice it to say that the definition of biblical "exegesis" has not been in greater disarray for over a century. The relationship of biblical studies to theological interpretation is being reformulated in ways completely foreign to the older neoorthodox debates. I think immediately, for instance, of Phyllis Trible at Union Theological Seminary in New York City. James Muilenburg, her doctoral mentor, also formerly at Union, was a major figure in the Biblical Theology Movement. Muilenburg's traditio-historical approach led to his emphasis on "rhetorical criticism" as a corrective to the limits of form criticism. By contrast, Trible and many of Muilenburg's students have developed "rhetorical criticism" into a primary theological method of interpretation. In her *God and the Rhetoric of Sexuality* and *Texts of Terror*, Trible employs a hermeneutical strategy of profoundly literary close readings of biblical texts in order to claim biblical authority for a feminist hermeneutical perspective.[42] In this respect, one might argue that Trible seeks to discover the literal sense of Scripture in a manner fully compatible with earlier centuries of orthodox interpretation. In her effort, the older neoorthodox formulations regarding "history" and "revelation" no longer play a significant role.

From a different stance, Brevard Childs, Old Testament professor at Yale, began his career with the publication of *Myth and Reality* (1960) in the Studies in Biblical Theology Series.[43] In that study, Childs argued from a traditio-historical perspective that the mediators of biblical tradition consistently historicize the "myths" they appropriate. In the 1970s he used entirely new terms—the "canonical context" of Scripture and the "canonical shape" of biblical passages and whole books.[44]

Although he had fully established his reputation as a form critic and tradition historian of the Bible, he had become suspicious that the whole conception of Scripture was skewed by the tendency of historical criticism to establish some other context as a norm for biblical interpretation. His canonical approach to biblical interpretation and theology has largely abandoned the older neoorthodox categories in order to find a new direction, one justified in part by a reassessment of the entire history of biblical interpretation. For both Trible and Childs the distinction, so popular in the Biblical Theology Movement, between what a text "meant" and what it "means" no longer proves to be a useful way to describe the activity of biblical interpretation.

Cone, Frei, Lindbeck, Trible, and Childs illustrate in different ways that a radical shift has taken place in biblical and theological studies in the last two decades. Just as neoorthodoxy had moved beyond liberalism, all of these recent theological proposals look beyond neoorthodoxy to new horizons in the theology of late modernity. All of these approaches accept the validity of liberal historical criticism of the Bible but construe its implications in ways not explored by either liberalism or neoorthodoxy. A major argument of this chapter is that neoorthodoxy cannot be accurately understood if "orthodoxy" is uncritically identified with either modern fundamentalism or evangelicalism. For that reason, I have refused to assign "orthodoxy" or the interpretation of the "literal sense" of Scripture to the right wing of the modern church. Nevertheless, the highly confessional, post-neoorthodox—arguably "orthodox"—approaches here described do not come close to forming a unified theological movement. They move in very different directions and are often isolated, if not in open conflict with each other. Still, I find in each of them promising addresses to specific, different problems that were left unresolved by neoorthodoxy. Each in its own way points to a rich, confessional revitalization of faith and action in our churches. Whatever the future, we seem to be taking one more step away from the old polarities of liberalism and fundamentalism that, at least in the United States, have so sharply defined theological options since the opening decades of the twentieth century.

NOTES

[1]David Kelsey, "Method, Theological," *The Westminster Dictionary of*

Christian Theology, ed. A. Richardson and J. Bowden (Philadelphia: Westminster, 1983), 363–68.

[2]James Richmond, "Neo-Orthodoxy," *The Westminster Dictionary of Christian Theology*, ed. A. Richardson and J. Bowden (Philadelphia: Westminster, 1983), 395.

[3]For an excellent overview, see Walter M. Horton, "Systematic Theology: Liberalism Chastened by Tragedy," in Arnold S. Nash, ed., *Protestant Thought in the Twentieth Century* (New York: Macmillan, 1951), 105–24, and, on a more popular level, William E. Hordern, chapter 5, "Neo-Orthodoxy: The Rediscovery of Orthodoxy," in his *Layman's Guide to Protestant Theology*, rev. ed. (New York: Macmillan, 1968), 111–29.

[4]Harry Emerson Fosdick, "Beyond Modernism," *Christianity Today* (1935).

[5]Horton, "Systematic Theology," 117.

[6]David Tracy, *Blessed Rage for Order* (New York: Seabury, 1975), 10.

[7]Ibid., 27.

[8]Harold Lindsell, *The Battle for the Bible* (Grand Rapids: Zondervan, 1976).

[9]Mark Noll, *Between Faith and Criticism: Evangelicals, Scholarship, and the Bible in America* (San Francisco: Harper & Row, 1986), 23; George Marsden, *Fundamentalism and American Culture: The Shaping of Twentieth Century Evangelicalism 1870–1925* (New York: Oxford University Press, 1980), 212–21.

[10]E.g., the note on Qoheleth 9:10 in *The Scofield Reference Bible* (New York: Oxford University Press, 1909) and Charles C. Ryrie, chapter 5, "The Hermeneutics of Dispensationalism," in his *Dispensationalism Today* (Chicago: Moody Press, 1965), 86–109. For a scholarly appraisal regarding the complex nature of such "literal interpretation," see especially Timothy Webber, *Living in the Shadow of the Second Coming: American Premillennialism 1875–1925* (New York: Oxford University Pres, 1979); also, Kathleen C. Boone, *The Bible Tells Them So: The Discourse of Protestant Fundamentalism* (New York: SUNY, 1989).

[11]Bernard Ramm, *Protestant Biblical Interpretation* (Boston: Wilde, 1956), 89–102.

[12]Jack Rogers and Donald McKim, *The Authority and Interpretation of the Bible* (New York: Harper & Row, 1979), 238–47, 289–98.

[13]Ernst Troeltsch, *Protestantism and Progress: The Significance for the Rise of the Modern World*, trans. B. A. Gerrish (Philadelphia: Fortress, 1986), 21.

[14]I owe this use of "submodern" to conversations with James Washington, professor of church history at Union Theological Seminary, New York City. He uses the term in an effort to find an accurate description within the dominant intellectual climate of opinion for large segments of the black church and other Christian groups that were marginalized from these debates. See his *Frustrated Fellowship: The Black Baptist Quest for Social Power* (Macon: Mercer University Press, 1986).

My own work illustrates a similar assessment for holiness and Pentecostal churches, including black churches. See, for example, "Pentecostalism and the Hermeneutics of Dispensationalism: The Anatomy of an Uneasy Relationship," *Pneuma* 6,2 (1984):1–26; "The Nicean Creed, Filioque and Pentecostal Movements in the United States," *Greek Orthodox Theological Review* 31,3–4 (1986):171–85 (reprinted in T. Stylianopoulous and S. Mark Heim, eds., *The Spirit of Truth: Ecumenical Perspectives on the Holy Spirit* [Brookline: Holy Cross Orthodox Press, 1986]); and "An Overview of the Hermeneutical Situation of Biblical and Theological Studies in the United States," in M. Branson and R. Padilla, eds., *Conflict and Context: Hermeneutics in the Americas* (Grand Rapids: Eerdmans, 1986), 11–21.

[15]David Kelsey, *The Uses of Scripture in Recent Theology* (Philadelphia: Fortress, 1975), 158–81.

[16]Webber, *Living in the Shadow*, 160–9.

[17]Sydney E. Ahlstrom, *Theology in America: The Major Protestant Voices from Puritanism to Neo-Orthodoxy* (New York: Bobbse-Merrill, m.d.), 589.

[18]Horton, "Systematic Theology," 119.

[19]G. Ernest Wright, *God Who Acts* (Naperville: Allenson, 1964); idem, *The Old Testament and Theology* (New York: Harper & Row, 1969).

[20]James Robinson, "The Historicity of Biblical Language," in B. W. Anderson, ed., *The Old Testament and Christian Faith* (New York: Harper & Row, 1963); Langdon Gilkey, "Secularism's Impact on Contemporary Theology," *Christianity and Crisis* 25 (1965–66):65.

[21]Sydney E. Ahlstrom, *A Religious History of the American People* (New Haven: Yale University Press, 1972), 961.

[22]Richard Quebedeaux, "The Evangelicals: New Trends and New Tensions," *Christianity and Crisis* 36 (1976–77): esp. 199; Donald Dayton, "Where Now, Young Evangelicals?" *The Other Side* (March/April 1976), 33–35; and Gerald T. Sheppard, "Biblical Hermeneutics: The Academic Language of Evangelical Identity," *USQR* 32,2 (1977):81–94. Cf. Noll, *Between Faith and Criticism*, 162–85.

[23]See n. 13 and Lindsell's sequel, *The Bible in the Balance* (Grand Rapids: Zondervan, 1979).

[24]Noll, *Between Faith and Criticism*, 153.

[25]Cf. in Ronald J. Sider, ed., *Karlstadt's Battle with Luther: Documents in a Liberal-Radical Debate* (Philadelphia: Fortress, 1978).

[26]Krister Stendahl, "Biblical Theology, Contemporary," *The Interpreter's Dictionary of the Bible* (Nashville: Abingdon, 1962), 1:419.

[27]Kelsey, "Method, Theological," 365.

[28]In David Kelsey, *The Uses of Scripture in Recent Theology* (Philadelphia: Fortress, 1975), the author showed that the "translation" model for biblical interpretation creates its own profound theological problems. In my view, this critical model works best with the more liberal examples such as Tillich and Bultmann.

[29]Daniel Fuller, "What Is a Theological Liberal?" *The Opinion* (student publication of Fuller Seminary) 10,4 (1971): 6.

[30]Cf. overview and bibliography in Brevard S. Childs, *Biblical Theology in Crisis* (Philadelphia: Westminster, 1970) and Henning G. Reventlow, *Problems of Biblical Theology in the Twentieth Century*, trans. John Bowden (Philadelphia: Fortress, 1986), 1–9.

[31]G. Ernest Wright, "The Study of the Old Testament," in Nash, ed., *Protestant Thought*, 18, 22–23.

[32]Floyd Filson, "The Study of the New Testament," in Nash, ed., *Protestant Thought*, 67.

[33]E.g., Gerhard Hasel, *Old Testament Theology: Basic Issues in the Debate* (Grand Rapids: Eerdmans, 1972).

[34]Childs, *Biblical Theology*, 61–87.

[35]James Cone, *My Soul Looks Back* (New York: Maryknoll, 1986), 48.

[36]Cone, Ibid., 45, 57–59; idem, *Black Theology and Black Power* (New York: Seabury, 1969); idem, *God of the Oppressed* (New York: Harper & Row, 1975).

[37]Cone, *My Soul Looks Back*, 168.

[38]Cf. Hans Frei, *The Eclipse of Biblical Narrative: A Study in Eighteenth and Nineteenth Century Hermeneutics* (New Haven: Yale University Press, 1974);

idem, *The Identity of Jesus Christ: An Inquiry into the Hermeneutical Bases of Dogmatic Theology* (Philadelphia: Fortress, 1974); George Lindbeck, *The Nature of Doctrine: Religion and Theology in a Post-liberal Age* (Philadelphia: Westminster, 1984).

[39]Cf. Cornel West, *Prophetic Fragments* (Grand Rapids: Eerdmans, 1988), 236–39, a review of Frei, *Eclipse.*

[40]Lindbeck, *Nature of Doctrine,* 18.

[41]Ibid., 67–69.

[42]Phyllis Trible, *God and the Rhetoric of Sexuality* (Philadelphia: Fortress, 1978); idem, *Texts of Terror* (Philadelphia: Fortress, 1984).

[43]Brevard S. Childs, *Myth and Reality in the Old Testament* (Philadelphia: Fortress, 1960).

[44]For an overview of changes in his position, see my "Canon Criticism: The Proposal of Brevard Childs and Its Implications for Evangelical Theology," *Studia Biblica et Theologica* 4,2 (1974): 3–17.

Part IV

DOING THEOLOGY TODAY: THE APPROACH OF KENNETH S. KANTZER

19

A SYSTEMATIC BIBLICAL DOGMATICS:[1] WHAT IS IT AND HOW IS IT TO BE DONE?[2]

KENNETH S. KANTZER
TRINITY EVANGELICAL DIVINITY SCHOOL,
DEERFIELD, ILLINOIS

Systematic biblical dogmatics is an eminently practical science. It is practical because it seeks to help me as a sinner and other sinners like me, come to know God, find acceptance with him, learn how we can please the One we love supremely and find usefulness in his great kingdom. It seeks to answer the question, What must I think and say and do about God, human beings, and the created universe in their interrelationships?[3]

The discipline of systematic theology goes by many names. Until modern times it was most frequently called Christian doctrine or teaching.[4] Calvin called it "instruction."[5] My favorite term for it is systematic biblical dogmatics. It is *systematic* because it organizes the material in whatever way will be most helpful and readily usable to set forth the whole of the instruction God has given to his church to enable his church collectively and in its individual members to be obedient and useful in his kingdom.[6] It is *biblical* because it is derived from the Bible.[7] And it is *dogmatics*[8] because it seeks to understand and communicate the commands of the sovereign God—commands that we are to accept, believe, and obey.[9]

EXEGETICAL THEOLOGY

Systematic biblical dogmatics differs from exegetical theology in that the latter seeks to answer the question, What does this particular passage of Scripture say?[10] Since Scripture is embedded in history, its human author speaks in a historical language and culture that he or she necessarily reflects. In addition, the biblical author sometimes makes statements about events reflecting an earlier history and culture (for example, Moses makes statements about patriarchal times). What he says, then, reflects a delicate combination of his own historical culture and the historical culture of the events he describes. We can determine what he says only to the degree that we understand these cultures, and the author's language is a part of the culture.

Most of this historical and cultural background the biblical authors themselves communicate to us, but we can also be grateful for the contribution of nonbiblical data that often throw further light on the meaning of the text. (The archaeological data from ancient Nuzi, for example, shed beautiful light on the significance of the household gods in Haran; and this increases our understanding of the story about Rachel and her theft of Laban's household gods.)[11]

Moreover, if we reflect a moment, we realize that we, too, employing our own language and thought forms, stand in a quite different history and culture. To know what the biblical author says, we must interpret it from the culture or cultures in which it was originally embedded into language symbols that are meaningful to us and to the readers or hearers within our culture.[12]

This cultural relativism does not need to lead to skepticism or massive uncertainty. On the contrary the right way to find the truth begins with a full recognition of cultural relativism. In fact, the only really devastating aspect of this relativism arises when we are ignorant of, or ignore, how deeply and thoroughly and necessarily all we think or say is enmeshed in our culture. This is true of the biblical writer, ourselves, and those to whom we wish to communicate.[13]

Moreover, cultural relativism is not a brand new discovery of the twentieth century and liberal theologians. Without using the term, the fathers of the ancient church knew about it and took it into account in their interpretations.[14] And so has the church since that day.[15] We have simply become more self-consciously aware of it and of its vast importance in interpreting any piece of literature, including the Bible.[16]

BIBLICAL THEOLOGY

Biblical theology grows out of exegesis. It seeks to summarize and organize the historical unfolding of revelation in time by individual author or by groups of related books. For instance, we have a biblical theology of the early nonwriting prophets, of the Synoptic Gospels, of the Johannine corpus, a theology of 1 Corinthians, a Pauline theology, and a theology of the Pastoral Epistles. Biblical theology is organized generally on an authorial or chronological basis or by treating books together according to some perceived similarities of style or genre rather than treating the Bible as a whole on a thematic basis.

Some students of the New Testament argue that we cannot speak of a biblical theology but only of biblical theologies.[17] From one point of view this is correct. The various biblical segments do not lend themselves to neat, unified theologies. The theology of Deuteronomy is different from that of Leviticus, and both are different from that of Jeremiah. Similarly in the New Testament, there are significant differences between the theology of the synoptics and that of John or Paul or the book of Hebrews. What was noted earlier of the cultural relativism of the various parts of the Bible certainly is applicable here.[18]

Revelation is progressive, and what is right for one person in one age, for example, is not necessarily right for quite a different person in a different age. Differences are not necessarily contradictions. And traceable through the Bible there is a unifying "scarlet thread" of a sovereign God who is holy, gracious, and redemptive in his relationship to weak and fallen humankind.[19] The differences are not to be ignored or flattened out but are to be seen in all their sharpness as truly reflecting the many-splendored complexity of the infinite God of the Bible in his relationship to sinners. The very angularity of the separate "theologies" of the Bible only displays to us a more complex and comprehensive picture of God and his universe.[20]

THE ROLE OF CHURCH HISTORY OR TRADITION

The word *tradition* has been used in two quite different senses. In the quarrels stemming from the Reformation period, tradition was often used to refer to apostolic or prophetic teaching authentically preserved in the church outside Scripture.[21] Of this I can only say that what is truly apostolic and can be known to be such I would accept as Spirit-guided instruction from God on the authority of Christ. Yet the authenticity of such nonenscripturated apostolic teaching is so utterly unreliable that I do not find this a serious problem. Moreover, Scripture itself is so clearly insistent on the authority and adequacy of what is written that it seems to imply quite clearly that the written apostolic teaching alone is to serve as the normative and permanent guide for the church.[22]

In any case, more and more the term *tradition* is used to refer to the voice of the historical church handed down to us through the past. This is not apostolic or prophetic revelation but the church's interpretation and application of the biblical teaching.[23] The value of this tradition I gladly acknowledge and take it with immense seriousness. While it is not infallible, it must be acknowledged as God's guidance of his people in accordance with his promise to the church of all ages.[24] To disregard it would display the sheerest egotism as though we were to say, I want to do this all by myself. I don't need any help from anyone.[25]

The role of church tradition is like that of an elder brother in the faith.[26] It not only helps us interpret biblical passages but also shows how the Scriptures were applied to the historical and cultural situations of the past so the people of God could be obedient to God in their day. By observing the changing situations to which Scripture has been applied across the centuries, we are aided in our own application of Scripture to our day. We can profit from the mistakes and learn from the godly insights of the believers of previous centuries. Even where our culture is different, as is always the case to some extent, we can profit from this repeated application of Scripture to diverse historical situations and cultures.

Contemporary Americans whose denominations began to exist in this century are prone to assume that the church started with them: they have no history. Evangelicals sometimes sound as though the church began with Wesley or Calvin or Luther, and from there they must jump back immediately to the apostles. Not so. We have a long and precious heritage that can warn us of mistakes, guide us to the truth, and make available to us today the manifold wisdom of the past. We need to acknowledge our heritage and take advantage of it.[27]

CONTRIBUTION OF THE LIVING CHURCH

In addition to the church of the past, I have the living church to disciple me, warn me, comfort me, encourage me, and exhort me to see the truth and do the right. Scripture was given to the church, and theology is a necessary work of the church, by the church, in the church, and for the church.[28] We live out our Christianity as part of that church. Our Lord promised special guidance for the assembled churches over against the individual believer. To seek to do theology in isolation is for the Christian to forfeit the ministry of the Holy Spirit promised to the living fellowship of the body of Christ.[29]

THE HOLY SPIRIT

Above all, in seeking to understand and apply the Scripture to our thought and life, we have the immediate and active power of the Holy Spirit who illuminates our minds to understand it rightly and to apply it faithfully to our lives and who exhorts us to do the right, convince us of sin, and warns us against the wrong.

The term "witness of the Holy Spirit" has engendered a great number of varied meanings.[30] Among evangelicals there are three generally recognized ways of interpreting it. The first is a kind of illumination.[31] The Holy Spirit enables us (or persuades us) to think rightly about the reasons for accepting Scripture as the Word of God, for accepting Jesus Christ as divine Lord and Savior, for interpreting Scripture faithfully, and for applying it honestly and rightly to our own lives.[32] Warfield, particularly in his analysis of Calvin's theology, stands as the greatest exponent of this view in our century.[33]

A second way of interpreting the witness is to understand it as religious and Christian experience both before the new birth, particularly in the sense of conviction of sin, and after the new birth in answer to prayer or in the changed life and attitudes wrought by the inworking, sanctifying Holy Spirit.[34]

Lewis French Stearns, in his work *Evidence of Christian Experience*, and many other scholars have stressed the role of the witness as a work of Christian experience performed by the Holy Spirit upon the soul of the individual Christian and in the community of believers.[35] This creates an experiential body of evidence that we do not otherwise have. Seeing what the Spirit has done, we are able to draw conclusions as to the truth of the

Christian faith and of its right application to our own hearts and minds. This is undoubtedly the view of the witness held by most simple Christians in our day.[36]

For my part, I agree that each of these is a significant and extraordinarily important function of the Holy Spirit. Both are recognized in Scripture. In 1 Corinthians 2:8ff. Paul stresses the illuminatory work of the Holy Spirit to enable us to see that what we formerly thought was merely human wisdom is really divine wisdom. The Holy Spirit opens up our mind so that we are able to think properly and draw the right conclusions.[37]

Moreover, in John 3:3ff. Scripture recognizes the experiential work of the Holy Spirit. Our Lord notes that the wind blows wherever it pleases, and even though you can't see it, you do see its effects. Similarly, you see the effects of answered prayer or the regenerating work of the Holy Spirit. And it is possible to draw conclusions from this as to his presence and active work in our behalf. How many times in a city mission we have heard a believer give his testimony that whereas he was blind, now he can see! He has no other explanation than that the Gospel is true. It has proved itself true in his own experience.[38]

Yet in spite of the reality of the illuminating work of the Holy Spirit and his work to act immediately upon us to change us and thus to provide us with a new body of experiential evidences, I do not believe that either of these is what is meant by the scriptural term "witness of the Holy Spirit." Rather, each of the biblical passages referring to the witness seems to reflect a divine judgment, never completely explainable as a human judgment that historical or experiential evidences are valid. The role of the witness is to seal truth upon the heart and mind. Its function is neither to illuminate so that a person can weigh the evidences better nor to provide a new sort of evidence so that the person can make his or her own judgment. It is rather to provide assurance, to create a conviction in the mind of the believer.[39]

The object of this biblical witness is essentially the Gospel, or, more specifically, the conviction that I, a sinner, have been forgiven and accepted as a full son or daughter into the favor of God solely on the ground of Jesus Christ and what he has done on my behalf, and on condition of personal faith or commitment to him.[40]

Indirectly, of course, the knowledge of Scripture and the complete doctrine of Christ rests on the witness to the Gospel; but directly and immediately the object of the Spirit's witness is not Scripture as a whole, but the Gospel and our acceptance with God through Christ.[41]

This does not mean that evidence is either invalid or worthless. Of course, history and experience may lead toward saving faith.[42] They may confirm the faith already sealed in the heart by the Spirit.[43] But the witness itself is a creative work of the Holy Spirit to provide a divine judgment, which God forms in the believer and seals on the whole soul by his Spirit.[44]

THE STEPS FROM BIBLICAL TEXT TO SYSTEMATIC THEOLOGY

So far we have seen that the Bible is the final authority and is normative over all other norms in doing theology.[45] But how do we get from the biblical text to the answer to our question, What should I think and do today? We cannot just translate the text. Systematic theology is not merely the translation of Scripture into our own cultural situation and thought forms.

Kelsey in his volume *The Uses of Scripture* reckons B. B. Warfield, of all those whose thought he analyzes or surveys, to be closest to this.[46] But such a view would make any coherent theology impossible. Abel built an altar, killed a lamb, and offered the lamb as a sacrifice to God. If the Bible were my guide by simply translating, I should go out in my backyard, redo the stone grill that I had used for frying hamburgers, buy myself a lamb from some farmer, and offer it on my ex-hamburger grill.

Most biblical passages are addressed to a specific group or to an individual living in a particular culture. To tear a verse out of its own historical and cultural context and assume that it is God's directive for everyone in all cultures and in all circumstances makes the Bible say what it never said at all. That is not being obedient to the Bible; it is to make up our own and quite unbiblical theology. That is why what is often called proof-texting is so objectionable.[47]

It is true that some biblical instruction sets forth universal rights and wrongs—like, perhaps, the Ten Commandments and certainly like the law of love. But we don't put our disobedient children to death. Model young ladies would not seek a husband the way Ruth did. I don't traipse off to Troas in mid-winter to fetch an overcoat when a dear friend is suffering from the cold. We don't insist that all women everywhere always keep silent in the church. I don't even talk in a completely unknown language, though my German friends think I come close to doing so when I speak German.

In addition to its truly universal principles, the Bible contains a great many applications of what is right (approved by God) and many more subapplications, as well as a few isolated and individual commands that pertain only to the one addressed in Scripture. A necessary part of our exegetical problem is to determine which passages are to be understood in Scripture as of universal application and which are restricted in their force to a particular individual, to a particular group, or even to a particular culture. And if the application is not universal, then we must ask ourselves in what sort of cases each passage applies.

Incidentally, I am not saying that the Holy Spirit cannot give direct revelation beyond what is contained in the Scripture or that he does not give specific revelations as to how a biblical passage is to be applied. I am only saying that our Lord has never promised that he will always give such extrabiblical revelations. If we wish to be guided by the whole of Scripture rather than by fragmented pieces of it, we must note not only all that Scripture commands but also to whom in its context each command is addressed.[48]

By no means does this imply that specifically restricted passages are useless. We know that is not the case, for "all Scripture is profitable." The many specifically addressed passages give me divinely approved applications of the law of love that should guide my application today. Of course, the judgment that God's approval of an act recorded in Scripture means that I in my similar situation should do likewise is a human judgment and is thus fallible as all merely human judgments and all systematic theology are.

In doing theology, therefore, I try to understand what all the biblical passages in their context really say on each subject. That gives me not just what God instructed Abel or Timothy to do; it also provides me with all the instruction God has given for the guidance of his people in dealing with the issue at hand. And each passage must be examined not only in the light of its immediate context but also in the light of the whole of Scripture. Then I take this divinely given instruction and apply it to myself. In the light of the universal commands of God— love everyone, worship only God, do not make idols, etc., and in the light of the many applications of these principles found in the Scripture, I can see what I in my day and in my situation must do to please God and to be useful in his kingdom. Thus even those passages not directly and immediately addressed to me provide me the profit promised in Scripture.

SYSTEMATIC OR NARRATIVE THEOLOGY[49]

Students sometimes ask me mighty tough questions. A few days ago a student in class raised his hand and without warning asked, "You say you believe the Bible is really the Word of God, but why do you put your theology into a system so different from the Bible? Don't you like the way God does theology?" Now I had been telling my students all along that we get our theology out of the Bible. It's God's instruction book for thinking and living. So why wasn't I following the biblical order? After a lifetime of teaching theology with the avowed purpose of doing it according to the Bible, I structured my systematic class under the time-honored rubrics: God, Trinity, Creation, Man, Sin, Christ, Atonement, Salvation, Authority, on down to Ecclesiology and Eschatology—just the way you don't find it in the Bible.

My answer is that when I must make a decision, I need to know right then and there all that God has revealed to us bearing on that decision. Most heresies in the past have started because people have failed to take into account the teaching of Scripture in its wholeness. They latched onto a piece of truth in the Bible and became so enamored with their brand-new discovery that they never bothered to learn what else the Bible had to say on that same subject. And when they did bother to look at the rest of the Bible, they twisted the other passages all out of shape to make them say just what the first passage said.[50]

Well, then, if we do theology right by forming it into a system, why didn't God do it that way? Why hasn't he given us a system or ordered sequence of instruction by category? All you need to know about God. All you need to know about Christ. All you need to know about salvation, and so on. The fact is, God really did give us his revelation in a system. It's just a different system for a different purpose.[51]

There are many reasons why the Bible was given to us in a sort of narrative unfolding of God's dealing with our race. The most obvious is that he didn't want to throw the whole book at us at one time. He knew it was best to give it a bit at a time— because we are "slow of heart to believe" (Luke 24:25).

Moreover, by revealing himself in history, God showed us

in the most convincing way that he is a personal God who lives and acts in and through history. We, too, must live and act and grow (or fail to grow) in history. The Bible, therefore, does not usually spell out its guidelines for us in general universal propositions, but in instruction specifically honed to meet the tensions of real life such as we face in making our decisions.

We can never forget the integrity of Joseph who faced and overcame the stressful kind of life temptations we too must face. This biblical narrative, with its strong pedagogical value, helps us far more than the general command "You shall not commit adultery." Narrative theology, therefore, is not antithetical to systematic theology. All truly biblical systematic theology must also be narrative theology. Systematic theology simply pulls together all the narrative theology, piece by piece as it is set forth in Scripture, so that we have in purview the whole of the relevant narrative pieces pertinent to the immediate question we are facing in life.

The Bible and systematic theology serve different purposes. We need both. The Bible is God's instruction spelled out in real life. It comes to us in the way we can best use it as we face life's problems. Theology or Christian teaching (and theology need not be written) represents our putting it all together in a single focus to enable us to know what we must think or do. The study of systematic theology is specially helpful for immature Christians who are not familiar with the broad scope of narrative instructions contained in the Bible. For example, when they read 1 Corinthians 14, they need to be reminded of 1 Corinthians 11. If we would be obedient to God, we must seek the comprehensiveness of divine instruction when we face a decision. Yet we grasp Bible truths most powerfully in the narrative setting of the Bible.[52]

I urge my students, therefore, not to preach a theological system from the pulpit or in a Sunday school class. They need a theology, and they should encourage every believer to have a theology; but they should preach and teach the Bible, because that is the way we are best able to absorb biblical instruction and use it to solve the tensions of life.

The heart of biblical preaching, therefore, ought to be the exposition of Scripture, not systematic theology. But the best of such preaching must always be biblically informed, and to be truly profitable exposition of Scripture it must inform those who are being instructed. It must set the content of a particular passage against the content of the comprehensive biblical teaching on that subject. That is, it must be set in the context of the relative branch of systematic theology, even though the control and emphasis are determined by the biblical text.[53]

THE RELATIONSHIP OF NATURAL REVELATION TO SYSTEMATIC THEOLOGY

In his famous diatribe against the value of natural revelation entitled *Nein*, Karl Barth repudiated any natural theology.[54] While he camped on 1 Corinthians 1 and 2, most expositers of the book of Romans agree that he failed to do justice to Romans 1 and 2.[55] In any case, on the basis of the Romans passage, I must disagree with his total rejection of any rational case for theism. In the Bible one can find examples of most of the major theistic arguments set forth with approval. The Bible does not present these as proofs in the usual sense of that word, however, but rather as references to a body of data to which we need to respond. These data, so the Scriptures claim, make sense—that is, they can be fitted into a coherent view—only if we posit a supreme Power in the universe to whom we are responsible. They do not tell us all we need to know about God, but they are the basis for a valid conclusion.[56]

Moreover, these data represent a useful evangelistic tool. They are to be presented to the unbeliever to lead him or her toward faith in God and in Christ.[57] Standing alone, they never lead a sinner into a saving knowledge of God. But God uses our presentation of the data, and we are to challenge unbelievers with this evidence.[58] If they reject the existence of God in the light of these data, they are morally reprehensible for failing to accept the truth. And in the light of who God has revealed himself to be, he judges those who fail to honor their Creator and worship him.[59]

In addition, these evidences confirm the faith of the believer. And as believers we are encouraged to contemplate the heavens and to give glory to God because of what we see there.[60]

On the other hand, I agree with Barth and with most evangelicals that natural revelation does not add to our understanding of the knowledge of God beyond what is contained in the Scripture. In Scripture God has given us all the instruction about himself we need for the living of the Christian life.[61] If we attempt to add content *not based on the Bible* to our understanding of who God is and what he does, that attempt will only lead us to what is false or what is useless or both. It is what Calvin would have called empty speculation.[62]

Yet the confirming of the faith may be intellectually and emotionally of extraordinary value to us as we contemplate with awe the starry heavens above us. The Psalms give us a pattern for the value of the natural revelation.[63]

THE ROLE OF REASON IN DOING SYSTEMATIC THEOLOGY

From our discussion of theological methodology so far, it has become apparent that reason plays a significant role when we do theology rightly and in accordance with biblical instruction.[64] We cannot rightly rule reason out as alien to doing theology, whether out of despair as exemplified by many modern deconstructionists[65] or on the biblical grounds of 1 Corinthians 1.[66] Nor can we take the stand of Karl Barth that logic can be used when it helps us and rejected when it does not. I remember a seminar in which I read a paper for Karl Barth showing that in his *Kirkliche Dogmatik* he had on numerous occasions employed a straightforward Aristotelian syllogism—major premise, minor premise, and conclusion. Some of his students objected to my presentation, but Barth's response was: "No, I use logic whenever it helps me; but when it doesn't, I ignore it. That's the trouble with you fundamentalists. You make yourselves slaves to logic."[67]

To trust the laws of logic is not to put law or logic above God.[68] Rather, it is to recognize that the laws of logic are an expression of the rational nature of the God of Truth.[69] He created humans in his own image so that we, like him, can think rationally. He also created an objective world that conforms to the reason of God and to our own reason so that we can trust our senses and arrive at the truth. And it is only by the use of reason in dependence on the basic laws of thought that we are able to know the truth and rest in our knowledge of it. This is true of our Christian faith and of all else as well. If we deny the basic laws of thought and particularly the law of noncontradiction, all so-called knowledge becomes mere nonsense.[70] Our dependence on them is a necessary guide to warn us of error and to lead us to the truth. Consequently, the Scriptures call us to make judgments on the basis of the laws of thought—as, for example, in the tests of a prophet (Deut. 13,

18), in the necessity of rejecting a false gospel (Gal. 1:3), and in the application of scriptural truth (Isa. 1:18).

What, then, is the role of reason in systematic theology? It is the instrument by which we can judge the credibility of faith. What is truly contradictory does not belong to faith. The God of the Bible is a consistent God. We contradict ourselves, but God does not contradict himself. Unfortunately, the acceptance of paradox[71] is widespread in evangelical circles and in much of modern thought.[72] This is a mistake and leads us to accept uncritically meanings of Scripture that are not what God wishes us to have. Scripture warns us emphatically not to accept as a revelation from God what contradicts previous revelation. And Paul condemns the Galatians for not rejecting what contradicted true faith. Paradoxes within the faith are not to be embraced and believed by the faithful Christian. The presence of a paradox warns me that I do not have the truth on that point.

Of course, I find apparent paradoxes in Scripture, for it is God who is always consistent, not I. When I do find a paradox, my first task is to examine my exegesis carefully. I check my data to make sure that I have not drawn an erroneous view of what Scripture really teaches in one passage or another. Having checked my exegesis, I examine what I have found to see if it really does involve a contradiction. If I still find what seems to be a paradox, my only rational conclusion is to admit that I do not know. The evangelical who believes a paradox believes too much. For example, he knows exactly what the Scripture teaches in one passage. He knows exactly what it teaches in another. And he knows that these two conflict and contradict each other. On the basis of Scripture itself I must conclude in such a case that I am ignorant either of exactly what Scripture means or of how the various passages of Scripture are to be fitted together. Hence, I must reserve judgment.

Naturally, the removal of logical (as opposed to literary) paradox is only a negative test of truth. We are not obligated either rationally or morally to accept the truth of every idea that is merely free from internal contradiction. For example, that a grapefruit-sized submoonlet is circling our planet presents no internal contradiction, but I neither believe it nor argue that it is impossible. I simply do not have sufficient grounds to believe that it is so. To accept a matter as true, we need to note not only that no contradiction is involved but also that we have a critical body of related and relative information that presents no contradiction where a contradiction would be likely were the matter not true. This is essentially what we mean when we speak of systematic coherence or internal freedom from contradiction and an external fitting of relevant facts.[73]

IS HUMAN KNOWLEDGE OF GOD VALID?

But granted that we can glean from the Bible a generally coherent view of what God and the universe are like, it is certainly legitimate to inquire further if this biblical world-and-life view has any ultimate validity. From a Christian point of view how could any finite, sinful, earth-bound being place any confidence in our human ability to know the infinite God? That "the finite is incapable of the infinite" has a long and honorable standing in the history of human thought.[74]

Many modern theologians, not to mention dominant philosophical thinkers since the days of Hume, reckon this to be an utterly insurmountable obstacle to any valid knowledge of God. They have given up the idea of a God active in the universe; of man made in the divine image with a capacity, like God's, to know the truth; of a universe created by a rational God in accordance with the structure of his own mind and, therefore, knowable by man made in the divine image; of a loving God who cared for his creation enough to enter a fallen race to win it back to himself and to goodness; of the best man who ever lived, who claimed to be God, come down to seek and to save us who are lost; of a Jesus Christ who died and rose again in triumph over death; and of a universe moving toward a meaningful and good goal. And having rejected these Christian postulates, they have, not surprisingly, ended up despairing of our ability to know God, ourselves, and our destiny. In all honesty, I confess that I must consider it highly irrational when a theologian calls us to make a commitment to We-Know-Not-What. The capital letters represent merely a concession to labeling an unknown something by the exalted name of God. But capital letters do not add knowledge content to a god who is essentially unknown and unknowable.[75]

For my part I cannot accept these negative judgments. In each case my assumptions are just the opposite. And I end up with a coherent picture of a great God who is personal and rational, who loves me and cares for me, and whom I can know and trust. This coherent view of God and the universe fits the facts we are able to know—from the big bang of creation, to the order and arrangement of the physical universe, to the ability of my mind to predict the future, to the otherwise inexplicable figure of Jesus of Nazareth, to the human conscience and moral law within, and to the meaningfulness of everything. Biblical Christianity makes sense out of an otherwise senseless universe and meaningless life.

BIBLICAL THEOLOGY IS CHRISTOCENTRIC

Finally, a systematic theology that is truly biblical is also Christocentric. Rightly interpreted, the whole Bible, both Old and New Testaments, reveals to us Jesus Christ, the holy and loving redeeming God. It instructs us as to who he is and what he means to sinful human beings and the universe. For the Bible this is a hermeneutical principle, not a limiting principle.[76] We do not put the Bible through a sieve, tossing out what does not bear to us Christ and accepting only what refers to Christ and his benefits. The whole Bible spells out for us the message of the gracious God. Insofar as we understand all that is taught in Holy Scripture, we thereby understand adequately who God is and what he means to us.[77]

The Christocentric focus of the Bible, however, must not be reckoned as antithetical to its theocentric focus. Jesus Christ is the God-man, who reveals to us God and brings us into a right relationship to the triune God of the Bible. He is the divine mediator between God and man—noetically and existentially. So we turn to the whole Bible, knowing that in the whole and in all its parts it reflects to us the sovereign, loving, holy, redemptive God who loves us and gives himself for us. And in it we find the true meaning of our own life and our true role in the universe of which we are a part.[78]

Christocentric and theocentric, therefore, are not contradictory ways of understanding the Bible. Rather, they are two ways of looking at the same thing. The Christocentric focus of the Bible is God's own way of leading us to the theocentric knowledge of the triune God.

What, then, shall we think? And what, then, shall we do? To answer these questions the church of our day most desperately needs to pay attention to the Holy Scripture and to build and teach a systematic theology based on this infallible Word of God.

NOTES

[1]I have chosen to address the text of this chapter to theological students at the Master of Divinity level, but in the footnotes I have responded in some preliminary way to a variety of theological perspectives, including those represented by the contributors to this volume. Full and detailed interaction with the contributors would require a book and, in any case, would not adequately reflect my appreciation of their work or my gratitude to them for honoring me in this way.

[2]Traditionally, this topic has been assigned to prolegomena. Answering this question is not, however, what we need to do before we get into theology. It is the first part of theology. From a Christian point of view, God has revealed how we should do theology as well as other aspects of the subject. Unfortunately, in today's contemporary theological forum, many never get beyond prolegomena. This comes as no surprise to anyone who holds, as I do, that any valid theology is dependent on divine revelation. If we are convinced that God has given no clear revelation or if we are not sure that he has, then we certainly cannot build a theology on the basis of revelation. Before we can proceed to elaborate a rounded systematic theology, we must first answer the fundamental question: How can we know anything about God?

[3]Note that I have not attempted to define theology as such. See Schubert Ogden, "What Is Theology?" in *The Journal of Religion* 52 (1972): 22–24. Roman Catholics, even at the most basic level, cannot agree as to what they mean to do when they "do theology." See John J. Connelly, "The Task of Theology" in *The Catholic Theological Society of America: Proceedings of the 29th Annual Conference* (Chicago: Catholic Theological Society of America, 1974), 1–58. Protestants are still less agreed. See, for example, Maurice Wiles, *What Is Theology?* (Oxford: Oxford University Press, 1976), 42ff., and John M. Frame, *The Doctrine of the Knowledge of God* (Phillipsburg, N.J.: Presbyterian and Reformed, 1987), 76–77.

[4]See Emil Brunner, *The Christian Doctrine of God*, trans. Olive Wyon (London: Lutterworth, 1949), 89–90, and especially the extraordinarily valuable study by Wolfhart Pannenberg, *Theology and the Philosophy of Science*, trans. Francis McDonagh (Philadelphia: Westminster, 1976). The section: "Part Two: Theology as Science," 228ff. is particularly helpful.

[5]John Calvin, *Institutes of the Christian Religion*, ed. John T. McNeill, trans. Ford Lewis Battles, 2 vols. (Philadelphia: Westminster, 1975): 1:xxxiv.

[6]The sense in which theology is systematic is a crucial issue. I understand theology to be systematic in the sense that it is orderly. One may have a reason for putting together its various parts, but that reason need not be that each part logically requires every other part. To conceive of systematics in this latter sense (what is often referred to as a "logical" system) would destroy the freedom of God and require a completely determined God and a completely determined universe—both of which seem to me flatly to contradict the nature of God and the universe as revealed in Scripture. In quite a different sense of the word *logical*, any valid systematic theology would be logical. See below, 468ff.

[7]This necessarily raises the issue of natural revelation and the role of reason in doing systematic theology. I believe there is a natural revelation and also a necessary role for human reason in the construction of biblical dogmatics. How I harmonize these tenets with the statement in the text will appear as we continue. See below in the section discussing *sola Scriptura*, 467ff., especially fn. 61.

[8]I am using the word *dogmatics* in its etymological sense of decree or

command. Of course, the term has highly undesirable overtones in modern English. Usually it implies that an assertion is to be accepted unquestioningly and without adequate grounds presented for it. Obviously, that is not the sense in which I am using the term here. For an excellent justification of the word as legitimately applied to systematic theology, see Karl Barth, *The Doctrine of the Word of God (Church Dogmatics*, I/1, trans. G. T. Thomson [Edinburgh: T. & T. Clark, 1936]), 305ff. Hereafter the *Church Dogmatics* will be cited with the notation of volume, part, and page—e.g., II/ 2 /350. Pannenberg defends the use of dogmatics in this same sense: Wolfhart Pannenberg, "What Is a Dogmatic Statement?" in *Basic Questions in Theology*, vol. 1, trans. George H. Kehm (Philadelphia: Westminster, c. 1970), 1:182–210. There is a hidden ambiguity in Barth's title *Church Dogmatics.* Barth opts for a dogmatics *by* the church (though under the norm of Scripture). I opt for a dogmatics that represents a study of the "decrees" of Scripture *over* the church. There is a sense in which it is both over and by the church, but the overall direction of authority is clarified by understanding it as dogmatics to or over the church.

[9]Gordon Clark objects that we don't obey much of Scripture, we just believe it. See Gordon Clark, *Karl Barth's Theological Methodology* (Philadelphia: Presbyterian and Reformed, 1963), 132–36. I agree with Karl Barth that all Scripture demands a response. *Church Dogmatics*, I/ 1 /235 and passim. In some cases our appropriate response is to do as the Scripture requires. In other cases, it is to respond by believing and worshiping.

[10]Exegesis, of course, means many different things in the world of contemporary biblical scholarship. I am using the term in the traditional sense of the attempt to understand the meaning intended by the biblical author as expressed in the text as it stands written. The first task of biblical exegesis is to determine the final form of the literary piece we are seeking to interpret—in short, textual criticism. This is not to denigrate the rights of historical criticism, source criticism, redaction criticism, form criticism, or other allied ways of examining a text and its background. In practice, these studies can be ways of helping us to interpret better the text we have. See especially, E. D. Hirsch, *Validity in Interpretation* (New Haven: Yale University Press, 1967). See also Tremper Longman, III, *Literary Approaches to Biblical Interpretation* (Grand Rapids: Zondervan, 1987); and Anthony C. Thiselton, *The Two Horizons: New Testament Hermeneutics and Philosophical Description* (Grand Rapids: Eerdmans, 1980).

I am also interested in the historical background of biblical statements and how these ideas came to find their way into the final text, but exegesis seeks the author/editor's meaning in the literary text in its final form as a literary piece. At worst, these studies can be means by which we reject the meaning of the text in its final form in favor of a quite different idea—an idea we conjecture to lie behind the meaning set forth in the final form of a literary piece.

In a significantly different sense, many theologians distinguish between the meaning of what the text says (the task of exegesis, as I perceive it) and what the text means (which is often quite different from what it says). In this case the modern interpreter is turning away from the meaning of the text to his own idea of what the reading of the text means and what he deems profitable. Krister Stendahl, the former dean of Harvard Divinity School, notes that what the text means is often far more important to the modern exegete than what the text says. See his illuminating piece in "Biblical Theology: Contemporary" in *The Interpreter's Dictionary of the Bible*, ed. George Arthur Buttrick et al. (Nashville: Abingdon, 1962), 4:418–32. This replaces any "authority" of the biblical text with the ability of the biblical text to stimulate ideas in the mind of the reader. Such ideas may be quite different from those of the biblical text.

For a valuable analysis of the quite varied understanding of what it means to "exegete" or to "use" Scripture, see David Kelsey, *The Uses of Scripture in Recent Theology* (Philadelphia: Fortress, 1975).

[11]Ignace J. Gelb, Pierre M. Purves, and Allan A. Macrae, *Nuzi Personal Names* (Chicago: University of Chicago Press, 1943).

[12]For theologians who take seriously the authority of the Bible, the task of doing systematic theology becomes awesome. See the comment of Karl Rahner in "Theology," *Sacramentum Mundi* (New York: Herder and Herder, 1969), 239: "The mass of material in exegesis and history of dogma is such that no single individual can take in and master theology even as it is at present."

[13]Unfortunately, cultural relativity is frequently appealed to in support of complete skepticism regarding our ability to recreate a biblical teaching in our culture and thought forms. We cannot know what the Scripture (or any writing from another culture than our own) meant, but only what it means to us today. Deconstructionists, for example, seem to take a far too skeptical view of our ability to secure in our own culture and thought forms what the biblical author meant in his ancient culture and thought forms. See the so-called "deconstructionists" P. Du Man, *Allegories of Reading: Figurative Language in Rousseau, Nietzsche, Rilke, and Proust* (New Haven: Yale University Press, 1979); C. Hartman, *Beyond Formalism* (New Haven: Yale University Press, 1979); and R. Barthes, *A Lover's Discourse*, trans. Richard Howard (London: Jonathan Cape, 1979). Barthes writes, "The text is plural. This does not mean just that it has several meanings, but rather that it achieves plurality of meaning, and irreducible plurality" (p. 76).

The logical corrollary of such an extreme view, of course, is solipsism; for after all, the difference in culture between any two people of the twentieth century and that between us and an eighth-century prophet or a first-century gospel writer is only one of degree. No one really acts on this skeptical basis, and it seems inconsistent to hold to such skepticism about our ability to understand what a person from another culture meant to say.

On the other hand, the careful student needs to preserve a proper caution about the ease of grasping what someone from an earlier culture really meant to say. The best treatment of this hermeneutical problem, I believe, is to be found in Hirsch, *Validity in Interpretation*. See also the articles by Donald Carson and Richard Muller (above, pp. 39–76 and 77–97). A related but still fundamentally important issue to the theologian and to the ordinary believer is the question of whether any finite human can know anything about the truly infinite God (should he exist). See below, page 470.

[14]In the ancient church it was quite clearly recognized that there was a significant difference between the way the Alexandrian theologians from Egypt understood the text and the way it was understood by the Antiochians only a few hundred miles away. The Latin theology of Augustine displayed its own distinctive African flavor, reflecting the culture in which it was developed. See R. P. C. Hanson, "Biblical Exegesis in the Early Church," in P. R. Ackroyd and C. F. Evans, eds., *The Cambridge History of the Bible* (Cambridge: Cambridge University Press, 1920), 1:412–53.

[15]Cultural distinctives are so thoroughly and obviously imbedded in the biblical text that any serious exegete could hardly avoid recognizing them. Calvin, for example, notes the cultural difference in marriage customs while exegeting the second chapter of Matthew. In his commentaries he struggled

with the problem of cultural relativism in seeking to understand biblical passages that he recognized as coming from a culture quite different from his own. See also David C. Steinmetz, "The Superiority of Pre-Critical Exegesis," *Interpreter's Dictionary of the Bible* (Nashville: Abington, 1962); and Beryl Smalley, *The Study of the Bible in the Middle Ages* (New York: Philosophical Library, 1932).

[16]The sheer bulk of literature dealing with problems of cultural relativity in the last decade or two has become astronomical. It stems from both the most conservative and the most liberal students of human language and of biblical exegesis and from all who theologically fall between the extremes. Mission theology probes the differences among African, Western, liberation, and feminist theologies, each of which brings new insights that those in other traditions were less able to see clearly. Recognition of this helps us better understand the true meaning of biblical texts and how they can best be applied to our contemporary situation no matter which culture we come from. The danger lies when differences no longer open up new ways of seeing what the text really says and the obvious meaning of the text is simply rejected on the basis of culturally determined presuppositions. Rosemary Reuther, for example, sets aside (altogether too easily) biblical texts and espouses on her own a theology that she deems more helpful to humankind. (See above, pp. 359–76.) As an evangelical, I do not so much object to her understanding of what is appropriate for the freedom of women as I do to her quite erroneous (and quite wooden) understanding of the biblical text.

[17]Perhaps the most articulate defender of this view, at least in English, is J. D. A. Dunn in his volume *Unity and Diversity in the New Testament* (London: SCM, 1977). He argues that we have different and contradictory theologies embedded in the New Testament. Sometimes he seems to suggest that these theologies are contradictory; but he is tolerant, and it is quite okay with him if others choose one of the poorer alternatives. More frequently, he argues that they contradict each other, but really all of them are basically and equally satisfactory. For a careful analysis of this position, see Donald A. Carson, "Unity and Diversity in the New Testament: The Possibility of Systematic Theology," in D. A. Carson and John D. Woodbridge, eds., *Scripture and Truth* (Grand Rapids: Zondervan, 1983), 65–95. Note especially his treatment of J. D. A. Dunn on pages 72–77.

[18]Naturally, these various "biblical theologies" are quite different from one another. Although some are different because of internal differences lying within the Bible itself, many are different because of the philosophical, theological, or hermeneutical presuppositions of the biblical scholar who is doing biblical theology. Many of these scholars would see serious contradictions between one or another of the various biblical theologies. Of course this would rule out any possibility of building a coherent theology on the basis of the Bible. Interestingly enough, one of the strengths of fundamentalist dispensational theology is its recognition of a quite radical discontinuity between Old and New Testaments and even within the Testaments. I would rather speak of a complementary relationship between the various parts of the Bible. Differing facets of truth are presented in different ways for different times and different purposes. Yet there is a golden thread of continuity that runs throughout the whole Bible and both Testaments. For example, those who find a radical discontinuity between Jesus and Paul often forget that both were Jews and fought the same opponent—theological and ethical legalism.

[19]For a defense of the inner unity of the various segments of biblical theology, see Walther Eichrodt, *Theology of the Old Testament*, trans. J. A. Baker

(Philadelphia: Westminster, 1951). Eichrodt organizes Old Testament theology around the "covenant," but other arrangements are surely possible. See also Jacob Jocz, *The Covenant: A Theology of Human Destiny* (Grand Rapids: Eerdmans, c. 1968); Herman N. Ridderbos, *Paul and Jesus: Origin and General Character of Paul's Preaching of Christ,* trans. David H. Freeman (Philadelphia: Presbyterian and Reformed, 1968); Walter C. Kaiser, *Toward an Old Testament Theology* (Grand Rapids: Zondervan, 1978); F. F. Bruce, *Paul and Jesus* (Grand Rapids: Baker, 1974); and George E. Ladd, *A Theology of the New Testament* (Grand Rapids: Eerdmans, 1974).

[20]Some differences, but by no means all, are "resolved" on the basis of the complexity of God. The outstanding example of this is, perhaps, the Christian doctrine of the Trinity or three-oneness of God. God's "psychology" is simply more complex than our own or anything we know. The same could be said of God's knowledge of future free acts and of his relationship to what we call space and time. Some of the unity we seek is achievable on a "before and after" basis; some is due merely to cultural expression; others are "markers" in the divine redemptive plan—that is, they have an anticipatory function, and so they resolve themselves when that to which they point arrives.

[21]Whether oral apostolic tradition is to be considered on a par with the canonical Scripture or only a trustworthy aid in the interpretation of Scripture is still a matter of dispute among contemporary Roman Catholic scholars, though both Meyendorff, representing Eastern Orthodoxy (see above, pp. 339–58), and Bevans, representing Roman Catholicism (above pp. 321–28), give prominence to the role of tradition as the consensus of the community of faith. Both, therefore, tend to subsume oral apostolic tradition under the rubric of the authority of tradition in the second sense. It should be noted that within the New Testament, *paradosis* simply means "that which is handed on." In different contexts, therefore, the term can also refer to apostolic truth that is "passed on," including what is contained in Scripture, or to negative traditions that set themselves against the divine self-disclosure in Scripture. Not all traditions are bad, and not all that are good possess the divine authority of Scripture. For a contemporary evangelical understanding of the role of tradition in evangelical theology, see above, pp. 171–94, David Wells, "The Theologian's Craft"; and see especially his article "Tradition: A Meeting Place for Catholic and Evangelical Theology," *Christian Scholar's Review,* no. 5 (1975), 50–61.

[22]We often forget that *graphē* means "writing." Our Lord stresses in most emphatic terms the authority of what "stands written" by contrast with the oral tradition of the Jews who opposed his teaching, and he commended those who adhered to the Scripture alone.

[23]After acknowledging the function of Bible and church in the sense that God mediates his blessing "through the ordinary, the material, the human," Bevan makes the astounding assertion that "it is a small but logical step for Catholics to understand that the church's Tradition, particularly as articulated in the papal and episcopal ministry of teaching (magisterium), must be taken with utmost seriousness both as a source and a judge of theology" (See above, pp. 321–38). Most evangelicals would grant that the church has a "sacramental" (Bevan's word) function in this sense; but that this would give special authority to the Roman Catholic papacy and bishops and particularly the kind of exclusive authority that the Roman church claims for its bishops, is hardly a "small step."

[24]See Karl Barth, *Church Dogmatics* (I/ 2 /487ff.). Here Barth traces brilliantly the *horizontal* authority from Christ through his prophets and apostles to us.

This is an aspect of Barth's theology that, unfortunately, is overlooked by his more liberal followers and by evangelicals who understand Barth only in terms of his liberal followers.

[25]Roland E. Murphy and Carl J. Peter analyze the contemporary Roman Catholic view of biblical authority in near Protestantlike style: "In principle the Bible remains the ultimate authority and holds the first priority within the total context. None of the other lines has a specified standing. They are all an 'input' into the current way in which the church is understanding the Bible." Roland E. Murphy and Carl J. Peter, "The Role of the Bible in Roman Catholic Theology," in *Interpretation*, 1971, 82. Of course one would need to scrutinize carefully what is meant by "first priority" and analyze the nature of "input." It should also be noted that this view hardly includes either the so-called "left wing" or the near medieval "right wing" of Roman Catholic pluralism since Vatican II.

[26]See Karl Barth, *Church Dogmatics*, I/ 2 /603–60.

[27]See Richard Muller, "Scholasticism, Protestant and Catholic: Francis Turretin on the Object and Principles of Theology," in *Church History*, 1986, 193–205.

[28]See H. O. J. Brown (above, pp 147–69). It is no accident that evangelical H. O. J. Brown entitles his contribution to his volume "On Theological Method: Faith and Tradition." His emphasis, like that of Augustine in the ancient church, is on tradition as the source of the living church that mediates faith to him, but a source tested by the written Word of God. Protestant disagreement with traditional Roman Catholic methodology on this point focuses first on the latter's exclusive identification of the church with those who are submissive to the pope. Evangelicals or traditional Protestants insist, rather, that the true church is composed of believers only; and the local visible church may be recognized as those who make a believable profession of faith in Christ, meet regularly for the preaching of the biblical Gospel and the right celebration of the sacraments (or ordinances), and, some would add, who commit themselves to obedience to Jesus Christ and practice church discipline. The most fundamental objection of Protestants or evangelicals to the traditional Roman Catholic view of tradition is its basic domestication of the Word of God. The Roman Church is not only the channel through which Scripture comes, but it also determines what Scripture is and what it means.

[29]This represents a major weakness in contemporary evangelicalism. Undoubtedly, it is too much to say that evangelicals have no developed doctrine of the living church. Yet emotionally we all too often consider the church not an essential element of our Christianity, but a sort of serendipity (or, sometimes, the cross we are called to bear). No doubt this attitude has been greatly encouraged by liberal takeovers of historic evangelical churches. Leaders of the church, whom we tend to identify with the church, not only reject the Gospel but fail altogether to nourish church members on the Word of God. Godly believers, starving for spiritual food and fellowship, turn to whatever source they can find—a new charismatic preacher of the Gospel, a parachurch organization, or perhaps the public radio or television. They so appreciate the fresh breath of life they receive that they do not always realize the impoverishment of soul that comes from a failure to participate in the church as a full member with the right celebration of the sacraments, the steady diet of instruction in the Word, and the blessings promised by our Lord to his body in the church. Too often the visible representatives of the church seem to function less like elder brothers eager to strengthen and encourage faith than like ravenous wolves seeking to destroy the sheep.

As constituting a movement, evangelicals may be defined as orthodox Protestants adhering to the "material" or content principle of salvation through personal faith in Jesus Christ and the "formal" or formative principle of the final authority of Holy Scripture. Representing the orthodox within all the diverse Protestant bodies, evangelicals have formulated quite different ecclesiologies, each reflecting its own tradition. In the United States evangelicals have often opted for the "gathered church" or "believers church" concept, but this is not true in Europe. And in drawing together across denominational barriers, evangelicals have tended not to accentuate ecclesiologies that divide them and, in some cases, have failed even to spell out an ecclesiology, viewing it as relatively unimportant. Gerald Sheppard (see above, pp. 437–59) is quite right, of course, when he argues, "Fundamentalism should never be identified uncritically with a defense of premodern orthodoxy." Much depends on how carefully he defines "fundamentalism." What he chooses to overlook is that contemporary evangelicalism, whatever may be its faults, stands, as does no other modern movement, with their evangelical predecessors of the sixteenth century and their evangelical successors since then, in adherence to both the material and the formal principles of Reformation and Protestant thought. Contemporary evangelicals do battle for the Gospel and justification by faith alone through a Nicean and Chalcedonian Jesus Christ and for the complete and final authority of the sacred Scriptures, which bear to us this Jesus Christ and what he means for our thought and life.

While making allowance in each case for their characteristic denominational distinctives, this includes also the main streams of the varied Mennonite groups (see above, John Yoder, "Thinking Theologically From a Free Church Perspective," pp. 251–65) and the even more varied Pentecostal bodies (see above, Russell F. Spittler, "Theological Style Among Pentecostals and Charismatics" pp. 291–318). The major exceptions are the United Pentecostal Church and some (though not by any means all) of the Roman Catholic charismatics. See also J. Rodman Williams, *Renewal Theology: God, the World, and Redemption: Systematic Theology from a Charismatic Perspective* (Grand Rapids: Zondervan, 1988).

[30]See Klaiber, "Die Lehre der altprotestantischen Dogmatiken von dem Testimonium Spiritus Sanctis und ihre dogmatische," *Jahrbücher für Deutsche Theologie*, ed., Liebuer, Dorner, et al, Second Series (Stuttgart: 1857), 1–54; and Jacques Pannier, "Essai sur l'Histoire du Dogme dans la Théologie reformée," in *Le Témoignage du Saint Esprit* (Paris: Librarie Fischbacher, 1893). For more recent studies of the witness, see Theo Preiss, *Das Innere Zeugnis des Heiligen Geistes*, trans. Georges Kaible (Zolliken-Zurich: Evangelischen Verlag, 1947); Bernard Ramm, *The Witness of the Spirit: On the Contemporary Relevance of the Internal Witness of the Holy Spirit* (Grand Rapids: Eerdmans, 1959); and John Frame, "The Spirit and the Scriptures" in *Hermeneutics, Authority and Canon*, ed. D. A. Carson and J. D. Woodbridge (Grand Rapids: Zondervan, 1986), 217–35. Frame's understanding of the role of the witness presents a needed caution to presuppositionalists who hover dangerously close to a fideistic irrationalism. Carl F. H. Henry in his *God, Revelation and Authority*, 6 vols. (Waco: Word Books, 1976–1983), represents the finest overall evangelical apologetic in the last half of the twentieth century. In this work he presents a carefully nuanced and guarded presuppositional approach, clearly avoiding any suggestion of fideism.

[31]As used here, the word *illumination* is a category in systematic theology, not a tightly defined biblical category. The New Testament frequently uses

apokaluptō and cognates for various aspects of the process by which humans come to know God and his truth. I refer here to one particular aspect of that process—the enablement of the mind, handicapped by its finiteness and earthbound limitations and blinded by sin, to draw correct conclusions from data.

32Note passages like 1 Corinthians 2 (especially v. 14).

33See B. B. Warfield's discussion of the witness in his article, "John Calvin's Doctrine of the Knowledge of God" in *Calvin and Calvinism* (New York: Scribners, 1950), 29–130. To secure a clear picture of Warfield's view, this article needs to be supplemented by his articles "Mysticism and Christianity" in *Studies in Theology* (New York: Oxford University Press, 1932), 649–66 and "St. Paul's Use of the Argument from Experience," in *The Expositor*, 5th Series, i (1895), 226–36.

34In a somewhat different sense, Friedrich Schleiermacher (so-called father of liberalism) defends a theology based on Christian experience and the human sense of ultimate dependence. See his *Christian Faith*, English translation edited by H. R. Mackintosh and J. S. Stewart (Edinburgh: T & T Clark, 1928).

35See Lewis French Stearns, *The Evidence of Christian Experience* (New York: Charles Scribner's Sons, 1890). See also the introduction to this volume by B. B. Warfield. A similar defense is found in John DeWitt, "The Testimony of the Holy Spirit to the Bible," *The Presbyterian and Reformed Review* (January, 1895), 69–85. More recently note Sverre Norborg, *Varieties of Christian Experience* (Minneapolis: Augsburg, 1937).

36Note the approval of the argument from experience by evangelical theologian Allen Coppedge (above pp. 267–89) and by Donald A. Thorsen, *The Wesleyan Quadrilateral: Scripture, Tradition, Reason, and Experience as a Model of Evangelical Theology* (Grand Rapids: Zondervan, 1990). Both Coppedge and Thorsen rightly describe it as a traditional Methodist and Wesleyan emphasis. Note, however, that it is common to all major divisions of the church. DeWitt and Stearns (see above) were Calvinists. Norborg was a Lutheran.

Experience is not the final (and it certainly is not an infallible) test of religious truth; but, when legitimately used, it leads to faith and confirms faith.

37Frederick Robert Tennant rejects the evidence of Christian experience, but he fails to place it in its proper theistic context. See his *Philosophical Theology*, 2 vols. (Cambridge University Press, 1928–1930), 1:306–32, where he dismisses lightly the argument from Christian experience on the grounds that it is impossible to show whether the observable, moral effects are due to the divine action or merely psychologically due to our human belief in the truth of those teachings. The same objection can be leveled against the moral argument for God as set forth in C. S. Lewis, *Mere Christianity* (New York: Macmillan, 1952), 17ff. Yet, if one combines these experiential data with the cosmological data and the teleological data, which seem to demand a supreme being guiding the universe, then the moral data and the data of conscience give evidence that the supreme being guiding the universe is concerned about moral values. The data of Christian experience are, thereby, raised to a new level. It becomes much more difficult to slough off the conscience as an accidental evolutionary quirk that simply proved useful in the struggle for survival, or to hold that the moral growth induced by believing these doctrines can be attributed merely to the effect of believing them.

38The average untaught Christian is not in a position to evaluate the theistic arguments of Thomas Aquinas or even the popular arguments of C. S. Lewis. With the blind man whose story is told in John chapter nine, however, he can say with conviction: "Whether he is a sinner or not, I don't know. One thing I do know. I was blind but now I see" (v. 25).

[39]For some illuminating insights on the value and object of the witness of the Spirit, see Karl Heim, *Das Gewissheits Problem in der systematischen Theologie bis zu Schleiermacher* (Leipzig: Hinricht, 1911).

In this discussion of the nature of the witness, Karl Barth seems to waver between the divine creation of knowledge in the human mind and the immediate sight of the glorified Lord who presents himself personally to a person and overwhelms him with the reality of his divine being. (*Church Dogmatics* I/ 2 /16, 203, and passim).

The biblical references explicitly discussing the witness of the Spirit are Galatians 4:4–6; Romans 8:15–16; and 1 John 5. In each of them, the focus of the witness is certainly on the central core of the Gospel—the good news that sinners are accepted by God into his forgiveness and favor through faith in Jesus Christ.

[40]Calvin interpreted the witness of the Spirit more broadly as certifying not only the central core of the Gospel, which, as he sees it, is the primary object of the witness, but also the Scripture and many of the major elements of Christian doctrine. At this point Fred Klooster is a true follower of John Calvin. See his article entitled "How Reformed Theologians Do Theology in Today's World," above, pp. 227–49.

[41]The biblical texts indicate that the direct object is only our sonship (forgiveness and acceptance) through faith in Christ. For an excellent treatment of this question, see Bernard Ramm, *Witness of the Spirit*, 53 passim. Ramm makes the distinction between the direct object (Calvin's primary object) of the witness of the Holy Spirit, which comes with certainty as a divine judgment impressed on the human mind, and the indirect objects, or those things that we are able to trust with assurance on the basis of the divine witness (when we have become convinced that the gospel is true).

[42]This is certainly the point of Paul's missionary preaching at Lystra (Acts 14) and at Athens (17:17ff.). See also Romans 2:14–15. It was presumably the point of our Lord in his conversation with Nicodemus (John 3).

[43]Note the so-called nature psalms; for example, Psalm 19:1–6.

[44]The witness seems to be referred to also by the biblical term *sealing*, the imprint by which God marks his own as a part of his forgiven family.

[45]Some theologians hold that the acceptance of normative divine revelation precludes the possibility of ever understanding theology as a science (G. Moran, *The Present Revelation* [New York: Herder and Herder, 1972] and *Theology of Revelation* [New York: Herder and Herder, 1966]). Why we can have a scientific study on the teachings of Plato or Shakespeare but not on the Bible completely eludes me. This is not to deny that faith may contribute to or detract from our understanding of the Bible. It is important here to note that biblical revelation does not come down to us in a totally other language of heaven but in a human language and, for the most part, in the "lip of Canaan"—one of the most earthy languages and, from the point of view of the Bible, a language of one of the most wicked people who ever dwelt on the face of this globe.

The question as to whether systematic biblical dogmatics is a science is not one of the most crucial issues of our day. Yet if by science we mean an organized body of knowledge in a particular area of study and open to the public, I see no necessary reason why it should not be called science. To deny it the right to the name science suggests that it does not provide knowledge or is unorganized or doesn't relate to any specific area or isn't open to public inspection. None of these is true. Moreover, the term *science* reminds all theologians that (1) theology, too, is a human endeavor and, like all other human sciences, very fallible; and (2) science itself, like theology, is a noble work divinely approved and, when rightly pursued, of immeasurable blessing to humankind.

[46]Kelsey interprets Warfield as most nearly exemplifying a theologian who builds theology on the basis of translating the Bible. See David H. Kelsey, *The Uses of Scripture in Recent Theology* (Philadelphia: Fortress, 1975), 191. At times Warfield certainly makes statements that lend themselves to this interpretation. Analysis of his methodology, however, quickly reveals that he does not depend simply on translation, but on a far more complex synthesizing of the varied texts relevant to the subjects he discusses.

[47]Proof-texting is not necessarily bad. In fact, all truly Christian theology must depend on proof-texting. To be sure, we are to use each text for the facet of truth that God is revealing in it. If we are to understand precisely what a given passage really teaches, however, not only must the passage be placed in the setting of its immediate context, but the biblical author and the culture in which that biblical author lived as well as the situation he is addressing must also all be considered. Then the truth from each particular text must be compared with that of other texts throughout the whole of the Bible, each in turn understood in its context to enable us to know what is the will of God for us according to the whole counsel of our God. Karl Barth objects to the fundamentalists' way of doing theology on this ground: they build their theology on isolated texts of Scripture rather than on the teaching of the Bible as a whole (*Church Dogmatics*, I/ 2 /608–9 and passim and especially III/ 1 /24). Barth is really interpreting their theory in terms of their practice. Fortunately, the theory of fundamentalists (and of evangelicals) is much better than their practice. Fortunately also, Karl Barth's practice is usually better than his theory. One needs to probe the difference for Barth between "the Bible as whole" and "the whole Bible."

[48]Naturally, it is not always easy to discern exactly to whom a particular passage is addressed, and, if it is not a universal, to what categories it applies. Does it, in fact, apply to me in my situation, right now? Here particularly the past traditions of the church and the Spirit's guiding of the church today are of help. By observing how God has guided his church in the past, I can secure insight as to how the passage may be properly applied to me in my day. Moreover, I rest in confidence that what I truly need to know, God will show me through his Word. Sometimes the nature of the immediate context discloses the unique reference of the passage to the original context alone (e.g., Paul's calling for his cloak from Troas). Sometimes the context makes unequivocally clear its universal reference (e.g., the law of love). Most frequently, neither of these is the case, and we must determine whether a passage that is not clearly universal or clearly unique is rightly to be applied to the situation we face. In such cases, the broader context of other passages is helpful. For example, in 1 Corinthians 14:35, Paul tells women to keep silent in the church. We can know that this is not a universal because three chapters earlier he approves of a woman praying and prophesying in what is clearly a public worship service. The very fact that all *right* applications are examples of pure love helps us. This is very different from Joseph Francis Fletcher's attempt to apply love rationally in flat disregard of explicit instruction in Holy Scripture. See his defense of so-called situational ethics in *Situation Ethics: The New Morality* (Philadelphia: Westminster, c. 1966). In some instances, however, I simply cannot be sure

whether a passage of Scripture applies in a given situation. In such cases I can often learn what is the truly loving act by listening to the Spirit-guided wisdom of my brothers and sisters in the church—clearly related to what the older Quakers referred to as the "sense of the meeting."

[49]Hans W. Frei is the most influential proponent of so-called narrative theology. See his *Eclipse of Biblical Narrative: A Study in Eighteenth and Nineteenth Century Hermeneutics* (New Haven and London: Yale University Press, c. 1975), and the more recent symposium edited by Stanley Hauerwas and L. Gregory Jones, *Why Narrative: Readings in Narrative Theology* (Grand Rapids: Eerdmans, 1989). The basic thrust of Frei is that we should allow the authors of biblical narrative to say what they want to say and not force their writings through the meat grinder of our post-enlightenment viewpoint. If the narrative tells of angels and demons and miracles and a God who acts immediately in human affairs and other matters obnoxious to our twentieth-century worldview, we should not insist on a hermeneutic that puts what they say through our grid so as to make them say what will be useful and meaningful to us. An honest hermeneutic must allow the biblical writer to state what he has to say in his own thought forms as best we can understand what he intended to say and according to our own thought forms—*not* to make the biblical narrator say what we can accept as valuable and true according to our worldview. In the first step we are asking what the biblical author meant to say as best we can understand it in our thought forms. In the second, we are asking, What do I believe or what ought I to think? The tie between these two steps is very close. They cannot be separated, but they can be distinguished. In the first instance we are functioning as exegetes. In the second, as theologians.

[50]Clear examples of this tendency can be seen in the "health and wealth" gospel (for those who usually fall within the larger group of those restricting the gospel to personal salvation) and in the so-called liberation theology (for those who concentrate on a social salvation). Both are clear instances of "overrealized" eschatology. The Bible promises complete health and total blessing for the individual (though hardly in terms of "health and wealth" values), but these promises will be fulfilled in the *eschaton*. Likewise, the Bible promises a rejuvenated earth—but in the *eschaton* (see Orlando Costas, above, pp. 377–96). As an evangelical, of course, Costas qualifies the unrealistic promises of nonevangelical liberation theology. A biblically rooted evangelical is committed, as a citizen, first to order, for without order there is neither freedom nor justice. Second, he or she is committed to radical freedom with boundaries that stop where one person's freedom infringes on the freedom and justice of another. Third, he or she is committed to justice with the goal of securing to each one and to each social group its due and all the good that will not infringe on that person's or that group's freedom or the just treatment of others.

[51]The danger of "narrative theology" lies neither in its understanding of biblical narrative as theology imbedded in narrative nor in the desire or even necessity of preaching the gospel as story. Its danger lies in its unwillingness to accept the trustworthiness of the biblical record of these narratives as truth coming from God for our guidance. By what strange alchemy can we accept the authority of the biblical author's narrative and yet feel quite free to reject his stated meaning of the narrative? I must confess I do not feel quite so strongly as Frei does in devaluing the work of the postenlightenment exegetes/theologians. For example, I owe a great deal to my own New Testament professor (Henry Joel Cadbury), who was not a theist and certainly would have to be labeled postenlightenment. He exegeted the biblical texts in Matthew and Luke as

teaching that the final texts of the biblical authors/editors were saying that Jesus was biologically born of a virgin. He then also understood that by their commitment to the biological virgin birth the first-century writers intended to exalt Jesus. Cadbury then rejected both the biological virgin birth and the exalted divine Jesus Christ. Emil Brunner agreed with Cadbury's exegesis at both points but rejected the biological virgin birth and accepted the divinely exalted Jesus Christ. As a conservative evangelical, I agree with their exegesis in both cases and also accept as true what the biblical authors said in both cases. In a similar way I rely on Nestles Greek text (26th edition), value the RSV English translation of the New Testament, and find fruitful exegesis in liberal and radical commentaries on the New Testament text. Like the liberals and radicals, I also am interested in what to believe about the Virgin Birth. Is it something that actually happened in our space-time universe, or is it a parable or a mythological truth or pure fiction? In this latter case, however, I am functioning not simply as an exegete but also as a twentieth-century theologian—but quite obviously not as a disciple of the enlightenment.

⁵²Biblical preaching, however, cannot ignore the complex ways that parts of the Bible are related to each other. We dare not preach as though the bits and pieces of the Bible need only to be juxtaposed so that no piece is omitted from our theology or our preached message. For example, parts of Scripture are rendered obsolete because of covenantal relationships (Heb. 8:13). The "befores" and "afters" of Scripture greatly affect all attempts to teach Christian ethics, Christian worship, and even Christian beliefs.

⁵³The alternatives to such a relationship between preaching and systematic theology are unthinkable: (1) the pastors alone—who receive a theological education—will be exposed to systematic theology and thus become the initiated, the elite of the elect, or (2) the ordinary lay Christians in the pew must develop their own systematic theology with no help or modeling when such help would prove enormously stabilizing in their own lives. The strength of the church depends on such preaching informed by and informing systematic theology.

⁵⁴See Emil Brunner, *Natural Theology, Comprising "Nature and Grace" by Emil Brunner and the Reply, "No" by Karl Barth*, trans. Peter Fraenkel, introd. by John Baillie (London: G. Bles, 1946). "Nature and Grace" in the same volume illustrates Brunner's qualified acceptance of a natural theology. See also the introduction to Barth's Gifford lectures, *The Knowledge of God and the Service of God According to the Teaching of the Reformation Recalling the Scottish Confession of 1560*, trans. J. L. M. Haire and Ian Henderson (New York: Scribner's, 1939), i-xxiv.

⁵⁵See Adolph Schlatter, *Gottes Gerechtigkeit: ein Kommentar zum Römerbrief* (Stuttgart: Calwer Verlag, c. 1967), 46ff.; F. F. Bruce, *The Epistle of Paul to the Romans: An Introduction and Commentary* (Grand Rapids: Eerdmans, c. 1963), 82ff.; and William Sunday and Arthur C. Headlam, *A Critical and Exegetical Commentary on the Epistle to the Romans*, 5th ed. (Edinburgh: T. & T. Clark, 1902), 39ff.

⁵⁶Among the Reformers, both Luther and Calvin agreed to the validity of a natural revelation (that there are valid natural arguments for believing in God apart from special supernatural revelation) though they rejected a natural theology (that on the basis of natural arguments alone unregenerate humans can arrive at a permanent trustworthy and adequate knowledge of God as Creator). This is frequently denied, as in Peter Barth, *Das Problem der Natürlichen Theologie bei Calvin: Theologische Existenz Heute*, 18 (München: Chr. Kaiser, 1935),

but its denial rests on a very selective induction from the works of both Luther and Calvin. For Calvin, see John Newton Thomas, "The Place of Natural Theology in the Thought of John Calvin," in *Journal of Religious Thought* 15 (1958), 107–36; and Gunter Gloede, *Theologie Natural bei Calvin* (Stuttgart: Kohlhammer, 1935). For Luther, see Julius Koestlin, *The Theology of Luther in Its Historical Development and Inner Harmony*, 2 vols., trans. Charles E. Hay (Philadelphia: Lutheran Publication Society, 1897), 2, 218ff., and Paul Althaus, *The Theology of Martin Luther*, trans. Robert C. Schultz (Philadelphia: Fortress, 1966), 16–17.

From the sixteenth to the twentieth century most evangelicals generally followed the lead of the Reformers except that the noetic effects of sin came to be emphasized less and less even among some evangelicals; and among liberals, natural theology often came to replace any theology based on special revelation. Liberal theology, in fact, took two paths to the knowledge of God—the path of Schleiermacher, exemplified par excellence by Adolph Harnack, *What Is Christianity?* trans. Thomas Bailey Saunders, introd. by Rudolph Bultmann (New York: Harper and Bros., 1957), and the path of the philosophers, exemplified by Immanuel Kant, *Religion Within the Limits of Reason Alone* (New York: Harper and Bros., 1960).

[57]See, for example, Acts 14 and 17 referred to previously.

[58]Peter calls for an *"apologia"*—a reasoned defense or apologetic for the hope that we have as Christians (1 Peter 4:16).

[59]This is the point of Romans 1:21ff. and Romans 2.

[60]Biblical encouragement to contemplate the heavens is exemplified in many of the Psalms. Note specially Psalm 19:1ff.

[61]Scripture appeals to itself as the adequate source (though not necessarily the exclusive source) from which we secure our knowledge of God and of the Christian life. See, for example, 2 Timothy 3:14–17. *Sola Scriptura* in Christian doctrine does not mean that Scripture is our only source of truth about God available to the regenerate mind. It means, rather, that Scripture is the only source of truth that is binding on the Christian conscience; and it is the sufficient source of truth about God, for it tells us all we need to know. Scripture is also the only infallible source of truth about God. That holding to *sola Scriptura* does not rule out all use of reason should be self-evident. See the following section, "The Role of Reason in Doing Systematic Theology."

[62]Note *Institutes*, I,11,1 and passim.

[63]For a fine presentation of the role of natural revelation from an evangelical viewpoint see Bruce A. Demarest, *General Revelation: Historical Views and Contemporary Issues*, foreword by Vernon C. Grounds (Grand Rapids: Zondervan, c. 1982).

[64]To see how one contemporary evangelical seeks to relate reason (philosophy) and theology, see above, Kevin J. Vanhoozer, "Doing Theology and the 'Ministry' of Philosophy," pp. 99–145.

[65]See above, fn. 13.

[66]See, for example, Søren Kierkegaard and his modern followers, the most influential of whom, Karl Barth, has already been cited. Søren Kierkegaard, *Concluding Unscientific Postscript*, trans. David F. Svenson, introd. and notes by Walter Lowrie (Princeton: Princeton University Press, 1944), 504 and passim.

[67]English seminar in the winter of 1955, Basel, Switzerland.

[68]Bertrand Russell, *Why I Am Not a Christian* (New York: Simon and Schuster, 1957), 8–9, 12.

[69]Both Luther and Calvin have often been interpreted as thoroughgoing

voluntarists. Note Calvin's explicit rejection of this view, however (*Institutes*, III/23 /3, 4). See also footnote 6 on page 950 of the *Institutes*, edited by Ford Lewis Battles (Philadelphia: Westminster, 1960).

[70]To say that I believe in God without assuming the law of noncontradiction is to destroy the meaning of that statement. It is the equivalent of saying "I believe in God" and allowing the possibility that in the same sense and at the same time I may legitimately say, "I do not believe in God."

[71]In this context, I am referring not to literary paradoxes in which Scripture and the teaching of our Lord abound. Rather, I speak of logical paradox—two contradictory ideas, both of which are believed to be true. Professional philosophers do not always use the term "logical paradox" for what I am rejecting. See George I. Mavrodes, *Belief in God: A Study in the Epistemology of Religion* (New York: Random House, c. 1970), especially 104ff.

[72]Tertullian is the church father to whom the acceptance of logical paradoxes by faith is frequently attributed. Luther added support for this view in his now famous opposition to the Sorbonne's rejection of double truth (but see Julius Koestlin, *Theology of Luther*, 265–66). In modern times the great proponent of Christian paradox is the Danish philosopher-theologian Søren Kierkegaard. Some have interpreted Kierkegaard as using paradox only as a literary tool or teaching device. According to them, he taught a fideistic approach to Christianity but not an acceptance of logical paradox. See Walter Lowrie, *Kierkegaard*, 2 vols. (New York: Harper, 1962), 2:295ff. I must say that I conclude from his writings that he is both a fideist and one who accepts logical paradoxes into his system of thought. In recent years, Cornelius Van Til stands out as an evangelical who holds to the validity of logical paradoxes though he insists that God is coherent and all valid paradoxes are such only for the finite sinful minds of earth-bound humans. To acknowledge that we are ignorant in the face of contradictions is rational. To rest our minds in contradictions is irrational. For a defense of the position of Van Til, see John M. Frame, *Van Til: The Theologian* (Phillipsburg, N.J.: Pilgrim, 1976).

[73]See E. J. Carnell, *Introduction to Christian Apologetics* (Grand Rapids: Eerdmans, 1948), 56–62.

The theological methodology of Schubert Ogden represents a rational apologetic to place Christian faith in a position where modern man can believe it. To do so, Ogden finds it necessary to reject two great obstacles to traditional Christian faith posed by many contemporary intellectuals: (1) that belief in Christianity entails holding to a God who acts in the universe directly (by alleged miracles) in ways not verified by science and history and (2) that the God of "classical theism" is absolute and thus free from time and change and growth. Such a God would be "totally unaffected by man and the world." Schubert M. Ogden, *The Reality of God and Other Essays* (New York: Harper & Row, c. 1964). See especially section 1, "The Reality of God," and section 6 "What Sense Does It Make to Say 'God Acts in History'?" To put it simply: Ogden's way of saving Christianity is to eliminate miracles and give up an absolute God. Whatever else might be said in response to this, this much seems obvious to any evangelical: (1) To give up all miracles is not to defend Christianity but to destroy it and replace it by a quite different religion—even if the new religion retains many ethical insights of the old Christianity—and (2) Christians have never adopted an "absolutist" view of God without the most serious qualifications and never without implying, if they did not state so directly, that in reality God is the *most related* of all beings. What they have insisted on as the bottom line is that the essential nature and character of God are unchangeable. In fairness to Ogden, we should note his statement "While all talk of miracles can be treated as a misguided effort at scientific explanation," their right use is "logically quite different." He then explains, "Therefore the real meaning of the Christian doctrine [of miracles] is the illumination each presents regarding the meaning of our actual existence as an existence within and under the all-embracing love of God . . . as represented in Jesus Christ." Miracles are, however, completely divorced from "the full autonomy of science and history." In unvarnished English, the miracles of biblical Christianity— creation, incarnation, death of Christ, second coming, or final judgment—have no significant relationship to events in our time-space world; nevertheless, they present a beautiful picture of God's wonderful yet mysterious love for us. We cannot help but wonder how Ogden can be so sure of this. I am sure, were he to read this, he would ask, "*Et tu, Brute*"? And my first response would be: "To the law and to the testimony!" (Isa. 8:20). My second response would be: "And it all makes sense to hold these miracles to be real events in our space-time world. It hangs together in systematic coherence."

[74]See the discussion of Christian theologians who accept logical paradox as necessary because of "the infinite qualitative difference between God and man"—to use a phrase of Søren Kierkegaard. See above, pp. 468–69.

[75]Kaufman seems to me to come dangerously close to this position in such statements as the following: "To regard God as some kind of desirable or knowable object . . . is at once a degradation of God and a serious categorical error", and "It was assumed that God or the divine exists or has reality out there; . . . it was taken for granted that the name God refers to a real being." Gordon D. Kaufman, *An Essay on Theologica Methodology* (Missoula, Mont.: Scholars Press, 1975), 35ff. Kaufman's "perspectival theology" presents a fine study in the sociology of religion but simply gives up the impossible task of "uncovering man's true nature, his situation in the world, and the ultimate reality with which he has to do." *God the Problem* (Cambridge, Mass.: Harvard University Press, 1972), 28. Note also ibid., 169: "What is ultimately real remains always a mysterious and unfathomable x." My question is, How then can Gordon Kaufman warrant prayer to God or worship such an "x"?

[76]Barth writes, "The Bible says . . . in truth only one thing . . . Jesus Christ" (*Church Dogmatics* I/ 1 /124ff. and everywhere throughout his writings). Barth, of course, not only holds to a Christocentric theology, but also to Christomonism. Emil Brunner agrees with Barth's Christocentrism: *The Christian Doctrine of God: Dogmatics*, trans. Olive Wyon (London: Lutterworth, 1949), 1:15 and passim. Without defining precisely what they mean by the term, a whole host of recent theologians have insisted that we must interpret the Bible Christocentrically. For Brunner this is not really a hermeneutic principle but a limiting principle. For example, as we noted earlier, he is convinced that the biblical texts teach the virgin birth of Christ; but he is not convinced of the biological miracle of parthenogenesis. He, therefore, refuses to commit himself to the virgin birth of Christ even though he admits it is clearly stated in the Scripture. Emil Brunner, *The Mediator: A Study of the Central Doctrine of the Christian Faith* (London: Lutterworth, 1934), 322–27. Barth comes closer to a genuinely Christocentric hermeneutics. He specifically warns against picking and choosing from Scripture what we are willing to believe in the hope that we can find truth apart from the text or behind the text. We dare not assume, he argues, that we can sovereignly stand in judgment over Scripture. Karl Barth, *Evangelical Theology: An Introduction*, trans. Grover Foley (New York: Holt, Rinehart and Winston, 1963), 31–32.

Yet Barth allows that it is the Christ aspect of each word of the text that determines the authoritative meaning we are to discover from the Bible. This is a delicate issue. Barth is infinitely better than most of his professed followers. No evangelical person questions (or ought to question) that the biblical prophets and apostles were fully imbedded in their own culture and spoke from their own perspective. For example, as Barth points out, the apostles wrote as first-century Jews and betray in every word that they did so. (*Church Dogmatics*, I/ 2 /509–10, and passim.)

The question is, Did they tell the truth? Evangelicals also acknowledge Jesus Christ as Lord and insist that we are bound by all that the Scriptures really affirm when rightly interpreted.

⁷⁷This is what evangelicals mean by the various terms they use to describe their view of biblical authority. The traditional terms are plenary, verbal, infallible, and inerrant. None of these terms, as used by evangelicals, implies dictation or denies the full involvement of the personality, thought forms, and personal idiosyncrasies of individual biblical authors. Typical is the view of Calvin, who reckoned it blasphemous to suggest that the biblical writers would teach what is not so (*Commentaries on the Twelve Minor Prophets*, trans. John Owen [Edinburgh: Calvin Translation Society, 1856–1858], 1:506); but he also allowed for mistakes in the text, thus accepting the validity of textual criticism (*Commentary on the Acts of the Apostles*, trans. Christopher Fetherstone, ed. Henry Beveridge [Edinburgh: Calvin Translation Society, 1854], 1:506); held that Peter did not compose 2 Peter but gave his apostolic testimony through an amanuensis (*Commentaries on the Catholic Epistles*, trans. and ed. John Owen [Edinburgh: Calvin Translation Society, 1955], 276–77, 363); and acknowledged that gospel accounts often present events in an apparently chronological order that was not correct. Calvin believed the gospel writors were not squeamish about the order, for it was not their purpose to give an exact order (*Commentary on a Harmony of the Evangelists Matthew, Mark, and Luke*, trans. William Pringle [Edinburgh: Calvin Translation Society, 1854], 1:258, 449; 2:89–90). In his view, they often did not write precisely, for they wished only to sketch the general picture. Calvin's point is that when you derive from the text what the biblical author is really saying, you have truth you can trust.

⁷⁸The principle here is illustrated by the older theologians' employment of "the analogy of faith." Unfortunately, in practice this often meant that Scripture was to be interpreted in harmony with the creeds and confessions of the church. Any interpretation that conflicted with confessions had to be rejected on the assumption that the creeds and confessions represented precisely the teaching of Scripture. This is to set up the creeds as normative over the Bible. I prefer to speak of the analogy of Scripture. See Walter C. Kaiser, Jr., *Toward an Exegetical Theology: Biblical Exegesis for Preaching and Teaching* (Grand Rapids: Baker, 1981), 134–40.

BIOGRAPHY OF
KENNETH S. KANTZER

Dr. Kenneth S. Kantzer is an outstanding theologian and educator whose achievements extend into numerous areas of Christian ministry. He has left a mark on the evangelical world in a way that few others have. He is presently Chancellor of Trinity College in Deerfield, Illinois, and Dean Emeritus and Distinguished Professor of Biblical and Systematic Theology at Trinity Evangelical Divinity School, Deerfield, Illinois. He is a member of numerous boards and committees across the nation.

The oldest of five children, Kenneth Kantzer was born in Detroit, Michigan, on March 29, 1917, and was raised in a nominally religious home. During his freshman year in college, he came to assurance of faith in Christ, making his first profession of faith in 1935 at the baccalaureate service of Wheaton College—the commencement of Ruth Forbes, who later became his wife.

Kantzer received a B.A. in 1938 from Ashland College and the following year a M.A. From Ohio State University. On September 21, 1939, he married Ruth Forbes, who had been instrumental in leading him to Christ.

Kenneth Kantzer's decision to attend Faith Theological Seminary marked his first step along the road of theological education. At Faith he began to think seriously about teaching at the college level. In fact, he taught at The King's College from 1941 to 1943 while pursuing his seminary studies. He graduated from Faith Theological Seminary in 1942 with the B.D. degree and in 1943 with the S.T.M. degree. For the next two years he taught Hebrew at Gordon College and Gordon Conwell Theological Seminary and held a pastorate in Rockport, Massachusetts.

Deeply committed to Christian liberal arts education and to impacting the church through college teaching, Kantzer spent the next seventeen years of his life (1946–1963) at Wheaton College as professor of biblical and systematic theology and as chairman of the department of Bible, Philosophy, and Religious Education. During his early years at Wheaton, he completed a Ph.D. degree in philosophy and religion at Harvard University (1950). His dissertation focused on the knowledge of God in the writings of John Calvin. In 1954 he headed the Wheaton Holy Land Tour and remained in Europe for a year of postdoctoral studies at the University of Göttingen in Germany and the University of Basel in Switzerland. He also taught theology at the Fuller Summer School of Theology from 1956 to 1963 and at the Young Life Institute in Colorado Springs.

Dr. Kantzer planned to remain at Wheaton College and to follow Merrill C. Tenney as Dean of the Graduate School. In 1963, however, the opportunity arose for him to become Dean of Trinity Evangelical Divinity School. He chose to leave Wheaton to serve at Trinity, which at the time had barely forty students. The decision was a costly one. Dr. Kantzer forfeited a full-year sabbatical in which he had planned to write a monograph on the theology of Karl Barth.

Kantzer's decision to forego this opportunity for scholarly production is an example of his consistent and sacrificial commitment to the cause of Christ. Kantzer chose to limit his time for writing so that he might devote his efforts to administering the divinity school and building a quality faculty.

As Dean and as Vice-President of Graduate Studies at Trinity Evangelical Divinity School, Kantzer poured himself into the formation and growth of the school. He gathered a quality faculty, and the school's student population expanded dramatically (presently there are 1,600 students associated with the divinity school). Throughout his years at Trinity, he sought diligently to act as a servant-leader, entrusting his co-workers with responsibility and then enabling them to complete their tasks. In 1973 students gave Dr. and Mrs. Kantzer a trip to Hawaii—a token of their fondness and respect for this remarkable couple.

In 1978 Dr. Kantzer was named Dean Emeritus of Trinity Evangelical Divinity School and became editor-in-chief of *Christianity Today*. As editor of the magazine, he strove to evaluate critically the evangelical establishment, to promote healing rather than alienation while keeping the magazine committed to radically biblical Christianity. He served for five years as editor of *Christianity Today*, returning to Trinity Evangelical Divinity School in 1982 fully intending to teach and write for the pastor and lay person. In 1984 he was appointed senior editor and dean of the research institute of *Christianity Today* and continues to hold both positions.

Almost immediately upon his return to the divinity school, Dr. Kantzer again faced diverging paths—one of which would lead to continued teaching and writing, and the other, to becoming President of Trinity College, which in 1982 was near collapse. Committed to Christian liberal arts education and convinced that no one else would take the risk, he opted to serve as President of the college for two years (1982–1983). During those years, Trinity College became reaffiliated with the Evangelical Free Church of America (in which Dr. Kantzer has served as an ordained minister since 1948). Under his leadership the college has experienced renewed growth. Since 1983 Dr. Kantzer has been Chancellor of Trinity College.

In 1984 Dr. Kantzer returned to Trinity Evangelical Divinity School to continue teaching—an activity he never completely abandoned even as President of Trinity College. Two years later, however, in 1986 when the divinity school initiated its Ph.D. program, he was asked to serve as Director—a position he undertook for what he thought would be a few months and actually held until 1990. Even with his dedication to the Ph.D. program, he remained involved in teaching and in writing prolifically for *Christianity Today*, recently contributing to and co-editing with Dr. Carl F. H. Henry the significant volume *Evangelical Affirmations* (1990).

Dr. Kantzer is a man committed to his family. The encouragement of his wife, Ruth Forbes, who had been a Greek major at Wheaton and studied alongside him in seminary and who still types the manuscripts that he dictates, has been a key influence in his maturation as a Christian. The Kantzers have two children, each of whom has given them two grandchildren. Their daughter, Mary Ruth, born in 1942, ministers on a farm for troubled couples with her husband, Dr. Loren Wilkinson, professor of literature and philosophy of religion at Regent College in Vancouver, B.C. Their son, Dick, born in 1947, is married to Huai-Ching. He formerly pastored an Evangelical Free Church and continues to pursue a Ph.D. at Yale University.

Despite a very busy life, Dr. Kantzer has managed to pursue and excel in several hobbies. An enthusiastic gardener, he enjoys cultivating a variety of flowers, among them African violets, impatiens plants, and begonias. He is an avid listener to baroque music and has a substantial classical music collection, which he considers his one luxury in life. He also reads extensively, frequently spending the last hour of each day absorbed in a book that might be a theology text, a classic of

English literature, a study of astronomy, or perhaps an old-fashioned Western novel for sheer relaxation.

Kantzer holds four honorary doctorates—from Ashland Theological Seminary, Gordon College, John Brown University, and Wheaton College. He has served as the consulting editor for *His* magazine and as book review editor for the *Journal of the Evangelical Theological Society* and is listed in *Who's Who in the Middle West*, *Who's Who in Education*, and *Outstanding Educators in America*. He is a member of the Evangelical Philosophical Society and the Evangelical Theological Society (of which he is a former president).

Dr. Kantzer has remained deeply interested in missions. Upon graduation from seminary, he applied to a missions agency to teach theology in Manchuria, but his plans were thwarted by the onset of the war. He served on the board of the Chinese Graduate School of Theology and presently sits on the boards of Columbia Bible College and Seminary, The Evangelical Alliance Mission (TEAM), and Pioneer Ministries.

His wisdom, personal warmth, and modeling as a humble servant of Jesus Christ have endeared him to generations of students and the colleagues with whom and for whom he worked so diligently. Indeed, Kenneth S. Kantzer has left a mark on the evangelical world in a way that few others have. Evangelical Christians are greatly in his debt.

PARTIAL BIBLIOGRAPHY—
KENNETH S. KANTZER

1957
"Calvin and the Holy Scriptures." In *Inspiration and Interpretation.* Edited by J. F. Walvoord. Grand Rapids: Eerdmans, 1957, 115–55.

1958
"The Christology of Karl Barth." *Bulletin of the Evangelical Theological Society* 1, no. 2 (Spring 1958): 25–28.
"The Christology of Karl Barth." *Asbury Seminarian* 12, no. 2 (Summer 1958): 24–28.
"Revelation and Inspiration in Neo-Orthodox Theology, Part I: What Is Revelation?" *Bibliotheca Sacra* 115, no. 458 (April 1958): 120–27.
"Revelation and Inspiration in Neo-Orthodox Theology, Part II: The Method of Revelation." *Bibliotheca Sacra* 115, no. 459 (July 1958): 218–28.
"Revelation and Inspiration in Neo-Orthodox Theology, Part III: Contemporary Thinking About Revelation." *Bibliotheca Sacra* 115, no. 460 (October 1958): 302–12.

1959
"Protestantism." In *Religions in a Changing World.* Edited by Howard F. Vos. Chicago: Moody Press, 1959, 407–37.
"Neo-Orthodoxy and the Inspiration of Scripture." *Bibliotheca Sacra* 116, no. 461 (January 1959): 15–29.
"Evangelical Theology and Paul Tillich." *Asbury Seminarian* (Spring-Summer 1959).

1960
"The Authority of the Bible." In *The Word for This Century.* Edited by M. C. Tenney. New York: Oxford University Press, 1960, 21–51.
"Error," "Expediency," "Purpose," "Stoics," "Wisdom." In *Dictionary of Theology.* Edited by E. F. Harrison. Grand Rapids: Baker, 1960.

1963
"Revelation and Inspiration in Neo-Orthodox Theology, Part II: The Method of Revelation." (Reprint from *Bibliotheca Sacra,* July 1958) In *Truth for Today: Bibliotheca Sacra Reader.* Edited by J. F. Walvoord. Chicago: Moody Press, 1963, 87–97.

1966
"The Christ-Revelation as Act and Inspiration." In *Jesus of Nazareth.* Edited by Carl F. H. Henry. Grand Rapids: Eerdmans, 1966, 241–64.

"Christ and Scripture." *His* 26, no. 4 (January 1966): 16–20.

"Human Wish vs. Divine Revelation." *His* 26, no. 8 (May 1966): 15–22.

1967

"Evangelicals and the Evangelistic Dialogue." *Christianity Today* (hereinafter *CT*) 11, no. 20 (July 7, 1967): 34–35.

1969

"What's Wrong With the Neo-Orthodox View of Scripture?" *Moody Monthly* 69, no. 9 (May 1969): 28–29.

1974

"Christian Higher Education for the Last Quarter of the 20th Century." *Monograph of Christian Concern, no. 3.* Miami Christian College, November 22, 1974.

1975

"Unity and Diversity in the Evangelical Faith." In *The Evangelicals: What They Believe, Who They Are, Where They Are Changing.* Edited by D. Wells and J. D. Woodbridge. Grand Rapids: Baker, 1975, 58–87.

1976

"A Theological Brief." In *The American Academy of Religion: Philosophy of Religion and Theology.* Compiled by Peter Slater. Missoula, Mont.: Scholars Press, 1976, 184–87.

"Buswell as a Theologian." *Covenant Seminary Review* (Spring-Fall 1976).

1978

Evangelical Roots: A Tribute to Wilbur Smith, editor. Nashville: Thomas Nelson, 1978.

"Charismatic Renewal: Threat or Promise?" In *Theology and Mission.* Edited by D. J. Hesselgrave. Grand Rapids: Baker, 1978, 17–37.

"Evangelicals and the Doctrine of Inerrancy." In *The Foundations of Biblical Authority.* Edited by J. M. Boice. Grand Rapids: Zondervan, 1978, 147–56.

"Evangelicals and the Inerrancy Question." In *Evangelical Roots.* Edited by K. S. Kantzer. Nashville: Nelson, 1978, 83–100.

"The Future of Evangelicalism." In *Evangelicals Face the Future.* Edited by D. E. Hoke. South Pasadena: William Carey Library; BGC, Wheaton, 1978, 127–46.

"Of Prophetic Robes and Weather Vanes" (an interview). *CT* 22, no. 13 (April 7, 1978): 21–26.

"Evangelicals and the Inerrancy Question" (adapted reprint). *CT* 22, no. 14 (April 21, 1978): 16–21.

"The Way Up Is Down: A Theology of Christmas." *CT* 23, no. 5 (December 1978): 20–24.

"Born in a Barn." (E) *CT* 23, no. 6 (December 15, 1978): 7.

1979

Perspectives on Evangelical Theology: Papers From the 30th Annual Meeting of the Evangelical Theological Society, editor (with S. N. Gundry). Grand Rapids: Baker, 1979.

"The Alternative to the People's Temple." (E) *CT* 23, no. 7 (January 5, 1979): 11.

"What's on the Menu?" (E) *CT* 23, no. 7 (January 5, 1979): 11.

"Human Engineering: Trouble Ahead." (E) *CT* 23, no. 8 (January 19, 1979): 12.

"WCC: An Uncertain Sound?" (E) *CT* 23, no. 10 (February 16, 1979): 12.

"Israeli-Egyptian Peace Treaty." (E) *CT* 23, no. 14 (April 20, 1979): 8.

"Resurging Islamic Orthodoxy." (E) *CT* 23, no. 15 (May 4, 1979): 14–15.

"Divorce and Remarriage." (E) *CT* 23, no. 16 (May 25, 1979): 8–9.

"In Search of Africa." (E) *CT* 23, no. 19 (July 20, 1979): 8–9.

"The Graham Image: A Parable of America's Blindness." *CT* 23, no. 26 (November 16, 1979): 26–31.

"The IYC: More Harm Than Help to the Family." (E) *CT* 23, no. 27 (December 7, 1979): 14–15.

1980

"Gaining Perspectives After a Decade of Change." (E) *CT* 24, no. 1 (January 4, 1980): 12.

"To Be All Things to All Men, Even the Iranians." (E) *CT* 24, no. 3 (February 8, 1980): 17–18.

"The Charismatics Among Us." *CT* 24, no. 4 (February 22, 1980): 25–29.

"Homosexuality: Biblical Guidance Through a Moral Morass." (E) *CT* 24, no. 8 (April 18, 1980): 12–13.

"Profile of US Pentecostal-Charismatics." (Excerpted from "The Charismatics Among Us." *CT* [February 22, 1980]). *Emerging Trends* 2, no. 4 (April 1980).

"Demands of an Aging Population." (E) *CT* 24, no. 9 (May 2, 1980): 12–13.

"Church and State: Playing Fair with Prayer." (E) *CT* 24, no. 11 (June 5, 1980): 12–13.

"Proper Pay for Pastors." (E) *CT* 24, no. 13 (July 18, 1980): 12–13.

"COWE: 200,000 by the Year 2000." (E) *CT* 24, no. 14 (August 8, 1980): 10–11.

"Being on the Board—and Getting Off." (E) *CT* 24, no. 15 (September 5, 1980): 14–15.

"Getting God's Kingdom into Politics." (E) *CT* 24, no. 16 (September 19, 1980): 10–11.

"Tax Support for Christian Colleges: Balancing the Ledger." (E) *CT* 24, no. 19 (November 7, 1980): 10–11.

1982

"Christ and Scripture." *His* 42, no. 9 (June 1982 [reprint from *His*, 1966]).

"Was Augustine Too Harsh?" *Leadership* 3, no. 3 (Summer 1982): 110.

"A Christian Education Worthy of the Name." (E) *CT* 22, no. 18 (November 12, 1982): 22–25.

"Reflections, Five Years of Change" (an interview). *CT* 26, no. 19 (November 26, 1982): 14–20.

"It's Too Soon to Quit!" (E) *CT* 26, no. 20 (December 17, 1982): 10.

1983

"Evangelicalism: Midcourse Self-Appraisal." (E) *CT* 27, no. 1 (January 7, 1983): 10–11.

"What Shall We Do About the Nuclear Problem?" (E) *CT* 27, no. 2 (January 21, 1983): 9–11.

"Documenting the Dramatic Shift in Seminaries from Liberal to Conservative." (E) *CT* 27, no. 3 (February 4, 1983): 10–11.

"Why Does Harvard Want an Evangelical Connection?" *CT* 27, no. 3 (February 4, 1983); 17–18.

"Liberalism's Rise and Fall." (E) *CT* 27, no. 4 (February 18, 1983): 10–11.

"When Should Christians Stand Against the Law?" (E) *CT* 27, no. 5 (March 4, 1983): 10–11.

"Why Is Easter Unattractive?" (E) *CT* 27, no. 6 (March 18, 1983): 7–9.

"Should Government Subsidize the Church?" (E) *CT* 27, no. 7 (April 8, 1983): 8–10.

"Homosexuality and the Church." (E) *CT* 27, no. 8 (April 22, 1983): 8–9.

"Planned Parenthood Attacks a Parent's Need to Know." (E) *CT* 27, no. 9 (May 6, 1983): 11–13.

"A New Solution to the Crisis in Our Prisons." (E) *CT* 27, no. 10 (June 17, 1983): 12–13.

"The Central American Powder Keg: How Can Christians Keep It from Exploding?" (E) *CT* 27, no. 11 (July 15, 1983): 12–13.

"Drunken Driving: Are We Angry Enough to Stop It?" (E) *CT* 27, no. 12 (August 5, 1983): 10–11.

"The Bob Jones Decision: A Dangerous Precedent." (E) *CT* 27, no. 13 (September 2, 1983): 14–15.

"What Book Has Influenced You Most: Twelve Christian Leaders Respond." *CT* 27, no. 13 (September 2, 1983): 27.

"Can Christian Colleges Survive the 80's?" (E) *CT* 27, no. 14 (September 16, 1983): 8–9.

"Biblical Authority: When Both Fundamentalists and Nonevangelicals Are Right." *CT* 27, no. 15 (October 7, 1983): 10–13.

"A Christian Response to the Korean Airline Disaster." (E) *CT* 27, no. 17 (November 11, 1983): 12–13.

"Gambling: Everyone's a Loser." (E) *CT* 27, no. 18 (November 25, 1983): 12–13.

1984
"Six Hard Questions for Evangelicals and Jews." In *Evangelicals and Jews.* Edited by M. Tanenbaum, M. Wilson, and A. Rudin, 1984.
"Orwell's Fatal Error." (E) *CT* 28, no. 1 (January 13, 1984): 10–11.
"The Good News the Resurrection Brings." (E) *CT* 28, no. 6 (April 6, 1984): 10–11.
"That Controversial Appointment." (E) *CT* 28, no. 5 (March 16, 1984): 12–13.
"Winds of Change in the World Council?" (E) *CT* 28, no. 7 (April 20, 1984): 10–12.
"The Separation of Church and State?" (E) *CT* 28, no. 8 (May 18, 1984): 10–11.
"Revitalizing World Evangelicalism: The Lausanne Congress Ten Years Later." (E) *CT* 28, no. 9 (June 15, 1984): 10–12.
"American Civil Religion." (E) *CT* 28, no. 10 (July 13, 1984): 14–15.
"A Theologian Looks at Schuller." (E) *CT* 28, no. 11 (August 10, 1984); 22–24.
"Our November Call to Conscience." (E) *CT* 28, no. 13 (September 21, 1984): 12–13.
"What Jews Need to Know About Christians." *Christian Life* 46, no. 7 (November 1984): 46–50.
"The Miracle of Christmas." (E) *CT* 28, no. 18 (December 14, 1984): 14–15.

1985
"Beyond 1984: An Evangelical Agenda." (E) *CT* 29, no. 1 (January 18, 1985): 14–15.
"Pastoral Letters and the Realities of Life." (E) *CT* 29, no. 4 (March 1, 1985): 12–13.
"Within Our Reach." (E) *CT* 29, no. 7 (April 19, 1985): 20–23.
"Christianity Today Institute: The Christian As Citizen" (with Gilbert Beers). *CT* 29, no. 7 (April 19, 1985): 1–32.
"Summing Up: An Evangelical View of Church and State." (CTI) *CT* 29, no. 7 (April 19, 1985): 28–31.
"The Issues at Hand: 'The Christian As Citizen'" (CTI) *CT* 29, no. 7 (April 19, 1985): I:2–3.
The Cut-Rate Grace of a Health and Wealth Gospel." (E) *CT* 29, no. 9 (June 14, 1985): 14–15.
"Bitburg: Must We Forgive?" (E) *CT* no. 10 (July 12, 1985): 14–15.
"A Man Under Orders: Where Is Pope John Paul II Taking the Roman Catholic Church?" (E) *CT* 29, no. 12 (September 6, 1985): 14–15.
"A Man of Zeal and Contradiction." *CT* 29, no. 13 (September 20, 1985): 36–38.

"Redaction Criticism: Handle with Care." (CTI) *CT* 29, no. 15: I-11, 12 (October 18, 1985): I:11–12.
"Varsity Racism?" (E) *CT* 29, no. 16 (November 8, 1985): 17–18.
"In Search of Heroes." (E) *CT* 29, no. 16 (November 8, 1985): 16–17.
"Don't Start the Revolution Without Me!" (SE) *CT* 29, no. 17 (November 22, 1985): 16.
"Disturbing the Peace." (E) *CT* 29, no. 18 (December 13, 1985).

1986

"The Priorities of Love." (CTI) *CT* 30, no. 1 (January 17, 1986): I:29–31.
"The Power of Porn." (E) *CT* 30, no. 2 (February 7, 1986): 18.
"Can Conservatives Find a Home in the National Council of Churches?" (interview with Arie Brouwer). *CT* 30, no. 2 (February 7, 1986): 42–45.
"Do You Believe in Hell?" (SE) *CT* 30, no. 3 (February 21, 1986): 12.
"Nightmare of the '80's." (E) *CT* 30, no. 4 (March 7, 1986): 14–15.
"Biomedical Decision Making: We Dare Not Retreat." (CTI) *CT* 30 no. 5 (March 21, 1986): I:15–16.
"Saving Public Education." (E) *CT* 30, no. 6 (April 4, 1986): 14–15.
"Tough Is Not Enough." (E) *CT* 30, no. 8 (May 16, 1986): 14.
"Building Faith: How a Child Learns to Love God," editor. (CTI) *CT* 30, no. 9 (June 13, 1986): 11–16.
"One Cheer for Carl Sagan." (SE) *CT* 30, no. 9 (June 13, 1986): 10.
"Final Thoughts." (CTI) *CT* 30, no. 9 (June 13, 1986): I:16.
"The Day of Salvation in the Third World." (E) *CT* 30, no. 11 (August 8, 1986): 14–15.
"Fixing History: A New Ideal in Race Relations." (E) *CT* 30, no. 12 (September 5, 1986): 16–17.
"On the Road with Kenneth Kantzer." (SE) *CT* 30, no. 14 (October 3, 1986): 10.
"Thank God for Karl Barth, But . . . " (E) *CT* 30, no. 14 (October 3, 1986): 14–15.
"Women in Leadership: Proceed with Care." (CTI) *CT* 30, no. 14 (October 3, 1986): I:14–15.
"Time to Look Ahead: As the 21st Century Beckons, the Church Faces a Dual Challenge." *CT* 30, no. 15 (October 17, 1986): 16–17.
"Church on the Move." (E) *CT* 30, no. 16 (November 7, 1986): 16–17.
"A Most Misunderstood Woman." *CT* 30, no. 18 (December 12, 1986): 19–21.

1987

Applying the Scriptures: Papers From ICBI Summit, III, Editor. Grand Rapids: Zondervan, 1987.
"Inerrancy and the Humanity and Divinity of the Bible." In *The Proceedings of the Conference on Biblical Inerrancy*. Edited by J. Gregory et al. Nashville: Broadman, 1987, 153–63.
"Parameters of Biblical Inerrancy." In *The Proceedings of the Conference*

on Biblical Inerrancy. Edited by J. Gregory et al. Nashville: Broadman, 1987, 111–25.

"Agreement Is Not Required." (CTI) *CT* 31, no. 2 (February 6, 1987): I:13–14.

"Problems Inerrancy Doesn't Solve." (E) *CT* 31, no. 3 (February 20, 1987): 14.

"Turning Down the Heat." (SE) *CT* 31, no. 4 (March 6, 1987): 11.

"Universalism: Troublesome Questions." (CTI) *CT* 31, no. 5 (March 20, 1987): 45.

"The Real Sex Ed. Battle." (E) *CT* 31, no. 7 (April 17, 1987): 16–17.

"Reclaiming Our Honor." (CTI) *CT* 31, no. 8 (May 15, 1987): 40.

"American Evangelicalism: What Does the Future Hold?" *UEA* 46, no. 3 (May-June 1987): 7–8.

"Decadence American Style." (E) *CT* 31, no. 11 (August 7, 1987): 12–13.

"Vacation by Objectives." (SE) *CT* 31, no. 12 (September 4, 1987): 15.

"For Once We Knew When to Quit." (SE) *CT* 31, no. 16 (November 6, 1987): 11.

"The Road to Restoration." *CT* 31, no. 17 (November 20, 1987): 19–22.

"A Farewell to Harms." (E) *CT* 31, no. 18 (December 11, 1987): 14–15.

1988

"Confidence in the Face of Confusion." (CTI) *CT* 32, no. 2 (February 5, 1988): 38.

"What Happened in 586 B.C.?" (SE) *CT* 32, no. 4 (March 4, 1988): 11.

"Fine-tuning Televangelism." (CTI) *CT* 32, no. 5 (March 18, 1988): 42.

"Lead! Lead! Lead!" (SE) *CT* 32, no. 9 (June 17, 1988): 11.

"Why I Still Believe the Bible Is True." *CT* 32, no. 14 (October 7, 1988): 22–25.

"Words About the Word." *CT* 32, no. 14 (October 27, 1988): 25.

"The Freedom of Jealousy." (SE) *CT* 32, no. 15 (October 21, 1988): 11.

"The Evangelist of Our Time." (E) *CT* 32, no. 17 (November 18, 1988: 14–15.

1989

"Militant Against Mediocrity." *CT* 33, no. 2 (February 3, 1989): 13.

"Listening to America's Ethnic Churches: Has the Melting Pot Stopped Melting?" *CT* 33, no. 4 (March 3, 1989): 40–42.

"Visions, Voices, and Choices." *CT* 33, no. 7 (April 21, 1989): 8.

"Rich Wisdom: NT Teachings on Wealth: The Christian Ideal." *CT* 33, no. 8 (May 12, 1989): 39–40.

"Prolife: What Does It Really Mean?: If Both Sides Would Listen." (CTI) *CT* 33, no. 10 (July 14, 1989): 37–38.

INDEX

Doing Theology in Today's World was typeset by the Photocomposition Department of Zondervan Publishing House, Grand Rapids, Michigan on a Mergenthaler Linotron 202/N. Compositor is Susan Koppenol Imprint Editor for Academie Books is Leonard G. Goss

The text was set in 10 point Palatino, a face designed by Herman Zapf in Germany in 1948. He used this face often in designing his exquisite manuale Typographicum *(1954). The italic of this face was originally called medici italic. Palatino is admired for its penlike, calligraphic strokes, and is popular for bookwork. This book was printed on 50-pound Lyons Falls Pathfinder paper by R.R. Donnelley & Sons, Harrisburg, Virginia.*